National Advisory Board

Novels for Students

Presenting Analysis, Context, and Criticism on Commonly Studied Novels

Volume 17

David Galens, Project Editor

Foreword by Anne Devereaux Jordan

GALE®

THOMSON

GALE

Detroit • New York • San Diego • San Francisco • Cleveland • New Haven, Conn. • Waterville, Maine • London • Munich

THOMSON

★

GALE

™

Novels for Students, Volume 17

Project Editor
David Galens

Editorial
Anne Marie Hacht, Ira Mark Milne, Pam Revitzer, Kathy Sauer, Timothy J. Sisler, Jennifer Smith, Carol Ullmann, Maikue Vang

Research
Nicodemus Ford, Sarah Genik, Tamara Nott

Permissions
Shalice Shah-Caldwell

Manufacturing
Stacy Melson

Imaging and Multimedia
Dean Dauphinais, Leitha Etheridge-Sims, Mary Grimes, Lezlie Light, Luke Rademacher

Product Design
Pamela A. E. Galbreath, Michael Logusz

For permission to use material from this product, submit your request via Web at http://www.gale-edit.com/permissions, or you may download our Permissions Request form and submit your request by fax or mail to:

Permissions Department
The Gale Group, Inc.
27500 Drake Rd.
Farmington Hills, MI 48331–3535
Permissions Hotline:
248-699-8006 or 800-877-4253, ext. 8006
Fax: 248-699-8074 or 800-762-4058

Since this page cannot legibly accommodate all copyright notices, the acknowledgments constitute an extension of the copyright notice.

While every effort has been made to ensure the reliability of the information presented in this publication, The Gale Group, Inc. does not guarantee the accuracy of the data contained herein. The Gale Group, Inc. accepts no payment for listing; and inclusion in the publication of any organization, agency, institution, publication, service, or individual does not imply endorsement of the editors or publisher. Errors brought to the attention of the publisher and verified to the satisfaction of the publisher will be corrected in future editions.

ISBN 0-7876-6029-9
ISSN 1094-3552

Printed in the United States of America
10 9 8 7 6 5 4 3 2 1

Table of Contents

The Informed Dialogue: Interacting with Literature

When we pick up a book, we usually do so with the anticipation of pleasure. We hope that by entering the time and place of the novel and sharing the thoughts and actions of the characters, we will find enjoyment. Unfortunately, this is often not the case; we are disappointed. But we should ask, has the author failed us, or have we failed the author?

We establish a dialogue with the author, the book, and with ourselves when we read. Consciously and unconsciously, we ask questions: "Why did the author write this book?" "Why did the author choose that time, place, or character?" "How did the author achieve that effect?" "Why did the character act that way?" "Would I act in the same way?" The answers we receive depend upon how much information about literature in general and about that book specifically we ourselves bring to our reading.

Young children have limited life and literary experiences. Being young, children frequently do not know how to go about exploring a book, nor sometimes, even know the questions to ask of a book. The books they read help them answer questions, the author often coming right out and *telling* young readers the things they are learning or are expected to learn. The perennial classic, *The Little Engine That Could, tells* its readers that, among other things, it is good to help others and brings happiness:

"Hurray, hurray," cried the funny little clown and all the dolls and toys. "The good little boys and girls in

the city will be happy because you helped us, kind, Little Blue Engine."

In picture books, messages are often blatant and simple, the dialogue between the author and reader one-sided. Young children are concerned with the end result of a book—the enjoyment gained, the lesson learned—rather than with how that result was obtained. As we grow older and read further, however, we question more. We come to expect that the world within the book will closely mirror the concerns of our world, and that the author will *show* these through the events, descriptions, and conversations within the story, rather than *telling* of them. We are now expected to do the interpreting, carry on our share of the dialogue with the book and author, and glean not only the author's message, but comprehend how that message and the overall affect of the book were achieved. Sometimes, however, we need help to do these things. *Novels for Students* provides that help.

A novel is made up of many parts interacting to create a coherent whole. In reading a novel, the more obvious features can be easily spotted—theme, characters, plot—but we may overlook the more subtle elements that greatly influence how the novel is perceived by the reader: viewpoint, mood and tone, symbolism, or the use of humor. By focusing on both the obvious and more subtle literary elements within a novel, *Novels for Students* aids readers in both analyzing for message and in determining how and why that message is communicated. In the discussion on Harper Lee's *To*

Kill a Mockingbird (Vol. 2), for example, the mockingbird as a symbol of innocence is dealt with, among other things, as is the importance of Lee's use of humor which "enlivens a serious plot, adds depth to the characterization, and creates a sense of familiarity and universality." The reader comes to understand the internal elements of each novel discussed—as well as the external influences that help shape it.

"The desire to write greatly," Harold Bloom of Yale University says, "is the desire to be elsewhere, in a time and place of one's own, in an originality that must compound with inheritance, with an anxiety of influence." A writer seeks to create a unique world within a story, but although it is unique, it is not disconnected from our own world. It speaks to us *because* of what the writer brings to the writing from our world: how he or she was raised and educated; his or her likes and dislikes; the events occurring in the real world at the time of the writing, and while the author was growing up. When we know what an author has brought to his or her work, we gain a greater insight into both the "originality" (the world of the book), and the things that "compound" it. This insight enables us to question that created world and find answers more readily. By informing ourselves, we are able to establish a more effective dialogue with both book and author.

Novels for Students, in addition to providing a plot summary and descriptive list of characters—to remind readers of what they have read—also explores the external influences that shaped each book. Each entry includes a discussion of the author's background, and the historical context in which the novel was written. It is vital to know, for instance, that when Ray Bradbury was writing *Fahrenheit 451* (Vol. 1), the threat of Nazi domination had recently ended in Europe, and the McCarthy hearings were taking place in Washington, D.C. This information goes far in answering the question, "Why did he write a story of oppressive government control and book burning?" Similarly, it is important to know that Harper Lee, author of *To Kill a Mockingbird,* was born and raised in Monroeville, Alabama, and that her father was a lawyer.

Readers can now see why she chose the south as a setting for her novel—it is the place with which she was most familiar—and start to comprehend her characters and their actions.

Novels for Students helps readers find the answers they seek when they establish a dialogue with a particular novel. It also aids in the posing of questions by providing the opinions and interpretations of various critics and reviewers, broadening that dialogue. Some reviewers of *To Kill A Mockingbird,* for example, "faulted the novel's climax as melodramatic." This statement leads readers to ask, "Is it, indeed, melodramatic?" "If not, why did some reviewers see it as such?" "If it is, why did Lee choose to make it melodramatic?" "Is melodrama ever justified?" By being spurred to ask these questions, readers not only learn more about the book and its writer, but about the nature of writing itself.

The literature included for discussion in *Novels for Students* has been chosen because it has something vital to say to us. *Of Mice and Men, Catch-22, The Joy Luck Club, My Antonia, A Separate Peace* and the other novels here speak of life and modern sensibility. In addition to their individual, specific messages of prejudice, power, love or hate, living and dying, however, they and all great literature also share a common intent. They force us to *think*—about life, literature, and about others, not just about ourselves. They pry us from the narrow confines of our minds and thrust us outward to confront the world of books and the larger, real world we all share. *Novels for Students* helps us in this confrontation by providing the means of enriching our conversation with literature and the world, by creating an *informed* dialogue, one that brings true pleasure to the personal act of reading.

Sources

Harold Bloom, *The Western Canon, The Books and School of the Ages,* Riverhead Books, 1994.

Watty Piper, *The Little Engine That Could,* Platt & Munk, 1930.

Anne Devereaux Jordan
Senior Editor, TALL
(Teaching and Learning Literature)

Introduction

Purpose of the Book

The purpose of *Novels for Students (NfS)* is to provide readers with a guide to understanding, enjoying, and studying novels by giving them easy access to information about the work. Part of Gale's "For Students" Literature line, *NfS* is specifically designed to meet the curricular needs of high school and undergraduate college students and their teachers, as well as the interests of general readers and researchers considering specific novels. While each volume contains entries on "classic" novels frequently studied in classrooms, there are also entries containing hard-to-find information on contemporary novels, including works by multicultural, international, and women novelists.

The information covered in each entry includes an introduction to the novel and the novel's author; a plot summary, to help readers unravel and understand the events in a novel; descriptions of important characters, including explanation of a given character's role in the novel as well as discussion about that character's relationship to other characters in the novel; analysis of important themes in the novel; and an explanation of important literary techniques and movements as they are demonstrated in the novel.

In addition to this material, which helps the readers analyze the novel itself, students are also provided with important information on the literary and historical background informing each work. This includes a historical context essay, a box comparing the time or place the novel was written to modern Western culture, a critical essay, and excerpts from critical essays on the novel. A unique feature of *NfS* is a specially commissioned critical essay on each novel, targeted toward the student reader.

To further aid the student in studying and enjoying each novel, information on media adaptations is provided, as well as reading suggestions for works of fiction and nonfiction on similar themes and topics. Classroom aids include ideas for research papers and lists of critical sources that provide additional material on the novel.

Selection Criteria

The titles for each volume of *NfS* were selected by surveying numerous sources on teaching literature and analyzing course curricula for various school districts. Some of the sources surveyed included: literature anthologies; *Reading Lists for College-Bound Students: The Books Most Recommended by America's Top Colleges;* textbooks on teaching the novel; a College Board survey of novels commonly studied in high schools; a National Council of Teachers of English (NCTE) survey of novels commonly studied in high schools; the NCTE's *Teaching Literature in High School: The Novel;* and the Young Adult Library Services Association (YALSA) list of best books for young adults of the past twenty-five years.

Input was also solicited from our advisory board, as well as from educators from various areas.

From these discussions, it was determined that each volume should have a mix of "classic" novels (those works commonly taught in literature classes) and contemporary novels for which information is often hard to find. Because of the interest in expanding the canon of literature, an emphasis was also placed on including works by international, multicultural, and women authors. Our advisory board members—educational professionals—helped pare down the list for each volume. If a work was not selected for the present volume, it was often noted as a possibility for a future volume. As always, the editor welcomes suggestions for titles to be included in future volumes.

How Each Entry Is Organized

Each entry, or chapter, in *NfS* focuses on one novel. Each entry heading lists the full name of the novel, the author's name, and the date of the novel's publication. The following elements are contained in each entry:

- **Introduction:** a brief overview of the novel which provides information about its first appearance, its literary standing, any controversies surrounding the work, and major conflicts or themes within the work.

- **Author Biography:** this section includes basic facts about the author's life, and focuses on events and times in the author's life that inspired the novel in question.

- **Plot Summary:** a factual description of the major events in the novel. Lengthy summaries are broken down with subheads.

- **Characters:** an alphabetical listing of major characters in the novel. Each character name is followed by a brief to an extensive description of the character's role in the novel, as well as discussion of the character's actions, relationships, and possible motivation.

  Characters are listed alphabetically by last name. If a character is unnamed—for instance, the narrator in *Invisible Man*—the character is listed as "The Narrator" and alphabetized as "Narrator." If a character's first name is the only one given, the name will appear alphabetically by that name.

  Variant names are also included for each character. Thus, the full name "Jean Louise Finch" would head the listing for the narrator of *To Kill a Mockingbird,* but listed in a separate cross-reference would be the nickname "Scout Finch."

- **Themes:** a thorough overview of how the major topics, themes, and issues are addressed within the novel. Each theme discussed appears in a separate subhead and is easily accessed through the boldface entries in the Subject/Theme Index.

- **Style:** this section addresses important style elements of the novel, such as setting, point of view, and narration; important literary devices used, such as imagery, foreshadowing, symbolism; and, if applicable, genres to which the work might have belonged, such as Gothicism or Romanticism. Literary terms are explained within the entry but can also be found in the Glossary.

- **Historical Context:** This section outlines the social, political, and cultural climate *in which the author lived and the novel was created.* This section may include descriptions of related historical events, pertinent aspects of daily life in the culture, and the artistic and literary sensibilities of the time in which the work was written. If the novel is a historical work, information regarding the time in which the novel is set is also included. Each section is broken down with helpful subheads.

- **Critical Overview:** this section provides background on the critical reputation of the novel, including bannings or any other public controversies surrounding the work. For older works, this section includes a history of how the novel was first received and how perceptions of it may have changed over the years; for more recent novels, direct quotes from early reviews may also be included.

- **Criticism:** an essay commissioned by *NfS* which specifically deals with the novel and is written specifically for the student audience, as well as excerpts from previously published criticism on the work (if available).

- **Sources:** an alphabetical list of critical material used in compiling the entry, with full bibliographical information.

- **Further Reading:** an alphabetical list of other critical sources which may prove useful for the student. It includes full bibliographical information and a brief annotation.

In addition, each entry contains the following highlighted sections, set apart from the main text as sidebars:

- **Media Adaptations:** a list of important film and television adaptations of the novel, including source information. The list also includes stage adaptations, audio recordings, musical adaptations, etc.

- **Topics for Further Study:** a list of potential study questions or research topics dealing with the novel. This section includes questions related to other disciplines the student may be studying, such as American history, world history, science, math, government, business, geography, economics, psychology, etc.

- **Compare and Contrast Box:** an "at-a-glance" comparison of the cultural and historical differences between the author's time and culture and late twentieth century/early twenty-first century Western culture. This box includes pertinent parallels between the major scientific, political, and cultural movements of the time or place the novel was written, the time or place the novel was set (if a historical work), and modern Western culture. Works written after 1990 may not have this box.

- **What Do I Read Next?:** a list of works that might complement the featured novel or serve as a contrast to it. This includes works by the same author and others, works of fiction and nonfiction, and works from various genres, cultures, and eras.

Other Features

NfS includes "The Informed Dialogue: Interacting with Literature," a foreword by Anne Devereaux Jordan, Senior Editor for *Teaching and Learning Literature* (*TALL*), and a founder of the Children's Literature Association. This essay provides an enlightening look at how readers interact with literature and how *Novels for Students* can help teachers show students how to enrich their own reading experiences.

A Cumulative Author/Title Index lists the authors and titles covered in each volume of the *NfS* series.

A Cumulative Nationality/Ethnicity Index breaks down the authors and titles covered in each volume of the *NfS* series by nationality and ethnicity.

A Subject/Theme Index, specific to each volume, provides easy reference for users who may be studying a particular subject or theme rather than a single work. Significant subjects from events to broad themes are included, and the entries pointing to the specific theme discussions in each entry are indicated in **boldface.**

Each entry may have several illustrations, including photos of the author, stills from film adaptations, maps, and/or photos of key historical events, if available.

Citing Novels for Students

When writing papers, students who quote directly from any volume of *Novels for Students* may use the following general forms. These examples are based on MLA style; teachers may request that students adhere to a different style, so the following examples may be adapted as needed.

When citing text from *NfS* that is not attributed to a particular author (i.e., the Themes, Style, Historical Context sections, etc.), the following format should be used in the bibliography section:

"Night." Novels for Students. Ed. Marie Rose Napierkowski. Vol. 4. Detroit: Gale, 1998. 234–35.

When quoting the specially commissioned essay from *NfS* (usually the first piece under the "Criticism" subhead), the following format should be used:

Miller, Tyrus. Critical Essay on *Winesburg, Ohio. Novels for Students.* Ed. Marie Rose Napierkowski. Vol. 4. Detroit: Gale, 1998. 335–39.

When quoting a journal or newspaper essay that is reprinted in a volume of *NfS,* the following form may be used:

Malak, Amin. "Margaret Atwood's *The Handmaid's Tale* and the Dystopian Tradition," *Canadian Literature* No. 112 (Spring, 1987), 9–16; excerpted and reprinted in *Novels for Students,* Vol. 4, ed. Marie Rose Napierkowski (Detroit: Gale, 1998), pp. 133–36.

When quoting material reprinted from a book that appears in a volume of *NfS,* the following form may be used:

Adams, Timothy Dow. "Richard Wright: Wearing the Mask," in *Telling Lies in Modern American Autobiography* (University of North Carolina Press, 1990), 69–83; excerpted and reprinted in *Novels for Students,* Vol. 1, ed. Diane Telgen (Detroit: Gale, 1997), pp. 59–61.

We Welcome Your Suggestions

The editor of *Novels for Students* welcomes your comments and ideas. Readers who wish to suggest novels to appear in future volumes, or who have other suggestions, are cordially invited to contact the editor. You may contact the editor via e-mail at: **ForStudentsEditors@gale.com.** Or write to the editor at:

Editor, *Novels for Students*
Gale
27500 Drake Road
Farmington Hills, MI 48331–3535

Literary Chronology

1819: George Eliot (born Mary Anne Evans) is born on November 22 at South Farm, Arbury, Warwickshire, England.

1860: George Eliot's *The Mill on the Floss* is published.

1866: H. G. Wells is born on September 21 in Bromley, England.

1871: Theodore Dreiser is born on August 27 in Terre Haute, Indiana.

1875: Thomas Mann is born on June 6 in Lubeck, Germany.

1880: George Eliot dies of a respiratory infection on December 21 in London.

1888: Raymond Chandler is born on July 23 in Chicago, Illinois.

1895: H. G. Wells's *The Time Machine* is published.

1902: John Steinbeck is born on February 27 in Salinas, California.

1903: Evelyn Waugh is born on October 28 in Hampstead, London, England.

1912: Thomas Mann's *Death in Venice* is published.

1920: Frank Herbert is born on October 8 in Tacoma, Washington.

1925: Theodore Dreiser's *An American Tragedy* is published.

1935: Thomas Keneally is born on October 7 in Sydney, Australia.

1937: John Steinbeck's *The Red Pony* is published.

1938: Evelyn Waugh's *Scoop* is published.

1939: Raymond Chandler's *The Big Sleep* is published.

1945: Theodore Dreiser dies of a heart attack on December 28 in Los Angeles.

1946: H. G. Wells dies on August 13 in London, England.

1948: Pearl Cleage is born on December 7 in Springfield, Massachusetts.

1951: Oscar Hijuelos is born on August 24 in New York City.

1955: Thomas Mann dies of phlebitis on August 12 in Zurich, Switzerland.

1957: Peter Høeg is born on May 17 in Copenhagen, Denmark.

1959: Raymond Chandler dies on March 26 in La Jolla, California, after a bout of pneumonia following a period of heavy drinking.

1966: Evelyn Waugh dies on April 10 in Combe Florey, Somerset, England.

1966: Sherman Alexie (born Sherman Joseph Alexie, Jr.) is born on October 7 in Wellpinit on the Spokane Reservation in eastern Washington.

1968: John Steinbeck dies of a heart attack on December 20 in New York City.

1972: Frank Herbert's *Soul Catcher* is published.

1982: Thomas Keneally's *Schindler's List* is published.

1986: Frank Herbert dies of complications following cancer surgery on February 11 in Madison, Wisconsin.

1989: Oscar Hijuelos's *The Mambo Kings Play Songs of Love* is published.

1990: Oscar Hijuelos receives the Pulitzer Prize for fiction for *The Mambo Kings Play Songs of Love*.

1993: Peter Høeg's *Smilla's Sense of Snow* is published.

1993: Sherman Alexie's *The Lone Ranger and Tonto Fistfight in Heaven* is published.

1997: Tessa Bridal's *The Tree of Red Stars* is published.

1997: Pearl Cleage's *What Looks Like Crazy on an Ordinary Day* is published.

Acknowledgments

The editors wish to thank the copyright holders of the excerpted criticism included in this volume and the permissions managers of many book and magazine publishing companies for assisting us in securing reproduction rights. We are also grateful to the staffs of the Detroit Public Library, the Library of Congress, the University of Detroit Mercy Library, Wayne State University Purdy/ Kresge Library Complex, and the University of Michigan Libraries for making their resources available to us. Following is a list of the copyright holders who have granted us permission to reproduce material in this volume of *Novels for Students* *(NfS)*. Every effort has been made to trace copyright, but if omissions have been made, please let us know.

COPYRIGHTED MATERIALS IN *NfS*, VOLUME 17, WERE REPRODUCED FROM THE FOLLOWING PERIODICALS:

The Explicator, v. 55, Spring, 1997. Copyright (c) 1997 by Helen Dwight Reid Educational Foundation. Reproduced with permission of the Helen Dwight Reid Educational Foundation, published by Heldref Publications, 1319 18th Street, NW, Washington, DC 20036-1802.—*Meanjin*, v. 42, March, 1983 for "The Ned Kelly of Cracow: Keneally's *Schindler's Ark*," by Michael Hollington. Reproduced by permission of the author.—*PMLA*, v. 87, January, 1972. Copyright (c) 1972 by the Modern Language Association of America. Reprinted by permission of the Modern Language Association of America.—*Scandinavian Studies*, v. 69, Winter, 1997 for "A House of Mourning: *Frøken Smillas fornemmelse for sne*," by Mary Kay Norseng. Reproduced by permission of the publisher and the author.—*Southern Folklore*, v. 57, 2000. Reproduced by permission.—*Studies in English Literature, 1500–1900*, v. xiv, Autumn, 1974 for "Maggie Tulliver's Long Suicide," by Elizabeth Ermarth. (c) 1974 William Marsh Rice University. Reprinted by permission of the publisher and the author.

COPYRIGHTED MATERIALS IN *NfS*, VOLUME 17, WERE REPRODUCED FROM THE FOLLOWING BOOKS:

Perez Firmat, Gustavo. From *Everynight Life: Culture and Dance in Latin America*. Edited by Celeste Fraser Delgado and José Esteban Muñoz. Duke University Press, 1997. (c) 1997 Duke University Press. All rights reserved. Reproduced by permission.—Shatzkin, Roger. From *The Modern American Novel and the Movies*. Edited by Gerald Peary and Roger Shatzkin. Frederick Ungar Publishing Co., 1978. Copyright (c) 1978 by Frederick Ungar Publishing Co., Inc. Reproduced by permission.—Speir, Jerry. From *Raymond Chandler*. Frederick Ungar Publishing Company, 1981. Copyright (c) 1981 by Frederick Ungar Publishing Co., Inc. Reproduced by permission.—Swales, Martin. From *Thomas Mann: A Study*. Rowman and Littlefield, 1980. (c) Martin Swales 1980. Reproduced by permission.

PHOTOGRAPHS AND ILLUSTRATIONS APPEARING IN *NfS*, VOLUME 17, WERE

RECEIVED FROM THE FOLLOWING SOURCES:

Alexie, Sherman, photograph by Jim Cooper. AP/Wide World Photos. Reproduced by permission.—Andresen, Bjorn, as Tadzio and Dirk Bogarde as Gustav von Aschenbach in the 1971 film based on the novella by Thomas Mann, photograph. The Kobal Collection / Alfa. Reproduced by permission.—Banderas, Antonio, and Armand Assante, in the film "Mambo Kings," 1991, photograph. The Kobal Collection. Reproduced by permission.—Bogart, Humphrey, as Philip Marlowe, with Lauren Bacall, scene from the film "The Big Sleep," directed by Howard Hawks, based on the novel by Raymond Chandler. The Kobal Collection/Warner Bros. Reproduced by permission.—Bridal, Tessa, photograph by Eloise Klein. Courtesy of Milkweed Editions. Reproduced by permission.—Castro, Fidel. Portrait of Fidel Castro. AP/Wide World Photos. Reproduced by permission.—Chandler, Raymond, photograph. The Library of Congress.—Cleage, Pearl, photograph. (c) Barry Forbus. Reproduced by permission of Pearl Cleage.—Clift, Montgomery, and Shelley Winters in the film "A Place in the Sun," 1951, photograph. The Kobal Collection. Reproduced by permission.—Dreiser, Theodore, photograph by Pirie MacDonald. The Library of Congress.— Egede, Hans, holding a staff, statue, photograph by Wolfgang Kaehler. Corbis. Reproduced by Corbis Corporation.—Eliot, George, drawing. The Library of Congress.—Fitzgerald, Geraldine, being consoled by Griffith Jones, in a scene from the film version of George Eliot's novel, "The Mill on the Floss," directed by Tim Whelan. The Kobal Collection. Reproduced by permission.—Fleet Street in London, England, during the 1930s, photograph by E. O. Hoppe. Corbis. Reproduced by Corbis Corporation.—Guevara (Serna), Ernesto, photograph. AP/Wide World Photos. Reproduced by permission.—Herbert, Frank, photograph. AP/Wide World Photos. Reproduced by permission.— Hijuelos, Oscar, photograph. AP/Wide World Photos. Reproduced by permission.—Høeg, Peter, in Rockefeller Plaza, photograph by Marty Reichenthal. AP/Wide World Photos. Reproduced by per-

mission.—Keneally, Thomas, sits in an Eritrean cafe, photograph. AP/Wide World Photos. Reproduced by permission.—Large crowd of workers and students gathering in downtown Montevideo, Uruguay, in support of a general strike against President Juan M. Bordaberry's government, photograph. AP/Wide World Photos. Reproduced by permission.—Large group of Ethiopian fighters gathered together during the Italian invasion of Abyssinia. (c) Hulton-Deutsch Collection/Corbis. Reproduced by Corbis Corporation.—Mann, Thomas, photograph. The Library of Congress.— Means, Russell (addressing crowd, standing near statue), 1970, photograph. AP/Wide World Photos. Reproduced by permission.—Miles, Peter, Robert Mitchum, in the film "The Red Pony," based on the book by John Steinbeck, photograph. The Kobal Collection. Reproduced by permission.— Neeson, Liam, Ben Kingsley (Neeson, holding hand over typewriter as Kingsley types), in the film "Schindler's List," 1993, photograph. The Kobal Collection. Reproduced by permission.—Ormond, Julia, as Smilla Jasperson, in a scene from "Smilla," directed by Billie August, based on a novel by Peter Høeg, photograph. The Kobal Collection/ Constantin Films. Reproduced by permission.— Poster informing people of the precautions they can take to avoid infection from the AIDS virus, photograph by Sue Ford. Ecoscene/Corbis. Reproduced by Corbis Corporation.—The profiles of various primates illustrate the evolution of anthropomorphic facial features, photograph. National Institutes of Health/Corbis. Reproduced by permission.—Scene from the film "Mill on the Floss" by George Eliot, engraving. Hulton Archive/Getty Images. Reproduced by permission.—Schindler, Oskar, and a group of Jews he rescued, photograph. Prof. Leopold Pfeffergerg-Page/USHMM Photo Archives.—Silverheels, Jay, sitting next to Clayton Moore (The Lone Ranger), photograph. Corbis. Reproduced by permission.—Steinbeck, John, photograph. National Archives and Records Administration.—Waugh, Evelyn, photograph. Mark Gerson Photography. Reproduced by permission.—Wells, Herbert George, photograph. AP/Wide World Photos. Reproduced with permission.

Contributors

Bryan Aubrey: Aubrey holds a Ph.D. in English and has published many articles on twentieth-century literature. Entry on *Scoop*. Original essays on *Scoop*, *The Tree of Red Stars*, and *What Looks Like Crazy on an Ordinary Day*.

Jennifer Bussey: Bussey holds a master's degree in interdisciplinary studies and a bachelor's degree in English literature. She is an independent writer specializing in literature. Entry on *What Looks Like Crazy on an Ordinary Day*. Original essay on *What Looks Like Crazy on an Ordinary Day*.

Alison Leigh DeFrees: DeFrees is a writer and editor living in Brooklyn, New York. When not writing reviews for Gale, she writes grants for a Brooklyn non-profit organization, and works on novels and screenplays. Original essay on *Soul Catcher*.

Joyce Hart: Hart has degrees in English literature and creative writing and focuses her writing on literary themes. Entries on *The Red Pony* and *The Tree of Red Stars*. Original essays on *The Red Pony*, *Soul Catcher*, *The Tree of Red Stars*, and *What Looks Like Crazy on an Ordinary Day*.

Diane Henningfeld: Henningfeld is a professor of English literature and composition who has written widely for educational and academic publishers. Entry on *Smilla's Sense of Snow*. Original essay on *Smilla's Sense of Snow*.

David Kelly: Kelly is an instructor of creative writing and literature at several colleges in Illinois.

Entry on *The Mambo Kings Play Songs of Love*. Original essays on *The Mambo Kings Play Songs of Love*, *Scoop*, and *The Tree of Red Stars*.

Laura Kryhoski: Kryhoski is currently working as a freelance writer. She has also taught English literature in addition to English as a Second Language overseas. Original essay on *Schindler's List*.

Uma Kukathas: Kukathas is a freelance writer. Entry on *Schindler's List*. Original essay on *Schindler's List*.

Daryl McDaniel: McDaniel is a writer with a bachelor's degree from the University of Michigan. Original essay on *Scoop*.

Candyce Norvell: Norvell is an independent writer who specializes in literature. Entry on *An American Tragedy*. Original essay on *An American Tragedy*.

Ryan D. Poquette: Poquette has a bachelor's degree in English and specializes in writing about literature. Entry on *Soul Catcher*. Original essays on *Schindler's List* and *Soul Catcher*.

Chris Semansky: Semansky is an instructor of English literature and composition and writes on literature and culture for several publications. Entries on *The Big Sleep*, *Death in Venice*, *The Lone Ranger and Tonto Fistfight in Heaven*, and *The Time Machine*. Original essays on *The Big Sleep*, *Death in Venice*, *The Lone Ranger and*

Tonto Fistfight in Heaven, and *The Time Machine*.

Kelly Winters: Winters is a freelance writer. Entry on *The Mill on the Floss*. Original essay on *The Mill on the Floss*.

Paul Witcover: Witcover is an editor and writer whose fiction and critical essays appear regularly in magazines and online. Original essay on *Soul Catcher*.

An American Tragedy

Theodore Dreiser

1925

Theodore Dreiser's massive novel *An American Tragedy* was published in December 1925 in two volumes. Coming in the middle of Dreiser's long career, it was the first novel to earn him fame and wealth, though not the first to be controversial.

An American Tragedy is a detailed portrayal of the dark side of the American Dream—the story of what can happen when an ordinary man's desire for wealth and status overwhelms his moral sense. Dreiser built the novel around a real-life crime after spending years researching incidents in which men murdered women with whom they had been romantically involved but who had become inconvenient for one reason or another (often because of an unwanted pregnancy, as in the novel). Dreiser chose as his starting point the case of Chester Gillette, who drowned his pregnant girlfriend in a New York lake in 1906. Like the novel's Clyde Griffiths, Chester Gillette was electrocuted for his crime.

An American Tragedy is widely considered Dreiser's best novel and an important work of American naturalism. Naturalism, which began in Europe and flowered in America, is a literary style that explores the premise that individuals' fates are determined by a combination of hereditary and environmental constraints that leave no room for free will or true individual choice. Some scholars and critics consider *An American Tragedy* one of the greatest American novels of any style or period.

Theodore Dreiser

Author Biography

Theodore Dreiser was born in Terre Haute, Indiana, on August 27, 1871. He was the twelfth of thirteen children of John, a German immigrant, and Sarah Dreiser. The family was poor, quarrelsome, and prone to scandal. John suffered permanent injury in an accident, which made it difficult for him to provide for his family. The children, however, were never told about his health problems and thought their father was simply a failure. In *Dictionary of Literary Biography*, Philip L. Gerber writes that Dreiser's niece, Vera Dreiser, described the household in which her uncle grew up as being characterized by "superstition, fanaticism, ignorance, poverty, constant humiliation." In addition, the family was constantly on the move, and Dreiser's formal education was spotty. The echoes of this chaos and humiliation are clearly heard in Dreiser's fiction.

Dreiser left home and moved to Chicago when he was fifteen. He filled in the gaps in his education by reading, especially classic literature, and survived by working at low-paying jobs in stores and restaurants. In 1889 and 1890, he attended Indiana University, but this was his last attempt at formal education. He returned to Chicago and was able to get a job as a reporter. Over the next few years, Dreiser wrote for newspapers in St. Louis, Pittsburgh, and New York. He married Sara Osborne White in 1898; the marriage ended in divorce in 1910.

As a journalist, Dreiser observed two disparate elements of American society: the few who were becoming fabulously wealthy, and the many who spent their lives laboring in poverty. Just as American ideas of equality and opportunity began to ring false for Dreiser, he discovered European writers and philosophers who gave voice to his disillusionment. Among these were novelists Emile Zola, Honoré de Balzac, Thomas Hardy, and Leo Tolstoy and philosopher Herbert Spencer.

Reading the works of these novelists showed Dreiser a new form in which he, too, could express his views on society. His first novel, *Sister Carrie*, published in 1900, drew on his family experiences, including that of his sister, Emma, who, like the novel's main character, ran away with a married man. *Sister Carrie* and *An American Tragedy*, published in 1925, are Dreiser's most lasting and important works. Many critics and scholars consider Dreiser the foremost author of American naturalism, a literary movement that adopted ideas popular in science at the time, especially the idea that each human being's fate is wholly determined by heredity and environment, leaving no room for individual will. *An American Tragedy* is widely considered the signature novel of American naturalism.

In 1930, Dreiser was nominated for the Nobel Prize in literature, but the award went to Sinclair Lewis, who praised Dreiser in his acceptance speech. Dreiser married Helen Patges Richardson on June 13, 1944. In 1945, the American Academy of Arts and Letters presented him with its Award of Merit. Dreiser died of a heart attack on December 28 of that year in Los Angeles.

Plot Summary

Book 1

An American Tragedy opens on a summer evening in Kansas City, Missouri, in the early years of the twentieth century. Dreiser introduces twelve-year-old Clyde Griffiths along with his family: his father, Asa, and mother, Elvira, poor evangelists who run a mission in a shabby part of the city; and his two sisters and one brother. From the beginning, Clyde is antagonistic toward his parents' beliefs and activities. He is entranced by the material world that his parents shun. As a teenager, Clyde gets a series of jobs in increasingly glamorous settings—from streetcorner (as a newsboy) to department store basement to drugstore to upscale hotel—that take him farther and farther from his parents' dingy life. All the while, Clyde daydreams about his rich Uncle Samuel who owns a factory in Lycurgus, New York.

In his bellhop job at the Hotel Green-Davidson, Clyde makes friends with other young men whose desires match his own. Together they indulge in alcohol, prostitutes, and other illicit pleasures. Clyde lies to his parents about his activities.

Clyde has a relationship with Hortense Briggs, a coarse girl who uses her sexuality to manipulate Clyde. The two go on a car trip with friends. A young man named Willard Sparser has stolen the car and, driving recklessly, he hits and kills a pedestrian, flees the accident scene, and finally crashes into a pile of lumber. Clyde runs away from the crashed car to avoid sharing responsibility for these crimes.

Book 2

Book 2 opens three years later. Clyde is now living in Lycurgus. He fled to Chicago after the car accident and, at his job at the Union League Club, encountered his wealthy uncle, who was on a business trip. Samuel Griffiths gave his nephew a job in his shirt factory.

Clyde's cousin Gilbert resents him. Being the nephew of the factory owner makes Clyde the social superior of the workers, but most of his relatives see him as an inferior. Clyde is briefly attracted to a lascivious factory worker named Rita Dickerman. When his uncle promotes him, though, he shifts his sights higher. He meets and is infatuated with the wealthy and beautiful Sondra Finchley; but she is out of his reach. Clyde then begins an affair with Roberta Alden, a poor but pretty and sensitive factory worker.

Clyde soon loses interest in Roberta. Meanwhile, Sondra pretends that she is attracted to Clyde, using him to punish Gilbert for acting cool toward her. Clyde hopes to marry Sondra, and she develops some degree of real interest in him. Roberta soon finds that she is pregnant and presses Clyde to marry her.

Desperate at the thought of losing his opportunity for wealth and status, Clyde agrees to marry Roberta but instead plans to kill her. He takes her out in a boat intending to capsize it and make Roberta's drowning look like an accident. Things

Media Adaptations

- *An American Tragedy* was first adapted to film in a 1931 production with the same title directed by Josef von Sternberg and starring Phillips Holmes as Clyde. The 1951 film *A Place in the Sun* is also an adaptation of Dreiser's novel, although the characters' names have been changed. The film stars Montgomery Clift and Elizabeth Taylor and also features appearances by Shelley Winters and Raymond Burr.

- The novel also has been adapted in play form as *An American Tragedy*, by Patrick Kearney, in 1927, and as *An American Tragedy: The Trial of Clyde Griffiths*, by Erwin Piscator, in the 1920s.

do not happen as Clyde has planned. He changes his mind about killing Roberta, and when the boat overturns and hits Roberta on the head, it really is an accident. Roberta comes to the surface and cries out for help, but Clyde does not help her.

Book 3

Clyde flees the scene of Roberta's death, but circumstantial evidence, including letters to Clyde from both Roberta and Sondra, leads to his arrest for first-degree murder. Sondra leaves town, and her identity is never publicly revealed. Samuel Griffiths hires attorneys for Clyde, and they devise a complex defense strategy for a client whom they view as extremely inept. Clyde lies to everyone, including his attorneys, about his intentions and actions.

After a long trial, a jury finds Clyde guilty. His mother's efforts to have his death sentence overturned or commuted fail. Clyde tells the truth about his plan to murder Roberta to only one person, the Reverend Duncan McMillan. When McMillan shares this confession with the governor, Clyde's last hope is extinguished. Clyde is executed. He goes to the electric chair bewildered as to why McMillan was not willing to lie for him. Clyde also dies unsure of the extent of his own guilt and of the line between truth and untruth, reality and fantasy.

Characters

Roberta Alden

Roberta is a poor, shy, somewhat naive girl who works in the factory where Clyde is a supervisor. She is prettier and more sensitive than most of the "factory girls," but these qualities do not help her prospects in life; her poverty and her position as a factory worker consign her to a low position in society.

Although Roberta hopes to improve her lot in life by getting an education and by marrying as well as she can, she repeatedly breaks the rules of social conduct. She talks with the foreign workers at the factory, which is considered taboo. She enters into a romantic relationship with Clyde, her supervisor, which is also taboo. Then, she has a sexual relationship with Clyde, breaking not only society's moral code but her own.

When Roberta becomes pregnant, she first tries to get an abortion and then considers killing herself. Finally, she coerces Clyde into agreeing to marry her. Clyde, however, decides to murder her instead and lures her to an outing on a lake, where she drowns.

Titus Alden

Roberta's father, Titus Alden is a poor farmer. He wants revenge for Roberta's death.

Alvin Belknap

Belknap is Clyde's defense attorney. It is Clyde's wealthy uncle, Samuel Griffiths, who hires Belknap.

Hortense Briggs

Hortense is an attractive but coarse Kansas City girl who manipulates Clyde's emotions to get him to buy things for her.

Burton Burleigh

The assistant district attorney in Lycurgus, Burleigh tampers with evidence in Clyde's case to ensure that he is convicted of first-degree murder.

Rita Dickerman

Rita is a promiscuous girl who pursues Clyde in Lycurgus.

Sondra Finchley

A wealthy and beautiful young woman who lives in Lycurgus, Sondra personifies all the things Clyde values and desires: money and luxuries, social status, and a life of carefree pleasure. Clyde so desperately wants Sondra and all that she possesses that he plots to murder Roberta when Sondra shows an interest in him.

When Clyde arrives in Lycurgus, Sondra quickly and correctly sizes him up as a poor relation of the local Griffiths, and she has no interest in him. However, when she becomes upset with Clyde's cousin Gilbert, she decides to feign interest in Clyde to irritate Gilbert. For reasons that are a mystery to her, Sondra develops some degree of real attraction to Clyde. Though she is young, she is sophisticated and careful enough to be suspect of these feelings for an unlikely suitor. In spite of the attraction she feels, she always maintains a certain teasing distance between herself and Clyde, and she never really treats him as an equal. Clyde, on the contrary, responds to Sondra's interest by being willing to sacrifice everything in order to gain her.

When Roberta drowns and Clyde is arrested, Sondra leaves town. Because of her father's wealth and position, her name is never made public during the trial. She writes Clyde one last letter, expressing some sympathy for him, but she types the letter and does not sign it, maintaining her social and emotional distance from him.

Asa Griffiths

Asa is Clyde's father, a poor evangelist who, with his wife, runs a mission and preaches on the streets of Kansas City. Asa is dull and ineffectual; he does not understand human nature or society, and he does not know how to respond to the tragedies that befall his children.

Bella Griffiths

Bella is the daughter of Samuel and Elizabeth Griffiths, Clyde's uncle and aunt. She is gregarious and willing to help Clyde enter her social circle.

Clyde Griffiths

The novel's main character, Clyde is driven all his life in pursuit of his idea of the American dream. He is materialistic and pleasure-seeking, and he lacks any strong moral center. He is willing to lie and to indulge in unethical and illegal behavior in pursuit of his goals, and he repeatedly runs from difficulties, especially those he creates for himself. For Clyde, there is no clear line between reality and fantasy, right and wrong. To escape his sordid life, he daydreams of wealth and luxury. To live with his acts of cowardice, he rationalizes them.

The son of poor, shabby evangelists, Clyde, even as a child, is much more attracted to the material than to the spiritual. As a teenager, he gets a series of jobs, from drugstore clerk to hotel bellhop, designed to take him out of his parents' world and into a society that revolves around money and pleasure. A dreamer, Clyde has vague hopes of being catapulted to wealth and status by some happy accident or beneficent relationship. It never occurs to him that he might gain all he wants through some combination of hard work and ingenuity. Clyde is too weak-willed to be the master of his own fate, so he dreams that circumstances will somehow transport him to a better life.

When Clyde runs into his rich uncle, Samuel, in Chicago, it seems that his dreams have begun to come true. Samuel Griffiths gives Clyde a job in his factory in upstate New York. Clyde's entry into upper-class society is not as automatic as he expects, but eventually he does gain the favor of the wealthy and beautiful Sondra Finchley. Clyde sees Sondra as his ticket to the life he has always wanted. So desperate is he to gain money and status through her that he plans to murder Roberta, his pregnant girlfriend, so that he can avoid scandal (the scandal of abandoning the woman he has impregnated and of having an illegitimate child) and be with Sondra.

Although Clyde has planned Roberta's death, when it comes it is as much a product of chance and circumstance as it is of Clyde's will. Clyde is actually trying to apologize to Roberta for striking her when he inadvertently overturns the boat and it hits Roberta's head. True to character, Clyde at this moment chooses to run away; although Roberta cries out to him for help, he swims away and lets her drown.

Clyde is captured, convicted of first-degree murder, and electrocuted, although he testifies that Roberta's drowning was an accident. He rationalizes that it is true to say it was an accident because Roberta's death did not happen exactly has he had envisioned it. Even in the last moments of his life, the line between truth and untruth—between reality and fantasy—is blurred in Clyde's mind.

Elizabeth Griffiths

Elizabeth is Clyde's aunt (Samuel's wife). She invites him to dinner out of a sense of obligation.

Elvira Griffiths

Elvira is Clyde's mother. She runs a Christian mission along with her husband. She stands by Clyde and tries to get his sentence commuted even though she doubts his innocence. Once Clyde's fate is sealed, his mother's desire is to see to the salvation of his soul, and she sends a minister to see him. In spite of her son's death, her faith in a kind and merciful God is unshaken.

Esta Griffiths

Esta is Clyde's older sister. She runs away with a touring actor, who makes her pregnant and then deserts her.

Gilbert Griffiths

Gilbert is Clyde's cousin, the son of Samuel and Elizabeth. He is not as good-looking as Clyde, and he resents Clyde's intrusion into the life of his family and into their business.

Russell Griffiths

Russell is the son of Clyde's sister Esta and the actor who deserts her. He looks much like Clyde, and Clyde's parents adopt him.

Samuel Griffiths

Samuel Griffiths is Asa's brother and Clyde's uncle. He is a successful businessman in Lycurgus, New York. When he meets Clyde in Chicago, he feels a familial obligation to his nephew and gives him a job in his factory in New York.

Oscar Hegglund

Oscar is one of Clyde's fellow bellhops at the Green-Davidson Hotel. He provides Clyde with opportunities to experience worldly pleasures that are new to him.

Fred Heit

The county coroner, Heit is the first person to suggest that Roberta may have been murdered.

Reuben Jephson

Jephson is Belknap's law partner. It is Jephson who comes up with the strategy the attorneys will use to defend Clyde. This complex and ultimately unsuccessful strategy is based on the premise that Clyde is too cowardly and inept to plan and carry out a murder. Jephson assures Clyde that he will be found innocent.

Orville W. Mason

Mason is the politically minded, self-serving district attorney who succeeds in getting a first-degree murder conviction in Clyde's case.

Reverend Duncan McMillan

McMillan is a good man who wants to save Clyde's soul but also contributes to his death. Clyde confides in McMillan that he intended to murder Roberta. McMillan later tells this to the governor, who, based on the information, refuses to commute Clyde's sentence. Clyde does not understand why McMillan did not lie for him, and McMillan feels some guilt over his role in Clyde's death.

Thomas Ratterer

Thomas is a bellhop at the Green-Davidson Hotel, along with Clyde. He eventually helps Clyde get a job at the Union League Club in Chicago, where Clyde runs into his wealthy uncle, Samuel.

Willard Sparser

Willard is a friend of Oscar Hegglund. He steals a car and, driving recklessly, hits and kills a girl. Clyde is a passenger in the car and runs from the scene along with the others to avoid taking responsibility for the death.

Themes

The American Dream as Illusion

The idea of the American Dream is that all Americans have the opportunity to improve themselves economically and socially. In America, it is said, a person's circumstances at birth place no limit on his or her potential; people can make of themselves whatever they choose and rise as high as they are willing to climb.

If Dreiser's message in *An American Tragedy* can be summed up in a sentence, it is: the American Dream is a lie. Dreiser creates a microcosm of America by introducing characters that represent every stratum of society and every point on the spectrum of humanity. Then, he shows that their lives reflect the opposite of the American Dream. Clyde Griffiths, the Everyman at the center of the novel, cannot make of himself anything other than what he was when he was born: poor and not particularly perceptive or resourceful. When he sees the glittering material things and the pleasures that comprise success, he desires them but lacks the attributes that would allow him to at-

Topics for Further Study

- At one point during the writing of *An American Tragedy*, Dreiser thought of entitling it *Mirage*. Why do you think he considered this title? Which of the two titles do you think better suits the book, and why?

- Do you agree with the jury that convicted Clyde of first-degree murder? Why or why not? If you disagree, what crime, if any, was Clyde guilty of, and what punishment did he deserve?

- Do some research to learn about the crime on which Dreiser based his book. Discuss similarities and differences between the true story and the fictional one, and speculate about why Dreiser made the changes he did.

- Do some research to learn about life in the United States in the early 1900s. Compare what you learn to Dreiser's portrayal. Does the author provide an accurate, balanced portrayal of this period of history?

- Learn about the writer Horatio Alger and read one or more of his stories. Write an essay explaining how Alger's view of American life differs from Dreiser's. Tell which author's view is more like your own, and explain why you share this view.

tain them legitimately. In addition, the deck is stacked against him; the "haves" are devoted to keeping the "have nots" in their place. Because of this, most of his wealthy relatives do not accept him as their equal.

Clyde becomes so obsessed with having what his own shortcomings and other people's prejudices prevent him from attaining that he is willing to commit murder for the sake of obtaining his dreams. Dreiser's point is not at all that Clyde comes to a bad end because he is a bad person. To the contrary, Dreiser conveys that Clyde comes to a bad end because he is an average person who believed in the American Dream and tried to make it come true.

While *An American Tragedy* is Clyde's story, Dreiser drives home his point in the lives of all his other major players. Roberta, whose dreams of improving her lot are much more modest than Clyde's, hopes to marry a man who is her social superior and, as a result, ends up dead. The "haves," Gilbert and Sondra, are born not only rich but also possessing a cleverness about manipulating their environment that is lacking in Clyde and Roberta. The "haves" easily retain the wealth and privilege to which they were born.

In Dreiser's America, the American Dream is an illusion. Each person's fate is decided before he or she is born. Attempts to move beyond one's circumstances at birth lead to disaster.

Moral Ambiguity

Morality is far from black-and-white in *An American Tragedy*. The most glaring example of moral ambiguity is in the novel's central event—Roberta's death. Although the jury's verdict is clear, the degree of Clyde's guilt is ambiguous, both in readers' minds and in Clyde's. While he coldly planned Roberta's murder, Clyde did not carry out his plan. The chain of events that led to Roberta's death really was an accident. Clyde's only purposeful act was to swim away after she cried for help. While it is clear that he should have tried to help her, it is not at all clear that he could have. He is guilty, but just how guilty is clear to no one.

Dreiser also telegraphs moral ambiguity through his religious characters, working from the premise that religion purports to set the highest moral standards. Clyde's parents are evangelists who shun worldly goods and attitudes for "higher" values. However, their lives are pathetic and ineffectual. They are unable to protect their daughter from betrayal and abandonment or their son from the electric chair. Perhaps even more telling, their lives of sacrifice and self-denial have not inspired even their own children to follow their example. Dreiser seems to say that renouncing the material world has no better results than embracing it.

Reverend McMillan provides a particularly poignant example of moral ambiguity. He is a well-meaning man who visits Clyde in prison hoping to save his soul. Trusting McMillan's intentions, Clyde admits to him what he has told no one else: that he did plan to murder Roberta. McMillan at first feels happy that he has helped Clyde "come clean." But, later, McMillan directly contributes to Clyde's death. The governor who could commute Clyde's sentence asks McMillan if Clyde is truly guilty, and McMillan tells him of Clyde's confession. McMillan's revelation leads to the execution of a man, who, while certainly guilty, may not be guilty of first-degree murder. McMillan's adherence to a high moral standard does not necessarily bring about a just result. In addition to ending Clyde's life, it also causes Clyde to go to his death regretting that he ever trusted anyone. Even McMillan is aware of this and later questions his action.

Style

Naturalism

Many scholars consider *An American Tragedy* the defining work of American naturalism, and the novel does incorporate all the hallmarks of the naturalist movement.

Naturalism emerged in France in the 1870s and 1880s in response to new philosophical and scientific ideas, especially Charles Darwin's theory of evolution. Émile Zola defined the movement in France. It flowered in the United States from the final years of the nineteenth century through World War I and into the 1920s. The standard-bearers of American naturalism, in addition to Dreiser, are Stephen Crane, Jack London, Frank Norris, O. Henry, and poet Edgar Lee Masters.

At the core of naturalism is determinism, the idea that an individual's course in life is wholly determined by some combination of animal instinct, heredity, and environment. The individual will is said to be incapable of operating outside the influence of these powerful forces. As in Darwin's theory, only those who are genetically suited to their environment will survive and prosper—a principle most often expressed as "the survival of the fittest."

Naturalist writers portray these principles by creating ordinary characters, placing them in extraordinary or challenging circumstances, and narrating their reactions in a dispassionate, reportorial style. Thus, Dreiser draws Clyde as an Everyman who is motivated by animal instincts (the drive for sex and for a desirable mate, for example). His challenge is that he is born poor in a society that values only money and the pleasures it can buy. The child of weak, ineffectual parents, Clyde is not equipped by heredity to succeed in this environment, where people compete for power, position, and wealth. He is not "fit," and his destiny is failure. The same is true of his female counterpart, Roberta. The children of the wealthy and powerful, however, inherit not only wealth but also the attributes they need to master their environment. Therefore, they succeed, usually with very little effort.

Doubling

Dreiser liberally uses the technique of doubling throughout *An American Tragedy*, creating doubles for both characters and events.

To highlight the contrasts between the lives of the poor and those of the rich, Dreiser creates his significant characters in pairs: Clyde's upper-class counterpart is his cousin Gilbert, and Roberta's is Sondra; Clyde's parents have doubles in his aunt and uncle; and so on.

Adding to the novel's complexity, Dreiser also pairs each significant character in the first part of the book (in Kansas City) with a double who appears later (in Lycurgus). Very early in the story, Clyde's sister Esta is seduced, impregnated, and abandoned by a traveling actor. Much later, Roberta appears as her double, seduced, impregnated, and abandoned in the most terrible and final way by Clyde, who is also an itinerant (neither from nor permanently settled in Lycurgus) and also an "actor" (a deeply and consistently dishonest man who lies about everything from his family background to his murderous intentions). In Kansas City, Clyde has a relationship with a woman of loose morals named Hortense Briggs; her counterpart in Lycurgus is Rita Dickerman.

Dreiser provides events in pairs as well. One striking example is that, in Kansas City, Clyde runs away from the wreckage of a car in which he has been a passenger and which has hit and killed a pedestrian. The double for this event is Clyde's swimming away from the capsized boat and Roberta as she cries for his help.

The doubling of events serves several purposes. First, the earlier event in each pair is a foreshadowing of the later one. Second, the doubling creates a predictable pattern and symmetrical structure for the novel. The perceptive reader comes to expect the second beat—a sensation similar to waiting for the other foot to fall. Third, the doubling of characters and events conveys Dreiser's message that Clyde cannot escape his predetermined fate. People and events are the same in Lycurgus and in Kansas City. Clyde may flee from one city and state to another, but he cannot bring about any meaningful change in his life. He is hemmed in by fate, and the many doubled events and characters of the novel seem to wall Clyde in, leaving him no room for escape.

Historical Context

The Roaring Twenties

The 1920s are variously known as the Roaring Twenties, the Jazz Age, and the Dance Age. They were a time of both success and excess. More Americans were rich than ever before, thanks to a booming stock market, rising land values, new inventions, and new ways of producing goods that made things affordable to more Americans. Even average-income Americans began to acquire conveniences that had been either unavailable or unaffordable just a few years before: cars, radios, indoor plumbing, electric refrigerators and washing machines, and more.

With so much money around and so many things to buy, many Americans focused on getting rich and having fun. Young women called flappers flouted traditional restrictions. They wore short skirts and short hair, and they spent their time dancing, going to movies, and drinking liquor. The use of illicit drugs and alcohol, illegal during Prohibition (1920–1933), surged along with the stock market.

The America of the 1920s produced countless young men like Clyde Griffiths, who found themselves excited by and obsessed with a world that glittered with a thousand new pleasures. Some of these young men—even some who, like Clyde, were born poor—did get rich, through some combination of intelligence, ambition, resourcefulness, hard work, and luck. Many others did not. Some who did not become fabulously wealthy nevertheless did well. The arts and sports thrived along with industry; writers (including Dreiser, of course), musicians, movie stars, and baseball players earned fame with their talents.

Not everyone got rich or famous, or even lived better than they had before. Farmers (like Roberta's father in the novel) struggled, as the prices they could get for their crops dropped. This was partly because the end of World War I meant less demand for food. The military downsized drastically and needed less food for troops, and European nations were able to begin growing their own food again. New mechanized production processes also threw many people out of work and into poverty.

Compare & Contrast

- **1920s:** Pregnancy outside of marriage carries a heavy social stigma for the woman, the child, and, to a lesser extent, the man involved. The woman is often labeled a "tramp" for life and discriminated against socially and economically. The child is tagged a "bastard" and subjected to similar discrimination and humiliation.

  Today: In most elements of American society, pregnancy outside of marriage carries no social stigma. In fact, a few women, including some high-profile celebrities, choose to have and rear children on their own, without the involvement of a partner.

- **1920s:** Most states have strict anti-abortion laws that make it extremely difficult for a woman to obtain an abortion from a qualified physician. As a result, some women entrust themselves to abortionists who do not have medical training, or some even attempt to end their own pregnancies, as Roberta does in the novel.

  Today: Abortion has been legal in the United States since the 1973 Supreme Court decision Roe v. Wade. While abortion is still politically controversial, and while many states have passed restrictions on the circumstances under which abortion may be performed legally, abortions performed by qualified physicians are still available.

- **1920s:** The United States is experiencing an economic boom in which industrialists and the capitalists who back them are amassing great wealth. The boom ends abruptly with the stock market crash of 1929.

  Today: The United States has just experienced an economic boom in which high-tech entrepreneurs and those who invested in their ventures became wealthy very quickly. The year 2000 marks the beginning of the end, as stock markets retreat significantly for consecutive years, wiping out the wealth of some, and adversely affecting most companies and investors.

The 1920s was a time in which American society rearranged itself. Some people made great gains, others suffered loss and deprivation, and few ended up where they had started.

Critical Overview

At every moment from the publication of *An American Tragedy* to the present, the novel has had both staunch supporters and vocal detractors. Consistently, supporters have noted the importance of the novel's themes and the power of the story, while detractors have criticized the philosophy that underlies the story and the author's prose style.

When *An American Tragedy* debuted in 1925, it was a bestseller and a critical success. Even some critics who had panned Dreiser's previous novels praised this one. Stuart Sherman was a critic of the New Humanism school, which held that society brings out the best in people and helps them curb animal instincts. This philosophy was contrary to that of Dreiser and the naturalists. In spite of this philosophical opposition and his harsh criticism of Dreiser's earlier work, Sherman lauded *An American Tragedy* for its effective presentation of a worthy theme. Most of Dreiser's fellow writers, who were faithful in defending him from critics throughout his career, also praised *An American Tragedy*. H. G. Wells dubbed it "one of the very greatest novels of this century," according to the article *Theodore Dreiser*, by Philip L. Gerber, in the Twayne's United States Authors series. Similar accolades came from H. L. Mencken, Sherwood Anderson, Sinclair Lewis, and other contemporaries.

New York Times reviewer Robert L. Duffus wrote that, while "the story is far too long," still,

Montgomery Clift and Shelley Winters in A Place in the Sun, *the 1951 film version of Theodore Dreiser's novel* An American Tragedy

"Mr. Dreiser gives us as fine and haunting a study of crime and punishment as he or any other novelist has written in America." The novel, he concluded, "demands attention."

Dreiser and *An American Tragedy* remained in favor until the 1930s, when some critics turned against the author's work because of the author's endorsement of communism (which, it must be acknowledged, is reflected in this and other novels). This politically based criticism continued throughout the rest of Dreiser's life. In addition, academics of the New Criticism school, which emphasized the importance of correct and elegant use of language, denounced Dreiser's prose style. *Atlantic* magazine writer Michael Lydon, in a 1993 piece that praises Dreiser highly, acknowledges the long history of complaints about his prose. Lydon quotes Arnold Bennett as having said in 1930 that "Dreiser simply does not know how to write, never did know, never wanted to know." Even Dreiser's supporters acknowledge certain weaknesses in his prose but minimize their importance. Alfred Kazin, in his introduction to *The Stature of Theodore Dreiser: A Critical Survey of the Man and His Work*, quotes Saul Bellow's defense of Dreiser: "I think . . . that the

insistence on neatness and correctness is one of the signs of a modern nervousness and irritability. When has clumsiness in composition been felt as so annoying, so enraging?" Kazin agrees with Bellow, concluding that "what counts most with a writer is that his reach should be felt as well as his grasp, that words should be his means, not his ends." Kazin notes his concurrence with Malcolm Cowley's statement, "There are moments when Dreiser's awkwardness in handling words contributes to the force of his novels, since he seems to be groping in them for something on a deeper level than language."

Dreiser's politics have become less an issue over time, and while there is still some disagreement about the quality of his writing, his reputation is strong and secure. Lydon writes in his *Atlantic* article, "Justice to Theodore Dreiser":

> As the centenary of Dreiser's emergence approaches, it is time to drop the barbs and acknowledge, without reservation, that Theodore Dreiser is an immortal, a giant who stands with Cooper, Hawthorne, Melville, Twain, and James among Americans. . . . Except for O'Neill and Faulkner, Dreiser's contemporaries stand in his shade.

Criticism

Candyce Norvell

Norvell is an independent writer who specializes in literature. In this essay, Norvell argues that Dreiser's own life is perhaps the strongest argument against his worldview as expressed in his novel.

The worldview that Dreiser sets forth in *An American Tragedy* is the deterministic view that a person's fate is sealed from birth, determined by his or her particular heredity and environment in tandem with the animal instincts that affect all humans. This philosophical and literary view is based on the observation of Charles Darwin and other scientists that only those animals that are born with attributes that make them well-suited to their environment are able to survive and thrive. This idea is often referred to as "the survival of the fittest."

Hence, Clyde Griffiths and Roberta Alden are destined to fail in their attempts to better themselves economically and socially. Born poor and powerless, they will die that way, and they can do nothing to change this. In fact, it is their efforts to improve their circumstances that bring about their deaths. It is as if nature punishes them for trying to subvert that natural order.

This worldview was not one that Dreiser merely explored in the novel; it pervades his work, and it was the driving force in his personal philosophy and political views.

Because the world is vast and highly diverse, it is not surprising that people hold wildly divergent ideas about it. Arguments can be made for and against any number of conflicting worldviews because examples can be found to support virtually any generalization one cares to make. One can offer convincing arguments against the worldview expressed in *An American Tragedy*. Nor does this completely invalidate the deterministic view. What is surprising, though, is that one rather powerful argument against the novel's worldview is the life of its author. Dreiser's own life is a clear contradiction of the explanation of human life and society offered in the book.

Like Dreiser's other novels, *An American Tragedy* contains many autobiographical elements. Dreiser, like Clyde, grew up poor. If anything, his circumstances were even more dire than those of his fictional counterpart. His family was not only poverty-stricken, it was combative and unstable. The household splintered, regrouped, careened

> **"** Where, in this real-life story, is the hopelessness and futility, the inexorable working out of cruel forces of determinism, found in the fictional one? Dreiser's life is an embarrassment to his worldview.**"**

from one place to another. Although religion played a role, as it does in Clyde's family, in Dreiser's family that role was no more predictable or dependable than anything else in the child's world. There was no emotional or moral center.

Dreiser modeled Clyde's parents partly on his own. His father was disabled and inept; his mother played the martyr. The episode in which Clyde's sister Esta is seduced, impregnated, and abandoned by an actor mirrors a similar event in the life of one of Dreiser's sisters. Like Clyde's family, Dreiser's family spawned multiple scandals.

Clearly, Dreiser's heredity—one of the three legs on which his theory of determinism stands— did not mark him for success in the competitive, fast-changing, industrialized society into which he was born. He did not even get a solid education, partly because of his family's instability and partly because of his own unwillingness or inability to profit from formal education. So far, Dreiser looks very much like Clyde Griffiths, the character he invented to show the futility of efforts at economic and social self-improvement.

The similarities do not end in family background or childhood. Like Clyde, Dreiser had a strong sex drive and lacked an equally strong moral orientation that might have controlled it. Dreiser was unfaithful not only to his wife but to his mistresses. In a dozen different ways, Dreiser flouted social convention and generally accepted ethics. He plagiarized the work of fellow writers (poetry and journalism, not fiction). He aligned himself with communism, a political system that the vast majority of Americans condemned. By behavior as well as by birth, then, Dreiser seemed destined for failure. Indeed, for lesser offenses than his own, he punishes his characters in *An American Tragedy*

What Do I Read Next?

- *Murder in the Adirondacks* (1986), by Craig Brandon, is a nonfiction account of the murder around which Dreiser built his novel. Brandon includes more than one hundred photographs in his detailed account.

- Although Dreiser is best known as a novelist, he also wrote short fiction. Editor Howard Fast collected some of Dreiser's best short works in *The Best Short Stories of Theodore Dreiser* (1989).

- Dreiser also wrote two volumes of autobiography, *A Book about Myself* (1922, published in 1931 as *Newspaper Days*) and *Dawn* (1931). These books detail the early experiences that shaped Dreiser's fiction and his view of life.

- Dreiser's niece, psychologist Vera Dreiser, wrote *My Uncle Theodore* (1976) with Brett Howard. For her biography, Vera Dreiser had access to family sources.

- Jack London is another American naturalist writer, and his short novel *The Call of the Wild* (1903) is widely acclaimed as an important text of the movement. Its wilderness setting makes it a stark contrast to *An American Tragedy*, demonstrating how the same ideas of determinism and survival of the fittest play out in a very different environment.

- *The Red Badge of Courage* (1895), by Stephen Crane, is still another important example of American naturalism. It relates the battlefield experiences of a young Civil War soldier.

---

because that is what his worldview predicts: Those who break the law of the jungle, whether the jungle is a jungle or a small town in New York or American society at large, pay the price. Clyde's relationship with Roberta makes them both lawbreakers, as he is her superior at the factory. Clyde is even more drastically out of line in his relationship with Sondra, by far his social and economic better. These missteps lead to bigger missteps with increasingly greater consequences. Clyde and Roberta are out of their depth (the latter in a literal as well as figurative sense). They lack the inborn wit and self-control to manipulate events to their benefit, and the results are disastrous.

Not so in real life. While Dreiser's worldview predicts that the author should come to as bad an end as does the character with whom he shares so much, that is not at all what happened. In spite of Dreiser's lack of formal education or credentials, he was able to build a successful career as a journalist. Rather than being denied opportunity because he was poor and uneducated, rather than being punished severely for his moral misdeeds, Dreiser found editors who were willing to hire him based solely on his ability to write articles that readers liked. Neither nature nor human prejudice leapt up to foil him. When he decided to write fiction, publishers were willing to read and publish his work. Eventually, Dreiser became wealthy by doing what he liked to do and by writing what he wanted to write. *An American Tragedy* was turned into a successful Broadway play, and Dreiser got what was at the time a fortune for the film rights to the book. His fellow writers, many of them higher born and better educated, not only welcomed him into their midst but praised his work effusively.

Where, in this real-life story, is the hopelessness and futility, the inexorable working out of cruel forces of determinism, found in the fictional one? Dreiser's life is an embarrassment to his worldview.

The next question, then, is why did Dreiser hold, and promote in his writing, a worldview that so baldly contradicted his own experience of the world? Many scholars have answered that all the success and money that eventually came to Dreiser failed to erase his bitter memories of childhood poverty, instability, and humiliation. Perhaps he repeatedly recreated them in his fiction as a way of making the world acknowledge his own earlier suffering. Perhaps he was more altruistic than self-centered and wrote this way to call attention to the similar suffering of others. In any case, by his very success, he did not help his cause of convincing others that human beings are pawns to nature and the merciless law of the jungle. In the long run, life and the American society that he indicts in *An American Tragedy* were both kind to Dreiser. He rose from beginnings that were shabby both materially and intellectually to become one of the most acclaimed writers of his generation. He lived well, and when he died, in Hollywood, the epitome of all that glitters, he was buried among other celebrities in Forest Lawn cemetery. He could hardly have been more successful.

There was one thing—one fact in Dreiser's life that casts a slight shadow over his gleaming achievements. He was denied first the Pulitzer Prize and later the Nobel, in spite of the fact that many of his influential contemporaries thought he deserved one or both. Interestingly, the man who in his fiction portrayed the futility of trying to change fate campaigned for the prizes, especially the Nobel. His personal correspondence provides a record of his unsuccessful attempts to gain the Nobel Prize, and these efforts provide, in a limited sense, a parallel to Clyde's desperate efforts to win the similarly unattainable Sondra Finchley.

Dreiser did not get everything he wanted, and quite possibly he did not get everything he deserved. To acknowledge that he was denied one success in a life studded with successes is hardly to capitulate to his view that fate is merciless and immutable. In the world as it really is, against all odds and his own mindset, Theodore Dreiser got money, fame, and the respect of his peers. In the fictional world Dreiser created, Clyde Griffiths got the electric chair. Given that the real man and the fictional man started so similarly but ended so differently, nature and society have cause to complain that they have been slandered in *An American Tragedy*. Surely, things are not all that bad.

In a 1993 *Atlantic* article, Michael Lydon describes Dreiser as "the great gawk of American literature . . . the poor-born, ill-educated German-American Hoosier from Terre Haute, an oaf with mud on his shoes who invaded the drawing rooms of the genteel . . . " According to Dreiser's worldview, he should never have gotten in.

Source: Candyce Norvell, Critical Essay on *An American Tragedy*, in *Novels for Students*, The Gale Group, 2003.

Sources

Duffus, Robert L., "Too Big to Write Smaller," in *New York Times*, January 10, 1926, p. 24.

Gerber, Philip L., "Chapter Six: 'Society Should Ask Forgiveness': *An American Tragedy*," in *Theodore Dreiser*, Twayne's United States Authors Series Online, G. K. Hall & Co., 1999.

———, "Theodore Dreiser," in *Dictionary of Literary Biography*, Vol. 9: *American Novelists, 1910—1945*, edited by James J. Martine, Gale Research, 1981, pp. 236–57.

Kazin, Alfred, Introduction, in *The Stature of Theodore Dreiser: A Critical Survey of the Man and His Work*, edited by Alfred Kazin and Charles Shapiro, Indiana University Press, 1955, pp. 3–12.

Lydon, Michael, "Justice to Theodore Dreiser," in the *Atlantic*, Vol. 272, No. 2, August 1993, pp. 98–101.

Further Reading

Elias, Robert H., *Theodore Dreiser: Apostle of Nature*, 1948, amended edition, Cornell University Press, 1970.
Elias's biography, though written more than fifty years ago, is still considered perhaps the best scholarly treatment of the author and his work.

Gogol, Miriam, ed., *Theodore Dreiser: Beyond Naturalism*, New York University Press, 1995.
The ten writers in Gogol's collection each take a different approach to Dreiser's work, analyzing elements from his female characters to film versions of his novels. This collection is rare in that it offers modern views on Dreiser's work.

Kazin, Alfred, and Charles Shapiro, eds., *The Stature of Theodore Dreiser*, Indiana University Press, 1955.
Kazin and Shapiro collected criticism of Dreiser's work published from 1900 to 1955.

Pizer, Donald, ed., *The Cambridge Companion to American Realism and Naturalism*, Cambridge University Press, 1995.
This volume provides analyses of important texts in American realism and naturalism along with historical context and critical approaches.

The Big Sleep

Raymond Chandler

1939

Raymond Chandler began writing his first novel, *The Big Sleep*, in 1938, and it was published in 1939. Critics consider it the best of the seven that he wrote. Before publishing the novel, Chandler wrote stories for pulp fiction magazines. He uses the plot and details from three of these stories, "Killer in the Rain," "The Curtain," and "Finger Man" in *The Big Sleep*. Alfred A. Knopf, Chandler's American publisher, promoted the book by linking Chandler with Dashiell Hammett and James M. Cain, two popular novelists of detective fiction also published by Knopf. Chandler's writing, however, was more hard-boiled than Cain or Hammett's. The narrator of the novel, private investigator Philip Marlowe, is a world-weary tough guy who nevertheless lives by a chivalric code of honor and retains a sense of professional pride in his work. He negotiates the decadent world of crime-ridden Los Angeles, trying to sort out the details of an increasingly complex scheme to blackmail the Sternwoods, a wealthy family that made its money in oil. The story is as much a character study of a certain male American mindset as it is a "who-dunnit" crime story. More than simply a mystery novel, *The Big Sleep* has become a classic of American literature, with Chandler praised for his deft handling of plot, as well as his terse style and acerbic wit. Avon Books brought out the novel in paperback in 1943. In 1946, a film adaptation of *The Big Sleep* was released, starring Humphrey Bogart and Lauren Bacall, two of the biggest movie stars of the day.

Author Biography

Raymond Thornton Chandler was born July 23, 1888, in Chicago, Illinois, to Maurice Benjamin Chandler, a civil engineer, and Florence Thornton Chandler, a British immigrant. Chandlers' parents divorced when he was seven years old, he and his mother moved to London, England, to live with her family.

Chandler was educated at Dulwich College preparatory school, which taught students the value of public service and gentlemanly behavior as much as it did academic subjects such as mathematics and literature. After graduating from Dulwich, Chandler studied French in Paris, and spent time as a tutor in Germany before returning to England, where he worked as a civil servant for a brief period before growing disgusted with bureaucracy. In 1912, after trying and failing to make a living as a writer, Chandler moved back to the United States, where he worked at a variety of odd jobs until joining the Canadian army in 1917. Chandler saw limited time at the Western front in France during World War I and was training to be an air force pilot when the war ended. In 1924, Chandler married Pearl Cecily Eugenia Hurlburt, a woman twice-divorced and eighteen years his senior; the marriage lasted thirty years until her death in 1954. By the time of the marriage, Chandler had been employed for two years by Dabney Oil Syndicate in Los Angeles, rising through the ranks to become a vice president. His affairs with office workers and his heavy drinking, however, led to his dismissal in 1932.

Chandler began writing stories for the pulp fiction market, publishing his work in outlets such as *Black Mask* and *Detective Fiction Weekly*, learning the trade as he went along. After years of what amounted to paid apprentice work writing for the pulps, Chandler published his first novel, *The Big Sleep* in 1939. It was a critical and popular success. Like Hammett, whose writing Chandler studied, Chandler set his stories in cities, and used the language of the streets. His meticulous attention to physical detail, complex plotting, and especially, his development of one of the greatest twentieth-century characters in American literature, private investigator Philip Marlowe, helped make Chandler one of the most popular mystery writers of his day. In Marlowe, Chandler created someone who, though exhausted and battered by the world's brutality and corruption, nonetheless lived by a code of honor and took pride in his work.

Raymond Chandler

In addition to his short stories and seven novels, which include *Farewell, My Lovely* (1940) and *The Lady in the Lake* (1943), Chandler wrote screenplays for Hollywood including *Double Indemnity* (1944), *The Blue Dahlia* (1946), for which he received an Edgar Award from the Mystery Writers of America and an Oscar nomination for best screenplay, and *The Lady in the Lake* (1947). After a bout of pneumonia following a period of heavy drinking, Chandler died on March 26, 1959. He was, at the time, working on a new novel called *Poodle Springs*. The novel was later finished by Robert B. Parker and published in 1989.

Plot Summary

Chapters 1–5

The Big Sleep opens with private investigator Philip Marlowe visiting General Sternwood's mansion. Marlowe muses on the house's art and the fact that the furniture looks as if no one uses it. He first meets Carmen Sternwood, a flirt who, at twenty years old, is the younger of the General's two daughters. Then he meets the General, who receives him in his hothouse, a jungle-like setting in which the old man grows tropical orchids. The

Media Adaptations

- Warner Brothers released the film adaptation of Chandler's novel in 1946. The movie, directed by Howard Hawks, stars Humphrey Bogart and Lauren Bacall and is considered a classic of film noir. It is available in most libraries and video stores. Chandler's novel was adapted once more in 1978 in a film directed by Michael Winner and starring Robert Mitchum and Sarah Miles.

General tells Marlowe he is being blackmailed by someone named Arthur Gwynn Geiger, who wants the General to pay for Carmen's alleged gambling debts. Marlowe agrees to visit Geiger and put an end to the General's troubles. On his way out of the house, Vivian Regan, the older of the General's daughters, meets with Marlowe and tries to find out what the detective and her father spoke about, suspecting that it was about her husband, Rusty Regan, who left her about a month previously.

Pretending to be shopping for a rare book, Marlowe visits Geiger's antique bookstore, but Geiger is not in. While Marlowe waits for Geiger, a man comes in and disappears into a back room and then reappears with a book that he pays for and then leaves. Marlowe follows him a few blocks until the man hides the book in a tree. Marlowe, however, finds the book. Attempting to find Geiger, Marlowe visits another bookstore in the neighborhood and is given a description of Geiger by a woman who works there. He surmises through his discussion with this woman that Geiger's shop is a front for something. He discovers what that something is when he opens the book he had retrieved from the tree and sees that it contains pornographic photographs.

Chapters 6–10

Marlowe follows Geiger home and sees Carmen Sternwood's car parked in front of Geiger's home. He hears shots, and then breaks in to find Geiger dead on the floor and Carmen drugged and naked in front of a camera, the plateholder (negative) of which is missing. While rummaging through the house for clues, he finds a notebook with entries written in code. Marlowe takes Carmen home. The next morning, Bernie Ohls, the District Attorney's chief investigator, calls Marlowe and the two of them drive to the Lido fish pier where a man had driven into the ocean. The dead man is Owen Taylor, the Sternwoods' chauffeur, who once proposed to Carmen. Investigators cannot decide if the death was a homicide or a suicide. Marlowe returns to the city and visits Geiger's store once more, only to see men in the back room packing up books. He follows one of the men to Geiger's house, where the same man is packing up yet more books, and then to the apartment of Joe Brody.

Chapters 11–16

Vivian Regan visits Marlowe and shows him a nude photograph of her sister taken at Geiger's house, claiming that someone is blackmailing her for $5,000 and will give the photo to the "scandal sheets" unless she pays up. She says that she can borrow the money from Eddie Mars, an owner of a gambling parlor that she frequents. Ohls tells Marlowe that all of the Sternwoods have alibis for last night. Hunting for more clues, Marlowe returns to Geiger's house, only to find Carmen Sternwood, who has gone there to retrieve the nude photographs taken of her. While Marlowe and Carmen are in the house, Eddie Mars arrives, telling Marlowe that Geiger is his tenant and threatening the private investigator with a gun. Marlowe heads to Joe Brody's apartment, and after a standoff that includes Agnes Lozelle, the blonde woman who works at Geiger's store and who is Brody's girlfriend, Marlowe learns that Brody was also at Geiger's the night Geiger was killed. Brody claims he saw Taylor running out of the house and he followed him, hit him on the head, and took the photographic plateholder Taylor himself had taken from Geiger's. Marlowe finally convinces him to give up the photographs and plateholder. Just then, Carmen knocks at the door, holding a gun to Brody and demanding the photographs. After a tussle, Brody gives the photos to Marlowe, and Carmen leaves. Shortly after she leaves, Carol Lundgren, the young man Marlowe had seen at Geiger's store, knocks on the door and shoots Brody dead when he answers. Marlowe chases him down and takes him back to Geiger's.

Chapters 17–19

Marlowe finds Geiger's body in a bed in Lundgren's room and learns that Lundgren had been living with Geiger. Marlowe, Ohls, and Lundgren visit Taggart Wilde, the District Attorney, who is meeting with Captain Cronjager when they arrive. The two tell the story of the last few days but leave out a few details, specifically Carmen Sternwood's visit to Brody and Marlowe's run-in with Eddie Mars. The story goes as follows: Owen Taylor, who had once proposed to Carmen Sternwood, killed Geiger in a fit of rage when he found out Geiger was taking nude photographs of her. Brody tried to capitalize on the death by taking over Geiger's pornography business. Lundgren came home and moved Geiger's body to the back room, so that he would have time to move his things out of the house before the police found out about Geiger's murder. Lundgren sees Brody moving Geiger's pornographic books, and so believes that Brody killed Geiger. Lundgren kills Brody. Cronjager is upset because he is just learning about all of this the day after it happened. The next day, the newspapers report the Brody and Geiger murders solved, with Brody accused of killing Geiger over a shady business deal involving a wire service and Lundgren accused of killing Brody. The Sternwoods, Mars, Marlowe, and Ohls were not mentioned, nor did the papers connect the Taylor death to any of the events. Mars calls Marlowe to thank him for keeping his name out of his report.

Chapters 20–25

In these chapters, Marlowe hunts for Rusty Regan, first visiting Captain Al Gregory of the Missing Persons Bureau, and then Eddie Mars's casino. Mars claims to know nothing. Marlowe "apparently" rescues Vivian Regan from a mugging outside the casino, and then takes her home. She attempts to seduce Marlowe, but he fends off her advances, asking her what information Mars has on her that she will not share with him. She says nothing. When Marlowe arrives home, he discovers Carmen in his bed and undressed. Again, Marlowe declines an invitation for sex and kicks Carmen out. The next day, Harry Jones, a two-bit grifter who had been tailing Marlowe, tells him that Eddie Mars had Regan killed and that Mona Grant, Eddie's estranged wife, is hiding out outside of town.

Chapters 26–32

Marlowe visits Puss Walgreen's insurance offices and overhears Jones talking to Lash Canino. He listens as Jones tells Canino where Lozelle is

hiding out and then listens as Canino poisons Jones by pouring him a cyanide-laced drink. Marlowe calls Lozelle and offers her two hundred dollars for information about Mona Grant's whereabouts. After paying her and receiving the information, Marlowe heads out of town, where he runs into Canino and Art Huck, who runs an auto repair garage. The two beat up Marlowe and handcuff him. He wakes up to see Grant in a silver wig guarding him. After Marlowe tells her that Mars is a killer, she lets him escape. Marlowe waits outside for Canino to return and then, with Grant creating a diversion, shoots Canino dead. The next day Marlowe visits General Sternwood and explains to him why he kept looking for Regan even after the General had told him the case was closed. The General first feigns anger and then offers Marlowe a thousand dollars to find Regan. On his way out of the house, Marlowe sees Carmen and she asks him to teach her how to shoot a gun. She takes Marlowe down an old deserted road and, during target practice, shoots at him, but does not kill him because he had loaded the gun with blanks. Carmen has an epileptic seizure and Marlowe takes her home. He tells Vivian what happened and finally discovers the truth from her: Carmen had killed Regan because he refused her advances. With Eddie Mars's help, they disposed of the body in an old oil well. Marlowe makes Vivian promise to take Carmen away and get professional help for her, threatening to report the details of Regan's murder if she does not. She agrees and Marlowe leaves, musing on death and how nothing matters when one is doing "the big sleep."

Characters

Joe Brody

Joe Brody is a small-time hood who was once involved with Carmen Sternwood; her father paid him to stop seeing his daughter. Brody's new girlfriend is Agnes, Geiger's employee. Brody has successfully blackmailed the General once and tries to do it again with nude photos of Carmen, which he took off Taylor after following Taylor from Geiger's home. Lundgren kills Brody because he believed that Brody had killed his lover, Geiger.

Lash Canino

Lash Canino is a cold and ruthless hit man who wears brown clothes and a brown hat and drives a brown car. He works for Mars as a bodyguard and all purpose thug. Canino helps to dispose of Rusty Regan's body after Carmen Sternwood kills him. He also poisons Jones after extracting information from him about Agnes's location. Marlowe kills Canino in a shoot-out.

Larry Cobb

Larry Cobb is a drunk and Vivian Regan's escort at the Cypress Club.

Captain Cronjager

Captain Cronjager, "a hatchet-faced man," is at Wilde's home when Marlowe and Ohls chronicle the events leading up to and including Geiger and Brody's murders. He is angry with Marlowe for not reporting the murders earlier and the two of them argue.

Arthur Gwynn Geiger

Arthur Gwynn Geiger is a pornographer who owns a rare book store on Hollywood Boulevard and rents a house from Mars. A middle-aged "fattish" man with a Charlie Chan moustache, Geiger is shot dead while taking photographs of a nude Carmen Sternwood. His lover is Lundgren, who also lives in the house.

Mona Grant

Mona Grant is a former lounge singer and Mars's estranged wife. She is also a former girlfriend of Rusty Regan. She is hiding outside of town and guarded by Canino, so that the police will think that she ran away with Regan. Initially, she is naive and gullible, refusing to believe Marlowe when he tells her that Mars kills people, but she lets Marlowe escape while she is guarding him, and then helps him kill Canino by creating a diversion.

Captain Al Gregory

Al Gregory is head of the Missing Persons Bureau. Marlowe describes him as "a burly man with tired eyes." He knows more than he lets on, initially presenting himself as a "hack," but later telling Marlowe that he is an honest man in a dishonest city. Gregory shows Marlowe a photograph of Regan and provides him with information about his history.

Art Huck

Art Huck, a gaunt man in overalls, owns a house and an auto repair shop outside of the city. He and Canino are protecting Grant, who is hiding out at Huck's place. Huck fixes Marlowe's flats and then helps Canino capture him.

Harry Jones

Harry Jones is a small-time criminal and friend of Brody and Rusty Regan's. He tells Marlowe that Mars had Regan killed. He is a small man with bright eyes. He sums up his philosophy of life when he tells Marlowe, "I'm a grifter. We're all grifters. So we sell each other out for a nickel." He is poisoned by Canino, after Jones tells the killer where Agnes is hiding.

Agnes Lozelle

Agnes Lozelle is Joe Brody's ash-blonde girlfriend who works in Geiger's store. She is surly and aloof when Marlowe visits the store, arousing his suspicions. She bemoans her luck at always attracting "half-smart" men. After Brody is killed, she connects with Jones, who tries to protect her from Canino. Marlowe gives her two hundred dollars for information about Mona Grant.

Carol Lundgren

Carol Lundgren worked for Geiger, was his lover, and lived with him. He is a good-looking, thin, blonde young man who Marlowe refers to as a "fag" and a "pansy." After Lundgren shoots Brody, Marlowe chases him down and brings him back to Geiger's house. He is arrested and charged with Brody's murder.

Philip Marlowe

Philip Marlowe, the novel's narrator, is a single, thirty-three year old private investigator. Marlowe had formerly worked for Wilde, the District Attorney, but was fired for insubordination. He is a handsome, charming, cynical, street-smart character who loves his work but shows contempt for women. When he is not smoking or drinking, he is nursing a hangover and working the Sternwood case. Marlowe has a high degree of professional pride and a general disdain for the rich. He puts work before romance and is loyal to his employer, General Sternwood, declining the amorous advances of both of Sternwood's daughters. Arrogant, witty, self-deprecating, and world-weary, Marlowe served and continues to serve as the inspiration for the characters of numerous private investigators in both fiction and film.

Eddie Mars

Eddie Mars is the middle-aged proprietor of the Cypress Club, a gambling house on the beach that Vivian Regan frequents. He also rents a house to Geiger. Impeccably dressed in expensive gray suits, Mars has a cool demeanor and rarely involves himself directly in crime, choosing instead to hire others such as Canino to do his dirty work. His wife, Grant, was once Rusty Regan's lover. Mars has connections in the police department and it is likely that he will not be charged with any crimes.

Mathilda

Mathilda is Vivian Regan's maid. Marlowe describes her as "a middle-aged woman with a long gentle face."

Vincent Norris

Vincent Norris is General Sternwood's butler. He is about sixty years old, with silver hair, an agile manner, and a quick wit. He holds a considerable degree of power in the Sternwood household, writing checks for the General and deciding what information the General should and should not have.

Bernie Ohls

Bernie Ohls is the chief investigator for Wilde and a friend of Marlowe's who had recommended Marlowe to General Sternwood. Ohls is tough, having killed nine men during his career. But he also takes pride in his work and has a degree of integrity. He takes Marlowe to see Owen Taylor's body and accompanies him to Wilde's to report the details of Brody and Geiger's murder and subsequently to report Jones's and Canino's deaths.

Terence Regan

Terence "Rusty" Regan is an Irish immigrant, former bootlegger, and late husband of Vivian Regan. Regan was a good friend of General Sternwood, who would listen to his stories of the time he spent in the Irish Republican Army. He was in love with Grant, Mars's wife, and becomes the object of Marlowe's investigation in the second half of the novel, after General Sternwood hires Marlowe to find him. Regan is killed by Carmen Sternwood after he spurns her advances.

Vivian Regan

The oldest Sternwood daughter, Vivian is in her 20s and almost as hard-boiled as Marlowe, spending most of her time at the roulette table at the Cypress Club gambling or drinking and attempting to seduce men like Marlowe, who describes her as "tall and rangy and strong-looking." Her escort is Larry Cobb, a slobbering drunk for whom she has no affection but considered marrying at one point. She has been married three times, most recently to Rusty Regan. She helps to cover up the truth of Regan's death by deceiving Mar-

lowe to protect her sister. She finally tells Marlowe the details of his death at the end of the novel.

Carmen Sternwood

Carmen Sternwood is the younger of the two Sternwood sisters. She is twenty years old, beautiful, relentlessly flirtatious, spoiled, and epileptic. She is also at the center of the blackmailing scheme that includes Geiger and Brody. She spends most of the novel sucking on her thumb or playing with her hair, or telling Marlowe that he is cute. After being sexually rejected by Marlowe a number of times, she attempts to shoot him while Marlowe is showing her how to use a gun. Her sister tells Marlowe that Carmen had killed Regan for the same reason. Marlowe makes Vivian promise to seek professional help for her sister as a condition for him to remain silent about the details of Regan's death.

General Gus Sternwood

General Sternwood is the elderly millionaire father of Carmen and Vivian, who initially hires Marlowe to "take care" of someone who is attempting to blackmail him. He fell off a horse when he was fifty-eight years old and is paralyzed from the waist down. Sternwood now lives through others, spending most of his time in a wheelchair in his hothouse growing orchids. He loved Rusty Regan because Regan told him stories and kept him company, and he hires Marlowe to find him. Norris and the daughters keep the truth of Regan's death from him.

Owen Taylor

Taylor was "a slim dark-haired kid" from Dubuque, Iowa who worked as a chauffeur for the Sternwoods. His body is found in a car off the Lido pier and his death is ruled a suicide. Marlowe speculates that Taylor killed Geiger when he found out he was taking nude photographs of Carmen Sternwood, to whom Taylor had once proposed.

Taggart Wilde

Taggart Wilde is the District Attorney and Marlowe's former boss. He comes from an old Los Angeles family and his political connections are many and deep. His father was a friend of General Sternwood's. Marlowe describes him as "a middle-aged plump man with clear blue eyes that managed to have a friendly expression without really having any expression at all." He determines what will be reported in the newspapers regarding Brody and Geiger's killings and helps keep the Sternwood name out of the papers.

Topics for Further Study

- Divide the class into four groups and assign each group eight chapters from the novel. Each group should compile a list of terms from their respective chapters that Marlowe and other characters use that are peculiar to the detective-story genre. Such terms might include words like "gat" (gun) or "peeper" (private investigator). Compile all of the terms into a dictionary for the class.

- Watch the 1946 film adaptation of Chandler's novel and list the differences between the film and the novel. Discuss possible reasons for those differences as a class.

- Rewrite the last chapter in the book, resolving the Rusty Regan mystery in a different way. Exchange your chapter with a classmate and discuss in pairs.

- While screenwriters were working on adapting Chandler's novel to film, they sent him a note asking how Owen Taylor really died. Chandler responded, saying he did not know. On the board, brainstorm possible theories of Taylor's death and vote as a class on the best theory.

- In pairs, make a list of your favorite similes in the novel and then put them on the board and as a class discuss what makes them effective.

Themes

Privilege and Entitlement

Although Marlowe works for General Sternwood, a millionaire, his loyalty to the man is not based on Sternwood's wealth but on his age, infirmity, and honesty. Throughout the novel, Marlowe treats people as they treat him, rather than as they expect to be treated by virtue of their class standing or social position. This is demonstrated in the way he responds to the Sternwood sisters, both of whom are privileged and behave as if they are entitled to special treatment. Vivian Regan is shocked by Marlowe's "rude manners" during their first en-

counter, and Carmen Sternwood is so disturbed by Marlowe's sexual rejection of her that she attempts to kill him. Marlowe is also discourteous to Captain Cronjager during his visit to Wilde's office, refusing to defer to Cronjager's position as police captain when discussing the Geiger and Brody killings. Marlowe's behavior in this instance has as much to do with his own sense of entitlement regarding what he can and cannot do in his job as a private investigator as it does with Cronjager's arrogance.

Meaning of Life

In the early twentieth century, the sheer horror and scale of atrocities during the first World War caused many people to lose faith in God and organized religion. Combined with the increasing acceptance of scientific theories such as evolution, many no longer believed in a higher benevolent intelligence to provide meaning to their lives, and so, struggled to find purpose. Some, like the Sternwood sisters, spent their time pursuing pleasure gambling, drinking, and engaging in promiscuous sex. Others, like Marlowe, found meaning in their work and in adherence to a code of honor. Still others, such as General Sternwood, who had lost control of much of his body, survived by living through people like Marlowe and Rusty Regan. Death, however, hovers just above the heads of all the characters, as Marlowe reminds readers at the end of the novel: "What did it matter where you lay once you were dead? ... You just slept the big sleep, not caring about the nastiness of how you died or where you fell."

Law and Order

Laws are meant to ensure a safe environment for citizens, to maintain social order, and to instill a sense of justice in the populace. The rampant corruption and disregard for the law in Chandler's novel demonstrates that the social fabric has begun to fray in 1930s Los Angeles. Police protect pornographers and gamblers, women destroy men for sport, the wealthy buy their way out of trouble, and appearances inevitably belie reality. Characters routinely manipulate each other for personal gain. The spirit of Chandler's novel can be summed up by small-time criminal Harry Jones, who says to Marlowe, "We're all grifters. So we sell each other out for a nickel."

Style

Dialogue

Dialogue, the conversation between two or more characters, is a primary tool writers use for characterization and to drive plots. Writers use dialogue to reveal the desires, motivations, and character of the players in their stories, helping to create an idea and an image of them in readers' minds. Chandler is known as a master of vernacular dialogue. His characters talk the way that 1930s thugs, cops, and private investigators talk on the job, in language studded with slang such as "loogan" (a man with a gun), "peeper" (private investigator), and "centuries" (hundred dollar bills). His characters, especially Marlowe, are also known for their use of biting similes to describe someone or thing. Similes are comparisons that employ "as" or "like." For example, in describing the way Brody's cigarette dangles from his mouth, Marlowe states: "His cigarette was jiggling like a doll on a coiled spring." This is also an example of Marlowe's wit, which he uses to ward off sentimentality and to demonstrate his self-awareness.

Description

The bulk of Chandler's novel is objective description. Marlowe spends a long time describing the physical settings of individual scenes, thus making a kind of character out of place. This strategy creates vivid images in readers' minds, helps to develop characterization, and prepares readers for the ensuing action. Marlowe's elaborate description of Geiger's house as a virtual palace of tackiness, for example, emphasizes Geiger's sordid behavior as a pornographer and (to Marlowe) as a homosexual. Chandler was heavily influenced by Ernest Hemingway's use of description in his novels of the 1920s.

Plot

Plot refers to the arrangement of events in a story. In Chandler's novel, details of the events come fast. However, the interpretation of the events change as Marlowe receives new information, causing readers to rethink what they believe as well. For example, at first Ohls and Marlowe believe that Taylor had committed suicide. However, when they discover a bruise on his forehead, they believe he was hit by a blackjack and murdered. Later however, Brody claims to have hit Taylor but not to have killed him with the blow. The truth of what actually happened to Taylor is never revealed. Unlike conventional mystery novels where all loose ends are tied up, *The Big Sleep* leaves many questions unanswered and plot details unresolved.

Historical Context

1930s

While Chandler was penning his novel in the late 1930s, the United States was attempting to recover from the depression that had economically devastated the country since 1929. Marlowe, who charged millionaire General Sternwood twenty-five dollars a day plus expenses, was not only working, he was making well over the average national salary, which stood at $1,368. Unemployment during the 1930s reached a high of 25%. To help alleviate the economic suffering of many Americans, President Roosevelt signed the Social Security Act and the Wagner Act in 1935, ensuring the elderly an income, and ensuring workers the right to unionize, respectively.

Farmers were especially hard hit during the 1930s, and many from Midwestern "Dust Bowl" states such as Oklahoma and Missouri (so named because of the drought and dust storms that hit that area in the 1930s) moved to California hoping for work and a better life. On the outskirts of Marlowe's Los Angeles and in the fertile valleys of the state, migrant workers picked lemons, potatoes, cotton, peas, and other crops, going wherever there was work. The Works Progress Administration, a huge government job program, was also created in 1935. Over its seven-year life span the WPA spent eleven billion dollars employing more than eight million people for 250,000 projects that involved rebuilding the country's roads, bridges, and public buildings. The WPA also provided work for artists, writers, and musicians, as the federal government broadly sponsored the arts for the first time.

Sternwood, who made his millions in oil, would have been interested in the Public Utility Holding Company Act of 1935. The Act created a new federal agency, the Federal Power Commission, which regulated electricity prices, while the Federal Trade Commission did the same for natural gas prices. Many business people fought against components of Roosevelt's New Deal, claiming that they hindered job creation and development of markets, but Roosevelt remained resolute.

The literature of the 1930s explored issues of integrity and honor. Ernest Hemingway's novels, *To Have and Have Not* (1937) and *For Whom the Bell*

Compare & Contrast

- **1930s:** The economy of the United States continues to slump after a massive downturn in the stock market, which began in 1929 and led to the Great Depression.

  Today: After a massive boom, the economy of the United States slumps after a massive downturn in the stock market, which began in 2000.

- **1930s:** To combat widespread crime in the United States various federal government agencies within the Department of Justice are consolidated to form the Federal Bureau of Investigation.

Today: After the attacks on the World Trade Center and the Pentagon, President Bush forms the Office of Homeland Security to strengthen protection against terrorist threats and attacks in the United States.

- **1930s:** Although gambling is illegal, many gambling houses exist, and often have police protection.

  Today: State lotteries are commonplace and many states have legal gambling casinos, many of them operating on Native-American reservations.

Tolls (1939), for example, both featured characters who pitted themselves against larger forces such as corporations and fascism. John Steinbeck's *Grapes of Wrath* (1939) chronicled the struggles of the Joad family, tenant farmers crippled by the depression and the effects of corporate capitalism. Hollywood, on the other hand, where Chandler would make his mark during the 1940s writing screenplays, offered less weighty fare, providing escapist entertainment for the masses. Films popular during this time include *Topper* (1937), *Bringing Up Baby* (1938), and Frank Capra's *Mr. Smith Goes to Washington* (1939). Film noir, elements of which Chandler helped to define in his novels and screenplays, was just beginning to take shape in movies such as *The Maltese Falcon* (1941), featuring Humphrey Bogart playing Hammett's Sam Spade, and *This Gun for Hire* (1942). The 1940s, of course, was noir's heyday, with Chandler writing the screenplays for classics such as *Double Indemnity* (1944) and *The Blue Dahlia* (1946), and seeing his novels *Farewell My Lovely*, *The Big Sleep*, and *The Lady in the Lake* adapted for the big screen.

Critical Overview

Knopf published *The Big Sleep* in America in 1939 and Hamish Hamilton published the first English edition the same year. The novel received brief but favorable reviews in publications in both countries, with reviewers likening Chandler's work to that of Dashiell Hammett's, the foremost writer of detective novels in the 1920s and 1930s. The first American printing of 5,000 copies sold out quickly, and a second printing was ordered immediately in both the United States and England. Chandler's publishers were so pleased with his success they offered him a 20 percent royalty for the first 5,000 copies of his next novel, and 25 percent on any copies sold beyond that.

After Chandler's death, his reputation as a serious writer grew, with many critics claiming *The Big Sleep* as his best novel. In his biography, *The Life of Raymond Chandler*, Frank MacShane argues that although the novel was in reality a stitching together and elaboration of three short stories, the completed product was more than the sum of its parts. MacShane writes, "It is as if the creation of the original images required the sort of emotional energy that makes a poet remember his lines years after he first wrote them down." Other critics consider Chandler's use of Marlowe as the first-person narrator the key ingredient in the novel's success. Russell Davies, for example, in his essay, "Omnes Me Impune Lacessunt," claims Marlowe's self-mockery and "the balance of ironies" in the novel "is really the secret of Chandler's success."

Lauren Bacall as Vivian Sternwood Rutledge and Humphrey Bogart as Philip Marlow in the 1946 film rendition of The Big Sleep

Critic Clive James agrees, noting, "In *The Big Sleep* and all the novels that followed, the secret of plausibility lies in the style, and the secret of the style lies in Marlowe's personality." Jerry Speir also focuses on Marlowe in discussing the novel. However, instead of treating Marlowe as a knight-errant as have many other critics, Speir argues, *"The Big Sleep* might be read as a *failure* of romance." Daniel Linder draws attention to the linguistic irony in the novel in his essay for *The Explicator*, arguing that Carmen Sternwood's repeated use of the words "cute" and "giggle" have an "echoic" effect on readers that demands interpretation.

Criticism

Chris Semansky

Semansky is an instructor of English literature and composition and writes on literature and culture for several publications. In this essay, Semansky considers the appeal of Marlowe in Chandler's novel.

At the heart of Chandler's first novel and at the heart of all of his novels is Phillip Marlowe, a man of contradictions, who has served as a kind of prototype for private investigators in films and novels over the last sixty years. Rather than alienating readers with his homophobia, his machismo, and his seeming disdain for women, Marlowe has helped Chandler attract a large readership, as he also embodies professional and personal integrity, speaking his mind without worrying about being politically correct or offending the powers that be.

Marlowe, however, is also a cynic, who distrusts others and their motivations, and in general experiences the world of appearances as masking a darker, corrupt reality. This is readily apparent in his description of himself to General Sternwood during their initial meeting. Marlowe tells him: "I'm thirty-three years old, went to college once and can still speak English if there's any demand for it. . . . I'm unmarried because I don't like policemen's wives." Marlowe's comment about speaking English underscores his own contempt for pretentious talk and formal education in general. He learns what he knows from the streets and from his job, and has honed his powers of observation through hard work. His comment about "policemen's wives" also shows his disregard for convention, as he stereotypes the kind of women that

> " Being true to a professional code of conduct sustains him through the ever-changing landscape of right and wrong that marks the world of the private investigator."

policemen marry. It is also a jab at police, who are at times Marlowe's adversaries.

Historically, cynicism emerged in ancient Greece and was popularized by Antisthenes, a pupil of Socrates, and Diogenes. Cynics were disgusted by ostentation, wealth, and the behavior of the leisure class. Cynics today retain those qualities, but also find fault with almost all institutions and individuals, believing that the former are corrupt and the latter selfish. This kind of attitude was easy enough to develop for someone like Marlowe who fought crime in the 1930s, when police corruption in the United States ran rampant and when those who displayed wealth were generally scorned by the masses, which were still suffering under the long shadow of the Great Depression. Marlowe's cynicism, however, was tempered by idealism and a belief that doing his job well and with integrity gave value and meaning to his life. In a revealing speech mid-way through the novel, Marlowe tells Wilde, the District Attorney, that he is willing to risk alienating half of the Los Angeles police force to be true to his values:

> I'm on a case. I'm selling what I have to sell to make a living. What little guts and intelligence the Lord gave me and a willingness to get pushed around in order to protect a client. It's against my principles to tell as much as I've told tonight, without consulting the General. As for the cover-up... they come a dime a dozen in any big city. Cops get very large and emphatic when an outsider tries to hide anything, but they do the same things themselves every other day, to oblige their friends or anybody with a little pull.... I'd do the same thing again, if I had to.

It is this sense of loyalty that makes Marlowe an attractive character, and the quality that makes him vulnerable. Without it, his wisecracks and put downs would ring hollow, come off as mere vaudeville. Marlowe's loyalty to the General, though, does not come at the expense of his obligation to

obey the law, for the law itself was little more than groups of self-interested parties battling for turf among Los Angeles's criminal elements. Captain Gregory, head of the Missing Persons Bureau, sums up the state of the law when he talks to Marlowe the day after the private investigator kills Canino:

> Being a copper I'd like to see the law win. I'd like to see the flashy well-dressed muggs like Eddie Mars spoiling their manicures in the rock quarry at Folsom, alongside of the poor little slum-bred hard guys that got knocked over on their first caper and never had a break since. You and me both lived too long to think I'm likely to see it happen. Not in this town, not in any town half this size, in any part of this wide, green and beautiful U.S.A. We just don't run our country that way.

Gregory's comment is a dig at the idea that truth and justice for all exists in the United States. The cynicism of cops and of politicians such as Wilde makes Marlowe's cynicism easier to take, for on him it serves as a weapon with which to fight the deception he encounters every day in his job. Blind allegiance to the law for Marlowe would make him complicitous in the web of deceit and lies. Being true to a professional code of conduct sustains him through the ever-changing landscape of right and wrong that marks the world of the private investigator. Chandler's description of Marlowe's character in his well-known essay, "The Simple Art of Murder" puts it thusly: "He will take no man's money dishonestly and no man's insolence without a due and dispassionate revenge."

He will also take no woman's "insolence." Though he exhibits the sex appeal of a man's man with his tough talk and rough manners, Marlowe is no easy mark for a woman intent on seducing him. He first rejects Vivian Regan when she offers herself to him after he saves her from a mugger outside the Cypress Club, attempting to use her desire for him as an opportunity to extract information from her. He then refuses Carmen Sternwood's offer of sex, literally throwing her out of his bedroom, after telling her, "It's a question of professional pride.... I'm working for your father. He's a sick man, very frail, very helpless. He sort of trusts me not to pull any stunts." The morning after this incident, Marlowe wakes up groggy and remarks, "You can have a hangover from other things than alcohol. I had one from women. Women made me sick." Many critics have noted Marlowe's adherence to a chivalric code and some of them have labeled him a failed knight, a reading buttressed by the knight imagery in the stained-glass entrance of the Sternwood house and, later, in Marlowe's apartment, while he is puzzling a chess problem. "It wasn't a game for knights," Marlowe says, after making a move about which he thinks twice. More to the point, the world, and Carmen Sternwood, did not deserve knights. Marlowe does not turn in Carmen for killing Rusty Regan because of his loyalty to her father and his desire not to add more pain to his dying days.

This decision has consequences, for in the end, the line between Marlowe's behavior and those he condemns throughout the novel has grown thinner. He takes an odd solace, however, in the idea of Regan's death, depicting it as an escape from the morally corrupt jungle he lives in and the tangle of conflicting desires that marks his life: "Me, I was part of the nastiness now. Far more a part of it than Rusty Regan was. But the old man didn't have to be." Coupled with the realization that he has been swallowed by the very kind of corruption he has sought to battle, Marlowe's description of General Sternwood on his death bed feels almost like the private investigator's own death wish: "His heart was a brief, uncertain murmur. His thoughts were as gray as ashes. And in a while he too, like Rusty Regan, would be sleeping the big sleep."

Source: Chris Semansky, Critical Essay on *The Big Sleep*, in *Novels for Students*, The Gale Group, 2003.

Jerry Speir

In the following essay, Speir offers a detailed analysis of the plot of The Big Sleep, *focusing on Marlowe's emotional transformation and the events that influence it.*

> "I'm not joking, and if I seem to talk in circles, it just seems that way. It all ties together—everything."
> *The Big Sleep*

Philip Marlowe crackles to life on a cloudy October morning in the first paragraph of *The Big Sleep* (1939). "I was wearing my powder-blue suit, with dark blue shirt, tie and display handkerchief, black brogues, black wool socks with dark blue clocks on them. I was neat, clean, shaved and sober, and I didn't care who knew it. I was everything the well-dressed private detective ought to be. I was calling on four million dollars." Already he exhibits the wry self-mockery which occupies us throughout the novels. The tone is self-assured, even cocky, but it also maintains the ironic detachment of a man conscious of his own pose. By the end of the novel, however, these high spirits will have changed dramatically. And it is precisely in such alterations of Marlowe's mood and in the revelations which precipitate them that Chandler imbeds the meaning of his stories. To appreciate this transformation in *The*

> " Even if we still possess the idealistic, romantic sensibilities that can drive us to noble actions, the consequences, like the motives, are never really unadulterated. And finally, like Marlowe, we are impotent to untie the knots of our lives."

Big Sleep, we must first understand the events which prompt it—the plot, that element about which Chandler claimed to have little concern.

The plot of this novel has drawn considerable, undeserved criticism. One critic, Stephen Pendo, has gone so far as to assert that it is "a confused tangle that demonstrates Chandler's problem of producing a cohesive story line," expressing a fairly common judgment. Part of the problem here may derive from what one is willing to accept as cohesive. And part of the problem, particularly as relates to the public's general misconceptions about this story, no doubt relates to interpretations of the popular 1946 film version of the novel rather than to the book itself. While the film is quite successful within its own limits—and Chandler was very pleased with Bogart's portrayal of Marlowe—it achieves much of its mystery and suspense by omitting many of the subplots and explanations of motivation which are critical concerns for Chandler and which he so carefully details in the novel. A general caution is perhaps in order here concerning the use of any of the movies based on Chandler's works as guides for interpreting the novels or the novelist. Most, in fact, stray further from their sources than does the Bogart-Bacall version of *The Big Sleep*.

But, to return to the question of cohesiveness, as relates to Chandler's plots, we should bear in mind his remark that he was always "more intrigued by a situation where the mystery is solved more by the exposition and understanding of a single character . . . than by the slow and sometimes long-winded concatenation of circumstances." It is to character, then, and to the motivations of character that we must look in Chandler if we are to

What Do I Read Next?

- Another popular Chandler novel chronicling the adventures of Phillip Marlowe is *The Long Goodbye*, published in 1953. This novel was made into a Hollywood film (1973) directed by Robert Altman and starring Elliot Gould.

- Al Clark's *Raymond Chandler in Hollywood* (1982) explores Chandler's life when he was writing screenplays for films such as *Double Indemnity* and *The Blue Dahlia*.

- In 1994, Robert Parker, considered by many to be Chandler's successor as king of the hardboiled detective novel, wrote *Perchance to Dream*, a sequel to *The Big Sleep*. Parker also finished the novel Chandler was working on when he died: *Poodle Springs* (1986).

- Edward Thorpe's *Chandlertown: The Los Angeles of Philip Marlowe* (1983) examines the role Los Angeles plays in Chandler's detective fiction.

untangle the confusion. And, since the confusion among readers and critics is so widespread, a fairly detailed analysis of the plot seems in order.

The characters who occupy center stage in *The Big Sleep* fall into two echelons: the members and associates of the wealthy Sternwood family and a loosely associated group of racketeers with whom the Sternwoods have inevitably become involved.

The Sternwood family consists of an aging, dying patriarch known as "the General," and his two daughters, Carmen and Vivian, "still in the dangerous twenties." Wrapped in a rug and bathrobe, sitting in a wheelchair amidst the orchids of his sweltering greenhouse, the General describes himself to Marlowe as "a very dull survival of a rather gaudy life" who seems "to exist largely on heat, like a newborn spider." His complaint is that he is "being blackmailed again." As he explains, he has recently "paid a man named Joe Brody five thousand dollars to let my younger daughter Carmen

alone;" he then proceeds to show Marlowe a new demand for $1,000 from a man named Geiger for what Geiger says are gambling debts. Geiger's stationery indicates that he is a dealer in "Rare Books and DeLuxe Editions."

In the course of their conversation, Marlowe gets the General's opinion of his children: "Vivian is spoiled, exacting, smart and quite ruthless. Carmen is a child who likes to pull wings off flies." Marlowe also learns about another member of the family, Rusty Regan, Vivian's third and most recent husband who has disappeared under mysterious circumstances. Regan's past accomplishments include work as a bootlegger and service as an officer in the I.R.A. The General has in fact been quite taken by the young man's tales of the Irish revolution, and Marlowe is soon amused and perplexed to learn that virtually everyone, daughters and police included, assume he has been hired to find Regan.

But, sticking to his primary suspect, Marlowe soon learns that Geiger's real business is a rather high-class lending library of dirty books. He locates Geiger's house and parks outside in the dying light to perform a little surveillance. The rain which has been threatening all afternoon drips through the leaking top of his convertible, and, typically, he turns to a pocket flask in his glove compartment for comfort. Carmen arrives and enters. Shortly afterward a flash of "hard white light" comes from the house in conjunction with a scream—a scream that "had a sound of half-pleasurable shock, an accent of drunkenness, an overtone of pure idiocy. It was a nasty sound." By the time Marlowe gets to the house, three shots have been fired and there is the sound of someone fleeing.

Marlowe's discovery of what has happened is revealed in a manner that is virtually a trademark of Chandlerian exposition. After building suspense with mysterious flashes, sudden gunfire, and an unidentified person running away, Chandler opens our first look at the scene with one of Marlowe's characteristically deadpan remarks: "Neither of the two people in the room paid any attention to the way I came in, although only one of them was dead." As we begin to read that statement, we sense that at least some of the suspense is about to be resolved. But its last phrase brings us up abruptly with the recognition that our expectations were too simplistic. Thus chastened, and with a smile for the author's almost perverse sense of comic relief, we attend more warily to Marlowe's typically dispassionate survey of the room and its every detail:

It had a low beamed ceiling . . . brown plaster walls decked out with strips of Chinese embroidery and Chinese and Japanese prints . . . a thick pinkish Chinese rug . . . bits of old silk tossed around, as if whoever lived there had to have a piece he could reach out and thumb . . . a black desk with carved gargoyles at the corners and behind it a yellow satin cushion on a polished black chair with carved arms and back . . . the pungent aftermath of cordite and the sickish aroma of ether.

Only after that exhaustive catalogue do we get any information about what most interests us, the people.

On a sort of low dais at one end of the room there was a high-backed teakwood chair in which Miss Carmen Sternwood was sitting on a fringed orange shawl. She was sitting very straight, with her hands on the arms of the chair, her knees close together, her body stiffly erect in the pose of an Egyptian goddess, her chin level, her small bright teeth shining between her parted lips. Her eyes were wide open. The dark slate color of the iris had devoured the pupil. They were mad eyes. She seemed to be unconscious, but she didn't have the pose of unconsciousness. She looked as if, in her mind, she was doing something very important and making a fine job of it. Out of her mouth came a tinny chuckling noise which didn't change her expression or even move her lips.

She was wearing a pair of long jade earrings. They were nice earrings and had probably cost a couple of hundred dollars. She wasn't wearing anything else.

Geiger, we are told after a similarly lengthy description, "was very dead."

This very calculated pacing serves several functions. First of all, it impresses us with the detective's method: having access only to objective data, he must weigh all details equally if he is to avoid overlooking one that might prove critical. But, more importantly, for Marlowe himself such pacing and apparent concern for objectivity provide a necessary check on his own subjective sensibilities. This kind of emotional control is further related to Chandler's notion of an "objective method" of writing in which dialogue and description become vehicles of emotion (see Chapter 7). That is, Chandler—and Marlowe—recognize that subjectivity is the ground of human experience and motivation, rather than objective reality. But, any one individual—Marlowe or the reader—has only the external indications of that subjectivity, that inner activity, from which to draw conclusions about any particular person. It was Chandler's desire to convey emotion and character not by *describing* them, but by *demonstrating* them through dialogue and physical details. A continued analysis of the plot

and of Chandler's manner of relating it should enlighten the point.

Following Geiger's death, Marlowe discovers that the books from his store are being moved to the apartment of Joe Brody, the man whom the General mentioned as a recipient of $5,000 of his blackmail money. Agnes, the woman who worked in Geiger's store, is evidently assisting Brody in his plot to take over the business.

Back at Geiger's house, Marlowe runs into Eddie Mars, whom he describes with the same detached thoroughness as he had the furniture. He is

a gray man, all gray, except for his polished black shoes and two scarlet diamonds in his gray satin tie that looked like the diamonds on roulette layouts. His shirt was gray and his double-breasted suit of soft, beautifully cut flannel. Seeing Carmen he took a gray hat off and his hair underneath it was gray and as fine as if it had been sifted through gauze. His thick gray eyebrows had that indefinably sporty look. He had a long chin, a nose with a hook to it, thoughtful gray eyes that had a slanted look because the fold of skin over his upper lid came down over the corner of the lid itself.

His "colorlessness" is also a characteristic of Chandler's descriptive technique and, as we will see later (Chapter 7), another device by which he imparts meaning.

Mars is the operator of The Cypress Club, a local gambling establishment, and considers himself just a businessman. He claims to own the house in which Geiger was living and says he was just passing by to check on his tenant. But Marlowe is skeptical. He has already learned that Mars is also a good friend of Vivian Sternwood and that he has, in fact, financed some of her gambling sprees. It also appears that there was more connection between Mars and Geiger than the simple tenant-landlord relationship. If nothing else, Geiger's was a business that needed protection and Mars was the man with the contacts and power to deliver it. But the exact nature of their relationship must await further development.

Marlowe shortly finds his attention occupied by a small man with "tight brilliant eyes that wanted to look hard, and looked as hard as oysters on the half shell." His name is Harry Jones and he is selling information. His information concerns Eddie Mars's wife, Mona. Mona Mars, it is generally agreed, disappeared about the same time as Rusty Regan and popular consensus has it that they left together. Mona's presumed relationship with Regan is also believed to be the primary impetus behind Eddie Mars's relationship with Vivian. But

Harry Jones has information which suggests otherwise. Harry is a mouthpiece for Agnes, the bookstore clerk assumed to be allied with Joe Brody, and their association represents yet another fragmented piece of the local rackets organization at war with itself, a primary subplot. Agnes has recently seen Mona and is willing to divulge her whereabouts for sufficient cash.

Harry is too loyal to Agnes to convey the information himself and insists that Marlowe meet him later with the money, and he will take him to her. When Marlowe arrives at the appointed rendezvous, he discovers that Lash Canino, one of Eddie Mars's enforcers, has gotten there ahead of him and is trying to get Harry to tell him where Agnes is and what she knows. After Harry finally relents and gives him a false address to placate him, Canino offers whiskey to seal their "friendship." Harry dies quickly from the cyanide in the liquor as Marlowe stands by helplessly on the other side of the wall. He must wait until later for his chance at this embodiment of evil whom Harry had described simply as the "brown man": "Short, heavy set, brown hair, brown eyes, and always wears brown clothes and a brown hat. Even wears a brown suede raincoat. Drives a brown coupe. Everything brown for Mr. Canino."

With the aid of a chance phone call from Agnes, Marlowe makes contact with her, gets her information, and heads out into the hills where Mona Mars was spotted. The rain that has pervaded the book is now very heavy, and as Marlowe nears the appointed site, in his words, "Fate stage-managed the whole thing." His car skids off the slick roadway, and he finds himself near Art Huck's Garage, a hot-car processing establishment associated with Eddie Mars's rackets. Canino is there and, without much ado, Marlowe is overpowered and knocked unconscious.

When he comes to, Marlowe finds himself handcuffed, bound, and alone in a room with a woman. The woman is Mona Mars. Despite his condition, Marlowe manages to amuse her with his bright chatter. She is particularly amused that he thinks she is being held prisoner. She even removes her platinum wig, disclosing her bald head which she claims to have had shaved herself "to show Eddie I was willing to do what he wanted me to do—hide out. That he didn't need to have me guarded. I wouldn't let him down. I love him." Eventually, Marlowe's tireless talk manages to persuade her to help him escape rather than wait to see what his fate might be when Canino returns.

But before Marlowe can get well outside the house, Canino is back. When Canino goes inside, Marlowe starts his car and provokes him to fire from the window. Finally, the ruse draws Canino from the house and, with a bit of cooperation from Mona, Marlowe manages to get the drop on him. After Canino has fired six wild shots, Marlowe steps calmly from his hiding place, asks simply "Finished?" and fires four shots of his own into "the brown man," thus ending his reign of terror—and marking Marlowe's only killing in the novels.

Next morning, the sun is shining and Marlowe makes his way first to the police and then to General Sternwood to explain his findings and activities. General Sternwood is quite distressed that the police have been revolved at all. Marlowe more or less apologizes by explaining that he has assumed from the beginning that there was more to the General's interest in the case than the simple matter of blackmail over debts. As he explains, "I was convinced that you put those Geiger notes up to me chiefly as a test, and that you were a little afraid Regan might somehow be involved in an attempt to blackmail you." Marlowe further elaborates that his disposition of the case has been based on the assumption that the police are not likely to overlook anything obvious in the course of their investigations. He sets himself distinctly apart from the more traditional detective of fiction:

> I'm not Sherlock Holmes or Philo Vance. I don't expect to go over ground the police have covered and pick up a broken pen point and build a case from it.... if they overlook anything ... it's apt to be something looser and vaguer, like a man of Geiger's type sending you his evidence of debt and asking you to pay like a gentleman.

His explanations are sufficient to restore the General's confidence. The old man allows that he is just "a sentimental old goat" and tacitly admits that Regan has indeed been his primary concern all along; he offers Marlowe $1,000 to "Find him.... Just find him."

On his way out of the house, Marlowe spots Carmen and returns the little pearl-handled pistol which he had taken away from her in a scene where she tried to kill Joe Brody. "I brought you back your artillery," he tells her. "I cleaned it and loaded it up. Take my tip—don't shoot it at people, unless you get to be a better shot. Remember?" Carmen's immediate reaction is, "Teach me to shoot." And giggling in her strange way, she persuades him to drive her to an old abandoned oil field on the family property. Here, amid these reminders of the family fortune and its corruption, Marlowe sets up a target. But as he is walking back from it, "she showed me all her sharp little teeth and brought the gun up and started to hiss. . . . 'Stand there, you son of a bitch,' she said." Marlowe laughs and she fires at him—four times before he takes the gun from her. He has anticipated the scene and loaded the gun with blanks. Carmen makes a whistling sound in her throat and passes out.

After Marlowe has taken her home, he engages her older sister Vivian in conversation. From this encounter, then, we finally gather enough details to begin to make sense of this curious and deadly family tragedy. What we discover is that Carmen stands at the center of the troubles. She suffers, among other things, from epileptic attacks, as her behavior at the scene where Geiger was killed, and the strange hissing, giggling noises she frequently utters have already warned Marlowe.

When Regan disappeared, it was because Carmen killed him—in the very same fashion in which she tried to kill Marlowe. Marlowe explains her actions, conjecturally, as a combination of her epilepsy, adolescent lust, and the almost inevitable neurosis fostered by the circumstances in which she was reared. As he tells Vivian, "Night before last when I got home she was in my apartment. She'd kidded the manager into letting her in to wait for me. She was in my bed—naked. I threw her out on her ear. I guess maybe Regan did the same to her sometime. But you can't do that to Carmen."

Vivian admits that Carmen killed Regan and explains her own actions and motivations:

> She came home and told me about it just like a child. She's not normal. I knew the police would get it all out of her. In a little while she would even brag about it. And if dad knew, he would call them instantly and tell them the whole story. And sometime in that night he would die. It's not his dying—it's what he would be thinking just before he died. Rusty wasn't a bad fellow. I didn't love him. He was all right, I guess. He just didn't mean anything to me, one way or another, alive or dead, compared with keeping it from dad.

Vivian, of course, is not the type to approach reality head on; none of the Sternwoods are. As she perceived the situation, her only option was to try to cover up the matter, and the only person she knew powerful enough to help her do that was her gambling acquaintance Eddie Mars. Mars, of course, was only too glad to be of service; the incident clearly gave him leverage on the Sternwood fortune. Canino, no doubt, did the dirty work of stashing the body. But Mars's commitment to service went even further. When the police appeared to be coming too close to the truth, he had his own wife, Mona, hide out to make it appear that she and Regan had left together, thus giving the police a reasonable explanation for Regan's disappearance.

But Mars's greed was finally stronger than his patience. Geiger's whole blackmailing scheme appears, in fact, to have been a ploy sponsored by Mars. As Marlowe theorizes to Vivian:

> Eddie Mars was behind Geiger, protecting him and using him for a cat's-paw. Your father sent for me instead of paying up, which showed he wasn't scared about anything. Eddie Mars wanted to know that. He had something on you and he wanted to know if he had it on the General too. If he had, he could collect a lot of money in a hurry. If not, he would have to wait until you got your share of the family fortune, and in the meantime be satisfied with whatever spare cash he could take away from you across the roulette table.

But this plan did not account for the unpredictable influence of youthful passions. Owen Taylor, the Sternwood chauffeur, had his own romantic interest in Carmen. He was violently affected by her association with Geiger and when he discovered Geiger taking nude pictures of her, pictures that were to be a part of the blackmail plot, he killed him. It was Taylor's fading footsteps that Marlowe heard in that first scene at Geiger's house. Geiger's death then triggered a series of subplots. One of these involved his smut-lending business. With Geiger gone, Joe Brody moved to take over the trade, largely with the help of Agnes, Geiger's former assistant. This move persuaded Carol Lundgren, Geiger's young homosexual roommate, that Brody had been responsible for Geiger's death, so Lundgren killed Brody. Harry Jones was then killed by Canino when Harry tried to work a scheme with Agnes to sell information about Mona to Marlowe. And Mars, without his front man, was forced into covering his own tracks.

Such is the mushrooming effect of one poorly conceived decision. Even an apparently well-intentioned act, such as Vivian's effort to cover up Carmen's murder of Regan, can become the initial stone from which an expanding circle of evil radiates. Four deaths result from Vivian's actions. Owen Taylor kills Geiger because he does not approve of his relationship with Carmen. Carol Lundgren kills Joe Brody because he thinks Brody killed Geiger. Canino kills Harry Jones because he is getting too close to the truth and killing is Canino's job. And Marlowe kills Canino.

But curiously enough, Marlowe must also share, at least partially, in the blame for Harry's death. It was Marlowe, after all, who mentioned to Mars that he was being followed; this tip called Mars's attention to Harry's involvement in the story and led ultimately to his death. Indeed, Marlowe must finally recognize himself to be more subtly and pervasively involved in this very complex story than even he at first imagined. Part of his realization comes when he asks the butler, concerning the General, "What did this Regan fellow have that bored into him so?" The answer he gets is, "Youth, sir. . . . And the soldier's eye. . . . If I may say so, sir, not unlike yours." Understanding the similarity of Marlowe and Regan, at least in the General's eyes, is central to understanding the story. As readers, we, like Marlowe, begin to perceive that Vivian's decision to hide Carmen's murder of Regan may not, in fact, have been motivated solely by a desire to protect her sister or even to protect her ailing father. Rather, she may well have surmised that Regan was more important to the General than his own daughters. Thus, she may—rightly—have been more fearful of the unknown consequences of the discovery of the murder by her father than of opening herself to the blackmailing demands of Eddie Mars. Marlowe must feel more than a little uneasy as he realizes that he has been drawn into this family saga as a substitute for Regan, one surrogate son hired to ascertain the whereabouts of another, while the daughters slip ever further into the grips of gangsters.

But a sixth death in the book, that of Owen Taylor, may help illuminate our search for "first causes," for a place to lay ultimate responsibility for the chain of murders chronicled here. Shortly after the scene in which he kills Geiger, Taylor's car is found in the surf off Lido pier with him still in it. The hand throttle had been set halfway down, and he was apparently sapped before the car plunged through the barricades into the sea. But this case is never solved, although Joe Brody is a prime suspect. When the first film version of *The Big Sleep* was being prepared, the screenwriters even sent a query to Chandler: "Who killed Owen Taylor?" Chandler's response was a simple "I don't know."

The incident is important because it calls attention to Chandler's general distaste for the typical demand that detective stories should tie up every loose end. Furthermore, it underscores his deep-seated aversion to strictly rational explanations for human actions. If we look closely at Vivian's decision to cover Carmen's deadly act, for example, we simply can not devise a purely rational account of it. Given the implied strife between the two sisters, Vivian's less-than-loving relationship with her father, and the fact that Carmen's victim was her own husband (even if she did not love him), Vivian's act simply can not be circumscribed within rational bounds. Nevertheless, given Vivian's character, her environment, and an emotionally-charged situation, we can readily *believe* that she might make such a decision. The deeper we penetrate the motives of Chandler's characters, the deeper we find the morass of human passion and unpredictability.

But if Chandler is not interested in constructing neatly rational puzzles, what exactly is he up to here? We can glean at least a partial answer to this perplexing question from a close examination of the opening scene and some related passages. When Marlowe first comes to call on the Sternwood millions, his attention is arrested by a curious drama in glass:

> Over the entrance doors, which would have let in a troop of Indian elephants, there was a broad stained-glass panel showing a knight in dark armor rescuing a lady who was tied to a tree and didn't have any clothes on but some very long and convenient hair. The knight had pushed the visor of his helmet back to be sociable, and he was fiddling with the knots on the ropes that tied the lady to the tree and not getting anywhere. I stood there and thought that if I lived in the house, I would sooner or later have to climb up there and help him. He didn't seem to be really trying.

Critics have often complained that Chandler was overly concerned with sentimentalism and the tropes of the chivalric romance; the kind of elements on which this glass panel focuses. But even a cursory look at Chandler's overt references to the romance and knight-errantry within the novel, as here, indicates a decided touch of irony in his treatment of the subject. Indeed, *The Big Sleep* might be read as a chronicle of the *failure* of romance. In the midst of one of his confrontations with Carmen, for example, Marlowe turns to his chess board for distraction. He makes a move with a knight, then retracts it and comments, "the move with the knight was wrong. I put it back where I had moved it from. Knights had no meaning in this game. It wasn't a game for knights." And near the end of the book, he comments again on the knight in the stained-glass window saying, he "still wasn't getting anywhere untying the naked damsel from the tree."

Carmen, of course, *is* the naked damsel in distress in this book, and finally we and Marlowe must ask ourselves if he has really been any more successful in aiding her than has the knight in armor trapped forever in the glass. And we must agree that he has not.

About all that can be said for Marlowe here as the "romantic hero" is that he does, at least, keep Carmen from killing anyone else while he is on the scene. And he keeps her from being killed or from facing the harsh justice of the legal system—rather, he advises Vivian to "take her away. . . . Hell, she might even get herself cured, you know. It's been done." But he has been totally ineffectual in penetrating the mystery of this family and its seemingly inexorable involvement with the world of crime. He has achieved no ennobling resolution. He has had no success in getting at the heart of this saga which is finally the story of two women, two sisters, Carmen and Vivian, and the last days of a dying old patriarch. Marlowe's understanding is hardly less limited than Vivian's, and she can not bear to probe her actions very deeply:

> I knew Eddie Mars would bleed me white, but I didn't care. I had to have help and I could only get it from somebody like him. . . . There have been times when I hardly believed it all myself. And other times when I had to get drunk quickly—whatever time of day it was. Awfully damn quickly.

In Vivian's reluctance to face her relation to evil squarely, Chandler reminds us all of the limits of our ability to approach and comprehend the truth. Even if we still possess the idealistic, romantic sensibilities that can drive us to noble actions, the consequences, like the motives, are never really unadulterated. And finally, like Marlowe, we are impotent to untie the knots of our lives. He tries, like Vivian, simply to avoid seeing, to deaden his sensibilites; in the book's last paragraph he "stopped at a bar and had a couple of double Scotches." But, as he recognizes, "they didn't do me any good." Avoiding complexity does not resolve it.

As he walks out of the Sternwood house for the last time, Marlowe comments: "Outside, the bright gardens had a haunted look, as though small wild eyes were watching me from behind the bushes, as though the sunshine itself had a mysterious something in its light." At the end, there is still mystery—the mystery of the human condition, of life and death in a world of fate and chance and evil.

Source: Jerry Speir, "The First Novels: *The Big Sleep, Farewell My Lovely, The High Window*," in *Raymond Chandler*, Frederick Ungar Publishing Co., 1981, pp. 19–31.

Roger Shatzkin

In the following essay, Shatzkin compares the novel and film versions of The Big Sleep, *finding that in both confusion and illogicality are natural parts of the terrain.*

Raymond Chandler's *The Big Sleep* appears to fit that category of novel critic Edmund Wilson identified as capable of being "poured . . . on to the screen as easily as if it had been written in the studios . . ." ("The Boys in the Back Room" [1940]). In many respects, director Howard Hawks and his collaborators did succeed in pouring the essence of Chandler into their 1946 film. Most notably, they recreated the novel's atmosphere of evanescent corruption and emphasized character at the expense of formal considerations of plot. Nevertheless, the glibness of Wilson's metaphor disguises the "filtering" process operant in any transfer of narrative from one medium to another: Chandler's story of his hero's failed individualistic and Romantic quest became on screen a dark romantic comedy that explores the feasibility of human and sexual commitment between a man and a woman, in this case the film's stars and real-life lovers, Humphrey Bogart and Lauren Bacall. (In practical terms, Hawks was making a sequel to *To Have and Have Not* [1944], which first starred the pair.)

For *The Big Sleep*, there are added problems with Wilson's simple-minded notion of adaptation: Chandler's rather loosely plotted and crowded narrative (synthesized ingeniously out of four pulp magazine stories) became even more complex on screen. The reason for this was a seemingly straightforward filtering mechanism: the Hollywood Production Code's objection to "censorable" aspects of the novel. "Much of the illogic of the film," James Monaco has written, "is simply due to cuts which were made to conform to the Code." But let us take a closer look at some of the misconceptions surrounding the novel and the film, and the apparently intertwined issues of incomprehensibility and censorship.

The first misconception: *The Big Sleep*, both as novel and film, defies comprehension. True, Raymond Chandler confessed to suffering "plot-constipation," wished to possess "one of these facile plotting brains, like Erie [Stanley] Gardner or somebody," and admitted that *The Big Sleep* "happens to be more interested in people than in plot . . ." And granted, director Hawks persisted in glorifying the illogic of his adaptation: in interview after interview he insisted that he "never could figure the story out . . ." that he "can't follow it," and

> "Though their events and characterizations may be ultimately deciphered, novel and film are texts *about* confusion; impenetrability, if not their final result, is at their core."

so on. What is more, one of the oft repeated anecdotes about a film's production links author and *auteur* in mutual confusion: during the filming, Bogart, the picture's Philip Marlowe, apparently asked Hawks just who killed one of the minor characters, a chauffeur named Owen Taylor. (Taylor turns up in his employer's Buick, awash in the Pacific.) Since neither Hawks nor his screenwriters William Faulkner and Leigh Brackett knew, they cabled Chandler. And Chandler wired back: "I don't know."

For the record: with a little effort, novel and film *can* be comprehended, if what is meant by that is that their plots can be linearized, sorted out. (Paul Jensen deserves credit for mentioning this in his article on Chandler in *Film Comment*, November-December, 1974.) But to shift perspective, the popular myths about *The Big Sleep* are important. Though their events and characterizations may be ultimately deciphered, novel and film are texts *about* confusion; impenetrability, if not their final result, is at their core. So the question becomes, not "who killed Owen Taylor?" but, more properly (to echo Edmund Wilson's skepticism about detective fiction), "who *cares* who killed Owen Taylor?"

Neither Chandler, nor Marlowe, the novel's detective-narrator, seems to have cared. Hired by the elderly, infirm General Sternwood to investigate some gambling debts his younger daughter, Carmen, has incurred, debts which in turn may become the basis for blackmail, Marlowe plunges into intrigue more complex than circumstances would seem to warrant. For one thing, the General's son-in-law, "Rusty" Regan is missing, and his older daughter, Regan's wife Vivian, suspects that Marlowe has been engaged to find him. As is clear in Chandler: Carmen's ostensible blackmailer, Arthur Geiger, runs a pornographic lending library; Geiger

is murdered at his home in the presence of a stupefied Carmen; he has provided drugs and photographed her nude for future extortion schemes. Marlowe rescues Carmen, entering Geiger's place after hearing shots and observing two men leaving in quick succession. The first man turns out to be Taylor, who drives off to his mysterious death.

Marlowe (and Chandler) forget about Taylor. Attention shifts instead to the second man out of the house, Joe Brody, who, like Taylor, is an ex-boyfriend of Carmen's. Brody somehow obtains the negatives of Carmen and proceeds to blackmail her. Marlowe goes to Brody's apartment to recover the negatives and pictures; he first disarms Brody and then Carmen, who has come to retrieve the blackmail materials herself. After Carmen leaves, Carol Lundgren, Geiger's valet and lover shoots Brody, mistakenly thinking that Brody has killed Geiger. As Marlowe later explains, Taylor, chivalrously defending his old flame Carmen, had actually done the deed.

Either William Faulkner or Leigh Brackett (Hawks's original screenwriters) was the person concerned about what happened to Taylor. One of them wrote some dialogue for a scene, patterned after one in the novel (but cut from the final film), that sums up, more neatly than Chandler, what happened. In this scene, mid-way through the novel and screenplay, Marlowe is explaining his involvement in the affair to the district attorney. In the novel, Marlowe merely alludes to the events that have transpired and then responds to the D.A.'s queries. In the screenplay, the D.A., in dialogue never filmed, adds his own summation:

> So Taylor killed Geiger because he was in love with the Sternwood girl. And Brody followed Taylor, sapped him and took the photographs and pushed Taylor into the ocean. And the punk [Lundgren] killed Brody because the punk thought he should have inherited Geiger's business and Brody was throwing him out.

Although no one involved with the production seems to recall this unshot speech, the screenwriters' D.A. would have settled the question of Taylor's demise once and for all, tying up a "loose end" over which Chandler himself apparently never fretted.

Faulkner or Brackett's dialogue here strives for order (despite Hawks's recollection that "there was no sense in making [the story] logical. So we didn't"). And the dialogue, in changing Lundgren's motivation from a lover's revenge also manifests another tendency toward "logic." And this brings us to the second misconception about the film: how it censored the novel.

Throughout the two drafts of the script, the screenwriters anticipated that many sections of the novel might offend the Production Code—matters of sexual conduct, police misconduct, Marlowe's final decision to let a murderer go free—and they took steps to circumvent possible problems. Many of the novel's "objectionable" aspects did have to be cut from the final film. Geiger's pornography racket is nowhere mentioned (we just see some posh clients skulking about his "bookstore"), nor is the homosexual relationship between Geiger and Lundgren. Both of these omissions cause confusions (as does the film's ending to a degree, but for reasons other than censorship). But other changes, such as presenting a clothed Carmen at Geiger's and later at Marlowe's apartment, do not alter the final quality of the film. A recent assessment, such as Gavin Lambert's that the movie "seems badly hobbled by censorship" (*The Dangerous Edge*, 1975), hardly seems appropriate.

Prior censorship was the rule in the screenplays. The screenwriters transformed Geiger's business from pornography and extortion to the vaguer endeavor of blackmail alone (late in the second script draft Marlowe actually finds packing cases of "manilla filing envelopes, ledgers, etc."). Lundgren's relationship to Geiger becomes all business. Even Carmen Sternwood's nymphomania is de-sexed (though one wonders how Martha Vickers sultry performance in the film could have possibly jibed with the script's conception). Carmen's psychotic and homicidal behavior is brought on by jealousy. She murders Regan and attempts to murder Marlowe, according to Faulkner and Brackett, because she has lost the affections of both of them (at least in her mind) to her sister Vivian, and *not* because they are the only two men who refuse to sleep with her. And though Hawks has credited the Production Code office with rejecting the novel's ending and, when prodded, providing their own, Faulkner and Brackett had already altered Chandler's denouement in their first script. (In letting Carmen go free to be "cured" in the book, Marlowe violates the Code's provision against unpunished crimes. The film's ending is actually a *third* script revision of the novel's ending.)

But Faulkner and Brackett's careful anticipation of the Code and their finely wrought "logic" were to no avail. Hawks excised a number of scenes from their screenplay as he shot. And the filming, done from the second draft or Temporary script,

had run too long. So "Jules Furthman was called in," according to Leigh Brackett, "for a rewrite to cut the remaining or unshot portion [of the script] into a manageable length...." Whatever coherence the original screenwriters had concocted (or preserved from Chandler) was eradicated in shortening an overlong screenplay; it was not the direct evisceration of the novel for the censors, as Monaco and other critics have averred, that cause the movie's notorious incomprehensibility.

But the film, in its final and less "coherent" form, becomes—in the best Hawks tradition—a type of Rorschach test in which the elipses can be filled in by the audience. And, paradoxically, it moves closer to the novel as a result. In the minds of viewers imbued with the requisite imagination, the spirit of the book's censorable content remains, albeit sometimes between the lines. As Charles Gregory has written, despite the fact that the movie had to avoid "explicit references to sex, dope and pornography that are woven into the novel ... somehow the film reflects all this to the sophisticated viewer without ever drawing the ire of the censors or even the notice of the prudes."

Typical of the cuts made to shorten the script was the removal of a shot in the first scene showing Owen Taylor washing the Sternwood Buick as Marlowe passes from the General's mansion to his hothouse (a direct transposition from the novel intended to identify the chauffeur and foreshadow his complicity in Geiger's murder). In the film, Marlowe simply walks from the mansion's hallway into the greenhouse—the magic of film editing has connected the two edifices. And Taylor gets whisked away to the limbo of legend.

But as Leigh Brackett observed: "Audiences came away feeling that they had seen the hell and all of a film even if they didn't rightly know what it was all about. Again, who cared? It was grand fun, with sex and danger and a lot of laughs...." Again, who cared? Let us turn to the novel and film in more detail to see if we can decipher what they are all about—and if it matters if they are *about* anything.

For that matter, what *is* Raymond Chandler's *The Big Sleep* about? The novel functions as an entertainment, a sometimes self-satiric, self-contained world of double-cross, moral and political corruption in which our confusion as readers helps engender our involvement and our identification with the hero, Philip Marlowe. The central movement of the novel, though, focuses on its protagonist's quest, not for the solution to a puzzle or a mystery (though that is necessarily accomplished), but primarily for his double, his *doppelganger*. It is this covert quest—which informs the bulk of Chandler's novels but is most prominent in *The Big Sleep* and *The Long Goodbye* (1954)—and its requisite failure that create many of the novel's strong, if fugitive, resonances.

Marlowe's search for Terence "Rusty" Regan is the hidden energizing force of the novel (hidden, in some ways, from Chandler himself). It is also the genesis of the novel's seeming confusion and impenetrability. But the pattern of Marlowe's search for Regan does not emerge readily from the narrative. Throughout roughly the first half of the novel, questions about Regan, Vivian Sternwood's missing husband, keep surfacing, but Marlowe's chief preoccupation lies with keeping Carmen safe and the Sternwood's family name unbesmirched through the three deaths that touch on them (i.e., Geiger's, Taylor's, and Brody's). Marlowe's identification with Regan is established at his initial visit to the General (where he replaces Regan as the old man's sensual surrogate—drinking and smoking for Sternwood's vicarious enjoyment—and is hired for a job that Regan, the General's confidant as well as son-in-law, would probably have undertaken). But Marlowe does not turn his attention to the missing man until the mystery that propels the beginning half of the action, concerning Carmen's blackmail, has ostensibly been resolved. And all along, he denies various allegations that he *is* looking for Regan, even though, ironically, they are true.

At this point, to better understand Regan's place in the novel, it will help to clarify the structure of *The Big Sleep*. Writing on the film, James Monaco has offered a helpful description that applies equally well to the novel. He notes in the movie's construction a "dual structure: a 'surface' mystery (usually the client's) and a 'deep' mystery (the metaphysical or political problem which presents itself to the detective)." Fredric Jameson views Chandler's dual structure slightly differently, noting a tendency for the novels to mislead readers because a Chandler work "passes itself off as a murder mystery." Jameson points out that "In fact Chandler's stories are first and foremost descriptions of searches . . ." Here the "murder mystery" corresponds to Monaco's "surface" enigma, the "search" to the "deep" structure. Jameson later expresses the double nature of the narrative in terms of time:

The final element in Chandler's characteristic form is that the underlying crime is always old, lying half-forgotten in the pasts of the characters before the book begins. This is the principal reason why the readers attention is diverted from [the underlying crime]; he assumes it to be a part of the dimension of the present. . . .

Relating this to *The Big Sleep* then, this is what happens: the crime in the past that generates the whole novel, yet which is unknown to Marlowe or the reader at the outset of the book, is the murder of Regan by Carmen Sternwood. Regan, like some entombed character in Poe, lies mouldering in a sump in the oilfield below the Sternwood mansion while four more deaths result from the unrecognized cover-up of his demise. And Marlowe spends all his initial energy treating the symptoms of the case, the surface of the present, before turning to their cause in the past.

I do not believe that Chandler was in complete touch with the metaphysical significance of Regan for his protagonist. Chandler, as is most clearly exemplified in his *Atlantic* essay, "The Simple Art of Murder," written five years after *The Big Sleep*, tended to conceive of his hero in extremely idealized terms:

. . . Down these mean streets a man must go who is not himself mean, who is neither tarnished nor afraid. . . . He must be the best man in his world and a good enough man for any world!

Despite Chandler's notion of the hero as knight in a corrupt world (a conception taken up too uncritically by many who have written about him), Marlowe is a far from simplistic character. In the beginning of *The Big Sleep*, he does literally project himself into a tableau on a stained-glass panel in the Sternwood home, depicting "a knight in dark armor rescuing a lady . . . [who] didn't have any clothes on . . ." "I would have to climb up there and help him," Marlowe says to himself. "He didn't seem to be really trying." However, later in the novel, when a naked Carmen invades his bedroom, he looks down at his chessboard and concludes that "Knights had no meaning in this game. It wasn't a game for knights." The thought is reemphasized when he enters the Sternwood house for the last time and observes the knight, who "still wasn't getting anywhere. . . ."

In short, a dialectic exists within the novel: Marlowe begins as knight, but is forced to cope in a sordid world: to do so he must be willing to summon a darker side of himself. Chandler's idealization represses this darker side. This is where Regan as "double" comes in: Chandler fractionalizes his hero into two characters. Regan, missing and dead (ultimately repressed!) throughout the entire novel represents the potentially corruptible side of his protagonist which Chandler cannot brook. Regan has crossed the line. He is beyond the law all the way—a successful gangster-bootlegger. He commits himself sexually to women: he marries Vivian Sternwood; he (probably) has an affair with Mona Mars, before and after she is married. He commits himself to public social causes: he fought for the I.R.A. in 1922. He commits himself to having (if not coveting) money: he carries fifteen thousand dollars in bills at all times. In fact, the D.A. surmises that the real reason Sternwood hired Marlowe in the first place was to find out if Regan had betrayed his trust by being the real force behind the blackmail instigated by Geiger (ironically, he is). In sum, Regan is Marlowe's alter ego, an adult version of the detective's adolescent, solipsistic Romantic, who in "growing up" has taken the fall.

Throughout the novel we are given hints of the Marlowe-Regan bond. Marlowe resembles Regan: the D.A.'s man Bernie Ohls describes Regan as a "big guy as tall as you and a shade heavier." Both men are in their thirties. Their relationships to women intersect completely. Vivian Sternwood and Mona Mars are both attracted to Marlowe as they were to Regan, and Carmen tries to shoot Marlowe, as she did Regan, because he too would not sleep with her. (The link of the two men through the women is possibly covert evidence of Marlowe's repressed homoerotic attraction to Regan.) General Sternwood's butler explicitly compares the two men, and the General takes a paternal (and perhaps homosexual) interest in both. And when Marlowe confronts a photograph of Regan, the detective describes his impressions in terms he might as easily use for himself. It was "Not the face of a tough guy and not the face of a man who could be pushed around much by anybody ... [It was] a face that looked a little taut, the face of a man who would move fast and play for keeps...." Marlowe concludes portentously, "I would know that face if I saw it."

So Marlowe's search for Regan represents maximally an investigation into his own identity, into his own soul's potential weaknesses and arrested tendencies. In his final soliloquy Marlowe intones the following famous lines in speaking of his entombed "brother" Regan:

Where did it matter where you lay once you were dead? In a dirty sump or in a marble tower on top of a high hill? You were dead, you were sleeping the big sleep, you were not bothered by things like that.

Oil and water were the same as wind and air to you. You just slept the big sleep, not caring about the nastiness of how you died or where you fell. Me, I was part of the nastiness now. Far more a part of it than Rusty Regan was....

Marlowe, who when captive at one point made macabre jokes about his choice of casket and about Eddie Mars's henchman digging *him* a grave, finally comes face to face with his own mortality only through Regan. In so doing, he begins to understand his corruptibility, as well (on the ethical level as "knight" he has let murderess Carmen go unpunished). He is "part of the nastiness now ..." and that is the full import of his search. For the reader, as Fredric Jameson has put it, the end of the novel "is able to bring us up short, without warning, against the reality of death itself, stale death, reaching out to remind the living of its own mouldering resting place."

Paradoxically, Faulkner, Brackett, and Hawks's screen version immediately makes the Marlowe-Regan connection much more explicit than in the novel. In the Hawksian tradition of professional equals, Marlowe's first dialogue with the General reveals that he and Regan have been respectful opponents during prohibition, each on a different side of the law ("We used to swap shots between drinks, or drinks between shots—whichever you like."). But if anything, Regan (mysteriously now named "Shawn") is invoked quickly only to be exorcised. Though the surface mystery in the film remains the same, still concerning Carmen's blackmail, the deep mystery will ultimately concern, as Monaco has pointed out, what gambler Eddie Mars "has" on Vivian Sternwood Rutledge (Lauren Bacall), here a divorcee. (In the novel, Mars is blackmailing Vivian over Carmen's murder of Regan; he has helped her dispose of Regan's body.) The question of what Mars "has" on Vivian masks the real thrust of Hawks's film, which is to determine with whom Vivian will ultimately side, and as in his best comedies whether or not she and Marlowe will realize their mutual romantic attraction.

To emphasize leading lady Bacall as Vivian, Hawks and his writers placed her in three scenes in which she does not appear in the novel (Marlowe returning Carmen to her home, his visit to Brody's apartment, his incarceration in Realito at the hands of Mars's man Canino); they lengthened one encounter from the book (Vivian's visit to Marlowe's office), and added one long scene that appears only in the film. This scene, the famous Cafe/Horserace double entendre sequence (mandated by Warners' front office a full year after the rest of the movie was in the can, to give the stars yet more exposure together) is indicative of a pattern of attraction-repulsion between Vivian and Marlowe that firmly establishes as the center of the film the question of their eventual fate together.

In almost every scene in which they appear together, up until the penultimate one, Marlowe and Vivian begin a wary, but cordial verbal sparring. But each encounter ends in witty vitriol ("Kissing is nice, but your father didn't hire me to sleep with you."). The first mode of verbal skirmishing is the substitute for and correlative of a romantic language founded on emotion that Hawks employs throughout his romantic "screwball" comedies. Though Hawks took this convention from his comedies, in *The Big Sleep* he left its significance open ended. The dialogue between Marlowe and Vivian can end in romance or—in keeping with Chandler, the tradition of the *femme fatale* in general and of *film noir* in particular—in betrayal.

Near the end of the film, an obligatory "lay off the case" scene with Bernie Ohls (Regis Toomey) was written into the film; it confirms that Marlowe's vacillating relationship with Vivian has become the film's deep structure and raison d'être. After Ohls has conveyed his message instructing Marlowe to desist, the detective recapitulates the case so far and indicates why he must go on:

> "Bernie, put yourself in my shoes for a minute. A nice old guy has two daughters. One of them is, well, wonderful. And the other is not so wonderful. As a result somebody gets something on her. The father hires me to pay off. Before I can get to the guy, the family chauffeur kills him! But that didn't stop things. It just starts them. And two murders later I find out somebody's got something on wonderful."

So the film comes down to Marlowe's endeavors to "clear" and win "wonderful."

When the ending does come, it makes little plot sense. Marlowe and Vivian are united after the detective forces Mars, his only serious "rival," out of a door into a hail of machine-gun fire. In Jules Furthman's reworking of the conclusion, the only logical extra-textual explanation for Mars's death is that he, not Carmen, killed Regan, and that he is blackmailing Vivian by making her think Carmen did it.

If the narrative logic is flawed, the emotional logic is not. We care about Marlowe/Bogart and Vivian/Bacall; they have earned our respect through their mutual (and mostly verbal) abilities to cope with a hostile environment. And it is satisfying to see their compatibility, which we have

sensed all along, romantically vindicated. Likewise, in the novel, despite his limitations, we care about Marlowe. His voice unifies the quicksilver and chaotic world in which he operates, a world in which almost all events can never be known but only hypothesized about. And that extends to one misplaced chauffeur, at sea in the depths of illogic, about whom one ultimately need not care. Peace to you, Owen Taylor.

Source: Roger Shatzkin, "Who Cares Who Killed Owen Taylor?" in *The Modern American Novel and the Movies*, edited by Gerald Peary and Roger Shatzkin, Frederick Ungar Publishing Co., 1978, pp. 80–94.

Sources

Chandler, Raymond, *The Big Sleep*, Vintage, 1992, pp. 114, 204.

———, "The Simple Art of Murder," in *Atlantic Monthly*, December 1944, p. 59.

Davies, Russell, "Omnes Me Impune Lacessunt," in *The World of Raymond Chandler*, edited by Miriam Gross, Weidenfeld and Nicolson, 1977, pp. 32–42.

James, Clive, "The Country behind the Hill," in *The World of Raymond Chandler*, edited by Miriam Gross, Weidenfeld and Nicolson, 1977, pp. 116–26.

Linder, Daniel, "The Big Sleep," in the *Explicator*, Vol. 59, Issue 3, Spring 2001, p. 137.

MacShane, Frank, *The Life of Raymond Chandler*, Hammish Hamilton Ltd., 1986, p. 68.

Speir, Jerry, *Raymond Chandler*, Frederick Ungar Publishing, 1981, p. 30.

Further Reading

Durham, Philip, *Down These Mean Streets a Man Must Go: Raymond Chandler's Knight*, University of North Carolina Press, 1963.
    Durham examines Marlowe's code of chivalric behavior in this ingenious study.

Hiney, Tom, *Raymond Chandler: A Biography*, Atlantic Monthly Press, 1997.
    Hiney draws on Chandler's papers and letters to construct this engaging biography.

Marling, William, *Raymond Chandler*, Twayne, 1986.
    Marling provides a solid and accessible introduction to Chandler's fiction in this study.

Van Dover, J. K., ed., *The Critical Responses to Raymond Chandler*, Greenwood, 1995.
    This collection of essays covers a wide range of critical approaches to Chandler's novels.

Death in Venice

Thomas Mann
1912

Thomas Mann's initial inspiration for his novella, *Death in Venice* (1912), came from German writer Johann Wolfgang von Goethe, who fell in love with a teenage girl when he was seventy-four years old and vacationing in Marienbad. However, Mann's own trip to Venice supplied many of the details for the story. The story concerns Gustav von Aschenbach, an accomplished middle-aged writer who has dedicated his life to his art and the pursuit of beauty, and his love for Tadzio, a fourteen-year-old Polish boy vacationing with his family in Venice. Although Tadzio escapes the cholera epidemic engulfing the city, von Aschenbach does not, and he dies on the beach the day Tadzio leaves. Mann uses the story to explore the relationships between death and beauty, life and art, chaos and order—all recurring themes in his writing. Mann gives von Aschenbach German composer Gustav Mahler's first name and physical appearance, and Tadzio evokes the Greek gods Eros and Hermes, the latter of which is Mann's favorite Greek god. The "actual" Tadzio, the boy Mann saw in Venice and on whom he based his character, was identified years later as Baron Wladyslaw Moes.

Von Aschenbach also bears a remarkable similarity to Mann himself. Both live in the same Munich neighborhood, both summer in the Bavarian Alps, and both share the same work habits. Both are also heavily influenced by the classics. The novella itself, full of allusions to Greek mythology, is indebted to the *Odyssey* and Erwin Rohde's *Psyche*, an influential book on Greek religion. *Death*

Thomas Mann

in Venice remains one of Mann's most popular works, appearing in numerous anthologies and in Mann's *Collected Works* (1960). It has also become a classic of gay literature, even though the story does not explicitly address homosexuality.

Author Biography

A master of refined and tightly structured prose, and arguably one of the most important literary figures of twentieth-century Germany, Paul Thomas Mann was born June 6, 1875, in Lubeck, Germany, the second son of Thomas Johann Heinrich Mann and Julia da Silva-Bruhns, a wealthy Brazilian and daughter of a former citizen of Lubeck. Although pampered by his mother, Mann strove during childhood to please his father, a grain exporter who wanted his son to take over the family business. When his father died in 1891, the family dissolved the business and moved to Munich, where Mann attended the University of Munich, pursued a writing career, and studied the philosophy of Arthur Schopenhauer and Friedrich Nietzsche. He published his first book, a collection of stories titled *Little Herr Friedemann* in 1898, when he was just twenty-two years old. Following in the footsteps of

his older brother, Luiz Heinrich, who was developing his own career as a respected writer, Mann established a reputation as a leading writer of his generation with his next book, the sprawling family saga, *Buddenbrooks* (1901), a thinly veiled account of his own family history and Lubeck, his home town and a port in the southwest corner of the Baltic Sea.

Though he was strongly attracted to young men, Mann adhered to social convention, marrying Katja Pringsheim in 1905. Pringsheim, a wealthy Munich-born woman, managed Mann's career and finances and bore him six children. In 1912, Mann published *Death in Venice*, a novella exploring the obsessive love of a middle-aged writer for a young boy. Like his other stories from this period, *Death in Venice* ends tragically, as the protagonist, Gustav von Aschenbach, falls into the moral and emotional abyss of his own unchecked desires. The inner turmoil of von Aschenbach mirrored the political turmoil of Europe at this time, which was consumed with the Ottoman Empire's desperate attempts to retain power. Mann supported Kaiser Wilhelm's policies and urged other German intellectuals to do the same, claiming that liberalism was contributing to the increasing decadence in Germany and Europe. Mann's political views are on display in his 1924 novel, *The Magic Mountain*, which explores the conflicts between liberal and conservative values. With the rise of Hitler and the Nazis, Mann fled to Switzerland in 1933, and in 1938 moved to the United States, where he was named an honorary faculty member at Princeton University. That same year the German government revoked his citizenship and denounced Mann for his political activism.

Mann's numerous books include the four-volume *Joseph and His Brothers* (1934–44), *Doctor Faustus* (1947), and *The Confessions of Felix Krull, Confidence Man* (1954). Recipient of the Nobel Prize for Literature in 1929 and internationally acclaimed for his essays as well as his stories and novels, Mann died in 1955 in Switzerland.

Plot Summary

Chapter 1

In the opening chapter of *Death in Venice*, von Aschenbach, physically and emotionally exhausted by his work, takes a walk by a cemetery on the outskirts of Munich and sees a red-haired stranger with a rucksack. The man wears a straw hat and has the "appearance of a foreigner, of a traveler from afar." Seeing the man awakens wanderlust in von Aschenbach, and he determines to leave Munich for a vacation. Von Aschenbach had previously shunned travel, doing so only for his health and not for any passion or desire to visit exotic places. This desire was different, however, representing an urge to get away from his work, the very thing that has consumed him his entire life.

The date of the story is unspecified, but the narrator writes that the opening scene takes place, "On a spring afternoon in 19—, a year that for months glowered threateningly over our continent . . . ." Mann refers here to the numerous diplomatic crises throughout Europe that would eventually lead to World War I.

Chapter 2

In this chapter, the narrator provides an extended character description of von Aschenbach, noting his early success as a writer, his fragile health, and his illustrious family background. All of his ancestors "had been officers, judges, and government functionaries ... devoted to the service of king and country." Von Aschenbach's devotion to his art is a way to control the destructive, darker emotional impulses that can easily overwhelm one's appetites. Von Aschenbach's disciplined nature, his adherence to will and rationality, and the life of the mind, is symbolic of middle-class Europe's repression and fear of the body's desires.

Chapter 3

Von Aschenbach leaves for a resort on the Adriatic about two weeks after seeing the traveler in the cemetery in Chapter One, but soon tires of its "provincial flavor" and journeys to Venice. On the boat, he sees a group of young people accompanied by an old fop with dyed hair and rouge in his cheeks, whose appearance disgusts the writer. Arriving in Lido, von Aschenbach is taken to Venice by a disturbed gondolier who disappears once he has dropped off von Aschenbach. At dinner, von Aschenbach first sees Tadzio and his family, and is overcome by Tadzio's beauty, noting how the boy reminds him of a Greek sculpture, and of Eros, the Greek god of love. After contemplating his own aging face, von Aschenbach walks through the city and falls sick. He determines to leave the city for Trieste, but after his luggage is mistakenly shipped to a different destination he decides to stay and wait for it to return. He recognizes his joy in having to stay, for it means he can be around Tadzio.

Media Adaptations

- Luchino Visconti's 1971 film adaptation of *Death in Venice* starring Dirk Bogarde and Bjorn Andresen is available at most video stores. In Visconti's film, Aschenbach is a composer instead of a writer.

Mann's story is rife with symbolism. The black gondola carrying von Aschenbach to Venice is coffin-like, and its ominous gondolier evokes the traveler from the cemetery and suggests the mythical Charon, who ferried Greek heroes such as Hercules and Odysseus to the Underworld across the River Styx. Venice, like Italy and southern Europe, symbolizes the passionate and the sensuous, in contrast to the orderly and disciplined Germany, a northern European country.

Chapter 4

Von Aschenbach decides to stay in Venice, even though his luggage has returned. He spends his days watching Tadzio and reflecting on his beauty and the similarity between his own love for the boy and Socrates's love for Phaedrus. Von Aschenbach believes that both he and Socrates see in beauty a path to the spiritual. Tadzio inspires von Aschenbach to write, and using the boy's body as a model the writer pens an essay that he believes "would soon amaze many a reader with its purity, nobility, and surging depth of feeling." The next morning, von Aschenbach follows Tadzio to the sea determined to strike up a casual conversation, but is overcome with fear and walks past him. Obsessed with the boy, von Aschenbach falls deeper into a kind of dream world, in which he sees daily events such as the sunrise in terms of Greek mythological figures such as Eos, goddess of dawn, and her brother Helios, god of the sun. Tadzio himself reminds von Aschenbach of Hyacinthus, a beautiful Spartan boy loved by Apollo.

After Tadzio smiles at von Aschenbach while the latter is reading on the terrace, the writer becomes enraptured with the boy, comparing the smile to that of Narcissus, a Greek god who spurned the advances of the nymph Echo, who subsequently died of grief. The gods punished Narcissus by having him fall in love with his own reflection in the river and drown. Von Aschenbach flees the terrace and retreats to the rear of the hotel park whispering to himself: "You must not smile so! Listen, no one is allowed to smile that way at anyone!" The chapter ends with von Aschenbach whispering, "I love you!" As von Aschenbach's infatuation with Tadzio grows, the distance between narrator and von Aschenbach also grows. Whereas the two were previously intertwined, they are now more easily distinguished.

Chapter 5

Cholera grips Venice and the number of tourists declines. Von Aschenbach stalks Tadzio's family through Venice's labyrinthine streets, convincing himself of the dignity of his feelings, and that his pursuit of Tadzio is noble. One night, while watching musicians perform at the hotel, von Aschenbach sees Tadzio nearby, and notes, "He is sickly; he will probably not live long." The following day, a British travel agent confirms that Asiatic cholera is spreading through the city, and warns von Aschenbach to leave, as a quarantine will be instituted soon. Because Venice's economy is based on tourism, however, no one has told travelers the truth or the severity of the situation. Crime, public drunkenness, and all forms of vice skyrocket in this crisis atmosphere. Von Aschenbach consoles himself with the thought that if the epidemic leads to a quarantine, he would be quarantined with Tadzio. That night he dreams of an orgiastic ritual in which animal-skin clad people dance madly while worshipping a huge wooden phallus. "His soul tasted the lewdness and frenzy of surrender."

The city gradually empties of remaining tourists, and von Aschenbach feels relieved because he no longer has to disguise his passion for Tadzio. He begins dressing extravagantly, wearing jewelry, makeup, and perfume, and dyeing his hair. He now resembles the traveler in the first chapter and the foppish man he despised in the third. Von Aschenbach also develops fever after eating infected strawberries. When he discovers that Tadzio's family is leaving after lunch, he walks to the beach to watch Tadzio play with his friends one more time. After wrestling with his friend, Yashu, who had pushed his face in the sand, Tadzio stands up and walks into the water, rebuffing any attempts of an apology. He looks back at the shore after reaching a sandbar and makes eye contact with von

Aschenbach, who imagines the boy is beckoning him. This is von Aschenbach's last thought as he slumps in his chair and dies.

Characters

Cemetery Traveler

Von Aschenbach sees the traveler in the cemetery at the beginning of the story. He is carrying a rucksack and a walking stick, and wearing a yellow suit with a straw hat. To von Aschenbach, he looks like a foreigner. "His posture conveyed an impression of imperious surveillance, fortitude, even wildness." Like the gondolier and the old fop, the traveler displays his teeth "menacingly." The traveler makes hostile eye contact with von Aschenbach, but von Aschenbach turns away. However, the sight of the stranger induces the writer to reflect on his youth and dream of traveling to exotic places; von Aschenbach resolves to go on a vacation. When von Aschenbach snaps out of his reverie and heads for the train, he discovers that the traveler has disappeared.

Gondolier

The gondolier who takes von Aschenbach from Lido to Venice resembles both the traveler in the cemetery and the foppish old man from the boat. He has a "brutal appearance," wearing brightly colored clothes and a straw hat "tilted rakishly on his head." He has blonde hair, a moustache, and an upturned nose, and at first ignores von Aschenbach when the writer asks to be taken to San Marco. When von Aschenbach asks him what he charges, the gondolier replies mysteriously, "You will pay." After dropping von Aschenbach off at the dock, he disappears, and von Aschenbach learns from officials that the gondolier is unlicensed and "a bad man." The gondolier represents Charon, who ferries the dead to the Underworld across the River Styx.

Old Fop

Von Aschenbach first sees the foppish old man on the steamer to Italy. He is traveling with a group of young clerks from Pola and dressed in a panama hat and a yellow summer suit with a red tie. Von Aschenbach is repelled by the man's attempt to look young. His rouged cheeks, dyed hair, loud clothes, false teeth, and exaggerated behavior disgust him. As von Aschenbach disembarks, the "ghastly old imposter" drunkenly and lasciviously addresses him, and as he does his upper set of teeth falls out. The old fop is linked by appearance to the traveler in the cemetery, the gondolier, the street performer, and von Aschenbach himself at the end of the story.

Street Performer

The street performer appears in the last chapter during the onset of Asiatic cholera, and carries the smell of carbolic acid authorities are using to disinfect the city. He stands apart from the other performers in his band and has similar features as the traveler in the cemetery, the gondolier, and the old fop. He has a large Adams apple, a snub nose, red hair, and moves his tongue suggestively around his lips. Like the other three figures, he is out of place. "He seemed not to be of Venetian stock, more likely a member of the race of Neapolitan comics, half pimp, half actor, brutal and daring, dangerous and entertaining." He assures von Aschenbach there is no disease in the city, just the normal health hazards that come with the sirocco. The singer symbolizes decadence and death, and portends von Aschenbach's fate.

Tadzio

Tadzio is a fourteen-year-old Polish boy on vacation at the same hotel as von Aschenbach. His curly blonde hair, slight body, pale skin, and aquiline features remind von Aschenbach of "Greek statues from the noblest period of antiquity." At various points, von Aschenbach compares the boy to Narcissus, Hyacinthus, and Phaedrus. He is also a sickly youth and headed for an early death. Tadzio is aware of von Aschenbach but never communicates with him. On the boy's last day in the city, he plays with his friend, Yashu, on the beach, and then wades out into the sea after their playing turns rough. Von Aschenbach's last sight before he dies is of the boy looking towards him from a sandbar. The author interprets the look as Tadzio beckoning him towards him.

Tadzio's Sisters

Tadzio's sisters range from fifteen to seventeen years old, and von Aschenbach infers from their plain appearance and dull expressions that they were raised differently than Tadzio. The sisters represent the qualities that von Aschenbach prized during his life, but the sisters do not appeal to him, aesthetically or sexually.

Gustav von Aschenbach

Von Aschenbach is a widowed, middle-aged, internationally celebrated German writer who has dedicated his life to his art and to the pursuit of artistic beauty. The son of a career civil servant and part of a family of judges and government officials, von Aschenbach wins fame with his writing early in his life. He strives, under pressure, to meet the expectations of a public that counts on him to produce work of intellectual brilliance. Von Aschenbach takes pride in his disciplined lifestyle and austere work habits, but is exhausted at the story's opening and in need of inspiration.

His trip to Venice is the first excursion he has taken in years. When he first sees Tadzio, he tells himself his response to the boy's beauty is purely aesthetic, but as the story progresses, von Aschenbach's feelings become obviously sexual. As his obsession with the boy grows, von Aschenbach throws away all of the dignity and discipline he has cultivated throughout his life. He succumbs to his desires, dressing like the old fop from whom he earlier turned away in disgust, debasing himself, and staying in Venice to be around Tadzio even though he knows deadly cholera is sweeping through the city. Von Aschenbach represents the willful and rational northern European who has repressed his deeper, instinctual nature only to see it return with a vengeance later in life. Symbolizing the decline of Europe at the beginning of the twentieth century, as well as embodying the consequences of living a sexually repressed life, von Aschenbach remains one of Mann's most fully realized characters.

Yashu

Yashu is Tadzio's close friend and companion who plays with him on the beach in Venice. With dark black hair and a husky build, Yashu is a bigger and more masculine boy than Tadzio and appears to idolize his friend.

Themes

Art and Society

The idea of the artist as a hero with a noble calling to pursue beauty has a rich tradition in western literature, especially romantic and modern literature. Mann describes von Aschenbach as an artist who has sacrificed his emotional life and distanced himself from the sensuous world to create beauty with his stories. In the second chapter, the

Topics for Further Study

- Analyze Mann's use of color in describing the traveler in the cemetery, the gondolier, the old fop, and the street musician. Write a short essay interpreting the symbolic significance of color in this work.

- Does Mann's novella have a moral? If so, what is it? Back up your response with evidence from the text.

- Break up into five groups. Each group should rewrite one chapter, telling von Aschenbach's story from a first person point of view. After reading your chapter to the class, discuss the choices you had to make and how they changed the meaning of the story.

- Compare Euripides's play, *The Bacchae*, with Mann's novella and make a list of all similarities you can find between the two works.

- Research the history of Venice and its relationship to the arts. Then present your findings to your class.

- Are beauty and art as corrupting today as they were in Mann's time? Illustrate your response with specific examples.

- Von Aschenbach becomes more aware of his own age the deeper he falls in love with Tadzio. As a class, brainstorm what you fear most about ageing and then discuss your responses. Have social attitudes towards ageing changed since 1911 when Mann wrote the novella? Be specific with your responses.

- Write a short essay examining Mann's use of ethnic and sexual stereotypes in the novella.

---

narrator says of von Aschenbach, "Even as a young man ... he had considered perfectionism the basis and most intimate essence of his talent, and for its sake he had cooled his emotions." As a writer consumed by ideas and a moral obligation to pursue beauty at all costs, even his physical health, von Aschenbach likens himself to heroic figures such as Socrates and St. Sebastian, an early Christian martyr, both of whom lived their lives in pursuit of a higher good. A critic in Mann's novella claims that the kind of hero von Aschenbach favored in his stories was based on the idea of "an intellectual and youthful manliness which grits its teeth in proud modesty and calmly endures the swords and spears as they pass through its body." Von Aschenbach was proud of this description, and felt it accurately portrayed his work. Mann shows what happens when von Aschenbach loses control over his passions and can no longer distinguish between art and life.

Sexuality

Death in Venice has become a central text in the canon of gay literature, even though the novella depicts no sexual acts and never explicitly mentions homosexuality. However, von Aschenbach's love for Tadzio, which he tells himself is based on the young boy's beauty, is quite obviously sexual as well, and the passion he feels for the boy is evident in his physical responses to the sight of the boy. Mann develops the theme of same sex love primarily through his use of Greek mythology, particularly when he makes comparisons between von Aschenbach's love for Tadzio with Socrates's love for Phaedrus and Apollo's for Hyacinthus. Ancient Greek culture was well known for its homosexual relationships, especially older Greek men's love for boys. *Death in Venice* is not, however, a cautionary tale about the dangers of homosexual love. Rather, Mann uses the relationship to point out the danger of letting emotions override reason and to underscore the relationship between desire and death.

Death

In *Death in Venice*, Mann shows how the pursuit of erotic beauty, at the expense of reason and restraint, can lead to degradation and death. Before his trip to Venice, von Aschenbach clearly embodies reason and the pursuit of an austere artistic beauty in his writing. Once in Venice, however, he encounters Tadzio who, for the writer, clearly embodies erotic beauty and sexual possibility, something the writer has denied himself throughout his life. Von Aschenbach's obsession with the boy causes him to rationalize or ignore behaviors that previously would have been repugnant to him. He begins wearing jewelry, dyes his hair, and dons flamboyant clothes in an effort to attract Tadzio's attention. And by remaining in Venice when he knows of the cholera epidemic, von Aschenbach risks death. Mann also underscores the relationship between erotic beauty and death by packing his story with symbolic imagery such as von Aschenbach's jungle dream of primitive people worshipping a huge phallus in a Bacchean orgy, and by setting the story in Venice, a sensuous, yet decaying city, as corrupt and dangerous as it is beautiful.

Style

Mythology

Myths are anonymous and traditional stories that cultures tell to explain natural phenomena. Mann makes broad use of Greek mythology to structure his story and to emphasize the timelessness of his tale. At various points von Aschenbach compares Tadzio with Cupid, Hyacinthus, Narcissus, and Phaedrus, all Greek characters and gods. He describes the sunrise in terms of Greek mythology, and laces his story with references to figures such as Kleitos, Kephalos, Semele, Zeus, Orion, and others. Episodes such as when von Aschenbach rides in the coffin-like gondola with an unlicensed gondolier are used to evoke motifs in Greek literature such as heroes' journey to the Underworld on Charon's boat across the River Styx. Such allusions help to characterize von Aschenbach as a learned man of refined sensibilities and to link von Aschenbach's fate with that of mythological characters.

By liberally dosing his story with implicit and explicit allusions to Greek mythology, and by incorporating Platonic dialogues into a realistic story, Mann highlights von Aschenbach's love of classicism and antiquity. Such references also make the story, for a 1912 readership, more palatable, as they lessen the impact of Mann's exploration of same sex, inter-generational erotic love.

Symbolism

Symbols are images or actions that stand in for something else. Mann packs his story with symbols to imbue details and characters with deeper meaning and to create a modern myth out of von Aschenbach's tragic decline. The image of the cemetery at the start of the novel, for example, foreshadows von Aschenbach's own death, and the appearance of the foppish drunken man on the boat to Venice symbolizes the very kind of person von Aschenbach will become after he abandons his moral and aesthetic ideals. Venice itself, perhaps, is the most significant symbol in the story.

Setting

Setting refers to the time period, the place, and the culture in which a story takes place. Mann chose Venice as his setting because of its rich tradition as a European cultural center, and because of its symbolic significance. Like von Aschenbach, Venice, a once venerable old European city, is in decline. Although on the surface it is a sensuous, cosmopolitan city that people still visit in droves, it is also rotting from within, slowly sinking into the swamp on which it is built, and has lost much of its allure and become primarily a tourist destination. Public officials and merchants are corrupt, conspiring to hide the news of the cholera sweeping the city from visitors, and almost all Venetians that appear in the story are disingenuous, desiring only to extract money from von Aschenbach and other visitors. The cholera infecting the city represents the decadence into which not only Venice has fallen, but von Aschenbach himself and, at the beginning of the twentieth century, much of Europe. Mann traveled to Venice extensively during his life, saying that it reminded him of his hometown, Lubeck. He also set his 1896 story, "Disillusionment," in Venice.

Although Venice is the primary external setting for most of the story, Mann sets a good deal of the story in von Aschenbach's mind as well. The description of the city and of Tadzio and other characters are all filtered through von Aschenbach's perceptions, and serves to chronicle the deterioration of his mental and emotional health.

Historical Context

Early Twentieth Century

A number of events occurred in 1911 inspiring Mann to begin work on *Death in Venice*. One of these was the death of Czech-Austrian composer Gustav Mahler on May 18, 1911, a brooding modernist who made his living as a conductor. Mahler's fierce and uncompromising dedication to his art, and demand for perfection from his musicians, appealed to Mann, who had met him a few years before his death. Mann not only gives von Aschenbach Mahler's first name, but he also models his hero's physical description on the composer. Mann was no stranger to Venice either. In fact, he was vacationing there when Mahler died, and followed reports of the composer's last days in the local papers.

Compare & Contrast

- **1910–1915:** In 1912, the *Titanic*, a sprawling 892-foot ocean liner and the world's largest ship, sinks off the coast of Newfoundland during its maiden voyage after hitting an iceberg. More than 1,500 people die.

  Today: James Cameron's film of the disaster, *Titanic* (1997), smashes box office records and is an international blockbuster, winning eleven Academy Awards, including one for Best Picture.

- **1910–1915:** In 1914, Archduke Franz Ferdinand, heir to the Austro-Hungarian throne, is assassinated in Sarajevo, the capital of the Austro-Hungarian empire, setting in motion the conflict that would become World War I.

  Today: After many of it buildings and streets are destroyed and many of its citizens killed during the 1990s war against Serbia, Sarajevo is now being rebuilt.

- **1910–1915:** In 1913, D. H. Lawrence publishes *Sons and Lovers*, a novel that literally illustrates Freud's theory of the Oedipus Complex and shocks many readers.

  Today: Graphic sex is a staple feature of the contemporary novel, both literary and popular.

In addition to the shock of Mahler's death, Mann was influenced by the deterioration of the political situation in Europe at this time. In 1911, Germany sent its battleship, *The Panther*, into the southern Moroccan port of Agadir after France occupied the country during a prolonged bout of tribal unrest. France, Britain (France's ally), and Germany geared up for war as negotiations dragged on. Germany eventually accepted more than 100,000 square miles of the Congo in exchange for relinquishing any claims to Morocco, but Kaiser Wilhelm continued to fan the flames of war, declaring that European countries were conspiring against Germany. In 1912, the Balkan states were also in crisis. Shelving their differences temporarily, these countries united against the Ottoman Empire. Bulgaria signed a treaty with both Serbia and Greece, and shortly after with Montenegro, forming the Balkan League. They were responding to the Turks' forced "Ottomanization" of parts of their countries. In October, Montenegro attacked the Turks in Macedonia, defeating them, and in a short time Balkan troops had ousted almost all Ottoman forces from Europe. As a result of the war, Albania gained independence. However, Bulgaria remained dissatisfied with how the spoils were divided and in June they launched an attack on their own allies. Europe was bracing itself for the inevitable outbreak of world war.

The political deterioration of Europe during this time was matched by an increasing cultural decadence and moral decline, a theme Mann explores, and one that was popular in literature during the turn of the century. A chief influence on the decadence movement in literature was Algernon Charles Swinburne, whose erotic poetry, written during the 1870s and 1880s, paved the way for writers to be more frank in writing about sexuality. Oscar Wilde, a gay Irishman, is perhaps best known among those exploring themes of sexuality, decadence, and aestheticism at the end of the nineteenth century. His novel, *The Picture of Dorian Gray* (1891), examines ageing, homoeroticism, and the role of art and the artist in society, all themes in Mann's novella as well. Responding to the notion that art should have a moral purpose, figures such as Wilde, Arthur Symons, and Ernest Dawson underscored their belief in art for art's sake in their novels, poems, plays, and essays. It is important to note that Mann's novella, rather than participating in the decadence movement, was a response to it.

Mann, like many artists during this time, was especially influenced by the theories of Sigmund Freud. Freud's theories on infantile sexuality and the unconscious had a profound effect on writers,

Bjorn Andresen (forefront) as Tadzio and Dirk Bogarde as Gustav von Aschenbach in the 1971 film version of Death in Venice

providing them with new material and ways of thinking about character development and human behavior. In 1900, Freud published *The Interpretation of Dreams*, followed in 1901 by *The Psychopathology of Everyday Life*, and in 1905 by *Three Essays on the Theory of Sexuality*. As Mann illustrates in his story about von Aschenbach and Tadzio, the sexual instinct provides humanity with its drive and creative force, but can also be a destructive force if not channeled.

Critical Overview

Death in Venice has occasioned numerous essays by critics exploring its thematic and stylistic richness, and is even more popular today than it was in 1912 when it was published. In "Myth Plus Psychology," an essay appearing in *Germanic Review*, André von Gronicka examines the structural "ingredients" of Mann's formula for his novella. In detailing how myth and psychology inform the work, von Gronicka expands upon conventional definitions of myth, arguing that it "encompasses legend, history, and the literary traditions of the more recent past." This allows him greater freedom to

show how mythic elements, apart from Greek stories and characters, operate in the story.

Manfred Dierks also seeks to pin down Mann's use of myth, by making connections between *Death in Venice* and two texts that heavily influenced Mann: Nietzsche's *The Birth of Tragedy* and Euripides's *The Bacchae*. In his essay, "Nietzsche's Birth of Tragedy and Mann's *Death in Venice*," in *Studies of Myth and Psychology in Thomas Mann*, Dierks argues, "Mythological and other classical themes ... can be grouped according to intensity and breadth of acquisition. This sort of differentiation by degree usually corresponds to their relative value as a textual element." Rita A. Bergenholtz focuses on the question of genre, asking if von Aschenbach indeed is a tragic character, a question that continues to vex critics. In her essay, "Mann's *Death in Venice*," for *The Explicator*, Bergenholtz argues that because the story focuses on von Aschenbach's fall rather than his rise, "Mann presents us with a parody of tragedy, which satirizes the romantic assumptions that enable such an exalted view of humankind." Constance Urdang also considers the story a parody. In her essay, "Faust in Venice: The Artist and the Legend in *Death in Venice*," in *Accent*, Urdang claims the story parodies the Faustian legend. Brendan Lemon is more concerned with the real-life implications of Mann's story and how accurately, or not, it reflects an ageing gay man's sexual desire. Writing for *The Advocate*, Lemon concludes in his essay, "Beached," "What most distinguishes von Aschenbach and his kind . . . may be the fact that sex for them is primarily mental."

Criticism

Chris Semansky

Semansky is an instructor of English literature and composition and writes on literature and culture for several publications. In this essay, Semansky examines the polarities in Mann's story.

In *Death in Venice*, Mann exploits polarities for characterization, to underscore his themes, and to drive the plot. These polarities are most easily seen in the setting for the story and in his descriptions of Tadzio, von Aschenbach, and the mysterious men who appear in key scenes. Since his story is structured this way, Mann's descriptions accrue meaning and help to develop the novella's central polarity, the relationship between life and art.

In moving von Aschenbach from the rainy, gray streets of Munich, Germany to the sunny, hot climate of Venice, Italy, Mann symbolizes the differences between temperament and sensibility in northern and southern Europe. Von Aschenbach, a German, epitomizes the austere, hardworking, methodical, and rational Teutonic character, priding himself on his intellect, focus, and self-restraint. Venice, for von Aschenbach, signifies adventure, a place he thought of as "incomparable, someplace as out of the ordinary as a fairy tale." Approaching it from the sea, von Aschenbach describes "that dazzling grouping of fantastic buildings that the republic presented to the awed gaze of approaching mariners; the airy splendor of the palace and the Bridge of Sighs." A city built upon a swamp, with canals for streets, Venice is an international center for the arts and a tourist haven, known for its beaches, warm climate, and sensuous decadence. By describing it from the perspective of the port, Mann utilizes the sea's symbolic link to sex, death, and chaos to show how von Aschenbach is drawn inexorably towards it, and away from the solid footing of land.

The polarity of the two cities is only one of many Mann uses to highlight the battle raging in von Aschenbach's mind and body. This battle, part of what Mann presents as a universal one, entails the conflict between the emotions and the intellect or, more specifically, in the mythic terms that implicitly frame the story, between Apollonian and Dionysian principles. Apollo and Dionysus are Greek gods, the former god of the sun, the latter, god of wine. In his study, *The Birth of Tragedy*, Nietzsche uses these terms "Apollonian" and "Dionysian" to symbolize principles of classical Greek culture. The Apollonian principle corresponds to ideas of form, individuation, and rational thought, whereas the Dionysian principle suggests the opposite, corresponding to drunkenness, ecstasy, and unrestrained emotion. Tragedy, in Nietzsche's view, results from the tension between these two principles. Mann, a student of both Nietzsche and Schopenhauer, from whom Nietzsche derived some of his ideas, dramatizes von Aschenbach's tragedy by showing him devolving from a person of refined tastes and discerning judgment into an obsessive and self-deluded would-be pedophile who can no longer control his desires. Von Aschenbach, who initially embodies the Apollonian principle, in the end literally loses himself to the Dionysian principle, surrendering all pretense towards worshipping Tadzio for his form and giving full rein to the lustful impulses that consume him. Venice and Munich are not the only settings in the story. Mann also characterizes von Aschenbach by showing what he is thinking. By moving back and forth between von Aschenbach's thoughts and perceptions of the physical world, Mann underscores the writer's growing self-deception, and also emphasizes the growing distance between the narrator and von Aschenbach as von Aschenbach's mania deepens.

The polarity that undergirds the story, of course, is that between the modern world and ancient Greece, with all of its literary figures and mythological characters. Most of the characters in the story have a counterpart in myth. Tadzio, for example, is referred to variously as Hyacinthus, Eros, Narcissus, etc. for qualities he exhibits that resonate with von Aschenbach. Von Aschenbach also participates in these fantasies he has of the boy. For example, after his luggage is misdirected and he decides to stay in Venice he watches Tadzio play on the beach, daydreaming of playing Socrates to Tadzio's Phaedrus. Cribbing from the Platonic dialogues, von Aschenbach-Socrates dreams of saying to the boy, "My dear Phaedrus, beauty alone is both worthy of love and visible at the same time; beauty, mark me well, is the only form of spirit that our senses can both grasp and endure."

The mysterious men—the traveler in the cemetery, the gondolier, the old fop, and the street musician—that von Aschenbach encounters at crucial points in the story also have their counterparts in myth, and serve as a link between antiquity and the modern world. In their lascivious appearance, their foreign [to von Aschenbach] appearance, and the responses they elicit from von Aschenbach, the men symbolize the Dionysian principle, which both attracts and repels von Aschenbach. In his essay, "Nietzsche's *Birth of Tragedy* and Mann's *Death in Venice*," Manfred Dierks suggests the men are "corybantes from his [i.e., Dionysus's] swarm." Corybantes are Dionysus's guardians, charged with inspiring terror and frenzy during sacred rites and rituals. They function in Mann's novella to foretell von Aschenbach's descent into mania, and in their foreign appearance, they are linked to the object of von Aschenbach's desire, Tadzio, a Pole. Foreignness itself is a leitmotif in Mann's story, that is, a recurring image or idea helping to structure the composition and draw readers' attention to Mann's themes. By making Tadzio and the men foreign, Mann can make them all the more inscrutable to von Aschenbach, who can then project upon them his own desires. It is noteworthy that von Aschenbach never talks with Tadzio, but when he hears him speak, the boy's voice captivates him:

> Von Aschenbach understood not a single word he said, and though it may have been the most ordinary thing in the world it was all a vague harmony to his ear. Thus, foreignness raised the boy's speech to the level of music, a wanton sun poured unstinting splendor over him, and the sublime perspectives of the sea always formed the background and aura that set off his appearance.

The mysterious men, Tadzio and von Aschenbach, and other polarities, Dierks argues, are derived from parts of the tragedy, *The Bacchae*, by the Greek playwright Euripides. The play details Dionysus's anger at King Pentheus of Thebes, who has challenged his divinity by questioning his parentage. The women of Thebes are possessed by Dionysus's power, wearing animal skins, dancing ecstatically, and copulating on Mt. Cithaeron. Dionysus defeats Pentheus easily, in large part because of the latter's hubris and ambivalent sexual identity, leading him to his death at the hands of the Bacchae (Dionysus's worshippers, led by Pentheus's mother), who literally rip him to shreds. Mann incorporates his own scene of bacchic mania in his novella in two ways. At the macro level, the inhabitants of cholera-infected Venice are beginning to act out their baser instincts as the plague progresses, displaying drunkenness and lewdness.

> Von Aschenbach, who initially embodies the Apollonian principle, in the end literally loses himself to the Dionysian principle, surrendering all pretense towards worshipping Tadzio for his form and giving full rein to the lustful impulses that consume him."

At the micro level, von Aschenbach, after deciding not to warn Tadzio's family of the plague, experiences an intense dream of such a ritual, in which men, women, and animals swarm together in a frenzy of sex and violence:

> With foam on their lips they raved; they stimulated each other with lewd gestures and fondling hands; laughing and wheezing, they pierced each other's flesh with their pointed staves and then licked the bleeding limbs. Now among them, now a part of them, the dreamer belonged to the stranger god.

Mann uses the dream to symbolically mark von Aschenbach's final capitulation to the Dionysian principle. With von Aschenbach's fall, Mann cautions those who would choose the life of unrestrained passion over that of reasoned behavior. As a neoclassicist, Mann was as interested in instructing his readers as he was in entertaining them. Von Aschenbach's tragedy, Mann suggests, is as old as the myths upon which his story is built.

Source: Chris Semansky, Critical Essay on *Death in Venice*, in *Novels for Students*, The Gale Group, 2003.

Rita A. Bergenholtz

In the following essay, Bergenholtz suggests that Death in Venice *is a parody of tragedy, citing the novel's focus on Aschenbach's "bathetic decline and fall" as evidence.*

One of the persisting critical questions regarding Gustave von Aschenbach, the protagonist of Thomas Mann's *Death in Venice* (1912), is whether or not he is a tragic character. Like numerous critics, Erich Heller argues that he is, and describes the novella as the "tragic story of Aschenbach's

> Numerous critics have suggested that tragedy is no longer possible in the twentieth century because, in general, we no longer believe in ideas of the heroic and noble. When we can no longer tell straightforward tragic tales, we must turn, as Thomas Mann does in *Death in Venice*, to parody."

disillusion and downfall." In sharp contrast, Martin Travers insists that "it is not on a note of exaltation that Aschenbach is granted his exit, but rather on one of banality. . . . It is not the noble genre of tragedy but that hybrid form of doubtful status, tragi-comedy, that provides the medium for his valediction." I would go further and argue that Mann presents us with a parody of tragedy, which satirizes the romantic assumptions that enable such an exalted view of humankind. Consequently, Aschenbach is not a romantic artist-hero but a parody of one. His literary career is described as a "conscious and overweening ascent to honour." However, the novella focuses not on his so-called rise but on his bathetic decline and fall. Indeed, from the outset Aschenbach's supposed pilgrimage of artistic renewal moves relentlessly downward.

Michel Butor notes that the word "pilgrimage" designates, "first of all, the journey to the tomb of a saint, next to the spot of a vision, an oracular site; one carries his question there and expects a response, a curing of the body or soul." In a parodic pilgrimage, however, there is no revitalization of artistic powers or regeneration of body and soul. Indeed, in Mann's novella, Aschenbach's physical decline, evident from the beginning, becomes increasingly apparent as the story progresses. He suffers from a "growing fatigue"; his strength is "sapped." In fact, long before his fatal journey to Venice, Aschenbach's life is "on the wane." By forty, he is "worn down by the strains and stresses of his actual task." Nevertheless, he endures. At fifty-something he is still holding fast—until, of course, he falls in love in Venice.

However, in a satiric narrative such as *Death in Venice*, "falling in love" is not merely a metaphorical expression. As Frank Palmeri explains, "The plot and the rhetoric of narrative satire cohere in accomplishing the same movement of lowering or leveling." Palmeri continues: "The reduction of spiritual to physical in satiric narrative corresponds to the rhetorical reduction of metaphors to literal meanings." This displacement "works to satirize hidebound characters . . . who live within the confines of clichés and received ideas." In a letter to Carl Maria Weber (4 July 1920), Mann explained how the fall motif was originally connected with Aschenbach's story:

> Passion as confusion and as a stripping of dignity was really the subject of my tale—what I originally wanted to deal with was not anything homoerotic at all. It was the story—seen grotesquely—of the aged Goethe and that little girl in Marienbad whom he was absolutely determined to marry.
>
> . . . this story with all its terribly comic, shameful, awesomely ridiculous situations, this embarrassing, touching, and grandiose story which I may someday write after all.

Walter Stewart offers this apposite conclusion: "Mann sees the actual fall of Goethe in the presence of a child as the very essence of degradation. . . . That Gustav Aschenbach collapses in exhaustion following his frantic chase after Tadzio must therefore be considered something less than a coincidence."

Writing to Karl Kerenyi (20 February 1934), Mann says, "I am a man of balance. I instinctively lean to the left when the boat threatens to capsize on the right, and vice versa . . . " In sharp contrast to Mann, Aschenbach is an extremist. He is off balance and destined to fall. Thus, instead of reaching a climax, Aschenbach's story continues to wind down, as "(o)ne afternoon he pursue(s) his charmer deep into the stricken city's huddled heart." There he literally "lose(s) his bearings. He did not even know the points of the compass; all his care was not to lose sight of the figure after which his eyes thirsted." Then, when Aschenbach realizes that his mad quest to locate his beloved Tadzio is fruitless, he "(sinks) down on the steps of the well and lean(s) his head against its stone rim." Ironically, the narrator's description of Venice as a "fallen queen" applies to Aschenbach as well. Indeed, our final view of Aschenbach emphasizes this fallen state: Gazing at Tadzio from his beach chair, Aschenbach's tired head falls upon his chest, and he expires.

Numerous critics have suggested that tragedy is no longer possible in the twentieth century because, in general, we no longer believe in ideas of the heroic and noble. When we can no longer tell straightforward tragic tales, we must turn, as Thomas Mann does in *Death in Venice*, to parody. Mann's predisposition toward the parodic mode is made clear in his essay "Sufferings and Greatness of Richard Wagner" (1933):

> It is well to understand that the artist, even he inhabiting the most austere regions of art, is not an absolutely serious man . . . and that tragedy and farce can spring from one and the same root. A turn of the lighting changes one into the other; the farce is a hidden tragedy, the tragedy—in the last analysis—a sublime practical joke. The seriousness of the artist—a subject to ponder.

Source: Rita A. Bergenholtz "Mann's Death in Venice," in *Explicator*, Vol. 55, Spring, 1997, pp. 145–47.

Martin Swales

In the following excerpt, Swales posits two levels on which Mann's Death in Venice *advances critical understanding as virtue—the "metaphorical," and the "realistic, psychological."*

Der Tod in Venedig (Death in Venice) (1912) tells the story of how Gustav von Aschenbach, a writer famous for the chiselled perfection of his work and for the values of order and self-discipline which it enshrines, decides to break out of his routine existence in Munich by taking a holiday in Venice. In Venice he becomes increasingly fascinated by a Polish boy, Tadzio, who is staying with his family at the same hotel. Aschenbach persuades himself that his interest in the boy is purely the disinterested one of aesthetic appreciation, but gradually it becomes clear that he has succumbed to a homosexual infatuation. Aschenbach's decline is echoed in disturbing events which occur in Venice: the weather is oppressive, the city smells of carbolic. Aschenbach finally discovers the true state of affairs: there is a cholera epidemic in the city. But he is no more able to leave than he is to warn Tadzio and his family. Not long afterwards he is found dead in his deck chair on the beach.

One of the central problems which *Der Tod in Venedig* poses for the reader is the whole question of motivation and causality in the story. The opening few pages raise the issue with particular clarity. The weary, jaded Aschenbach is standing by a tram stop in Munich. Across the road there is 'das byzantinische Bauwerk' (the byzantine edifice) of a cemetery. In the doorway of this building Aschenbach suddenly notices a tramp, a strange, exotic figure whose long white teeth are bared in a curious grimace. The narrator continues: . . .

> At a metaphorical level it is the tragedy of the creative artist whose destiny it is to be betrayed by the values he has worshipped . . . At a realistic, psychological level, the story is a sombre moral parable about the physical and moral degradation of an ageing artist who relaxes the iron discipline of his life . . ."

Whether the strange man's appearance with its suggestion of wandering and travel had stirred his imagination, or whether some other physical or psychological influence was at work—to his surprise he was aware of a strange opening up of his inner life, a kind of disquiet and restlessness.

The narrator can, it seems, only conjecture as to what is going on. Is it simply the image of a wanderer that fills Aschenbach with thoughts of travel? Or are there other factors at work? A few lines later the narrator puts an end to all speculation with the terse phrase . . .

it was the urge to travel, nothing more.

But this need for a change of scenery quickly assumes fantastic proportions in the protagonist's fevered imagination: he sees a vision of an exotic, sultry jungle, . . .

amongst the knotted trunks of a bamboo thicket he saw the baleful eyes of a crouching tiger gleam.

The vision fades—but the decision to travel remains. As he boards the tram Aschenbach looks around for the tramp but he is nowhere to be seen.

The opening scene swiftly establishes what are to become key motifs and images for the story as a whole. The mysterious tramp will recur in two figures who appear later on: in the unlicensed gondolier and in the street musician who entertains the hotel guests. All three have certain physical features in common: the snub nose and the bared teeth. All three figures suggest an exotic, forbidden realm existing outside the familiar world: particularly the episode with the gondolier makes clear the metaphorical significance of these figures. They

What Do I Read Next?

- In 2001, Gilbert Adair's study, *Inspiration for "Death in Venice"—The Real Tadzio 1900–1962*, was published. Adair examines the life of Wladyslaw Moes, the person on whom Mann based his character Tadzio.

- German writer Herman Hesse was a good friend of Mann. His novel *Siddhartha* (1922), the story of the Buddha's quest for enlightenment, reflects Hesse's interest in Indian philosophy and culture.

- In *Buddenbrooks*, a semi-autobiographical family saga published in 1901, Mann details the history of the Buddenbrook family and the town in which they lived.

- Mann was deeply influenced by German philosopher Friedrich Nietzsche, who elaborates on his ideas about Apollonian and Dionysian principles in *The Birth of Tragedy*, published in 1871.

- John Julius Norwich's 600-page-plus 1982 tome, *A History of Venice*, chronicles the history of Venice from the Middle Ages to its capture by Napoleon.

represent death (the bared teeth, glimpsed first outside the cemetery, suggest the skull). Does this then mean, we ask ourselves, that we are to take this story on a supernatural level? Do we take the title literally: that it is about Death summoning the ageing artist? It is, of course, a possible reading. But what of the psychological argument—what of that phrase about 'Reiselust nichts weiter'? Perhaps Aschenbach is simply jaded, in need of a change. Perhaps for this reason his subconscious generates the dream of rampant, anarchical living: the jungle. The images of untrammelled life harbour a certain threat—the eyes of the crouching tiger. Aschenbach seems aware of the threat . . .

> to travel then . . . but not too far, not as far as the tigers.

But, within the symbolism of the story, the tigers do catch up with him. For the clerk at the travel agent in Venice will tell Aschenbach about the movement of cholera epidemics in recent times. And the cholera is born in that . . .

> jungle of primeval islands in whose bamboo thickets the tiger crouches.

Is cholera then purely the contingent outward embodiment of an essentially metaphysical process? Aschenbach has repudiated his orderly, contained existence: he seeks experience of anarchic, dionysian fury, and the very intensity of rampant life will overwhelm his weary body and mind. Does the strange God, Dionysus, follow the course of the cholera in order to seek out his destined victim? It is certainly suggested, at the metaphorical level. But there is also the meticulously sustained level of psychological realism to the story. And, accompanying and articulating this level of motivation we have the narrator's stern comments of moral judgement on Aschenbach. Particularly towards the end epithets such as 'der Verwirrte', 'der Betörte', 'der Starrsinnige' abound, epithets which spell out Aschenbach's self-deception, blindness, and obstinacy. And the moral viewpoint is not simply a matter of brief phrases. It culminates in a bitter paragraph that highlights the horror and degradation of Aschenbach's condition . . .

> He sat there, the master, the artist made respectable, the author of *The Wretched*, that work which in such exemplary and clear form had renounced any sympathy with bohemianism, with the lurking depths, the abyss, which had reprehended the reprehensible; he who had climbed so high, who had gone beyond all knowledge and irony, who had accommodated himself to the responsibilities that go with fame and public trust, he whose renown was officially recognized, whose name had been ennobled, whose style was taken as a model for schoolboys to follow—he sat there, his eyelids closed: occasionally there was a sidelong glance, scornful and embarrassed, but then swiftly hidden, and his slack lips their colour heightened by rouge, formed single words . . .

The very rhythm of this sentence with its complex of relative clauses ('er saß dort . . . der Meister . . . der Autor . . . der Hochgestiegene . . . er, dessen Ruhm . . . dessen Name . . . er saß dort') gives a passionate, rhetorical feel to the narrator's disgust as he contrasts Aschenbach, the man of orderliness and control, with the pathetic wreck crumpled against the fountain.

The story works on two levels. At a metaphorical level it is the tragedy of the creative artist whose destiny it is to be betrayed by the values he has worshipped, to be summoned and destroyed by the vengeful deities of Eros, Dionysus, and Death. At a realistic, psychological level, the story is a sombre moral parable about the physical and moral degradation of an ageing artist who relaxes the iron discipline of his life, who becomes like the pathetic dandy on the boat to Venice, an older man desperately trying to recapture his lost youth. Both these levels of the story—and the kind of reader response which they elicit—co-exist in Thomas Mann's text. One can illustrate this co-existence by examining the function of those passages in the story which draw on a whole tradition of aesthetic philosophy from Plato onwards. I have in mind those paragraphs where we are given discursive reflections about art and beauty, quotations from and allusions to the Platonic dialogues. In one sense, such passages supply a philosophical and metaphysical context for Aschenbach's experience which makes his story illustrative of larger problems. Beauty, so the argument runs, is the one absolute that is perceivable by the senses. When man encounters the Beautiful he is visited almost by a shock recognition that he has come face to face with an intimation of his higher spiritual destiny. Yet Beauty is a subversive value: the very fact that the senses are involved in its perception means that man's excited response may be not spiritual but sensual. The higher love may, on examination, prove to be nothing more than a sexual infatuation. And this is true particularly of homoerotic experience. Because a homosexual attraction cannot lead to physical creation, to procreation, it may promise the higher creativity of the mind, of art. Yet equally the homoerotic can be the source of furtive, degraded and degrading relationships. Such considerations as these figure in the text of *Der Tod in Venedig* in two ways. Clearly they function in their own right as philosophical reflections on the ambiguous nature of Beauty. And this philosophical scheme gives Aschenbach's story the dignity of a metaphysical drama. But equally these reflections are inseparable from the particular psychological context of Aschenbach, the ageing artist. He himself uses such considerations to justify—and, ultimately, to deceive himself about—the nature of his feelings for the boy Tadzio. The metaphysical argument is of a piece with the realistic, psychological argument. The Platonic musings on Beauty are vital ingredients of Aschenbach's psychology: they are *his* thoughts—and yet they are also the thoughts enshrined in a major philosophical tradition of the West.

What, then, is the effect of this coexistence of meanings? T. J. Reed has shown how the story has its roots in what was initially a local problem: Mann

disliked the enthusiasm in contemporary art circles for work that was sensuous, plastic, 'sculptured', rather than reflective, critical, analytical. From this came the impetus to a moral tale about the degradation that awaits the man, the artist who denies scruple and reflection in the name of a cult of formal beauty and perfection. But the ideas and values that are implicated in Aschenbach's decline are, as we have seen, part of a longer cultural and philosophical tradition with which Mann has to take issue if he is to understand the forces that mould and shape his hero's thinking. And any such cultural tradition is not simply a stable, timeless entity: it is transmitted through the specific sensibility of a particular man, of a particular time, of a particular culture and society. The story makes clear that Aschenbach is very much part of the historical ambience around him. The narrator reflects: . . .

> In order for a significant product of the human mind to make instantly a broad and profound impact there must be a secret affinity, indeed a congruence between the personal fate of its creator and the general fate of its contemporary audience.

In what does this sympathy consist which makes Aschenbach the spokesman of a generation? The narrator answers: . . .

> Once—in an unobtrusive context—Aschenbach had directly suggested that any major achievement that had come about stood as an act of defiance: it had been made in defiance of grief and torment, poverty, destitution, bodily weakness; vice, passion and a thousand other obstacles.

Aschenbach speaks, then, for a generation of 'Moralisten der Leistung' (moralists of effort), a generation which identifies moral good with spiritual struggle and attrition. Virtue is to be found in the 'Trotzdem', in the overcoming of difficulty, scruple, doubt in an exercise of willed self-assertion. This is a Nietzschean legacy, what J. P. Stern has called 'the morality of strenuousness'. The narrator, in a passage of explicit commentary, goes on to imply a critique of the cast of mind that identifies morality with an entity that has, strictly speaking, no room for moral values. . . .

> Does form not have two faces? Is it not moral and immoral at one and the same time? Moral as the result and expression of discipline, but immoral and indeed anti-moral in so far as it is of its very nature indifferent to moral values; in fact it is essentially concerned to make morality bow before its proud and limitless sceptre.

Here the narrator comments upon an aspect of Aschenbach's personality as artist, but such is the 'sympathy' that binds *this* artist to his time that the aesthetic credo implies the cultural and intellectual temper of its age. *Der Tod in Venedig* appears some two years before the outbreak of the First World War. It is a text which suggests how the ethos of discipline and order is a questionable value, one which, in its very repudiation of scruple, reflection, analysis, lays itself open to the seductions of untrammelled, orgiastic experience, thereby confusing self-transcendence with self-abasement. Mann's story acquires a particularly sombre colouring when we remember the waves of collective enthusiasm with which a whole European generation acclaimed the outbreak of war in 1914. Significantly, in his essay *Bruder Hitler (Brother Hitler)* of 1939 Mann wrote the following: . . .

> *Death in Venice* knows a great deal about the repudiation of contemporary psychologism, about a new decisiveness and simplicity in the psyche—all this, admittedly, I brought to a tragic conclusion. I was not devoid of contact with tendencies and ambitions of the time, with what was felt to be—and proved to be—the coming mood: twenty years later it was to be hawked through the streets.

It would, however, be too easy to see *Der Tod in Venedig* as simply a cautionary tale. For it is too perceptive in its understanding of the ethos of form, too implicated in the cast of mind which it diagnoses, to be a work of straightforward didacticism. Indeed, it is one of the profoundest ironies of the book that its own formal control, its deliberately 'classicizing' style is of a piece with the artistic and human ethos which it criticizes. And this gives the work an authority richer than unambiguous denunciation could ever achieve. To borrow the term applied to Aschenbach's achievement, Mann's tale is bound to its time by complex ties of sympathy. And sympathy implies 'suffering with', a 'suffering with' which, in this case, embraces analytical understanding and critique.

Source: Martin Swales, "The Vulnerable Artist," in *Thomas Mann: A Study*, Rowman and Littlefield, 1980, pp. 29–45.

Sources

Bergenholtz, Rita A., "Mann's *Death in Venice*," in the *Explicator*, Vol. 55, No. 3, Spring 1997, p. 327.

Dierks, Manfred, "Nietzsche's *Birth of Tragedy* and Mann's *Death in Venice*," in *Studies of Myth and Psychology in Thomas Mann*, Vittorio Klostermann, 1972, pp. 18–37.

Lemon, Brandon, "Beached," in the *Advocate*, No. 767, September 1, 1998, p. 64.

Luke, David, Introduction, in *Death in Venice and Other Stories*, by Thomas Mann, translated by David Luke, Bantam, 1988, pp. xxxii–xlv.

Mann, Thomas, *Death in Venice*, translated and edited by Clayton Koelb, Norton, 1994, pp. 1–65.

Reed, T. J., *Thomas Mann: The Uses of Tradition*, Oxford, 1974, pp. 44–78.

Urdang, Constance, "Faust in Venice: The Artist and the Legend in *Death in Venice*," in *Accent*, Vol. XVIII, No. 4, Autumn 1958, pp. 253–67.

von Gronicka, André, "Myth Plus Psychology," in *Germanic Review*, Vol. 31, 1956, pp. 191–205.

Further Reading

Braverman, Albert, and Larry David Nachman, "The Dialectic of Decadence: An Analysis of Thomas Mann's *Death in Venice*," in *German Review*, Vol. XLV, No. 4, November 1970, pp. 289–98.

  Braverman and Nachman analyze von Aschenbach's change from an idealist to a sensualist.

Brennan, Joseph Gerard, *Thomas Mann's World*, Russell & Russell, 1962.

  Brennan examines how Mann's aesthetic sensibility is reflected in his writing.

Burgen, Hans, and Hans-Otto Mayer, *Thomas Mann: A Chronicle of His Life*, Translated by Eugene Dobson, University of Alabama Press, 1969.

  Burgen and Mayer's book chronicles Mann's life year by year, providing links between his writing and events in his life.

Leppmann, Wolfgang, "Time and Place in *Death in Venice*," in the *German Quarterly*, Vol. XLVIII, No. 1, January 1975, pp. 66–75.

  Leppmann examines the "timelessness" and "classical" quality of Mann's novella through a discussion of Venice as it was in 1911, the year Mann began writing his story.

Mann, Erika, *The Last Years of Thomas Mann: A Revealing Memoir by His Daughter, Erika Mann*, translated by Richard Graves, Farrar, Straus and Cudahy, 1958.

  Mann's daughter reminisces about her father's last years.

Ritter, Naomi, ed., *Thomas Mann: "Death in Venice": Case Studies in Contemporary Criticism*, Bedford Books, 1998.

  This collection of essays utilizes a range of critical strategies to interpret Mann's novella. Each essay is prefaced with a history and description of the school of thought to which it belongs.

Syppel, Joachim H., "Two Variations on a Theme: Dying in Venice (Thomas Mann and Ernest Hemingway)," in *Literature and Psychology*, Vol. VII, No. 1, February 1957, pp. 8–12.

  Syppel describes how the themes of beauty and death in Mann's novella compare with Ernest Hemingway's representation of them in *Across the River and into the Trees*.

The Lone Ranger and Tonto Fistfight in Heaven

Sherman Alexie

1993

The Lone Ranger and Tonto Fistfight in Heaven, published in 1993 by Atlantic Monthly Press, was Sherman Alexie's breakthrough book. Comprised of twenty-two interconnected stories with recurring characters, the work is often described by critics as a short-story collection, though some argue that it has novel-like features similar to Louis Erdich's *Love Medicine*. The book's central characters, Victor Joseph and Thomas Builds-the-Fire, are two young Native-American men living on the Spokane Indian Reservation, and the stories describe their relationships, desires, and histories with family members and others who live on the reservation. Alexie fuses surreal imagery, flashbacks, dream sequences, diary entries, and extended poetic passages with his storytelling to create tales that resemble prose poems more than conventional narratives.

The book's title is derived from one of the collection's stories, which details the experience of a Native American who leaves the reservation to live in Seattle with his white girlfriend and then moves back. The Lone Ranger and Tonto are symbols for white and Native-American identity, respectively. The names are taken from a popular radio and television show of the 1950s in which a white man, the Lone Ranger, teams up with an Indian, Tonto, to battle evil in the old west. Alexie, who claims the title came to him from a dream, studs his stories with other references to popular culture to underscore the ways in which representations of Native Americans have played a part in

Sherman Alexie

constructing the image they, and others, now have of them. The book's popularity, in part, stems from James Kincaid's effusive praise of Alexie's collection of poetry and stories, *The Business of Fancydancing* (1992), in *The New York Times Book Review*. With Kincaid's review, Alexie, who had published with small presses, was thrust into the national spotlight. He deftly depicts the struggles of Native Americans to survive in a world that remains hostile to their very survival, and he does so in an honest and artful manner. *The Lone Ranger and Tonto Fistfight in Heaven* won a PEN-Hemingway nomination for best first book of fiction and was adapted into a feature film, *Smoke Signals* in 1998, for which Alexie wrote the screenplay.

Author Biography

Poet, novelist, and screenwriter, Sherman Alexie has helped to reshape conventional images of Native Americans through his lyrical, yet blunt portrayals of life on the reservation. Born Sherman Joseph Alexie, Jr. October 7, 1966, in the tiny town of Wellpinit on the Spokane Reservation in eastern Washington, to Sherman Joseph, a Coeur d'Alene Indian, and Lillian Agnes Cox, a Spokane Indian, Alexie almost did not make it out of childhood. At

six months old, he was diagnosed with hydrocephalus, which required surgery. Although doctors were not hopeful of his recovery, Alexie did recover, though he suffered from seizures during childhood. Alexie credits his difficult childhood with helping him to develop his imagination. He became a voracious reader and excelled at math. Later, and like many of his friends, he also developed a problem with alcohol. However, after a series of increasingly self-destructive episodes, Alexie quit drinking at age twenty-three.

Although he initially planned to pursue a career in medicine, Alexie changed his mind after taking a poetry workshop with Alex Kuo at Washington State University. With Kuo's encouragement, he began writing in earnest, and in 1991 when he graduated from WSU with a bachelor's degree in American Studies, he received a Washington State Arts Commission Poetry Fellowship. In 1992, he was awarded a National Endowment for the Arts Poetry Fellowship and published two collections of poems, *I Would Steal Horses* and *The Business of Fancydancing: Stories and Poems*. The latter was favorably reviewed in the *New York Times Book Review*, and Alexie's reputation as a fresh and vital voice in literature was established. His first book of prose, a collection of linked stories titled *The Lone Ranger and Tonto Fistfight in Heaven*, published in 1993, was highly praised and won Alexie a wide audience. Alexie adapted the book into a feature-length film called *Smoke Signals* in 1998, which won awards from the Sundance Film Festival. Alexie received a Lila Wallace-Reader's Digest Writers' Award and a Washington State Governor's Writers Award for the book, and it was also a PEN/Hemingway Best First Book of Fiction Citation Winner. Alexie is a prolific writer who also works hard at marketing his work; his recent projects include the novels *Reservation Blues* (1995), which received the Before Columbus Foundation: American Book Award for 1996 and the Murray Morgan Prize, and *Indian Killer* (1996), which was a New York Times Notable Book; his short-story collection, *The Toughest Indian in the World* (2000), was awarded the 2001 PEN/Malamud Award. Alexie lives in Seattle, Washington, with his wife, Diane, and their son, Joseph.

Plot Summary

Every Little Hurricane

This first story of *The Lone Ranger and Tonto Fistfight in Heaven* introduces Victor, his parents, and his uncles, Arnold and Adolph, who are quarreling during a New Year's Eve party when Victor is nine years old in 1976. The weather forecast is for a hurricane, and the narrator surveys the bizarre behavior of many of the Indians on the reservation, many of them drunk and angry, recalling some wrong that had been done to them. The story also contains a flashback to when Victor was five years old and his parents could not afford to buy him anything for Christmas. Alexie introduces the themes he will develop throughout the book such as the relationship between the real and the imaginary, reservation poverty, and the idea of memory as an index of social and individual identity. Victor is a fictionalized version of Alexie, as the author has admitted.

A Drug Called Tradition

In this story, Thomas Builds-the-Fire is hosting the "second-largest party in reservation history." The first was the New Year's Eve party in the first story. Thomas, Junior, and Victor take a ride to Benjamin Lake, where they ingest an unspecified drug and proceed to have visions during which they earn their adult Indian names by stealing horses. Events from the past frequently bleed into the present during this story, illustrating Victor's claim that "Your past is a skeleton walking one step behind you, and your future is a skeleton walking one step in front of you."

Because My Father Always Said He Was the Only Indian who Saw Jimi Hendrix Play "The Star Spangled Banner" at Woodstock

In this story, Victor recounts memories of his father coming home drunk during the 1960s and listening to Jimi Hendrix play "The Star Spangled Banner." As a child, Victor would share in his father's drunken ritual, putting the song on the stereo as he walked in the house, and then curling up and sleeping at his feet after he passed out. Jimi Hendrix, part Cherokee Indian, was a Seattle-born rock and roll star who gained fame for his masterful guitar playing. He died in 1970 at 27, choking on his own vomit while being taken to the hospital, purportedly due to drug abuse. Victor recounts that his father's love of Hendrix played a role in the breakup of his parents' marriage, as did his alcoholism and desire to be alone.

Crazy Horse Dreams

In this very short story, Victor relates an experience he had with a woman at a powwow. He draws on the image of Crazy Horse, a famous Sioux

Media Adaptations

- Directed by Chris Eyre and winner of two Sundance Film Festival awards, *Smoke Signals* (1998) is adapted from stories in *The Lone Ranger and Tonto Fistfight in Heaven*. It is available at most video stores and many libraries.

warrior, to show how contemporary Indian men cannot measure up to the ideal of Crazy Horse. The woman Victor meets at a fry bread stand and seduces wants him to be something he is not. "His hands were small. Somehow she was still waiting for Crazy Horse."

The Only Traffic Signal on the Reservation Don't Flash Red Anymore

In this story, Victor and Adrian, reformed alcoholics, sit on their front porch, drink Pepsi, and discuss basketball and the reservation's rising star, Julius Windmaker, who, like Victor and other rising stars before him, eventually succumbs to alcoholism. The story ends with the two having a similar conversation about a talented young Indian girl named Lucy. Adrian and Victor hope that she can develop her talents and not begin drinking.

Amusements

In this story, Sadie and Victor play a prank on an old drunk Indian called Dirty Joe, putting him on a carnival ride when he passes out. A security guard chases Victor, who runs into the Fun House and sees his image distorted in "crazy mirrors."

This Is What It Means to Say Phoenix, Arizona

This is one of the stories adapted for the film *Smoke Signals*. After learning that his father has died in Phoenix, Arizona, Victor decides to retrieve his belongings and his ashes. Thomas Builds-the-Fire offers to give Victor the money to make the trip if he can go with him. The two retrieve Victor's father's ashes, a photo album, and his father's pick-up truck. Along the way, the two reminisce about Victor's father and reach an understanding of one another. At the end of the story, Victor offers Thomas some of his father's ashes.

The Fun House

In this character sketch of his Aunt Nezzy, Victor recounts an episode during which a mouse crawls up his aunt's leg, and her son and uncle mock her. Nezzy becomes fed up with her son and her husband's ingratitude, and leaves the house to swim naked in Tshimikain Creek, refusing to leave even when her husband and Victor plead with her. At sundown, she leaves the creek, but she also knows that her life will be changed as a result of the day.

All I Wanted to Do Was Dance

Victor recounts a number of drunken episodes from his life and how drinking destroyed his relationships and led to an all-consuming despair. He ends the story by describing the day he decided to stop drinking.

The Trial of Thomas Builds-the-Fire

In this fabulous story, Thomas Builds-the-Fire is put on trial for unspecified crimes, after he begins speaking following twenty years of silence. A man from the Bureau of Indian Affairs describes Thomas's behavior: "A storytelling fetish accompanied by an extreme need to tell the truth. Dangerous." The story contains passages from the court transcripts in which Thomas tells stories of white injustices to Indians from the nineteenth century, including an incident in 1858 in which Colonel George Wright steals 800 horses from the Spokane chief Til-coax. In this story, Thomas speaks as if channeling the voice of one of the ponies. In other stories, he speaks in the voice of those involved in the ensuing battle between the settlers and the Indians. Thomas Builds-the-Fire was sentenced to two concurrent life terms for his "crime."

Distances

In a collage of scenes, Victor describes the differences between "Urbans," Indians who left the reservation to live in the city, and "Skins," Indians who stayed on the reservation. He also describes burning down houses because white people had inhabited them, dancing with Tremble Dancer, an Urban, and assorted dreams about Indians from the past.

Jesus Christ's Half-Brother Is Alive and Well on the Spokane Indian Reservation

Containing elements of parable and allegory, this story covers the years 1966–1974 and chronicles the relationship between the narrator and an orphaned baby he adopts who takes on Christ-like characteristics. The baby's mother is Rosemary Morning Dove, who claimed she was a virgin when the baby was born, around Christmas. After a fire kills her and her lover, Frank Many Horses, the narrator adopts the baby, named James. A heavy drinker, the narrator quits in 1971 in order to keep James. The last three years of the story detail his life as a sober man and his growing relationship with James, whom he hopes will take care of him when he grows old.

A Train Is an Order of Occurrence Designed to Lead to Some Result

On his birthday, Samuel Builds-the-Fire, grandfather to Thomas Builds-the-Fire, is laid off from his job cleaning rooms at a motel. Although he has never had an alcoholic drink his entire life, Samuel Builds-the-Fire drinks this day. He drinks so much he passes out on railroad tracks as a train approaches.

A Good Story

Quilts are used as a metaphor for the story's structure. Junior's mother, who is making a quilt, tells him all of his stories are sad, so Junior tries to tell one that is not. He relates a tale about Uncle Moses, and his nephew, Arnold, which ends with Uncle Moses beginning the very tale that Junior just told. This self-reflexive story underscores how storytelling helps to ensure the continuity of Indian identity.

The First All-Indian Horseshoe Pitch and Barbecue

This densely poetic story, the most upbeat in the entire collection, describes the event of its title. There are hot dogs, Pepsi, Kool-Aid, a horseshoe pitch competition, and talk of making basketball the new tribal religion.

Imagining the Reservation

Alexie explores the ways in which Indians use their imaginations to battle their culturally and physically impoverished lives on the reservation. His symbolic descriptions dart between "what if" fantasies of the past, memories of an impoverished childhood, and the reality of the present. As in other stories in the collection, Alexie peppers this one with allusions to popular culture such as television shows and rock and roll music. Addressing Adrian and writing, "I am in the 7-11 of my dreams, surrounded by five hundred years of convenient lies," the narrator underscores his belief that "imagination is the only weapon on the reservation."

The Approximate Size of My Favorite Tumor

The narrator, Jimmy Many Horses, who has cancer, describes his on-again, off-again relationship with his wife, Norma. She leaves him because he cannot stop joking about the terminal illness, saying that it is the size of a basketball, and that in an X-ray he could see the stitches on it. His wife returns to live with him at the end of the story because the person she was living with was "too serious."

Indian Education

This story is structured as a series of short descriptive vignettes, each depicting a grade in Victor's education, from first grade through twelfth. Recounting representative incidents from each grade that illustrate his life on the reservation, battles against discrimination, and hopes for the future, Victor describes himself as intelligent, athletic, and despairing.

The Lone Ranger and Tonto Fistfight in Heaven

In this title story, Victor leaves the reservation to live in Seattle with his white girlfriend, who plays out the role of the Lone Ranger to Victor's Tonto. When the relationship sours, Victor returns to the reservation, stops drinking and finds a job answering phones for a high school exchange program.

Family Portrait

This story describes Junior's family members and their propensity for storytelling. It bears a remarkable similarity to the story Alexie tells about his own life. Alexie structures the story by "translating" what people say into what he heard. Superficially, he blames the sound from the always-on television as distorting words. However, the television itself acts as a metaphor for how popular culture and European ways have ruined Indian traditions.

Somebody Kept Saying Powwow

In this story, Junior, an alter ego of Victor and Alexie, describes his experiences with Norma Many Horses. For Junior, she is a role model who epitomizes the right way to live. She neither drinks nor smokes, is honest to a fault, is confident of her Indian identity, and acts as a caretaker for other Indians on the reservation, who respectfully call her "grandmother." She calls Junior "Pete Rose," comparing Junior with the baseball player who is remembered more for his gambling than he is for his record-setting career.

Witnesses, Secret and Not

Victor is thirteen in this story, and he and his father are driving to the police station so that the police can ask his father questions about a missing Indian, Jerry Vincent, who was supposedly killed ten years earlier. His father narrowly escapes crashing the car, after skidding on the icy road. At the police station, Victor's father repeats what he has told the police numerous times before: he knows nothing about Jerry Vincent other than what he has already told them. The father admits to Victor on the drive home that he was involved in a car accident once in which a white man was killed, but he was never arrested because the white man had been drinking. The story ends when the two return home and Victor's father cries into his food.

Characters

Adrian

Adrian appears in a few stories but figures prominently in "The Only Traffic Signal on the Reservation Don't Flash Red Anymore." In this story, he and Victor sit on their front porch and discuss how drinking has ruined so many members of the reservation and cut short the dreams of many Indian teenagers, like Victor, who aspired to play basketball.

Samuel Builds-the-Fire

Samuel Builds-the-Fire is the grandfather of Thomas Builds-the-Fire and the main character in the story, "A Train Is an Order of Occurrence Designed to Lead to Some Result." In this story, Samuel loses his job on his birthday and begins drinking alcohol, something he has avoided his entire life. Like his son and his grandson, he is a storyteller, but younger tribal members on the reservation have tired of him and do not have time to listen to his stories, and his children have all moved away. Samuel leaves the reservation to live in the city and takes a job cleaning motel rooms.

Alexie illustrates the idea that the Spokane Indians are becoming more like Americans in abandoning their elders, and he suggests they are losing touch with their tradition of storytelling. The final image in the story is of Samuel passed out drunk on the railroad tracks.

Thomas Builds-the-Fire

Thomas Builds-the-Fire is a visionary and compulsive storyteller whom most people on the reservation ignore. He is a central figure in "A Drug Called Tradition," "This Is What It Means to Say Phoenix, Arizona," and "The Trial of Thomas Builds-the-Fire." In the latter story, readers learn he once held the postmaster hostage with the idea of a gun. He is being tried for speaking the truth, after remaining silent for twenty years. During the trial he speaks in the "voice" of a young pony that survived a horse massacre in 1858, in the voice of the warrior Qualchan, who was hanged, and in the voice of sixteen-year-old warrior Wild Coyote at the Battle of Steptoe. Thomas Builds-the-Fire represents the Spokane Indian's link to the past and the traditions they are losing.

Crazy Horse

Crazy Horse was a mid-nineteenth-century Lakota Indian known for his courage in battle and for his fierce resistance to white encroachment on Lakota lands. He appears in "Crazy Horse Dreams" as a symbol of what male Indians had once been.

Lester Falls Apart

Lester Falls Apart is a comical figure who appears in a number of stories.

Victor Joseph

Named after two famous Nez Perce chiefs, Victor Joseph narrates a number of stories in Alexie's collection and is a primary character in others. Along with Junior Polatkin and Thomas Builds-the-Fire, he is an alter ego of Alexie, who often uses events from his own life as a basis for Victor's stories. Readers first meet him in "Every Little Hurricane," when he is nine years old and waiting for a hurricane to descend upon the reservation on New Year's Eve. The subjects he presents in this story—drunken tribe members fighting, poverty, unemployment, and humiliation—recur throughout the collection. He was once a basketball star on the reservation, drives a garbage truck for the BIA, and like other characters, he drinks to excess. However, he quits drinking after realizing the damage it has done to himself

and others.

James Many Horses

James Many Horses is the central character in "The Approximate Size of My Favorite Tumor." In this story, he is dying of cancer but cannot stop telling jokes about it. As a result, his wife, Norma Many Horses, leaves him, only to return later because the next man she is with was "too serious." Like most of Alexie's characters, James is sarcastic, self aware, and fatalistic, joking with his doctor about his impending death.

Norma Many Horses

Norma Many Horses is a primary character in "Somebody Kept Saying Powwow" and "The Approximate Size of My Favorite Tumor." She is married to James Many Horses, does not drink, and loves to dance. For Victor, she is a kind of ideal Indian woman, who is deeply committed to her people and undaunted by the problems they face. People refer to her as "grandmother" out of respect.

Aunt Nezzy

Aunt Nezzy, a middle-aged cousin of the narrator who sews buckskin dresses, appears in "The Fun House." After her son, Albert, and husband laugh at her when a mouse crawls up her leg, she leaves the house in disgust to go swimming naked in a local creek. She is disgusted by the way her family has taken her for granted, and is taking steps to change her life. At the end of the story she tries on a beaded dress that is too heavy and buckles from its weight. Refusing help, she rises. The dress is a symbol of salvation. At the beginning of the story, Nezzy says about the dress: "When a woman comes along who can carry the weight of this dress on her back, then we'll have found the one who will save us all."

Junior Polatkin

Junior Polatkin, named after a Spokane chief from the nineteenth century, is another of Alexie's alter egos, and readers first meet him in the story, "A Drug Called Tradition," when he, Victor, and Thomas (all of Alexie's alter egos in one story) take a drug and experience a number of visions during which they steal horses to win their Indian names.

Sadie

In "Amusements," Sadie helps Victor put Dirty Joe on an amusement ride when he is passed out drunk.

Victor's Father

Victor's father appears in a number of important stories in the collection including, "Because My Father Always Said He Was the Only Indian Who Saw Jimi Hendrix Play 'The Star-Spangled Banner,'" "This Is What It Means to Say Phoenix, Arizona," and "Witnesses, Secret and Not." He is a hard-drinking, and at times emotionally distant man who nonetheless loves his family, and is idolized by his son. After he dies in "This Is What It Means to Say Phoenix, Arizona," Victor flies to Phoenix with Thomas Builds-the-Fire to retrieve his father's ashes.

Julius Windmaker

Julius Windmaker appears in "The Only Traffic Signal on the Reservation Don't Flash Red Anymore." A rising fifteen-year-old basketball star, he begins drinking and loses interest in the game. His character is symbolic of how other reservation Indians have ruined their lives and dreams with alcohol.

Themes

Postcolonialism

Postcolonial literature seeks to describe the interactions between European nations and the peoples they colonized. Alexie's stories focus on this type of interactions, showing, for example, the United States government's attempt to control Native Americans by occupying their land, and then placing them on reservations that are run with the "help" of the Bureau of Indian Affairs. Alexie's stories illustrate the emotional complexities of living in a community torn apart by alcoholism, stripped of its larger social purpose, yet unwilling to assimilate the values and purposes of a culture that has oppressed its people for centuries. Characters such as Junior, Victor, and Thomas Builds-the-Fire are frequently humiliated during their interactions with whites, especially the police, and often respond with anger and black humor. In the allegorical and Kafka esque story "The Trial of Thomas Builds-the-Fire," Alexie illustrates the absurdity of his tribe's, and all Native Americans', situation as Thomas is sent to jail for life for a "murder" that occurred more than one hundred and forty years earlier. Alexie underscores the continued victimization of Native Americans in this story by symbolizing the unfairness of the American system of justice.

Topics for Further Study

- Read Leslie Marmon Silko's "The Storyteller," and then compare and contrast it with stories from Alexie's collection. Describe how each of them describes the value of storytelling as a tradition and a survival skill. Provide specific examples from the respective texts.

- Research the relationship between the Coeur d'Alene Indians and the Spokane Indians and present your findings to your class.

- Alexie's characters often respond to the way in which Native Americans have been stereotyped in popular culture. Research films and novels for illustrations of these stereotypes and list them on the board. Next, construct a list of the ways in which Alexie's stories respond to these stereotypes. Discuss as a class.

- Alexie frequently describes how the Bureau of Indian Affairs has humiliated Native Americans. Research the BIA, and write a short essay about the ways it has changed in the last twenty years.

- Argue for or against the idea that *The Lone Ranger and Tonto Fistfight in Heaven* can be considered a memoir.

- The idea of the "authentic Indian" appears frequently in Alexie's stories. What does this term mean, and how is Alexie using it? Discuss as a class.

- Analyze the films *Dancing with Wolves* and *The Last of the Mohicans* in terms of how they do or do not perpetuate stereotypes of Native Americans. Discuss as a class.

- Research the Native-American ritual of the Ghostdance, and write a short essay about how it functions as a symbol in Alexie's stories.

- Compare *The Lone Ranger and Tonto Fistfight in Heaven* with its film adaptation, *Smoke Signals*. Discuss what is left out and what is included in the film and the possible reasons behind these decisions.

Language

Alexie uses colloquial dialogue, paradox, and zeugma to effect an ironic, though realistic voice. He studs the speech of his characters with "enit," which means, "ain't it," and "eh," and other colloquialisms to illustrate how Indians speak on the Spokane Reservation. Alexie's use of paradox to show the contradictions of reservation life is evident in statements such as this one about Norma Many Horses: "Norma, she was always afraid; she wasn't afraid." Zeugma, the yoking together of two or more words in a grammatical construction to achieve a surprising effect, appears throughout the stories, and Alexie uses it for dazzling poetic effect. One example occurs when Victor says: "I walked back in the house to feed myself and my illusions." In this instance, he is using "feed" literally to suggest food, and figuratively to mean, "sustain his self-deception."

Psychological Abuse of Native Americans

Alexie details the various kinds of abuse Native Americans have endured living under the United States government. Not only have Native Americans had their lands taken from them, but they have also been forced to live in reservations and to give up their entire way of life. By forcing them to live on government handouts and labor at jobs that have little meaning to them, the federal government, in effect, has ensured that Native Americans will continue to live impoverished lives—emotionally, spiritually, and psychologically. Victor's numerous and ironic references throughout the stories to "five hundred years," alludes to the length of time that Europeans have occupied Native-American lands and reshaped how Native Americans see themselves and their relationship to others. Alexie especially focuses on the damage done to Native-American males who, because of their compromised traditions and the loss of their fathers to alcoholism, have no good role models. Many of the males in Alexie's stories are proud, but desperate. The bitterly ironic story, "Indian Education" illustrates how the educational system on the reservation, run by the BIA and missionaries, tries to strip young Native-American children of their identity by forcing them to cut their braids and punishing them for not knowing their place. Alexie also sprinkles his stories with anecdotes of racial discrimination against Native Americans outside the reservation.

Imagination

In "Imagining the Reservation," Alexie writes, "Survival equals Anger X Imagination. Imagination is the only weapon on the reservation." What he means by that is that Native Americans have to be emotionally and psychologically resourceful to keep their sense of humor and their traditions alive in conditions hostile to their existence. Much of the imagination in his stories comes in the form of dark humor, a response to desperate straits in which many of his characters find themselves. Alexie himself demonstrates imagination and resourcefulness in the very way he has constructed the book as a kind of fictional memoir of his own life on the reservation. In an interview with John and Carl Bellante in *Bloomsbury Review*, Alexie refers to the characters Victor Joseph, Junior Polatkin, and Thomas Builds-the-Fire as " the holy trinity of me." And indeed, the stories are peppered with details and events from Alexie's life. For example, 1966, the year of Alexie's birth, is also the year of Victor's birth and of another of his narrators.

Style

Style

Alexie employs postmodern practices of writing to tell his stories. Some of these practices include weaving historical figures and figures from popular culture with characters created by Alexie. For example, in "Crazy Horse Dreams" he uses the Sioux warrior Crazy Horse as a symbolic presence to explore how the imagination effects ways in which people in the present respond to one another. In other stories, he uses Jesus Christ, Jimi Hendrix, the Lone Ranger, and Pete Rose as cultural icons that serve as touchstones of personal meaning. Alexie also challenges readers' ideas as to what makes a story by cobbling together diary entries, dream sequences, aphorisms, faux newspaper stories, multiple narrators and stories within stories to tell his tales. One of the most obvious examples of this occurs in the story, "The Trial of Thomas Builds-the-Fire," in which Thomas takes on the persona of a number of historical figures, human and animal, to relate events occurring more than a century earlier.

In postmodern writing such as Alexie's, the lines between fiction and fantasy, reality and dream are erased, and the storyline—if there is one—is often blurred. Alexie also mixes tones, moving from comedy in one sentence to tragedy in the next. Such rapid shifts of tone create a playful linguistic surface that at times mocks the very story he is telling. Alexie mocks whites and Native Americans alike. For example, in "Indian Education," Victor parodies the Spokane Indian tradition of naming children, writing, "I was always falling down; my Indian name was Junior Falls Down. Sometimes it was Bloody Nose or Steal-His-Lunch. Once, it was Cries-Like-a-White-Boy, even though none of us had seen a white boy cry." This ironic stance towards tradition, genre, and self permeates the collection.

Narrator

The narrator is the person through whose eyes the story is told. Sometimes that person is a character in the story and sometimes not. Alexie uses a number of narrators in this collection including Thomas Builds-the-Fire, Jimmy Many Horses, Victor Joseph, and Junior. Though he primarily uses the latter two, by varying narrators, and using both first and third-person point of view, Alexie creates a complex portrait of Native-American life as filtered through multiple sensibilities.

Setting

Setting refers to the place, time, and culture in which the characters live and the story occurs. Alexie's primary setting is the world of the Spokane Indian Reservation in Wellpinit, Washington, though he occasionally sets part of a story in Spokane or Seattle. He represents the reservation as a seedy and poverty-stricken place where despairing inhabitants spend their days drinking and playing basketball. If characters work, they use their hands, driving trucks, sewing quilts, or clerking. Their diet consists of commodity beef and cheese supplied by the federal government, beer, and fry bread, a traditional Indian food, and they live in houses built by HUD (Housing and Urban Development). Most of the stories take place in the 1960s and 1970s, when reservation life was particularly bleak, but also when many tribes began to assert their rights and lobby for more self-governance and compensation for lands taken from them. Characters both work for and loathe the Bureau of Indian Affairs (BIA), the arm of the federal government responsible for administering reservation life.

Historical Context

History and Culture of the Spokane Indians

As an enrolled Spokane Coeur d'Alene Indian, Alexie draws on his experience on the reservation in Wellpinit, Washington, to craft his stories. Approximately 1,100 Spokane tribal members live on the Spokane Indian Reservation located about 50 miles northwest of Spokane, which includes a school and offices of the Bureau of Indian Affairs (BIA). The Spokane Indians belong to the Interior Salish group, who had made their home in northeastern Washington, northern Idaho and western Montana. "Spokane" means "Sun People." White settlers who moved into the Spokane's territories in the middle of the nineteenth century often skirmished with the Indians, and many from both sides were killed. In 1881, the Spokane Reservation was established by executive order of President Rutherford B. Hayes, and in 1906 land allotments were made to the inhabitants. In 1940, by an act of Congress, the United States acquired tribal land along the Spokane River for the construction of Grand Coulee Dam, affecting both the Spokane Indians' and the Coeur d'Alene Indians' ability to fish for salmon. The tribes had few avenues through which to challenge the government until 1946, when the Indian Claims Commission was created to settle claims filed by Indian tribes against the United States. The Spokane tribe filed a claim arguing that the government under-compensated them for land in an 1887 cession of land agreement. In 1967, the tribe was awarded a $6,700,000 settlement. Currently, the tribe owns 104,003 acres of land.

1960s–1970s

Many of the stories in *The Lone Ranger and Tonto Fistfight in Heaven* take place in the 1960s and 1970s. These decades were rife with conflict between the federal government and Native Americans. Alexie refers to abuses by the BIA numerous times in his stories, including "Indian Education," in which he describes the blatant attempts by government teachers to humiliate him and strip him of his Indian appearance. Although Native Americans were, and remain, among the poorest people in the United States, their population doubled between 1945 and 1975, from 500,000 to more than one million. A number of activist groups emerged during this period demanding autonomy from the federal government and redress for past injustices. In 1969, a group of militant Native-American activists occupied Alcatraz Island in San Francisco Bay for eighteen months, calling for the creation of a Native-American educational center. In 1972, thousands of Native Americans participated in the "Trail of Broken Treaties" march to Washington, D.C.,

Sherman Alexie's Lone Ranger and Tonto Fistfight in Heaven *was influenced by the popular 1950s television show*

where they occupied the offices of the BIA. In 1973, the American Indian Movement (AIM), a group founded to help tribes assert their rights to their heritage and lands, seized the town of Wounded Knee, South Dakota, where United States troops slaughtered more than 300 Sioux in 1890. Arguing that the Oglala Sioux tribal government had been corrupted by its association with the BIA and that the Sioux had been cheated in the 1868 Sioux treaty of the Black Hills, AIM took hostages and demanded the United States reopen treaty negotiations. AIM leaders Russell Means and Dennis Banks pressed the United States to give back 1.3 million acres in the Black Hills the government had taken from the Sioux. They also argued that 371 treaties between the Native Nations and the Federal Government had been broken by the United States, and demanded an investigation. The occupation ended after 71 days, after a violent confrontation between AIM and United States Armed Forces who had surrounded the Pine Ridge Indian reservation. A few AIM members were killed and the government arrested 1,200 people. During the next few years, the Pine Ridge reservation became a hotbed of unrest and violence, as the BIA and the Federal Bureau of Investigation sought to root out "instigators" and quell Indian activism.

Critical Overview

The Lone Ranger and Tonto Fistfight in Heaven is Alexie's first full-length collection of prose and has been universally praised, both by reviewers and by academic critics. Reviewing the collection for *Whole Earth Review*, Gramyo Tokuyama describes the book as "twenty-two masterfully crafted stories of the human potential to pull oneself up from dark humiliating circumstances." Sybil S. Steinberg, of *Publishers Weekly*, claims "Alexie writes with simplicity and forthrightness, allowing the power in his stories to creep up slowly on the reader." Steinberg notes the inter-relatedness of the stories, and praises Alexie's ability to depict the rich complexities of modern Native-American life. Of Alexie's unblinking representation of life on the reservation, Steinberg writes, "He captures the reservation's strong sense of community and attitude of hope tinged with realism as its inhabitants determine to persevere despite the odds."

Comparing Alexie to other Native-American writers such as Louis Erdich, N. Scott Momaday, and James Welsh, all of whom have written both poetry and novels, Alan Velie writes, *The Lone Ranger and Tonto Fistfight in Heaven* "establishes him not only as one of the best of the Indian writers but as one of the most promising of the new generation of American writers." In an essay for *The Review of Contemporary Fiction*, Brian Schneider argues that it is Alexie's voice that holds the stories together as a coherent narrative. Schneider writes: "Alexie's remarkable collection deserves a wide audience because of his original narrative voice, which mixes mythmaking with lyrical prose and captures the nation-within-a-nation status of American Indians and the contradictions such a status produces."

Criticism

Chris Semansky

Semansky is an instructor of English literature and composition and writes on literature and culture for several publications. In this essay, Semansky considers the role of storytelling in Alexie's stories.

In oral cultures, storytelling is the primary means by which history and tradition are passed from generation to generation. Alexie foregrounds the role of storytelling in his writing, however, not only as a means by which Native Americans can keep their collective memories alive, but also as a way that individuals can survive the daily assaults of Eurocentric culture on their imaginations and sensibilities. More often than not, rather than presenting a chronological narrative of events as one expects in conventional stories, Alexie's "stories" evoke states of mind and grapple with the numerous and conflicting representations vying for attention in the contemporary mind.

In her review of the collection in *American Indian Quarterly*, Denise Low writes, "Sherman Alexie's short stories in *The Lone Ranger and Tonto Fistfight in Heaven* could not have been written during any other period of history." Low is alluding not only to the numerous references Alexie makes to popular culture such as 7-11 stores, television shows, and baseball celebrities such as Pete Rose, but also to the peculiar condition in which Native Americans find themselves in the late twentieth century, having to constantly renegotiate their identity among the welter of conflicting signs that saturate their lives.

These signs are everywhere, in the image of Indians on television shows such as *The Lone Ranger*, in history books and in popular movies like

> By mythologizing James as someone who is more interested in helping Indians survive this world than he is in saving their souls for the next world, Alexie responds to the Christian missionaries who were so prevalent on reservations and who helped run their schools."

Dances With Wolves, that attempt to portray "real" Indians, and they exist in the tribal lore that inhabits the imagination of Native Americans themselves. Living on the reservation, segregated from white American culture at large, but vulnerable to its relentless sign system and its (mis)representations of Indians, Alexie's characters battle to achieve some sense of authenticity in a world where that very notion has become suspect. The fractured narratives and stories inside stories emphasize the desperation and urgency that drive these characters in their search for meaning.

One way his characters cultivate meaning is by mythologizing the reservation and its inhabitants. In "The Only Traffic Signal on the Reservation Don't Flash Red Anymore," Victor and Adrian practice this brand of storytelling in their discussions of basketball talent on the reservation. They focus on Julius Windmaker, "the latest thing in a long line of reservation basketball heroes," who "had that gift, that grace, those fingers like a goddam medicine man." In his study of Alexie in *Contemporary American Literature*, Kenneth Millard writes that this story "establishes the reservation in terms of a community of shared hardship where stories of survival help to protect Indians from erosion and disappearance." Erosion comes from within and without. As more and more Indians leave the reservation, ties to community and family are broken, and those who remain must battle alcohol, a crippling sense of stagnation, and an increasing isolation from the "outside" world. Adrian and Victor retain hope for life on the reservation by building myths around gifted individuals. Seemingly insignificant events such as a few minutes of a high school basketball game take on epic proportions each time Julius's story is retold. By creating contemporary myths around living Indians, the two keep alive the hope that conditions can change and that individuals can transcend their bleak circumstances.

Mythologizing takes on other forms as well. In "Jesus Christ's Half-Brother Is Alive and Well on the Spokane Indian Reservation," the narrator adopts a baby, James, after its parents have died in a fire. The baby does not walk or talk until the Christmas of his seventh year. When he finally speaks, he speaks with the wisdom of an elder:

> He says so many things and the only thing that matters is that he says he and I don't have the right to die for each other and that we should be living for each other instead. He says the world hurts. He says the first thing he wanted after he was born was a shot of whiskey. He says all that and more. He tells me to get a job and to grow my braids. He says I better learn how to shoot left-handed if I'm going to keep playing basketball. He says to open a fireworks stand.

Full of practical advice that counter ideas often associated with Christianity, James directly responds to the Christian notion that Christ died for the sins of humankind so that human beings may live, by telling the narrator that "we should be living for each other instead." By mythologizing James as someone who is more interested in helping Indians survive this world than he is in saving their souls for the next world, Alexie responds to the Christian missionaries who were so prevalent on reservations and who helped run their schools. It is James who literally saves the narrator from the ravages of alcoholism, as he is forced to give up the bottle if he is to keep custody of the child. Even Alcoholics Anonymous, which the narrator joins, is built upon the act of storytelling, as members meet to tell stories about how alcohol has ruined their lives and how they are going to stop drinking and change their lives. By listening to the stories of others and telling one's own story, members of AA derive the strength to stay sober.

The idea of salvation is at the heart of storytelling in Alexie's stories—salvation from one's own destructive impulses, salvation from the appropriation of Native-American history and traditions by others, salvation from the onslaught of technology that supplants human connectedness and colonizes family life. A year after he quits drinking, the narrator of "Jesus Christ's Half-Brother Is Alive and Well on the Spokane Indian Reservation," says, "Every day I'm trying not to drink and I pray but I don't know who I'm praying to." Storytelling is akin to praying in these stories. The act alone is enough. In "The Trial of Thomas Builds-the-Fire," inspired by Franz Kafka's novel, *The Trial*, Thomas, after being convicted of absurd charges, finds himself on a bus with convicts heading to prison. After being prodded, he begins to tell his stories, just as he had done at his trial. Thomas is both a tribal visionary and a walking archive of Spokane Indian history, and in Alexie's ironic representations of Indian culture, a parody of the modern Indian who cannot stop talking about his Indian identity and his tribal past. In "Family Portrait," the narrator describes television as a force that eats into his family's emotional life, and something they need to be saved from:

> The television was always loud, too loud, until every emotion was measured by the half hour. We hid our faces behind masks that suggested other histories; we touched hands accidentally and our skin sparked like a personal revolution. We stared across the room at each other, waited for the conversation and the conversion, watched wasps and flies battering against the windows. We were children; we were open mouths. Open in hunger, in anger, in laughter, in prayer. Jesus, we all want to survive.

There are so many similarities between the characters in Alexie's stories and Alexie's own life that the collection can also be seen as Alexie's attempt to tell the story of his life by mythologizing it. Such self-mythologizing has become a staple of postmodern writing and can be seen in writers as diverse as John Berryman, Mark Strand, Ann Sexton, Gerald Vizenor, and Mark Leyner. At a time when many consider literary realism to be antiquated and an insufficient way to depict how people live now, creating mythologies around and of oneself has become an effective and provocative way to depict reality.

Source: Chris Semansky, Critical Essay on *The Lone Ranger and Tonto Fistfight in Heaven*, in *Novels for Students*, The Gale Group, 2003.

Jacqueline L. McGrath

In the following essay, McGrath examines The Lone Ranger and Tonto Fistfight in Heaven *as both a literary work and as an artistic cultural representation.*

In Sherman Alexie's story, "A Drug Called Tradition," from his story collection, *The Lone Ranger and Tonto Fistfight in Heaven*, Victor, the narrator, speaks about what he calls the skeletons of the past and the future: "There are things you should learn. Your past is a skeleton walking one step behind you, and your future is a skeleton walking one step in front of you . . . Now, these skeletons are made of memories, dreams, and voices. And they can trap you in the in-between, between touching and becoming. But they're not necessarily evil, unless you let them be. What you have to do is keep moving, keep walking, in step with your skeletons . . . no matter what they do, keep walking, keep moving . . ."

This idea about skeletons, or the hauntings and the remnants of tradition, and the bones absent of flesh, but animate and manifest, is metonymic of the larger ideas and questions Alexie grapples with in this work: that is, how can a member or a performer of a tradition negotiate the seemingly incompatible drives of that tradition—the desire to perpetuate, to conserve, to maintain an idiom and its meaning, but at the same time, to accommodate the need to innovate, to create, and to move forward in a tradition, and explode and shape its word power? How can a participant in a tradition walk with the skeletons and traditions, but walk and innovate at a pace that avoids being trapped by their embrace?

My discussion of Alexie's work challenges the dogmatic and conservative insistence that, while a written, authored work can be considered a folklore text, it is not and cannot be called folklore. This essay is directed toward both scholars entrenched in the study of literary texts and to academic folklorists who insist on conventional and conservative parameters for what constitutes folklore. My aim is to articulate an approach to this particular authored text which would prevent the incorrect and casual identification of folklore in literature, as well as any preemptive dismissal of its presence in this novel. By reading Sherman Alexie's *The Lone Ranger and Tonto Fistfight in Heaven* as a literary construction as well as a work born of a particular culture and artistic tradition, I insist on a more complicated understanding of its content, shape, and meanings in a critique of folklore theories which limit and confine our concepts of the power and dimensions of shaped words. I also challenge the popular but simplistic notion that Native American writing is somehow more "oral" than other texts, and I combat in part the increasingly useless distinction between the written and oral manifestation of verbal art by relying on some ideas of Dell Hymes as well as John Miles Foley. Foley, who considers text a medium for representing parts of an oral traditional performance, argues in *The Singer of Tales in Performance* (1995) that a text (or the material written representation of folk-

> " Alexie's writing strives to subvert and critique stereotypes about Indians that are maintained by mainstream culture. At the same time, the artistic features of his work undermine the traditional forms of the novel and traditional character types and themes of literature."

lore) cannot be declared something "different in species" from the oral tradition to which it is related, asking instead "how a given text continues the tradition of reception?" We can achieve an understanding of Alexie's text's reception and its place in a tradition, of course, by understanding the written representation on its own terms, by relying on textual indications of performance, and by learning or understanding the "institutionalized meanings" within the register of the tradition. That is, we can examine Alexie's text for its literary practices which represent those signals of performance, and then we can begin to seek a truer understanding of traditional meanings and ideas. Alexie, of course, relies on our readerly knowledge that we inscribe into his text, and then he uses literary devices that are both conventional and which subvert and d disrupt western literary principles. I assert, however, that besides easily dissecting Alexie's story collection and recognizing textual indications of meaning and performance, and beyond identifying keys to performance which indicate how this text might register with people in Alexie's folk group, I also contend that there is a kind of living dimension to the authored, printed word that cannot be summarily discounted unless we are unwilling to examine and enflesh our understanding of word power and a living tradition, and I argue for a more expansive notion of how folklore processes can be exchanged and represented.

Sherman Alexie, a Spokane and Coeur D'Alene American Indian, is an academically trained writer and political activist who wrote and produced the

What Do I Read Next?

- Alexie's novel *Reservation Blues* (1995) solidified his reputation as one of America's strongest writers. Alexie draws on the Faust legend in telling the story of an Indian blues band called Coyote Springs.

- N. Scott Momaday's Pulitzer Prize–winning first novel, *House Made of Dawn* (1968), helped pave the way for other Native-American writers such as Alexie. The novel tells the story of a Tano Indian named Abel who returns from World War II army service to his home in New Mexico. Momaday charts Abel's struggles to reaffirm the ways of his people while living in a world often antagonistic towards those ways.

- *Megatrends 2000: Ten New Directions for the 1990s* (1990), written by John Naisbitt and Patricia Aburdene, provides a social forecast for the 1990s, describing trends and their contexts, including the emergence of free-market socialism, global lifestyles, and cultural nationalism.

- *American Indian Myths and Legends* (1985), edited by Alfonso Ortiz and Richard Erdoes, gathers 160 tales from 80 tribal groups to survey the rich Native-American mythic heritage.

- *Manners & Customs of the Coeur d'Alene Indians* (1975), by Jerome Peltier, is a useful introduction to the customs of Alexie's tribe.

film *Smoke Signals*, based upon his work *The Lone Ranger and Tonto Fistfight in Heaven*. Born in 1966, Alexie grew up on the Spokane reservation in central Washington, and attended Gonzaga State and Washington State University, where he earned a BA in 1991. Alexie, who cites Adrian C. Louis, Simon Ortiz, Joy Harjo, and Linda Hogan as models, has published thirteen books, including seven collections of poetry. He asserts that his writing is primarily autobiographical: "It's fiction as autobiography, or autobiography as fiction, I'm not sure which one." This self-described life writing,

accompanied by a skewering humor and scathing wit, earned Alexie a reputation as an ego-driven and opportunistic writer. In a feature interview on National Public Radio, Liane Hansen quotes a woman who grew up knowing the author: "What people on the reservation feel is that he's making fun of them. It's supposed to be fiction, but we all know whom he's writing about. He has wounded a lot of people." He has also been criticized by other Native American and non-native novelists for his position that only Native Americans can write characters who are Indian, and he is known for vilifying white authors for attempting to do so, particularly Barbara Kingsolver. Kingsolver insists she resents his attitude because it would "limit the scope" of most authors; presumably she resists confining authors to composing characters of their own ethnic and cultural background. Alexie explains, "I write what I know, and I don't try to mythologize myself, which is what some seem to want, and which some Indian women and men writers are doing, this Earth Mother and Shaman Man thing, trying to create these "authentic, traditional" Indians. We don't live our lives that way." I find myself torn between agreeing with his criticism of writers such as Kingsolver or Tony Hillerman, who capitalize on the popularity of the Native American novel genre and perpetuate romantic stereotypes in their characterizations of Indian people, and my own rejection of the impossibility of non-Natives studying, reading, and writing about Native American people and culture in ways that are not colonizing and destructive. I think, however, that Alexie's own work is important because of its consumption by a variety of audiences, and I attribute the variety of response to his work to the confluence of traditions and multiple registers he taps in the creation of his art.

Alexie has earned critical acclaim from the literary establishment, but I find book reviews typically misunderstand the forces at work in his writing. Critics frequently praise his work as lyric, humorous and comic, and, of course, make use of the fabulous catch-all phrase critics use for any phenomena they can't easily categorize, "magical realism." In one review titled, "The Despair and Spirit of American Indians," Lawrence Thornton criticizes Alexie's work without considering its Native culture and political context, dismissing all its phenomena as postmodernism. Another critic, Michael Castro, says, "Plot and character, the classical main elements of fiction and drama, do not stick with us after reading these stories," clearly an example of a critic working from a Western literary aesthetic. Another critic, Gramyo Tokuyama, writes, "Using poignant humor he exposes the cultural demise of a nation steeped in sacred tradition and surrounded by a passionless society." Tokuyama, by identifying this as a central theme of the book, seems to venerate the romantic notion that pure and true Native American cultures would still be gloriously uncorrupted if isolated from the surrounding "passionless" society. Of course, Alexie provides a sharp critique of stultifying and isolationist traditional practices as he simultaneously skewers disconnectedness and apathy, demonstrating how these factions consistently intermingle. In Alexie's books, one society doesn't surround another—rather, societies disintegrate together.

Native American author Leslie Marmon Silko is the only critic who calls *The Lone Ranger and Tonto Fistfight in Heaven* a set of interlinked short stories, and examines its folkloric qualities, especially its traditional referentiality; nearly all the other critics treat each stow as a separate piece and judge it using purely literary vocabulary. Silko wrote a review for *The Nation* in which she explains how traditions of Native American oral narratives demonstrate a legacy of "lengthy fictions of interlinked characters and events" as commonplace. Silko's comment indicates the importance of tradition to the writing of Alexie's work, and she contextualizes his authored literature in relationship to oral tradition and composition, for, as Silko points out, the structure and chronology of Alexie's book does not reflect standard components of Western literature, because Native American literature has traditionally taken a different shape which does not necessarily include features like Castro's "plot and character." Silko also points out that Alexie is, in fact, drawing on a canonical Western tradition as well as a native tradition, and she argues that he uses ghosts sometimes in the same way as Henry James or Shakespeare, as symbols instead of real beings, as well as images from Indian culture. She suggests the way he writes about a small town is within the tradition of communities evoked in literary works like *The Scarlet Letter*, *Babbitt*, *Sanctuary*, and *The Last Picture Show*. I think the vast majority of critics cannot arrive at the same combination of Western and non-Western literary criticism Silko uses to read this work, as the relies on some aspects of folklore theory as well as her training as a literary critic to review Alexie's novel more responsibly.

Louis Owens, another Native American literary critic who examines the construction of third-

wave Native literatures, relates the syncresis of Alexie's work to what he calls the initial problem confronting any Native American author. Owens argues that a Native American writer's art is initially problematized by its complicity with linguistic colonization. Owens writes about the complexity of the task confronting a novelist who would write about Indians and Indian concerns: "every word written in English represents a collaboration of sorts as well as a reorientation (conscious or unconscious) from the . . . world of oral tradition to the . . . reality of written language." While seemingly falling into the trap of polarizing the solely written and the solely oral composition of word art, Owens focuses on the political ramifications of negotiating these multiple registers. Indeed, after understanding the implications of incorporating one cultural form of expression—that is, Native American verbal art—with a literary genre that has historically and contemporarily dominated and oppressed it, we can more thoroughly comprehend how Alexie simultaneously disentangles himself from what Owens calls a collaboration with a tool of colonization.

Furthermore, Alexie's writing strives to subvert and critique stereotypes about Indians that are maintained by mainstream culture. At the same time, the artistic features of his work undermine the traditional forms of the novel and traditional character types and themes of literature. Alexie creates art that successfully exposes interrupts, and unsettles Western patriarchal notions about Indians and Indian beliefs. Scott B. Vickers explains this artistic innovation: "The most successful Native American writers have adopted the forms, but not necessarily the traditional motifs, of the Western cannon, and have often brought to these genres the distinctive story-telling traditions of their own culture." Alexie syncretically innovates on myriad traditions to produce work that is revolutionary and transformative, shifting the idiom of his work away from static fiction and toward a tradition of dynamic and audience-altering art. If his work is not conventionally a living performance and communal exchange, its deeply powerful and weighted expressive nature propels his work into an expression that defies containment, definition, and the limitations of existing scholarship to dissect its expressive and affective communicative ability.

Certainly, by relying on current folklore scholarship, we can demonstrate that Alexie's work is undoubtedly a folkloric text. While authored by an individual writer, inked and seemingly fixed, it contains idiomatic and metonymic words, "old-time" stories, themes, and characters, as well as keys to performance, including special codes, figurative language, parallelism, special paralinguistic features, special formulae, and appeals to tradition. We can sort through his work and pick out multiple demonstrations of this text's relationship to the folklores in which the author participates. Furthermore, we can uncover how Alexie percieves his authorial role in relationship to his membership in his American Indian community; Alexie is a master of literary convention, and the confidence he displays in interviews indicates he is in fact comfortable with the primacy of authorship; however, he explains his complicated role as one which depends on more than singular individuality: "I'm a Spokane Indian who just happens to be a writer. I'm proud of who I am, and it defines everything I do. I think all too often, brown people buy into the Western civilization idea of looking at the artist as the individual. That's only part of it. We are also members of tribes. Nothing gets me madder than a brown person who says, 'I just want to be a writer.' It's denying who you are simply because of the pressures white culture puts upon you."

Alexie refuses to extricate his art from its traditional and community context, and repeatedly claims his creative contribution and his tradition's creative contribution are equitable. Indeed, we can examine his content for the hallmarks of Native American literature and traditional narrative themes, including repetition, the "recasting of tribal narratives into modern day story lines, a certain admixture of sacred and profane influences, and the enunciation of tacitly Indian worldviews and personal experiences." These are certainly all elements Alexie incorporates in *The Lone Ranger and Tonto Fistfight in Heaven*, and though the end product is a marketable literary work which conforms to canonical values (in that it is shaped like prose, has characters, plot events, a beginning and ending, literary symbolism and metaphor), the actual stories undermine many western literary conventions, in both content and the literary tactics employed.

To outline the work briefly, *The Lone Ranger and Tonto Fistfight in Heaven* is composed of twenty-two short stories; there is no conventional plot connecting them, but they are interlinked, much like Louise Erdrich's *Love Medicine*, a storytelling style some critics characterize, because of the additive development, as inherently oral traditional. This collection is narrated from multiple points of view and replicates traditional pan-Indian myths such as trickster and metamorphosis tales, in addition to many other "old-time" themes and motifs. Alexie, who has also published two novels and one other story collection (*Indian Killer* 1996, *Reservation Blues* 1995, and *The Toughest Indian In the World 2000*), blurs the chronology of the stories and the collection itself does not have a dominant narrative or story frame, causing many critics to label this a collection of short stories (a term Alexie does not use). Two of the characters appearing most frequently, Thomas Builds-the-Fire and Victor Joseph, became the protagonists of the film *Smoke Signals*. Thomas is a nerdy storyteller who tells stories and seems to serve as a surrogate for Alexie while providing a running commentary on oral tradition in tribal culture. Victor, caught between reservation community and his own individuality, tries to present himself as the stereotypical warrior Indian, and is a habitual persecutor of Thomas and a harsh critic of his stories. However, and despite himself, Victor often enjoys, or is at least fascinated by, Thomas's stories, and on one occasion he wonders whatever happened to "a sense of community."

As for replicating orality in a text, Alexie consistently tries to evoke oral performance by addressing the reader and marking the beginning of a performance with page breaks and snippets of poetry or related traditional narratives. These tactics are Alexie's attempts at ethnopoetics, and change the appearance of the text on the page, dividing the prose into a form that is interrupted and perhaps even conversational. For instance, one performative technique Alexie repeats is addressing commentary or questions toward the reader. In "The First Annual All-Indian Horseshoe Pitch and Barbecue," the story is told in first person, but at the end, a series of questions are posed to the audience by the narrator, a device repeated in several stories: "Can you hear the dreams crackling like a campfire? Can you hear the dreams laughing in the sawdust? Can you hear the dreams shaking just a little bit as the day grows long? Can you hear the dreams putting on a good jacket that smells of fry bread and sweet smoke? Can you hear the dreams stay up late and talk so many stones?"

Alexie addresses the reader throughout the work, informing us: "Now, I'll tell you that I haven't used the thing . . ."; commanding us: "Believe me, there is just barely enough goodness in all of this . . ."; questioning us: "Didn't you know?" These questions are intended to elicit my participation in the telling of the story, as I pause and respond, in my mind or out loud. The call for reader response goes far beyond the provincial "dear reader" that Western canonical writing invokes.

Alexie also incorporates specialized language that is reflective of current Indian lexicon, but is also recognizable to readers who are outside the tradition, including the formula "enit," a word used to punctuate sentences which has multiple meanings depending on context, including "true," "yes," "alright," among others. But Alexie refuses to define or explain this usage, insisting that we decode it by visiting for a time in the presence of his Indian characters.

Besides picking out the keys to performance articulated by oral traditional theories, we can locate other evidence that Alexie is pushing toward a kind of "new" tradition. Evidence of innovation on both traditional narratives and the traditions of print journalism is developed by Alexie in newspaper stories throughout the work. First, after the murder trial of Thomas Builds-the-Fire, the text offers us an article describing his conviction, a straight news story in the *Spokesman Review*, presumably written by a non-Native journalist, with quotes from all parties and conforming to the style and expected uninterpreted content of conventional journalism. Later, we are given another news clipping, this time written by Norma, a reservation Indian, about a basketball game. She reports, "He hit a three thousand foot jumper at the buzzer . . ." "I think he was Crazy Horse for just a second," said an anonymous and maybe-just-a-little-crazy-themselves source . . ." Alexie seems to be innovating, through Norma, on both the conventions of print journalism and the traditional hero motif. The contrast between the "straight" news and the more mythic rendering of the Indian-created news suggests the latter is a socially created text which changes between event and transmission, a representation of a dynamism not present in the straight news. Perhaps Alexie recreates a newspaper article in two separate stories to demonstrate the differences between two disparate traditions for recording an event. These two versions indicate that the community news story is a kind of folklore, based on an event and interpreted in a traditional manner by a storyteller who is a member of the oral collective.

The most interesting innovation on a traditional figure is the development of the character Thomas Builds-the-Fire, for as Alexie himself explains in an interview, "Thomas explodes the myth and stereotype about the huge, stoic, warrior Indian. He's the exact opposite of what people have come to expect—the idea of an Indian geek just doesn't happen. He's something of a trickster figure, sort of a coyote figure, and he's mythological

in that sense. He's always subverting convention, not only Indian conventions about Indians but white conventions about Indians." Thomas is in many ways very humorous, and the fact that he is a disregarded storyteller who cheerfully tries to maintain the oral tradition of his community, but who frequently offers stories which incorporate new themes, figures, and formula in traditional material, seems to be Alexie's vehicle for commenting on and manifesting the complications of oral tradition. Certainly, the work suggests that Thomas Builds-the-Fire is NOT a valued conduit of tradition; as Victor explains to us, "Thomas was a storyteller that nobody wanted to listen to . . . Nobody talked to Thomas anymore because he told the same damn stories over and over again."

In his innovative creation of a literary work Alexie has crafted stories which illustrate the tensions within living traditions (both the oral tradition in which he participates, as well as the literary tradition of authored text). Through his "new-time" storyteller, Thomas Builds-the-Fire, Alexie complicatedly both rages against and replicates what is static and conservative about an oral tradition and what results from that stasis in his Native American community. Through his treatment of Thomas he suggests that stasis of tradition is part of what continues to oppress and cripple American Indians socially and economically. At the same time, Alexie offers ideas about both the value and the problematic nature of innovation according to tradition— the very innovation needed to overcome the results and effects of stasis is frightening because it is change, and it is new and unrecognizable. This is a fear illustrated in the characters of Norma, an American Indian woman who rejects alcoholism and unemployment, and who fancydances as well as she boogies. The innovation according to tradition in her own life makes her declare, "Every one of our elders who dies takes a piece of our past away . . . and that hurts more because I don't know how much of a future we have." This fear of the new and its impact is manifest in the character of one unnamed narrator, who hopes for innovation but questions its possibility: "Driving home, I heard the explosion of a house catching fire and thought it was a new stow born. . . . But. . . . it's the same old story, whispered past the same false teeth. How can we imagine a new language . . . and a new life when a pocketful of quarters weighs our possibilities down?" The question for Alexie often seems to be whether the risk and the imperative of innovation on tradition, and the radical and revolutionary disruption his work can wreak on readers who belong to the dominant culture as well as on American Indians is worth the seeming loss or decay of oral tradition and traditional meaning.

In his article "Custer and Linguistic Anthropology," Dell Hymes declares, "One can believe, I do believe, that about the dry bones of print, words heaped up in paragraphs, something of the original spirit lingers. That spirit need not be lost to comprehension, respect, and appreciation. We are not able to revive by singing, or stepping over a text five times, but by patient surrender to what a text has to say, in the way it has to say it, something of life can again become incarnate." Hymes, of course, is arguing for the value in reading and studying the textual remnants of folk traditions, believing that manuscript forms may retain certain keys to performance which allow us to tap into how a text means.

This same idea can be applied to literary works like Sherman Alexie's *The Lone Ranger and Tonto Fistfight in Heaven*, but I would venture to say that beyond the embodiment of literature or collected texts with traditional meaning lies the prospect that the revivification of the "dry bones" of words incarnates more than the spirit of a living tradition. Those words, I assert, are more than dry bones, but are important genetic material, if you will—those words contain something of the humanity of the person who commits those words to text. I challenge us to expand—to explode—our ideas about what the word is and how it means. I assert that an electronic medium, or inked, printed text retains some essence or skeleton of the human being who committed the text to fixity. We must wonder if the medium of printed text is as limited as we insist. Native American literary critic Scott B. Vickers explains that, "For Native Americans, writing is an opportunity to re-invoke the poetry of the oral tradition, and thus a whole new cultural ethos, so that oral tradition can once again flourish in a new medium and even change the medium itself." I think, as writers like Sherman Alexie try to innovate on the medium of printed, fixed literature, so too can folklorists innovate on their conventional understanding of the power of text on a page.

Can we argue, then, that when writers like Alexie innovate on both literary conventions and oral traditional narrative conventions, his work becomes caught in "flux," much as, perhaps, our understanding of folklore in literature is? I challenge us to make room for a vision of folklore as a phenomena so powerful and ephemeral that it can transcend the confines of written text in ways we cannot collect and explicitly describe, but the recognition of that possibility, that step over the bones, may open a world of life incarnate that exists too deeply to be seen or touched, but can only be known.

Source: Jacqueline L. McGrath, "'The Same Damn Stories': Exploring a Variation on Tradition in Sherman Alexie's *The Lone Ranger and Tonto Fistfight in Heaven*," in *Southern Folklore*, Vol. 57, No. 2, 2000, pp. 94–105.

Sources

Alexie, Sherman, *The Lone Ranger and Tonto Fistfight in Heaven*, Atlantic Monthly Press, 1993.

Bellante, Carl, and John Bellante, "Sherman Alexie, Literary Rebel," in *Bloomsbury Review*, No. 14, May–June 1994, pp. 14–15, 26.

Low, Denise, Review of *The Lone Ranger and Tonto Fistfight in Heaven*, in *American Indian Quarterly*, Vol. 20, No. 1, Winter 1996, p. 123.

Millard, Kenneth, *Contemporary American Fiction*, Oxford University Press, 2000, pp. 96–103.

Schneider, Brian, Review of *The Lone Ranger and Tonto Fistfight in Heaven*, in the *Review of Contemporary Fiction*, Vol. 13, No. 3, Fall 1993, pp. 237–38.

Steinberg, Sybil S., Review of *The Lone Ranger and Tonto Fistfight in Heaven*, in *Publishers Weekly*, Vol. 240, No. 29, July 19, 1993, p. 235.

Tokuyama, Gramyo, Review of *The Lone Ranger and Tonto Fistfight in Heaven*, in *Whole Earth Review*, No. 86, Fall 1995, p. 57.

Velie, Alan R., Review of *The Lone Ranger and Tonto Fistfight in Heaven*, in *World Literature Today*, Vol. 68, No. 2, Spring 1996, pp. 407–408.

Further Reading

Cline, Lynn, "About Sherman Alexie," in *Ploughshares*, Vol. 26, Issue 4, Winter 2000, pp. 197–202.
    Cline's essay succinctly covers the major developments in Alexie's life and writing career.

Donahue, Peter, "New Warriors, New Legends: Basketball in Three Native American Works of Fiction," in *American Indian Culture and Research Journal*, Vol. 21, No. 2, Spring 1997.
    Donahue discusses the significance of basketball in Native-American culture in *The Lone Ranger and Tonto Fistfight in Heaven* and *Reservation Blues*.

Hirschfelder, Arlene, and Martha Kreipe de Montano, *The Native American Almanac: A Portrait of Native America Today*, Prentice Hall General Reference, 1993.

This useful reference book includes history of Indian and white relations, Native Americans today, treaties, tribal governments, languages, education, religion, games and sports, and Native Americans in film and video.

McFarland, Ron, "Sherman Alexie," in *Dictionary of Literary Biography*, Vol. 206: *Twentieth-Century American Western Writers*, First Series, edited by Richard H. Cracroft, The Gale Group, 1999, pp. 3–10.
McFarland provides a thorough overview of Alexie's writing and life.

Waldman, Carl, *Who Was Who in Native American History*, Facts on File Publications, 1990.
Alexie occasionally makes references to Native-American heroes from history. This book provides biographies of Indians and non-Indians important in Indian history, from early contact through 1900.

The Mambo Kings Play Songs of Love

Oscar Hijuelos

1989

Oscar Hijuelos's novel *The Mambo Kings Play Songs of Love* was published in 1989, and soon became a huge international bestseller. It tells the story of Cesar Castillo, an aged musician who once had a small amount of fame when he and his brother appeared on an episode of *I Love Lucy* in the 1950s. The book chronicles Cesar's last hours as he sits in a seedy hotel room, drinking and listening to recordings made by his band, the Mambo Kings. Events and characters whirl through his mind, evoking what he has lost over the years: his brother and collaborator, Nestor, who spent his adult life constantly rewriting one song about a lost love; the many lovers who gave themselves up to him as he rose triumphantly through the mambo music craze of the early fifties; and the way of life that disappeared for all Cubans after that country was overthrown by an insurrection led by Fidel Castro in 1959. In telling Cesar's story, Hijuelos weaves in cameo appearances by several real-life mambo musicians, including Desi Arnaz, Tito Puente, Pérez Prado, Machito and Mongo Santamaría.

This novel, Hijuelos's second, won the Pulitzer Prize for fiction in 1990, marking the first time that that prize was awarded to a Hispanic author. Hijuelos has published four more novels since then, frequently touching on the theme of immigrants and how they adjust to coming to America.

Oscar Hijuelos

Author Biography

Oscar Hijuelos (his last name is pronounced "E-*way*-los") was born in New York City on August 24, 1951. His parents came from the Oriente province of Cuba, emigrating in 1943 to the Spanish Harlem section of New York, which is where the author grew up. As a teenager in the 1960s, Hijuelos played guitar in Top 40 bands. He attended City College of New York, receiving a bachelor of arts degree in 1975 and a master's degree in creative writing in 1976. After college, he worked for Transportation Display, Inc., an advertising firm, for seven years. During that time, he continued writing.

In 1978, his short story "Columbus Discovering America" received a Pushcart Press citation for "outstanding writer." Following that, he won an Oscar Cintas fiction writing grant for 1978–1979; a Bread Loaf Writers Conference scholarship in 1980; a fiction writing grant from Creative Artists Programs Service in 1982; and a grant from the Ingram Merrill Foundation in 1983.

His first novel, *Our House in the Last World*, was published in 1983. It concerns a Cuban couple, Alejo and Sorrea, who, like the author's parents, emigrate from Cuba to New York in the

1940s. It won several awards, including the American Academy in Rome Fellowship in Literature, which allowed him to live in Rome for a while. While in Italy, he developed an interest in archeology, a hobby which has affected the historical curiosity of his books.

The Mambo Kings Play Songs of Love, published in 1989, was Hijuelos's second novel, and is by far his most famous to date. Along with other honors, it won the Pulitzer Prize for fiction in 1990, making Hijuelos the first Hispanic novelist to take that award. He followed this up with *The Fourteen Sisters of Emilio Montez O'Brien* in 1993; *Mr. Ives' Christmas* in 1995; and *Empress of the Splendid Season* in 1999. Although Hijuelos has been an American citizen all of his life, his books are rich in images of Cuba that he gained from research and from the memories of older family members. This makes him distinct from other Cuban-American writers, whose works often contain a strong political element that draws on the sharp contrast between the two countries' systems.

Hijuelos's latest novel, his sixth, is *A Simple Habana Melody*, published in 2002. He still lives in New York City, near the Spanish Harlem apartment where he grew up.

Plot Summary

It Was a Saturday Afternoon on LaSalle Street

The first few pages of *The Mambo Kings Play Songs of Love* are narrated by Eugenio Castillo, who is the nephew of the book's main character, Cesar Castillo. He describes an afternoon in his childhood, sometime in the early 1960s, when the landlady called up to the apartment where his family lived to let Cesar know that they were rerunning the episode of *I Love Lucy* that he and his brother had appeared on, performing the song that Eugenio's father Nestor wrote, "Beautiful María of My Soul." When Eugenio goes to the kitchen to get him, Cesar has a difficult time rising from the table, having been out until four or five in the morning playing the trumpet. With Eugenio's help, Cesar makes it to the couch, and Eugenio brings him a drink of whisky as he watches the most important moment of his life repeat once more.

Side A: In the Hotel Splendour, 1980

Cesar has checked into a room at the Hotel Splendour with his record player, a stack of records,

Media Adaptations

- This novel was adapted to a movie in 1992, starring Armand Assante and Antonio Banderas as the Castillo brothers. It was directed by Arne Glimcher. It was produced by Warner Brothers and is available on videocassette from Warner Home Video.

- An audiocassette version of the book was read by E. B. Marshall and released by NewStar Media in 1991.

- Although most movie soundtracks have little to do with the novels the movies are adapted from, the soundtrack for *The Mambo Kings* brings to life the music that is so important to the book. It features songs by legendary musicians such as Tito Puente and Celia Cruz, as well as works by contemporary Cuban artists such as Arturo Sandoval. The album includes two versions of the Mambo Kings' signature song "Beautiful María of My Soul": one in English (performed by Los Lobos) and one in Spanish (performed by one of the movie's stars, Antonio Banderas). It is available on cassette and compact disc from Elektra.

and several bottles of liquor. He wonders if this is the room in the same hotel where he used to take girls in the old days. He recalls arriving with Nestor in New York in 1949 and forming the band. They were from a farm in Cuba and had been playing with a small combo in Havana before moving to New York, where they moved in with their cousin Pablo and his family at 500 LaSalle Street.

The early days of the band Cesar and Nestor formed, the Mambo Kings, were slow. They worked in a meat factory during the days and wrote songs, in particular "Beautiful María of My Soul," which Nestor eventually rewrote forty-four times. Cesar remembers that, before moving to Havana, he was with an orchestra run by Julián García in Santiago de Cuba. He married Julián's niece, Luisa, and she moved to Havana with him, but one of his many girlfriends told Luisa about their affair, and Luisa left Cesar while she was pregnant. They reconciled for a few months, but then she left him for good. Over the years he sent presents to their daughter, Mariela.

In 1950, Nestor met Delores Fuentes and they started an affair that made Nestor think back to his tragic affair with María. It had occurred several years earlier, in Havana: walking down the street one day, he heard a man and woman fighting, and, investigating it, found a man beating on María. He chased the man away, and he and María started a passionate love affair. Eventually, though, Nestor turned to his brother Cesar for advice about how to behave toward his woman, and Cesar recommended that he assert his manliness and abuse María. She left him and went back to her home village. When he eventually followed, he learned that she had just married the man he had seen beating her in Havana. In America, his affair with Dolores led to her being pregnant with Eugenio, so they got married. A daughter, Leticia, was born three years later, in 1954. Nestor was a distant father and husband, always dreaming about María: writing her letters, and working on his song about her.

The Mambo Kings became one of the most popular bands in New York. One night in 1955, Desi Arnaz and Lucille Ball came to see them. After the show, Cesar struck up a conversation with Arnaz. They were from the same area of Cuba, and they had both sung in the Julián García band. Cesar remembers conversing into the night with Arnaz and Ball and inviting them back to his and Nestor's apartment, although he is not sure if that is how it went. Three months later, they went out to Hollywood to film the *I Love Lucy* episode in which the Castillo brothers play Ricky Ricardo's cousins who have just arrived from Cuba. They became wealthy from that appearance, as several singers, including Arnaz, recorded "Beautiful María of My Soul," and the Mambo Kings did their one and only national tour.

Nestor died in a car accident in 1957, sliding on an icy road into a tree while driving back from a performance. Cesar stayed in the apartment with Dolores and the children for a while, but he found himself too attracted to Dolores. He joined the Merchant Marines and traveled the world for two years. After a while of inactivity, he took a job as the maintenance man for the building at 500 LaSalle.

Side B:Sometime Later in the Night in the Hotel Splendour

During the night, a man from the next room at the Hotel Splendour comes over to borrow some liquor from Cesar. He invites Cesar back to his room to meet the woman he is with. Back in his own room, Cesar hears the couple through the wall, making love, and he is disappointed about what his own life has come to.

He remembers the doctor who told him that his body is incapable of processing alcohol, that it is like poison to him, and he pours himself another drink.

His mind drifts back to the early 1960s when he began to perform again, in order to make money to send to his family, which was suffering in Cuba because of the Communist revolution. With the backing of a local gangster, Fernando Pérez, he opens a small nightclub, the *Club Havana*, but he loses money because he hires too many friends, and the gangsters take control of it, using it as a place to sell drugs in the neighborhood.

Toward the End, While Listening to the Wistful "Beautiful María of My Soul"

Cesar recalls his most recent affair, when he was nearly sixty. Her name was Lydia Santos. She was in her mid-thirties, and had two children. Cesar began taking her out and buying presents for her children. Even after he determined that he was truly in love with her, he was insecure, always expecting her to leave him for a younger man.

As his health deteriorated, his doctor gave him prescription pain killers, which made him angry and disoriented. He said offensive things to Lydia, and later wondered why he said them. They finally broke up when she had to miss a date with him: she called later to explain that she had taken a child to the emergency room, but Cesar would not accept her excuse.

One final memory Cesar has is from his childhood: he wanted to be a musician so badly that he would pay a local musician for lessons with rum that he stole from his father. His father always beat him mercilessly for stealing, and treated him badly the rest of his life. Cesar also remembers his mother, who was at her happiest when dancing in the kitchen. Then he says goodbye to a succession of people who have been important in his life. He is found the next morning with a drink in his hand, a smile on his face, and a handwritten copy of the lyrics to "Beautiful María of My Soul."

When I Called the Number

Like the first section, the last section is told by Eugenio. He talks about going to see Desi Arnaz about a year after Cesar's death. Mr. Arnaz remembers Cesar and Nestor well, and has a photograph of himself with them on his wall, along with photos of other celebrities. He starts singing "Beautiful María of My Soul," which he admires, but forgets some words. When he is out of the room, Eugenio has a fantasy that combines the appearance of the ghost of his father, Nestor, and the famed *I Love Lucy* episode.

Characters

Desi Arnaz

Desario Arnaz is a real-life person who plays a crucial role as a character in the book. He was born in the Oriente province of Cuba and became a famous television star. When he hears the Castillo brothers in a nightclub, he invites them to perform on his television sitcom, *I Love Lucy*. Cesar remembers having Desi and his wife, Lucille Ball, to their apartment for some Cuban food, spending the night eating and drinking with them, but he questions whether his memory is accurate. In the last section of the book, Nestor's son Eugenio goes to visit Mr. Arnaz, and finds that he remembers the Castillos very well and has a picture of them on his wall.

Lucille Ball

Lucille Ball is a real person as well as a character in the novel. She was the star of the show *I Love Lucy*, which, in the book, the Castillo brothers appear on in the 1950s. Lucy is hardly mentioned in *The Mambo Kings Play Songs of Love*. In her few scenes, she is gracious but slightly impatient with her husband, Desi Arnaz, who wants to spend time talking about Cuba with Cesar and Nestor.

Cesar Castillo

Cesar is the focus of this novel. Except for a few pages at the beginning and a few at the end that are narrated by his nephew Eugenio, the book concerns Cesar sitting in a room at the Hotel Splendour in 1980, drinking and listening to the recordings he and his group, the Mambo Kings, made in the 1940s and 50s. He is sixty-two years old, depressed because his health is failing him, and purposely drinking himself to death because he can no longer drink or have sex, which were his main pursuits in life.

Cesar's reminiscences bounce around in no particular order, covering how he was abused by his father back in Cuba, how he left home to be a musician, working first in the capital city of Oriente province and then in Havana, before emigrating to New York City in 1949. As the leader of the Mambo Kings band, he lived the good life, meeting famous people, drinking and playing music all night, and having sexual encounters with dozens of women, some of which he thinks may have occurred in the same room he currently occupies, before the Hotel Splendor became run down. The high point of his professional career was the brothers' appearance on *I Love Lucy*, which made them famous and led to high sales figures for their most popular album, *The Mambo Kings Sing Songs of Love*, which sold ten thousand copies. After that, his life had a few problems, but for the most part he was where he wanted to be.

When his brother Nestor died in 1957, Cesar's life fell apart. He became uninterested in performing music, eventually taking a job as the superintendent of his building. He became sexually infatuated with his brother's widow. He lets his health decline, drinking recklessly, to the point where a doctor admitted him to into the hospital, warning that he faced a breakdown of his ravaged digestive system if he did not change his lifestyle. In his sixties, he had a love affair with a woman in her thirties, Lydia Santos. While mixing medication and alcohol, Cesar became abusive to her, and she stopped seeing him. With nothing to live for, he gave away prized possessions and came to the Hotel Splendour for a night of drinking and reminiscing. He is found dead in the morning with a drink in his hand and a smile on his face, having written out the lyrics to the haunting song Nestor worked his whole life on, "Beautiful María of My Soul."

Delores Castillo

Although he cannot forget María, whom he fell in love with in Cuba, Nestor marries Delores in New York, and they have two children together. She is a voracious reader and something of an introvert, having come to New York from Cuba when she was thirteen and taken care of her hardworking and hard-drinking father until he died. When she marries Nestor, she moves into the apartment the Castillo brothers share; after Nestor's death, she becomes uncomfortable because Cesar keeps trying to make love to her, and so she asks him to

move out. When the children are grown up and her second husband dies, she goes back to school, something that Nestor had prevented her from doing. She has an affair with a young man who is also a student, and when he breaks off their relationship she wanders home through a bad neighborhood and is mugged and almost raped.

Eugenio Castillo

Eugenio is the son of Nestor Castillo. He is the narrator of the book's brief introduction, in which he remembers being a child and watching his father and uncle on an *I Love Lucy* rerun with Cesar, and of the last section, in which he goes to visit Desi Arnaz in California. Throughout the story, he is mentioned from Cesar's perspective as a moody art student and briefly as a trumpet player, although he gives up music early.

Leticia Castillo

Leticia is Nestor's daughter. She is seldom mentioned in the book except when, as a young woman, she develops a crush on one of the young Cuban musicians whom Cesar helps, and has her heart broken by him. Later she marries and has children.

Mariela Castillo

Mariela is Cesar's daughter in Cuba. Mariela's mother, Luisa, leaves him soon after the baby is born because he is having affairs with other women. He constantly sends gifts to his daughter from America, and returns to Cuba to visit her when she is thirteen, but he never sees her after that. They nearly meet in the 1970s, when she is in her thirties and appearing in Montreal with a Cuban ballet troupe, but Cesar is old and finds himself too ill to travel to Montreal, so they talk on the phone for one last time.

Nestor Castillo

Nestor is the more sensitive of the two Mambo Kings, younger than Cesar by ten years. As a boy, he has a strong bond with his mother, but he leaves to follow his older brother's success. He meets María in Havana. They have a brief but tempestuous affair, during which Nestor follows Cesar's advice to be more *macho*, ordering her around. She leaves him and goes back to her home village. Heartbroken, he writes a song about her, which eventually evolves into "Beautiful María of My Soul." Over the rest of his lifetime, Nestor writes forty-four versions of the song.

After moving to New York, Nestor joins Cesar in forming the Mambo Kings, but he is shy and for the most part just follows his outgoing brother. He meets Dolores Fuentes at a bus stop, falls in love with her, marries her and has two children with her, but still he cannot help thinking about María. One afternoon he buys a book called *Forward America!* at a newsstand and for the rest of his life he reads and rereads it, marking passages in the margins. It is an inspirational book, meant to tell readers how to lead happy, fulfilled lives. Even when the Mambo Kings make a fortune on the recording of the song they played on the *I Love Lucy* show, Nestor keeps his job at the meat packing factory.

Nestor dies in 1957, while driving Cesar's car back from a coming-out party in New Jersey, with Cesar and his date in the back seat. His funeral is attended by some of the most important Mambo musicians, and others send floral bouquets. Thoughts of Nestor haunt Cesar throughout his life.

Ana María Fuentes

Ana María is Delores' sister, and remains a part of Cesar Castillo's life throughout the decades.

Delores Fuentes

See Delores Castillo

Julián García

Julián is the leader of the band in Santiago de Cuba. He gives Cesar his first break in music when he is just nineteen. In one of Cesar's drunken memories, he thinks that he may have met Desi Arnaz when he came to audition for Julián's band, that Arnaz was the singer who was leaving on the day that he came to audition, but he soon questions whether that was the way it happened at all.

Luisa García

Luisa is the niece of Julián García, the orchestra leader whom Cesar works with in Cuba. Cesar marries her in 1943, and they have a daughter, Mariela. When one of Cesar's lovers confronts Luisa, she divorces him and eventually remarries.

Dr. Victor López

Dr. López is the person who puts Cesar in the hospital for a few weeks, and tells him he will be dead soon if he does not quit drinking.

Bernardito Mandelbaum

A lifelong friend of Cesar, Bernardito is neither a musician nor a Cuban, but an artist who is enraptured with Cuban culture. He designs the covers for several of the Mambo Kings albums. He has an extensive collection of Latin music. When he meets a woman, Fifi, at a Mambo Kings party, he falls in love with her. He moves in with her, but does not marry her for twenty-five years, because his parents disapprove.

Miguel Montoya

The pianist for the Mambo Kings and their musical arranger, Miguel Montoya is described as "elegant," and as a sharp dresser. In later life, Montoya makes a fortune by moving to Hollywood and playing with the commercial orchestra "Ten Thousand Strings," and also writing scores for cheap Mexican horror films.

Fernando Pérez

Fernando is an old friend of Cesar's, a gangster. When Cesar is poor, Fernando offers to back him financially in opening a bar. The place that they open is the *Club Havana*. It is successful, but it loses money because of Cesar's freewheeling practices, so Fernando buys him out. Under the control of Fernando's organized crime associates, the place gains a reputation for selling drugs in the neighborhood, until, after Fernando's death, it closes down.

Frankie Pérez

Frankie is from the New York neighborhood where Cesar and Nestor live. They meet him when he is dancing at a hall where the Mambo Kings are playing early in their career. He remains a friend of Cesar's throughout his life, after the band has broken up.

María Rivera

María is the subject of Nestor's song "Beautiful María of My Soul." When he meets her, she is a dancer in the chorus line at the Havana Hilton. He first sees her when, walking down the street, he finds a man abusing her and fights with the man. Nestor and María have a torrid love affair, but after a while Nestor takes his brother's advice and starts treating her badly, being verbally and physically rough. Soon after, she disappears from town. He goes to the village where she grew up and finds that she has married the man whom she was fighting with when they met. Through the years, Nestor continues to write María letters, proclaiming his love.

Lydia Santos

When Cesar is sixty-two, he begins an affair with Lydia Santos, who is thirty-five. She has two children, works at a menial job, and lives in a bad neighborhood. Cesar spends money on her and her children, but he finds it difficult to believe that she is actually interested in him romantically. He becomes jealous, and the medication that he takes as his health fails him makes him say rude things to her. One night Lydia does not show up for a date, explaining that she spent the night in the emergency room because her son was ill; Cesar refuses to believe her, and, with his feelings hurt, he quits seeing her.

Mrs. Shannon

Mrs. Shannon is the landlady of the building that Cesar lives in from 1949 to 1980. At first, she dislikes him, but after his appearance on the *I Love Lucy* show she becomes susceptible to his flirting, and gives him a job as the building's supervisor.

Vanna Vane

The Castillo brothers meet Vanna Vane when she is a cigarette girl at the Palm Nightclub. Cesar has an affair with her, and he has her photographed for the cover of one of the group's records. Through the years, he continues to date Vanna, and throughout his night in the Hotel Splendour he thinks of her, wondering if they ever had sex in that same hotel room. Vanna becomes pregnant by him, and he takes her to get an abortion. Eventually, she marries a man named Friedman who works for the post office, living with him and her two sons in Co-op City in the Bronx, wondering whatever happened to Cesar.

Themes

Ideal Love

In *The Mambo Kings Play Songs of Love*, Nestor Castillo is characterized by his devotion to the memory of María, with whom he had a love affair during his early twenties. Their affair was over after only a few months, and Hijuelos gives readers several reasons to doubt that the love between Nestor and María was really as deep as he remembers it to be. For one thing, the book refers to several uncomfortable moments between them, probably because she is trying to conceal her relationship with the man she eventually marries. Nestor does not really know much about her. Also,

he does not seem to understand his own motive for being attracted to her. The novel leads into their first meeting with a description of Nestor wandering among the prostitutes along the waterfront and thinking how he could only sleep well, comfortably, in the arms of his mother, who was also named María. He is not aware of the simple psychological fact that he might be projecting onto María the dancer a purity that he associates with his mother, missing the fact that he does not really understand her at all.

The clearest indicator that Nestor's love for María is idealized and not actual can be seen in the way that he cannot relate his romance to real life. As a composer, he is limited to writing just one song, going back to rewrite it over and over, obsessed. He stays up nights rewriting his song about María and writing letters to her, neglecting the relationship that he should have with his wife and two children. He lives in a fantasy, consistently reliving a love that never was as solid and true as he has made it to be in his mind.

Machismo

Both of the Castillo brothers struggle to project a sense of machismo, which is especially important to men in Spanish-speaking countries such as Cuba. Machismo is a personality that emphasizes traits that are generally associated with masculinity, such as physical strength, aggression, and sexual virility. The term often has a negative connotation, because macho behavior often entails dominating and abusing women. It is also negative because it is often achieved through presenting a false front or adapting a macho pose, rather than being an honest characteristic that occurs naturally as part of one's true personality.

The insincerity often associated with machismo is clearly shown in the way that Nestor treats, and loses, María. On their first night together, Nestor tells her "everything about his short life, his childhood illnesses, his sense of unworthiness, his fears that he could never be a real macho in the kingdom of machos." Later, his uncertainty about her grows and Cesar advises him to be more macho with her: "A little abuse never hurt a romance. Women like to know who's the boss." Soon after, Nestor adapts a macho approach, María leaves him, going back to her old abusive fiancé.

Cesar's long life is spent pursuing machismo. Much of the novel bounces from one description to the next of his sexual conquests or graphic thoughts about women as conquests. Cesar's constant focus on affirming his machismo through sexual activity becomes increasingly tragic as he grows older and realizes that women do not see him as a lover anymore. When he falls in love, at age 60, with a woman in her thirties, his need to be macho defeats him: Lydia appears to be happy with Cesar, but he is insecure, focusing on any sign that she lacks respect for him and breaking up with her over a minor issue because his masculine pride is offended.

Success and Failure

The two sections of this novel narrated by Cesar's nephew Eugenio show readers the different fates that can befall musicians. The first, at the beginning of the book, shows the once-great Cesar Castillo as a failure, a washed-up has-been. Readers can tell that he once held some degree of fame because a neighbor sees him on the television (on a show taped so long ago that she has not entirely certain that it is him) and because the stacks of records that he knocks to the floor are ones that Cesar recorded. Still, the Cesar Castillo presented in this section, stumbling drunkenly around his apartment in the middle of the afternoon, shows no sign that he might once have been a television or recording star. Because this section is in Eugenio's eyes, Cesar looks like more of a failure than he does in the sections that present his life from his point of view.

At the end of the book, Eugenio meets Desi Arnaz, who shows all of the signs of commercial success. He has a large, expensive home, with horses and several gardens that overlook the Pacific Ocean. He is still involved in business deals, which is indicated by the fact that he excuses himself to "take care of some telephone calls."

Success and failure intersect in a shared wistfulness about the past. Cesar, drunk in a hotel room, listens to his old songs and reminisces about the people he has known, while Arnaz wanders around his huge estate singing phrases from his old songs, thinking briefly about the fact that his life will soon end, but then going on with his business.

In drawing the connection between the two, Hijuelos does nothing to diminish Arnaz's success, but instead he sheds a new light on Cesar's apparent failure. Eugenio feels comfortable in Arnaz's house, recognizing, for the first time in his life, the common denominator between Cesar, Nestor, and Arnaz, connecting Arnaz's graciousness with the modesty of his father and uncle. Once he learns to

Topics for Further Study

- Explore the life and career of one of the musicians mentioned in the book, such as Celia Cruz, Pérez Prado, Tito Rodriguez or Machito, and report on the similarities and differences between that person's experiences and those of the fictitious Cesar Castillo.

- In the 1940s and 1950s, Cuba was a popular resort destination for American vacationers. After doing some research, design a mock travel brochure for Havana in 1948, describing what tourists could expect to see there and what things cost in the actual prices of the time.

- Watch the movie *For Love or Country: The Arturo Sandoval Story*, about the famed jazz trumpeter who left Cuba in 1990. Based on the movie, explain how the political world and the musical world have changed since the Castillo brothers in the novel emigrated in the 1940s.

- A central point in the Castillo brothers' lives is their few minutes on the *I Love Lucy* program. Watch a current sitcom, and write a short story about what you imagine old age will be like for one of the minor actors who is not a regular on the show.

- Contact the Congress person representing your district and ask them to explain the current United States policy toward Cuba.

- Research Latin American dance, then teach your class how to dance the mambo. Use recordings done in the 1950s, or even the soundtrack from the movie *The Mambo Kings* for the music.

see beyond success and failure, he is able to accept their love in a way that he could not before.

Self-Destruction

Both of the Mambo Kings, Cesar and Nestor Castillo, are responsible for the ends of their own unhappy lives. Nestor's death occurs because of an accident that could have happened to anyone, a car sliding on a patch of ice. Still, there is no doubt that he had little value for his life, skulking around in sadness and barely involved in his surroundings. The accident that causes his death is presented as a logical conclusion for Nestor who, at thirty-one, has nothing left to live for anyway, with his days and nights spent writing the same song over and over.

Cesar's self-destruction takes longer, and it is more deliberate. After Nestor's death he turns away from the best things in his life and begins a thirty-year downward spiral. He quits music for several years, drinks constantly, and finds more desperation than pleasure in sex. As the narrative points out, he tries "to keep his brother alive by becoming like him."

Knowing that his doctor has forbidden him to drink liquor, likening it to poison, Cesar gives away his most valuable possessions and spends his last night in the Hotel Splendour drinking himself to death. After thirty years of decline, Cesar, like Nestor, finds himself left with nothing but memories. When he is found dead in the morning, there is a "tranquil smile" on his face, indicating that his death has been a release from a life that he wanted to escape.

Style

Point of View

The Mambo Kings Play Songs of Love is told from two points of view. The first is that of Eugenio, who tells of his experiences in the first person, using "I" and "me." Eugenio is the narrator of the book's opening and closing sections, starting with a childhood memory that he has of his uncle Cesar and ending with a fantasy of the Castillo brothers' hearts being reunited after death.

Most of the book is from Cesar's point of view. The sections that concern him are told in the third person: not using Cesar's voice, but still relating the details of his experience as he would have observed them. From Cesar's point of view, women are described in terms of their sexual attributes, musicians in terms of their talent, and political events in terms of how they affect Cuban farmers. Readers are therefore given a biased view of the world, and can only experience unbiased reality in brief glimpses. An example of this is the way that Cesar's daughter Mariela shows little interest in him, even though he feels that he is going to great

lengths to be a good father. There are also places where his memory of events is questioned, such as when, after describing his first meeting with Desi Arnaz and Lucille Ball, the narrative explains that it may not have happened that way after all.

The point of view of the book is inconsistent, often relaying information to readers that Cesar would not know. At Nestor's funeral, for instance, the narrative gives a long paragraph of Dolores' thoughts, setting it off in parentheses to indicate that it is outside of the normal narrative flow. There are, however, no parentheses around the details given about Nestor's romance with María, details that would have been outside of Cesar's range of experience. Background about characters, such as the story of Dolores' encounter with the man who put on the beauty pageant and Mrs. Shannon's growing attraction to Cesar, are told directly to readers, despite the fact that Cesar would not have been aware of these details.

Structure

This book is divided into five sections. The first and last balance each other: each is short, less than ten pages, and consists of Eugenio Castillo discussing influential musicians, one who has sunk into obscurity and another who revels in fame. Between these two sections, there are two parts that are also balanced against each other. "In the Hotel Splendour, 1980" and "Sometime Later in the Night in the Hotel Splendour" are referred to, like an old vinyl record, as "Side A" and "Side B."

The symmetry of these two sets of pairs is broken, however, with the inclusion of a fifth section, titled "Toward the End, While Listening to the Wistful 'Beautiful María of My Soul.'" This section is conspicuous because it does not have a corresponding section to balance out against, as the other sections do. It follows the narrative thread that runs through "Side A" and "Side B," but, following the "record" symbolism, it could not be "Side C," since records are flat and do not have a third side.

The events that Cesar thinks about in this uneven section cover his physical decline, which leads to his decision to drink himself to death, and the fulfillment of that plan. The fact that it extends beyond the "Side A" and "Side B" structure could mean that Cesar's life has gone beyond his musical identity, that he has transcended the Mambo King personality he once made for himself and risen, or sunk, into the realm of human reality.

Antihero

Cesar Castillo is not the sort of character that most readers would consider a hero. He spends most if his time drinking, thinking about his own sexual prowess, objectifying women and avoiding responsibility. He allows himself to wallow in self-pity rather than taking advantage of the opportunities made available to him. At one point in the novel, he thinks about a woman that he raped one Christmas day, puzzled at her tears because he feels he has done her a favor, taking her virginity at age forty: "It was about time for you," he tells her. He does not remember her name. And he dies at the end of the book without even regretting his crime.

Still, many readers end up feeling sympathy for Cesar. Musicians respect him for his talent, and this novel is steeped in the world of mambo music. Readers adapt the values of this small, specific society over the values that they might hold in the real world. The novel does not necessarily promote Cesar's perspective, which can be seen by the contrasting sections at the beginning and the end, which have Eugenio coping with a hopeless Cesar and a collected Desi Arnaz. In spite of his faults, the book respects Cesar, along with his weakness and self-destructiveness.

Historical Context

Recent Cuban History

After Cuba gained its independence from Spain at the turn of the century, the Cuban government was marred by political instability, incompetence, and corruption. Throughout the 1930s, 1940s and 1950s, the most powerful politician was Fulgencio Batista y Zaldívar. Batista served as elected president from 1940 to 1944, and then, as the 1952 election was underway, led a military coup that seized power, suspending the constitution and declaring himself president. Under his control, rich politicians became increasingly richer, while poverty grew among Cuba's poor. Social services were ignored: disease and illiteracy ran rampant. Resistance to the government, in the form of labor strikes and demonstrations, grew. In 1956, Fidel Castro, a young lawyer who had been exiled to Mexico for participating in a failed revolt after Batista's coup, returned to Cuba, and under his direction, the people's discontent grew into an uprising. With few soldiers supporting him but with military brilliance, Castro was able to stand up against the unmotivated, corrupt Batista army. The

United States became impatient with the Cuban government's neglect of its own people, and in 1958 withdrew its military support. This gave Castro's supporters their chance to press their revolution. On January 1, 1959, the government toppled: Batista left for exile in the Dominican Republic, and Castro, then thirty-one years old, took control.

The Castro government's first order of business was undoing the economic turmoil the country had fallen into. Castro ordered reforms that gave the government control over land and industries that had been privately owned. Political opponents were executed and imprisoned, and the country was declared a one-party socialist state. Relations with the United States went downhill throughout 1960 and 1961, as the Cuban government nationalized major industries such as sugar and oil production, seizing control of the property of American investors. The United States severed diplomatic relations and began concocting plans to overthrow Castro. The most conspicuous of these plans was the Bay of Pigs invasion in April of 1961. Fifteen hundred Cuban exiles, financed by the U.S. Central Intelligence Agency, left Miami for Cuba. They were captured as soon as they arrived, having been given insufficient military or tactical support. Shortly after, Castro declared himself a Marxist-Leninist and announced a formal alliance with the Soviet Union, America's adversary in the Cold War.

Since the early 1960s, relations between the United States and Cuba have been at a standstill. Travel between the two countries is restricted, and a trade embargo continues. Over the decades, different occasions have occurred to nearly break the status quo. In the 1970s, President Jimmy Carter supported a softer stance, loosening the embargo and giving Cubans access to American goods, but the next president, Ronald Reagan, took a hard-line anti-Communist stance which assured continued antagonism. After the collapse of the Soviet Union in the late 1980s, when Hijuelos's novel was published, the Cuban economy plummeted, and political observers expected to see the Castro regime crumble. The economy rebounded in the mid-90s, however. Today, Castro is in his seventies and showing signs of failing health: he has announced that plans have been made for a successor to his nearly-fifty-year reign. But Cuban exiles in America await the opportunity for political unrest that will come once he is gone.

Compare
&
Contrast

- **1950s:** Cuba is a popular vacation resort for American tourists, who enjoy the benefits of the strong U.S. dollar and a foreign government that welcomes U.S. businesses.

  1980s: Cuba is an ally of the Soviet Union, the communist superpower that rivals America. American citizens are not allowed to travel to Cuba or to do business there.

  Today: Despite the collapse of the Soviet Union in 1991, Cuba is still a communist country, and the American travel and trade embargo against Cuba still exists.

- **1950s:** America is undergoing a Mambo craze. Even mainstream orchestras are including works with a Latin flavor into their repertoires.

  1980s: America is undergoing alternative music craze to replace Mambo music, among others. Mambo music and dance are relics of the simpler times and are considered old-fashioned.

  Today: Mambo music is taken seriously by jazz musicians. Some of the old mainstream Latin acts, like Pérez Prado and Xavier Cugot, are ap-

  preciated by young listeners as kitsch or "lounge music."

- **1950s:** Dancing to live music is an ordinary way to spend an evening out.

  1980s: The importance of live music is diminishing. Dance clubs rely more and more on recordings, and only feature live bands on special occasions.

  Today: Disc jockeys become major entertainment celebrities on the basis of how they choose to mix recorded songs together.

- **1950s:** New York City is considered a city of ethnic neighborhoods, each based upon the population of immigrants that settled there.

  1980s: New York City is mostly thought of as an exciting but dangerous place, where crime in the streets runs rampant.

  Today: Although it still has the elements that characterized it in the past, New York City's international reputation is mainly built on the strength of character and cooperation shown in the aftermath of the destruction of the World Trade Center in 2001.

The Mambo

The mambo was developed in Cuban ballrooms in the 1940s, when the traditional rumba was infused with Afro-Cuban rhythms that were becoming popular at that time in American jazz music. The word "mambo" comes from a Bantu instrument that was originally used in religious rituals. In the late 1930s, Cuban composer Orestes Lopez wrote a traditional *danzon*, or dance song, which he called "Mambo": it included elements of the *son*, a folk song style that is native to Oriente province, which the novel identifies as the home of the Castillo brothers and of Desi Arnaz. In Lopez's song, the orchestra leader would call for musicians to start their solos by shouting out, "Mil vices mambo! (A thousand times mambo!)."

The musical style first became popular in the United States through the work of flamboyant band leader Pérez Prado, who billed himself as the Mambo King. Prado, who worked as a piano player and arranger for the famous Orquestra Casino de la Playa, left Cuba in 1947. Settling in Mexico City, he released a string of recordings that made it onto the American charts, including "Mambo No. 5" and "Cherry Pink and Apple Blossom White." With his trademark goatee beard and showy style, Prado was identified with the mambo by audiences in the 1950s, even though music historians tend to downplay his significance in the development of the music itself.

A more lasting musical significance of the Americanization of mambo music is its fusion into

American jazz. In the 1940s, trumpeter-arranger Mario Bauza introduced jazz trumpeter Dizzy Gillespie to Cuban music. Gillespie is one of the most important and influential musicians in jazz history, credited with being one of the driving forces in the creation of bebop. Gillespie's collaboration with Cuban percussionist Chano Pozo in 1947–1948 created a musical style known as Afro-Cuban jazz, or, sometimes, as Cu-bop.

Mambo music achieved the height of its glory in the early- to mid-1950s in New York, particularly at the Palladium Ballroom on Broadway, often referred to as the "Temple of Mambo." Among the mambo dancers who became famous there were Mambo Aces, "Killer Joe" Piro, Paulito and Lilon, Louie Maquina and Cuban Pete. Many of the musicians who worked regularly at the Palladium are mentioned in *The Mambo Kings Play Songs of Love*, including Tito Puente, Tito Rodriguez, and Machito.

In 1954 the mambo's popularity was challenged by a new dance craze, the *chachacha*, created by Cuban violinist Enriqué Jorrin. It was a simpler dance that was easier for non-professional dancers to master. The *cha-cha* was so close in nature to the mambo that Pérez Prado put out an open offer of $5000 to anyone who could demonstrate how the two musical styles differed. In the 1960s, the *chachacha* gave way to the *pachanga* and the *boogaloo*. Eventually, all music coming out of the Latin New York scene has come to fall under the general blanket term of *salsa*.

Critical Overview

The Mambo Kings Play Songs of Love was a popular and critical success as soon as it was first published in 1989. It was heavily promoted by its publisher, Farrar Straus and Giroux, a fact that Nicholas Kanellos made note of in his review for *The American Review*: "a 40,000 copy first hardcover printing, a $50,000 national marketing campaign, 100% national co-op advertising, rights sold in advance to England, France, Finland, Germany, Holland and Italy, extensive exposure at the American Booksellers Association..." Kanellos went on to observe that this extensive promotion "has paid off, with glowing reviews in all the right places, from *Time* and *The New York Times* to *Publishers Weekly* and *Kirkus*; and the first Pulitzer prize for fiction to a Latino. And," he added, "*The Mambo*

Fidel Castro

Kings is worth it. This is the best Hispanic book ever published by a large commercial press."

While the book is generally praised, critics have also found fault with it. Critical difference regarding the book's quality have generally centered around two subjects: Hijuelos's success in rendering the central character, Cesar Castillo, as a rounded and believable human, and the book's loose, repetitive, almost plotless structure. Both views have supporters and detractors. In the *Time* magazine review that Kanellos mentioned, for instance, R. Z. Sheppard noted that Cesar's "flamboyant plumage and mating behaviors seem dated and may not appeal to readers who now find machismo to be a dirty word." But Sheppard went on to dispute that charge: "Hijuelos deflects this prejudice with sensitivity and a charged style that elevates stereotype into character." Cathleen McGuigan made nearly the same point in *Newsweek* when she noted that Cesar "is a classic portrait of machismo," and then explained that the book is so well written that the familiarity of the character type does not diminish it: "Fortunately Hijuelos has a tender touch with his characters, and Cesar is more than a stereotype." The most direct criticism of Hijuelos's characterizations came from novelist Nick Hornby, who reviewed the book in

The Listener. Hornby's review, "Cuban Heels," proposed that *The Mambo Kings Play Songs of Love* is actually about three main characters: "Nestor, Cesar and Cesar's penis." About the last, he wrote, "Its exploits are detailed with alarmingly loving care and though there are hints that Hijuelos has an ironic perspective on all this machismo, they come none too frequently."

Hornby also brought up Hijuelos's rambling, formless method of presenting the story. "Its other major disadvantage is that it is wildly under-edited," he wrote, "at just over 400 pages one is left with the feeling that there is a great short story in here struggling to get undressed." The same criticism came from Sven Birkerts, who, reviewing Hijuelos's follow-up book (*The Fourteen Sisters of Emilio Montez O'Brien*) for *The New Republic*, commented that *The Mambo Kings Sing Songs of Love* had been "overweight by at least 100 pages." Acknowledging the absence of plot, Birkerts opined that "the true glory of the book was its prose, which was energetic, detailed, able to modulate from the silky to the percussive in the space of a line." Margo Jefferson noted the same effect in *The New York Times Book Review*: she praised Hijuelos's prose with the observation that the book "alternates crisp narrative with opulent musings—the language of everyday and the language of longing." Immediately following this praise, though, she wrote, "When Mr. Hijuelos falters, as from time to time he does, it's through an excess of self-consciousness: he strives too hard for an all-encompassing description or grows distant and dutiful in an effort to get period details just right."

Several reviewers compared the novel's twisted, indirect form to the style of music that is its focus. In "Fascinatin' Rhythm," her review in *Newsweek*, McGuigan admitted that "The novel isn't conventionally plotted; it slides back and forth in time and meanders into dreams and fantasies." She found this to be an asset: "Like an album of mambo tunes, some of the sequences begin to sound alike, but the rhythms and colors are hard to resist." Hornby, too, took note of the similarities between the prose style and the Castillo brothers' profession. "Hijuelos seems to be trying to capture at great length the rhythms and resonances of the music in the writing," he pointed out. He, however, found this "improvisational" narrative theory easy to resist: "in practice the effect is more Black Sabbath than Charlie Parker, and phrases and incidents are repeated over and over without any discernible modulation."

Criticism

David Kelly

Kelly is an instructor of creative writing and literature at several colleges in Illinois. In this essay, Kelly explores the idea that The Mambo Kings Play Songs of Love *would have been a more powerful novel if the character of Nestor had been edited out.*

Oscar Hijuelos's novel *The Mambo Kings Play Songs of Love* offers readers a rich, vibrant concoction of characters and details, as hot and lively as the music at the core of the story. The narrative, in fact, may be a little too rich for its own good: readers come away from it knowing little more about the central character, Cesar Castillo, than they do about such arcana as the types of underwear women wore in the 1950s through the 1980s, or the plumbing in old buildings, or the costs of 78 r.p.m. records, or the books that were popular at the middle of the century. With so much information volleyed at the reader, it takes some concentration to see, at the end of the novel, how little Cesar develops as a character. Readers can turn to any page, in the beginning, middle, or end of the novel, and be assured that Cesar likes being drunk and having sex, and can reasonably guess that the possibility of a lengthy description of either is at hand. Cesar's true personality has very little below the surface, a fact that is obscured by the constant, attention-drawing parade of exotic minor characters like René stabbing Elva, Bernardito waiting twenty-five years to marry Fifi, gay Enrique marrying Teresa, Mr. Stein owning books in Hebrew and German and Angie Pé, who only shows up to record a message at Coney Island in 1954, and Leticia's crush on Rico Sánchez. Good novels fill in all of the corners with details, but there is also such a thing as being too detailed, distracting readers from what is really important by making everything seem important.

This book is well in need of a thorough editing job, in order to give some sense of perspective to its hundreds of details. It simply has too much going on. This is, of course, almost impossible to prove, since "too much" is a subjective judgement. Millions of readers have found *The Mambo Kings Play Songs of Love* to be just fine the way it is. To them, there is no reason for the novel to be anything more than a simple story of two brothers, one introverted and one extroverted, one romantic and the other physical: *un macho grande* and *un infeliz*, in Hijuelos's words. The book could be taken at face value and accepted this way, but there really is no reason to not think about its weaknesses.

Although the two Castillo brothers, Cesar and Nestor, are talked about throughout the course of the novel, neither is developed as a complete, convincing character. They just ride through the Cuban-American culture of the 1940s through the 1970s, each holding on to his own solitary personality traits. When Nestor dies he is the same insecure mother's boy that he has been all along, and Cesar dies listing the women, family and friends who have passed by him without his having formed an attachment to any of them. There is no progress, no result, for all of the minutiae that the narrative heaps on.

In streamlining Cesar's story, there are thousands of details that could be left out. Many that are less closely related to plot or character can be justified as necessary for establishing the world that Cesar lives in; this makes them, in a roundabout way, important for establishing his character. Many other stories, though, do not establish their importance, and instead focus on things and people that Cesar merely encountered along the way in his sixty-two year life. Having been encountered is not enough to earn them a place in his story; the fact that these events happened, even in a fictitious sense, does not in itself make them worth snaring part of the reader's attention. After accepting that some of the details presented in *The Mambo Kings Play Songs of Love* must go—a fact that many critics take for granted, but one that Hijuelos, his publisher nor many of his readers seem to find essential—it becomes necessary to sort through all of the colorful information and decide which tell Cesar's story best. For instance, easily half of the sex scenes, and quite a few of the club dates that the Mambo Kings attend, draw their pay, then leave, could have been removed from this book without in any way altering anyone's sense of who Cesar is. The problem with editing would be deciding which scenes are truly telling of who he is, and which are just routine.

In trying to determine which parts of this story could be done without, one large, surprising element draws attention to itself: there would really be very little loss to the story if the character of Nestor Castillo had just been left out. This might at first seem to require a huge structural overhaul of the novel, which advertisers and critics alike, not to mention the screenwriters who adapted the novel to a movie, have defined as the story of two brothers whose combined life experiences make up the

" Nestor has their mother's traits, Cesar their father's: why are there even two main characters in this novel, when all of their experience could be encompassed by one character?"

author's point. Actually, though, the brothers' significance in the book is in no way equal: Nestor is such a pale shadow that he has little use in the story of Cesar.

Cesar and Nestor are written as distinctly different characters, but their differences are not clear enough to justify more than one character. Nestor has just two or three salient characteristics. For one, he is fixated on his mother, who nursed him back to health when he was young. The second is the most notable character trait, but it might just be a continuation of the first: his infatuation with María. He loses sleep thinking about María, tries unsuccessfully to politely pay some attention to his wife and children, but ends up writing new versions of "Beautiful María of my Soul" in the middle of sleepless nights. He signs letters to his mother "your *hijito*" (baby boy). At one point, Nestor himself notices that his mother and María are linked by having the same name, but he never does become aware that his fixation on a woman whom he knew for just a few months goes beyond sweeping romance to a routine Oedipal attachment. As Hijuelos notes when talking about Nestor's insomnia, "Cubans then (and Cubans now) didn't know about psychological problems."

Nestor's third trait is his vague desire to assimilate. He totes around the book *Forward America!* by a certain D. D. Vanderbuilt, underlining passages about aggression and self-assurance. It never has much effect, though. After being unfaithful to his wife, he turns to the book's philosophy that "the confident, self-assured man looks to the future and never backward to the past," but, except for momentary lapses, the book shows no sign of easing his longing for the past.

After Nestor's death, Cesar inherits *Forward America!*, as well as his brother's predilection for

What Do I Read Next?

- Oscar Hijuelos's first novel, *Our House in the Last World* (1982), concerns a New Yorker who is haunted by the stories his parents tell of Oriente province in Cuba, where they emigrated from before his birth. A re-issue of this novel with a new afterward by Hijuelos was published in 2002 by Persea Press.

- In Hijuelos's novel *A Simple Habana Melody: From When the World Was Good* (2002), Cuban music and nostalgia again are major themes: a Cuban composer, travelling in Europe in the 1940s, ends up mistakenly interred in the concentration camp at Buchenwald.

- Jamaica-born poet Claude McKay, who was one of the leading figures of the Harlem Renaissance in the 1920s, captured the spirit of exile that is felt in this book in his poem "The Tropics in New York." That poem is now available in *Claude McKay: Selected Poems* (1999).

- In 1996, American musician Ry Cooder went to Cuba and made a documentary about a group of traditional Cuban musicians, some of whom have been playing since the 1950s. *The Buena Vista Social Club*, directed by Wim Wenders, had an impressive theatrical run for a documentary, and its soundtrack album was a best-seller. *Buena Vista Social Club: The Companion Book to the Film*, published by te Neures Pub-

lishing Company in May of 2000, tells the story of how these musical talents, who were neglected for decades, came to worldwide attention.

- Critics have pointed out the debt that Hijuelos's flowing, descriptive style owes to Gabriel García Márquez's 1969 novel *One Hundred Years Of Solitude*. García Márquez's book, which described a century in the history of a fictional South American town, is considered one of the most important and influential books in all of Latin American literature. The most recent edition, by Harper Perennial, was published in 1998.

- Like *The Mambo Kings Play Songs of Love*, Christina Garcia's novel *Dreaming in Cuban* (1993) concerns a family that emigrated from Cuba to New York, only to find their roots cut off by the Communist revolution that has made it difficult to go back.

- Popular Cuban-American author Beatriz Rivera's novel *Playing with Light* (2000) concerns a modern-day reading group of Cubans living in Miami and discussing a novel set in Havana in the 1870s, and a group of Cubans in the 1870s discussing a futuristic novel about Havana in the late 1990s. It was published by Arte Publico Press in 2000.

---

turning to it in his spare time for advice. In his hands, it has no more power than it does in Nestor's. Hijuelos mentions the book occasionally, but not with any consistency. As a symbol of Cesar's taking on his dead brother's traits, this is a particularly weak one: since readers do not see the book affecting Nestor's personality, having Cesar carry it around does not show any hint of his becoming like Nestor, it just shows that he has a sentimental attachment to one of Nestor's belongings. If this book is supposed to represent something more sweeping, such as the immigrant's struggle to suppress his tradition and adapt an American

way of looking at things, then it could just as easily have been written as Cesar's book to begin with. The idea of Nestor looking to the past and not the future is so dwarfed by his melancholy that *Forward America!*'s significance is hardly noticeable. In Cesar's hands, the book could at least represent a struggle to find his place in the world.

Cesar is, of course, crudely drawn as a macho figure, one who derives his self-esteem from sex. While Nestor's memories of childhood involve his mother comforting him, Cesar's memories focus on beatings from his father. The story draws so many

---

distinctions between the two Castillo brothers that it seems almost eerie that each should remember only one parent. Since these are two different views of two different parents, it would make sense for these memories to exist in just one person, dividing the masculine and feminine aspects of the Castillo farm in Oriente so neatly and simplistically.

Nestor's main function in the book is to represent the hopeless romantic, who is so in love with a beautiful woman whom he cannot have that he allows himself to waste away. In theory, this is the reverse image of Cesar's boisterous, life-affirming carnality. In practice, however, Hijuelo does not show enough real difference between the two brothers to make readers feel the differences of their two personality types. When Nestor meets María, he defends her from a bully, a thing that one could easily imagine Cesar doing. When they begin their sexual relationship, though, any distinction between the two brothers becomes seriously blurred: Nestor and María's scenes together are indistinguishable from the book's many sex scenes involving Cesar. They are, in fact, indistinguishable from Nestor's lovemaking with Dolores.

This may well be the book's point—that Nestor turns sensual like Cesar when he meets the woman he loves and that Cesar turns mournful like Nestor after the death of his brother. The book puts them in situations meant to show they are not that different from one another. The problem is that the book never establishes their differences well enough to make their sameness worth noting. Nestor has their mother's traits, Cesar their father's: why are there even two main characters in this novel, when all of their experience could be encompassed by one character? Without Nestor in the book, readers would be focused on Cesar and his experiences, and the threshold for which descriptions and peripheral characters are relevant to his life would be lower. Without the distracting plot line of the two brothers switching personalities, the significance of all of Hijuelos's fine detail would be easier to grasp.

Of course, this is all speculation. The book is finished, and has proven itself extremely popular with audiences and critics just as it is. It is fine to imagine what the book would be like with a major change like the removal of one of the two main characters, all the while bearing in mind that this is just a hypothetical exercise in literary criticism. There is no reason to pretend that there ever would be a version of the book like the one described here, with the character of Cesar Castillo embodying all of the traits and experiences given to himself and

his brother in the novel. Besides, if such a book did exist, some critic somewhere would immediately comment on how much better it would have been if the Mambo King's passive and aggressive traits had been divided into two different main characters, perhaps brothers.

Source: David Kelly, Critical Essay on *The Mambo Kings Play Songs of Love*, in *Novels for Students*, The Gale Group, 2003.

Gustavo Perez Firmat

In the following essay, Perez Firmat examines Mambo Kings *within the context of the recent wave of Cuban culture in the United States, identifying how the novel both embraces and drifts from Hispanic influences.*

In the summer of 1990, the cover story of the June 25 issue of *People* magazine was devoted to Gloria Estefan, who, as you know, is the most important moving part of the Miami Sound Machine. At the time Estefan was staging what the magazine termed an "amazing recovery" from a serious traffic accident that had left her partially paralyzed; Estefan herself was upbeat about her prospects, and the point of the story was to reassure all of the rhythm nation that little Gloria would conga again.

I begin with this anecdote for two reasons: first, because it gives fair indication of the prominent role that Cuban Americans play in the increasing and inexorable latinization of this country— by now, few Americans will deny that, for better or for worse, the rhythm is going to get them. My other reason for bringing up the *People* story has to do with the photograph on the cover, which showed Gloria holding two puppies whose names happened to be Lucy and Ricky. Like one of the Miami Sound Machine's last records, the photograph cuts both ways: it suggests not only the prominence but also the pedigree of Latino popular culture. After all, if Gloria Estefan is one of the most popular Hispanic figures in this country today, Ricky Ricardo is certainly her strong precursor. Surprising as it may seem, Desi Arnaz's TV character has been the single most visible Hispanic presence in the United States over the last forty years. Indeed, several generations of Americans have acquired many of their notions of how Hispanics behave, talk, treat or mistreat their wives, by watching Ricky love Lucy. And just last semester I had a Cuban-American student who claimed that he had learned how to be a Cuban male by watching *I Love Lucy* reruns in his home in Hialeah.

> In subject matter, intention, and design, *Mambo Kings* places itself in the line of descent of some central works in the canon of contemporary Latin American fiction. At the same time, however, the novel's translational drift distances it from its Hispanic pedigree."

But the connection between Estefan and Ricky goes further than this. The Miami Sound Machine's first crossover hit was "Conga"—the song that contained the memorable refrain, "come on, shake your body, baby, do the conga, / I know you can't control yourself any longer"; well, the person who led the first conga ever danced on North American soil was none other than Desi Arnaz, who performed this singular feat in a Miami Beach nightclub in 1937. Alluding to this historic (and quite possibly, hysteric) event, Walter Winchell later said, in a wonderful phrase, that a conga line should be called instead "a Desi-chain." It is well to remember, then, that a few years ago when Gloria Estefan entered the Guinness Book of World Records for having led the longest conga line ever (119,984 people), she was only following in Desi's footsteps, only adding another kinky link to the Desi-chain.

I can summarize the significance of this photograph by saying that it illustrates in a particularly clear manner the two forces that shape ethnic culture, which I will call *traditional* and *translational*. As a work of tradition, the photograph points to the genealogy of Cuban-American culture; it reminds us that Gloria Estefan is only the latest in a fairly long line of Cuban-American artists to have come, seen, and conga'd in the United States. As a work of translation, it reminds us of the sorts of adjustments that have to occur for us to be able to rhyme "conga" and "longer." In this the photograph is typical, for ethnic culture is constantly trying to ne-gotiate between the contradictory imperatives of tradition and translation.

"Tradition," a term that derives from the same root as the Spanish *traer*, to bring, designates convergence and continuity, a gathering together of elements according to underlying affinities or shared concerns. By contrast, translation is not a homing device but a distancing mechanism. In its topographical meaning, translation is displacement, in Spanish, *traslación*. This notion has been codified in the truism that to translate is to traduce (*traduttore, traditore*); inherent in the concept of translation is the sense that to move is to transmute, that any linguistic or cultural displacement necessarily entails some mutilation of the original. In fact, in classical rhetoric *traductio*—which is, of course, the Spanish word for translation—was the term to refer to the repetition of a word with a changed meaning. Translation/*traslación*, traduction/*traducción*—the mere translation of these terms is a powerful reminder of the intricacies of the concept.

What I should like to do here is explore these notions a bit further by discussing *The Mambo Kings Play Songs of Love*, a recent novel by Oscar Hijuelos that has been termed "the best Hispanic book ever published by a commercial press." Although only a couple of years old, *Mambo Kings* is already becoming something of a contemporary classic. Not only is Hijuelos the first Cuban-American writer to receive the Pulitzer prize for fiction; he is the only one of a tiny group of *Latino* writers to be published successfully by a major North American publisher. Just to mention one contrasting example: within a few months of the publication of *Mambo Kings*, William Morrow brought out another novel by a Cuban-American writer, Virgil Suárez's *Latin Jazz*. Yet Suárez's novel elicited only moderate interest and quickly sank from sight. One major difference between the two novels is that, unlike Suárez, Hijuelos writes from what may be termed a "translational" perspective. Like *Latin Jazz*, *Mambo Kings* divides its attention between Cuba and the United States, as it tells the story of a Cuban family that migrates to this country. Unlike *Latin Jazz*, however, *Mambo Kings* does not pledge allegiance to its Cuban roots, for it is very much a novel written *away* from Spanish and *toward* English; this drift is already visible in the title, which also moves from Spanish to English, from "mambo" to "songs of love." One reason for Hijuelos's success may well be the savvy—and even the *sabor*—with which he translates tradition. In subject matter, intention, and design, *Mambo Kings* places itself in the line of descent of some central works in the canon of contemporary Latin American fiction. At the same time, however, the novel's translational drift distances it from its Hispanic pedigree. Although *Mambo Kings* invites a general reading as a product of Hispanic culture and specifically as part of its literary tradition, it makes such a reading virtually impossible. In rhetorical terms *Mambo Kings* may be regarded as a sustained traduction, that is, a transfigured repetition of certain elements in Spanish American literature and culture.

The novel follows the lives of two Cuban brothers, César and Nestor Castillo, who emigrate to New York in the late forties and form an orchestra called the Mambo Kings, achieving ephemeral fame one night in 1955 when they make an appearance on the *I Love Lucy* show as Ricky's Cuban cousins. In talent as well as temperament, Nestor and César are worlds apart. César, the leader of the band, is a consummate ladies' man with slicked-back hair, a mellifluous voice, and an irrepressible libido. He remarks that he had only three interests in life: rum, rump, and rumba. His brother Nestor is moody and melancholy; his main claim to fame is having written the Mambo King's greatest hit, "Bellísima María de Mi Alma," "Beautiful María of My Soul," a sad ballad about the girl who broke his heart in Cuba. For years Nestor works tirelessly on this tune, coming up with twenty-two different versions of the lyric; only his death in a car accident puts an end to his scriptural obsession. The story of the Castillo brothers is told in flashbacks by the agonizing César, who by 1980 has ended up broke and broken in a New York tenement and who spends his last hours replaying records of *recuerdos*.

The novel's debt to Hispanic literary tradition is evident in two principal ways. Given the episodic plot and the explicitness with which César's sexual exploits are recounted, one cannot read *Mambo Kings* without thinking of the genre of the picaresque, a subgenre that in Cuba includes such texts as Carlos Loveira's *Juan Criollo* (1927) and Guillermo Cabrera Infante's *La Habana para un infante difunto* (1979). Like the protagonist of Loveira's novel, César is a Don Juan *Criollo*, a creole translation of the Spanish literary type. In the classical picaresque, the protagonist is driven by hunger and spends a large part of his life in the service of successive masters. In the erotic picaresque, the moving force is a different kind of appetite, and instead of going from master to master the protagonist goes from mistress to mistress—not *de amo en amo* but rather *de amorío en amorío*.

This is perhaps the aspect of the novel that has elicited the strongest response from its readers, for the narration's attention to the nature of things erotic verges on the pornographic. This is not to say, however, that the text unequivocally endorses its protagonist's phallocentrism, for César's recollections are filtered through his nephew Eugenio, who puts distance between the reader and César's view of himself. Eugenio's mediating presence helps to turn the novel into something other than a celebration of the Castillos' not-so-private members. As César's closest relative and the author of the book's fictional prologue and epilogue, Eugenio occupies a position halfway between the narrating "I" and the narrated "he." In fact, as I will argue a bit later, Eugenio is best seen as César's translator, which means that their two voices are formally separate but often hard to tell apart. In this respect *Mambo Kings* is what one might call a "hetero-autobiography"—a text whose narrator and protagonist are in some ways distinct, in other ways indistinguishable.

Even though César's recollections are given in the third person, Eugenio's presence at the beginning and end makes him the medium for the interior story—so much so that some of his sentences are repeated verbatim in the interior text; thus, for example, his description of the Castillos' cameo on *I Love Lucy* matches word for word the description that the supposedly impersonal narrator had provided earlier. It's not entirely clear what one should make of this duplication, which is inexplicable unless one posits that the *entire* account is Eugenio's invention—an intriguing possibility that the text insinuates but does not confirm. Without going this far, however, one can at least venture that Eugenio "underwrites" César's memoirs. I use this verb in both of its meanings: to write beneath something and to guarantee. Even if Eugenio is not responsible for the specific verbal shape of César's recollections, he is at least generally responsible for the memoirs as a whole. As the novel begins, Eugenio is watching a rerun of *I Love Lucy*. After the episode is over he remarks, "the miracle had passed, the resurrection of a man." Since the "resurrection of a man" is precisely the novel's own miracle, *Mambo Kings* can be regarded as a type of rerun whose origin is Eugenio. As his name already suggests, Eugenio is the source, the progenitor of the account.

The other token of tradition in the book is music, for Hijuelos's novel also connects with a spate of recent works of Spanish American fiction that derive inspiration from popular music. I am thinking generally of books like Sarduy's *De donde son los cantantes* (1967), Lisandro Otero's *Bolero* (1986), and even Manuel Puig's *El beso de la mujer araña* (1976), with which Hijuelos's novel shares also the practice of providing explanatory footnotes. More concretely I am thinking of two specific novels: Luis Rafael Sánchez's *La guaracha del Macho Camacho* (1980) and Guillermo Cabrera Infante's *Tres tristes tigres* (1965). Like *La guaracha del Macho Camacho*, which centers on a tune by the same name, *Mambo Kings* revolves around one song, "Beautiful María of My Soul," whose lyric is finally transcribed in the last chapter; as in Sánchez's novel, Hijuelos's text establishes a counterpoint between music and text, or *música y letra*. Cabrera Infante's novel, which also gives high visibility to forms of popular music, includes a section entitled "Ella cantaba boleros" (She sang boleros), a phrase that Hijuelos seems to be transposing in his title, since the "songs of love" in the title is a translation of the Spanish *boleros*.

With its juxtaposition of mambo and bolero, Hijuelos's title alerts the reader to the importance of these two musical genres in the novel. The mambo was a mixture of Afro-Cuban rhythms and North American big-band instrumentation popularized by Dámaso Pérez Prado, whose nickname was in fact "el rey del mambo." Championed also by such orchestras as Tito Rodriguez and the Mambo Devils, Tito Puente and the Picadilly Boys, and Eddie Carbia y los mamboleros, the mambo enjoyed a remarkable popularity during the early and mid-fifties, giving rise to such mamboid compositions as "Papa Loves Mambo," with which Perry Como had a number-one hit in 1954; Vaughn Monroe's "They Were Doing the Mambo (But I Just Sat Around)"; Mickey Katz's "My Yiddishe Mambo" (about a woman who's "baking her challes for Noro Morales"); Rosemary Clooney's "Italian Mambo" (sample lyric: "you calbrazi do the mambo like a-crazy"); and Jimmy Boyd's "I Saw Mommy Doing the Mambo (With You Know Who)." This last song is a yuletide ditty about a little boy who catches his mother mamboing with Santa on Christmas eve (and it wasn't the only yuletide mambo—there was also a "Santa Claus Mambo," a "Jingle Bells Mambo," and a "Rudolph the Red-Nosed Mambo").

By the latter part of 1954, the whole country had fallen under the Afro-Cuban spell of the mambo. That fall, Tico Records organized "Mambo U.S.A.," a fifty-six-city tour that took the mambo to America's heartland and which Hijuelos's recounts; the troupe of forty mambists included Ma-

chito, Joe Loco, Facundo Rivero, and many others (as well as César and Nestor Castillo, of course). In December stores were full of mambo gifts: mambo dolls, mambo nighties, and mambo "kits" (a record, maracas, and a plastic sheet with mambo steps to put on the floor.) And that same month Paramount released *Mambo*, with Silvana Mangano in the role of a dancer who has to choose between marriage and mambo. As a headline in the December 1954 issue of *Life* put it, with more than a tinge of racism, "Uncle Sambo, Mad for Mambo."

Pérez Prado himself was enormously successful. He appeared on American television and was booked in the best nightclubs. When he opened at the ritzy Starlight Roof of the Waldorf Astoria in July of 1954, his was only the second Latin orchestra ever to play that venue (the other was Xavier Cugat's). A year later his band was picked as the most popular orchestra in this country; that same year one of his songs, "Cherry Pink and Apple Blossom White," stayed on the Billboard charts for twenty-six weeks; surprisingly, only one other song in the history of U.S. popular music has enjoyed a longer run on the charts—Elvis Presley's "Don't Be Cruel," which became a hit the following year. "Cherry Pink" also became the theme for a highly successful RKO movie, *Underwater!* (1955), in which Jane Russell, accompanied by Pérez Prado, dances a modest mambo—in a bathing suit.

Most of Pérez Prado's mambos are instrumental compositions characterized by Afro-Cuban percussion and dissonant sax and trumpet riffs. (Pérez Prado's favorite composer was Stravinsky.) The laconism of Pérez Prado's mambo was proverbial; typical in this respect is the lyric of the first famous mambo, the *ur*mambo as it were, whose title is "Qué rico el mambo," and which ran in its entirety: "mambo, qué rico el mambo, mambo, mambo, qué rico é é é é." Even the apopé of the "es" to "é" betrays Pérez Prado's penchant for verbal minimalism. It is not accidental, thus, that another of his hits was entitled "Ni hablar." In Pérez Prado's hands, the mambo was a medium for sound, not sense. Indeed his signature became the guttural grunts with which he punctuated the breaks in the music and which the jazz historian Marshall Stearns has compared to the cries of an "excited muledriver." I mention this because the mambo's lovely inarticulateness makes it an odd choice as a model for literary composition. To the extent that *Mambo Kings* derives inspiration from the mambo, it tends toward a kind of expressiveness whose medium is *not* language. Most literary transpositions of popular songs focus on their lyrics—thus it is, for example, with

La guaracha del Macho Camacho. But with the mambo, literary transposition is difficult because of the form's instrumental nature.

It is not surprising, for this reason, that what the mambo kings play are not mambos but "songs of love," for in the novel the bolero fills the void left by the mambo. Unlike the mambo, most boleros are sad, even whining ballads whose distinctiveness has less to do with the music than with the words. In the bolero, rhythm and melody take a back seat to verbal elaboration, as is suggested by Nestor's twenty-two versions of the lyrics to "Beautiful Maria of My Soul." The narrator describes Nestor's bolero as "a song about love so far away it hurts, a song about lost pleasures, a song about youth, a song about love so elusive a man can never know where he stands; a song about wanting a woman so much death does not frighten you, a song about wanting a woman even after she has abandoned you." The repetitive intensity of this description, which echoes Nestor's own obsessive rewriting, gives some idea of the bolero's involvement with language. In the novel, the bolero modulates the narrator's voice, providing him with structures of feeling and forms of expression. This identification is evident in the fact that the title of the book is also the title of one of the mambo king's LPs—the scriptive record merges with the musical recording.

Not only does the bolero's wordiness contrast with the mambo's laconism; the two genres also serve as vehicles for discordant emotions. If the central preoccupation of the bolero is loss, the central impulse of the mambo is conquest. Both as music and as dance, the mambo is aggressive, uninhibited, seductive: wham, bam, thank you, mambo. It is no accident that one of the central numbers in the movie *Dirty Dancing* was a mambo ("Johnny's Mambo"). By contrast, in a bolero the speaker is typically passive and mournful. Like Nestor's "Beautiful María of My Soul," the bolero is a medium for bemoaning unhappiness in love, for questioning the injustice of fate. For this reason, the novel as a whole becomes a musical agon between mambo and bolero, lust and loss, conquest and relinquishment. And the musical question the novels asks is ¡la vida es mambo? ¡o la vida es bolero? Is life a chronicle of conquest—or is life a dirge?

This question is answered, of course, in the lives of the two brothers. César, with his "king-cock strut", is the mambo king; Nestor is the spirit of the *letra* of the bolero. As the narrator puts it

1992 film depiction of Mambo Kings *with Antonio Banderas as Nestor Castillo and Armand Assante as Cesar Castillo*

succinctly, "César was *un macho grande;* Nestor *un infeliz*". The irony is that, in the end, the great macho turns out to be no less of an *infeliz* than his brother. Indeed, the plot narrates how, after Nestor's death, César gradually takes on his brother's temperament; early in the novel Nestor is described as "the man plagued with memory, the way his brother César Castillo would be twenty-five years later." The gradual merging of the two brothers culminates with César's last act, which is to transcribe the lyrics of his brother's composition, "Beautiful María of My Soul." When he writes down the lyrics as if they were his own, César becomes Nestor, remembrance becomes impersonation. César merges with his brother, becoming another man "plagued by memory."

César's final impersonation summarizes the drift of the book. Like the title itself, the novel moves from mambo to bolero, from conquest to loss. César lives in frenetic mambo time only to discover that life actually follows the languid measures of the bolero. The account of his many conquests is modalized by the reader's awareness that these chronicles of conquest are actually a derelict's last words. If Nestor composes his bolero in order to get María back, César reminisces in order to recapture his life as a *macho grande;* and the narration explicitly plays on the punning relationship between "member" and "remember"—at one point César "remembered a whore struggling with a thick rubber on his member." For César, remembering is a way of re-membering himself, a way of sleeping with the past. And like the bolero composed by Nestor, the novel itself is very much "a song about lost pleasures, a song about youth." Not one to avoid extremes, the narrator carries the mourning into the most unlikely places. Loss is so ubiquitous that even penises weep: "By evening they were sitting out on a pier by the sea necking, the head of his penis weeping semen tears."

My discussion thus far is intended to give some idea of the ways in which *Mambo Kings* incorporates Hispanic literary and musical culture. Having said this much, I should now like to reflect briefly on how the novel distances itself from this same culture. That is to say, I should like to reflect on the text's translational impulse, which is evident, first of all, in the ambivalence that Hijuelos's novel demonstrates toward the Spanish language. In one sense, Spanish is everywhere in the text: in the place and character names, in the characters' hispanicized diction, and in the constant references to Cuban music. In another sense, however, Spanish is nowhere, for Hijuelos has of course rendered in English all of the characters' thoughts and words. Indeed, since César's memories make up most of the novel, and since these memories were almost certainly framed in Spanish, the text we read presupposes an invisible act of translation, somewhat in the manner of *Don Quixote.* The source of this translation must of course be Eugenio, who is both narrator and translator; indeed, Eugenio's genius, his *ingenio*, is to filter César's recollections in such a way that the reader tends to overlook Eugenio's responsibility for the text's language.

Significantly, the only sustained Spanish passage in the book is the lyric of "Beautiful María of My Soul," which appears at the very end. One cannot overlook the overdetermination of its appearance: Nestor's song of love, the book's preeminent statement on loss, is transcribed in a language that itself has been lost. The Spanish lyric is a testament to what is lost in translation. And Nestor's beautiful María may then be the emblem for the maternal language that was left behind in Cuba. Moreover, since César's last act is to transcribe this lyric, this Spanish interpolation is literally a testament. When readers finally come upon these words, they find themselves at a loss. For Anglophone

readers, the loss is more acute—since they cannot understand what they read. The bolero, which is one of the novel's principal links to Hispanic culture, is also the novel's figure for the loss of that culture, a loss whose most fundamental manifestation is linguistic.

In a narrow but significant sense, this linguistic loss has been present throughout the novel in the surprisingly large number of misspellings of Spanish words and names. For example, Antonio Arcaño, who is one of the seminal figures in the early history of the mambo, becomes Antonio Arcana; the famous singer Bola de Nieve is strangely transformed into a Pala de Nieve; the equally famous Beny Moré loses his accent and becomes Beny More—a notable example of how "more" can be "less." These errata and others like them may be evidence of sloppy editing; nonetheless, they also constitute typographical reminders of translation as loss, displacement, as traduction.

But perhaps the best example inside and outside of the novel of traductive translation is Desi Arnaz, who is an important secondary character. In fact, the book ends with Eugenio's account of his visit to Desi's house in California, where Desi and Eugenio reminisce about the mambo kings. Think for a moment about the name of the character that Desi played on TV: Ricky Ricardo. The name is a bilingual text that contains both original and translation, since Ricky is a familiar American rendering of the Spanish Ricardo. But it is a translation that distances, a traductive translation: the Germanic Ricardo (which, incidentally, means "king") is not only anglicized but turned into a diminutive: it does not become Richard, or Dick, or Rick, but Ricky—a child's name (much as, one may add, Desiderio became Desi). And of the two given names—Ricky, Ricardo—it is the North American one that comes first. Ricardo—which in Spanish is seldom a last name and at that time was the first name of one of Hollywood's leading Latin lovers, Ricardo Montalbán—becomes the last name. It is as if Ricky has pushed Ricardo into the lastname position, with the consequence that Ricardo's "real" last name, say, "Rodriguez," drops out of the picture entirely. In a sense, Ricky Ricardo is an orphan's name, one that reveals nothing about Ricky's parentage. Still, what matters about Ricky's ancestry is that he is Hispanic, and Ricardo functions well enough as a marker of ethnicity. Ricardo signifies that the subject is Hispanic; Ricky signifies that the Hispanic subject—the "I" in *I Love Lucy*—has been acculturated, domesticated, maybe even emasculated. Ricardo is the Latin lover, Ricky is the American husband.

The contrast between Ricky and Ricardo may well boil down to the different connotations of the final letters in each name, "y" and "o." In English, the suffix "y" is used in forming diminutives, nicknames, and terms of endearment or familiarity. By attaching a "y" to a proper name we establish an affective relation with the name's holder, we make the name contingent or dependent on us—an effect that may have to do with the other function of the suffix "y," which is to turn a noun or a verb into an adjective, as when we turn "touch" into "touchy" or "feel" into "feely." By contrast, the final "o" is a marker not of familiarity but of foreignness, and not of endearment but of distance. Think, for a minute, of the words in English that end in "o." Once we get past the names of some instruments— piano, cello—and a few fruits and vegetables— potato, tomato, avocado, mango—we run into such words as psycho, weirdo, tyro, bimbo, Drano, Oreo, buffo. The fact that in Spanish "o" is a masculine ending probably also acts on our sense of the suffix in words such as macho, mambo, Latino, Gustavo. The story of "o" is a tale of estrangement, for the English language treats o-words like foreign bodies. Thus by replacing the "o" in Ricardo with the "y" in Ricky one removes the unfamiliarity, and perhaps the threat, of the foreign body. (One might recall here that the radical spelling of "women" is "womyn, where the "y" feminizes, takes the "men" out of "women.") Replacing Ricardo with Ricky is, at the very least, an acculturating gesture, a way of turning the resident alien into a naturalized citizen. Ricky is the price that Ricardo pays for sleeping with Lucy—the price he pays for being allowed to enter Lucy's bedroom and America's living rooms. Lucy and Ricky—the "y" that ends their names is not the least significant thing they have in common.

Ricky Ricardo's name alerts us, therefore, to the schisms that bisect what Michael Fisher has called the "ethnic I." For me a handy emblem of the erosion of Ricky's subject position is the transition from the initial "I" of the show's title to the final "y" of his Americanized name (Desi Arnaz once remarked that he wanted to be remembered as the "I" in *I Love Lucy*). This is a transition from agency to contingency, from activity to passivity, from visibility to invisibility. It would be easy to ridicule the stereotypical elements in the portrayal of Ricky, who like Desi himself used to do, ends each rendition of the Afro-Cuban song "Babalú" with an entirely un-African "olé." But it may also be possible to see Ricky Ricardo (name and character) as a moving emblem for what is lost—and perhaps what is gained—in translation. Every time Ricky breaks into his nearly unintelligible Spanish or says "wunt" for "won't" or "splain" for "explain," his words, beyond whatever comedic value they may have, remind us of the risks—and also of the rewards—of loving Lucy.

I propose something similar happens in Hijuelos's novel. At one point in the *Mambo Kings*, during an interview on a radio show, César Castillo praises Desi Arnaz. The emcee replies. "But no one has ever considered him very authentic or original." To which César counters: *"Bueno,* but I think what he did was difficult. For me, he was very Cuban, and the music he played in those days was good and Cuban enough for me." "Good and Cuban enough"—this statement may apply equally well to Hijuelos's novel, a dance to the music of time that, like Desi and Ricky, loses and finds itself in translation. As a Hispanic product repackaged for North American consumption, *Mambo Kings* clearly illustrates the predicament of ethnic culture, which is that it must walk a narrow line between the danger of co-optation on the one hand and of unintelligibility on the other. In this also it resembles the mambo, whose big-band sound was similarly criticized for not being Cuban enough, but whose success was due in some measure to its impurities.

In a fine book, *Chicano Narrative: The Dialectics of Difference*, Ramón Saldívar has argued that what distinguishes Chicano narrative is the power to demystify relations between hegemonic and minority cultures. I do not think that *Mambo Kings* is demystifying in this sense; rather than dealing with relations between hegemonic and minority cultures, *Mambo Kings* focuses on the transactions between two cultures, each of which asserts its own particular kind of hegemony. Even if the novel's very existence in English seems to tilt the balance in favor of Anglo-American culture, the novel's content, suffused as it is with Hispanic culture, tends to rectify the scales. Indeed, as we have seen, even the text's English betrays a Spanish accent. Hijuelos's own version of the "dialectics of difference" faces off Spanish American culture on one hand and North American culture on the other, but without treating the former as a subaltern or "minority" culture. Their relation is "appositional" rather than "oppositional." It may be, in fact, that Cuban-American literature differs from Chicano literature in conceiving of culture contact as appositional. Apposition may more accurately reflect the nature and history of Cuban-American participation in the Anglo-American mainstream.

In any event, Hijuelos's considerable achievement is to stage the negotiation between cultures in such a way that the novel neither forsakes nor is enslaved by its family resemblance to things and texts Hispanic. Spanish American culture figures in the novel as a distant relation—much as César and Nestor appear on *I Love Lucy* as Ricky's Cuban cousins. The art of the *Mambo Kings* resides in knowing how to cultivate distant relations, which means also knowing how to put them in their place. By taking distance from its ancestry, the novel is able to occupy an eccentric space somewhere between Havana and Harlem, a kind of make-believe border ballroom where North meets South, where Ricky loves Lucy, and where mambo kings play songs of love forever.

The preceding sentences may sound like a conclusion, but they are not. I would like to end on a more personal note. Most Latino writers of my acquaintance have thoroughly detested this novel, considering that it sacrifices genuine Hispanic flavor in order to cater to the tastes of a North American readership. For them, *Mambo Kings* is a sort of literary Taco Bell: inauthentic and even indigestible. For me, however, the issue is whether authenticity, or a certain kind of authenticity, is really worth pursuing. As one who has feasted more than once on a Double Beef Burrito Supreme, I am less quick to dismiss fast food, however hyphenated. Hyphens are curious creatures; they connect, they separate, and above all, they are elastic. *Mambo Kings* is a study in the elasticity of hyphens; the novel distends the hyphen inside "Cuban-American" to the breaking point, but without letting it snap. To my mind, this is Hijuelos's most important lesson: he teaches us to stretch the hyphen, to get lost in translation. Sometimes you can even stretch the hyphen so much that it becomes a conga line.

And how about the phrase "lost in translation?" What does *this* phrase evoke? In what kind of a place does one end up if one gets lost "in translation?" When I try to visualize such a commonplace, I imagine myself, on a given Saturday afternoon, in a shopping center in Miami called the Town and Country Mall. Since I'm thirsty, I go into a store called Love Juices, which specializes in nothing more salacious or salubrious than milk shakes made from tropical fruits; having quenched my thirst, I want to buy some Liz Claiborne jeans, and I head for a boutique called Mr. Trapus, whose name— *trapo*—is actually the Spanish word for an old rag; undaunted by the consumerist frenzy that has possessed me, I then purchase a hand-painted Italian tie in another store nearby called Cachi Bachi—a

name that, in spite of its chichi sound, is a Spanish slang word for junk, *cachibache*. And then, for dinner, I go to Garcia's Caribbean Grill, where I have something called a Tropical Soup, the American version of the traditional Cuban stew, *ajiaco*. In this way, I spend my entire afternoon lost in translation—and loving every minute. Translation takes you to a place where cultures divide to conga. My effort here has been to show you the way to such a place. Now, enter at your own risk. Who knows, you might end up becoming the missing link in the Desi-chain.

Source: Gustavo Perez Firmat, "I Came, I Saw, I Conga'd," in *Everynight Life: Culture and Dance in Latin/o America*, edited by Celeste Fraser Delgado and José Esteban Muñoz, Duke University Press, 1997, pp. 239–54.

Sources

Birkerts, Sven, "The Haunted House," in the *New Republic*, March 22, 1993, pp. 38–41.

Hornby, Nick, "Cuban Heels," in the *Listener*, Vol. 123, No. 3158, March 29, 1990, p. 33.

Jefferson, Margo, "Dancing into the Dream," in the *New York Times Book Review*, August 27, 1989, pp. 1, 30.

Kanellos, Nicholas, Review of *The Mambo Kings Play Songs of Love*, in the *Americas Review*, Vol. XVIII, No. 1, Spring 1990, pp. 113–14.

McGuigan, Cathleen, "Fascinatin' Rhythm," in *Newsweek*, August 21, 1989, p. 60.

Sheppard, R. Z., "Hail Cesar," in *Time*, August 14, 1989, p. 68.

Further Reading

Carpentier, Alejo, *Music in Cuba*, University of Minnesota Press, 2001.
   Originally published in 1946 (before the time when this novel begins), Carpentier's study of the roots of Cuban music shows how West Indian, European, and African influences came together to form the unique Cuban sound in writing that is intellectual in style and content but accessible to the common reader.

Salazar, Max, *Mambo Kingdom: Latin Music in New York*, Omnibus Press, 2002.
   Salazar is a respected historian who has written on several facets of Latin American music. In this new book, he explores the significance of the New York scene in bridging the cultural gap between European and Latin traditions.

Suchlicki, Jaime, *Cuba: From Columbus to Castro and Beyond*, 4th ed., Brasseys Inc., 1997.

This study is one of the most thorough analyses written on Cuban history by an American, updated to reflect the post-Soviet world.

Sweeney, Philip, *The Rough Guide to Cuban Music*, Rough
Guides, Inc., 2001.
This in-depth analysis of the country's music traces
its development, with hundreds of short biographies
of musicians who have had international influence.

Yanow, Scott, *Afro-Cuban Jazz: Third Ear–The Essential
Listening Companion*, Backbeat Books, 2000.
This book traces the connection between American
jazz and Cuban music back to the early twentieth-
century. As part of the "Third Ear" music series, it
presents a respected overview, and includes recom-
mendations of important recordings.

The Mill on the Floss

George Eliot

1860

The Mill on the Floss, published in 1860, is based partially on Eliot's own experiences with her family and her brother Isaac, who was three years older than Eliot. Eliot's father, like Mr. Tulliver in the novel, was a businessman who had married a woman from a higher social class, whose sisters were rich, ultra-respectable, and self-satisfied; these maternal aunts provided the character models for the aunts in the novel. Like Maggie, Eliot was disorderly and energetic and did not fit traditional models of feminine beauty or behavior, causing her family a great deal of consternation.

By the time Eliot published *The Mill on the Floss*, she had gained considerable notoriety as an "immoral woman" because she was living with the writer George Henry Lewes, who was married, though separated from his wife. Social disapproval of her actions spilled over into commentary on the novel, and it was scathingly criticized because it did not present a clear drama of right and wrong. Perhaps the most offended reader was Eliot's brother Isaac, who was very close to her in childhood but who had become estranged from her when he found out about her life with Lewes; he communicated with her only through his lawyer. In the book, Eliot drew on her own experiences with a once-beloved but rigid and controlling brother to depict the relationship between Maggie and her brother Tom.

Author Biography

George Eliot was the pen name of Mary Anne Evans, born November 22, 1819, at South Farm, Arbury, Warwickshire, England. She was the youngest child of Robert Evans and his second wife, Christiana Pearson, and had four siblings, two by her father's first marriage and two by his second. Eliot was her father's favorite child and was brought up to follow his Protestant beliefs. However, in her early twenties, she told her father that although she admired Jesus and his teachings, she rejected the idea that the Bible was of divine origin, and she refused to go to church. This shocked her family and many others, but she refused to attend services she did not believe in. This emphasis on following her own inner promptings rather than social convention would become a marked feature of her character and her life.

After her father's death in 1849, she had little money and little chance of getting married because she did not fit the contemporary ideal of beauty. A meeting with John Chapman, a family friend, led her to write for the quarterly *Westminster Review*. Through this work, she met the writer George Henry Lewes in 1851. Lewes was married with five children, though separated from his wife, and he and Eliot fell in love and began openly living together, a scandalous act for the times. As a result, Eliot was ostracized by many "respectable" people for most of her life.

In September 1856, Eliot began to write fiction. Her first work, a story titled "Amos Barton," was published anonymously in the January 1857 issue of *Blackwood's Magazine*. More stories followed, and her first novel, *Adam Bede*, was published in 1859. It received immediate critical acclaim as "a work of genius" in the periodical *The Athenaeum* and was called "the highest art" by the writer Leo Tolstoy.

Eliot followed this with the semi-autobiographical *The Mill on the Floss* (1860), which was highly successful, earning her four thousand pounds in one year, a huge sum for the time. In the next ten years, she published *Silas Marner* (1861), *Romola* (1863), and *Felix Holt the Radical* (1866). From 1871 to 1872, she published her masterpiece, *Middlemarch*. This was followed by *Daniel Deronda* (1876) and *Impressions of Theophrastus Such* (1879).

Lewes died in 1879, leaving Eliot grief-stricken. In 1880, she married John Walter Cross, who was about twenty years her junior, but she died

George Eliot

of a respiratory infection only seven months later, on December 21, 1880, in London.

Eliot's books are notable for their realistic portrayal of preindustrial English society, her interest in scandal and gossip, and her emphasis on political and social reform. They often feature female protagonists who struggle against social convention, but who, in the end, must accept it or be ostracized by their families and friends.

Plot Summary

Book 1: Boy and Girl

The novel begins with a description of the rural area where the action takes place, near the town of St. Ogg's and the River Floss. The narrator reminisces about a February many years ago and begins to tell the story of the Tulliver family.

Mr. Tulliver, who is the fifth generation in his family to own and run Dorlcote Mill on the River Floss, tells his wife that he will send his son Tom to a school where Tom can learn to be an "engineer, or a surveyor, or an auctioneer ... or one of them smartish businesses as are all profit and no outlay." His wife advises him to ask her wealthier

Media Adaptations

- *The Mill on the Floss* was adapted to film in a Carnival Films production, in association with UGC D.A. International and Canal Plus. It was produced by Brian Eastman and directed by Graham Theakston. The film starred Emily Watson as Maggie, Ifan Meredith as Tom, James Frain as Philip Wakem, and James Weber-Brown as Stephen Guest.

sisters and their husbands for their opinion, but Tulliver says he will do whatever he wants. However, he does decide to ask Mr. Riley, an auctioneer, who is somewhat educated, for his opinion. The two parents discuss their other child, Maggie, who takes after her father. She is as dark as Tom is fair and is clever but headstrong, uninterested in her appearance and in social niceties. True to her nature, Maggie comes to tea late with her hair mussed up, and when her mother urges her to do patchwork, she refuses. Her mother is bothered by the fact that Maggie is nothing like her and by the fact that she is much smarter than a woman "should" be.

Riley visits Tulliver, who says that he wants Tom to have an education but that it should be in a different field from his own, as he does not want Tom to grow up and take the mill away from him. Maggie, hearing this, is quick to defend Tom, and she distractedly drops the book she has been reading, *The History of the Devil*, a surprising choice for a young girl. Tulliver explains to Riley that he bought the book without knowing what it was about, because it had an interesting cover. Maggie discusses the book with them, but when she begins to discuss the devil, Tulliver tells her to leave the room. He tells Riley that she is too smart for a woman—unlike her mother, who is not noted for her intelligence. He tells Riley that he chose her as a wife for this very reason.

Riley advises Tulliver to send Tom to the son-in-law of a businessman he knows. This teacher is Reverend Walter Stelling; Riley offers to contact Stelling for Tulliver and says that Stelling can teach Tom anything he needs to know.

Tom is coming home from his current school, but Maggie is not allowed to go out and meet him. Angered, she dunks her freshly brushed hair in water and then beats up a doll she keeps in the attic. Bored, she heads out to talk to Luke, the miller. He is not interested in her clever talk and reminds her that she has forgotten to feed and water Tom's rabbits while he was gone, and they have all died. This upsets her, but she forgets about it when Luke invites her to visit his wife. They have an illustration of the biblical parable of the Prodigal Son in their home, and she is fascinated with it and happy that his father took him back. However, she is upset when Luke reminds her that perhaps the son did not deserve it.

Tom gives Maggie the gift of a new fishing line and promises to take her fishing. The narrator, in introducing him, mentions that his fresh-cheeked, fair, and open appearance belies his character, which is rigid, inflexible, and unmodifiable. When he goes to see his rabbits, Maggie confesses that she has neglected them. He is angered by this and not affected by her remorse. He leaves her alone to cry, but they soon make up. The next day they go fishing together, and she hopes that they will always be close like this.

Mrs. Tulliver plans to invite her sisters and their husbands over to discuss Tom's education. Mrs. Tulliver wants Tom and Maggie to make a good impression on them, while Tulliver does not care what they think. Tom and Maggie, bored with the visit and all the rules imposed by the presence of their rigid relatives, run off with some pastry that their mother has made for the relatives. Tom heads out to see Bob Jakin, a poor boy who is headed to see a rat-catching at a farm nearby. Bob tosses a coin and asks Tom to call it but then will not hand it over when Tom calls it correctly. They fight, and Bob throws a knife that Tom once gave him on the ground to show his contempt for Tom. When Tom does not pick it up, though, Bob takes it back.

The aunts arrive. Mrs. Glegg complains about others being late, refuses to eat cheesecake, because she never eats between meals, and tells Mrs. Tulliver she should have dinner earlier, as her family has always done. Mrs. Pullet arrives in tears over the death of someone who is not related to the family; this elicits Mrs. Glegg's scorn, as she only cares about immediate relatives. Pullet defends his wife and discusses details of the dead woman's will. Mrs. Pullet and Mrs. Tulliver go upstairs to see a bonnet until Mrs. Deane arrives with her daughter, Lucy. Lucy, who is fair, pretty, and well behaved, is contrasted with the wild, dark Maggie. Mrs. Pullet in particular criticizes Maggie's dark, heavy hair. Maggie, who is sick of hearing her hair discussed, goes upstairs and cuts it off but regrets it when Tom laughs at her and the adults discuss her even more.

When Tulliver reveals his plans for Tom's education, Mrs. Glegg is shocked. Mr. Deane says that Wakem, a prominent lawyer, is also sending his son to Stelling. Mrs. Glegg comments that she has lent money to Tulliver, reminding him that he owes her. They argue, and Mrs. Glegg leaves in a huff.

The Tullivers discuss their debt of five hundred pounds to Mrs. Glegg. Tulliver realizes that the only way he can pay it is to ask his brother-in-law, Moss, to whom he has loaned three hundred pounds, to pay him back. The next day he rides over to Moss's. Moss, who is a poor farmer, is not home, but Tulliver's sister Gritty is. They live in a rundown hovel and have eight children. Gritty speaks admiringly of Maggie and says she hopes Tom will be good to Maggie in the future. This softens Tulliver, reminding him that Gritty is his own sister and he should be good to her.

Moss comes home and Tulliver asks him about the money. Moss says he would have to sell his house and everything he owns to pay it back, but if he must, he will do so. Tulliver says he must, but after leaving them, he thinks twice about it and rides back to tell Gritty that they can forget about the debt. Tulliver is glad he did this and thinks that somehow his example will result in Tom helping Maggie someday.

Maggie visits the Pullets. Maggie and Lucy like each other despite their differences in character; Tom says he likes Lucy more than Maggie. The house is fussy and overly neat, and when Maggie accidentally steps on a sweet cake and spills Tom's wine, her aunt Pullet sends the children outside. Meanwhile, Mrs. Tulliver discusses finances and convinces Mrs. Pullet to ask Mrs. Glegg to forget about the five hundred pounds Tulliver owes her.

Maggie becomes angry at Lucy, who is so perfect and clean and who is getting all of Tom's attention. She pushes her into the mud, and Tom decides that it is only just to throw Maggie in, too. However, he is in trouble, too, because they were not supposed to go anywhere near the mud. In order to save himself, he drops the issue and does not

tell the adults on Maggie. Meanwhile, Maggie has disappeared.

Maggie, who has been told often that she looks like a gypsy, runs off to join them. She assumes they will be glad to see her and be enlightened by her education. She finally finds their camp but is not happy there; the gypsies frighten her and steal her silver thimble. One of the gypsy men eventually takes her home on his donkey, and Tulliver pays him for returning Maggie. Maggie regrets her headstrong decision, and Tulliver does not punish her for it.

The narrator describes the town of St. Ogg's, a town that cherishes respectability above all else. The Gleggs live there. Mr. Glegg, a retired wool merchant, spends most of his time in his garden. His wife, who is thrifty like him, is less likable and more prone to arguing. He tells her that she should not make Tulliver pay his debt now, since anyone else who borrows it would not pay as much interest as Tulliver. They argue about this until Mr. Glegg tells her he has left a lot of money to her in his will. The thought of future riches distracts her and pleases her, and she decides to let Tulliver keep the loan for the time being.

Mrs. Pullet tries to convince Mrs. Glegg to let Tulliver keep the money. She succeeds, because Mrs. Glegg has already decided to do so. However, Tulliver has already written to Mrs. Glegg, saying that he will pay the money in the following month. He still needs the money, of course, and he decides to borrow it from a client of his longtime enemy, Lawyer Wakem.

Book 2: School-Time
Tom turns out to be the only pupil of Reverend Stelling, and he is bored without friends. In addition, he is not very bright, so studying Latin and geometry is torture to him. Stelling turns out to be an ambitious man who spends far more than he makes, and he is unable to adapt his teaching to Tom's abilities; Tom is good at business and has common sense. Bored, Tom plays with Stelling's baby daughter and starts to miss Maggie's company.

Maggie visits, and she is very interested in his studies; she shows that she can pick up the topics much more quickly than he can, even though she is a girl. She stays there two weeks and learns Latin and geometry, largely on her own. Despite this, when she asks Stelling if she can study as Tom does, Stelling and Tom both tell her women are too stupid to "go far into anything."

Tom goes home for Christmas, but life at home is unpleasant. His father, who likes to argue and sue people, has a new feud going with Pivart: a new neighbor who lives upstream from the mill wants to use water from the Floss to irrigate his fields. Tulliver feels this is an infringement on his own water rights, and he is sure that Lawyer Wakem is behind it. Meanwhile, Wakem is planning to send his son Philip to Stelling. Even though Tulliver hates Wakem, he is secretly pleased about his son having the same education as Wakem's.

Tom meets Philip Wakem. Philip is deformed as the result of a childhood accident. He is shy, well educated, and proud. Tom is disgusted by his deformity and hates him, until he discovers that Philip is a skilled artist, an ability Tom lacks. They begin to talk, and Philip, who is good at Latin, tells Tom stories about the ancient Greeks and Romans. In return, Tom brags about how he beat up all the other boys at his old school.

Tom continues to do poorly at schoolwork, but he is good at military drills, which he practices with the drillmaster, Poulter. Tom is fascinated by Poulter's combat stories and gets Poulter to lend him his sword.

Philip and Tom get into a fight, and Tom calls Philip's father a rogue. Hurt, Philip cries.

Tom assumes his fight with Philip is over, and he acts friendly. However, Philip will not let the insult go. Maggie comes to visit. She is fascinated by Philip, because she has a "tenderness for deformed things." She also admires his ability in music and drawing.

Tom gets out the sword and swaggers to impress Maggie, but he drops the sword and cuts his foot.

Philip is kind to Tom, telling him the injury will not make him permanently lame. After this they become friendlier. Philip asks Maggie if she would love him if he were her brother, and she says yes, she would, because she would be sorry for him. However, this incident makes her realize that Philip cares for her, and she tells him she wishes he really were her brother. She tells her father how she and Tom have become friends with Philip, and Tulliver advises them both not to get too close.

Maggie goes to a girls' boarding school with her cousin Lucy. In the meantime, her father has begun a lawsuit against Lawyer Wakem, so she cannot be too friendly to Philip. Eventually, he loses the suit and must sell everything he owns, including the mill, to pay for it. What is more, when

Tulliver received this news, he fell off his horse and has been out of his mind ever since. Tom and Maggie head home, and the narrator notes that "the golden gates of their childhood . . . [had] forever closed behind them."

Book 3: The Downfall

Tulliver looks for someone who will buy the mill and let him run it. He is also troubled because he has already scheduled a sale of his household goods in order to raise the money to pay back Mrs. Glegg's five hundred pounds. He decides to send Mrs. Tulliver to the Pullets to ask them to lend him five hundred pounds.

When Mrs. Tulliver asks her sisters for help, they see Tulliver's failure as a sort of divine judgment against him, and they refuse to help. Tom decides the whole thing is Lawyer Wakem's fault and decides that someday he will make Wakem pay for it.

Tom and Maggie get home and find the bailiff waiting in the parlor. He has come to sell all their things. Mrs. Tulliver is upset over the impending loss of her belongings. Her sisters are coming to buy a few things but only the ones they want for themselves; otherwise they will not help. Tom says he will get a job and help the family. Maggie is appalled by her mother's emphasis on things and her lack of caring about Tulliver, who is still out of his mind, and she goes to take care of him.

The following day, all the aunts and uncles gather to decide what must be done. They have no sympathy for Mrs. Tulliver's now-destitute state or her desire to keep some of her old things, and they tell her she must make do with a few meager necessities. Tom tells them that if they were planning to leave money to him and Maggie, they could simply give it out now and save the family. Mrs. Glegg refuses to do so, because she would have less to leave after she died and people might think she was poor when they heard of her small legacy. Maggie, angered, asks why they came to interfere if they do not plan to help. Tom is annoyed by her outburst.

Mrs. Moss, the poorest of all the relatives, arrives and tells the children that she has three hundred pounds but cannot repay it without herself becoming bankrupt. Tom tells the other relatives that Tulliver did not want the money back. Mr. Glegg says that if there is any proof of the loan, the authorities will insist that it be paid back anyway. Tom and Mr. Glegg decide to find the loan note and destroy it, leaving the Mosses free of any obligation.

While they search for the note, Tulliver wakes from his coma and is surprisingly lucid. He tells Tom to take care of Maggie and Mrs. Tulliver, verifies that he does not want his loan back, and reminds Tom to make Wakem suffer for the trouble he has supposedly brought to the family. Then he lapses into unconsciousness again.

Tom visits his uncle Deane, a successful businessman for Guest and Company, and asks for a job. Deane tells him that his fancy education is useless and that he is qualified for nothing. He will try to get Tom a job but cannot promise anything. Back at home, Maggie suggests that she learn bookkeeping so she can teach it to Tom. He thinks this is mighty presumptuous for a mere woman and becomes angry at her.

The Tulliver household is finally sold. A visitor appears later that day: Bob Jakin. He shows Tom the knife Tom once gave him and tells Tom it is the only thing anyone has ever given him. In return, he says, he wants to give the family ten sovereigns that he received for putting out a fire at another mill. Tom refuses the money, but Maggie says that if they ever need help in the future, they will call on Bob.

In the meantime, Deane has found Tom a job in a warehouse. Mrs. Tulliver goes to Lawyer Wakem and asks him not to buy the mill, because it will upset her husband. Instead, she asks him to let Deane's company buy the mill. His company, Guest and Company, is thinking of buying it and letting Tulliver run it. Wakem says he could buy it and let Tulliver run it, but Mrs. Tulliver says her husband would never agree to this. In truth, Wakem never intended to buy the mill, but now he decides it is a good idea to do so.

Wakem buys the mill, and Tulliver, who sees that he has no choice, agrees to run it. Gradually, he becomes strong again, but he chafes under Wakem's ownership. One day he makes Tom write in the family Bible that he has agreed to run the mill for Wakem but that he will never forgive him, that he wishes "evil may befall him," and that one day Tom will make him suffer for it. Maggie says that it is wrong to write such a curse in the Bible, but Tom writes and signs it.

Book 4: The Valley of Humiliation

The narrator discusses the Dodson family and their idea of religion, calling it "simple, semipagan," and noting that they worship "whatever is customary and respectable." They are egotistical people who serve their own interests. The Tulliv-

ers are similar but have a little more impetuosity and warmth.

Tom is fully employed at the warehouse, but Maggie, at thirteen, is bored, with nothing to do. She is full of energy and drive, qualities considered deplorable in a girl, but the same qualities make young Tom "manly" despite his emotional immaturity.

Bob Jakin drops by one day. He is a traveling salesman, or packman, and he drops off some books he bought as a gift for Maggie. One is a religious book by Thomas à Kempis, which advocates renunciation and asceticism, and this grabs her imagination. She tries to lead an ascetic, spiritual life.

Book 5: Wheat and Tares

Philip Wakem comes to the mill with his father one day. Although Maggie is home, she does not want to see him with his father there, because she cannot be friendly to him in front of his father. She is now seventeen and is stately and very beautiful. On a walk to the woods near her house, she meets Philip, who has been waiting for her. They agree to meet there periodically. He is in love with her, but as yet she does not think of him that way.

Meanwhile, Tom has done well in his work. He gives all his money to his father, saving up to buy back the mill someday. Bob Jakin tells Tom that he can make much more money if he invests in some goods, which Jakin will give to a sailor friend of his to sell on his voyages. Tulliver is unwilling to give up any money, so Tom borrows fifty pounds from Mr. Glegg to invest in the venture. Mrs. Glegg, who has fallen for Bob Jakin's sales talk, also lends him twenty pounds of her own. By the time Maggie meets Philip, Tom has made 150 pounds and plans to pay off the entire mill debt by the end of the following year.

Maggie and Philip meet some more. He draws her and plays music for her, both of which arouse her love of art and beauty. They agree to keep meeting, even though their families would be against it. Philip is deeply in love with Maggie, even though he knows she feels sorry for him because of his deformity.

A year later, they are still meeting secretly. Maggie returns a book she borrowed from Philip, saying she disliked it because the author, like so many others, had the fair-haired girl win over one who was dark, like Maggie. Philip tells her that one day soon she may triumph over her fair-haired cousin Lucy in love. This annoys Maggie, who had been speaking metaphorically and does not like to think of being Lucy's rival. Philip tells her he loves her, but she says she could never upset her father by returning that love.

One day Maggie's aunt Pullet comments that she has often noticed Philip Wakem in a particular spot in the woods. Maggie blushes, and when Tom sees her, he knows she has been meeting Philip. Tom corners Maggie, asks what she thinks she is doing, and says their father would be driven mad if he knew. He makes her promise that she will never see Philip again. She says she would never promise this for Tom, but in respect for her father, she agrees.

Three weeks later, Tom comes home and tells his father that he has enough money to buy back the mill. Tulliver is thrilled and dreams of the revenge he will have on Lawyer Wakem. He goes to dinner with his creditors and tells them he can pay them off. This fills him with pride, and when he meets Wakem in the street, he tells him he will not work for him anymore and knocks Wakem off his horse and whips him furiously. The next morning, Tulliver asks Tom to try to get Wakem to sell him the mill and tells him to take good care of his mother and Maggie. He dies without forgiving Wakem, and Tom and Maggie promise they will always be good to each other.

Book 6: *The Great Temptation*

Stephen Guest, son of the main partner of Guest and Company, is courting Maggie's cousin Lucy Deane. He is good-looking and a smooth talker, and he is marrying Lucy largely because she fits a description of the perfect wife: good looking, but not too much; thoughtful of other women, but not too much; gentle and "not stupid." When Maggie visits, he is fascinated with her dark beauty and intelligence. He is attracted to her but acknowledges that she is not the sort of woman he would want to marry.

That night, Maggie cannot sleep, because she keeps thinking of how well Stephen can play music and sing and remembering the passionate way he looked at her. When Lucy asks what Maggie thinks of Stephen, however, Maggie says she thinks he is too self-confident. Lucy says that Philip is going to visit the next day, but Maggie says she cannot see him without her brother's permission. Lucy asks why not, and Maggie tells the whole story of her past connection with Philip. Lucy finds this very romantic and decides that she will find a way to bring them together again.

Maggie goes to visit Tom, who is living at Bob Jakin's house. He agrees to release her from her promise not to see Philip but says she will have to live without a brother if she sees him. Maggie says that she does not want to lose her brother, so she will not love Philip but will only be a friend to him. Tom finally agrees that she can see him.

Uncle Deane tells Tom he has done good work and that he and Mr. Guest are going to give him a share in their business. Tom is grateful but suggests that the company buy Dorlcote Mill and let him run it and eventually buy it from them by working off the price. He says that Wakem may be interested in selling it, because the current manager has been drinking too much. Deane says he will investigate.

Maggie, who is now under Lucy's wing and socializing with the high society in St. Ogg's, is enjoying her new leisure. The men and women of St. Ogg's are all fascinated with her: the men because of her beauty, the women because of her unpretentiousness. One of the men is Stephen Guest, who is understood to be Lucy's fiancé. There is a chemistry between him and Maggie, of which Lucy is unaware.

The following day, Philip comes to visit Maggie and Lucy. He and Maggie are nervous about meeting again but secretly glad. Maggie tells him that Tom has agreed that they can be friends but that she is planning to go away to a "new situation." Stephen arrives, and Philip is annoyed by his presence and by the fact that Maggie is evidently swayed by him.

Later, Deane tells Lucy that his company might buy the mill from Philip's father. Lucy says that if he lets her, she will talk to Philip to get him to convince his father to go along with the deal.

Lucy talks about it with Philip. Philip asks his father to talk to him in his room, where there are several drawings he has made of Maggie. His father asks about them, and Philip explains that he would marry her if he could but that he has never been taught a skill that would allow him to support himself and her. Wakem is enraged that his son wants to marry a Tulliver, and when Philip says that Maggie never got involved in the family feud, Wakem says that it does not matter what a woman does; what matters is whom she belongs to. They argue, but in the end Wakem, thinking about his own deceased wife and the happiness she gave him, agrees to sell the mill and allow Philip to marry Maggie if she agrees.

At a bazaar in St. Ogg's, Maggie attracts a lot of attention because of her looks. There is tension between Maggie, Stephen, and Philip. Maggie thinks she would prefer Stephen as a husband, but she is not sure. Lucy tells her that now that Tom will own the mill, there is no reason why she cannot marry Philip. Maggie reminds her that Tom still hates him.

At a dance at Stephen's house, Stephen kisses Maggie, and she is offended at his boldness. The next morning, she is supposed to visit her aunt Moss. Philip arrives before she leaves and asks if they can ever be together again. She says that Tom is the only factor keeping them apart.

After four days of her visit to Aunt Moss, Stephen visits and asks her to forgive him. She does, and he asks her to marry him. She says no, because he is engaged to Lucy, and he cannot convince her that it would not be wrong. She convinces him that it is time for them to go their separate ways, because she is going away to work.

A few days later, Maggie visits her aunt Pullet, who is having a party to celebrate Tom's purchase of the mill. Aunt Pullet is annoyed that Maggie is going to go away and get a job as a governess, but on the other hand, she refuses to do anything to help her. Lucy gets Tom to take her home from the party and asks him to allow Maggie to marry Philip. Tom refuses to bless their union but says Maggie can do what she wants.

Maggie stays with her aunt Glegg, but Stephen sees her each evening at dinner. They are still interested in each other, although Maggie fights it. Still, she thinks it is harmless if they show their love to each other, because she will soon be leaving anyway. A series of mishaps result in Maggie and Stephen going on a boating trip down the Floss together; although the trip is only supposed to last an afternoon, Stephen does not stop where they had planned to but keeps on going until the tide makes it impossible to return that day. This is crucial, because in their society staying away overnight would ruin Maggie's reputation as a virtuous woman; people will assume that she is loose. Stephen tells her their only alternative is to run away and get married, but Maggie refuses. More mishaps ensue, and Maggie does not get home until five days later.

Tom is angry with her for shaming the family, and he will not let her stay in the mill. Bob Jakin takes her and Mrs. Tulliver in. Bob wonders why Maggie is not married, but he does not ask.

The narrator comments on this state of affairs, saying that if Maggie had gotten married, society would have found it a romantic story. However, since she is not, all the blame falls on her as an un-

wed woman, and people assume she has been promiscuous and that Stephen then refused to marry her; they do not think badly of him at all, even though the event was his fault. Meanwhile, Stephen has gone abroad and has written a letter to a local clergyman, Dr. Kenn, saying that Maggie is not to blame. The local opinion is not swayed by this. Dr. Kenn thinks Maggie should marry Stephen, but he realizes that Maggie's feelings must be taken into account. He promises to find a job for Maggie.

Aunt Glegg scolds Tom for assuming the worst of his sister; Mr. Glegg takes Lucy's side and is against Maggie; Mrs. Pullet is undecided; and Mrs. Glegg takes Maggie's side and offers to take her in. Maggie thanks her but says she would rather be independent.

Philip writes a letter saying he believes in Maggie's innocence, that she is meant for him, and that he wants to help her in any way he can.

Dr. Kenn has not been able to find a job for Maggie, so he hires her as a governess for his children. However, after a while, rumors fly that he is going to marry her. Lucy visits Maggie, and Maggie tells Lucy that she never meant to deceive her and that Stephen will come back to Lucy eventually. Lucy tells Maggie that Maggie is a better person than she is.

Dr. Kenn finally has to fire Maggie because the gossip about her position in his house has become too slanderous. He tells her it's best if she leaves St. Ogg's. Maggie gets a letter from Stephen, saying he still loves her and wants her, but she resists her desire for him and burns the letter.

Meanwhile, it's been raining for two days, and the river is rising in a flood. Maggie gets into a boat and is swept out in the flood and paddles to the mill, where the water is up to the second story. She rescues Tom, and he finally realizes how paltry and futile their disagreements were. They both drown in the flood, but the narrator notes that, in death, they went down in "an embrace never to be parted: living through again in one supreme moment, the days when they had clasped their little hands in love, and roamed the daisied fields together."

Characters

Lucy Deane

Lucy, Maggie's cousin, is her opposite: as fair as Maggie is dark, well-behaved, quiet, and proper where Maggie is boisterous. The Dodson sisters all consider her to be the perfect little girl, but surprisingly, Maggie likes and admires her instead of hating her. She is not stupid, but neither is she notably intelligent. However, she is kindhearted, innocent, and sweet, never seeing evil in anyone. Even when Maggie and Stephen are obviously interested in each other, Lucy trusts that they are merely friends.

Mr. Deane

Mr. Deane is a shrewd businessman, who is proud of himself and scornful of frivolous learning, such as the Latin and geometry Tom studies; he believes in the value of hard work and useful skills such as bookkeeping. He began as a lowly worker and rose to his present position as a new partner in the firm of Guest and Company. He gives Tom a warehouse job and lends him money, which allows Tom to invest in a scheme that makes enough money for him to buy back the mill.

Mrs. Deane

Mrs. Deane is the third Dodson sister; she values propriety and appearances. Her character is not well defined, but she is respected by all because her husband, Mr. Deane, is a wealthy businessman. At first, her sisters thought she was marrying beneath her, but time has shown her to have been the most successful, at least in terms of marital prosperity.

Mr. Glegg

Mr. Glegg is a retired businessman who did well but who now spends most of his time working in his garden and trying to figure out the puzzling ways of women.

Mrs. Glegg

Of all the Dodson sisters, Mrs. Glegg is perhaps the most rigid and strict; she is obsessed with proper behavior and the way things look. She is the oldest and demands that the other sisters live up to her standards, which are impossible to meet and often senseless. She is the most interested in money of all the sisters and is not noted for her charity or understanding, but in the end she values her family over the opinions of other people. When Maggie is disgraced at the end of the book, Mrs. Glegg offers to take her in.

Mr. Guest

Mr. Guest is the main partner of Guest and Company, a wealthy trading firm. He has recently taken Mr. Deane on as a partner.

Stephen Guest

The son of a wealthy businessman, Stephen is good-looking, self-assured to the point of being somewhat cocky, and rather thoughtless. He is unofficially engaged to Lucy Deane, but that does not stop him from flirting with Maggie and, eventually, trying to run off with her. He does not seem to have much drive and ambition, and his main prospects in life derive from the fact that his father has already made a fortune, which he will inherit. Stephen falls in love with Maggie, but he is thoughtless and impetuous in his courting of her, not stopping to think about the consequences of running away or to consult with her before he takes her down the river. He is selfish but is somewhat redeemed by the fact that he is truly in love with Maggie; when she refuses him, he suffers intensely.

Bob Jakin

Bob Jakin has known Tom since childhood, when they occasionally played together. He grows up to be an amusing talker and canny trader who travels with a pack, selling items door to door. He is generous and kind and, unlike Tom who can carry a grudge forever, never forgets a kindness. He is often kind to others, offering to give Tom all his money, bringing books to Maggie, and setting Tom up with a lucky investment opportunity. After Maggie's disgrace, he and his wife take her in when Tom refuses to.

Dr. Kenn

Dr. Kenn is an Anglican clergyman. He believes that Maggie should marry Stephen after their disgraceful disappearance, but when he talks to her, he realizes the situation is too complex to fit simple rules of right and wrong. He shows kindness in taking her in but is overwhelmed when the tide of social opinion turns against him. In the end, he has to let her go from her post as governess to his children.

Luke

Luke works for Mr. Tulliver, running the mill. He is a simple man, religious and practical, without much use for education. He is not impressed by Maggie when she tries to show him how much she knows.

Gritty Moss

Mrs. Moss is Mr. Tulliver's sister. She is married to a poor farmer; they have eight children, and her kindness and warmth is shown by the fact that despite their poverty, she is still sad over the loss of her twins who died in infancy. She is honest and responsible, and when Mr. Tulliver comes to her asking her to pay back three hundred pounds he lent her, she does not become angry at him but resignedly says that her family will have to sell everything they have, but they will do it.

Mr. Moss

Mr. Moss is a poor farmer who lives with his large family in a decrepit hovel. He works hard but never seems to do well.

Mr. Pivart

Mr. Pivart moves into a farm upstream from Tulliver's mill and gets into a legal battle with Tulliver when Tulliver learns that Pivart will be using river water to irrigate his fields; Tulliver believes this infringes on his own right to use the water in his mill, but he loses the case.

Mr. Poulter

Mr. Poulter is Tom's drillmaster at school. He is fond of recounting war stories and impressing Tom with his military action. Foolishly, he lets Tom have his sword for a week in exchange for a small fee, and Tom wounds his foot with it.

Mr. Pullet

Mr. Pullet is a gentleman farmer who farms as a "hobby"; he is thin and is described mainly in terms of his memory for his wife's many prescriptions and his liking for lozenges.

Mrs. Pullet

Mrs. Pullet, one of the Dodson sisters, is Mrs. Tulliver's sister. Like her sisters, she is insistent on propriety and traditional codes of behavior. She is very careful of her personal belongings and also tends to be somewhat morbid and hypochondriacal.

Mr. Riley

Mr. Riley is an auctioneer, much admired by Mr. Tulliver for his business sense and for his wide circle of acquaintances, who recommends that Mr. Tulliver send Tom to Reverend Stelling for school.

Reverend Walter Stelling

Reverend Stelling is a clergyman who lives far above his means; he is ambitious but not very intelligent. He is unable to adapt his program of Latin and geometry to Tom's needs or to see that Tom, although not bright at these subjects, has other talents. He is shallow and not particularly spiritual despite his position.

Bessy Tulliver

Mrs. Tulliver, like her older sisters, values appearances, propriety, and tradition, but she is not very intelligent. She does not know what to do with Maggie, who is extremely smart and energetic and who does not fit the traditional expectations of female appearance or behavior.

Edward Tulliver

Mr. Tulliver, who is the fifth generation of his family to own Dorlcote Mill, is a hardheaded, stubborn man who remembers every slight and fiercely holds on to grudges. However, he is warm with his family. He is not very bright and has little insight into any character, including his own. He is continually becoming caught up in petty arguments that eventually escalate into lawsuits. He chose his wife because she was not very intelligent, and he is puzzled by Maggie because she is so smart and because she does not fit the traditional ideals of feminine appearance and behavior. He is not very close to his sister, Mrs. Moss, but occasionally he realizes how important family is and tries to be kind to her; this reminds him to tell Tom and Maggie to remain close and take care of each other.

Maggie Tulliver

Maggie is more like her father's family than her mother's. She is impetuous, warm, and highly intelligent, but she is also forgetful and impulsive. She has olive skin and untidy black hair, traits that upset her mother's family, and she is continually bothered by their obsession with her looks.

Unlike Tom, she is not sure of herself, and other people can easily make her feel bad about herself. When her father goes bankrupt, she is so ashamed that she turns to an ascetic life, where she can hide from the world that has been so cruel to her family. However, her sensitivity extends to other people's feelings as well. It leads her to become close to Philip Wakem, because she feels pity for his deformity. Philip, who is as interested in books and music as Maggie is, gets her interested in life again. She reenters the social world, where she meets Stephen Guest, and her urge to avoid hurting either Stephen or Philip by choosing between them leads her to make many mistakes.

Tom Tulliver

Maggie's older brother Tom is very much like his mother's family, the Dodsons. He is bossy and convinced that he always knows what's good for everyone else, traits he displays in childhood and continues throughout the book. He is not very concerned about other people's feelings as long as he's satisfied with himself, and if other people are hurt by his actions, he believes that's their fault for not adhering to the standards he has set. He is ambitious, but not very intelligent; although he studies geometry and Latin, he does not retain them and is more interested in "cutting a fine figure" in front of other people than in learning. He has a very high opinion of himself but does not stop to think how he will impress other people without skills or knowledge, so when he goes to get a job, he is surprised that he is suitable only for the most menial labor.

Like his father, Tom is stubborn and unyielding, and the more other people argue with him, the more tenaciously he clings to his own opinion. He never lets go of a grudge, is not forgiving, and does not comprehend what love or kindness is. When his father tells him to take care of Maggie, he thinks of this purely in the monetary sense, not in the sense of loving her. Just before he and Maggie die in the flood at the end of the book, he realizes that his view of life has been too narrow and that he has not loved her as he should have, but by then it's too late: after this realization, they die together.

Lawyer Wakem

Lawyer Wakem is Mr. Tulliver's archenemy because in the past he has been involved in many lawsuits that brought trouble to Tulliver, who habitually takes others to court. The enmity grows when Wakem is hired by Mr. Pivart to mediate a water dispute, and the case is decided in favor of Pivart. When Wakem buys Tulliver's mill, this brings Tulliver's hatred to a high pitch. However, Wakem is not as evil as Tulliver believes he is: when his son Philip explains that he loves Maggie Tulliver, Wakem remembers his own happy relationship with his deceased wife and tells Philip that he can marry Maggie if she will have him.

Philip Wakem

Philip is the son of Lawyer Wakem and thus an archenemy of the Tulliver family, according to Tom and Mr. Tulliver. An accident around the time of his birth resulted in his having a deformed back; as a result of this injury and his difference from most other people, he is sensitive, kindhearted, and aware of suffering. He is also a talented artist and musician. When Tom injures his foot while playing with a sword, Philip is the only one who understands Tom's fear that he will be crippled forever, and Philip reassures him despite their previous fights. Of all the characters, Philip is the most sensitive to other people and their needs and has the greatest insight into others' behavior. Philip and Maggie have an affinity through their mutual love of books, music, and art, but Philip's isolation, and the fact that he has not been taught any kind of useful occupation, makes him unsuitable as a husband. Indeed, the other characters often consider him effeminate and weak.

Themes

Ordinary People's Lives

At the time of its publication, *The Mill on the Floss* received critical attention, both good and bad, because it was one of the first novels to consider the lives and problems of middle-class English country people and to present their lives in great detail. Some readers of the time found this fascinating; others were repelled by the amount of time Eliot spent exploring the lives of "common" people. For example, Leslie Stephen, writing in *Cornhill Magazine* in 1881, wrote that no other writer had so clearly presented "the essential characteristics [of quiet English country life]" and that she "has shown certain aspects of a vanishing social phase with a power and delicacy unsurpassed." On the other hand, W. L. Collins, writing in *Blackwood's Edinburgh Magazine* in 1860, wrote that the novel was drawn "from the worst aspect of the money-making middle class—their narrow-minded complacent selfishness, their money-worship, their petty schemes and jealousies."

What all critics agreed on, however, was that Eliot drew a very accurate portrait of middle-class country people. No one in the book is wealthy, with the exception of Lawyer Wakem and Mr. Guest, and the characters' money is derived from their own work, not passed down from upper-class parents. Bob Jakin, the lower-class packman, is vividly portrayed, largely through his entertaining dialogue, but also through his generosity. When Eliot describes the Tullivers sitting down to tea or a conference of all the aunts and uncles, she shows them interacting and lets readers hear their conversation, which is presented with great wit and accuracy and sums them up by noting:

> There were particular ways of doing everything in [the Dodson] family: particular ways of bleaching the linen, of making the cowslip wine, curing the hams, and keeping the bottled gooseberries. . . . Funerals were always conducted with peculiar propriety in the Dodson family: the hatbands were never of a blue shade, the gloves never split at the thumb, everybody was a mourner who ought to be, and there were always scarfs for the bearers. . . . A female Dodson, when in 'strange' houses, always ate dry bread with her tea, and declined any sort of preserves, having no confidence in the butter, and thinking that the preserves had already begun to ferment for want of the sugar and boiling.

Later, she describes the materialistic and shallow people of St. Ogg's:

> One sees little trace of religion [among these people], still less of a distinctively Christian creed. Their belief in the Unseen, so far as it manifests itself at all, seems to be rather of a pagan kind; their moral notions, though held with strong tenacity, seem to have no standard beyond hereditary custom.

Eliot also portrays the life of the countryside: farmers, like the Mosses, working to survive; Luke, the simple miller; housewives buying goods from packmen like Bob Jakin; more prosperous people building up their businesses; and boatmen on the river.

Individual versus Society

Maggie Tulliver is an extremely intelligent and energetic girl who by nature is perpetually at odds with the narrow-minded, conservative, and restrictive culture she lives in. Throughout the book, she is torn between resisting social conventions and obeying them. Even as a child, she does not fit the model of the proper girl: she is untidy, disobedient, hot-tempered, and highly intelligent. There's really no place for her; her mother is embarrassed by her and despairs of ever getting her to behave like other girls, and, as Mr. Tulliver makes clear, most men want to marry a woman who is, if not exactly stupid, at least not intelligent enough to challenge them. Both her parents regard her as somewhat "unnatural" because of her unusual traits.

Maggie's brother Tom is the personification of the family and social values Maggie struggles against. She tries to reconcile her own personal freedom and inner nature with Tom's narrow and controlling ideas about what is right for her and the family. Unlike her brother, she is interested in

Topics for Further Study

- In the book, Maggie is torn between obeying her brother's often selfish wishes and choosing her own happiness. Which do you think is more important: obeying the wishes of parents and family or choosing your own life, even when they disagree with it? If your parents or brother threatened to disown you because of a choice you made, what would you do?

- Research the use of water-powered mills, like the one in the book, to grind grain. When were such mills invented? How did they work? When did their use begin to fade, and why?

- In the book, Maggie is highly intelligent, yet instead of being considered smart, she is viewed as "unnatural" by her father and others. How have attitudes toward women's education and intelligence changed over the years since 1860?

- Tom makes money by investing in goods, which a sailor then sells on his voyages overseas. Investigate seafaring trade practices of the mid-1800s. Was this sort of investment common? Was it risky or a sure thing for Tom to do this?

books and learning and is sensitive to music and art. However, these interests are not much encouraged by her family or others.

When Maggie visits Tom's school, she asks Reverend Stelling if she could study geometry and Latin, as Tom is doing. Although it's obvious to the reader that she has a natural gift for learning and is much more intelligent than Tom, Stelling says scornfully that although women "have a great deal of superficial cleverness . . . they couldn't go far into anything." Maggie is crushed by this comment, and Tom is triumphant. Maggie is also confused because she has been called "quick" all her life and has thought this quickness desirable but now, because of Stelling's remark, thinks that perhaps this "quickness" is simply a mark of her female shallowness and inferiority of mind: she's doomed never to succeed. Eliot writes, "Maggie was so oppressed by this dreadful destiny that she had no spirit for a retort."

Later in the book, Maggie gets into trouble because of her deep desire to love and be loved. No one in her family, least of all Tom, truly understands her or loves her unconditionally, so she is deeply gratified by the attention Philip and Stephen give her. However, she is also conflicted about their attention because her relationship with Philip is considered shameful by her family and, in the case of Stephen, it's considered scandalous by everyone.

By the end of the book, she is so trapped by these conflicting urges—to give in to others, do what they want, and live an unfullfilling life, or to do as she pleases and lose her family and friends—that there is seemingly no way out except death. When she dies in the flood, the conflicts are over, and she is united with her brother again. However, this is not a real solution; if she had survived the flood, it's obvious that her unity with Tom could never have lasted.

Style

Dialect

A notable feature of Eliot's writing is her use of local dialect in dialogue to express her characters' educational and social class. For example, Mr. Tulliver tells his wife, "What I want is to give Tom a good eddication. . . . I should like Tom to be a bit of a scholard, so as he might be up to the tricks o' these fellows as talk fine and write with a flourish." Mr. Riley, who is an auctioneer and somewhat better educated, does not use dialect when he tells Tulliver, "There's no greater advantage you can give him than a good education. Not that a man can't be an excellent miller and farmer, and a shrewd sensible fellow into the bargain, without much help from the schoolmaster."

Bob Jakin, who is of an even lower class than the Tullivers, uses more marked dialect; for example, when he is discussing a reward he received for putting out a fire, he says, "It was a fire i' Torry's mill, an' I doused it, else it 'ud ha' set th' oil alight; an th' genelman gen me ten suvreigns—he gen me 'em himself last week."

Mrs. Tulliver uses dialect when she says that Maggie seems crazy or stupid, because when she sends Maggie upstairs to get anything, "She forgets what she's gone for, an' perhaps 'ull sit on the floor i' the sunshine an' plait her hair an' sing to herself like a Bedlam creatur.'"

However, Eliot shows the reader that Maggie is actually acutely intelligent. Maggie never uses dialect, even in the beginning of the book when she is very young, is not yet educated, and would be expected to talk like her parents. Her first comment in the book, after her mother asks her to sit and sew, is "Oh, mother, I don't *want* to do my patchwork." She adds, "It's foolish work—tearing things to pieces to sew 'em together again. And I don't want to do anything for my aunt Glegg—I don't like her." This clarity of expression in such a small child is clearly meant to show Maggie's notable intelligence as well as her difference from her family.

Dialect was often used by writers in Eliot's time, but as Lynda Mugglestone wrote in *Review of English Studies*, Eliot's use of dialect to characterize speakers is particularly notable for its accuracy, subtlety, and clarity.

Foreshadowing

Throughout the novel, Eliot repeatedly refers to the river, reminding the reader of its power and hinting at the catastrophic flood to come in the final chapters. She describes its many moods and repeatedly cautions that the river has flooded before and may flood again; when the flood does occur at the end of the book, it is almost expected.

In the book's first sentence, Eliot describes the river "hurrying between its green banks to the sea, and the loving tide, rushing to meet it, checks its passage in an impetuous embrace." The contrast between the placid countryside and the power of the river, which runs the mill where much of the action is centered, makes the reader aware that the river is tamed, but perhaps not perfectly.

Later, Eliot mentions "the rushing spring-tide, the awful Eagre, come up like a hungry monster," and describes how Maggie thinks of "the river over which there is no bridge" described in Bunyan's *Pilgrim's Progress* as a symbol of death. In addition, in this chapter, Mrs. Tulliver fears that Maggie has drowned when she is late coming home.

Eliot also presents a legend of the patron saint of St. Ogg's, a boatman who operated a ferry on the Floss. One stormy night, a woman carrying a child wanted to cross the river, but no one would take her because of the danger. Ogg ferried her across, and when she reached shore, her clothes became flowing white robes and she was revealed to be the Blessed Virgin. She blessed Ogg, giving him the ability to save many lives when the river flooded. When he died, his boat floated out to sea, but his ghost could still be seen during floods, ferrying the Blessed Virgin over the water. However, Eliot notes that the people of St. Ogg's have largely forgotten this tradition, as well as their faith; they are more interested in money and image. This implies that they have also forgotten how dangerous the river is and in their arrogance assume that nothing can touch them.

Later, Eliot writes that the river "flowed and moaned like an unresting sorrow." This hints at the sorrow to come.

Near the end of the novel, when Stephen has taken Maggie too far down the river to respectably return without being married, he tells her, "See, Maggie, how everything has come without our seeking—in spite of all our efforts. . . . See how the tide is carrying us out—away from all those unnatural bonds that we have been trying to make faster round us—and trying in vain. It will carry us on. . . . and [we will] never pause a moment till we are bound to each other, so that only death can part us."

Maggie is swayed by this argument, thinking that she might "glide along with the swift, silent stream, and not struggle any more." This view of the results of marriage sounds more like a description of death than matrimony and foreshadows later developments, when Maggie and Tom are carried away in the flood; instead of being parted by death, as Maggie and Stephen would have been, they are forever united in it.

Historical Context

Education

Schools run by the state did not exist in England until 1870. Before that time, parents could send their children to any of four different types of school: private, endowed, church, and ragged. Anyone could open a private school, and no particular qualifications were required, so these schools varied greatly depending on the skill of the teachers. In *The Mill on the Floss*, the Reverend Stelling's school is a private arrangement, and as Eliot shows, Stelling is obviously not a very gifted teacher. Endowed schools were provided money by wealthy people, often as charity ventures and usually had more supervision of teachers. The Church of England, as well as other religious groups, also ran schools. Ragged schools were established by the

Ragged School Union, founded in 1844, to educate the poor.

Women often did not attend school, but those in the wealthier classes had private governesses who schooled them in ladylike "accomplishments" such as painting, drawing, and music.

Roles of Women

In the mid-nineteenth century, women were expected to marry and have children. Because they were not allowed to enter any jobs other than menial ones, they were dependent upon either their parents or husbands for money. In addition, because money and property were inherited only through males, it was almost impossible for a woman to be single and financially independent even if she had wealthy parents, because her brothers or male cousins would inherit everything from them, leaving her without an income. Those who, like Maggie, did not have wealthy parents and were not married had to find work, but their need to work was regarded as somewhat shameful, both for them and for their families. Maggie planned to become a governess; other work available to women included washing clothes, factory work, farm labor, domestic service, sewing, and prostitution.

Women were considered the property of men; a girl belonged to her father until she married, after which she belonged to her husband. A woman had no legal rights; even if someone committed a crime against her, she could not prosecute. Instead, her husband would prosecute the crime as an offense against his property. Women did not have parental rights, so a husband could take his wife's children and send them to relatives or elsewhere to be raised without her consent. If a woman entered the marriage with an inheritance, it became her husband's when they married, and he could spend it on anything he pleased. Women could not obtain divorces, even if their husbands were abusive or unfaithful, and if they ran away, they could be arrested, brought back to their husbands, or imprisoned.

All of these laws and customs made life very difficult for women who, like Maggie Tulliver, found it hard to fit the mold of quiet and submissive womanhood. Nevertheless, some women did rebel against these strictures; George Eliot, who lived with George Henry Lewes without being married to him, was one of them.

The Industrial Revolution

Beginning in the mid-eighteenth century, new inventions in agriculture, textile spinning and

Compare
&
Contrast

- **1860:** Most professions are closed to women, who are expected to marry and have children. Those in the poorer classes must do menial labor, and any money they make is legally their husbands' property.

  Today: Women can choose almost any career they desire, including professions such as law and medicine; they can join the armed forces and can expect to see combat; and they are free to enter traditionally male-dominated fields, such as business, construction, and many others.

- **1860:** Women are given less education than men, or are educated in vastly different subject areas than men, and are not allowed to attend universities.

  Today: Women and men have equal educational opportunities.

- **1860:** Women do not have the right to vote.

  Today: The Twentieth Amendment to the Constitution, giving women the right to vote, was passed in 1920.

- **1860:** When a woman marries, all her property becomes her husband's, and in her wedding vows, she must promise to obey her husband in all things.

  Today: Women retain legal access to their own property after marriage, and the word "obey" is not a requirement in wedding vows.

---

weaving, iron making, and energy generation led to immense changes in the economy and society. By the mid-nineteenth century the Industrial Revolution was transforming England from a rural economy and culture to an urban one based on factories and industry. The growth in factories led to more jobs for working-class people, but it forced them to move to the cities, where the factories were located. This resulted in a population drain in rural areas and unhealthy overcrowding in cities, where sanitation, housing, and medical facilities were often inadequate for the growing masses of workers. Because there were so many potential workers, employers paid very low wages, did not pay sick or injured workers, and fired anyone who complained. Children as young as six years of age worked long hours in the factories, side by side with adults, but received much lower wages. In addition, because parents and children of poor families often worked, children received little or no supervision and family life suffered. In the countryside, the old system of village and church community began to break down as people moved to the cities to find work.

The Industrial Revolution resulted in a huge growth in the goods that were available to poor and middle-class people, because factory production made textiles, pottery, and other items affordable. In addition, the boom in jobs meant that some people were able to learn useful skills, get some education, save money, and become members of the expanding middle class.

Critical Overview

In an 1860 issue of the *Saturday Review*, a reviewer commented that *The Mill on the Floss*, in comparison to Eliot's earlier novel *Adam Bede*, "shows no falling off nor any exhaustion of power." The reviewer also compared Eliot's "minuteness of painting and a certain archness of style" to the work of Jane Austen and the "wide scope of her remarks, and her delight in depicting strong and wayward feelings" to the work of Charlotte Brontë. According to this reviewer, Eliot's greatest achievement in the novel is that "for the first time in fiction, [she has] invented or disclosed the family life of the English farmer, and the class to which he belongs." By using local dialect, vivid characterization, and occasional comedy, Eliot engenders trust in the reader. In addition, the reviewer commented, she "is full of

Griffith Jones as Stephen Guest and Geraldine Fitzgerald as Maggie Tulliver in the 1937 film portrayal of The Mill on the Floss

meditation on some of the most difficult problems of life," such as the destinies, possibilities, and spiritual situation of all her characters. However, the reviewer disliked Eliot's emphasis on painful circumstances, her occasional overemphasis of moral issues, and her occasional discursiveness.

In that same year, a reviewer wrote in *Blackwood's Edinburgh Magazine* that the novel was "incontestably superior" to *Adam Bede*, because readers are brought to know the characters so intimately that they cannot help reading steadily to the end of the story. The reviewer noted, "And the interest, when once fairly started, though not rapid, never flags." The reviewer praised Eliot's characterization, use of middle-class protagonists, and her unobtrusive moral message.

I. M. Luyster wrote in *Christian Examiner* in 1861 that "since half the book is devoted to the childhood of the principal characters, it loses with some readers a portion of its interest as a romance." He also objected to Eliot's occasional use of "gratuitous vulgarity, for which the author is solely responsible," which, he noted, was "a great blemish, especially in a woman's book." However, he wrote, this vulgarity seldom appears in *The Mill on the Floss* and then only in some of the characterizations.

Leslie Stephen wrote in 1881 in *Cornhill Magazine* that Eliot was "one of the very few writers of our day to whom the name 'great' could be conceded with any plausibility."

By 1901, however, Eliot's reputation had declined. In *Victorian Prose Masters*, W. C. Brownell wrote that this was probably because turn-of-the-century readers were not interested in Eliot's psychological analysis of characters, and he remarked, "We have had a surfeit of psychological fiction since George Eliot's day." Thus, even though Eliot was "at the head of psychological novelists," her work did not garner the praise it deserved. He summed up, "No other novelist gives one such a poignant . . . sense that life is immensely serious, and no other . . . is surer of being read, and read indefinitely, by serious readers."

In *Reference Guide to English Literature*, Walter Allen wrote that Eliot "is probably over-rated" in England but remarked that "in critical estimation she leads all other Victorian novelists and is seen as the one nineteenth-century English novelist who can be mentioned in the same breath as Tolstoy."

Lettice Cooper, in *British Writers*, wrote that the book "has both the strength and the weakness of an autobiographical novel. There is no more vivid picture in English fiction of the sorrows and sufferings of a child." The book's weakness, according to Cooper, is that in depicting Maggie, Eliot did not have enough objectivity about Maggie's character, but at the same time, this gives her portrait of Maggie increased "freshness and intensity." However, Cooper praised the novel's "superb setting of English family life, narrated . . . with humor and shrewd observation." She also noted, "The Dodsons are the very marrow of the English middle class of the last century, a tradition that still survives."

Criticism

Kelly Winters

Winters is a freelance writer. In this essay, Winters considers the conflict between self-realization and acceptance in Eliot's novel.

In *Studies in the Novel*, June Skye Szirotny commented that, of all Eliot's works, only in *The Mill on the Floss* does she "explore the conflict between self-realization and acceptance that makes for the ambivalence at the heart of all her fiction—ambivalence that she will set herself to resolve in the rest of her fiction."

This ambivalence runs, like the River Floss, throughout the novel and is the heart of Maggie's conflict with her family and society. It is made worse by the fact that "acceptance" or "love" is rarely given freely by the other characters in the book; it is always conditional. In effect, her family lets Maggie know that "[o]nly if you behave as you're supposed to will we love and accept you."

When Maggie can't or won't behave as her family wants her to, they label her as "unnatural" and threaten to stop loving her. When Mrs. Tulliver insists that Maggie curl her hair, Maggie douses her head in a basin of water, putting an end to the question of curls. Her mother threatens that if her aunts hear about this, "they'll never love you any more." When Tom finds out that she has forgotten to feed his rabbits, he says, "I don't love you, Maggie" and becomes cold to her. In fact, whenever she does anything that displeases him, either he tells her he doesn't like her any more and that he likes someone else (usually their cousin Lucy) instead or he simply walks away from her. Later in the book he goes farther, saying he will hate her if she doesn't do as he says. Arrogantly,

he tells her, "You might have sense enough to see that a brother, who goes out into the world and mixes with men, necessarily knows better what is right and respectable for his sister than she can know herself. You think I am not kind; but my kindness can only be directed by what I believe to be good for you." In other words, his love is conditional; he will only love her if she obeys him. In addition, it is purely self-serving; in the first section of the book, Eliot makes this very clear when she comments:

> Tom, indeed, was of [the] opinion that Maggie was a silly little thing—all girls were silly.... Still he was very fond of his sister, and meant always to take care of her, make her his housekeeper, and punish her when she did wrong.

In fact, there is almost no one in the world who loves Maggie as she is, rambunctious behavior, intelligence, and all; everyone around her is constantly trying to mold her and withdrawing from her when they are unable to do so. Only Bob Jakin, who chivalrously brings Maggie gifts and takes her in after her disastrous boat ride, and Lucy, who kindly schemes to bring her and Philip together, have no self-serving motives when it comes to Maggie. They are truly her friends and are only interested in helping her find happiness.

However, her family has a big impact on her, and these two friends can't make up for her family's lack of understanding. Because of her family's attitude toward her, Maggie lives under a constant threat of disapproval and abandonment. This is especially hard for her because she has a loving nature; she is described as being "as dependent on kind or cold words as a daisy on the sunshine or the cloud." Because of her strong need to be loved and her sadness when any love is withdrawn, she is often willing to do anything to gain approval from Tom and others. Eliot comments at the beginning of the novel:

> It is a wonderful subduer, this need of love—this hunger of the heart—as peremptory as that other hunger by which Nature forces us to submit to the yoke, and change the face of the world.

Maggie loves Tom far more than he loves her, and she falls into despair when he does not approve of her. He, on the contrary, does not care what she thinks of him; it would never even occur to him to wonder what's on her mind.

Eliot writes that Tom was the one person of whom Maggie was most afraid:

> . . . afraid with that fear which springs in us when we love one who is inexorable, unbending, unmodifiable—with a mind that we can never mould our-

selves upon, and yet that we cannot endure to alienate from us.

She is thus placed in a no-win situation: if she does as he wants, she will be miserable; if she goes against him, she will suffer through losing him.

In addition to her fear of losing Tom's love, Maggie also has a hearty dose of self-blame; she blames herself for the estrangement and strife between her and Tom, even though, to the reader, he appears to be largely responsible for it because of his narrow-minded and controlling nature. Maggie has been taught to see herself as selfish when she seeks love and companionship with Philip, simply because her family would be upset to know she was associating with a Wakem. They demand that she sacrifice this chance for love, or even friendship, so that they can remain strong in their feud with the Wakem family. Like Tom, they never consider how this will affect her. Interestingly, Maggie never becomes angry at Tom or her family for trying to run her life or preventing her from seeing Philip; she simply assumes that they are right and she is wrong.

When Maggie goes down the river with Stephen, few people are sympathetic to her. Although she is actually blameless, she is vilified for shaming her family and Tom. Few people are particularly interested in finding out whether or not she is actually guilty of any illicit behavior. For example, Eliot writes that as Tom awaits news from her, he assumes she is guilty without knowing any facts:

> His mouth wore its bitterest expression, his severe brow its hardest and deepest fold.... Would the next news be that she was married—or what? Probably that she was not married; Tom's mind was set to the expectation of the worst that could happen—not death, but disgrace.

It is fascinating to note that Tom believes that "disgrace" would be worse than death; in effect, he would rather have Maggie die than have her be disgraced. Disgrace would reflect badly on him and his family, whereas death would not. This is yet another example of his extreme selfishness and rigidity.

When Maggie does return, Tom will have nothing to do with her, telling her she has disgraced the entire family and that she has been "a curse" to her best friends. He then disowns her, saying, "You don't belong to me," and he won't listen to her explanations and apologies. Although he says he will provide for her, he will not allow her to associate with him or to come under his roof.

> " In other words, his love is conditional; he will only love her if she obeys him."

This rejection is what Maggie has been dreading for her entire life. Typically, she does not defend herself; Eliot explains her behavior by saying she is "half-stunned—too heavily pressed upon by her anguish even to discern any difference between her actual guilt and her brother's accusations, still less to vindicate herself." Instead, she says weakly, "Whatever I have done, I repent it bitterly," and she apologizes. However, Tom will have none of it. "The sight of you is hateful to me," he tells her.

When a massive flood carries part of the mill away and leaves Tom stranded in their old house, Maggie is the only person who shows up to save Tom. For the first time in his life, he realizes that he has underestimated her and their relationship. Eliot writes that he was "pale with a certain awe and humiliation." It is the first time in the story that he has been deeply beaten or humiliated by anything. He calls her by his childhood nickname for her, "Magsie," and they come to an unspoken forgiveness and understanding, similar to the one they shared as children. They are close again, allies in the fight against the flood, instead of the adversaries they had become.

When a giant mass of debris rushes toward them on the fast-flowing river, their boat is smashed and driven under, and they both drown as they are holding each other "in an embrace not to be parted: living through again in one supreme moment, the days when they had clasped their little hands together and roamed the daisied fields together."

This "solution," with which Eliot wraps up Maggie's problems with her brother, her family, and society, is false, because it depends on Maggie's death. If Maggie and Tom had lived through the flood, he might have retained his new respect for her, but it's likely that he would not have. By nature, Maggie simply could never get along with Tom, no matter how self-sacrificing she tried to be; Eliot makes this very clear throughout the novel. Suppose Maggie had lived: what then? Would she have become Tom's housekeeper, as he had planned when they were children? If so, she would never marry, never have children, and would remain a servant to him for the rest of her life. This was Tom's dream, but was never hers. She could not marry Philip, or Stephen, and society's gossip and slander about her character would still remain, even though Stephen has written a letter explaining that she was not guilty of any misdemeanor. Victorian society was strict and unforgiving of girls and women who became involved in any scandal; as Eliot notes, even when she became a governess to Dr. Kenn's children, everyone in town slanders her, despite the knowledge of Stephen's exonerating letter. As Dr. Kenn tells her, "There is hardly any evidence which will save you from the painful effect of false imputations." He also advises her that human nature being what it is, people will never believe she is innocent.

Maggie's story is destined to be tragic: because of her perhaps mistaken love for her brother and her deep regard for her family, she stunts herself. When Maggie dies in the flood, she and her brother are united in a way they haven't been since childhood. However, it is not an adult connection of equals but a return and regression to a time when they were so young and their experiences so limited that they had no reason to quarrel. What Eliot does not do, and perhaps cannot do, given the society she lived in and her own struggles against slander and gossip, is provide an ending to the story in which Maggie lives through the flood and has a happy and productive life. Throughout the book, Maggie struggles with balancing self-realization and acceptance, but the ending of her story, instead of leading her to a solution of that problem, is a simple regression to a time when these problems did not exist.

Source: Kelly Winters, Critical Essay on *The Mill on the Floss*, in *Novels for Students*, The Gale Group, 2003.

Elizabeth Ermarth

In the following essay, Ermarth discusses the reality of the norms Maggie struggles to achieve throughout the novel.

George Eliot makes it clear in *The Mill on the Floss* that the social norms of St. Oggs exert a heavy influence on Maggie's development. This fact has long been obvious but less obvious, perhaps, is that fact that the norms Maggie struggles with are sexist. They are norms according to which she is an inferior, dependent creature who will never go far in anything, and which consequently are a denial of her full humanity. Years of such de-

nial teach Maggie to repress herself so effectively that she cannot mobilize the inner resources that might have saved her. By internalizing crippling norms, by learning to rely on approval, to fear ridicule and to avoid conflict, Maggie glows up fatally weak. In place of a habit of self-actualization she has learned a habit of self-denial which Philip rightly calls a "long suicide." Both she and Tom feel the crippling influence of these norms but we will focus here on Maggie and on how being female is an important key to her tragedy.

George Eliot said several times that the first part of this novel, which deals with Maggie's childhood development, had such importance for her that she devoted an amount of time to it that might seem disproportionate. Maggie's fate develops out of her social experience, particularly out of the local attitudes toward sex roles and out of the assumptions behind those attitudes. We can begin with the Dodsons' emphasis on rules and measuring and with their correlative faith in the clear difference between right and wrong.

The Dodsons' "faithfulness to admitted rules" results in two equally dangerous habits: an utter inability to question themselves and a correlative habit of questioning everybody else. The Dodson sisters have codified their need to feel "right" into a whole social and economic position. I am what I am, they say, because I am not that inferior thing. One is either a Dodson or not a Dodson, but the category of not-Dodson contains no valid or interesting possibilities. To be not-Dodson is simply to be wrong or at best unfortunate. Of course, the harmony established on the basis of such narrow exclusiveness is constantly threatened both from within by atrophy and from without by excluded forces. It is Mr. Tulliver's keen consciousness of being "right" that prompts him always to be "going to law" with his neighbors and finally to ruin himself and his family; it is Maggie's sense of being continually "wrong" and her need always to measure up to standards not her own, that encourages the disaster. However, during Maggie's childhood at least, the family and communal rules are strong by their very negations. Nearly everyone is bent on being "right": from little Lucy Deane with her perfect dress and demeanor to the Rev. Walter Stelling who teaches his pupils in the "right" way: indeed, the narrator tells us, "he knew no other."

This emphasis on rules and measuring connects naturally with a tendency to value the measurable, a tendency which is expressed in the materialism of St. Oggs, where most of the respectable citizens are in trade, and which finds its most grotesque elaboration in the Dodson sisters' household religion. Their peculiar view of human priorities puts a premium on physical manifestations and leaves little room for deviation. The important differences between people are usually physical, as with the Dodson kinship which is an affinity of blood not spirit. "There were some Dodsons less like the family than others—that was admitted; but in so far as they were 'kin' they were of necessity better than those who were 'no kin.'" In a similar way the correct appearance and behavior for little girls is already established, too rigidly to allow for the internal, individual imperatives Maggie feels. Maggie's physical characteristics—her unruly hair, her unruly manners, her physical robustness as a young woman—all inappropriate for a Dodson girl, generally convince her relations that she is a "mistake of nature": a deformity just as surely as Philip Wakem with his hunchback.

The same logic of right and wrong that holds in social and economic matters also holds for the sexes. If one is either right or not right, of course the second alternative merely means to be wrong. In St. Oggs one is either male or not-male, and while there may be a way to be a proper female, in a deeper way to be not-male means merely to be wrong or inferior in some essential way. For a woman in this society to be "right" means accepting a place that is defined for inferior creatures, always adjunct to the more significant activities of men. As the hard-headed Wakem says bluntly, "We don't ask what a woman does—we ask whom she belongs to."

Most men in the novel have a deep, unselfconscious belief that they are innately superior to women, even to the women they most care about. Although Maggie is Mr. Tulliver's favorite child, he deplores her acuteness. In discussing the important question of a child's education he says of her simply, it's a pity she wasn't a boy, she is "too 'cute for a woman. . . . It's no mischief while she's a little 'un, but an over-'cute woman's no better nor a long-tailed sheep—she'll fetch none the bigger price for that." Both Mr. Tulliver and Stephen Guest look for a certain weakness when choosing their spouses. Mr. Tulliver confides to Mr. Riley, "I picked the mother because she wasn't o'er 'cute—being a good-looking woman, too an' come of a rare family for managing; but I picked her from her sisters o' purpose, 'cause she was a bit weak, like; for I wasn't agoin' to be told the rights o' things by my own fireside." Mr. Stephen Guest, the

> "Potentially she could develop a strong, flexible character, given her inclinations and her gifts; but actually she is preparing for disaster because she never has an opportunity to make her own choices or to develop her own judgment."

"odiforous result of the largest oil mill and the most extensive wharf in St. Oggs" (316), is a "patronising" lover who finds charm in silliness. When Stephen directs Lucy to sing "the whole duty of woman—'And from obedience grows my pride and happiness,'" his banter has a point. He chooses the wife "who was likely to make him happy," which means that he has a norm Lucy happens to fit, not that he derives his norm from knowing her qualities. "He meant to choose Lucy: she was a little darling, and exactly the sort of woman he had always most admired."

As a growing boy Tom struggles anxiously to be superior. For him equality is confusing and inferiority insupportable. He is baffled by Bob Jakin's different ways and standards and by the fact that he cannot assert mastery because Bob does not care for Tom's approval. Tom makes the most of his opportunities with Maggie, who does care. He feels the flattery of her emotional dependence on him and he gives his affection chiefly as a reward for submission. "He was very fond of his sister, and meant always to take care of her, make her his housekeeper, and punish her when she did wrong." When Tom takes an equal chance with Maggie for the unevenly divided jam-puff, he cannot accept either the fact that she wins the big half or the fact that she offered it to him anyway, so he turns the incident into another instance of Maggie's inferiority. She is made to feel that she is somehow mysteriously at fault: a "fact" she knows for certain because Tom withdraws his affection as punishment.

Tom's affections for his absent sister are strongest when his ego is most in jeopardy, under

What Do I Read Next?

- Eliot's *Silas Marner* (1861) is a story of alienation and betrayal that nevertheless has comedic elements.

- *Adam Bede*, which was hugely successful when Eliot published it in 1859, tells the story of Hetty Sorrel—a young woman who is seduced, has a baby, and neglects it so that it dies—and of Adam Bede, who loves her.

- *Middlemarch* (1872), widely considered Eliot's most ambitious work, presents a clash between individuals' aspirations and the limitations imposed on them by society.

- Eliot's *Daniel Deronda* (1876) tells the story of Daniel, an early Jewish activist in England.

- Charlotte Brontë's *Jane Eyre* (1847) tells the story of an orphan girl who becomes a governess in a mysterious household.

- In Thomas Hardy's *Tess of the D'Urbervilles* (1891), a rural woman is seduced by an unworthy man and is subsequently abandoned by her husband.

---

his tutelage at Mr. Stelling's. His difficulties with Euclid and Latin and the long lonely evenings crush his spirit and give him a "girl's susceptibility." "He couldn't help thinking with some affection even of Spouncer, whom he used to fight and quarrel with; he would have felt at home with Spouncer, and in a condition of superiority." When Philip Waken arrives it is even worse for Tom since Philip is much more accomplished, and so Tom is delighted when Maggie arrives to visit. Now he can measure his ability in Latin against her non-existent one. How important condescension to "girls" is to Tom, and how readily he gets corroboration in this from adults, appears in this exchange with Stelling:

"Girls can't do Euclid: can they sir?"

"They can pick up a little of everything, I daresay," said Mr. Stelling. "They've a great deal of superfi-

cial cleverness; but they couldn't go far in anything. They're quick and shallow."

Tom, delighted with this verdict, telegraphed his triumph by wagging his head at Maggie behind Mr. Stelling's chair. As for Maggie, she had hardly ever been so mortified. She had been so proud to be called 'quick' all her little life, and now it appeared that this quickness was the brand of inferiority. It would have been better to be slow, like Tom.

"Ha, ha! Miss Maggie!" said Tom, when they were alone; "you see it's not such a fine thing to be quick. You'll never go far in anything, you know."

And Maggie was so oppressed by this dreadful destiny that she had no spirit for a retort.

At the end of a scene like this Tom's prophecy promises to be self-fulfilling. Mr. Stelling, so long as he can patronize her actually enjoys her talk; and Tom actually learns through Maggie to take more interest in Latin. But neither Tom nor his teacher can admit to themselves that she has intellectual potential, and when Maggie demands recognition they resort to that old and effective cruelty, ridicule: Tom with conscious delight and Mr. Stelling, at his more advanced stage of masculine development, without thinking.

The women in the novel accept their place willingly. Lucy knows her lover thinks her silly and that he likes insipid women, but she does not think of challenging this view of her character. She is complacent in her "small egoisms" and "small benevolences," fond in her turn of patronizing dependent creatures like Mrs. Tulliver and even Maggie. The most Lucy's talents run to, given the limits of her options, is to manage and manipulate people by strategem into better dealings with one another: not a bad cause, perhaps, but in her case pitifully circumscribed. "I'm very wise," she tells her papa, "I've got all your business talents." She probably does, poor thing. Within her scope she manages but her scope is small and her influence peripheral to the real business of people's lives. She derives her strength from her security and hence does not dream of asserting herself.

Like Lucy, Mrs. Tulliver was a good child. She never cried, she was "healthy, fair, plump, and dull-witted; in short, the flower of her sex for beauty and amiability." She is like the early madonnas of Raphael, says the narrator (reminding us of the venerable age of this tradition of feminine virtue) with their "blond faces and somewhat stupid expression" who were probably equally as "ineffectual" as Mrs. Tulliver and Lucy. Mrs. Tulliver's view of the whole duty of women befits a Dodson sister: it is to make beautiful elderflower wine; it is to keep her clothes tidy so no one can speak ill of her, for she does not "wish anybody any harm" (implying with her usual logic that if she keeps her clothes neat she will somehow be wishing her neighbors well); it is to make pie fit to "show with the best" and to keep her linen "so in order, as if I was to die tomorrow I shouldn't be ashamed." As she concludes with unwitting penetration, "a woman can do no more nor she can."

Maggie, too, learns the family pieties, though not so willingly. She is strong enough to be suffocated by her narrow life, but not strong enough to escape it. Responsive and flexible, she resents the narrow restrictiveness of her environment and she struggles valiantly against it. But because she is completely alone in this struggle her small force is too feeble to prevail. Her family's constant opposition to her aspirations gradually teaches her a habit of self-distrust which overpowers her better self and which perverts her energies. This habit is already well-developed on the morning she goes off to fish with Tom. "Maggie thought it probable that the small fish would come to her hook, and the large one to Tom's." Soon Tom sees she has one and he whispers excitedly,

> "Look, look Maggie", and came running to prevent her from snatching her line away.

> Maggie was frightened lest she had been doing something wrong, as usual.

The family pieties, unflattering though they are and in conflict with her inner imperatives, are inseparable from her sense of identity. She feels she must be wrong, not according to any standard of her own but according to some external authority which she barely understands and yet which, as a child, she implicitly trusts more than she trusts herself.

She has already learned to defer to others in place of developing a sense of her own authority; hence what she learns to fear most is the withdrawal of approval. In the jam-puff episode this is Tom's device for enforcing her submission and he has learned it from his elders. Maggie's mother uses the same device to control her troublesome daughter. On the morning Tom is to be brought home from school, for example, Maggie is prevented from going along because the morning was too wet "for a little girl to go out in her best bonnet." When Maggie tries to assert herself against these unfair restrictions by ducking her curls in water, she gets the following response: "'Maggie, Maggie,' exclaimed Mrs. Tulliver, sitting stout and helpless with the brushes on her lap, 'what is to become of you if you're so naughty: I'll tell your aunt Glegg

and your aunt Pullet when they come next week, and they'll never love you any more.'" Of course, Maggie and Tom are none too fond of their aunts—their mother says this is "more natu-ral in a boy than a gell"—but the important point is that Maggie is threatened with the withdrawal of approval or love as punishment for being the wrong kind of little girl. She is referred to a standard she does not accept or understand (the value of her aunts' love) and for which her own mother will betray her or "tell" on her.

Insulting behavior causes dependency, as Bernard Paris has shown in his "Horneyan analysis" of Maggie's neurosis. With her pride constantly knocked away from under her, Maggie responds by becoming self-effacing and dependent, buying her identity at the price of her autonomy. The narrator suggests in the first Book that "the dark-eyed, demonstrative, rebellious girl may after all turn out to be a passive being compared with this pink-and-white bit of masculinity with the indeterminate features." If Maggie wants to be accepted she must learn to submit to the control of others who will then reward her obedience with affection. Without this affection Maggie has no identity, and so it happens that "the strongest need in poor Maggie's nature" develops, the "need of being loved."

As a child Maggie has no adult reserve about her feelings so it is then that her need to be loved is most apparent. Tom has no sooner arrived from school than he is teasing her and she is having to beg, "*Please* be good to me". When he wants to punish her for not being sure his rabbits were fed, he says, "I'm sorry I brought you the fish-line. I don't love you". And Maggie begs: "'O, please forgive me, Tom; my heart will break,' said Maggie shaking with sobs, clinging to Tom's arm, and laying her wet cheek on his shoulder. . . . What was the use of anything, it Tom didn't love her?" Alone in her attic, just as "her need of love had triumphed over her pride" and she is going down "to beg for pity" she hears Tom's step on the stair. "Her heart began to beat violently with the sudden shock of hope. He only stood still at the top of the stairs and said, 'Maggie, you're to come down.' But she rushed to him and clung round his neck sobbing, 'O Tom, please forgive me—I can't bear it—I will always be good—always remember things—do love me—please dear Tom!'" Her need for love, inculcated by her bitter experience, overthrows her pride so completely that it also overthrows her integrity. She cannot exercise independent judgment. She will promise to be something she cannot be

Book illustration depicting Tom and Maggie being overwhelmed by the flood from Mill on the Floss

(always good, always remember things): anything, so long as the essential support is not withdrawn. Her need for love is a morbid dependency, and Tom uses it to master her, threatening to hate her if she is not just what he requires.

Maggie's dependency is re-inforced continually by ridicule and disapproval. When she shows her precious picture book to Mr. Riley she has the sense, not that he thinks the *book* silly but that *she* was "silly and of no consequence." No matter what Maggie does on her own initiative she usually regrets it. For example, on the visit to aunt Pullet, while Lucy characteristically waits without eagerness until she's told to eat, Maggie "as usual" becomes fascinated by a print of Ulysses, drops her cake underfoot, and earns the general disapprobation once again. The next minute, when the musical snuff-box excites her feelings, she runs to hug Tom and spills his wine.

> "Why don't you sit still, Maggie?" her mother said, peevishly.
>
> "Little gells mustn't come to see me if they behave in that way," said aunt Pullet.
>
> "Why, you're too rough, little miss," said uncle Pullet.

Poor Maggie sat down again, with the music all chased out of her soul, and the seven small demons all in again."

When she resolves on a "decided course of action" in regard to her troublesome hair and cuts it all off, she is again met with disapproval and ridicule. "She didn't want her hair to look pretty—that was out of the question—she only wanted people to think her a clever little girl, and not to find fault with her." But Tom's response brings an "unexpected pang" of regret. "'Don't laugh at me, Tom,' said Maggie, in a passionate tone, with an outburst of angry tears ...'" The impulsiveness of her actions and the rapidity of her regret seem to be consequences of her persistent sense of inferiority, a sense which is further re-inforced on this occasion. She is met in the dining room with "a chorus of reproach and derision" so that, when Tom unexpectedly adds his own, "her feeble power of defiance left her in an instant, her heart swelled, and, getting up from her chair, she ran to her father, hid her face on his shoulder, and burst out into loud sobbing." Nearly the only source of sweetness in her early life comes when she throws herself on this source of support, never from her own powers, which only bring her ridicule and shame. The love she gets is nearly always payment for humiliation. It is not surprising, then, that she learns to distrust her own powers and to develop a fatal sense of the sweetness of submission.

Maggie's rapid shift from defiance to despair suggest the fatal instability that is developing in her. Potentially she could develop a strong, flexible character, given her inclinations and her gifts; but actually she is preparing for disaster because she never has an opportunity to make her own choices or to develop her own judgment. Whatever she attempts, the withdrawal of approval is so great a threat—almost an ontological threat—that she cannot proceed in the face of contradiction. In her later struggles with St. Oggs Maggie does not struggle like Antigone to hold her own against social norms because, in a fundamental way, she has no force of her own. She has assimilated the social norms and if she fights against them she must fight against herself. *She* believes the lie, that she is inferior, or wrong, or not to be taken seriously. She has learned to collaborate in her own defeat.

The same self-defeating habits occur in the second stage of her life, when Maggie must face the family disaster and when she establishes important relationships outside her family (with Philip and Stephen). As a child Maggie gives up her will for the reward of acceptance and affection; after the downfall when her family seem like strangers and she is driven more into herself she develops a new rationale for the old habit, she gives up things on prinicple. It is perfectly in keeping with her childhood need to be loved that an adolescent Maggie resolves to meet the family misfortune by "plans of self-humiliation and entire devotedness" (notice the familiar connection between devotion and the necessity for self-humiliation). She succeeds so well that her mother is amazed "that this once 'contrary' child was become so submissive, so backward to assert her own will." But the motives are still what they were. As the narrator warned, her rebelliousness was weaker than her need to be loved and it has turned into a strange passivity. She *likes* to give up her will or, rather, to exert her will only against herself. She now can do to herself what others used to do to her, and it gives her the sense of being "right" for the first time in her life. Being "right" requires Maggie to turn against herself.

The morbidity of her so-called renunciation is obvious to Philip Wakem. She refuses even to read or hear music because "it would make me in love with this world again, as I used to be—it would make me long to see and know many things—it would make me long for a full life." Philip tells her she has "wrong ideas of self-conquest." "It is mere cowardice to seek safety in negations. No character becomes strong in that way. You will be thrown into the world some day, and then every rational satisfaction of your nature that you deny now will assult you like a savage appetite. . . . It is less wrong that you should see me than that you should be committing this long suicide." Philip's own self-interest in the matter does not invalidate the accuracy of his observations on her "wilful, senseless privation" and "self-torture." He perceives that the fatal weakness Maggie is cultivating is a form of suicide.

Of course self-privation suggests there is something of which to deprive herself. Unlike Lucy, who renounces personal desires so completely that she effectively has none, Maggie has desires that might be fulfilled. She is responsive to the appeal of books, of music, of conversation with Philip, and she feels her life growing again through these experiences. In particular she begins to feel need for a life outside love, as if she is beginning to understand that what she has called love is really a self-defeating, neurotic compulsion. "I begin to think there can never come much happiness to me from loving. I have always had so much pain mingled with it. I wish I could make myself a world outside it, as men do." A true prompting, this wish for a life outside affection. George Eliot wrote to her friend Mrs. Robert Lytton:

> We women are always in danger of living too exclusively in the affections; and though our affections are perhaps the best gifts we have, we ought also to have our share of the more independent life—some joy in things for their own sake. It is piteous to see the helplessness of some sweet women when their affections are disappointed—because all their teaching has been, that they can only delight in study of any kind for the sake of a personal love. They have never contemplated an independent delight in ideas as an experience which they could confess without being laughed at. Yet surely women need this sort of defense against passionate affliction even more than men.

The important themes of the novel are recapitulated here: the importance to a woman of a life outside love, the danger of ridicule in pursuing it, the unhealthiness of confinement to the affections. Maggie might have become a woman who, like Madame de Sablé, was a woman "men could more than love—whom they could make their friend, confidante, and counsellor; the sharer, not of their joys and sorrows only, but of their ideas and aims." But to make a life outside love one needs experience of actual dealings with the actual world, experience from which Maggie has always been cruelly "protected." Even in her statement to Philip it is clear that she has in mind vague hopes but no real alternative.

While Maggie's inner promptings to a wider life do exist, they are not stronger than her habit of self-denial as, I think, her rejection of Philip shows. Maggie obeys Tom's insistence that she break with Philip ostensibly out of duty to her father, but there may be some argument about her motives. She feels an unaccountable relief when her relations with Philip are cut off, a relief which seems to me to have reference to the demands Philip has been making on her: that she be herself and trust her interests. But responsibility for herself is something she has learned to avoid, and so her relief seems a clear assertion of an old reluctance to assert herself and not, as has been thought, a sexual repulsion to Philip. George Eliot has spent most of her time showing that Maggie is not chiefly a sexual creature but a social creature, and so it is plausible, given the whole direction of the novel, that Maggie is simply glad the inner conflict and need for decision are over.

Much as she may wish for a life outside love, the undertow of her dependency is too strong a force with her, preventing her from dealing with the conflicts of adult life. Her clandestine association with Philip, which by definition is a separate reality from her home life, inevitably results in a conflict with her family once the protection of secrecy disappears. Yet she is emotionally unprepared to accept the fact that her two worlds are separate and unreconcilable. Tom says that since she can do nothing in the world she should "submit to those that can," still assuming that it is her nature to depend and be capable of nothing. Maggie cries, "you are a man, Tom, and have power, and can do something in the world"; but these poignant words are lost on Tom Tulliver and, with Maggie's acquiescence he makes her choice for her, literally requiring her to speak the words he gives her: "'Do as I require,' said Tom. 'I can't trust you, Maggie. There is no consistency in you. Put your hand on this Bible, and say, "I renounce all private speech and intercourse with Philip Wakem from this time forth."'" Maggie gives her word, although in this context it hardly can be called hers. Her private reflections after this scene reveal how fully she wishes to escape from conflicts she cannot resolve:

> She used to think in that time that she had made great conquests, and won a lasting stand on serene heights above worldly temptations and conflict. And here she was down again in the thick of a hot strife with her own and others' passions. Life was not so short, then, and perfect rest was not so near as she had dreamed when she was two years younger. There was more struggle for her—perhaps more falling. If she had felt that she was entirely wrong, and that Tom had been entirely right, she could sooner have recovered more inward harmony....

She would rather be "wrong" and submit to the "right" than to continue in a struggle she is un-equipped for, or to support the painful consciousness that she is responsible for defending a valid position, but that, at the same time, she is without the resources necessary to the task.

Maggie seems to acknowledge that this promise she made for Tom was not really hers when she asks him to release her from it, two years later. But the scene in which Tom gives her her freedom has a bitterly ironic quality, since it actually confirms in other ways how little strength she has for bearing freedom. "When Maggie was not angry, she was as dependent on kind or cold words as a daisy on the sunshine or the cloud: the need of being loved would always subdue her, as, in old days, it subdued her in the worm-eaten attic." It subdues her again. Tom releases her, but with resentment and criticism. She sees the "terrible cutting truth" in Tom's remark that she has "no judgment and self-command" without seeing that

this is true because she has always been commanded, that even now she is seeking to be commanded to do what she herself wants to do. Her one clear response, through the confusion of inner voices which condemn both herself and Tom, is despair at being shut out from acceptance by Tom.

The same weakness for substituting another's will for her own plays a crucial role in her relationship with Stephen, when she falls in love with him as well as when she leaves him. Initially she feels a sense of relief at being able to depend on Stephen, first when she slips in the boat and is supported by his firm grasp, and later when he takes her arm in the garden. "There is something strangely winning to most women in that offer of the firm arm: the help is not wanted physically at that moment, but the sense of help—the presence of strength that is outside them and yet theirs—meets a continual want of the imagination." Being used to treatment that is indifferent and preemptive, Maggie is more at the mercy of such flattery which, when it comes "will summon a little of the too-ready, traitorous tenderness into a woman's eyes, compelled as she is in her girlish time to learn her life-lessons in very trivial language." Maggie's love for Stephen is traitorous dependence because it fulfills her need to be supported from without, rather than from within, and it thus acts as one further encouragement to deny herself.

In the light of her development it seems clear that Maggie rejects Stephen out of the same weakness that made her accept him. She rejects him, not out of moral principle, but out of the same, deep-rooted, unhealthy instincts that made her give up Philip and music and books. Both Philip and Stephen ask in different ways that she assert her will against the wills of others and that is what she cannot do (of course, Stephen also asks for a personal submission to himself that Philip does not ask). Now, far from being a virtue in Maggie this unassertiveness is perverse. George Eliot makes it crystalline in her novels and letters and essays that one must not only learn to renounce (i.e., submit to actual conditions that cannot be changed) but also to act (i.e., shape the conditions that can be changed). One must even "dare to be wrong." So when Maggie returns to St. Oggs for the third time, when she clings to those who ostracize her, saying—"I have no heart to begin a strange life again. I should have no stay. I should feel like a lonely wanderer—cut off from the past"—George Eliot is not praising Maggie out of Maggie's own mouth for acting on principle or for respecting the past. While George Eliot valued those things, she also valued realism. Maggie is merely expressing her insistence on having what, by definition, she cannot have: acceptance of herself by her brother and by St. Oggs.

The confusion and ambivalence we feel so keenly in the final chapters reflects accurately Maggie's own confusion and ambivalence at the painful conflict in her life between aspiration and fact: "It is no moral philosophy that determines her decision, but a far deeper moral sense, which turns out to be hardly distinguishable from a sense of what she *is*. It is a clear recognition that there is no escape from what she is, however bitterly she might wish there were." This interpretation makes clear the essential importance of the full portrait of Maggie's childhood. It is not the happiness of her childhood that finally brings her down but the intensity of it. She speaks to Stephen of Philip's claims, yet neither she nor Philip ever recognized the kind of formal relationship she implies; she speaks of the past that sanctifies one's life, but we know her past has hardly done that; and finally, when Stephen presses her, her reasons disappear and she responds just as she did to the prospect of leaving St. Oggs: her "heart" won't let her. "'O, I can't do it,' she said, in a voice almost of agony—'Stephen—don't ask me—don't urge me. I can't argue any longer—I don't know what is wise; but my heart will not let me do it.'" The past is her "stay": from which it does not follow that for her this is the best, but merely that it is for her the case. She is still looking to the same source for resolution of conflict, for rest from the too-feeble effort that always seems to turn back on itself and achieve nothing. When she leaves Stephen her mind is

> unswervingly bent on returning to her brother, as the natural refuge that had been given her. In her deep humiliation under the retrospect of her own weakness—in her anguish at the injury she had inflicted—she almost desired to endure the severity of Tom's reproof, to submit in patient silence to that harsh disapproving judgment against which she had so often rebelled.... She craved that outward help to her better purpose which would come from complete, submissive confession—from being in the presence of those whose looks and words would be a reflection of her own conscience.

Given other conditions these instincts might not be entirely wrong (although the masochistic note here is hard to miss), but she has chosen the wrong object in Tom, and she perseveres, like the goldfish still endeavoring to swim in a straight line beyond the glass, in spite of the actual condition.

When Tom rejects her, she looks for some other "sure refuge" or stay to "guarantee her from falling," and lacking any, she only continues to vacillate between her conflicting feelings. She denies Stephen and then is inclined to yield because she begins to "doubt in the justice of her own resolve"; then, having decided to accept him, "close upon that decisive act her mind recoiled; and the sense of contradiction with her past self in her moments of strength and clearness came upon her like a pang of conscious degradation. No—she must wait . . . for the light that would surely come again." The confusion in interpreting this part of the novel is owing partly to Maggie's confusion. Her course is as erratic as a boat loose on the flood. Philip does have a claim, and so does Tom and even Stephen; but their claims conflict and Maggie has not learned the strength to do what she must, which is to choose one particular course and let another go. Her only instinct is to wait passively for help.

"'O God, where am I? Which is the way home?' she cried out, in the dim loneliness." In the flood, at night, her boat leaves its mooring at Bob Jakin's and floats away: a "transition of death" which is only the last in a series of fatal transitions which began in her childhood and which in a few moments will finally carry her under. As she floats and then rows towards home she is finally able to see the "light" she waited for: "the dawning seemed to advance more swiftly, now she was in action." What seems to be a dawning is a fatal illusion, because it is death she is heading for. Maggie is looking for a "reconcilement with her brother: what quarrel, what harshness, what unbelief in each other can subsist in the presence of a great calamity . . . ?" The undertow of dependency carries her back, and only with it can she act decisively: "as if her life were a stored-up force that was being spent in this hour, unneeded for any future."

The final scene where Tom reverts to the "childish" nickname for his sister, the scene which ends in a recollection of "the days when they had clasped their little hands in love, and roamed the daisied fields together" seems not saccharine and sentimental but, in light of the present interpretation, harsh and grim. Such sentimentality as there is echoes Maggie's longing for an impossible reconciliation. (When did they ever roam the fields in love?) And the words suggest that, since she was shaped to be a child by the family pieties, it is fitting that her life ends in a reversion to childhood where her energies to be an adult, tragically, are "unneeded."

George Eliot, born the same year as Maggie, left her brother Isaac, who was born the same year as Tom; she left her home of thirty years for London and despite the hard and lonely beginning she never went back. Maggie went back and her fate is the strongest possible argument and justification for doing the opposite: for doing precisely what George Eliot did in leaving her home behind. George Eliot does not try to disguise the tremendous difficulties in making the endless, painful effort required of such a woman, nor does she disguise the importance to such a woman of some support in making the effort; but in counterpoint she offers a grim warning as to the consequences of avoiding that effort. For Maggie the price of "feminine" affection and "feminine" self-sacrifice is suicide. Just as a fully human life is constituted of mind, imagination, and feeling, not only biological conditions, so equally, human death comes not only with the deprivation of oxygen but with the deprivation of mental, imaginative, and emotional life. Maggie's literal drowning is merely physical corroboration of the more important disaster.

Source: Elizabeth Ermarth, "Maggie Tulliver's Long Suicide," in *Studies in English Literature*, Vol. XIV, No. 4, Autumn 1974, pp. 587–601.

John Hagan

In the following essay excerpt, Hagan discusses what he considers the questionable interpretation of polarity in Mill on the Floss *by various critics.*

One of the reasons the critics I have been considering offer a questionable interpretation of the novel's tragic central subject is that they narrow the range of George Eliot's outlook and thus create a polarization which does not exist in the novel itself. Each reading ignores the explicit indication of her perspective which she provides near the beginning of Book IV, where, after explaining that she has been depicting the "oppressive narrowness" of Tom's and Maggie's environment in order that the reader may understand "how it has acted on young natures in many generations," she identifies the young natures with whom she is specifically concerned as those "that in the onward tendency of human things have risen above the mental level of the generation before them, to which they have been nevertheless tied by the strongest fibres of their hearts." Applied to Maggie, this passage makes clear that the yearnings for a wider life which spring from the fact that Maggie has "risen above the mental level of the generation before" her and the love which ties her to her brother, her father, and her past by "the strongest fibres of her

heart are to be regarded as *equally* legitimate, *equally* worthy of fulfillment. By not allowing that both kinds of need deserve satisfaction, that it would be best for Maggie if neither had to be sacrificed, one misses either the fact that her life is a tragedy, or the fact that the essential nature of that tragedy is one of having to choose between goals that are equally good but incompatible.

This incompatibility is not inherent in the goals themselves (the desire to marry Philip and the desire to remain loyal to Tom, for example, are not intrinsically irreconcilable), but is the result of circumstance. Nor is this circumstance chiefly "social," for to whatever degree the narrowness of thought and feeling which is characteristic of Maggie's social environment thwarts her desires, it comes to play upon her chiefly through the characters and actions of Tom and Tulliver. Maggie has intense desires for a full and rich life which Tom and Tulliver can neither comprehend nor sympathize with, but she is, at the same time, bound to them by a noble love which makes her renunciation of those desires morally necessary. From this situation spring directly or indirectly all the decisive frustrations of her life and hence the tragedy which is at the center of the novel. A detailed analysis of the structure of the plot will I believe, demonstrate this.

The first segment, which comprises Books I and II, centers on Maggie's late childhood and establishes the premises about her psychology and her relations to Tom, her father, and her society in general on which the rest of the novel depends. The major emphasis is placed on precisely those two aspects of her character and situation which, as I have just noted, are explicitly singled out at the beginning of Book IV: that is, her intellectual and spiritual superiority to her environment and the fact that she is "nevertheless tied" to this environment by "the strongest fibres" of her heart. On the one hand, extensive, primarily satirical portraits of her mother and her maternal aunts and uncles, who lack Maggie's sensitivity, and who habitually misunderstand, criticize, and reject her, make clear the degree to which her position in this society is an isolated and painful one. On the other hand, George Eliot shows that Maggie is dominated by a great need to love and be loved by Tom and Tulliver, which impels her to turn to them in times of trouble, and enables her to find in this uncomprehending and otherwise intolerable environment a spiritual home. The essential fact is that, during this period of her life, her father and brother reciprocate her love. This is why at the end of Book II, when Maggie's childhood is coming to an end, George Eliot can refer to it as having been an Eden, and why at the end of the novel the last thing Maggie remembers before she drowns is the time when she and Tom, like a kind of Adam and Eve, "had clasped their little hands in love, and roamed the daisied fields together." The point is not that Maggie's childhood is an unadulterated idyll (it obviously is not), but that this is the time when her need to be loved and accepted by her brother and father is most fully satisfied. It is true, of course, that even in this period Tom's need to love Maggie is much less than hers to love him. But it is also true that, in comparison to the later periods of her life, Maggie's childhood is the period of least frustration and greatest fulfillment. It becomes for her the touchstone of what her loving relations to her brother and father should be.

The relations to her brother, in particular, are defined most clearly by a series of parallel episodes which give Book I its structural backbone (the episode on the dead rabbits, of the jam-puff, of the haircutting, of the mud, and, climactically, of the gypsies) and in nearly every one of which there emerges a sequence of actions which dramatizes Maggie's hunger for Tom's love, the frustration of that hunger, her rebellion, and the pleasure she receives from reconciliation. At this period of her life such reconciliation and the consequent fulfillment of her need to be loved by her brother satisfy Maggie's deepest instincts. Her need to rebel is decidedly secondary, and is primarily a response to her brother's rejections. When Maggie's craving to love and be loved by her brother asserts itself, as sooner or later it always does, her desire to rebel is suppressed; and when that craving is satisfied, as sooner or later it always is, she is reconciled to her otherwise hostile environment.

In Book III, however, with the father's financial and mental collapse, begins the process which results in the cruel frustration of that craving and in the tragic search for alternative sources of fulfillment. This Book is thus the pivot on which the central action of the novel turns. Its title, "The Downfall," refers not only to the misfortunes which befall Tulliver, but to the fact that those misfortunes expel Maggie from the "Eden" of her childhood by progressively alienating from her the father's and brother's love on which she has come so deeply to depend.

Her initial inclination is to seek escape from her daily miseries by retreating into "wild romances of a flight from home . . . to some great man," like

> To ask why Maggie's first quest fails is to ask what has brought these circumstances into being."

Walter Scott, who would understand and "surely do something for her." Such fancies led her in childhood to seek compensation for Tom's rejection by running away to the gypsies. But this kind of solution will no longer work, for by now Tulliver's plight has inculcated Maggie with a strong sense of moral responsibility. The object of her first quest becomes, therefore, a way not of fleeing her world, but of enduring it, and the key ready to hand turns out, of course, to be Thomas à Kempis, in the spirit of whose philosophy of renunciation and resignation Maggie hopes to solve the problem of her frustrated desire for her father's and brother's love and for the happiness of her childhood by crushing that desire itself. This quest is the main subject of Book IV, Chapter iii.

That it fails—as the two different quests which follow it in Books V and VI will also fail—is clear. The crucial question is why it fails. In one sense, obviously, the fault is Maggie's: her longings for a happiness which will compensate for the emptiness of her life after her father's downfall are so great that the effort of renunciation becomes for her a source of that very happiness which she is supposedly renouncing. George Eliot's ironical attitude toward this piece of self-deception is quite explicit. Yet it is also true, as I have shown, that Maggie's longings arouse George Eliot's deepest sympathies. To deny their legitimacy would be to insist absurdly that she alter her very nature and completely subdue herself to the oppressive narrowness of the provincial world around her. Thus, it might seem to follow that the fault lies instead in Kempis' philosophy itself: Kempis' demand that legitimate yearnings such as Maggie's be suppressed is unnatural. Yet, again as I have shown, George Eliot's sympathy for this philosophy is as great as her sympathy for the passions it would deny. Under the circumstances, Maggie's attempt to live by it—to endure suffering rather than to seek escape in romantic daydreams—not only makes good sense, but is even morally noble. The issue, therefore, comes down to the existence of the circumstances themselves—circumstances which decree that what is morally noble should also be unnatural. To ask why Maggie's first quest fails is to ask what has brought these circumstances into being.

And the answer to that can only be the flaws in the characters of her father and brother. Maggie's frustration and her struggles to endure that frustration by means of renunciation are the direct consequences of Tom's and Tulliver's failure, at this stage in her life, to perceive, to understand, and to reciprocate her love. Were they to respond to her now as they did in her childhood, Maggie's happiness would be restored, and any futile attempts to deny her need for happiness would therefore no longer need to be made. But such a response has become impossible for them: their mutual hatred of Waken, their acute sense of disgrace, and their grim determination to restore the family fortunes imprison them in a world of gloomy obsessions from which Maggie is wholly excluded. The conflict which thus results is the conflict which appears in all George Eliot's novels—that between two radically different kinds of characters: on the one hand, the large-souled, who, like "all of us" (as George Eliot puts it in *Middlemarch*, Ch. xxi), are "born in moral stupidity, taking the world as an udder to feed our supreme selves," but are sensitive and imaginative enough ultimately to transcend this limitation and see that others possess "an equivalent center of self," and, on the other hand, the narrow-souled, who are incapable of this kind of vision, and remain permanently trapped in the confines of the egoistic self.

The conflict between these two kinds of characters which begins to emerge as the novel's central tragic issue in Book IV becomes even more intense, however, in Book V, when Maggie begins her second quest for fulfillment, the result of which is her involvement with Philip Wakem. The futility of her attempt to live by Kempis' philosophy which was demonstrated in Book IV by her self-deception is demonstrated even more clearly now, three years later, by the flaring-up of her erotic passion for "the only person who had ever seemed to love her devotedly, as she had always longed to be loved." Her need to love and to be loved by her father and brother and to win their approval remains as compelling and legitimate as ever; she continues to be bound to them by "the strongest fibres" of her heart. But now, partly because Tom and Tulliver continue to frustrate her demand, and partly because Maggie is going through a natural process of maturation, which, in accord with "the onward

tendency of human things," enables her to rise even farther "above . . . [their] mental level" than previously, this need is balanced by an equally strong, legitimate, and autonomous desire to find additional fulfillment from sources beyond them. Both kinds of fulfillment have become essential to her. Yet, because of the "moral stupidity" of Tom and her father, she will get neither. This is the basic tragic situation of the novel which now definitely takes shape.

The obvious solution to Maggie's hunger for a new life in Book V is for her and Philip to marry; she is nearly seventeen by this time, and he is twenty-one. Near the end of a year of secret meetings in the Red Deeps, she kisses him, admits that she loves him, confesses that she has found in him the greatest happiness since her childhood with Tom, and implicitly tells him that, though the thought is new to her, she would willingly marry him if there were no obstacle. But the crux of the situation is precisely that there *is* an obstacle, and that because of it her second quest proves as futile as the first. Superficially, of course, that obstacle is in Maggie herself—in her profound attachment to her father and brother, both of whom oppose not only marriage but even friendship between Maggie and Philip because of their long-standing hatred of Philip's father. If Maggie's attachment to them were not so deep, she could disregard the voice of her guilty conscience which urges her to renounce Philip, defy their ban, and find an escape from her frustration. But it does not follow from this that her attachment is wrong. George Eliot explicitly states that Philip's arguments for continuing to meet Maggie in the Red Deeps are "sophistry" and "subterfuge"; and she calls Maggie's "prompting against a concealment that would introduce doubleness into her own mind, and might cause new misery to those [Tom and Tulliver] who had the primary natural claim on her" a "true" prompting. Given Maggie's deep loyalty to her father and brother, and given George Eliot's complete sympathy with that loyalty, Maggie's scruples of conscience are wholly justified. The real obstacle to her fulfillment lies, as in her first quest, in the flawed characters of Tom and Tulliver, whose opposition to Philip springs from their narrow prejudice against Wakem and their complete failure to appreciate the depth of Maggie's need for a fuller life. The most active opposition comes, of course, from Tom, who cruelly forces upon Maggie an absolute choice between Philip and himself. Were it not for Tom's fanaticism, Maggie could be loyal to him and marry Philip at the same time; in themselves both goals are completely compatible and completely desirable. The necessity of choosing between them is an artificial one forced upon Maggie by Tom's insensitivity. The situation is very similar, indeed, to that in *Middlemarch*, when Mr. Casaubon cruelly contrives his will so as to force Dorothea to choose between inheriting his property and marrying Ladislaw (Ch. 1). As George Eliot sums up at the end of Book VI, Chapter xii, Tom belongs to a class of minds to which

> prejudices come as the natural food of tendencies which can get no sustenance out of that complex, fragmentary, doubt-provoking knowledge which we call truth. . . . however it [a prejudice] may come, those minds will give it a habitation: it is something to assert strongly and bravely, something to fill up the void of spontaneous ideas, something to impose on others with the authority of conscious right: it is at once a staff and a baton. Every prejudice that will answer these prejudices is self-evident.

The nature of the tragic contrast between the two kinds of characters represented by Maggie and Tom and its decisive effect on Maggie's destiny could hardly be spelled out more distinctly

By the middle of Book VI, however, the situation has been complicated by an additional factor: Maggie is reluctant to marry Philip not only because of Tom's continued opposition, but because of her growing attraction to Stephen Guest, whom she met at Lucy's home upon her return to St. Ogg's after her two years' absence as a governess, and whose admiration has become one of the chief causes of her renewed discontent. The two things with which Stephen is most frequently associated—music and the river—come to epitomize the irresistible force of the intoxication which she increasingly feels in his presence. To satisfy her newly aroused yearnings for love and life by surrendering herself to Stephen has now become, in fact, her third and final quest.

This quest fails, of course, no less than did the others. Maggie has to renounce Stephen, just as she renounced Philip, and, as a result, the frustration of her life reaches its tragic climax. The pattern of futile quests which has been taking shape since the last chapter of Book IV is thus logically completed and the novel's true central subject is fully defined. The relation of this failure to the two preceding ones, however, needs careful clarification. The first two quests failed, as we have seen, because of the flaws in the characters of Maggie's father and brother, who were unable to reciprocate her love and opposed her marriage to Philip. But the third quest fails for a different reason: Maggie gives up

Stephen, not (as in Philip's case) because she is intimidated into doing so and wishes to avoid betraying Tom and her father, but because of her own free choice and her desire not to betray Philip and Lucy, to whom she and Stephen are tacitly engaged. In this decision Tom plays no role whatsoever. Nevertheless, he is decisively related to the failure of Maggie's third quest in other ways which keep the conflict between him and Maggie—and, by implication, the larger conflict between the kinds of characters which they respectively represent—the tragic focal point of the novel to the very end.

To begin with, though Maggie renounces Stephen of her own free will, both her involvement with him in the first place and the great intensity of that involvement are direct consequences of the earlier renunciation of Philip which Tom virtually forced upon her. Philip's warning at the time—namely, that "'You will be thrown into the world some day, and then every rational satisfaction of your nature that you deny now, will assault you like a savage appetite'"—is precisely what happens later when she meets Stephen. Had she been able to marry Philip with Tom's approval in Book V, this tragic development would presumably have been impossible. Tom has helped to create the very predicament for which Maggie herself must pay the tragic price.

Moreover, almost equally influential in Maggie's destiny is the continuation of Tom's ban on Philip not only to the beginning of Book VI, but even to the end. The obvious solution to her suffering after her renunciation of Stephen at the end of Book VI would be to return to Philip and marry him, just as this was the obvious solution at the beginning of this Book, when she came back to St. Ogg's. Philip's letter clearly implies that if Maggie were to return to him, he would accept her. But, even if she were able to overcome her remorse and the infatuation she still strongly feels for Stephen, the insuperable barrier of Tom's ban on Philip would still remain. Tom's "bitter repugnance to Philip" is the same after the trip down the river as it was before—the same at the end of her final quest as it was at the beginning. The "something" for which Maggie had earlier hoped "to soften him" has still not occurred.

But the most important way in which Tom is related to the failure of Maggie's final quest is through his reaction to her renunciation itself. This reaction is, indeed, the central subject of all but the last chapter and the brief "Conclusion" of Book VII, a fact which strikingly differentiates this Book from the three preceding ones (which are centrally concerned with Maggie's quests themselves), and thus makes clear the decisive thematic significance George Eliot wishes to attach to it. Maggie's renunciation of Stephen is climactic: uncompelled by anything but the voice of honor and conscience, and carried out in opposition to the strongest, most sensual passion for love and a rich life she has known, it represents the moment in the novel when her success in living by Kempis' philosophy is most complete. Only later, when temptation in the form of Stephen's letter assaults her again, does her hold on this philosophy slacken. Yet the point of the first four chapters of Book VII is that if Maggie's self-discipline has reached its height, so too, in ironic counterpoint, has Tom's blindness and opposition. The heroism of her renunciation of Stephen, instead of at last winning her brother's understanding, respect, and love, as it should, is powerless against the alienation of his sympathy which has been caused by the river journey itself. Completely oblivious to the moral grandeur of that renunciation, he rejects her more brutally than ever before, and Maggie, of course, is crushed.

With the exception of the malicious town gossips, no one else in her world is so cruel to her. In fact, after the rejection scene in Chapter i, nearly every other episode in the first four chapters of Book VII is carefully designed by George Eliot to emphasize the key importance of that scene by contrasting Tom with characters and actions which put him in the worst possible light: Bob Jakin climaxes an earlier series of benevolent actions by chivalrously taking Maggie into his home as a lodger; Dr. Kenn gives her sympathetic counsel, and, failing in his efforts to find her employment elsewhere, takes her on as a governess to his own children; Philip declares not only that he forgives Maggie and still loves her, but that in loving her he has attained to a new and enlarged life of selflessness; Lucy too has forgiven her; and even Aunt Glegg, although motivated by family pride, comes staunchly to her defense on the ground that she should be punished only in proportion to the misdeeds actually proved against her, rather than those merely alleged. Especially important is the contrast between Tom and Dr. Kenn. Whereas the latter can appreciate Maggie's spiritual conflicts because he is a man of "broad, strong sense" who can "discern that the mysterious complexity of our life is not to be embraced by maxims, and that to lace ourselves up in formulas of that sort is to repress all the divine promptings and inspirations that spring from growing insight and sympathy," Tom is the "man of max-

ims" par excellence—a representative of all those "minds that are guided in their moral judgment solely by general rules, thinking that these will lead them to justice by a ready-made patent method, without the trouble of exerting patience, discrimination, impartiality—without any care to assure themselves whether they have the insight that comes from a hardly-earned estimate of temptation, or from a life vivid and intense enough to have created a wide fellow-feeling with all that is human." This passage, echoing the earlier one on Tom as a man of prejudice, emphatically defines again the crucial distinction between the two types of human character which underlies the tragic contrast and conflict between Tom and Maggie herself.

But, if it is true that Tom's climactic rejection of Maggie is the central subject of most of Book VII, this has the crucial effect of placing the drama of her fall and recovery in Book VI in a wholly new perspective. What now becomes clear is that the struggle leading up to her renunciation of Stephen and the renunciation itself have been fully and emphatically rendered by George Eliot not because they themselves are the novel's central subject, but because they provide the occasion for the rejection which is the culminating revelation of Tom's insensitivity, and because only in relation to their nobility can the horror of that rejection and insensitivity be fully measured. The ultimate importance of the entire affair with Stephen which constitutes Book VI is not that it brings to a climax Maggie's efforts to live by Kempis' philosophy (though this does happen), but rather that it brings to a climax Tom's failure to understand his sister's needs and reciprocate her love. By the end of Book VII, Chapter iv, then, the drama of Maggie's tragic frustration is complete in all essentials, and has emerged as the true center of the novel. Each of her three vitally necessary quests for love and a wider life, which were originally incited by the alienation of her father's and brother's love at the time of the family downfall, and were later broadened and intensified by the natural process of her maturation, has ended in failure. And the failure in each case is related in some vital way to the flawed characters of Tom or Tulliver or both, who are far inferior to Maggie in spiritual sensitivity, but to whom she is nevertheless bound by the noblest feelings of loyalty and devotion.

There still remains, of course, the important question of how this drama is related to another one, namely, that of the flood and its aftermath, which comprises the main action of Book VII, Chapter v, and the "Conclusion." As is well known, this part of the novel has given critics more trouble than any other; there is almost universal agreement that for one reason or another it is unsatisfactory. That the action is melodramatic and indeed almost comic in its foreshortening and fortuity; that it is sentimental in the abruptness with which Tom at last awakens to Maggie's nobility and in the description of their death embrace; and that it has the defect of imposing a somewhat mechanical finality, a formal "ending," upon a struggle in Maggie's soul which, as long as Tom's opposition exists, can only remain inconclusive—all are points that can be conceded at once. But the question of the thematic relevance of this action to the rest of the novel may still be profitably reconsidered. For if the flood sequence is seen as functioning primarily to clarify and reinforce the tragic central theme of the novel I have been defining, its logic becomes inescapable. When Maggie begins her prayer to the "Unseen Pity" in Book VII, Chapter v, that theme has been developed as far as strict dramatic necessity requires: as a result of the attitudes of her father and brother various frustrations have been built up in her which there is no way of enduring except by struggling again, as we see her doing, to renounce all her desires. The flood sequence, though it carries the action farther, adds nothing new to this theme. But it does serve as a rhetorical device for giving it maximum final emphasis. A series of ironies focuses all the major issues. That the "something" which Maggie had earlier hoped would "soften" Tom has finally occurred, so that he begins to awaken to her greatness of soul and to reciprocate her love, accentuates the momentous significance of his earlier blindness and spirit of opposition; that this awakening occurs only because Maggie is sacrificing herself to save *him* highlights the importance of his selfishness; that now it comes too late to alter Maggie's destiny confirms our sense of the decisive difference for the better it could have made earlier; that she and Tom are killed by floating "machinery" symbolizes how destructive have been the effects on her of her father's and brother's prosaic materialism; and finally, that their epitaph reads "In death they were not divided" comments definitively on how much Maggie and Tom were divided in life. With this epitaph, indeed, as I suggested earlier, the thematic center of the novel is established conclusively: appearing as both the last words and again as the epigraph, it unmistakably implies that the whole of Maggie's story must be seen with reference to her tragic relationship with Tom—and, of course, by extension, her father. The key concept

of the novel, it emphatically announces, is "division"—the division between the large-souled woman, whose profound love for her father and brother is one of the proofs of her spiritual greatness, and the narrow-souled father and brother themselves, whose inability to reciprocate that love or grasp the validity and urgency of her other needs destroys her life.

Source: John Hagan, "A Reinterpretation of *The Mill on the Floss*," in *PMLA*, Vol. 87, No. 1, January 1972, pp. 53–63.

Sources

Allen, Walter, "Eliot, George," in *Reference Guide to English Literature*, 2d ed., edited by D. L. Kirkpatrick, St. James Press, 1991.

Brownell, W. C., "George Eliot," in *Victorian Prose Masters: Thackeray—Carlyle—George Eliot—Matthew Arnold—Ruskin—George Meredith*, Charles Scribner's Sons, 1901, pp. 99–145.

Collins, W. L., "A Review of *The Mill on the Floss*," in *Blackwood's Edinburgh Magazine*, May 1860, pp. 611–23.

Cooper, Lettice, "George Eliot," in *British Writers*, Vol. 5, British Council, 1982, pp. 187–201.

Levy, Emanuel, "*The Mill on the Floss*," Movie review, in *Variety*, June 2, 1997, p. 55.

Luyster, I. M., "The Eliot Novels," in *Christian Examiner*, March 1861, pp. 227–51.

Mugglestone, Lynda, "Grammatical Fair Ones: Women, Men, and Attitudes to Language in the Novels of George Eliot," in *Review of English Studies*, February 1995, p. 11.

"A Review of *The Mill on the Floss*," in *Saturday Review* (London), April 14, 1860, pp. 470–71.

Stephen, Leslie, "George Eliot," in *Cornhill Magazine*, February 1881, pp. 152–68.

Szirotny, June Skye, "Maggie Tulliver's Sad Sacrifice: Confusing but Not Confused," in *Studies in the Novel*, Summer 1996, p. 178.

Tufel, Alice L., "A Hundred Conflicting Shades: The Divided Passions of George Eliot," in *Biblio*, November 1998, p. 20.

Wiesenfarth, Joseph, "George Eliot," in *Dictionary of Literary Biography*, Vol. 21: *Victorian Novelists Before 1885*, edited by Ira B. Nadel, Gale Research, 1983, pp. 145–70.

Further Reading

Bodenheimer, Rosemarie, *The Real Life of Mary Ann Evans: George Eliot, Her Letters and Fiction*, Cornell University Press, 1996.

Bodenheimer uses Eliot's own writings, particularly her voluminous correspondence, to explore her life and work.

Giobbi, Giuliana, "A Blurred Picture: Adolescent Girls Growing Up in Fanny Burney, George Eliot, Rosamond Lehman, Elizabeth Bowen and Dacia Maraini," in *Journal of European Studies*, June 1995, p. 141.
Giobbi examines adolescent female characters in the work of several women writers and discusses their path to maturity.

Hughes, Kathryn, *George Eliot: The Last Victorian*, National Book Network, 2001.
In this combination of biography and critical work, Hughes examines Eliot's phenomenal celebrity in her own lifetime, as well as the Victorian society that nurtured it.

Ludwig, Mark, "George Eliot and the Trauma of Loss," in *Essays in Literature*, Fall 1992, p. 204.
Ludwig discusses the repeated portrayal of traumatic loss in Eliot's novels.

The Red Pony

John Steinbeck
1937

John Steinbeck's *The Red Pony*—which some critics believe represents one of Steinbeck's best works—is divided into four separate sections, unlike standard chapters. The sections are held together by common characters, location, and themes, and they follow a similar time line, but the continuation of story line is not as smooth as the transition between normal chapters of a novel. They all follow the trials of Jody Tiflin, however, as he progresses through the rites of passage from young boy to young man.

It is through the red pony, which Jody receives as a gift from his father, that he learns about death. This is a painful experience for a shy young boy who is so proud of his pony that he invites friends home from school just to look at the small horse. Likewise, it is through other animals that populate this book that Jody also learns about sex, old age, sickness, and birth. He is gently guided through his journey from boy to man with the help of a ranch hand named Billy Buck, who is reputed to know more about horses than any man around. However, even Billy cannot defy nature and must learn that he cannot make promises that he cannot keep. Through Billy and Jody's mother, Jody learns compassion and understanding. Jody's father is not as open to other people, but Steinbeck takes care not to depict Jody's father as a villain. Steinbeck treats all his characters fairly and fleshes out their personalities to their fullest extent possible within the confines of his stories.

John Steinbeck

Three of the sections of this novel were published separately before being collected in the book *The Red Pony*. The first two, "The Gift" and "The Great Mountains," were published in the *North American Review* in 1933, and the third, "The Promise," appeared in *Harper's* in 1937.

Author Biography

John Steinbeck was born in Salinas, California, on February 27, 1902, the son of John Ernst, a government employee, and Olive Hamilton Steinbeck, a schoolteacher. He grew up in the midst of an agricultural community on the east side of the coastal mountains, and when he turned seventeen, he began a six-year relationship with Stanford University, sporadically attending classes in literature and writing but never attaining a degree. In 1925, he gave up furthering his education and moved to New York City, where he worked for a time as a laborer on the construction project of Madison Square Gardens. He became discouraged about not finding a publisher for his writing, so one year later he returned to California.

He lived off and on at his parents' home, even after marrying Carol Henning, the first of his three

wives. He continued to write, and in 1929 *Cup of Gold*, his first novel, was published. It was not until 1935 that Steinbeck enjoyed commercial success with his fourth novel *Tortilla Flat*, and from that point on his career as a writer was set. In the next sixteen years, he would write eleven novels, numerous short stories, three plays, and five movie scripts. His most notable works include *Of Mice and Men* (1937), which was made into a play in the same year and adapted for film many times; *The Red Pony* (1937), which was made into a movie in 1949 and adapted for television in 1973; *The Grapes of Wrath* (1939), which was made into a movie in 1940 and 1991; *Cannery Row* (1945), which was adapted as a movie in 1984, and *East of Eden* (1952), which was adapted as a movie in 1954 and again in 1984.

During World War II, Steinbeck worked as a foreign correspondent for the *New York Herald Tribune*, first stationed in North Africa and then Italy. Later, during the Vietnam War, he also was a foreign correspondent, this time for *Newsday*.

Steinbeck's themes often revolved around what he saw as the evils of materialism, and his books were often his attempts to fight for human dignity and compassion in the wake of political and corporate corruption and rampant poverty. *The Grapes of Wrath*, probably his most famous work, was both widely read as well as banned and burned. Steinbeck spent two years living with farmers who had lost their lands in the Dust Bowl and migrated from Oklahoma to California in search of a better life, in order to gain firsthand experience in the hard luck of their lives. In 1940, he was awarded the Pulitzer Prize for his efforts.

Steinbeck would go on to win many more awards in his lifetime, including the Nobel Prize for literature in 1962. He also won an Academy Award nomination for best original story for his screenplay *Lifeboat*. After his success with *Grapes of Wrath*, however, critics maintained that Steinbeck had lost the passion in his writing, some even going so far as to state that he won the Nobel Prize mostly for his early works.

Steinbeck moved back to New York in his latter years, somewhat disappointed by the reaction of the citizens of his hometown of Salinas. This was a conservative group of people who found Steinbeck and his novels too liberal and thus too disruptive for their tastes. He married Gwyndolyn Conger by whom he had two sons, one of whom was tragically addicted to codeine at the age of seven and would go on to write his own book, criticizing his father as a parent. In 1950, Steinbeck married Elaine Scott. On December 20, 1968, while in New York, he died of a heart attack.

Plot Summary

The Gift

The story begins with a long description, focused on everyone who lives on the ranch getting up in the early morning. First to appear is Billy Buck, the only help on the ranch, who is presented as a very meticulous man, who rises from his bed in the bunkhouse. When he hears Mrs. Tiflin ringing the triangle, he walks slowly toward the house, not entering until he hears the sounds of Mr. Tiflin's boots on the kitchen floor. It would be impolite for him to sit down at the breakfast table before Mr. Tiflin, his boss.

Jody Tiflin, the young protagonist of the story, is the last one to get out of bed. He is portrayed as an obedient and somewhat shy son. Jody's father, Carl Tiflin, is described as stern. He is a man of few words. Jody does not bother to ask his father where he is going that morning, but because his father has boots on, Jody knows that his father and Billy will be riding their horses somewhere that day. Later, when he watches his father and Billy round up a bunch of old milk cows, Jody knows that they are driving the cattle to the butcher's.

Jody spends most of his day alone, playing with his dogs, wandering around the ranch. As he roams the land, he senses change in the air. He also notices two big black buzzards, a sure portent of death.

Mrs. Tiflin is always busy in the kitchen, cooking, cleaning, guiding Jody through his chores. When Jody's chores are finished, he heads outside with a rifle his father has given him, a rifle without bullets. Jody will have to wait two more years before he will be allowed to use live ammunition. "Nearly all of his father's presents were given with reservations which hampered their value somewhat," Jody thinks. When Carl and Billy return, Jody discovers that they have brought with them a red pony, a present for Jody.

Jody takes very special care of the red pony, whom he names Gabilan. The pony is somewhat wild, but it takes a liking to Jody, who slowly and gently teaches it to wear a bridle. One day, after a brief but cold rainstorm in which the pony gets

Media Adaptations

- Steinbeck wrote a screenplay for *The Red Pony*, and it was produced in 1949, starring Myrna Loy and Robert Mitchum. Noted American composer Aaron Copeland wrote the musical score. The story was rewritten for television in 1973 and starred Henry Fonda and Maureen O'Hara.

chilled, it develops an illness that Billy is unable to cure. The pony dies, leaving Jody devastated.

The Great Mountains

This section begins with Jody in a foul mood. He's looking for trouble and does not stop until he has killed a bird with his slingshot. He does not appear remorseful about the death and only hides the evidence because he does not want "older people" to find out what he has done. He knows they would not approve.

Jody stares at the mountain range in the distance and wonders who lives there. He asks his mother and father and Billy, but no one can tell him much about what exists in the far ranges. As Jody makes up stories in his head about who might live there, he notices the figure of a man walking toward the ranch. It turns out to be an old man, who tells Jody that his name is Gitano. The man has come back to his home to die. Gitano used to live on the same property where the Tiflins now live. As a matter of fact, Gitano's family claim to this land goes far back into history.

Mrs. Tiflin is surprised by the appearance of this old man. She remembers the old adobe house that used to exist on the property, but she knows nothing of this man or his family. Soon Mr. Tiflin and Billy come to Mrs. Tiflin's rescue and tell the man that he cannot stay there. There is no work available, and Mr. Tiflin cannot afford to feed anyone else. He does, however, invite Gitano to stay for dinner, sleep overnight in the bunkhouse, and have breakfast with them in the morning. That is the best he can do. Gitano accepts.

Jody shows Gitano to the bunkhouse and eventually gains enough nerve to ask the old man if he came out of the mountains. The man answers in the negative. Jody pursues his line of questioning, and finally Gitano tells him that once he did go into the mountains but he cannot remember much about them except that it was quiet and nice up there.

Jody invites Gitano to walk with him to the barn to see the horses that his father owns. Gitano is taken by an old horse that Jody refers to as Easter. It is the first horse that his father ever owned. "He's thirty years old," Jody tells Gitano. "No good any more," Gitano replies. "Just eats and pretty soon dies."

Carl overhears this conversation and adds, "Old things ought to be put out of their misery," taunting the old man. Billy tries to soften the tone by adding, "They got a right to rest after they worked all their life. Maybe they just like to walk around." Carl continues to search for sore points in Gitano, and Jody recognizes his father's harshness.

Before going to bed, Jody sneaks into the bunkhouse and watches Gitano go through a bag of his belongings. Included in the bag is a long, old sword, something that Gitano's father gave to him. In the morning, Gitano does not appear for breakfast. When Jody searches through Gitano's things, everything is there except the sword. They all soon discover that the old horse Easter is also missing.

The Promise

Carl's father decides to give Jody another chance at having a pony. He makes arrangements for one of his mares to be mated. Jody must take the horse to a neighbor, who owns a stallion. Just before arriving at the neighbor's, the stallion sees Jody bringing the mare and breaks free as Jody is walking the mare up the road. Jody hides, as the stallion is very big and acting strangely. He watches the two horses and fears that the stallion will kill his mare. Jess Taylor, the owner of the stallion, tries to convince Jody to go away, but Jody insists on watching the mating.

Much later, Jody becomes impatient while waiting for signs that his mare has been impregnated. Billy warns him that it will take a long time before they will see any signs. Jody asks a lot of questions of what it will be like to watch the birthing, and Billy explains a lot of the details. After they talk, Jody asks, "Billy, you won't let anything happen to the colt, will you?" Billy knows that Jody blames him for the loss of the red pony and tries to assure Jody that everything will be all right, but he says he cannot promise anything.

A year passes, and Jody almost gives up hope. One morning, his mother shows Jody how to make a warm mash for the mare. This signals that the mare is showing signs of pregnancy. From then on, Jody is ever watchful of the mare as she goes through her changes, growing wider with every day. When the time comes, Jody stands at Billy's side, watching everything that he does.

Billy grows restless and more serious as the mare becomes more and more uncomfortable in her attempts to deliver. Finally, Billy inspects the mare internally and discovers that the colt is turned the wrong way for delivery. The mare will not be able to push the colt out of her without tearing up her insides.

Billy tells Jody to go outside, but Jody insists on staying and watching. Billy picks up a hammer and tells Jody to at least turn his head away. Jody then hears the smash of hammer against bone as Billy kills the mare by bringing the hammer down on her head. When the mare falls, Billy cuts her belly and pulls out the colt. Although Jody tries to feel excited and happy about the birth of the colt, his feelings are tainted with the image of Billy covered in blood and the body of the dead mare.

The Leader of the People

Mrs. Tiflin receives a letter from her father stating that he will be visiting her soon. When Carl finds out that his father-in-law is coming, he immediately begins complaining. When Mrs. Tiflin asks what it is about her father that irritates him so, Carl states that he talks too much. Mrs. Tiflin tells Carl that he talks a lot, too, but Carl says that the real problem with his father-in-law is that he only talks about one thing. At this point, Jody breaks into the conversation with "Indians and crossing the plains!" These are the two topics that Mrs. Tiflin's father continually refers to. He craves telling stories about how he led a caravan of people across the plains and how they had to deal with the Native-American populations that they encountered. Carl is tired of the stories because he has heard them so many times.

When Grandfather finally arrives, every topic that someone else brings up seems to remind him of a story from his past. Soon, he is lost, recounting his own history and his adventures, telling stories that they all know by heart. Carl is the most impatient and most rude, interrupting his father-in-law, telling him that he'd already heard that story. Jody, contrary to his father, encourages his grandfather to tell more stories.

In the morning, everyone sits down at the breakfast table and wonders where Grandfather is. Mrs. Tiflin assures them that Grandfather will be coming soon. It's just that he is very particular about dressing himself in the morning. Carl begins to poke fun at his father-in-law. When Mrs. Tiflin criticizes Carl's insults toward her father, Carl gets angry with her. He raises his voice and complains about the stories, asking no one in particular why he has to listen to his father-in-law's stories over and over again. No one notices that Grandfather is standing at the doorway to the kitchen.

There is tension in the air. Carl tries to apologize, but in order to do so, he must lie. He tells his father-in-law that he was just trying to be funny. Grandfather does not really believe him. "An old man doesn't see things sometimes," he says. "Maybe you're right."

After breakfast, Grandfather seems to have lost all his energy. He tells Jody that maybe he will leave early. "I feel as though the crossing wasn't worth doing," he says, making a reference to the topic of all his stories. He confesses that it's not really the stories that are important but the way the telling of the stories makes him feel. He had hoped that other people in listening to the stories would feel just as he did. Grandfather had led many people out West. When they reached the ocean, they stopped. When Jody tries to cheer up his grandfather by saying that maybe one day he would lead people, Grandfather says, "There's no place to go." Then he adds, "There's a line of old men along the shore hating the ocean because it stopped them."

Characters

Billy Buck

Billy Buck is the ranch hand who is known for his gentle understanding of horses. He promises, at one point, that nothing will happen to Jody's red pony. Unfortunately, the pony becomes very sick, and Billy cannot save him. Billy feels very bad about having made a promise that he could not keep.

When one of the mares becomes impregnated, Billy knows better than to promise anything to Jody. He tells Jody that he will do his best to give him a healthy colt but that there are no guarantees. In order to deliver the colt, however, Billy must kill the mother, for the colt is turned the wrong way in her womb.

Billy's character is in stark contrast to Carl Tiflin's. Billy is more sensitive, more compassionate, less harsh, and more understanding. He listens to Billy, and he also listens to Grandfather's stories, just as he always listened to them. He is much more sensitive toward Gitano, who has worked hard all his life and, according to Billy, deserves time to rest.

Gitano

Gitano is an old man who comes back to the Tiflins' ranch to die. It was on this same property that he and his father were born. It is not explained how they lost their property, but Gitano insists that he is staying there until he dies.

Gitano is told that he is not welcome on the property, and because he does not have any other place that he wants to go, early in the morning he disappears with the old horse Easter and a sword that his father had left him.

Grandfather

Mrs. Tiflin's father comes to visit his daughter and her family. He is a proud man whose time has passed. He has nothing to look forward to, and so he lives in the past. The highlight of his life occurred while he led pioneers across the Plains into California. Once he reached the ocean, he had nowhere else to go. Since that time he has been angry at the ocean for having stopped him. To give himself a sense of worth, he constantly repeats his stories. He does not understand that other people do not get the same feelings that he gets in retelling them. His spirit is broken when his son-in-law tells him, indirectly, that he is tired of hearing the same stories over and over again.

Jess Taylor

Jess Taylor is the neighbor who owns the stallion that eventually impregnates Jody's mare. He rescues Jody when the stallion breaks loose to get to the mare that Jody is leading up the long driveway. Jess suggests that Jody wait in the house but understands Jody's desire to watch the mating.

Carl Tiflin

Carl Tiflin has very little about him that is likeable. He is a hard worker, and he recognizes that his son deserves to be rewarded for being so good. His saving grace is his sensitivity in knowing to bring home one of the most thrilling gifts he could give his son. However, after bringing home the red pony, Carl has very little to do with helping Jody raise the pony. Likewise, Carl knows that after the pony dies, he needs to replace it with something else. He offers Jody another try at raising a colt by having his mare impregnated. However, once again, it is Billy, not Carl, who helps Jody through the whole ordeal.

Carl is not very sympathetic when Gitano shows up at the ranch. He does not have any empathy for the old man, not even as much empathy as he has for his old horse Easter. When Gitano takes the horse into the mountains, Carl assumes that Gitano has stolen him. He has no awareness that Gitano has gone into the mountains to kill the horse and then to kill himself.

Carl's worst side appears in the last story when his father-in-law comes to visit. Carl is totally incapable of showing the old man any respect. He is bored with his stories and lets everyone, including his father-in-law, know it. Through his crudeness, his father-in-law's spirit is broken.

Jody Tiflin

Jody is the young boy on whom the stories in this novel focus. The stories follow a rite of passage for Jody as he learns how to be responsible for animals and to experience the pain of losing an animal to death, and he begins to show signs of maturing into a man.

Jody is often quiet and shy, but he soaks in all the conversations and emotions that are around him. He painfully watches his red pony grow more and more ill. In the end, he also finds his pony on top of the hill, having run away to die. He sees the buzzards come down and begin to consume the dead pony.

Later he watches his mare and a neighbor's stallion mate and then patiently awaits the new colt. The arrival of the colt is traumatic due to complications, and the mare must be killed. Jody learns about the cycles of death and birth through witnessing the lives of the animals around him.

It is not just the animals that teach him, though. Jody is very aware of Gitano's impending death, more so than anyone else around him. He is a curious boy and has deep insights into the emotions of those around him. When he sees Gitano's sword, he senses that he must keep a secret. When he hears that Gitano has gone up into the mountains, he knows why Gitano has gone there. Likewise, Jody is also very sensitive to his grandfather's feelings. He knows that his father has broken his grandfather's spirit, and Jody tries to repair it.

Mrs. Tiflin

Mrs. Tiflin is never given a first name, and she is seldom seen outside of the kitchen. Her character only comes to life in the last story, when her father comes to visit. She finally speaks back to her husband in this story, letting him know her true feelings about his impatience with her father. Other than that one moment, Mrs. Tiflin is either cooking or cleaning.

Themes

Rite of Passage

Over the course of the four sections of this book, the protagonist, Jody Tiflin, goes through several experiences that force him to encounter many difficult emotions. In the process of dealing with the harsh realities of life, Jody changes from a naive young boy into a responsible and maturing young man. Many ancient cultures have specific ceremonies for inducting a young boy into the realm of grown men. These ceremonies are often referred to as rites of passage. In modern cultures, even though the ceremony is less traditional or formalized, young boys and girls still experience, sometimes randomly, certain types of rituals that mark them for life. In urban settings, in the absence of strong family relationships, this rite of passage might be experienced through membership in a gang. Biologically, every young boy and girl goes through physical changes that signal the onset of adulthood.

Jody's rite of passage is expressed in his having to come to terms first with the care and development of a young, somewhat wild colt. Next, he must face the death of his colt, which makes him reflect on the brevity of life, including his own. This concept of death is further developed when Gitano appears in the second section and when Grandfather comes to visit in the last story. Jody becomes involved in the process of aging and the sense of loss of purpose when he takes an interest in both old men. Gitano is compared to the old horse Easter, both of them having worked hard in their youth and now being set out to pasture. Jody senses Gitano's need, like an old animal, to find some place to die. With his grandfather, Jody understands the loss of purpose that comes over some old people when they are no longer appreciated.

These experiences deepen Jody's respect for life. He thinks about emotions that as a child he had never considered before. He takes an interest in others, moving from the egocentric focus of his youth into the more compassionate stage of an adult. In addition, when he watches the mating of his mare with the neighbor's stallion, he gains a deeper understanding of procreation. He watches Billy deliver the colt at the expense of the mare's life. These are tough circumstances that mark Jody's entrance into adulthood.

Death

The theme of death looms over all the sections of this book. In the opening pages, Jody wanders out into the field and encounters buzzards, probably having found a dead cow out in the pastures. Shortly after receiving the red pony as a gift from his father, the pony becomes ill and runs away to die. Jody finds the dead pony with buzzards standing on the carcass. He kills one of the buzzards but later is reminded by Billy that the buzzards were not responsible for the red pony's death. Although Jody wants to vent his anger on someone or something, he learns that there is really no one to blame. He must accept death as a part of life.

The red pony's is not the only death that occurs. Gitano, the old ranch hand, returns to the place of his birth to die. Gitano shows Jody an old sword that he carries with him, a sword that was handed down to him by his father. Gitano does not have much to say about the sword, but Jody senses that it represents something very serious in Gitano's life and, possibly, in Gitano's reasons for being there. Jody tells no one about the sword, and the next morning when Gitano disappears with the old horse Easter and the sword, the reader is left to surmise that Gitano has gone into the mountains to die.

In the third section, there is the horrific death of the pregnant mare. Billy must kill the mare in order to save the colt. This is a hard decision that he must make. Either the colt or the mare must be sacrificed. Possibly because Billy feels guilty about the death of the red pony, he chooses to save the colt so that he can give the young horse to Jody.

In the last section of the book, although Grandfather is not near death or showing any signs of ill health, there is a sense that his life is over. Grandfather loses his sense of purpose. The greatest experience in his life ended many years earlier, and since then, he has remained stuck at the shore, unable to move ahead. Grandfather represents a more symbolic form of death.

Old Age

Tied in with death is the theme of old age. As presented in this book, old age has very little meaning. There is the old horse Easter who has been put to pasture after having served her master with many years of hard labor. Gitano is like Easter in many ways. He is very old, and he has worked many years. He cannot or does not choose to work any more and has decided to die. Although Billy argues that Gitano has a right to rest and be taken care of, Carl is not ready to take on that responsibility. Carl is more sensitive to his horse than he is to Gitano, who is a stranger. Carl even admits that it would be more humane to shoot his old horse than to let him suffer the aches and pains of aging. Although Gitano has family members to go to, he chooses not to burden them. He decides to go off into the mountains possibly to kill himself rather than to allow someone else to take care of him.

Grandfather, in the last section of the book, also has trouble dealing with old age. Carl is no more sympathetic toward his father-in-law than he was with Gitano. Carl is tired of hearing Grandfather's old stories. He makes Grandfather feel that his time has passed and that no one is interested in hearing about the old days and Grandfather's glory. Grandfather, feeling lost about his present situation, returns to the stories in order to return to a time when he felt worthwhile. He led many people out to the West Coast. He faced challenges and hardships that he feels his son-in-law does not understand. Modern life is too soft for him. However, Grandfather is too old for new adventures, or so he believes. There is no place left to be discovered, no place left to go to, no need for him to lead people anywhere. Old age is more a punishment for Grandfather than a reward for all the experiences of his youth.

Style

Linked Short Stories

Three of the four stories in this book were published as separate short stories. What holds these stories together so that they can be considered a book is the elements that they have in common. These are common characters, setting, and themes. Linked short stories are not as tightly connected as the chapters in a book. First of all, they stand on their own, each section completing a thought. Second, the connections between the sections are rather loose. There is no explanation of anything that was left unresolved in the previous section. For example, when Billy delivers the colt in the third section, there is nothing said about Jody's reaction or the care of the colt in the fourth section. It is almost as if the colt did not exist in the final chapter of the book.

Topics For Further Study

- Research the California trail across the plains to the West Coast. Draw a map of one of the major routes. Provide a mileage scale; highlight major natural formations that the pioneers might have seen along the way; mark major intersections and supply points; locate major tribes of Native Americans. Accompany this map with short diary excerpts from actual pioneers, to give a fuller understanding of the intensity of this trip.

- Write a coming-of-age short story of a young girl or boy who must face a specific challenge that changes her or him forever. This could be written as fiction or taken from your own experience.

- Shortly after writing *The Red Pony*, John Steinbeck left his hometown of Salinas, California, and moved to New York. Find out why Steinbeck became disgruntled about Salinas, and then write a story as if you were a local journalist covering his move to the East Coast.

- The last chapter in *The Red Pony*, "The Leader of the People," centers a major portion of its action on the decaying haystack. Reread this chapter and find as many symbols as you can that

are contained in the haystack and Jody's insistence in wanting to kill the mice that he finds there. How is the haystack connected to the grandfather? What is the significance of Jody wanting Grandfather to help him? Why do you think Steinbeck used the haystack in this chapter?

- Pretend that you are Gitano from the chapter "The Great Mountains." Write a poem expressing your feelings as you ride up into the mountains with the old horse Easter. How would you relate to Easter? What would be your thoughts at being rejected by the Tiflins? Come up with your own interpretation of why Gitano took the horse and his sword and left without telling anyone.

- Research how to raise a colt from birth to the point when a horse is old enough to be ridden. Write out a schedule, as if you were a trainer, for the steps to be taken at the appropriate ages of the horse to get it used to accepting a bridle through taking a saddle and being ridden. In your research, find out if this training has changed from the 1930s to the present time.

However, there's enough of a connection between the sections that the reader gets a sense of continuation. Jody continues to have similar experiences that move him forward into the world of adults. Personality traits of Carl, Jody's father, remain consistent from first section to the end. Billy feels sorry about Jody having lost the red pony in the beginning of the book and remains sensitive about this through the third portion, when he must decide to kill the mare in order to save the newborn colt.

Linked short stories might have been used in order for Steinbeck to publish each section separately and thus gain an audience for the novel. Choosing between linked short stories and chapters may just reflect a preferred style of writing. With

linked short stories, each section develops a theme and completes it. In writing chapters, themes are usually only slightly developed in each separate chapter and then more fully engaged throughout the entire work, coming to conclusions only in the last chapters.

Setting

The setting of this novel is at the ranch and in agricultural valleys of California during the early part of the twentieth century. It is a time of transition, when old ways are quickly vanishing. This is reflected in the characters Gitano, whose Spanish heritage has been wiped out by the white settlers, and Grandfather, whose mission in life has been exhausted because there is no more frontier to be discovered.

In placing the story on a western farm, Jody has the opportunity to witness the basic elements of life—procreation, birth, and death—by watching the animals around him. Because he lives in a somewhat remote area, he gains his knowledge from nature.

Although Grandfather believes there is no more frontier left, Jody eyes the mountains, where no one lives and few people that he knows have ever been, as a place of great mystery and possible future exploration. He also wonders about the ocean and what might lie beyond.

Symbolism

Steinbeck employs many different symbols in his writing. Most obvious is the ruined adobe house in which Gitano was raised. The adobe was a mud construction that demanded regular care. The structure eventually becomes all but washed away, similar to the Spanish culture that Gitano represents. Gitano comes back to die on his family's homeland. However, the Tiflins have taken over the property and do not welcome Gitano back. This symbolizes the taking over of the valley by white settlers, who eventually pushed the Spanish and Mexican cultures away.

The Gabilan mountains symbolize many things for different characters in the story. For Jody, they are wild and mysterious, and that is why he decides to call his red pony Gabilan. The mountains represent his adulthood, in some ways, as he knows he wants to explore them as soon as he is old enough. To Grandfather, the mountains are meaningless now. Previously, they had represented a challenge as he fought to traverse them on his way to the ocean when he first crossed from the Plains into California. Now, they are just in his way when he wants to visit his daughter. They represent nothing special. They remind Gitano of his youth, and they represent a place of death.

The haystack in the last section of the book symbolizes the past for Grandfather. Jody tells the story about the old boar (which could be construed as a pun for the word *bore*, as when Grandfather repeats his stories), in which the pig dug into the haystack to get the mice and the haystack smothered him. In much the same way, Grandfather continues to dig into the past, repeating his stories for anyone who has the patience to listen to him. Grandfather, too, is slowly smothered by his past, as he finds no way of living in the present.

Historical Context

Crossing the Plains to California

Many of the trails that lead across the Plains to the West Coast began along the Missouri River in such places as Independence and St. Joseph, Missouri. From here, pioneers heading either to Oregon or California would begin their long and treacherous treks across the wild lands.

The major routes followed the Platte River in Nebraska to the Sweetwater River in Wyoming, a nearly eight-hundred-mile-long section of the trail and a halfway mark for many of the pioneers. At the Sweetwater, the trails split, one taking a more northern route (like the Mormon Trail) and others taking a southern route.

The next major junction was the Snake River, which many people picked up at the Fort Hall trading post in Pocatella in southern Idaho. At this point, those people interested in going to California broke away from the groups that were crossing the mountains to Oregon.

Before the gold rush in 1849, the majority of people took the trail to Oregon to the Willamette Valley. Between 1841 and 1848, it is estimated that over eleven thousand people immigrated to the Oregon valley with less than three thousand continuing south to California. However, during the peak of the gold rush, almost two hundred thousand people are estimated to have taken the southern route to California, while only thirty-five hundred crossed over to the more northern territories.

Despite Jody's grandfather in *The Red Pony* declaring that there was no place for him to go at the end of the trail because the ocean stopped him when he reached the shores of the Pacific Ocean, Monterey, where he probably lived, was actually one of the major seaports on the Pacific Ocean in the late 1800s. He could have hopped onto any of the large trading/importing ships and traveled to any place in the world.

Salinas, California

Salinas, California is called the Salad Bowl of America for all the lettuces and other salad greens that are grown in this lush valley. Located just east of the coastal mountains that separate Salinas from the seaside town of Monterey on the Pacific Coast, Salinas enjoys the benefits of a dry, warm climate.

Salinas was not always an agricultural area. Initially, it was the home to several small tribes of Native Americans, who lived there for many

Compare & Contrast

- **1930s:** Migrant farm workers, most of them coming north from Mexico, are subject to the dictates of the farm owners and suffer poor wages and working and living conditions. In 1936, some of them go on strike for better wages, employing a former colonel of the army to lead them. They are equipped with machine guns and steal red flags from a highway crew, threatening the residents of Salinas by telling them that a communist army is about to take over the city.

  Today: Although working and living conditions still remain difficult for migrant workers, there are many support groups who have rallied for better wages, health facilities, and educational opportunities for those who work on California farms.

- **1930s:** Salinas, California, is still mostly a cattle-raising land, with wheat and lettuce grown

on some farms. The population of Salinas is about fifty thousand people.

  Today: Salinas is known as the salad bowl of America, providing most of the states with salad greens. The population has increased to almost five hundred thousand people.

- **1930s:** Steinbeck irritates most of the population of his hometown of Salinas by his proletariat views of workers' rights in his novels, such as *The Grapes of Wrath*. His books are burned in protest.

  Today: The citizens of Salinas have constructed a huge Steinbeck Center, which draws an average of one hundred thousand visitors a year. The city is planning a three-year celebration for the one-hundredth birthday of Steinbeck.

---

thousands of years before Spanish soldiers and missionaries arrived. Under Spanish rule, the main focus of the population was the coastal areas, and so the valley, where Salinas is located, was largely left on its own. However, when the Mexicans overthrew the Spanish rulers, the Mexican government began giving out land grants. From these land grants grew the communities that would eventually make up such towns as Salinas.

During the early stages of the gold rush, James Bryant Hill bought a large land grant in the valley and was one of the first people to plant crops there. It would not be until 1867 that a partnership between a few large farmers and cattle rancher Eugene Sherwood would be formed. These men laid out a plan for a half-mile square that would become the heart of Salinas City.

At the time of the writing of *The Red Pony*, wheat was still the main crop grown in the valley. Most of the land was still used for cattle. Today, Salinas is known for its crops of lettuce, artichokes, broccoli, sugar beets, and beans. Due to its rich valley soils, Salinas would eventually become one of the wealthiest cities per capita in the United States.

Critical Overview

John Steinbeck enjoyed a very long writing career. His first book was published in 1929, when he was twenty-seven years old, and his last book went to print in 1961, seven years before his death. However, he did not, despite his having won the Nobel Prize in literature in 1962, enjoy critical support throughout his entire writing career. As a matter of fact, many critics believed that his finest work was *The Grapes of Wrath*, which was published early in his career, in 1939. Similarly, some believed that the awarding of the Nobel Prize was actually a reflection on his early stage of writing and not for the works that he created after 1939.

Steinbeck's first three novels received very little attention. It was not until he published *Tortilla Flat* (1935) that he gained recognition. Over his long career he achieved great success, though some critics choose to give more weight to the works written in his early career. The works produced within this time frame include *The Red Pony*.

In general, Steinbeck's work was often praised for its positive view of life. When he used California as a setting, critics believed that his work flowed more naturally and clearly, such as in *The Red Pony*, *The Grapes of Wrath*, and *Of Mice and Men*. Although his male characters were often well developed and thus highly complimented by reviewers, Steinbeck was often criticized for neglecting the women in his stories, for leaving them flat and stereotypical.

A reviewer for the *Library Journal* praised a new edition of Steinbeck's collected works, which includes *The Red Pony*, calling it "something special" and "essential for all serious American literature collections." In an earlier review, a writer for the *Library Journal* referred to Steinbeck as belonging in "America's elite class of writers." In offering an overview of all of Steinbeck's works, Warren French, writing in the *Reference Guide to American Literature*, described *The Red Pony* as "Steinbeck's most popular and masterful work."

Peter Miles as Thomas Tiflin and Robert Mitchum as Bill Buck in the 1948 film adaptation of The Red Pony

Criticism

Joyce Hart

Hart has degrees in English literature and creative writing and focuses her writing on literary themes. In this essay, Hart examines Steinbeck's methods in creating the rites of passage theme in his novel.

John Steinbeck's *The Red Pony* was originally written as four separate short stories, with each story showing different stages of Jody Tiflin's rite of passage into manhood. In each story (or chapter), Steinbeck carefully and skillfully brings together specific circumstances that the young Jody must face. Through the use of explicit examples, as well as subtle metaphors, Steinbeck emphasizes certain character traits of Jody and shows how his personality matures from the first section to the last. By looking closely at Steinbeck's methods of demonstrating the changes in Jody, a greater appreciation of the author's writing skill is unveiled and a deeper appreciation of the story is gained.

The first section of *The Red Pony* is called "The Gift," and the first time that Jody is introduced to the reader, he is referred to as "the boy Jody." Immediately following this, Steinbeck writes: "He was only a little boy, ten years old." There is no doubt in the reader's mind, at this point, that Jody is young. Steinbeck makes sure that Jody is perceived as nowhere near being a man, not even a young man. Jody is also very obedient, Steinbeck

relates. When he hears his mother ring the triangle, a sign to get out of bed and down to the kitchen for breakfast, there is absolutely no hesitation. "It didn't occur to him to disobey the harsh note."

Jody washes his face and turns away from his mother "shyly." When he sits down at the table, he scrapes away "a spot of blood from one of the egg yolks." With these words, Steinbeck presents the innocence of Jody. Not only is Jody obedient and shy but he is unaware of mating; he is presexual. Billy Buck, the ranch hand, must inform Jody that the spot of blood is the sign of fertilization that the rooster has left behind. It's interesting to note that Steinbeck does not have Jody's mother or his stern father report this fact to Jody. Later on, the reader will discover that Billy is the one person most responsible for Jody's rite of passage. Steinbeck, at this initial stage, is foreshadowing these circumstances.

Next, Steinbeck has the young boy wishing to go along with his father and Billy as they prepare to take a herd of cattle to town to be butchered. This is a grown-up chore, and Jody longs to be included. So despite Jody's conscious innocence, something is stirring inside of him, something that

> " With these examples of rebellion, Steinbeck shows that Jody is straining at the reins, wanting to be rid of his father's restrictions but, at the same time, still in fear of them."

senses the changes that are about to take place that will push him into that world of men. In the meantime, however, Jody is patient and so in awe of his father that, even though he wants to go along, he does not even ask permission to accompany them.

To further insinuate the transition that Jody is about to experience, Steinbeck then has Jody climb up the hill and look back at the ranch from an elevated position, where "he felt an uncertainty in the air, a feeling of change and of loss and of the gain of new and unfamiliar things." At this same point in the story, Steinbeck brings in the image of two buzzards, which signal death. Although Jody may be unfamiliar with some aspects of nature, he is not unaware of the cycle of life and death. He is disturbed by the buzzards, but he understands that, ugly as they may be, they rid the land of carrion. Death brings life to the buzzards, and the buzzards, in turn, rid the land of contamination. Jody is old enough to understand this on a rational level. He has yet to experience loss and death on an emotional level. The events that are about to unfold will teach him those very lessons, and they will mark the first steps toward adulthood.

Slowly but surely, Steinbeck hints at a sense of revolt stirring inside of Jody, another of the initial signs that a child is beginning to move away from his parents, moving toward independence. The first mention of this occurs as Jody smashes a muskmelon with his heel. He doesn't feel good about his action. He knows it is wrong, and he tries to hide the evidence by burying the cracked melon. However, just a couple of paragraphs later, Steinbeck mentions that Jody was feeling "a spirit of revolt" once he joined his friends at school. After the school day has ended, Jody again goes up into the hills, this time with a shotgun, and aims it at the house. Although the gun is unloaded, Jody knows that if his father had seen him do it, he would have

to wait another two years before his father would give him any ammunition. With these examples of rebellion, Steinbeck shows that Jody is straining at the reins, wanting to be rid of his father's restrictions but, at the same time, still in fear of them.

The next big event, the gift of the red pony, marks yet another stage in the young boy's development. First of all, the pony cost money, which means that Jody's father, in giving Jody a valuable gift, is developing a trust in his maturing son. Jody has somehow shown his father that he is worthy of that investment, and now he must prove it. In caring for another living creature, Jody will also develop a sense of responsibility. In attending to the pony, Jody will hopefully develop a meaningful relationship that will open up his heart to more mature emotions.

The depth of those emotions is increased as Jody learns to take care of the pony. He is first exhilarated by the joy of owning the pony. Then, when the pony becomes ill, Jody's heart is wrenched by fear and worry. On top of being distressed about the pony, Jody's innocence is strained in another area. His complete trust that adults always know what they are doing is challenged when Billy promises that it won't rain on the day that Jody decides to leave the pony in the corral while he goes to school. It does rain that day, and the pony's illness appears to be a direct result of the inclement weather. Billy, with whom Jody has entrusted not only the care of his horse but also the care of his emotions, has disappointed him. This disillusionment with the adult world is another stage in the progression towards maturity. Children place all their faith in people who are older than they are when they believe that they themselves are not capable of making decisions. However, as they grow more experienced, the adult world appears in a more normal fashion; that is, men and women are seen as fallible. They are not the gods of wisdom and perfect understanding that children once believed them to be. In understanding that adults are capable of making mistakes, children gain courage to trust their own instincts and to reach their own conclusions about the world. Steinbeck demonstrates this stage in Jody's development by making Billy imperfect, by making him, despite all his wisdom, subject to at least an occasional error in judgment.

Before the first section of this novel ends, Steinbeck hurls Jody into a battle, a sure sign that the young boy is entering a sort of initiation rite into manhood. The pony has run away to die, and Jody finds the pony's dead body being attacked by a flock of buzzards. Angered by the death, Jody takes his frustration and pain out on one of the buzzards. Earlier, Jody smashed a muskmelon, something a young boy would do. Later, he slings rocks at small birds and rabbits. Here, in the final scene of this chapter, Jody takes on something that "was nearly as big as he was." The battle that Steinbeck describes is not a pretty sight, but it signifies an age-old scene. Jody faces death in defeating the buzzard. Now, Jody's feelings are fully bloomed, as noted by Billy's comment to Jody's father, who appears to be unaware of how much Jody has grown. When Carl Tiflin tries to comfort Jody by telling him that the buzzards didn't kill the pony, something that a father might tell a much younger son, Billy retorts: "Jesus Christ! man, can't you see how he'd feel about it?" Billy steps in as caretaker, sort of a cross between a father figure and an older brother. Carl appears unable to accept that his son is becoming a man, whereas Billy not only sees but welcomes the changes.

Each of the succeeding chapters reiterates the changes that Jody is going through. In "The Great Mountains," Jody holds a secret to himself when Gitano, the old man who comes to die at his birthplace, shows him an old sword that he carries with him. Holding onto a secret is a very difficult task, especially for a child. The fact that Jody is capable of doing this without being told to do so demonstrates a further example of his maturity. He senses that the sword represents something that must be kept in the realm of the unknown. "It would be a dreadful thing to tell anyone about it, for it would destroy some fragile structure of truth." At the end of the chapter, only Jody is capable of understanding why Gitano disappears with the old horse Easter. Steinbeck does not state the reasons, leaving the reader to manufacture the ending, just as he leaves his character Jody to do the same.

The third chapter, "The Promise," gives Jody another chance to raise a pony. However, if this were the only purpose of this section, it would be redundant, since the reader has already been exposed to Jody's ability to care for a pony. So "The Promise" takes on a more meaningful theme, leaving the raising of the colt to the imagination of the reader. The action of this section focuses on reinforcing two concepts already presented in previous chapters—the cycle of life and death and the realization that there are no guarantees in life. It also provides Jody with an up-close view of the mating process. Jody witnesses the impregnation of his mare, thus initiating him to sexuality, another important stage in the rite of passage. Jody not only

What Do I Read Next?

- Steinbeck wrote *The Pearl* (reissued in 2000) in a fable form, in which he relates the woes of a poor Mexican fisherman who finds a pearl one day and decides that it will change his life for the better. Unfortunately, the fisherman finds out that life is not so simple.

- Coming-of-age stories abound, and some of the best were written by Ernest Hemingway. His stories about Nick Adams have been collected as *The Nick Adams Stories* (1981) and follow the development of the main character from childhood to adulthood.

- In her book *Mona in the Promised Land* (reissued in 1997), Gish Jen writes her interpretation of adolescence, complicated by her Chinese-American teenager's decision to convert to Judaism.

- The setting of William Saroyan's novel *The Human Comedy* (reissued in 1991) is wartime America, and its protagonist is a young boy who is determined to become the fastest deliverer of telegrams. What he does not foresee is the effect that the telegrams will have upon the receivers, as wartime brings news of many deaths.

- Steinbeck's classic *The Grapes of Wrath* (reissued in 2002) was burned in his hometown because of its pro-labor elements. Most critics believe this was Steinbeck's greatest work.

- In a more humorous vein, David Sedaris's discussion of childhood is contained in *Me Talk Pretty One Day* (2001), in which he gives his readers an insight into what life was like for him growing up in North Carolina.

observes the mating, he monitors the complete development of the consequences of that encounter. He learns patience from having to wait for signs of pregnancy and eventually the delivery of the colt. He gains compassion from watching the suffering of the mare in the delivery, as well as the suffering of Billy when he must choose between the life of the mare and the survival of the colt. In the last chapter of this book, Jody transfers the compassion he has gained to a member of his family.

Compassion is one of the final stages of full maturity. In childhood, the world appears to revolve around the self. Everything is defined by how it affects the self. Only a fully mature adult is able to relinquish the need to think only of him- or herself in order to comprehend and empathize with the emotions of other people. In "The Leader of the People," the final chapter, Jody's maternal grandfather makes a visit. His grandfather lives in the past, and this annoys the other adults in the family. Grandfather is a storyteller; however, his stories have been repeated so many times that everyone knows them by heart. For the adults who lack compassion, Grandfather is a bore. In this chapter, Steinbeck sets Jody at odds with his father. Carl is the least compassionate person. He makes rude remarks and is, in the end, somewhat embarrassed when Grandfather overhears him complain about the stories.

Jody, on the other hand, who has been deemed "Big-Britches" by his father, a term meant to imply that he is growing up, but with negative connotations, is very sensitive to his grandfather's needs. He knows what it feels like to be the butt of his father's insults. Since Jody has gained the insight of compassion, he is able to transfer his feelings to his grandfather, whereas his father is unable to do this. Jody understands, maybe intuitively, that Grandfather needs to feel wanted. Grandfather's stories are not so much to glorify himself as to relive those feelings of people coming together and doing something magnificent. Once Grandfather reached the furthest edges of the West, there could be no more "westering" for him. He had reached his limits.

While Grandfather, in old age, finds life waning, Jody finds life just beginning. At the opposite ends of the spectrum, the young and the old meet and learn from one another. In the final lines of the story, Steinbeck demonstrates that Jody has passed the ritual, or rite of passage, from childhood to adulthood, by having him think not of himself but purely of someone else. He tries to console Grandfather in the best way that he can. When Grandfather tells him that the ocean stopped his progress, Jody tries to pick up the trail by stating that when he grows up, maybe he'll lead people. When Grandfather protests that the land has run out, Jody

tells his grandfather, "In boats I might, sir." When Grandfather further discourages him, Jody feels sad, but he is not defeated. Instead of giving in to his grandfather's depression, Jody offers a gift: "If you'd like a glass of lemonade I could make it for you." Grandfather gives in, and when Jody's mother discovers that she is mistaken in believing that Jody is doing this just to con a glass of lemonade for himself, she is astonished. Her surprise goes deeper than just realizing that Jody has made a very unselfish act; she is dumbfounded by the realization that her little boy has grown up.

Source: Joyce Hart, Critical Essay on *The Red Pony*, in *Novels for Students*, The Gale Group, 2003.

Sources

French, Warren, "Steinbeck, John," in *Reference Guide to American Literature*, 3d ed., edited by Jim Kamp, St. James Press, 1994.

Review of *The Grapes of Wrath & Other Writings, 1936–1941*, in *Library Journal*, September 1996.

Review of *Novels & Stories, 1932–1937*, in *Library Journal*, November 1, 1994.

Further Reading

Benson, Jackson J., *John Steinbeck, Writer: A Biography*, Penguin USA, 1990.

To better understand the writings of Steinbeck, it helps to understand his life, as much of the material of his books comes from his personal experience. Benson offers a comprehensive look into the life of Steinbeck.

Hill, Cherry, *The Formative Years: Raising and Training the Young Horse*, Breakthrough Publishing, 1988.

This definitive study of what it takes to raise a colt provides the information required to take on this task.

Steinbeck, John, *Working Days: The Journals of "The Grapes of Wrath," 1938–1941*, edited by Robert Demott, Penguin USA, 1990.

While creating the novel, Steinbeck kept a daily journal of his accomplishments and his frustrations. For an insider's look into the mind of an author, this book provides not only interesting background material for the novel but also a lesson for would-be writers.

Wallsten, Robert, ed., with Elaine Steinbeck, *Steinbeck: A Life in Letters*, Viking, 1975.

Steinbeck was a prolific letter writer. This collection is the next best thing to an autobiography.

Schindler's List

Thomas Keneally

1982

Schindler's List recreates the true story of Oskar Schindler, the Czech-born southern German industrialist who risked his life to save over 1,100 of his Jewish factory workers from the death camps in Nazi-occupied Poland. Thomas Keneally's "documentary novel," based on the recollections of the *Schindlerjuden* (Schindler's Jews), Schindler himself, and other witnesses, is told in a series of snapshot stories. It recounts the lives of the flamboyant profiteer and womanizer Schindler; Schindler's long-suffering wife, Emilie; the brutal SS (Nazi secret service) commandant Amon Goeth; Schindler's quietly courageous factory manager, Itzhak Stern; and dozens of other Jews who underwent the horrors of the Nazi machinery. At the center of the story, though, are the actions and ambitions of Schindler, who comes to Kraków, Poland, seeking his fortune and ends up outwitting the SS to protect his Jewish employees. It is the story of Schindler's unlikely heroism and of one man's attempt to do good in the midst of outrageous evil. The book explores the complex nature of virtue, the importance of individual human life, the role of witnesses to the Holocaust, and the attention to rules and details that sustained the Nazi system of terror.

Keneally's book was first published in Britain in 1982 under the title *Schindler's Ark* and released as *Schindler's List* in the United States the same year. When *Schindler's Ark* won Britain's Booker Prize in 1982, it stirred up controversy, with some critics complaining that the "documentary novel" did not deserve a prize normally reserved for fic-

Thomas Keneally

tion. The debate among critics did not affect the book's enormous popularity with readers, however. It enjoyed renewed interest after its adaptation into a feature film by Steven Spielberg in 1993. In part because of the success of the film, *Schindler's List* ranks as one of the most popular books ever written about the Holocaust.

Author Biography

Thomas Keneally was born in Sydney, Australia, in 1935 into an Irish Catholic family. He completed his schooling at various schools on the New South Wales north coast before starting theological studies for the Catholic priesthood in 1958. He abandoned this vocation in 1960, working first as a laborer and then as a clerical worker before becoming a schoolteacher. In 1964, he published his first novel, *The Place at Whitton*. He then left teaching and took a part-time job as an insurance collector while he continued to write. He married Judith Martin in 1965; their daughters were born in 1966 and 1967. In 1967, Keneally won the Miles Franklin Award for literature for *Bring Larks and Heroes*, and since then he has pursued writing as a full-time profession.

Four of Keneally's novels have been short-listed for the Booker Prize, Britain's most prestigious award for fiction writing. They are *The Chant of Jimmie Blacksmith* (1972), which explores the impact of the meeting of European and Aboriginal cultures from an Aboriginal point of view; *Gossip from the Forest* (1975), set during the First World War; *Confederates* (1979), about the American Civil War; and *Schindler's Ark* (1982; later published in the United States as *Schindler's List*), for which he won the prize. There was considerable controversy when *Schindler's Ark* won the Booker Prize, as many considered the book to be a work of journalistic reporting rather than a fiction novel. The following year Keneally was awarded the Order of Australia for his services to Australian literature. Keneally's other novels include *A Family Madness* (1985), *To Asmara* (1989), *Flying Hero Class* (1991), *Woman of the Inner Sea* (1993), and *A River Town* (1995). *The Great Shame* (1999), a nonfiction work, explores the fates of nineteenth-century Irishmen forced to emigrate to Australia.

Keneally also writes for the Australian press and travels widely, lecturing and presenting seminars and workshops. He lives in Sydney with his wife.

Plot Summary

Title

Schindler's List first appeared in Britain as *Schindler's Ark*. The word "ark" in the original title is in reference to the ark built by the biblical Noah, on God's instruction, to rescue people and animals from the Great Flood. Thus Schindler, simply from the original title of the work, is cast as a rescuer of men.

Overview

Schindler's List is made up of a series of stories about different people, which take place over a period of time. Keneally provides the details of the lives of many of the main characters. Events from their pasts, their experiences in the ghetto or labor camps, and their reactions to the history they witnessed are told in snatches over the course of the novel. But in the midst of these snippets there emerges the main story—of Oskar Schindler and his outrageous rescue of his Jewish workers. Keneally interrupts his storytelling periodically to offer historical commentary or to mention what happened to a character after the war was over.

Thus the action of the novel does not proceed chronologically but moves back and forth in time. The summary of the plot that follows for the most part outlines the main events of the story of Schindler's rescue of his workers in chronological time, omitting the other story lines.

Author's Note

Keneally prefaces *Schindler's List* with a note describing the nature of his nonfictional novel and acknowledging his sources. He explains how he came to hear about Schindler's story from Holocaust survivor Leopold Pfefferberg when the author was browsing Pfefferberg's luggage store in Beverly Hills.

Prologue

The prologue takes the reader to the heart of the story (it is Autumn 1943), setting the stage and providing a glimpse of some of the major characters. The scene takes place one evening in Goeth's quarters, as Oskar rubs shoulders with SS officers even while he is secretly undermining the Nazi system. He eats, drinks, and socializes with them but also offers kindness to Helen Hirsch, Goeth's mistreated maid. The author observes that, at this stage, Schindler is "in deep" in his "practical engagement in the salvation of human lives" but that he has no idea of what his rescue efforts will ultimately cost him.

Chapter 1

The novel opens with the conquest of Poland by the German troops. Schindler moves to Kraków to seek his fortune. Keneally provides a character sketch of the charming, flamboyant Schindler and outlines his background: his Czechoslovakian Catholic upbringing, his parents' troubled marriage, his wild streak as a youth, his difficulties with his fresh-faced country wife, Emilie, and his desire for success within the new regime.

Chapter 2

Schindler meets Itzhak Stern, whose advice he seeks about taking over a bankrupt business, Rekord, that produced enamelware. Stern advises Schindler to lease the estate. Schindler and Stern engage in conversation about the viability of Hitler's success and religion. Schindler says that it must be difficult for priests during this time to explain the biblical verse about God caring about the death of even a single sparrow. Stern says that the spirit of the verse may be summed up in the Talmudic verse that says that he who saves the life of one man saves the entire world. Stern always be-

Media Adaptations

- *Schindler's List* was adapted as a film by Steven Spielberg, starring Liam Neeson, Ralph Fiennes, and Ben Kingsley, Universal, 1993; available from MCA/Universal Home Video.

- *Schindler's List* is also available as an audiobook (abridged), read by Ben Kingsley, published by Simon and Schuster (1993).

lieved, Keneally points out, that it was at that moment that he planted a seed into Schindler's mind.

Chapter 3

Schindler takes over an apartment in Straszewskiego Street, once owned by a Jewish family, the Nussbaums. It was common practice for Jews to be removed from their homes without compensation, and Schindler is allocated this apartment by the Reich housing authorities. He goes to see Mrs. Mina Pfefferberg, who was recommended by the Nussbaums as a good decorator. At Mrs. Pfefferberg's house, Schindler meets Poldek (Leopold) Pfefferberg, who is ready to kill the German if he poses a threat to his mother. Pfefferberg and Schindler become friends and "business acquaintances," as Pfefferberg procures black market goods for Schindler.

Chapter 4

On December 3, the day he signs the papers to lease his enamelware factory (Deutche Email Fabrik, or D.E.F.; also known as Emalia), Schindler warns Stern of a pogrom that is to take place the next day. Kazimierz, the Jewish section of Kraków, is invaded. Some Jews flee in time, but others are killed in the terror that follows. Schindler feels a fundamental disgust at what happens, but not enough to do something to stop it.

Chapter 5

Schindler begins his affair with his Polish secretary, Victoria Klonowska. Around Christmas

1939, he meets and has drinks with a number of German police and other officials. They talk about the current "situation" and speculate about what is to be done to the Jews.

Chapter 6

Abraham Bankier, the former manager of Rekord and soon to be Schindler's office manager, helps Schindler to find Jewish investors for his enamelware factory. Emilie Schindler comes from Zwittau in Czechoslovakia to visit her husband. Schindler sets up his factory and employs 150 Jews; it is considered a haven in German-occupied Kraków, where Jews are routinely being thrown out of their homes.

Chapter 7

Stern tells Schindler the story of Marek Biberstein, the president of the *Judenrat*, the Jewish council set up by the Germans to administer Jewish affairs. Biberstein had offered a bribe to a German official to try to allow ten thousand Jews to remain at home, and he is now serving a jail sentence.

Chapter 8

In March 1940, a Jewish ghetto is set up. All Jews must live within its confines. Schindler's workers no longer receive wages but must live on their rations. Their payment goes to SS headquarters in Kraków. The Jews hear of Schindler's factory as a place where they will be well treated, and Schindler tells his workers that they will be safe with him and that if they work with him, they will survive the war.

Chapter 9

Schindler returns to his hometown of Zwittau and meets his estranged father.

Chapter 10

Conditions worsen in the Jewish ghetto, and there is great resentment towards the members of the *Judenrat*. Germany invades Russia, and the war intensifies.

Chapter 11

At the end of 1941, Schindler is arrested; he suspects one of his Polish workers has informed on him. He is questioned about his factory and released after his secretary contacts his police and SS friends, who intervene on his behalf.

Chapter 12

On April 28, 1942, his birthday, Schindler kisses a Jewish girl at the factory. He is arrested again. *Obersturmbannführer* Rolf Czurda, whom Schindler has met at cocktail parties, releases Schindler but warns him against this type of behavior.

Chapter 13

Pfefferberg, who had been working as a tutor, finds he cannot get a *Blauschein*, an identity sticker for Jews that provides some measure of security against arbitrary deportation. He receives one after declaring himself to be a metal polisher.

Chapter 14

Abraham Bankier and other workers are loaded into cattle cars and are about to be transported to labor camps. Schindler has them removed from the trains after threatening the officials in charge.

Chapter 15

In the pivotal scene of the novel, Schindler and his German girlfriend, Ingrid, are riding their horses on a hilly parkland, in full view of the Jewish ghetto. They witness the liquidation of the ghetto and the murder of countless men, women, and children. Schindler is particularly moved by the sight of a little girl in red. Later, the author says, Schindler would lay special weight on this day. Schindler says, "Beyond this day . . . no thinking person could fail to see what would happen. I was now resolved to do everything in my power to defeat the system."

Chapter 16

More details of the razing of the ghetto are revealed, as well as stories of escapes and resistance.

Chapter 17

Schindler has the reputation among Jews as a man who will assist them, and he helps the Jewish underground movement.

Chapter 18

Schindler travels to Hungary with Dr. Sedlacek, as Austrian dentist, to report the atrocities in Poland.

Chapter 19

Amon Goeth is installed as commandant of the forced labor camp at Plaszow. Examples of Goeth's brutality are described, including his execution of the Jewish engineer who is supervising the building of the barracks on the camp.

Chapter 20

Goeth and Schindler meet, and Schindler explains why his factory cannot be moved to Plaszow, as had been directed: for purely industrial reasons. Schindler is depressed after he sees the conditions at Plaszow. It is the last day of the existence of the ghetto, and the chapter ends with a description of Dr. H's nurses administering cyanide to the dying patients in the ghetto hospital to spare them being slaughtered by the German military.

Chapter 21

More than four thousand people who resisted deportation from the ghetto are found and executed in the streets. They are taken to Plaszow and buried in mass graves. Pfefferberg narrowly escapes death.

Chapter 22

Schindler makes plans to open his own factory camp outside Plaszow, and he obtains permission from *Oberführer* Julius Scherner and Goeth to do so, but he must foot the entire bill for the operation. The construction of the "subcamp" is approved.

Chapter 23

The Emalia camp is seen as a haven, and there is competition to get into it. Although the SS have some control over it, there are no beatings and the inmates are relatively well fed. Schindler is visited by Regina Perlman, who asks that her parents be moved from the labor camp to his subcamp. Schindler does not immediately consent, in case she is a spy, but her parents are eventually moved there. Stern brings a number of workers to the camp, including the Rabbi Menasha Levartov. While visiting the factory, Goeth finds that Levartov is not making hinges quickly enough and takes him out to shoot him. His pistol does not fire. He takes out another revolver to do the job, and it does not fire either.

Chapter 24

Schindler visits Goeth and tempts him towards being more restrained in his behavior towards prisoners—and to stop killing Jews at random from his balcony as he has been doing. Goeth likes the idea, and for a while he stops his arbitrary executions. But his clemency does not last long. It is also learned that Goeth and his clique are making personal fortunes through their corrupt dealings at the Plaszow Labor Camp.

Chapter 25

Schindler continues to spend vast sums of money to bribe officials and procure supplies to run his factory camp and take care of the inmates there.

Chapter 26

Details of the harsh living conditions of the Plaszow camp are given. Amid the suffering and routine executions, Josef and Rebecca Bau have a traditional courtship and get married in a Jewish ceremony. Schindler travels to Oranienberg to get assurances from officials that his subcamp will not be closed.

Chapter 27

Goeth is ordered to burn the dead bodies around the Plaszow camp. Schindler tells Stern that he is going to get all his Jewish workers out of their situation—or at least, he says, he will get Stern out.

Chapter 28

Goeth sends 1,400 adults and 268 children to Auschwitz as part of the "Health Action."

Chapter 29

Goeth tells Schindler that they must be aware of a Polish partisan attack from outside the camp. Later than evening Schindler is encouraged by news that Hitler has been assassinated, but it turns out not to be true. He becomes increasingly depressed. He gets word that the camps around Kraków will be disbanded.

Chapter 30

Schindler learns that Emalia must be disbanded and his workers sent to Plaszow for "relocation," which certainly means they will be sent to the death camps. Schindler approaches Goeth and says he wants to move his factory to Czechoslovakia. He would be "grateful" for any support—which means he will pay Goeth a bribe for allowing him to do so. Goeth agrees and says he will allow a list of people to be drawn up. Schindler "wins" Helen Hirsch from Goeth in a game of blackjack, and she is added to the list of skilled workers he will take to his factory.

Chapter 31

Goeth is arrested by the SS for his embezzlements, black-market dealings, and other illegal activities. Schindler drives to Brinnlitz in

Czechoslovakia to look at the site for his relocated factory camp. He spends one hundred thousand reichsmarks to grease the transfer to Brinnlitz. He draws up a list of names of prisoners. Marcel Goldberg, a personnel clerk, is in charge of the list and takes bribes to include names on it.

Chapter 32

The men on the Schindler list are transported by train to Brinnlitz. It is a three-day journey in freezing conditions.

Chapter 33

The Jewish male workers arrive in Brinnlitz. The women are transported from Plaszow and find themselves in the concentration camp at Auschwitz-Birkenau. Some are killed in the first days. The wretched conditions and the gassings in the camp are described. After more than ten days, Schindler manages to secure the women's return. Meanwhile, the Brinnlitz factory camp is set up. It ostensibly produces artillery casings, but this is simply a front; there is no production at the factory at all. The SS officers in charge of the camp are not allowed into the factory and may not hurt the prisoners without justification or a trial. Emilie Schindler works at the camp clinic.

Chapter 34

One of the camp workers, Janek Dresner, is accused of sabotage of the camp machinery by a German engineer supervisor. The officer in charge of the camp, *Untersturmführer* Liepold, wants to make an example of him. Schindler handles the problem by cursing and hitting the boy in front of the engineer, dismissing him as too ignorant to miscalibrate a machine, as he had been accused of doing. This is an example of the "stunts" pulled by Schindler to save the lives of his workers.

Chapter 35

Schindler manages to evade other inspections at his factory and hide the fact that it is producing nothing. He pays bribes to officials to maintain their silence. There are complaints from the townspeople about the prisoners and the state of the factory. During this time Schindler acquires an arsenal of weapons, and he trains some of the prisoners to use the firearms.

Chapter 36

Schindler pays the authorities for the prisoners from the Goleszow quarry, who arrive at his camp near death, to work for him. Goeth, released from prison, visits Schindler's new camp.

Chapter 37

On Schindler's thirty-seventh birthday, his workers present him with a small box crafted by one of the metalworkers. He makes a speech, saying that the tyranny will soon be over and that he will stay at Brinnlitz until they are free. He also arranges for the dismissal of Liepold from the camp. The war ends with the German surrender, and Schindler is happy but frightened by the news of the execution of German civilians. Schindler knows he must flee, and before he does, his workers present him with a ring on which is inscribed, "He who saves a single life saves the world entire." Schindler makes another long speech, urging the SS to leave quietly and for the workers to exercise restraint against their aggressors. The prisoners also present Schindler with a letter of introduction, written in Hebrew, explaining his extraordinary circumstances. The car is prepared for Schindler's departure; sacks of diamonds are inserted into the upholstery.

Chapter 38

The SS garrison leaves the factory camp, and Schindler, his wife, and eight prisoners leave Brinnlitz. They travel through Czechoslovakia, and in Prague the car is stripped of the diamonds. In Czechoslovakia they also encounter American troops, who treat them well. When they cross the Swiss border, they are arrested by the French police on suspicion on having been concentration camp guards. The Hebrew letter of introduction has been left with the Americans, and the group is afraid of what the Allies might do to Schindler if they find out he was the director of a camp. Schindler, his wife, and the prisoners are all interrogated and eventually decide to tell the truth. When the French hear their story, they weep and embrace them. In the meantime, the Soviets liberate the camp at Brinnlitz.

Epilogue

After the war, Schindler and his wife move to Munich, where they share lodgings with some of his former workers. Schindler takes on a Jewish mistress, and he clings to the company of "his Jews" who had come to Germany. He hears that Goeth had been condemned to death and hanged in Kraków in 1946. In 1949, Schindler receives $15,000 and a reference from an international Jewish relief organization to whom he had made reports during the war. He, Emilie, and other *Schindlerjuden* move to Argentina, where Schindler becomes a farmer. His business fails, and in 1957 he leaves Argentina, and Emilie, to return to Germany. He buys a cement factory, but that too fails, and by 1961 he is bankrupt again. In 1961, several *Schindlerjuden* invite him to Israel. He is honored by the municipality of Tel Aviv and in Jerusalem is declared a Righteous Person and invited to plant a carob tree in the Avenue of the Righteous leading to the *Yad Vashem* Museum. He spends some months of every year in Israel, living the rest of the time in cramped quarters in Frankfurt in a state of loneliness and depression and with almost no money. He continues to help with the effort to identify war criminals. In 1966, he is honored by the German government for his wartime efforts. In his sixties, Schindler begins working for the German Friends of Hebrew University raising funds in West Germany. In 1972, three *Schindlerjuden* dedicate a floor of the Truman Research Center at Hebrew University to Schindler. Schindler dies in 1974 in Frankfurt and is buried in Jerusalem.

Characters

Abraham Bankier

Abraham Bankier is the office manager of the defunct enamelware business that Schindler buys; he becomes the manager of Schindler's Deutsche Email Fabrik. He is one of a number of workers who is boarded onto a cattle car bound for a labor camp near Lublin before Schindler secures their rescue.

Josef Bau

Josef Bau is a young artist from Kraków who, while working at the Plaszow camp, falls in love with, courts, and marries Rebecca Tannenbaum in a Jewish ceremony.

Rebecca Bau

See Rebecca Tannenbaum

Oswald Bosko

Bosko is a German police *Wachmeister*, or sergeant, sympathetic to the Jews and who, early in the novel, has control of the ghetto perimeter. He is so rebellious against the regime that he lets raw material into the ghetto to be made into goods and then lets the goods out to be sold—without asking for a bribe. He is a "man of ideas" in contrast

to Schindler, who is a "man of transactions." Bosko eventually absconds from his police station and vanishes into the partisan forests, but he is found and shot for treason.

Wilek Chilowicz

The chief of the Jewish camp police, Chilowicz works in the Plaszow camp for Goeth and the SS. He is the "hander-out of the caps and armbands of authority in the debased kingdom" and "equates his power with that of the tsars." He is also used by Goeth as an agent of the black market, and since he knows so much about Goeth's dealings, Goeth eventually must get rid of him. The commandant does this by promising him and his family an escape from the camp and then has him found with a gun and executes him.

Rolf Czurda

Rolf Czurda is an *Obersturnbannführer*, or lieutenant colonel, and chief of the Kraków branch of the SD security service. Schindler meets him at a number of cocktail parties. Czurda releases Schindler after the latter is arrested and imprisoned for kissing a Jewish girl at his factory. Czurda warns Schindler that his behavior is no longer acceptable, saying, "That's not just old-fashioned Jew-hate talking. I assure you. It's policy." Goeth's Plaszow camp is under the authority of Czurda and his superior, Julian Scherner.

Danka Dresner

Danka is the daughter of the Dresners and cousin of "Red Genia." During an *Aktion* in the ghetto, she is hidden in the wall by an irrational woman who insists that she cannot fit Mrs. Dresner in also.

Mrs. Dresner

Mrs. Dresner is the mother of Danka Dresner. She and her daughter are on the list to go to Schindler's Brinnlitz camp, but they are sent to Auschwitz. Mrs. Dresner almost dies but is nursed back to health by Emilie Schindler.

Genia

"Red Genia," as she is called, is the young girl in red whom Schindler, from his horse, sees amid the confusion during the liquidation of the Kraków ghetto in March of 1943. Schindler does not know who she is, but it is learned that she is staying with the Dresners after the Polish couple living in the countryside find it too risky to look after her; her parents had been rounded up by the SS and taken away. "Redcap," as she is called by the Dresner boys, is a first cousin of Mrs. Dresner. She is schooled by her Polish caretakers to pretend not to be Jewish but Polish. Schindler wonders why the SS men do not execute her immediately but steer her back in line when she breaks free. He later realizes that this means that they recognize that she—like all witnesses—is to be executed.

Commandant Amon Goeth

Commandant Goeth is the SS *Untersturmführer*, or second lieutenant, who liquidizes the Kraków ghetto and takes command of the resultant forced labor camp at Plaszow. "Mad Amon," as he is called, is the embodiment of evil in the novel. He takes pride in extinguishing the Jewish ghetto and rules the labor camp without mercy. He also uses his position to do illicit business and make himself a fortune. Goeth is referred to as Schindler's "dark brother" because they are very similar in some ways. Like Schindler, Goeth is raised Catholic; in school he studied engineering, physics, and math; he is a practical man, not a thinker, but fancies himself something of a philosopher; he has a weakness for liquor and has a massive physique. But unlike Schindler, Goeth is a cruel man who is physically abusive—the Plaszow camp is a place of terror because Goeth shoots prisoners at random from the balcony of his villa overlooking the barracks. Schindler mistakenly thinks himself as a philosopher, but Goeth is completely deluded about his personality because he thinks of himself as a sensitive "man of letters." He is violent and unspeakably barbaric yet is sentimental about his children (from his second marriage), whom he has not seen for some time. He beats his Jewish maid, Helen Hirsch, but when he is arrested, he writes to her thinking she will give him a positive character reference. Goeth is a deeply troubled man, plagued with insomnia. There are allusions to him being a demented king or emperor whose sense of power has made him completely insane. Pfefferberg says of him, "When you saw Goeth, you saw death." Goeth is arrested by the SS on black-marketeering charges in 1944. After the war he is handed over to the Polish government, condemned, and hanged in 1946.

Marcel Goldberg

Goldberg is the personnel clerk at the Plaszow camp who takes bribes to put prisoners' names on the list of workers who will go to Schindler's relocated Brinnlitz camp. He is described as "a man of prodigious and accidental power" who keeps people in the dark about the list.

Helen Hirsch

Goeth's Jewish maid, whom he badly abuses and calls "Lena," is approached by Schindler in Goeth's villa, and she confides in him and tells him about Goeth's treatment of her, including the daily beatings. She gives Schindler her nest egg of 4,000 zloty to buy back her sister, who works in the camp kitchens, if she is ever put on the cattle cars; her sister's survival is Helen's "obsession." Schindler "wins" Hirsch from Goeth in a game of blackjack, and so she goes to work in his relocated camp factory.

Albert Hujar

Oberscharführer Hujar shoots Dr. Rosalia Blau while in the ghetto, and Diana Reiter after the foundations of the barracks collapsed. He falls in love with a Jewish prisoner.

Ingrid

Ingrid is Schindler's German girlfriend.

Victoria Klonowska

Schindler's beautiful Polish secretary works in his front office. Klonowska looks "like one of those lighthearted girls to whom the inconveniences of history are a temporary intrusion into the real business of life," but she is also hardheaded, efficient, and adroit. When Schindler is arrested, Klonowska negotiates with German dignitaries for her lover's release from the SS prison.

Rabbi Menasha Levartov

The young, scholarly city rabbi, masquerading as a metalworker in Plaszow, is brought by Stern to work at the Emalia camp. Stern tells Schindler that Goeth will certainly kill Menasha, as he was drawn to "people of presence." Goeth had attempted to murder the rabbi one day when he decided the latter was not making hinges quickly enough in the metalworks. The commandant fired his gun at Menasha, but it failed to go off. A second revolver also fails to fire. When Menasha is at his factory, Schindler urges him to leave work to honor the *Shabbat*, and the rabbi goes behind the barracks and recites *Kiddush* over a cup of wine.

Edith Liebgold

Edith, one of the Jewish women workers in Schindler's factory, finds herself believing Schindler's "godlike promise" when he tells her and other Jewish women on their arrival at the factory that "You'll be safe working here. If you work here, then you'll live through the war." Schindler, she says, infects her with certainty.

Josef Liepold

Liepold is the SS commanding officer at Schindler's Brinnlitz factory camp.

Julius Madritsch

Madritsch owns the uniform factory inside the Plaszow camp. He is a Viennese who managed to get himself released from the police force and took up the post of a *Treuhänder*, or supervisor, of a plant manufacturing military uniforms. Later, he opens a factory of his own in the suburb of Podgórze and, on Goeth's instructions, moves the camp to Plaszow. He is an "enterprising but humane" man who illicitly feeds and protects the four thousand workers in his camp.

Majola

Majola, Goeth's girlfriend, is a secretary at a factory. She has "sensitive manners," and it is rumored that she threatened not to sleep with Goeth if he continued arbitrarily gunning people down in the labor camp.

Mietek Pemper

Pemper is a studious young prisoner who works for Goeth as his typist. With his photographic memory, Pemper eventually contributes to Goeth's downfall by testifying against him—and remembering key facts of his illegal dealings at Plaszow.

Regina Perlman

Regina Perlman is a Jewish woman who lives in Kraków on forged South American papers. She visits Schindler and asks him if he would bring her parents to his camp. Schindler does not acknowledge her request, in case she is a spy, but within a month her parents come from Plaszow to his enamelware factory camp.

Leopold Pfefferberg

The colorful Leopold Pfefferberg—Polish war commander, teacher, black market dealer, and organizer—is the man from whom author Keneally first hears the story of Schindler. Before the war, Pfefferberg—young, confident, and "built like a wedge"—was a high school teacher. Before the action of the novel begins, he had been a company commander in the Polish army and had been taken prisoner by the Germans. He manages to escape by his wits, waving an official-looking document to some officials and taking the trolley home. Several times in the novel, Pfefferberg narrowly escapes death and imprisonment by thinking quickly on his feet. He has Aryan looks, so he sometimes roams through the ghetto freely, running illegal goods (for Schindler as well as others). He works for a time with the OD (Jewish Police) but leaves it after it becomes an instrument of the SS. During the *Aktion*, Pfefferberg encounters Goeth, who is almost certainly going to kill him. Pfefferberg tells the commandant he is under instructions to put the bundles together on one side of the road and so manages to live. He and his wife, Mila, get on the list to work at Schindler's Brinnlitz camp.

Mila Pfefferberg

Leopold Pfefferberg's wife, Mila, is a small, nervous girl in her twenties, a refugee from Lodz whom Pfefferberg had married in the first days of the ghetto. She is from a generation of physicians, lived a sweet childhood, and began medical education in Vienna the year before the war. She is the last surviving member of her family. She is quiet, clever, and wise; she has a gift for irony and is very different from her outgoing husband. Mila refuses to escape the ghetto by going into the sewers with Leopold.

Poldek Pfefferberg

See Leopold Pfefferberg

Philip

Philip is the *Waffen* SS *Standartenführer* (colonel) whom Schindler meets in prison and who had been arrested for being absent without leave after he and his Polish girlfriend "lose themselves in each other."

Diana Reiter

Diana Reiter is the architectural engineer and prisoner who is assigned to the construction of the barracks at Plaszow. She is ordered to be executed by Goeth when she argues with an officer, Albert Hujar, about the construction of the barracks. Before she dies, Goeth recognizes a "knowingness" in her eyes that say, *It will take more than that.*

Richard

Richard is the young German chef/manager who befriends Henry Rosner and helps to hide Rosner's son, Olek, during an *Aktion*.

Artur Rosenzweig

As the chairman of the *Judenrat* (Jewish council) and president of the OD (Jewish police), Rosenzweig sought to protect the interests of the Jews. "Decent" Rosenzweig is replaced by David Gutter, who does the bidding of the SS.

Henry Rosner

Henry Rosner is a violinist and prisoner at Plaszow. He and his family moved from Warsaw to the village of Tyniec before the Warsaw ghetto was sealed up. In Tyniec, and later in Kraków and the Plaszow camp, Henry and his brother Leopold, an accordionist, play for Goeth and the SS. While playing during a dinner party at Goeth's villa, Henry "fiddles up the death" of an SS officer. Goeth does not let Henry go to Schindler's camp because he appreciates his music too much. He is later transported to Auschwitz with his son, Olek, but they both survive.

Olek Rosner

Olek is the son of Henry and Manci Rosenberg. He is hidden by friends in Kraków and then brought unregistered to Plaszow and shipped off to Auschwitz with his father.

Julian Scherner

An SS *Oberführer* (rank above colonel) and the final authority for all Jewish matters in Kraków, Scherner is a middle-aged man who looks like a nondescript bureaucrat, likes to talk about business and investments, and is interested in liquor, women, and confiscated goods. He wears the smirk of his unexpected power "like a childish jam stain in the corner of the mouth" and is "always convivial and dependably heartless."

Emilie Schindler

Schindler's convent-schooled, fresh-faced wife, Emilie, marries at a young age and almost from the beginning puts up with her husband's infidelities. She knows her husband is not and will not be faithful, but she nonetheless does not want evidence of his affairs "thrust under her nose." One of Emilie's close friends as a girl was a Jew, Rita Reif, who is executed in 1942 by local Nazi officials. This might be an explanation for her willingness to help tend the sick Jewish workers at the Brinnlitz camp. Emilie nurses back to life several sick women and tends to the needs of dying patients. Some speculate that Emilie's kindnesses may have been "absorbed" into the legend of Schindler "the way the deeds of minor heroes have been subsumed by the figure of Arthur or Robin Hood." Emilie flees Czechoslovakia after the war with Schindler and eventually moves with him to Argentina. He continues to have affairs and finally leaves her and returns to Germany in 1957.

Oskar Schindler

Oskar Schindler, the subject of the novel, is a Czech-born industrialist who saves more than 1,100 of his Jewish factory workers from the death mills in German-occupied Poland. Schindler is flamboyant, a man of "magnetic charm," who uses his considerable skill to make friends with and grease the palms of SS officials so that he keeps his workers alive. Schindler is the unlikely hero of the novel: a womanizer and spendthrift, he comes to Kraków to make his fortune in wartime Poland (setting up an enamelware factory) and ends up performing a tremendously courageous act that saves the lives of hundreds of people. Schindler cheats on his wife with not one but two mistresses; he spends lavish amounts of money on liquor, cigars, and cars; and he comes to Kraków to become a tycoon off the free labor of Jews. But he risks his business to save his workers and eventually bankrupts himself by setting up a nonproductive factory so that they may be safe from the death camps. The author of the novel does not make very clear what Schindler's motivation is for his actions, but he does indicate that a turning point in his life was the liquidation of the Kraków ghetto, when he saw Jewish men, women, and children being murdered in the streets. "Beyond this day," Schindler says, "no thinking person could fail to see what would happen. I was now resolved to do everything in my power to defeat the system." Schindler is a complex character, the author says, because his is an unconventional type of virtue. Not only does he have indulgences, but he is a character of ambiguity. It is not clear *what* Schindler sees on the day of the ghetto liquidation that makes him act in the way he does. For sure, Schindler is not a thinking man (although he fancies himself a philosopher) but a practical one, and his methods are those of a man of action. But still there is a mystery as to what in him changed so that this congenial, apolitical man suddenly felt he needed to risk his life to save others. As his wife, Emilie, says, before and after the war Schindler's life was unexceptional, but in the short era between 1939 and 1945, he met people who "summoned forth his deeper talents." After the war, Schindler is honored by the Israeli government as a Righteous Person.

Dr. Sedlacek

Sedlacek is the Austrian dentist who works for a Zionist rescue organization in Budapest and who elicits Schindler's help to gather information.

Symche Spira

Spira is a new force in the OD (Jewish police) after it is controlled by the SS. He takes his orders from SS headquarters and rules the ghetto with a misguided sense of power. He extorts people and makes out lists for the SS of unsatisfactory or seditious ghetto dwellers. He is referred to as "high-booted" Spira, the "Napoleon" of the ghetto. He is eventually executed by the SS.

Itzhak Stern

Itzhak Stern is Schindler's accountant, friend, and "confessor." In contrast to Schindler, he is a thin, scholarly man who has the "manners of a Talmudic scholar and a European intellectual." Schindler meets him when he seeks advice about buying a factory. Stern thinks of Schindler as dangerous and resents his gestures of equality, and the first thing he tells Schindler is that he should know that he is "a Jew." Schindler responds that he is a German. During their first conversation, Schindler remarks on the difficulty that priests must have during these times talking about the verse in the Bible that talks about God caring about the death of even one sparrow. Stern replies that the sentiment may be summed up in the Talmudic verse that says that he who saves the life of one man saves the whole world—the verse that the prisoners later have inscribed on the ring they present to Schindler as a goodbye gift. Stern is well connected and practical besides being learned. He gets Jews into Schindler's factory and helps him with the details of the factory. He also, ironically, comforts Schindler before a coming *Aktion* and is Schindler's strength when he is depressed. Even when he works at the Plaszow camp, he is invaluable to Schindler's work and continues to be his confidant at Brinnlitz.

Rebecca Tannenbaum

Rebecca is the young woman who works as Goeth's manicurist and is courted by and marries Josef Bau in a traditional Jewish ceremony in the labor camp.

Raimund Tisch

The Madritsch supervisor in Plaszow, who smuggles in truckloads of food for prisoners in the uniform factory, is a quiet, clerkly Austrian Catholic man. He plays chess with Goeth (and loses) to improve the commandant's mood—and so save the prisoners' lives by preventing random executions. Tisch types the list of prisoners that will go to Schindler's camp. He is eventually honored by the Israeli government.

Themes

Virtue

In the opening pages of *Schindler's List*, Keneally says explicitly that it is the story "of the pragmatic triumph of good over evil" and of the story of a man who is not "virtuous" in the customary sense. Writing about evil, he goes on to say, is fairly straightforward, but it is more risky and complex to write about virtue. The hero of the novel, Oskar Schindler, is complicated because he seems to be at once virtuous *and* immoral. Schindler is married but keeps house with his German mistress and maintains a long affair with his Polish secretary. He is outgoing and generous but has even greater personal indulgences, including good cigars and cognac. He excels in profiting from shady dealings, procuring goods from the black market and bribing officials, through which he saves his workers' lives. From the beginning of the novel, Schindler seems to treat the Jews he encounters with respect, but for a long time he seems oblivious to the cruelties they face, being more interested in his business than the political situation around him. Also, after the war, and after his heroic rescue of his Jewish workers, Schindler leads an unremarkable life: he does not do good works or act as a champion of the powerless, but rather he again cheats on his wife, spends money lavishly, fails at his business ventures, and bankrupts himself. Yet, he is honored by the Martyrs' and Heroes' Remembrance Authority (*Yad Vashem*) Museum in Israel and declared a "Righteous Person." Perhaps the most difficult and interesting question raised by *Schindler's List* is, in fact, in what way Oskar Schindler is considered a "Righteous Person." Is he righteous simply because of his actions? His motivations? His personality?

Throughout the book, Keneally draws attention to the difficult nature of virtue (again, seen most obviously in the character of Schindler), to the not-so-obvious contrast between good and evil (Schindler is compared repeatedly to his "dark twin," the clearly evil Amon Goeth), and to what exactly constitutes morality. For example, the Austrian bureaucrat Szepessi has "a humane reputation even though he serviced the monstrous machine."

Topics for Further Study

- Research the "death camps" set up by the Nazis during World War II. Examine four in detail and compare them to the Plaszow labor camp described in *Schindler's List*.

- Research the lives of at least three other "righteous ones" honored by Yad Vashem, the Holocaust memorial in Jerusalem, for their rescue efforts during World War II.

- Compare the characters of Oskar Schindler and Amon Goeth. In what ways are they similar and in what ways different? How does Keneally use the similarities and differences between the two men to underscore the themes in his novel?

- Set up a mock trial for Amon Goeth, trying him for his crimes against the Jewish prisoners at Plaszow. What punishment should he receive?

- Compare Keneally's account in his novel to the treatment of Schindler's story in Steven Spielberg's movie. How do they differ?

- Why do you think Keneally wrote his book as a novel? Use textual evidence to explain the effects of Keneally's strategy and his possible motives.

Keneally also illustrates certain warped conceptions of goodness and morality that are entertained by various characters. The German prisoner Philip, whom Schindler meets after he is arrested for kissing a Jewish girl in his factory, complains about the corruptibility and thievery of the SS but seems unmoved by the fact that they routinely murder Jews. Goeth's conception of good and evil is perhaps most distorted, as seen when Goeth is "tempted" toward restraint and goodness by Schindler and entertains the idea the he might be seen as "Amon the Good."

Lists

Lists of various kinds figure throughout *Schindler's List*. The Nazis use lists to keep track of Jews, and they keep lists (such as invoices, man-

ifests, and vouchers) to sort the loot they plunder from their victims. When Schindler's office manager, Abraham Bankier, does not turn up at his factory and is put in a cattle car bound for a labor camp, Schindler confronts a young *Oberscharführer* who holds an enormous list of names of those who are to be transported. The official refuses to release Bankier and Schindler's other workers because "they're on the list." Schindler retorts that "it is not my place to argue with the list," demands to see the official's superiors, and thus gets around the system and frees his workers. It is through the use of such lists that the Nazis create a seemingly clean, orderly system to rid Europe of Jews. Lists make individuals seem less than human, like objects that can be counted, categorized, and dispensed with. Even the Jewish police, such as Symche Spira and other OD members, make out for the SS lists of unsatisfactory or seditious ghetto dwellers; in this way they aid the Nazi in their systematic annihilation of their brethren. Other Jews, such as Marcel Goldberg, a clerk in charge of lists ("labor lists and transport lists and the lists of living and dead"), receive bribes for putting Jews on favorable lists, including a list of those who work at Schindler's factory. Schindler, however, is not at all partial to lists. He does not like paperwork, preferring under-the-counter work and leaving details to his managers and secretaries. But, ironically, it is by creating a list of workers that he extricates and saves them from the labor camps and almost certain death. It is by creating this list, which Dolek Horowitz thinks of as "a sweet chariot which might swing low," that Schindler saves more than 1,100 Jews from the well-oiled German machinery whose purpose it was to exterminate them.

Witnesses

The importance of the testimony of witnesses is stressed in many discussions of the Holocaust. Witnesses are survivors who tell the world of the horrors they experienced so that perhaps history will not repeat itself. *Schindler's List* is a story that is reconstructed through the eyewitness accounts of fifty Holocaust survivors. As characters in the novel, many of them are represented as being distinctly aware of their status as witnesses. As Schindler observes the *Aktion* in which the Jewish ghetto is decimated, he has the sense of being a witness. It is at this stage, too, that he recognizes that the SS officer's leniency to the little girl in red means that the Nazis believe that all witnesses will perish—that is, that all Jews and Jewish sympathizers will be exterminated. Poldek Pfefferberg, too, when he moves among the dead bodies after an *Aktion*, "sensed why he had been placed there. He believed unshakably in better years to come, years of just tribunals." For many Jews, the need to recount their stories and to let the world know what happened helped them to continue to fight for survival. As one of the women at the Auschwitz camp says to Clara Sternberg as the latter looks for the electric fences on which to electrocute herself, "Don't kill yourself on the fence, Clara. If you do that, you'll never know what happened to you."

Style

Documentary Novel

Schindler's List is a "documentary novel," a novel that recreates events that actually took place in real life. The events described in the book are based on interviews with fifty Schindler survivors and enriched by extensive research as well as by the author's visits to Kraków, Plaszow, and Auschwitz-Birkenau. Keneally goes to great lengths to describe characters as they were in real life and to create a sense of realism. But he uses the texture and devices of the novel—a form normally used for fictional accounts—to tell the *true* story of Oskar Schindler because, he says, "the novel's techniques seem suited for a character of such ambiguity and magnitude as Oskar." Keneally stresses, though, that he attempts to avoid fiction in his work because "fiction would debase the record." He says that, although he has recreated some of the conversations, all events are based on detailed recollections of witnesses to the acts described. The result is a work that moves back and forth between simply telling a story and embellishing or commenting upon that story by examining how the author came to know the facts, how the facts may be disputed, or how the witnesses feel about certain events. For example, the author sometimes intrudes into a story to mention that another witness has a different account of those events, how a particular survivor says he or she felt about Schindler, and so on. The effect of this authorial intrusion is always to return the reader to reality, to make it plain that the events described are not merely a novelistic fantasy but a true account that impacted people's lives in ways that can barely be imagined.

The story of Oskar Schindler and the rescue of the "Schindler Jews" unfolds through a series of stories about dozens of characters. The narratives are pieced together by the author so that they are interesting anecdotes or character sketches on their own, but they also weave into the larger story about Schindler. The effect of this technique is that what becomes of most importance in the book is people, the minute details of their lives, the ideas they held and intimate moments they cherished. Unlike the film version of *Schindler's List*, Keneally's novel is memorable not so much for the backdrop of the labor camps and atrocities of war but for the realistic description of people and the personal sufferings or victories they experienced. There is, for example, the story of the courtship and marriage of Josef and Rebecca Bau in the barracks of the Plaszow camp, that of Henry Rosner playing the fiddle so magically that an SS officer kills himself, that of the young man who escapes Belzec by hiding for three days in the pit of the latrines, and that of young Janka Feigenbaum dying of cancer. That the novel is constructed in this way conveys a sense that the story of the Holocaust is made up of stories of individuals, each one a human life.

Symbols and Imagery

Despite its factual tone, *Schindler's List* uses a number of symbols and images, some of them recurring, to underscore its central questions and ideas. One of the most memorable scenes in the book is when Schindler, sitting on his horse, observes the destruction of the Jewish ghetto and, amidst all the turmoil, the figure of a small child wearing a red dress. It is after witnessing this event that Schindler vows to do everything he can to defeat the system. The red dress makes the young girl stand out, and it seems, for the first time, Schindler really understands that the Jews in the ghetto are individuals—humans—who are being subjected to the most inhuman treatment imaginable. The smallness of the child may be seen to represent innocence and the red to represent the blood of the Jewish people.

Other ideas that are used repeatedly in the book are those of gods, kings, and heroes. Oskar is referred to as a "minor god of deliverance, double-faced" who brings salvation to his Jewish workers. This ties in with the question of the complex nature of morality, for Schindler is not a conventional type of god. He is like Bacchus, the god of wine, who loves to indulge in good food and drink, but he also performs good acts. The imagery of kings is used often when describing Goeth, who fancies himself an emperor. He is compared to the Roman emperor Caligula, famed for his cruelty and excesses. Also, when he plays blackjack with

Schindler over the fate of Helen Hirsch, Goeth draws a king and loses the game. The notion of heroism is explored not only with the unlikely heroism of Schindler but in the description of many of the Jewish characters. During the *Aktion* in which the Jewish ghetto is razed, for example, Dr. H's nurse administers cyanide to his dying patients so that they can "escape" being murdered by the SS. "The woman is the hero of this," the doctor says to himself.

Historical Context

Hitler, WWII, and the Jewish Holocaust

The mass murder of European Jews and others under Nazi rule during World War II has come to be known simply as the Holocaust. "Holocaust" literally means "massive destruction by fire." It is thought that eleven million people were killed by the Nazis. These included political opponents (particularly Communists), Slavs, gypsies, mentally and/or physically disabled, homosexuals, and other "undesirables." An estimated six million men, women, and children were killed merely because they were Jews. The destruction of the Jews in Europe stands as the archetype of genocide in human history.

Jews had been the subjects of persecution in Europe at least since the seventeenth century. When Adolph Hitler, the charismatic, Austrian-born demagogue, rose to power in Germany during the 1920s and early 1930s, he rallied the German people with a message that included notions of "Aryan," or white, superiority and the inferiority of other races. The Jews were a special target of his hatred, and they were incorrectly represented during this time of social, political, and economic upheaval as being wealthy and in control of the country's economy. In 1932, Hitler ran for president of Germany. He did not win, but he did well, and when the party in power was unable to end the depression, its leaders turned to Hitler for help. He became chancellor, or prime minister, of Germany in 1933. Within weeks, he set into motion a series of laws that destroyed the nation's democratic government. He eliminated all opposition and launched a program of world domination and extermination of the Jews. His government, like all totalitarian regimes, established complete political, social, and cultural control over its subjects.

In Hitler's program for the "Aryanization" of Germany and world conquest, Jews were subjected first to discrimination, then persecution, and then state-condoned terrorism. This had as a turning point, the "night of the broken glass" also known as Kristallnacht, which took place in Munich, Germany, in November 1938. Nazi storm troopers burned down synagogues and broke into Jewish homes, terrorizing men, women, and children. Over twenty thousand people were arrested and taken to concentration camps. After Kristallnacht, Jewish businesses were expropriated, employers were urged to fire Jewish employees, and offices were set up to expedite emigration. Jews could buy their freedom and leave the country, but they had to abandon their assets when they left. By the outbreak of war in September 1939, half of Germany's five hundred thousand Jews had fled, as had many Jews from other German-occupied areas. When the Nazis invaded western Poland in 1939, two-thirds of Polish Jews—Europe's largest Jewish community—fell into their hands. As is described in *Schindler's List*, Polish Jews were rounded up and placed in ghettos, where it is estimated that five hundred thousand people died of starvation and disease.

After Soviet invasion in June 1941, the Nazis launched a crusade against the supposed Jewish-Communist conspiracy. Police battalions called *Einsatzgruppen* (operations groups) moved from town to town, rounding up Jewish men and suspected Soviet collaborators and shooting them. They then began to target Jewish women and children as well. The *Einsaztgruppen* murdered some two million people, almost all Jews.

While these massacres were taking place, Hitler's Nazi government was planning a "Final Solution" to the "Jewish question." Death camp operations began in December 1941 at Semlin in Serbia and at Chelmno in Poland, where people were killed by exhaust fumes in specially modified vans that were driven to nearby sites where bodies were plundered and burnt. At Chelmno and Semlin, 265,000 Jews were killed in this way.

More camps opened in the spring and summer of 1942, when the Nazis began clearing the ghettos in Poland and rounding up Jews in western Europe for deportation to labor and concentration camps such as those at Treblinka, Belzec, and Sobibor. The largest of the death camps was at Auschwitz. It was originally a concentration camp for Polish political prisoners but was expanded in 1941 with the addition of a larger camp at nearby Birkenau. Auschwitz-Birkenau and its subcamps held 400,000 prisoners, including 205,000 Jews. In the spring of 1942, gas chambers were built at

Compare & Contrast

- **1940s:** The dictator Adolph Hitler is the supreme ruler of Germany.

  1980s: The dictator Augusto Pinochet is the supreme leader of Chile.

  Today: The dictator Saddam Hussein is the supreme leader of Iraq.

- **1940s:** European Jews must carry passes and are marked by the Star of David so they may be identified as non-Aryans.

  1980s: Under apartheid, Black South Africans must carry "passbooks" to identify who they are.

  Today: Non-Muslims must wear markers to identify themselves as such under the Taliban government in Afghanistan.

- **1940s:** The Nazi regime carries out a program of genocide against European Jews, gypsies, and other groups.

  1980s: In the early 1980s, the Guatemalan military, acting on orders from the country's highest authorities, carry out genocide against the country's majority Mayan population.

  Today: The World Federalist Association and other human rights organizations campaign to end genocide forever, beginning in the twenty-first century, by reforming United Nations (UN) decision-making and by creating early-warning structures within the UN before the genocide starts.

Birkenau, and mass transports of Jews began to arrive there. Some were held as registered prisoners, but the great majority was gassed. These gassing operations were expanded in 1943, and four gas chamber and crematorium complexes were built. Before they were killed, the victims' valuables were stripped from them. Their hair was used to stuff mattresses, and any gold in their teeth was melted down. In total, about one million Jews died at Auschwitz-Birkenau.

The Final Solution moved into its last stages as Allied forces closed in on Germany in 1944. The camps were closed and burned down. Prisoners remaining at concentration camps in the occupied lands were transported or force-marched to camps in Germany. Thousands of prisoners on these death marches died of starvation, exhaustion, and cold, or they were shot. When the war ended and the concentration camps were liberated by Allied troops, thousands of unburied corpses and tens of thousands of sick and dying prisoners were found crammed into overcrowded barracks without food or water.

Much of Europe was destroyed in the war. Survivors of the camps were in terrible condition, both physically and psychologically. Trials were held in Nuremberg in 1945 at which top surviving Nazi leaders were tried for war crimes. Similar trials followed, but thousands of war criminals eluded justice. Israel was established as a state in 1948 and opened its doors to all Jews, and many of them who survived the Holocaust migrated there, as well as to the United States, Australia, and elsewhere.

Critical Overview

When it was published in Britain in 1982 as *Schindler's Ark*, Keneally's book was widely and prominently reviewed. Even before its publication, it had been short-listed for the Booker McConnell Prize, and there had been some mention in pre-publication reviews that the documentary style of the book made it an unusual contender for a fiction prize. The day after its official publication, *Schindler's Ark* won the Booker Prize, and a storm of controversy erupted. A number of critics felt that its deficiency in the fictional aspect undermined its quality. As Michael Hulse explains in "Virtue and the Philosophic Innocent: The British Reception of *Schindler's List*" in *Critical Quarterly*, Steven Glover, writing in the *Daily Telegraph* compared

Oskar Schindler in 1946 pictured with a group of Jews that he employed and rescued

it to a "tiresome television documentary" and D. J. Enright in the *Times Literary Supplement* found it to be on a par with second-rate adventure-style documentaries and "not a great literary novel." Many reviewers spent a great deal of time wondering whether the book was a novel, although others praised Keneally's considerable literary skill. One reviewer, Marion Glastonbury of the *New Statesman*, objected to the portrayal of Schindler as a man of virtue. Despite the controversy, however, *Schindler's Ark* was popular among British readers, selling forty thousand copies in two months.

American reviewers of *Schindler's List* also noted the book's documentary style but were less concerned with whether its nonfictional status meant it was or was not a novel. Paul Zweig in the *New York Times* declared that Keneally "has chosen a subject that art can contain," and numerous other writers found the work to be "remarkable." *Schindler's List* was soon an international bestseller, and the book cemented Keneally's status as a major writer and Australia's most prominent author.

Universal Pictures obtained rights for Steven Spielberg to turn Keneally's book into a film soon after it was published, but it did not reach development for about ten years. Before the release of

the film, Keneally's book continued to have modest success and sales. There was some interest in the work among academics, and a handful of articles appeared that discussed its status as fiction and the character of Schindler. However, after the release of the film version of *Schindler's List* in 1993 and particularly after it earned seven Academy Awards, the book enjoyed renewed popularity. Articles on the work appeared, many of them comparing Keneally's treatment of the story with that by director Steven Spielberg. But the phenomenal success of the movie has also overshadowed Keneally's accomplishment, and there are certainly more discussions in print on Spielberg's *Schindler* than on the work by the Booker Prize-winner. No volume of criticism has been devoted to Keneally's prose version of the work, for example, but there have been several books and countless articles analyzing the film, including the 1997 collection *Spielberg's Holocaust: Critical Perspectives on "Schindler's List,"* edited by Yosefa Loshitzky. The film also regularly appears in high school curricula as part of the study of the Jewish Holocaust. While Spielberg's work has certainly eclipsed Keneally's, it has also made the story of Oskar Schindler part of the American cultural imagination, and the novel has become a fixture on high school reading lists. It also continues to enjoy a wide general readership and has sold over a million copies since its publication.

Criticism

Uma Kukathas

Kukathas is a freelance writer. In this essay, Kukathas considers the narrative strategies Keneally uses in his novel.

When *Schindler's List* (under the title *Schindler's Ark*) won the Booker Prize in 1982, more than one critic objected to the fact that this work of nonfiction could win a major literary prize that had traditionally been awarded to the year's best book of fiction. Other critics complained that not only was the work not fiction, it was not good literature, mainly because of its documentary style. *Schindler's List* is an unusual novel, to be sure, because it moves back and forth between telling a story and reporting the facts of history—and people's very personal accounts of that history. It perhaps does not read like a literary novel because, in some sense, things are told too plainly. There are dozens of characters in the novel, but with the exception of Schindler and a few of his close associates, those characters are not "developed"; their complexities do not unfold in such a way that the reader begins to know them from their actions. Rather, the author explicitly tells their stories, narrates the events of their lives, reports what they are like, notes their characteristics, and offers a few key details about what they went through during the war and afterward. Also, because it is a true story, there is a certain lack of tension in the plot; from the beginning, the author makes clear exactly what will happen—that Schindler will rescue over a thousand Jews from the death camps through his own brand of ingenuity and charm. There are, then, few surprises in the sense that one usually expects from a novel; even in the thick of the main action of the story, Keneally offers information about who survives the war, how a particular character ultimately meets his or her end, and so on. However, while the narrative style of *Schindler's List* is different from traditional novels, it is far more than mere reportage and has characteristics not merely of a "good read" but of good literature. This is because of the techniques Keneally uses to suggest questions, present ambiguities, and offer layers of meaning even as he tells a straightforward, true story. Keneally uses devices found in more tradi-

> "Keneally offers surprisingly little in the way of commentary about the events that take place during the Holocaust, but he invites readers in other ways to think deeply about the meaning of what occurs."

tional works of fiction that make his documentary novel rise to the level of "literature," but at the same time his particular narrative technique has its own strengths for recounting the type of story he tells in *Schindler's List*.

In his author's note, Keneally says explicitly that his book is *not* fiction, because fiction would "debase the record" of the Holocaust. The stories he tells of the victims, survivors, and oppressors in *Schindler's List* are all based on eyewitness accounts, historical documents, and visits to the sites described in the novel. Thus, it can be assumed that Keneally does not embellish stories or infuse characters with his own authorial imagination, making them "stand for" or represent certain ideas he is trying to communicate to his reader. What Keneally does do is offer certain ideas and images throughout the novel that make the reader think about the significance of events or characters in a deeper way than might be suggested from only a strict reporting of the facts. Keneally offers surprisingly little in the way of commentary about the events that take place during the Holocaust, but he invites readers in other ways to think deeply about the meaning of what occurs.

One of the techniques Keneally uses is to repeat certain ideas and images over and over again. The most obvious one, of course, is that of the list. Nowhere does the author point out explicitly that the German war machine seems to run according to systematic directives and official lists, reducing its Jewish victims to subhuman status by cataloguing them—and their belongings—in order to dominate them. But as he describes repeatedly the German obsession with lists of various kinds, Keneally suggests that it is this type of impersonal, petty bureaucracy that enables the German military, from NCOs to SS authorities, to visit their terror upon the Jews, all the while retaining some notion of German "civilization." The members of the Jewish police, the OD, also use lists to pass information on to the SS, and they too seem to hide behind them in order to be able to betray their fellow ghetto dwellers. That Schindler finally rescues "his Jews" by drawing up a list of names of people to take to the relocated factory camp at Brinnlitz shows that he works within the confines of and by the rules of the German system, all the while undermining it. Throughout the novel, there is some sense that people can be judged by the way they use lists. Marcel Goldberg, the personnel clerk, keeps the Jews "in the dark" about the list of those to be sent to Schindler's factory; Raimund Tisch strains to remember names (he thinks of people as individuals) to add to the list and curses himself for not remembering more. The attitude toward the list thus also reflects characters' attitudes towards people as human beings. The list functions on various levels, including making readers think of these attitudes and of how people can hide behind bureaucracy and order to avoid recognizing the evil they may be engaged in.

Other ideas and images that recur in the novel are those of gods and kings. At the beginning of the novel, Keneally says that his book is about "virtue" and its unconventional representation in Oskar Schindler. In the rest of the book, the author offers no easy solutions about how to understand goodness—or, for that matter, evil. But he does explore the ideas in his descriptions of Schindler, his "dark brother" Amon Goeth, and others. Schindler, it is made clear, is far from virtuous in the traditional sense: he has mistresses, drinks heavily, and his ambition is to become a tycoon. Yet Schindler is repeatedly likened to a god. He is a "minor god of deliverance," a god like Bacchus, and he offers the "godlike promise" that his workers will survive the war if they stay at his factory. The image of Schindler as god suggests to the reader the complexity of this man who holds so much power and is, ultimately, a symbol of good despite the mystery that often shrouds his legend. Schindler's godlike qualities are often presented in contrast to Goeth's, who is often portrayed as a power-hungry king or emperor. Symche Spira, the Jewish policeman, is also referred to as a "Napoleon" and a "tsar." Both these men, with their king-complexes, do not understand the concept of mercy or goodness, but are corrupted by a misguided sense of power. Again, these ideas and images—and they

recur in the novel—explore the complexity and ambiguity of good, evil, and power, not by explicitly discussing them but by making readers think about them in their own terms.

Keneally thus uses these—and other—recurring images in *Schindler's List* to explore difficult ground, not to offer overt explanations but to allow readers to come to their own conclusions about people and events. Exploring ideas in this manner is a technique that is generally associated with works of fiction and imaginative literature, not of reportage. The author, by using these devices, adds a layer of complexity to his story, taking it out of the realm merely of history telling to the realm of story telling. He engages the reader in such a way that the reader must "fill in the blanks" and try to understand what certain types of behavior mean, why a character might be motivated in a certain way, and so on. The author takes readers to the heart of characters and events but then offers images as clues that the reader must interpret for him- or herself in trying to "understand" the story in a deeper way.

But while Keneally uses these "novelistic" methods and devices in *Schindler's List*, he also uses some devices that are not found in traditional novels. For example, as mentioned, many of the characters described in the book are undeveloped or "flat"; their characteristics are told to the reader by the author, but the reader does not get to "know" them from what they do or from an understanding of their psychologies or even their behavior. Rather, their characters emerge purely from a recounting of their stories, their histories. Also, throughout, Keneally "gives away" the ending of the story by flashing forward and explaining what happens after the war to certain characters, Schindler included. Keneally seems to do these things for a reason, however. It could be argued that what he is doing is presenting in the foreground the story of Oskar Schindler, a mysterious figure whose motivations and virtue are ambiguous. In contrast to Schindler is Goeth, a clear embodiment of evil and the worst of human nature. Schindler and Goeth thus represent good and evil, although not in altogether clear-cut terms. Schindler's story is the main thread of the novel, and Goeth's is told alongside it, his figure serving sometimes as a foil and sometimes as a mirror to that of Schindler. The rest of the novel is made up of the stories of the dozens of other characters, most of them Holocaust victims and survivors. Their stories and discussions of their personalities are told plainly, perhaps to emphasize the fact that it is ultimately *history* that is being recounted. By emphasizing the details of their lives and the facts of their personalities, Keneally stresses the fact that in this complex struggle between good and evil what was at stake were dozens of individuals, each with distinct histories that were changed forever.

Keneally, then, uses two different sets of techniques in *Schindler's List*. He uses novelistic techniques of "story telling" that involve using layers of meaning that his readers must uncover. He also uses techniques of "history telling" to hit home to the reader in no uncertain terms that the events described in his book took place and that the people described are flesh and blood. The two techniques complement each other and also leave readers with a sense that it is only through the use of the imagination, through trying to understand the deeper significances of events and people's behavior that history comes alive, and the horrors that people experienced become real.

Source: Uma Kukathas, Critical Essay on *Schindler's List*, in *Novels for Students*, The Gale Group, 2003.

Laura Kryhoski

Kryhoski is currently working as a freelance writer. She has also taught English Literature in addition to English as a Second Language overseas. In this essay, Kryhoski considers the power of images defining Keneally's text.

In *Schindler's List*, Thomas Keneally treats the subject of the Holocaust with sensitivity and grace in describing the account of Oskar Schindler, a German businessman whose "bottom line" in business was the successful rescue of Jews from the gas chamber. His account of the events surrounding such rescues is skillfully rendered by the employment of a series of images. As a good poet might, Keneally's use of imagery suggests ideas by "its vividness, emotional depth, psychological overtones, strangeness or familiarity, and connections to other images" in the work (excerpt taken from John Drury's "Creating Poetry"). The use of imagery is where Keneally's "poetic" genius lies—his presentation of images is powerful because the author has no need to draw conclusions that perhaps may discredit the sensitive subject to which he speaks. Instead, he lets these images speak for him, giving his novel voice as a powerful and historically-charged account of unthinkable horror.

The image of the scarlet child is a memorable image in Keneally's work and is a testimony to the power of the imagery inherent within the work. Little Genia, as she is initially referred to, is first in-

> " In a world of murderous, bloody red images, the one colorful image dominating the text is that of the scarlet child."

troduced as a small child that has been smuggled back into the Kraków area, into the ghetto, by a Polish couple. She appears in the image of the young child indulged by peasants in her red cap, red coat, and small red boots. She is a darling vision who, in reality, is indulged by those who would just as soon hunt her parents down as they would spoil her. Although Mrs. Dresner noticed "how strangely guarded the child was in all her answers" she, "had her vanities," and not unlike "most three year olds a passionately preferred color." The reader learns that this propensity or preference for red is the defining characteristic in terms of Genia's person. Her desire for the color is the one piece of childhood she is able to hold on to, the single indication that she is three years old outside of physical considerations. Insistent talk of the child's parents only leads to the rehearsed recitation of a string of lies little Genia has been fed as to any intimate and potentially discriminatory details surrounding her parents identity or location. The reaction to such an image, these deceptions of a small child, do not go unnoticed within the text, the narrator stating "the family frowned at each other, brought to a standstill by the unusual cunning of the child, finding it obscene." It is the idea of a child mastering the art of deception at a mere three years of age that is problematic; it goes against what seem to be fairly universal sentiments toward the very young. Any appreciation of honesty, innocence, and the freely expressive qualities children normally harbor has already been violated by cruel circumstances. Genia, in a very cruel and fundamental way, is the image of childhood and, by extension, life that has been debased by circumstance.

The image of red serves is a bright and compelling contrast to the dark activities of the ghetto for Oskar Schindler. Perched atop his horse and from some distance, he is able to make out a line of women and children being led by guards towards

What Do I Read Next?

- *Schindler's Legacy: True Stories of the List Survivors* (1994), edited by Elinor J. Brecher and with photographs by Jill Freedman, presents the stories of seventy-five real-life Schindler's list survivors, with personal accounts of the Holocaust, their encounters with Schindler, their experiences after the war, and their reunions with their unlikely savior.

- Hillel Levine's *In Search of Sugihara: The Elusive Japanese Diplomat Who Risked His Life to Save 10,000 Jews from the Holocaust* (1996) tells the story of Chiune Sugihara, a diplomat and spy who risked his career and saved as many as 10,000 Jews from deportation to concentration camps by issuing them transit visas.

- In his graphic narratives *Maus I: A Survivor's Tale: My Father Bleeds History* (1987) and *Maus II: Here My Troubles Began* (1991), Art Spiegelman blends autobiography with the story of his father's survival of the concentration camps. The characters here have the heads of animals—the Jews are mice, the Nazis are rats, and the Poles are pigs.

- William Styron's *Sophie's Choice*, published in 1979 and later made into a major motion picture starring Meryl Streep (1982), is the story of a Polish Catholic woman sent to Auschwitz for nonpolitical reasons, who struggles to survive her guilt about the past.

- *Survival in Auschwitz: The Nazi Assault on Humanity* (1947), by the Jewish writer and Holocaust survivor Primo Levi, is a narrative told with compassion and wit about the author's deportation from Italy to the concentration camp Auschwitz in Poland in 1943, where he spent ten months and witnessed unspeakable cruelty as well as miraculous endurance.

- *The Voice of Memory: Interviews 1961–1987* is a collection of thirty-six newspaper, journal, radio, and television interviews given by Primo Levi, providing new insights into Levi's complex character.

- *I Never Saw Another Butterfly: Children's Drawings and Poems from Terezin Concentration Camp 1942–1944* (1994) contains poems written by the few survivors of the fifteen thousand children under the age of fifteen who passed through the Terezin death camp. The poems record the young survivors' daily misery, courage, hopes, and fears.

Piwna Street. Schindler particularly notes "at the rear, dawdling . . . a toddler, boy or girl, dressed in a small scarlet coat and cap. The reason it compelled Schindler's interest was that it made a statement. . . . The statement had to do, of course, with a passion for red." The scene presenting itself to Schindler is laden with meaning. As a guard gently guides the scarlet child as she drifts away from the line, in a manner much like a concerned sibling, in the background looms the brutal image of SS teams working the streets with their dogs. A moment of tenderness against the backdrop of brutality presents a highly-charged emotive moment for Oskar. He aptly notes the ridiculousness of the situation, the presence of some sort of "moral anxiety" inherent in the proceedings, in the "meander-

ing" of the "scarlet toddler." The images are irreconcilable for the reader—how can a small moment of kindness emerge from such a whirlwind of violent confusion?

The violence of the scene is defined by suitcases hurled out of windows, their contents strewn on the street, or by people hiding, flushed out of their dwellings, and shot brutally on the street where they stood. These images resonate or take on a much deeper, darker meaning in light of the vision of Genia. As an observer, Oskar Schindler notes "they were doing it within a half block of her." Schindler is taken aback with the proceedings of the SS in front of such a young audience. Genia's presence is somehow compounding the killings on the sidewalk, somehow proving the seriousness of the murderous intent of the SS. Specifically, in a particularly jarring moment, "the scarlet child" as she is often referred to, is seen turning to watch a woman be shot in the neck by one member of the SS. The child then witnesses another SS man jam a young boy's head down to the ground before shooting him in the back of the head. A fellow guard's response to the child is again absurd amidst all of the bloodshed. After witnessing a moment of sheer horror, Genia is simply nudged back into the line gently. The absurdity of circumstance dominates the scene, wild variations of emotion expressed in the randomness of the brutality, the displays of affection, and the like. Similarly absurd images will be repeated within the text of the novel.

The insanity driving these actions gives a surreal quality to the proceedings. The nature of such crimes goes beyond admonition or mild reproof. These men have no limit to the horror they will inflict. These atrocities, which seem to defy human nature, become all the more scary or real to Schindler. In the world of this scarlet toddler, random acts of violence abound, and nothing is predictable. There is seemingly no refuge anywhere, nor is there any sympathy to be found. Observing the scene, Oskar can now define "the proposition" presenting itself—witnesses are permitted because such witnesses, like the red toddler, will all eventually perish. Clearly, then, killing had become an official act, allowing these men to act without a trace of shame and without even a thought to shielding a toddler from such violence. This realization also signifies a major turning point for Schindler. The tiny image of Genia in the ghetto ultimately leads him to conclude that "no thinking person could fail to see what would happen. I was now resolved in my power to defeat the system."

In a similarly poignant moment, Genia's uncle sees the scarlet child sitting among the shining boots of the SS. His eyes are met by hers, eyes clouding over, mute in the knowledge that reaching out to an uncle is not the sort of attention that will comfort or save her at this particular moment. As her uncle diverts the attention of the SS with a speech, he notices his niece move with a "dazzling speculator's coolness" as she steps out from between two guards nearest to her. Unlike their encounter at the Dresners', Genia is unable to respond to her uncle with the same childish enthusiasm demonstrated earlier in the text. Her escape is also described in a heart-pounding series of images:

> She moved with an aching slowness which, of course, galvanized her uncle's vision, so that afterward he would often see behind his closed eyes the image of her among the forest of gleaming SS knee boots.

Genia's performance again is strangely instinctual, that of a little toddler stumbling at a partly ceremonial "bluffer's pace" as she cautiously meanders or wanders by winding down the "blind side of the street." The image of the child also galvanizes or stimulates shock in the reader, precisely because of the conditions that give rise to it and define it.

Her story, however, proves to be a triumph in the colorless world of the ghetto. Unbeknownst to Schindler, Genia returns to the apartment safely. She then chooses to hide, and when her uncle discovers her, the scene is recorded with this image:

> It was just that he knew where to look, in the gap between the curtain and the window sash, and saw, shining in the drabness of the room, her red shoe beneath the hem of the bedspread.

There is a desire represented in the spirit of little Genia, who has an instinct for survival and a passion for life. In contrast to the drabness of the room, she is that one bright shiny moment, that one chance for the future, that one hope. The narrator is quick to point out Genia's victory, that she is able to return to the place where she was first discovered. What could have meant an end for her signifies the "triumph of red Genia's return." In a world of murderous, bloody red images, the one colorful image dominating the text is that of the scarlet child. Genia's survival is now dependent on "her precocious gift for maintaining silence and for being imperceptible in red." Considering her tiny stature, she is literally a small miracle.

The miracle of such an accomplishment, the image of a three-year-old infant triumphant in her escape, is one of many incomprehensible images characteristic of Keneally's text. It also mirrors a theme supported by similar images again and again throughout the course of the work. In the world defined by *Schindler's List*, seemingly so much depends on a scarlet child.

Source: Laura Kryhoski, Critical Essay on *Schindler's List*, in *Novels for Students*, The Gale Group, 2003.

Ryan D. Poquette

Poquette has a bachelor's degree in English and specializes in writing about literature. In the following essay, Poquette discusses the writing techniques that Keneally uses to underscore the profound sense of ambiguity in Schindler's List.

1993 film adaptation of Schindler's List *with Liam Neeson as Oskar Schindler and Ben Kingsley as Itzhak Stern*

Schindler's List, published in England as *Schindler's Ark*, is perhaps Thomas Keneally's most famous novel, in part because it was awarded England's prestigious Booker McConnell Prize for fiction in 1982. However, the book is even more famous because of the controversy surrounding its eligibility for the award. Michael Hollington, in his 1983 *Meanjin* article, summarizes the controversy: "Crudely put the question is, is it a novel or a true story?" Keneally based his story on a mountain of factual research and recollections from survivors, and yet used fictional techniques to embellish many parts of the story, so both positions can technically be supported. In reality, Keneally relies on both techniques, in an effort to create a sense of ambiguity or confusion in the reader, which manifests itself mainly in the moral ambiguity of Schindler and the physical ambiguity of the prisoners' survival chances.

Many critics have chosen to focus on the basic issue of whether the book is fiction or nonfiction. In a 1983 article for *Encounter*, A. N. Wilson says with conviction that "*Schindler's Ark* is not a novel. It is a highly competent, workaday piece of reportage." At the same time, Wilson is disap-

pointed that Keneally "shrunk from the task of turning it into a novel." From the other camp, Marion Glastonbury, in her scathing 1982 review of the book in the *New Statesman*, implies that the book is fiction, since Schindler is elevated "to a dignity unsustained by evidence." And in her 1989 essay for *Australian Literary Studies*, Irmtraud Petersson refers to the work as "a documentary novel."

Regardless of what category the book ultimately falls into, Keneally deliberately uses both of these contradictory writing styles to induce a sense of confusion and ambiguity in his readers. The book is filled with ambiguities. Graphic depictions of human depravity, told in a dispassionate, journalistic style that induces despair, are juxtaposed next to novelistic depictions of Schindler, who offers hope to both prisoners and readers that redemption can be found in the most unlikely of situations. But Schindler himself is an ambiguous hero.

In the first chapter, Keneally gives his initial description of Schindler as viewed from the outside. He notes Schindler's distinguished, aristocratic appearance, then warns that "it will not be possible to see the whole story under such easy character headings." Keneally proceeds to make a case that, under normal circumstances, Schindler would not be considered a moral man, for many reasons, the first of which is adultery. Although he is married, Schindler lives in Poland "with his German mistress and maintained a long affair with his Polish secretary," while his wife, a nun-like woman, lives in Oscar's hometown in Czechoslovakia. Although Keneally notes that Schindler "was a well-mannered and generous lover," he still says "that's no excuse," when considering the traditional idea of virtue. This point-counterpoint method of illuminating characters and situations continues throughout the novel.

Others note Schindler's adulterous tendencies. For example, when Poldek Pfefferberg goes to make a delivery of black-market goods to Schindler's apartment one day, Schindler's wife unexpectedly answers. Pfefferberg does not recognize her—being used to Schindler's German mistress answering the door—and so asks, "'Is Frau Schindler in?'" using the name that Pfefferberg reserves for Schindler's mistress. Oskar's wife corrects Pfefferberg, informing him that she is Schindler's wife, and invites Pfefferberg in for a drink. However, as the wife notes, "the young man was just a little shocked by Oskar's personal life and thought it indecent to sit and drink with the victim." It is telling that Keneally uses the word, "victim," at this point, since Schindler is later considered by many of the Jewish prison victims to be their savior. It is also a curious commentary that, while Pfefferberg does not approve of Schindler's promiscuity, he has no problem making black-market deliveries. In this story, there is an ambiguous morality among many characters, not just Schindler, although his morality—or lack thereof—is given the most detail.

Adultery is not Schindler's only vice; he is also a heavy drinker. In the beginning, Keneally notes that "some of the time he drank for the pure glow of it, at other times with associates, bureaucrats, SS men for more palpable results." These results include, as the novel progresses, increasing attempts to use alcohol in bribery and trickery, two of Schindler's other vices that Keneally explores during the story. Even though these traits are not technically virtuous, Schindler uses them to achieve great good. Once again, through Keneally's narrative, he never lets the reader get a solid foothold on whether they believe Schindler is inherently good or bad. Says Keneally, "And although Herr Schindler's merit is well documented, it is a feature of his ambiguity that he worked within or, at least, on the strength of a corrupt and savage scheme."

In the beginning of the story, Schindler uses bribery and trickery to maintain and increase his business, a very self-serving activity. When speaking of Schindler's unscrupulous bribes, Keneally lumps Schindler in with other power magnates like the demonic Amon Goeth, whom he often bribes in order to get his way: "Among men like Goeth and Oskar, the word 'gratitude' did not have an abstract meaning. Gratitude was a payoff. Gratitude was liquor and diamonds." Schindler lies to Goeth, pretending to like him, and bribes him continuously. However, ultimately, bribes are the method by which Schindler is able to achieve his greatest acts of redemption—saving his chosen Jewish prisoners. In fact, by the end, Schindler has given up all plans for making money, and has instead spent most of his fortune on an unprofitable business that is merely a front for saving Jewish prisoners from concentration camps.

As Keneally notes, Schindler himself contrasts the respective outputs of his moneymaking factory in Cracow—in which "enamelware was manufactured to the value of 16,000,000 RM," and "produced shells worth 500,000 RM"—to Brinnlitz, in which "the factory produced nothing." Schindler is happy about his second factory's lack of output,

> " Throughout the novel, Keneally alternately leads readers one way and then the other in their thought patterns. His combination of straightforward journalistic techniques with more literary embellishments serves to shake up readers, as the prisoners are shaken up."

however. On his birthday, he receives a telegram saying that the Brinnlitz shells have all failed their inspection tests, a message that he receives joyously. As Schindler notes, "'It's the best birthday present I could have got. Because I know now that no poor bastard has been killed by my product.'" But even here there are ambiguities. Schindler's earlier shells from the Cracow factory did pass their inspections, and were presumably used to kill people in battle. And the countless mess kits and other enamel cookware items that Schindler's Cracow factory produced were used to feed the German army, so while he has been helping Jewish prisoners, he has also been helping the Germans fight the war.

In the lives of the Jewish prisoners, the ambiguity goes beyond moral issues, extending to whether they will live the next day. When the prisoners are first rounded up and taken to Plaszów, many believe that this persecution will be no different than others in the past. They feel that all they have to do is wait it out until the war is over, and that in the meantime their services will be needed: "In the end the civil authorities needed Jews, especially in a nation where they were one in every eleven." However, this hope is soon crushed, when the prisoners see Goeth begin his killing spree at Plaszów, starting with a Jewish woman, Diana Reiter, who has professional training—in theory, a valuable asset to Goeth. When Goeth instructs his subordinate to kill Reiter instantly, in cold blood, for pointing out a mistake that the German subordinate has made, all of the prisoners start to question their own safety. After all, "if Miss Diana Reiter could not save herself with all her professional skill, the only chance of the others was prompt and anonymous labor."

As a result, the anxiety and ambiguity increases at the camp, and neither the prisoners nor the reader know when a certain person will live or die. Keneally underscores this feeling when calmly discussing Goeth's daily routine of random killing: "No one knew Amon's precise reason for settling on that prisoner—Amon certainly did not have to document his motives." In addition to the individual executions that are performed at Goeth's whim, the prisoners are also aware that he performs mass executions, when he need to make room for incoming inmates: "the Commandant's quick method was to enter one of the camp offices or workshops, form up two lines, and march one of them away." These cold, impartial descriptions of death are journalistic in style, merely reporting on the events and not commenting on them.

Then, in the midst of this cold despair, Schindler's Emalia factory in Kraków gives the prisoners, and readers, reason to hope. At Emalia, "no one collapsed and died of overwork, beatings or hunger." Schindler's factory becomes a goal for many in Plaszów, and "among prisoners who knew, there was already competition to get into Emalia." Later, this competition spreads to Schindler's famous list of prisoners that he is trying to save for work in his new Brinnlitz factory. However, even here, ambiguities are introduced. Just being on the list is not enough, since the SS officers do not bring the prisoners immediately to Schindler's factory. Instead, the men are shipped off to Gröss-Rosen, while the women are sent initially to Auschwitz-Birkenau. Both receive brutal treatment that saps their health and threatens to invalidate them for work in Schindler's factory.

Keneally plays on this fact, using his suspense-building ability as a novelist to offer several examples of how the men and women might not survive their respective stays in the concentration camps. For example, at Auschwitz, "the Schindler women went through frequent mass medical inspections." Some of the ultimate survivors are initially marked for death: "Mrs. Clara Sternberg found herself put aside in a hut for older women." The same anxious ambiguity is present in the Schindler men, who find out that the SS men lost Schindler's list. Goldberg, who originally typed up

the list, is asked by the SS men "to type out the list from memory." Even at this late point, when the prisoners have fought and bought their way onto the list, there is some ambiguity as to whether they will remain on it, and it comes down largely to Goldberg's memory. Once again, nothing is stable, nothing is guaranteed, and Keneally draws out the tension as long as possible to increase the sense of ambiguity.

Finally, the majority of the prisoners, both male and female, make it to Schindler's new factory in Brinnlitz, but, as noted earlier, their chances of survival are constantly threatened by the many factory inspections. Even after the war is over, many inside the Schindler factory worry that they will be attacked by retreating German military units, and there is tension and ambiguity until the camp is finally liberated, anticlimactically, "by a single Russian officer."

Even the ending is ambiguous. It is not a happy ending, in the traditional sense, because the overwhelming majority of Jewish prisoners die, including some of the Schindler Jews who could not be saved. Even Schindler himself dies relatively penniless and miserable. When all is said and done, Keneally's book does not give any pat answers. Throughout the novel, Keneally alternately leads readers one way and then the other in their thought patterns. His combination of straightforward journalistic techniques with more literary embellishments serves to shake up readers, as the prisoners are shaken up. Readers are not given a solid foothold either in their assessment of Schindler or in their expectations about the ultimate destiny of the Schindler prisoners. The two contradictory styles of writing force the reader to choose what aspects to focus on from the book and, ultimately, what message to take away from it. However, by unnerving the reader with ambiguities, Keneally, in the end, gives his readers a more heightened reading experience. Next to this fact, the question of whether the book is fiction takes on secondary importance.

Source: Ryan D. Poquette, Critical Essay on *Schindler's List*, in *Novels for Students*, The Gale Group, 2003.

Michael Hollington

In the following essay, Hollington discusses Keneally's novel as a predominantly Australian work, "owing more to the mythology of the bush than to that of central Europe."

The title of Thomas Keneally's Booker Prize winning text, with its overt Old Testament reference, may indicate that this book offers itself, as a consenting adult, to the kind of critical reading in which Christianity gets a large and sympathetic hearing. Keneally's Schindler, the Sudetan German who saved the lives of thousands of Jews in Poland between 1939 and 1945 is, like Noah, the 'one just man' of the dark and evil times of Nazi Germany—a type of Christ harrowing hell (Auschwitz, Gröss-Rosen, Plasów) to redeem the souls of the otherwise damned. Such a reading might construe him as a kind of Graham Greene hero, paradoxically bringing forth good out of the all-too-manifest corruption of his own flesh, so that in the end (in the words of the quotation that will obviously serve as a major exhibit for Christian interpretations of *Schindler's Ark*) it can be said of his urge to save Jews, 'that he desired them with some of the absolute passion that characterised the exposed and flaring heart of the Jesus that hung on Emiliés wall'.

Yet without dismissing such readings one notices a rather more secular paradox. For all its detailed, documentary striving after an accurate realist portrayal of wartime Poland—running to maps of Cracow, and plans of the concentration camp—*Schindler's Ark* is a peculiarly Australian book, owing more to the mythology of the bush than to that of central Europe. Although Australia figures overtly only once or twice in the text, the book seems to carry a subtext in which Australia functions as a discursive code to unlock the mysteries of the moral abyss of wartime Europe, explaining what it is that is lacking and why and how Schindler possesses it.

In a simple and general way, Keneally seems to imagine the issues at stake to be primarily personal and individual rather than social. He appears still to believe very much in the hero. There are other plausible 'just men' amongst the German inhabitants of the mad man's land of wartime Cracow They have rather absurd names, like Bosko, Madritch, and Titsch, and no attempt is made to interest us in their stories, or their interaction, either with each other or with Schindler. And it is not for purely technical reasons (because Keneally wanted to write a particular kind of novel, perhaps) that only one can be allowed to fly over the cuckoo's nest; it is rather that a particular kind of individual space is imagined for this hero to operate in, space which is more strictly Australian than European. Keneally's Schindler is a hero on the run, a kind of Scarlet Pimpernel charging about central Europe on a train, fixing deals and saving souls, even moving his *ersatz* concentration camp from Poland to Czechoslovakia at a stage of the war when this has

> **Although Australia figures overtly only once or twice in the text, the book seems to carry a subtext in which Australia functions as a discursive code to unlock the mysteries of the moral abyss of wartime Europe, explaining what it is that is lacking and why and how Schindler possesses it."**

become almost impossible. Like the Australian bush hero he's essentially an outlaw who doesn't belong to the society of the respectable and orderly: 'Oskar liked under-the-counter, liked the sport of it, the disrepute'; 'Oskar was by temperament an anarchist who loved to ridicule the system'.

It is repeatedly emphasised that Oskar is a kind of child of nature, with a residue of unfallen innocence. This doesn't imply that he's a simpleton: a kind of peasant cunning in his nature is invoked by the application to him of the Good Soldier Schweik stereotype. It is very much suggested, however, that Schindler is profoundly anti-intellectual, opposed in particular, to theories of individual heroism emanating from Paris. ('An existentialist might have been defeated by the numbers at Prokocim, stunned by the equal appeal of all the names and voices. But Herr Schindler was a philosophic innocent.') The anti-intellectualism is linked, both with a radical amorality, especially as far as sex is concerned—'To him sexual shame was a concept, something like existentialism, very worthy but hard to grasp'—and, just about simultaneously, with a fundamental morality of human kindness, stemming not from calculation but from spontaneous instinct: 'Oskar was a gambler, was a sentimentalist who loved the transparency, the simplicity of doing good.' Again, we are reminded of the babes and outlaws of the Australian bush.

I shall pass lightly over such relatively trivial aspects of Oskar's subterranean connection with Australia as his fondness, if not for the genuine amber nectar itself, then at least for such *ersatz*

European counterparts as cognac, and his capacity to drink with various mates until they (but never he) disappear beneath the table. It is during these essentially male occasions (the mistress of the camp commandant always absents herself, for they are 'offensive to her sensibilities') that Schindler's real business is transacted, climaxing as it does in the drunken poker game when he wins the right to bear off to the fake concentration camp the favourite Jewish female domestic slave of the commandant of the real one. Although such scenes are reminiscent of quintessentially European paradigms, like that in Mozart's *Die Entführung aus dem Serail* where Osmin the Turk is stupefied and duped with wine, so that the abduction can take place, they also evoke antipodean male mores and fantasies.

A final point about Oskar Schindler's Australian parallels is that he's represented throughout as the 'most apolitical of Capitalists'. A pragmatic entrepreneur, his achievements reflect an anti-ideological work upon the givens that are to hand, rather than any abstract or theoretical form of protest against his world. In this respect he is pointedly contrasted with Wachmeister Bosko. This former theological student wafted by an afflatus of enthusiasm into the SS, later attempted to expiate his mistake by joining the Polish partisans, and 'had contempt for partial rescues . . . wanted to save everyone, and would soon try to, and would perish for it'. It is apparent that Bosko cannot be the hero of this narrative; there are kinds of *theoretical* innocence that it discriminates against just as vigorously as it favours 'intuitive naturalness'. This could be put another way by observing that Bosko, unlike Schindler, appears incapable of negotiating that distinctive antipodean contradiction whereby outlaws and rebels may at the same time be highly successful 'captains of industry', despite, or perhaps because of, their inherently anti-social behaviour.

What kind of truth claims are put forward by *Schindler's Ark*? Crudely put the question is, is it a novel or a true story? Keneally is suitably disingenuous on this point:

> I have attempted to avoid all fiction . . . since fiction would debase the record, and to distinguish between the reality and the myths which are likely to attach themselves to a man of Oskar's stature.

The invitation, for any vaguely precise reader, is to see that whilst some kind of semi-plausible discrimination between reality and myth may be operative in the book, this in no sense implies that myth is disdained or eschewed. As the book will later tell us, 'the thing about a myth is not whether it is true or not, nor whether it *should* be true, but that it is somehow truer than truth itself'. According to such a measure of truth, it is possible, by the end of the book to say:

> Oskar had become a minor god of deliverance, double-faced—in the Greek manner . . . subtly powerful, capable of bringing gratuitous but secure salvation.

The notion of the author with which Keneally is working in this book is by no means dissimilar to this conception of its hero. The homology is proffered in the prologue, which comments that 'it is a risky enterprise to have to write of virtue'—phrasing that clearly borrows its terms from Oskar's *salto mortale* to describe a purely aesthetic adventurousness. The book itself 'constructs' a fake concentration camp out of the testimony of those whose memories, working intensely upon the most nightmarishly vivid experiences of their lives, inevitably construct myths. It too attempts a 're-demption' of those 'just men' whom memory immortalises and weaves into heroes or gods, and a damnation of those whose crimes it once more exposes. And in doing this the author himself appears, like Schindler, to play the role of a minor god who is Janus and Bacchus.

If we remember Sartre's existentialist dictum (in his critique of Mauriac's *Thérèse*), that the author must *not* play god with his own creation, an essential series of problems in *Schindler's Ark* are uncovered. In a supposedly documentary work, what validates the highly emotional, moralistic ironies that dispense grace and damnation? How can we be sure that these moralisings aren't some form of gloss upon yet another attempt to cash in on the holocaust, Janus-facedly pointing up these unspeakable horrors once again in order to catch that fat film contract? (There are frequent reminders that Oskar looks like Curt Jurgens and has 'the outrageous Charles Boyer charm'.) And—to return to the Australian subtext once more—why should we believe that the values of 'natural spontaneous goodness', derived from the bush or anywhere else, can offer any antidote to, or even a means of understanding, what happened in Poland between 1939 and 1945?

I'm not proposing here to try to answer any of these questions: they are intended to serve, instead, as gestures towards the kind of terms in which critical debate about *Schindler's Ark might* be conducted. Yet—to make a tentative start on the specifically Australian question—there are probably quite a number of occasions in the text where the voting is likely to run fairly heavily in Keneally's favour, where indeed (the Leavisite terminology seems unavoidable, for more than one reason) those values associated with Schindler, the bush outlaw, seem firmly and convincingly 'realised'. I shall select two.

Mieczyslaw Pemper, a Schindler protégé in the Janus-faced position of secretary to the commandant of the real concentration camp, is accused late one night of plotting an escape. The commandant Goeth is invariably trigger-happy: what is Pemper, literally at gun-point, going to do? Both he and the text rise to the occasion quite brilliantly:

> looking around him for some sort of inspiration, he saw the seam of his trouser leg, which had come unsewn. How could I pass on the outside in this sort of clothing? he asked.

Here we have an example or 'work on the given' that justifies both Schindler's realism and the author's pragmatic handling of the writing's testimony.

The other example is more extended and central; it is indeed earmarked on a number of occasions as *the* paradigmatic correct instinctual response to an impossible situation. It's the day of the SS Aktion to clear the Cracow ghetto. Men, women and children are slaughtered indiscriminately, while Schindler watches like a film camera with a panoramic lens. One child stands out because she wears bright scarlet: the most conspicuous and vulnerable colour, one might have thought. As it is, the colour saves her, for there is no such thing as camouflage in this world. The SS men seem to use her as a kind of audience for their killings, paying no attention to her brightness, for they don't believe that any witness will eventually survive. The unlivable situation is mastered through a flamboyant gesture. This too is a 'realisation' of Schindler's mode of operation, a kind of gaudy, vulgar 'Australian' strategy of coping, in which instinctive flair counts far more than calculation. It gets translated into Christian terms as a kind of *credo quia impossibile est* in the story of the man who escapes gassing at Belzec camp by hiding for three days in the pit of the latrines and walking out at night time, covered in shit; 'everyone understood that he got out precisely because he was beyond reason'.

All of this is in part a way of establishing, *pace* the Oxonian lobby, that *Schindler's Ark* is indeed a worthy Booker Prize winner, even if, for the sec-ond year running, the eminence of Günter Grass looms large. It's an ambitious book which cocks a snook at the metaphysical religiosity of Patrick White. Here we have Voss in the 80s, on the rebound from the Australian desert, back in his home patch, shorn of idealism. *Ach du lieber, rette mich nur!* is here rendered in a more prosaic and down-to-earth dialect.

But it's a pity that we still seem to have to be tossed into the great lap of God somewhere along the way. That flaming heart of Jesus on Emilia's wall, under certain lights in the book, looks a bit puce in colour, rather like a little something Dame Edna brought back from Cracow for the mantelpiece. 'Australia', read as the natural impulse of the heart, isn't ultimately an effective counterweight to 'Europe'. Whatever system it is that requires undermining underpins them both, and must be combatted, at least in part, with the weapons of intellect, intelligence and reason. Brecht's 'red statements' about Nazi Germany remain superior: his Schweiks are not heroes, but they do at least grasp that you get somewhere only when the office of 'just man' is abolished.

Source: Michael Hollington, "The Ned Kelly of Cracow: Keneally's *Schindler's Ark*," in *Meanjin*, Vol. 42, No. 1, March 1983, pp. 42–46.

Sources

Drury, John, *Creating Poetry*, Writer's Digest Books, 1991.

Gaffney, Carmel, "Keneally's Faction: *Schindler's Ark*," in *Quadrant*, Vol. 29, No. 7, July 1985, pp. 75–77.

Glastonbury, Marion, "Too Grateful," in *New Statesman*, Vol. 104, No. 2694, November 5, 1982, p. 25.

Hollington, Michael, "The Ned Kelly of Cracow: Keneally's *Schindler's Ark*," in *Meanjin*, Vol. 42, No. 1, March 1983, pp. 42–46.

Hulse, Michael, "Virtue and the Philosophic Innocent: The British Reception of *Schindler's List*," in *Critical Quarterly*, Vol. 52, No. 1, Spring 1996, pp. 163–88.

Johnson, Manly, "Thomas Keneally's Nightmare of History," in *Antipodes*, Vol. 3, No. 2, Winter 1989, pp. 101–104.

Keneally, Thomas, *Schindler's List*, Touchstone, 1993.

Kirby, Farrell, "The Economies of *Schindler's List*," in *Arizona Quarterly*, Vol. 52, No. 1, Spring 1996, pp. 163–88.

Loshitzky, Yosefa, ed., *Spielberg's Holocaust: Critical Perspectives on "Schindler's List,"* Indiana University Press, 1997.

Petersson, Irmtraud, "'White Ravens' in a World of Violence: German Connections in Thomas Keneally's Fiction," in *Australian Literary Studies*, Vol. 14, No. 2, October 1989, pp. 101–104, 160–73.

Pierce, Peter, "'The Critics Made Me': The Receptions of Thomas Keneally and Australian Culture," in *Australian Literary Studies*, Vol. 17, No. 1, May 1995, pp. 99–103.

Quartermaine, Peter, *Thomas Keneally*, Modern Fiction series, Edward Arnold, 1991.

Thornton, William H., "After the Carnival: The Film Prosaics of *Schindler's List*," in *Canadian Review of Comparative Literature*, Vol. 23, No. 3, September 1996, pp. 701–708.

Wilson, A. N., "Faith & Uncertainty," in *Encounter*, Vol. LX, No. 2, February 1983, pp. 65–71.

Zweig, Paul, "A Good Man in a Bad Time," in *New York Times Book Review*, October 24, 1982, pp. 1, 38–39.

Further Reading

Fensch, Thomas, ed., *Oskar Schindler and His List: The Man, the Book, the Film, the Holocaust and Its Survivors*, with an introduction by Herbert Stenhouse, Paul Eriksson, 1995.
   This casebook includes two postwar journalists' testimonies about Schindler, three pieces on Keneally's book, more than 140 pages of reviews of and reportage on Spielberg's film, and more than 50 pages of journalistic discussion on the Holocaust that the movie's success provoked.

Lengyel, Olga, *Five Chimneys: A Woman Survivor's True Story of Auschwitz*, Academy Chicago Publishing, 1995.
   This true story by a woman who lost her husband, her parents, and her two young sons to the Nazi exterminators tells of her work in the prisoners' underground resistance and her need to recount her story, which kept her fighting for survival.

Quartermaine, Peter, *Thomas Keneally*, Modern Fiction series, Edward Arnold, 1991.
   In this account of the work of Thomas Keneally, Quartermaine provides a wide-ranging introduction to Keneally's novels, including *Schindler's Ark*.

Roberts, Jeremy, *Oskar Schindler: Righteous Gentile*, Holocaust Biographies series, Rosen Publishing Group, 2000.
   This biography of Schindler ends by exploring the question of his status as a righteous man.

Schindler, Emilie, *Where Light and Shadow Meet : A Memoir*, W. W. Norton, 1997.
   Schindler's widow, Emilie, presents an unflattering portrait of her husband as erratic, immature, and self-serving to deflate the myth that has evolved around her husband's life since the phenomenal success of Spielberg's movie.

Scoop

Evelyn Waugh
1938

Evelyn Waugh's *Scoop* (London, 1938) is a satire on journalism. It is based on Waugh's stint as a war correspondent for the London *Daily Mail* in Abyssinia (now Ethiopia) in 1935, during which he covered the war between Abyssinia and Italy. Waugh admitted that he had no aptitude for war reporting, but he did observe closely the activities of his fellow journalists. The result was a satirical, farcical novel that takes lighthearted but deadly aim at the newspaper industry and the journalistic profession.

The plot rests on some comic twists of fortune. Lord Copper, the arrogant and ignorant owner of the *Daily Beast*, sends out by mistake a naïve writer of nature columns, William Boot, to cover the war in the fictional East African country of Ishmaelia. Geographically, at least, Ishmaelia is identical with Abyssinia. William gets some quick lessons in the devious way of journalists, who are always trying to outwit their colleagues and deliver a scoop. Helped by a series of lucky events, William gets several major scoops himself and returns to London as a world-renowned reporter. But it all means nothing to him, and he is happy to return to his country home, the isolated and dilapidated Boot Magna Hall, where his many eccentric relatives live.

Author Biography

Evelyn Waugh was born on October 28, 1903, in Hampstead, London, England, the son of Arthur

Evelyn Waugh

(an editor and publisher) and Catherine Charlotte (Raban) Waugh. He was enrolled at Lancing, a preparatory school, in 1917, where he wrote poetry, edited the school magazine, and was president of the debating society.

Waugh won a scholarship to Hertford College, Oxford, in 1922. At Oxford, he wrote poetry and stories for undergraduate magazines but, because of financial difficulties, he left the university in 1924 without graduating. He enrolled at Heatherley's Art School, and in 1925 he became a secondary school teacher in Wales and then in Buckinghamshire, England.

In 1927, Waugh married Evelyn Gardner. In 1928, his first novel, *Decline and Fall*, appeared. This was a satire on the English upper classes and the English educational system. While Waugh was writing his second novel, *Vile Bodies* (1930), he discovered that his wife was having an affair, so he filed for a divorce.

In 1930, he converted to Roman Catholicism, and he spent much of his time between 1929 and 1937 traveling. He visited the Mediterranean, Ethiopia (then known as Abyssinia), and North Africa, the West Indies and British Guiana, as well as Brazil, Mexico, and the Arctic. He reported on the Italian-Ethiopian war in 1935 and wrote sev-

eral accounts of his travels, including *Remote People* (1931), about his African journey, and *Waugh in Abyssinia* (1936).

Waugh's third novel, *Black Mischief*, was published in 1932 and cemented his reputation as a brilliant satirist. It was followed by the bleak *A Handful of Dust* (1934), before Waugh returned to light-hearted satire with *Scoop* (1938).

In 1936, the Catholic Church annulled his first marriage, and the following year Waugh married Laura Herbert. This inaugurated a more settled period in his life, although it was interrupted by the outbreak of World War II in 1939. Waugh was given an officer's commission in the Royal Marines; in 1941 he volunteered for service with the No. 8 Commando Forces in the Middle East, and he took part in several raids on the North African coast. In 1944, he joined the British Military Mission to Yugoslavia.

One of Waugh's best-known novels, *Brideshead Revisited*, was published after the war in 1945. It achieved international success, especially in the United States, where it was a Book-of-the-Month Club selection. In 1948, Waugh went on a lecture tour of Catholic universities in the United States.

In the 1950s, Waugh's literary output continued, although the satirist of the 1930s had now developed a deep dislike for contemporary society. His work from this period included the war novels *Men at Arms* (1952) and *Officers and Gentlemen* (1955), an autobiographical novel, *The Ordeal of Gilbert Pinfold* (1957), and a novella, *Love Among the Ruins* (1953). His last novel was another war novel, *Unconditional Surrender* (1961), which was published in the United States as *The End of the Battle*.

Waugh died on April 10, 1966, in Combe Florey, Somerset, England.

Plot Summary

Book 1: The Stitch Service

Scoop begins as the young novelist John Courteney Boot visits his aristocratic friend, Mrs. Julia Stitch, in London. She is in bed, her face covered in a mask of clay while she directs domestic operations. With her are her secretary, her maid, her precocious eight-year-old daughter, and a workman who is painting ruined castles on the ceiling.

Later, Boot explains to Mrs. Stitch as she drives to an appointment that he must leave London because his American girlfriend is driving him crazy. Mrs. Stitch suggests that he go as a war correspondent to Ishmaelia, East Africa, where there is a crisis. She convinces the head of the Megalopolitan Newspaper Corporation, Lord Copper, that Boot is the man to cover the war. But Mr. Salter, the Foreign Editor at the *Daily Beast*, wrongly assumes that the William Boot who writes a nature column for the *Beast* is the man to whom Copper refers.

The countryman Boot lives in the ancient, dilapidated Boot Magna Hall with a crowd of eccentric relatives. William has no desire to leave his home and has never met anyone at the *Beast*. But when he receives a cable from Salter summoning him to London, he assumes it is because of an error in his column the previous week. He goes to London expecting to be fired. The encounter between William and Mr. Salter is uncomfortable for them both. After a series of comic misunderstandings, Salter asks him if he will go to Ishmaelia as a war correspondent. William politely declines, but when Salter tells him that, unless he goes to Ishmaelia, he will be fired, William reluctantly agrees.

The following morning, William meets Lord Copper. Copper wants the war in Ishmaelia to be resolved quickly and in a way that will create good news copy. After the meeting, Salter tries to explain to William who is fighting and why, but William is none the wiser.

After a comical episode in which William visits two rival Ishmaelite legations in London to get a visa, he flies by private plane to Paris, kindly allowing a stranger to fly with him. Then he boards the train for Marseilles, where he meets the stranger again, who turns out to be an Englishman. The stranger promises to repay William's favor whenever he can.

William then has an uncomfortable journey by sea to Aden. He meets an English journalist named Corker, who is also going to Ishmaelia but knows no more about the place than William. Corker explains the fundamentals of journalism to William, including how to interpret cryptic cables he receives from London. In Aden, William meets up again with the mysterious Englishman, and Corker searches for a story for his news agency.

Book 2: Stones £20

The narrator explains the brewing conflict in Ishmaelia, a backward place that is corruptly run by the Jackson family, with General Gollancz Jackson as president. The capital city, Jacksonburg, receives much foreign investment, little of which

Media Adaptations

- An unabridged audiocassette tape of *Scoop*, narrated by Simon Cadell, is published by Cover to Cover Cassettes Ltd. (1998).

finds its way to the ordinary people. Six months earlier, trouble began when Smiles Soum, a lowly member of the Jackson family, quarreled with the leadership. He was perceived in London's liberal circles as a fascist, and support poured in for the president. Journalists flocked to the country, as war seemed imminent.

At the Hotel Liberty, a celebrated American journalist, Wenlock Jakes, is working on a book on English political and social life. There are journalists from many countries at the hotel, including the Englishmen Shumble, Whelper, Pigge, Sir Jocelyn Hitchcock, William, and Corker. The journalists are under pressure from their newspapers to cable a story, but little is happening. Eventually, Shumble makes up a story that a Russian spy has arrived disguised as a railway official. The story is treated as a world scoop but is soon killed by a chorus of denials.

William meets an old friend from school, Jack Bannister, at the British Consulate. Bannister tells him that there is, in fact, a Russian agent in Jacksonburg, but they do not know what he is up to. William is elated at getting such a tip-off, but Corker tells him it will not work after all the previous denials about the presence of a Russian agent.

More journalists arrive, and William moves to the Pension Dressler, run by a formidable German woman, Frau Dressler. There he meets Kätchen, a young German woman who is temporarily separated from her husband. They strike up a friendship, and she persuades him to buy her husband's collection of stones, which he later finds out is gold ore.

The journalists fall to quarreling amongst themselves, and then they all go on a trek to a place called Laku, where they have been led to believe there is some action. Laku, in fact, does not exist.

William receives instructions from his newspaper to remain in Jacksonburg. He is now the only correspondent left there, but he fails to send any news stories. The *Beast* office in London gets increasingly impatient with him and sends him a cable telling him he has been fired. Meanwhile, William has fallen in love with Kätchen. Kätchen persuades him to pay her to get news for him, since she knows some important people. She later informs him that the president has been locked up in his own palace, and William sends a cable with his first news item. The delighted *Beast* reinstates him.

At the British Legation, Bannister explains the political situation to William. He reveals that the Germans are backing the rebellion of Smiles, but the Russians are supporting the communist Young Ishmaelite Party. There is likely to be a communist-inspired coup, followed by a dictatorship. This is another scoop for William.

Kätchen's husband returns, as does Kätchen, who has been imprisoned because her papers were not in order. William is full of regret at losing her, but he cooperates in an escape plan. The two Germans escape down the river by using a canoe that William brought with him in his luggage.

When William returns from seeing them off, he discovers that the Young Ishmaelite Party has taken over the government, the Jacksons have been imprisoned, and a Soviet state has been declared.

As William despairs over his loss of Kätchen, the mysterious Englishman reappears, by parachute. He likes to be called Mr. Baldwin, and it turns out that he is a savvy businessman who has a large financial interest in Ishmaelia and has been manipulating events to his advantage. He explains the political situation, giving William yet another scoop, and then arranges a quick counterrevolution that topples the day-old Soviet state. President Jackson is reinstated. Mr. Baldwin then writes William's story for him and cables it to the *Beast*.

Book 3: Banquet

Back in London, Lord Copper recommends William to the prime minister for a knighthood. But by mistake the letter informing him of this is delivered to John Courteney Boot, the novelist.

William returns to England, covered in glory because of his journalistic successes. Other newspapers woo his services, and literary agents want his autobiography. But William wants only to return to his home at Boot Magna, from where he writes to Lord Copper declining his invitation to a banquet. Mr. Salter is sent to Boot Magna to bring William back, but he has a very uncomfortable time in the country and cannot persuade William to attend the banquet. The situation is saved when William's uncle Theodore shows up in the offices of the *Beast*, and it is agreed that he will be passed off as William Boot. At the banquet, Lord Copper goes along with the deception. Back at Boot Magna, William is free to continue writing his nature columns, which is all he ever wanted to do.

Characters

Mr. Baldwin

Mr. Baldwin is a small, mysterious man who, with his servant, joins William on his flight to Paris. He also turns up on the train to Marseilles. Later in the novel, he parachutes in to Jacksonburg and explains to William the political maneuverings going on in the country. It appears that Baldwin, which is simply the name he prefers to be known by, is a well-connected international businessman who is out to profit personally from the turbulent situation in Ishmaelia, whilst also preserving British economic interests. He owns the mineral rights in Ishmaelia, rights that the Russian and German governments are scheming to acquire. Eventually, it is Mr. Baldwin who writes the text of the final news story that William sends to the *Beast*. In that story, Baldwin refers to himself as a "mystery financier" and compares himself favorably to two of the great Englishmen of the past, Lawrence of Arabia and Cecil Rhodes, founder of Rhodesia (now Zimbabwe). Baldwin also arranges the counterrevolution that topples the day-old Soviet state in Ishmaelia.

Jack Bannister

Jack Bannister is a senior official in the British Legation in Ishmaelia. He is an old school friend of William Boot and passes on to him vital information about the country's political situation.

Doctor Benito

Doctor Benito is a rather sinister figure who is the Minister of Foreign Affairs and Propaganda in Ishmaelia. The journalist Pigge regards him as "creepy." Small and neatly dressed, suave and self-possessed, Benito allies himself with the Russian-backed Young Ishmaelite party and, when President Jackson is overthrown, he emerges as the new dictator. But his hold on power lasts only one day; he is toppled by the counterrevolution arranged by Mr. Baldwin.

Uncle Bernard

Uncle Bernard, one of William's uncles, spends his life conducting scholarly research on the family pedigree. Had he had more money, he would have made a claim to the vacant barony of de Butte.

Nanny Bloggs

Nanny Bloggs is William's old nanny at Boot Magna Hall.

John Courteney Boot

John Courteney Boot is a successful writer. He has written eight books, including novels, as well as travel and history books, and he is a well-known and respected name in intellectual circles. He accepts Mrs. Stitch's recommendation to become a war correspondent for the *Daily Beast* because he is desperate to get away from his American girlfriend. But there is a mix-up, and his remote cousin, William Boot, gets the coveted job. At the end of the novel, yet another bureaucratic mix-up ensures that a knighthood intended for William goes instead to John Courteney. Finally, still trying to evade his girlfriend, John Courteney Boot goes off to Antarctica as a reporter for the *Beast*.

Priscilla Boot

Priscilla Boot is William's sister. It is she who, as a joke, inserts all the references in William's article to the fictitious "great crested grebe."

William Boot

William Boot lives in the country at Boot Magna Hall, from where he writes a twice-weekly nature column for the *Daily Beast* called Lush Places. When a misunderstanding occurs, William is sent to Ishmaelia as a war correspondent, but he is a countryman and has little knowledge of the wider world. Even on the train journey to London, he makes a fool of himself, first in the dining-car, ordering whiskey when all they are serving is tea, and then in the carriage when he pays for a drink with an old sovereign, mistaking it for another coin, a shilling. Everyone stares at him.

William is an honest, good-natured man, but he is also very naïve and passive. He has no idea of how to do the job that has been assigned to him. Corker has to teach him the elements of journalism, but even then he shows himself to be an unpromising student, failing to understand the urgency with which he is required to gather news

at any cost. Then he foolishly falls in love with the German woman Kätchen and allows her to exploit him for money. It is only through a series of fortuitous events that William gets the scoops that make him famous. When he returns to London, he is unprepared for the glory and renown that now accompanies him, and he turns down all manner of offers from the literary and journalistic world that would have made him rich and even more famous. All he wants is to return home to the peaceful, unchanging world in the country that he knows and loves, and it is his good fortune that another misunderstanding involving the name Boot allows him to do just that.

Lord Copper

Lord Copper is the proprietor of the Megalopolitan Newspaper Corporation. He relishes his position of power and the trappings that go along with it, and he also possesses a grandiose sense of his own importance. This is suggested by the larger-than-life statue of him that stands in the entrance lobby of the Megalopolitan building in London's Fleet Street. Lord Copper claims that he allows his journalists to hold their own opinions, but, in truth, he has very pronounced ideas about the stories he is prepared to print. He is a powerful and ruthless man who likes to have his own way and usually succeeds in getting it. He dominates his staff, none of whom dares to contradict him, which means that Lord Copper is never made aware of the ignorance he displays on many topics. Nor does he realize that he is regarded as a bore, a fact that can be seen by the attitude of his guests at the banquet. The only person who enjoys Lord Copper's regular banquets is Lord Copper himself, largely because they give him the chance to give a long, uninterrupted after-dinner speech.

Corker

Corker is an English journalist whom William first encounters on the train to Marseilles. Gregarious, irreverent, and worldly wise, Corker is the opposite of William. Observing William's ignorance, he takes him under his wing, trying to teach him the basics of journalism. When Corker is pressed by Universal News, his news agency, to send a story, he concocts one based on the flimsiest research.

Frau Dressler

Frau Dressler is a German woman who runs a hotel, the Pension Dressler, which acts as center for the Germans in Jacksonburg. Frau Dressler has lived in Africa all her life. She is a large woman with a lot of energy who drives a hard bargain with the local peasants when they sell her their wares.

Sir Jocelyn Hitchcock

Sir Jocelyn Hitchcock is a famous English journalist who travels to Ishmaelia. He hides out by himself and, because of his reputation, all the other journalists are afraid that he is working on a big story somewhere that they have missed. Hitchcock eventually concocts a fake interview with the leader of the fascists, which supposedly took place in a town called Laku, a place that does not in fact exist. This piece of disinformation sends all the other journalists off on a wild goose chase to Laku, while Sir Jocelyn returns to Europe to work on his next assignment.

Wenlock Jakes

Wenlock Jakes is the highest paid journalist in the United States; his work is syndicated all over America. However, according to Corker, Jakes's methods leave a lot to be desired, since he tends to make his stories up. He even won a Nobel Peace Prize for his courageous reporting of a revolution in the Balkans but, according to Corker, that revolution only began because Jakes's story created such an unstable situation that within a week a revolution actually did occur. Jakes spends his time in Jacksonburg writing a book called *Under the Ermine*, a trashy exposé of English political and social life, for which has been paid a large advance by the publisher.

Kätchen

Kätchen is a young German woman who is temporarily separated from her husband and is staying at the Pension Dressler. Under her helpless exterior, Kätchen is amiably cunning, and she easily gets William, who falls in love with her, to fork over money to her from his expense account. She gets into trouble with the authorities in Ishmaelia because her immigration papers are not in order. As a result, she is briefly imprisoned. Kätchen is naïve in political matters and believes that a solution to her difficulties is to marry William. She thinks this will automatically make her a British citizen, safe from detention. Eventually, she and her returning husband escape down a river in William's canoe.

Erik Olafsen

Erik Olafsen is the resident Jacksonburg correspondent of a syndicate of Scandinavian news-papers. He plays many roles: he is also Swedish vice-consul, a surgeon at the hospital, and the proprietor of the Tea, Bible and Chemist shop. Olafsen is a large man with an eccentric character. He claims that he came to Ishmaelia as a refugee after he killed his grandmother in Sweden. It is Olafsen whom Mr. Baldwin chooses to put the counterrevolution into operation. The drunken Swede single-handedly routs the young Ishmaelite delegates as they listen to Doctor Benito.

Mr. Pappenhacker

Mr. Pappenhacker is the reporter for the communist newspaper *The Twopence*. He is more educated than the other journalists and tends to keep himself apart from them. He also makes a habit of being rude to waiters, since he thinks this will make them dissatisfied with the capitalist system and so hasten the communist revolution.

Pigge

Pigge is one of the English journalists in Ishmaelia.

Uncle Roderick

Uncle Roderick is the least eccentric of William's three uncles. He manages the financial affairs of the family estate and household.

Mr. Salter

Mr. Salter is the foreign editor at the *Daily Beast*. He does not like his hectic job, which he calls a "dog's life," and he knows little about foreign affairs. Nor did he like his previous job as editor of the women's page, which was much too difficult and stressful compared to the only job he really loved—the one at which he was able to choose the jokes in *Clean Fun*, one of Lord Copper's comic weeklies. However, Salter never expresses his discontent to Lord Copper. On the contrary, he is obsequious to his boss and never ventures to correct any of Lord Copper's errors or misstatements.

Mr. Salter lives an ordered, conventional life in London and regards the countryside as hostile territory. His visit to Boot Magna Hall confirms his worst impressions. He is forced to trek six miles across fields in his business suit to get there, and when he finds himself in the strange company of the Boot family, he is completely out of his depth. At the end of the novel, however, he has more luck. Lord Copper makes him become art editor for home knitting, a job he is sure to like.

Shumble

Shumble is one of the English journalists in Ishmaelia. He invents a story that there is a Russian spy in the country disguised as a railway official. At first the story is treated as a scoop, and Shumble is smug and self-satisfied at his success—but then the other journalists unite to kill the story by publicizing vehement official denials.

Algernon Stitch

Algernon Stitch is the husband of Julia Stitch. He is a minister in the British cabinet.

Mrs. Julia Stitch

Mrs. Julia Stitch, wife of Algernon Stitch, is a beautiful, well-connected, society lady. She is always busy with many things, and she specializes in solving the problems of people in her circle. It is Mrs. Stitch who persuades Lord Copper to hire John Courteney Boot as war correspondent. Mrs. Stitch has one notable eccentricity: she owns a small black car and has a habit of driving it on the sidewalk in order to beat the London traffic.

Uncle Theodore

Uncle Theodore is William Boot's eccentric, old-fashioned uncle who makes frequent, disastrous visits to London. When Mr. Salter visits Boot Magna, Theodore regales him with stories that he hopes are suitable for publication in the *Beast*, although Mr. Salter falls asleep and hears none of them. When Salter wakes, he makes the mistake of telling Theodore to contact the features editor of the *Beast*, which gives Theodore another excuse to make a trip to London. Theodore is taken on by the *Daily Beast* and, in the absence of William Boot, is passed off as the famous journalist Boot at the banquet organized by Lord Copper to honor him.

Themes

Journalism and the Truth

Waugh wrote that his main theme was "to expose the pretensions of foreign correspondents . . . to be heroes, statesmen and diplomats." In the novel, he pokes fun at the idea that the profession of journalism is characterized by a disinterested search for the truth. On the contrary, the only concern of the journalists is to file a story that will meet with the approval of their bosses at the newspaper. The goal is to keep one step ahead of the competition, which is why the journalists behave in such an unscrupulous manner toward one another. They steal their competitors' cables and lie about anything they think will give them an advantage. For example, they all say they will be leaving for Laku at "tennish" in the morning, but in fact they are all ready to leave at dawn. The talk of leaving later was simply to try to steal a march on the opposition.

Sir Jocelyn Hitchcock appears to be a past master at tricking his rivals. In Jacksonburg, he lies low so that a rumor will start about his "disappearance." This will make his story, that he has conducted an interview with an important political leader in the town of Laku, appear plausible. In fact, Sir Jocelyn could not have done what he claims, since the town of Laku does not exist. But his fabrication serves his purpose not only of getting out of Ishmaelia, a place he does not like (having filed the story, he is free to move on to his next assignment in Europe), but also of deceiving the other reporters.

This incident highlights a point Waugh wishes to emphasize: the question of whether a particular newspaper story is true or not is a secondary consideration, ranking well behind the need to interest readers and scoop the opposition. The famous American reporter Wenlock Jakes is typical in this respect. He won his reputation partly by filing stories that he simply made up. For example, he sent an eyewitness report of the sinking of the *Lusitania* (a passenger ship that was sunk off the coast of Ireland by the Germans in World War I). The only problem with Jakes's story was that he filed it four hours before the ship was hit. Similarly, Sir Jocelyn Hitchcock managed to give day-to-day reports about an earthquake in Messina without ever leaving the comfort of his desk in London. In Ishmaelia, Shumble takes a leaf out of their book by making up his own story about the presence of a Russian spy in disguise. The irony is that Shumble, although he never knows it, comes close to the truth, even though truth is not his main concern. (There really is a Russian agent in Ishmaelia, although it is not the railway official whom Shumble identifies.)

Much of the theme of the deviousness of the journalistic profession is brought out in William's interactions with Corker. When William receives his first cable from the *Beast*, he misinterprets it to mean that he should stay in Aden. Corker knows perfectly well that the cable does not mean this, but he declines to enlighten William. Only when Corker discovers that he and William are not rivals

Topics for Further Study

- In *Scoop*, the *Daily Beast* has a definite editorial position on the war in Ishmaelia. On the World Wide Web, examine the editorial pages of the *New York Times* and the *Wall St. Journal*. What can you tell about each paper's political position from its editorials? When both editorialize on the same issue, what differing positions do they take up, and what does this indicate about their underlying political philosophies? You can also try the same exercise with the *Washington Post* and the *Washington Times*.

- More people today get their news from television rather than from newspapers. What are the advantages and disadvantages of each medium as a source of news?

- Often in fiction, the protagonist grows and changes as a result of the experiences he undergoes. Does this happen to William Boot, or is he just the same at the end of the novel as he was at the beginning? If he has changed, how is he different?

- In recent wars, such as the Persian Gulf War of 1991 and the war in Afghanistan in 2001–2002, the American government has imposed restrictions on American reporters covering the conflict. This was not the case during the Vietnam War. Should the press have unfettered access to war zones and be free to report whatever is happening, or should restrictions be imposed in the cause of national security? Who should decide?

---

after all—since the *Beast* is accepting Corker's Universal News agency stories as well as William's—does he let William in on the secrets of the cryptic cables they receive.

When Corker is pressured by his agency to file a story about reactions in Ishmaelia to a proposed international police force, Corker's methods are revealing. He asks just one person, Mrs. Earl Russell Jackson, who runs the hotel where he is staying. She completely misunderstands the question, but

that does not stop Corker from inventing a story that the women of Ishmaelia are opposed to an interventionist police force.

It is Corker again who sets William straight about how the newspaper business is run. After Shumble's false story about the Russian spy, William suggests that they simply explain that the story was a mistake. But Corker tells him that such behavior would be "unprofessional"; newspapers do not like printing denials, since too many denials might lead the public to mistrust what they read; besides, it makes it look as if the reporters were not doing their job properly. Instead, Corker assures William that all the journalists must now find a Russian spy, whether he exists or not, so they can keep their newspapers abreast of the breaking story (which, of course, is not really a story at all). The way the process works seems to ensure that the real truth is unlikely to come out.

Style

Satire

Satire is literature that diminishes its subject by ridiculing it. A satire can evoke reactions such as amusement, contempt, or scorn. It can be aimed at an individual, a group of people, an institution, or a whole nation. The object of Waugh's satire is the entire newspaper industry, from the proprietor Lord Copper to the editors in Fleet Street and the foreign correspondents in the field.

An example of Waugh's method can be seen in the incident Lord Copper relates, in which he and his star reporter Sir Jocelyn Hitchcock quarreled over the date of the Battle of Hastings, as a result of which Hitchcock left the *Beast* for the *Brute*. The Battle of Hastings, when the invading Normans defeated the army of the Anglo-Saxon King Harold, took place in England in 1066. The date 1066 is known by every English schoolchild, but not, apparently, by England's most famous foreign correspondent. The incident suggests that Hitchcock is ignorant beyond imagination, and also implies that this kind of juvenile dispute is the level on which the newspaper business in Fleet Street is conducted. Even the titles of the newspapers, the *Beast* and the *Brute*, are satiric, mocking their pretensions to be the purveyors of news, information, and culture. Mr. Salter, the *Beast's* foreign editor, is almost as ignorant as Copper's view of Hitchcock. He cannot find Reykjavik on a map, nor can anyone else in his office. He is ill read, never having heard of the well-known novelist John Courteney Boot, and neither he nor the *Beast's* managing editor has the knowledge or ability to judge a writer's style, which is why they both think that William Boot's absurd, high-flown effort, "Feather-footed through the plashy fen passes the questing vole" is an example of good style.

Farce

Satire is usually distinguished from farce. Whereas satire may have a serious purpose in exposing vice or folly and pointing the way to something better, farce is comedy pure and simple. It is designed to make people laugh, using unusual situations or improbable events. Farce often makes use of physical humor such as slapstick or horseplay; it may also use practical jokes.

There are many farcical episodes in the novel. One of the funniest is when the aggressive goat at the Pension Dressler finally breaks the rope that fetters her and sends Dr. Benito's pompous emissary, who has just boasted to William that he was a college welterweight boxing champion, sprawling in the garbage.

Other examples of farce are the series of improbable events due to misunderstandings, such as the confusion over the two (and later three) Boots; the entry of Olafsen in a drunken frenzy to end the revolution almost before it has begun; the journalists' trek to a place that doesn't exist; and Salter's calamitous trek over six miles of country to Boot Magna Hall.

Farce is evident in the dialogue, too, as when Salter and William, when they first meet, talk at cross-purposes and so cannot communicate at all. William is expecting to be fired, while Salter has been instructed to offer him a job. To make matters worse, Salter has been given erroneous ideas about suitable topics of conversation when meeting a man from the country.

There is more farce nearer the end of the novel, when Salter is forced to travel to Boot Magna Hall. The Boots not only make the mistake of thinking that he walked the six miles from the railway station out of choice, but they also leap to the conclusion that his disheveled appearance is because of drunkenness. So, during dinner, when all the poor man needs to boost his flagging spirits is a little alcoholic refreshment, they refuse to give him anything other than water.

Historical Context

The Italo-Ethiopian War

The setting and many of the details in the novel derive from the historical situation in Abyssinia (now Ethiopia) in 1935 and 1936. Waugh covered the war as a foreign correspondent for the *Daily Mail*.

Italy invaded Ethiopia in October 1935. The pretext was an incident on the border between Ethiopia and Italian Somaliland. The Italians had superior weaponry and captured the capital city, Addis Ababa—Jacksonburg in the novel—in 1936. Italian fascist dictator Benito Mussolini proclaimed Italy's king Victor Emmanuel III emperor of Ethiopia. (In *Scoop*, the name of would-be dictator Dr. Benito is a deliberate reminder of Benito Mussolini.) The League of Nations opposed the Italian intervention but took only ineffective measures to end it. Britain had a stake in the region, but the other great European powers did not (unlike in the novel, where Britain, Germany, and Russia are all involved). The Italo-Ethiopian war, with its evidence that at least one of the totalitarian powers of Europe (the other was Nazi Germany) had imperialistic designs, contributed to the tensions that led up to World War II in 1939.

In *Waugh in Abyssinia* (1936), Waugh reported on his role as a journalist covering the conflict and offered his cautious support of the Italian intervention.

In 1936, civil war broke out in Spain, in which the nationalist, fascist forces of General Franco attempted to overthrow a socialist government. The socialists received much support from leftist intellectuals in England, some of whom, like George Orwell, even went to Spain to fight against Franco. In the Preface to *Scoop*, Waugh pointed out that, in his plot, he tried to combine elements from the Italo-Ethiopian war with some details drawn from the Spanish civil war. The Spanish element can be seen in the playful description of the government of Ishmaelia as "liberal and progressive" and in the names of some of its leaders. General Gollancz Jackson, for example, is intended to remind readers of Victor Gollancz, a left-wing publisher in England. When conflict breaks out, the Ishmaelian rebels are presented, like Franco's forces, as fascists. And the besieged government wins much support in left-wing circles in England: "In a hundred progressive weeklies and Left Study Circles the matter was taken up and the cause of the Jacksons restarted in ideological form." This passage could equally serve

Compare & Contrast

- **1930s:** Ethiopia (Abyssinia) is invaded by Italy in 1935. The Italians use poison gas, defying the Geneva Protocol that banned such weapons in 1925. The Italian occupation continues until 1941, when British forces liberate the country.

  Today: After rebels topple the socialist government of Ethiopia in 1991, multiparty elections are held in 1995 for the first time ever. In 1998, a border war breaks out with Eritrea, Ethiopia's northern neighbor. It is resolved by a peace treaty in 2000.

- **1930s:** Newspapers and radio are the only means by which people are informed about world events.

  Today: Most people use television rather than newspapers as their main source of news. However, more and more people are turning to the Internet as a news source. Because of the growth of the Internet, the old concept of a single daily edition of a newspaper is changing. The major

newspapers, such as the *New York Times* and the *Washington Post*, have websites in which the main stories are updated every few hours.

- **1930s:** Foreign correspondents such as H. R. Knickerbocker and John Gunther are well known in America for their vigorous and thorough reporting of world events.

  Today: Newspaper foreign correspondents are no longer household names to the American or British public. Their place has been taken by television reporters. Reporters such as MSNBC's Ashleigh Banfield make names for themselves by broadcasting from dangerous parts of the globe. Television and newspaper reporters take risks in doing their jobs, and occasionally there is a tragedy. The kidnapping and murder of *Wall St. Journal* reporter Daniel Pearl in 2002, as he pursued a story about terrorism in Pakistan, illustrates the dangers encountered by reporters in unstable regions of the world.

---

as a description of how the left in England rallied to the cause of the Spanish socialists.

Franco's fascists were victorious in 1939.

Foreign Correspondents

The 1930s were the heyday of the glamorous newspaper foreign correspondent, both in the United States and Britain. In the days before television, these were the men (and, in a few cases, women) who informed the public about the course of events in the trouble spots of the world. In the United States, the foreign correspondent fulfilled an important function because, at the time, the political landscape was dominated by isolationist thinking. As Arthur Schlesinger, Jr. writes of these correspondents, "[T]heir ardent dispatches brought home to Americans the personalities, ambitions, intrigues, and dangers that were putting the planet on the slippery slope into the Second World War."

Among the most famous American correspondents were John Gunther, Vincent Sheean, Ray-

mond Gram Swing, Dorothy Thompson, Edgar Snow, Harold Isaacs, Paul Scott Mowrer, Edgar Ansel Mowrer, and H. R. Knickerbocker. The latter was the model for Wenlock Jakes in *Scoop*. Knickerbocker was a Pulitzer Prize winner who during his career covered nearly every war front in the world, including the Italo-Ethiopian war, which he covered for Hearst International. He and Waugh struck up a cordial relationship there but quarreled over a remark Knickerbocker made and even came to blows over it.

Gunther, who was head of the *Chicago Daily News* bureau in Vienna in the early 1930s, and who was later transferred to London, wrote in his book *Inside U.S.A.* (quoted by Schlesinger) that the 1930s

were the bubbling, blazing days of American foreign correspondence in Europe. . . . Most of us traveled steadily, met constantly, exchanged information, caroused, took in each other's washing, and, even when most fiercely competitive, were devoted friends. . . . We were scavengers, buzzards, out to get the news, no matter whose wings got clipped.

One of the famous British correspondents was F. A. Voigt. In the 1920s and early 1930s, he was Berlin correspondent for the *Manchester Guardian*. His reporting angered the German authorities, and on one occasion in the early 1920s he was kidnapped; a wall around him was sprayed with bullets, but he escaped. Later, Voigt wrote fearlessly about the menace of Hitler's Nazi Party and had to leave Berlin hurriedly for Paris when Hitler came to power in 1933. Even then he continued to write in opposition to Hitler. Voigt's friends and colleagues used to say that he would rather be burned at the stake than be frightened off a story—an attitude that typified the foreign correspondent in the public mind, although such a glamorous view of the profession was not shared by Waugh, as *Scoop* makes abundantly clear.

A Scoop in Ethiopia

During the Italo-Ethiopian war in 1935–1936, there was one of the most famous journalistic scoops of the century. An Englishman named F. W. Rickett, negotiating on behalf of an American oil company, secured a huge oil and mineral concession from the Ethiopian emperor, Haile Selassie. Rickett (who is the original on which the character Mr. Baldwin in the novel is based) gave the information exclusively to three journalists, including Sir Percival Phillips of the *Daily Telegraph*. (Phillips is the model for Sir Jocelyn Hitchcock in *Scoop*.)

Waugh missed out on the scoop because, like the crowd of journalists in *Scoop*, he had been out of Addis Ababa chasing another story. The *Daily Mail* was not pleased with his performance and cabled him, "Badly left oil concession suggest your return Addis immediately."

Critical Overview

Scoop was well received by critics on publication in 1938, and this confirmed Waugh's reputation as a writer of humorous and effective satire on whatever subject he chose. Everyone agreed that the novel was amusing and entertaining. The anonymous reviewer for the *Times Literary Supplement*, for example, praised Waugh's "ribald wit" that "spurts in a brisk uninterrupted flow upon the caprices of sensational journalism." But the reviewer also found that the character William Boot "is too much the simpleton, too facile an instrument for satire," and he thought it fitting that the

London's Fleet Street quartered many of the major daily newspapers during the 1930s

knighthood at the end should go to John Boot rather than to William.

Novelist John Brophy, in an appreciative review in the *Daily Telegraph*, commented that Waugh as a writer was extremely good at making people laugh. But this alone did not make him a satirist, "for indignation founded on some belief is necessary to satire, and I have never been able from his books to discover what Mr. Waugh believes in."

In the *Spectator*, Derek Verschoyle declared *Scoop* to be an "enchanting book," admiring the calm way in which Waugh demolishes his satirical targets, without "surprise, sentiment or resentment." Verschoyle picked out the depiction of the Boot family as the highlight of the book: "[it] reveals an inventive power which it is little exaggeration to call that of genius."

Since its positive initial reception, however, *Scoop* has not usually been ranked with the very best of Waugh's achievements. It often takes a back seat to Waugh's earlier satires of the 1930s, especially *Vile Bodies* and *Black Mischief*. However, with the general reader, *Scoop* has been and remains one of Waugh's most popular novels.

Criticism

Bryan Aubrey

Aubrey holds a Ph.D. in English and has published many articles on twentieth-century literature. In this essay, Aubrey shows how Scoop *arose from Waugh's experiences as a journalist in Abyssinia in 1935.*

When Waugh writes of the ingenious but unethical feats of the likes of Wenlock Jakes and Sir Jocelyn Hitchcock, the reader might be forgiven for thinking that he exaggerates just a little for the sake of being satirical. After all, how could a reputable journalist write an eyewitness report of a revolution in a Balkan country that had not yet happened, as Jakes did? And how could Sir Jocelyn Hitchcock write eyewitness accounts of an earthquake in Messina without leaving his desk in London? Surely these things are not possible. Think again. In 2002, a British journalist working as New York correspondent for London's *Daily Mail* (the same *Daily Mail* that Waugh reported for in the 1930s and which was the model for the *Daily Beast*) seemed to be using Jakes and Hitchcock as his role models. The journalist, Daniel Jeffreys, wrote an eyewitness report for the *Mail* of the execution of a British citizen in Georgia (United States). It was a vivid account, including the condemned man's mouthing of the words "I love you" as he was about to die. The only problem with the story was that Jeffreys made it up. He was not a witness to the execution. No one at the time in London's Fleet Street knew this, and in an episode that could have been lifted directly out of *Scoop*, rival newspapers began berating their own foreign correspondents about why they had missed this scoop (exactly as happens in Waugh's novel when Shumble gets a scoop by making a story up). One British journalist commented (quoted by David Amsden in *New York* magazine), "It's very competitive being a foreign correspondent. But you can't compete with someone who makes things up."

Although the fabrication was later exposed, the *Daily Mail* never printed a correction or issued an apology. This was in keeping with British journalistic practice. Unlike their counterparts in the United States, such as the *New York Times*, British newspapers do not run a daily list of corrections to previous stories. They are no doubt aware of Corker's comment to William in *Scoop* that, if you print too many denials, readers will start to distrust the newspaper. This is an interesting example of the skewed logic that helps to give the novel its

Alice-in-Wonderland quality, where everything that happens seems to violate rational common sense but which is justified by its own curious form of logic.

If there were many more Daniel Jeffreys—one hopes there are not since this apparently was not the only story he is alleged to have made up—one might well understand the sentiment Waugh expresses in the Preface to *Scoop*: "Foreign correspondents, at the time the story was written, enjoyed an unprecedented and undeserved fame." Waugh was in a position to know, since for a while he was one himself. It is remarkable how much *Scoop* is based on his own experience of journalism. The book in which he wrote of his time as a war correspondent, *Waugh in Abyssinia*, although little read today, gives a very entertaining account of how journalists went about their business in Addis Ababa in 1935. It also provides insight into how a novelist takes the raw experience of his own life and turns it into the stuff of fiction.

One of the amusing episodes in *Scoop* is when William loads himself up with excessive supplies for his trip, including such items as a collapsible canoe, six suits of tropical linen, a camp operating table and a set of surgical instruments, and even a portable humidor, "guaranteed to preserve cigars in condition in the Red Sea." Courtesy of the *Daily Mail*, Waugh was given a similar opportunity to kit himself out before setting off to Abyssinia, an experience he describes in one of his memorable *bon mots*: "There are few pleasures more complete, or to me more rare, than that of shopping extravagantly at someone else's expense." Waugh also observed the excesses of others, especially those of a young reporter named William Deedes, of the *Morning Post*, whose equipment weighed a quarter of a ton and included clothing for every possible occasion and items such as snake-proof boots.

When Waugh reached Abyssinia, he soon found that life as a foreign correspondent was less glamorous than he might have expected. There was to be no "crouching in shell holes, typing gallantly amid bursting shrapnel." Since the war had not yet started, there was little hard news to report, and like the journalists in *Scoop*, Waugh went in search of local "color" (items such as descriptions of the landscape, the lives of the people, and native traditions). However, because of the high cost of cables, there was little opportunity for Waugh the writer to produce many worthwhile pieces. In *Scoop*, Waugh made a running joke of the cost of cables and the need to economize. In spite of some chiding from the *Beast*, William never grasps the sparse, elliptical style that saves words and money.

In many other details of *Scoop* that were based on Waugh's experiences in Abyssinia, one can see the imagination of the novelist at work. For example, like William of the *Beast*, Waugh stayed at a Deutsches Haus, run by a formidable German lady. The actual owners of the hotel were a Mr. and Mrs. Heft, but Waugh obviously thought he could make the character stand out more if she were unencumbered by a husband. Thus Frau Dressler is presented as a widow, Herr Dressler having met his end at some point in the past, details unknown.

Waugh applied a similar technique to the menagerie that he encountered at the Deutsches Haus. In *Waugh in Abyssinia*, he describes two geese there who chomped at the ankles of anyone unwise enough to go near them. In *Scoop*, the geese metamorphosed into a remarkable goat who "essayed a series of meteoric onslaughts on the passers-by, ending, at the end of her rope, with a jerk which would have been death to an animal of any other species." Eventually, of course, the rope breaks, providing Waugh with one of the funniest incidents in the novel.

Given the light, humorous tone of *Scoop*, it is perhaps surprising that Waugh was discontented and depressed much of the time he was in Abyssinia. Although he worked diligently, he was not an experienced journalist, and the *Daily Mail* regularly expressed disappointment with the material he sent them, which was judged to be inferior to that of his rivals. In this respect, Corker in *Scoop* represents Waugh. Corker receives a cable from his news agency that reads in part, "YOUR SERVICE BADLY BEATEN ALROUND LACKING HUMAN INTEREST COLOUR DRAMA PERSONALITY HUMOUR INFORMATION ROMANCE VITALITY." In this comic exaggeration, one senses the frustration of Waugh the gifted writer who nevertheless finds himself unable to please a few newspaper editors in London.

Perhaps partly because of his own frustration and lack of success, Waugh soon developed a contempt for journalistic ways. The scenes in *Scoop* in which the journalists of different nations quarrel with one other at the meetings of the Foreign Press Association seem to be based entirely on what Waugh himself witnessed. And he also comments in *Waugh in Abyssinia* that it was common for journalists to steal or destroy their rivals' stories.

For the celebrity American journalists he encountered, Waugh seems to have had nothing but

> Perhaps partly because of his own frustration and lack of success, Waugh soon developed a contempt for journalistic ways."

half-amused contempt. He comments that the American press had created in its readers such a desire for personal details about the correspondents that they made a habit of cabling "expansive pages of autobiography about their state of health and habits of life, reactions and recreations." He also claimed that the Americans would not hesitate in an emergency to invent a story, while the Europeans "must obtain their lies at second hand." What he meant was that the Europeans had to have a source to which they could attribute their information, even if that source was completely unreliable and the journalist knew the information was almost certainly false. The result of these lax standards was that the stories cabled by the press corps in Abyssinia were, according to Waugh, an amalgam of "fantastic rumour . . . trivial gossip, with, here and there embedded, a few facts of genuine personal observation."

Other elements of Waugh's satire in *Scoop* are based on actual events in London's Fleet Street. The move of star reporter Sir Jocelyn Hitchcock from the *Beast* to the *Brute* (a rival newspaper) after a dispute with Lord Copper is based on the departure of ace foreign correspondent Sir Percival Phillips from the *Daily Mail* to the *Daily Telegraph* after a dispute with the *Mail's* owner, Lord Rothermere. This took place just before the Abyssinian war, so Waugh found it easy to get the vacant job with the *Mail*, especially when his friend Diana Cooper (the model for Mrs. Stitch) had a word with Lord Rothermere. This is paralleled in the novel when Mrs. Stitch whispers in Lord Copper's ear about John Courteney Boot.

Is this, then, all there is to *Scoop*—a lighthearted riff on journalism, based on Waugh's own experiences and not to be taken too seriously? Waugh appears to have intended it so, and, indeed, the novel has not attracted as much critical attention as Waugh's earlier, darker, and more pessimistic satires. But *Scoop* cannot be dismissed without noting the kind of world it depicts. It is a chaotic, unpredictable one. No one has any control of his or her destiny because the world is ruled not by law or order as manifested in intelligible cause and effect relationships but by fickle fortune. In *Scoop*, however, fortune or fate is ultimately benign, because at the end of the novel, just as in a Shakespearean wish-fulfillment comedy, everyone receives what is dearest to his or her own heart. William returns to the country; Uncle Theodore gets the chance to saunter around London and even to get paid for it; Mr. Salter gets his dream job; and even Lord Copper, a man needing humbling if ever a man did, gets his desired future "full to surfeit of things which no sane man seriously coveted." So all's well that ends well, the trouble and strife that accompany everyone on the journey are just part of the game Lady Fortune plays, her purpose known only to herself.

Source: Bryan Aubrey, Critical Essay on *Scoop*, in *Novels for Students*, The Gale Group, 2003.

David Kelly

Kelly is an instructor of creative writing and literature at several colleges in Illinois. In this essay, Kelly explains that Waugh's humor is not based in deep understanding of social situations but in simple comic reversal of expectations.

Evelyn Waugh's novel *Scoop* is a social satire, making fun of the people who inhabit its world and of the moral values of the world itself. As most satires do, the book serves to comfort those who are not rich, powerful, or socially dynamic, by showing that the eminent members of society are no better than the average person, and are, in fact, usually worse. Waugh turns the common values of the real world on their head. In the real world, the privileged command what they want, while in *Scoop* the wealthy are so vague about their desires that they end up generally pleased with whatever results are reported to them. In the real world, political extremists are among the most dangerous people on the planet, whereas in the novel the guerillas' disregard for human life is far overshadowed by their lack of competence. In reality, there are media stars who manage to claim the best stories for themselves, whereas, in Waugh's version, the foreign correspondents who claim the most praise are those who ignore the facts of the situation they are covering and make up their own reality.

The success of a social satire is often attributed to the author's courageous handling of the truth. Deep down, readers and critics all suspect that luck and not talent rule the world and that coincidence is a more important force than cleverness; a novel like *Scoop* serves to support that suspicion. Critics tend to give credit to an author like Waugh for showing some sort of plain, unvarnished truth that most novelists are presumably too greedy or frightened to show, as if social satirists are blessed with some sort of x-ray vision that enables them to see through the pretensions that cloud ordinary vision.

In fact, Waugh's satiric method in *Scoop* is much simpler than that. The new reality that he awakens readers to in the novel is achieved by taking common expectations about the way the world operates and reversing them, and then, with a talented novelist's eye for detail, building a reasonable explanation for how the inverted events might happen. A satire like this depends less on the novelist understanding the subtleties of society than it does on making readers accept that which is most unlikely.

There are dozens of cases in which this effect can be seen played out, from the first page to the last. The book begins by introducing readers to a character who holds promise as a protagonist but who soon turns out to be quite minor in significance. John Courteney Boot is described as the sort of underappreciated literary wit and social gadfly that authors frequently use as stand-ins for themselves. He has never been a foreign correspondent before, and the early pages of the novel follow his effort to become one. His lack of experience is itself a factor that makes him an ideal protagonist for a novel about foreign correspondents, giving the author a chance to introduce readers to this world as John Courteney Boot is learning about it.

It is precisely because John Courteney Boot seems so perfectly designed to be the protagonist of this novel that he ends up relegated to a small supporting role. Readers no sooner settle in to the idea of him than he disappears, replaced in the novel by William Boot, a distant relation who is, not surprisingly, even more unqualified to report on a foreign war than John Courtney Boot. John at least has social connections and a respectable writing style, but William is about as socially maladjusted as a person could be (happily secluded in his family's country estate with his loony relatives and servants) and is, in addition, a bad writer.

There are several ways that the novel gains from the shift of focus from John to William. The most obvious is the sheer, joyous nonsense of having the least talented man get the job. Humor depends heavily on anarchy, on the sense that anything can happen.

Putting William at the center of the novel is more than just a reversal of expectation, however. This shift defines the shape that the rest of the novel is to take. The book has to manufacture a reality around William: those in power have to be a little more dense and those who are just following orders have to be just a little more bitter to present a convincing situation where someone so unsuspecting could suddenly find himself on a strange continent so quickly. William does not represent the sort of historic blunder that could happen in the real world: rather, he is so entirely inappropriate to the book's subject that Waugh constantly has to exercise his creativity to justify William's existence. Once William is firmly in position as the novel's protagonist, the other elements have to be equally, if not more, ridiculous. It is this nonsensical nature that is the source of the book's comedy, but it is a mistake to think that, just because the events are about world affairs and are funny, they are necessarily a reflection of political reality.

One aspect of the book that hints at satire of political intrigue but ends up playing as straight-out farce is the way that William's relationship with Kätchen is handled. Her character has aspects that are easily recognizable from any espionage story containing a femme fatale. She is foreign, mysterious, beautiful; she appears to be helpless; and she draws William close to her so subtly that he does not even seem to notice the burden that she is putting on him. In a more serious story, Kätchen would lead William into danger, while in a true social satire, she would represent an element of society that is dangerous to people like him. In this novel, though, she is benign. Her involvement is not an indicator of anything, just a harmless amusement unto itself. She ends up less a threat than an annoyance, costing William nothing but money, which he spends from his expense account. Even the return of Kätchen's husband, who early on presents a threat as one of the mysterious factions vying for control of Ishmaelia behind the scenes, ends up being laughably harmless: "the German," as he is referred to throughout the book, only wants to sleep and to brag about a previous disaster in which he carved a canoe with his own hands that promptly sank. Waugh uses readers' familiarity with characters like Kätchen and the German to make them seem threatening and more significant to the story than they end up being; as he does with other elements of *Scoop*, he then plays the situation for hu-

> Deep down, readers and critics all suspect that luck and not talent rule the world and that coincidence is a more important force than cleverness; a novel like *Scoop* serves to support that suspicion."

mor by presenting exactly the opposite of what is expected.

Exactly as good-natured and harmless as Kätchen are the journalists with whom William works. They range from Corker, who goes from war zone to war zone collecting souvenirs, to Wendell Jakes, who won a Nobel Peace Prize once for his reporting on a war that he himself created when he wrote lies about political strife in a calm country where he woke up after having fallen asleep on a train. While critics who read this novel as a social satire could make much of the ways that the journalists presented here reflect the callous professional detachment of real journalists, the connection is more playful than real. It may be true that the press is able to change the course of nations through frivolous mistakes, and it is almost certainly true that newspaper reports make journalists sound like they understand the complexities of foreign societies much, much more than they actually do. Still, after putting forth a convincing case that reporters have the power to create reality with their words, Waugh dismisses the entire press corps from the story, sending them off to the nonexistent town of Laku following a bogus lead. The book captures a sense of the herd mentality that dominates the foreign press corps but, by removing the journalists from the story, it surrenders any chance of examining the nuances of how the experienced war correspondents really operate.

Modern readers find themselves uncomfortable with the novel's treatment of Africans. The subject of colonialism is never a comfortable one now, as sensitivity toward racial prejudice has evolved. For Waugh's satire of the citizens of fictitious Ishmaelia to work, he would have to show respect for Africans. For modern readers to appre-

1934 invasion of Abyssinia by Italy, in which Evelyn Waugh served as a war correspondant and used his experience in writing Scoop

ciate his sense of humor, he would have to treat the African characters no differently than he would treat the European ones. Whether it is because he lacked the interest in the concerns of Africans or because he was too willing to give in to his own pride in being British, Waugh fails at satirizing the politics of Africa at the time.

The closest Waugh comes to successful political satire of the Ishmaelites is in the book's depictions of the two opposing consuls that William visits in London to obtain a visa to the presumed war zone. The fact that the Consul General is from Antigua and the rival legation is from Sierra Leone gives a nice, sharp commentary about outsiders poking into African politics. These two odd characters help to shed light on what was wrong with emerging African nations in the early 1900s. Their success as satiric characters is probably due to the fact that their roles in the book are so brief: they are both such minor, passing characters in William's life that the novel has no responsibility for granting them any semblance of reality.

Those in power in Ishmaelia, however, appear to be written more for humor than for political satire. As he does throughout the book, Waugh relies on the old pattern of simply inverting readers'

expectations of the political activists rather than working his satire out of any true sense of the people in this situation. Both the ruling Jackson party and the Communist insurgents are portrayed as lazy and incompetent. Political issues are not the defining points of this political struggle: greed is what motivates both Ishmaelite parties, as well as the Germans and Russians that are backing them. Greed is, if course, an important political motivator, and some have argued persuasively that it is the ultimate driving force behind any political stance. It is also more humorous to reduce political passions down to a base instinct, knocking down their pretensions. It is, however, dishonest to reduce whole categories of people to one simple motivation.

Scoop oversimplifies its African characters, straying too far away from satire. They do not have enough in common with real people in similar situations to reflect the real world but are instead played simply as buffoons. The cause does not seem to be racism, as the novel's narrative voice is generally evenhanded (although it does, notably, slip once, referring to the infuriatingly dense cab-driver as "the coon"). Of course, Waugh would have had the patronizing attitudes toward Africans that were common among Europeans in his time, and in light of those common attitudes his portrayal of Africans is not as harsh as one might expect. Still, he clearly favors the British. One striking example of this: in the real world, a patently incompetent newspaper reporter like William would not be able to walk away from the leader of a victorious political coup saying, as he does, "You're being a bore." In the end, all of the political intrigue between Russians and German and the various Ishmaelite parties turns out to play into the plans of one British manipulator, Mr. Baldwin, who appears to be the only person who has control over the whole situation.

To raise questions about the idea that *Scoop* is a political satire should not diminish the book's value or effectiveness. The novel's view of the world is far from a reflection of the political reality it is taken from; still, it is quite funny and often brilliant. There are things that remind readers of the way the world works and that is the core of political satire. The problem is that, when writing about a complex situation, Waugh resorts often to the comic device of playing against expectations rather than offering readers a comic view of what might really happen in such circumstances.

Source: David Kelly, Critical Essay on *Scoop*, in *Novels for Students*, The Gale Group, 2003.

Daryl McDaniel

McDaniel is a writer with a bachelor's degree from the University of Michigan. In the following essay, McDaniel discusses the subjects of power and the power of information in Waugh's novel.

Written in 1938, Evelyn Waugh's *Scoop* depicts a comic world of dishonest war journalists caught up in a rebellion in the fictional African country of Ishmaelia. The novel is based, in part, on Waugh's stint as a war correspondent in Abyssinia in 1935. On the surface, Waugh does not appear to take the subject of journalistic irresponsibility seriously. Though at times *Scoop* seems more farce than satire, the pointed comic criticism of a powerful press gone awry is more effective precisely because it is entertaining. Having been a correspondent himself, Waugh saw journalistic corruption first hand. In the foreword to Michael Brian Salwen's book *Evelyn Waugh in Ethiopia: The Story Behind "Scoop,"* Leonard Ray Teel writes of Waugh's time as a journalist: "The correspondents' conspiratorial competition for scoops disgusted him. Having missed a big story, he received a critical message by cable from his editors.

> In Waugh's world, the haphazard is often generated through people's ignorance, greed, and lack of attention to truth and detail."

He is said to have used that cable to light a cigar." In *Scoop*, Waugh has found a more creative way to burn the newspaper establishment by plucking the simple and unsuspecting country gentleman William Boot from his rural existence, where he writes a column titled "Lush Places," into the middle of a fictional war. *Scoop* explores the subjects of power and the power of information and demonstrates this in a number of ways during the course of the story.

Truth is in short supply and, more importantly in Waugh's world, nothing can be taken at face value. At the outset, Waugh leads readers down the garden path by focusing their attention on John Boot only for them to discover that William Boot is the main character. In *Scoop*, mistaken identity happens often and first impressions cannot be trusted as fact. Truth, reality, and facts are usually creations, or distortions, of man, with the press being the largest villain.

From the beginning of the story, the value of truth is irrelevant to Lord Copper, publisher of the newspaper not so subtly named the *Beast*. One might assume someone with the title "Lord" is an upstanding fellow, but it is quickly apparent that wielding the considerable power of the press is what drives him. As Lord Copper learns of the intrigue in Ishmaelia, he expresses his view of the role his paper should play: "The *Beast* stands for strong mutually antagonistic governments everywhere. Self-sufficiency at home, self-assertion abroad." This statement informs the reader of the enormous egotism of Lord Copper, a symbol of the press, and Waugh's view of the British Government as arrogant. Lord Copper also states: "I am in consultation with my editors on the subject. We think it a very promising little war. A microcosm of world drama. We promise to give it fullest publicity." Lord Copper's interests in the "little war"

What Do I Read Next?

- Waugh's *Brideshead Revisited: The Sacred and Profane Memories of Captain Charles Ryder* (1945) chronicles twenty years in the lives of the Marchmains, a wealthy English Catholic family. Unlike his earlier novels, this is not a satire but an exploration of love, politics, and the call of religion.

- English comic writer P. G. Wodehouse was one of the influences on *Scoop*, and his novel *Full Moon* (1947) is one of his most popular romantic farces. The setting of Blandings Castle is similar to Boot Magna in *Scoop*, and the intricate plotting, eccentric characters, and happy ending make the novel a classic of its kind.

- *Secrets of the Press: Journalists on Journalism* (1999), edited by Stephen Carter, is an entertaining collection of essays by British journalists on the state of the profession today. The essays by Christopher Munnion ("Into Africa"), Ann Leslie ("Female 'Firemen'"), and Emma Daly ("Reporting from the Front") describe, often amusingly, their experiences as foreign correspondents.

- Selina Hastings's *Evelyn Waugh: A Biography* (1994) was written with the full support of Waugh's family, who were dismayed at the negative portrayal of Waugh's personality in an earlier biography by Martin Stannard. Hastings presents a more balanced view that aims to give as close an impression as possible of what it was like to know the man.

is not about the people or politics involved but exploiting the inherent drama to sell newspapers.

The political conflict in Ishmaelia is derived out of a dispute among the current ruling family, the Jacksons. Smiles Soum, a distant family member of the Jacksons, is the fascist leader, upset by his minor post as "the Assistant Director of Public Morals." With such a title, one can only assume it is a low position, with little influence, within the government. Smiles Soum believes that the Ishmaelites, a race of whites, "must purge themselves of the Negro taint." Such words arouse international interest and the world's press soon arrives eager to spread future news, providing Soum the power he desires. Waugh mocks the ignorance of Europeans in Africa by having them equipped with "cuckoo clocks, phonographs, opera hats." The inclusion of such racial intolerance is undoubtedly a comment on the conflict between world powers at the time, but it is not the focus of this novel. While racism may be insidious, Waugh is determined to keep our attention on those who could tell us about it in detail but do not.

William is quickly indoctrinated into this treacherous world of journalism when a fellow journalist, Corker, tries to scoop him by refusing to decipher a message from the *Beast* to William written in "cablese." After learning that they will be working together, Corker agrees to teach William how to read the message. Corker also tells William that two of the great war correspondents, Sir Jocelyn Hitchcock and Wenlock Jakes, made their reputations on two dubious scoops. These two journalists of international prominence derived their celebrity from lies and deceit in what is commonly expected to be the most reputable of professions. The journalists' stories in *Scoop* are untrustworthy and gratuitous. Continuing his education of William, Corker advises him to wire "colour" stories when there is nothing to report: "Colour is just a lot of bulls-eyes about nothing. It's easy to write and easy to read . . . ," which is precisely what the editors desire.

Colour stories, lies, and deceit are the common tools of a journalist in Waugh's world. The power of misinformation is Waugh's theme. On one occasion, it is mistakenly believed that Hitchcock has traveled to the city of Laku to interview Smiles Saum. The world's correspondents at once follow in his footsteps, always afraid of being scooped. Readers soon learn that Laku is Ishmaelian for "I don't know." The city was, in fact, erroneously added to the map years ago by a European mapmaker who thought that a servant's answer of "Laku" to his question, "what is this place?" was the name of the city. In Waugh's world, the haphazard is often generated through people's ignorance, greed, and lack of attention to truth and detail. Not only does a servant have the power to name a city in the right set of circumstances but this misinformation leads the world's press on a goose chase. This is further emphasized as Hitchcock exits from his hotel room and readers learn that he never left for Laku. He tells William: "The job of an English special [correspondent] is to spot the story he wants, get it—then clear out and leave the rest to the [news] agencies." Waugh is continually building on the formidable power of the press, which is all too eager to supply misinformation in order to present stories the public will devour rather than focusing on the less entertaining facts.

One person who does actually supply accurate information to William is Kätchen. This down-on-her-luck woman exerts considerable power over the country journalist and is at the root of a major turning point in William's journalistic career, not to mention the novel. Captivated by her instantly, William is in love and cannot resist any request. Waugh presents Kätchen as selfish and manipulative, thus her influence over William is limitless. Kätchen persuades William to make her his secretary, which has unpredictable results. Just as all seems lost for William and he receives a wire stating that "LORD COPPER PERSONALLY REQUIRES VICTORIES," Kätchen takes female action. Through a series of shopping sprees, which says a lot about Waugh's view of what occupies a woman's time in the 1930s, Kätchen learns that President Jackson is being held hostage in an apparent coup d'etat. Before William can contact the *Beast*, he receives word that they have sacked him. Undeterred, William decides to send the information anyway. William Boot displays the same sarcasm as the author, only without the benefit of punctuation: "NOTHING MUCH HAS HAPPENED EXCEPT TO THE PRESIDENT WHO HAS BEEN IMPRISONED IN HIS OWN PALACE BY REVOLUTIONARY JUNTA HEADED BY SUPERIOR BLACK CALLED BENITO AND RUSSIAN JEW WHO [Jack] BANNISTER SAYS HE IS UP TO NO GOOD THEY SAY HE IS DRUNK WHEN HIS CHILDREN TRY TO SEE HIM BUT GOVERNESS SAYS MOST UNUSUAL LOVELY SPRING WEATHER BUBONIC PLAGUE RAGING . . . SACK RECEIVED SAFELY THOUGHT I MIGHT AS WELL SEND THIS ALL THE SAME."

Kätchen continues to figure largely in William's professional rise. Shortly after his first scoop, William learns that the Germans and Russians have been trying to mine gold ore. Dr. Benito, the minister of foreign affairs and propaganda for Ishmaelia, is working for the Soviets and imprisons Kätchen to try and keep William from wiring his latest scoop. However, this is not an effective deterrent and, suddenly, the world powers

have been altered. William Boot, Countryman, now has the power—whether he is cognizant of his new found influence or not. Scoring his second enormous scoop, William sends a 2,000 word telegram to the *Beast* informing them of the plot. The *Beast* is beyond thrilled and William's celebrity begins to grow. But there is no safety in this woman's arms for William. Having been involved with the failed German attempt to win the mine deal, Kätchen's previously absent husband returns and is now in grave danger. Ever the smooth customer, Kätchen bribes her way out of prison, reunites with her husband, and William, still powerless to Kätchen's desires, provides them with his canoe for their escape. Even though the inclusion of this scheming woman appears to the reader, like many of Waugh's plot points, to be arbitrary, her presence must lead us to conclude that he wishes us to come away with a certain view of the female sex. While one recognizes this characterization of Kätchen as a negative stereotype, there is another individual in *Scoop* who evades explanation and yet fills a pivotal role in this power play.

The revolution and counterrevolution in *Scoop* suggests that the overthrow of governments comes about through blundering, irrationality, and, finally, the unknown powers that lurk behind the scenes. In the case of Mr. Baldwin, whose true identity remains a mystery throughout the novel, the power of one individual can change the fate of a country. Mr. Baldwin is the greatest power in *Scoop*— intangible and thus unknowable. A powerbroker and manipulator of world events behind the scenes, Mr. Baldwin creates outcomes and then uses William to filter information to the world via newspapers. While Mr. Baldwin freely uses his power from unseen quarters, he chooses not to be recognized as the author of his own views. Instead, he shuns the spotlight while positioning William to be bathed in it even further. In another nod towards Waugh's ideas on British attitudes toward Africa, Baldwin tells William he has a message for the British public: "'Might' must find a way. Not 'Force' remember; other nations use 'force'; we Britons alone use 'Might.' Only one thing can set things right—sudden and extreme violence, or better still, the effective threat of it." Baldwin, like Waugh, understands the importance of well chosen words.

Because of the enigmatic Baldwin, the unassuming countryman, William Boot, returns to London an enormous celebrity and respected journalist. Lord Copper has orchestrated a tremendous banquet and has even used his influence to obtain a knighthood for William. William's absence cannot, however, prevent yet another mix-up—his invitation to the banquet is sent to John Boot and, as the banquet is about to begin, there is no Boot to congratulate. Uncle Theodore, William's eccentric relative, arrives at the paper to speak with the features editor about some of his "dirty stories" they might be interested in and is quickly shuffled in to take the place of honor. This mix-up makes Uncle Theodore the third Boot to be considered a war correspondent. Shakespeare, who used mistaken identities throughout many of his comedies, would be proud of the variety of ways Waugh finds to mistake identities in *Scoop*.

Shakespeare's characters often escaped into the woods where lines of reality are blurred. Conversely, William Boot journeys from his authentic country life to enter a game with the power brokers of the urban world that William is ill-equipped to play. *Scoop* is an escapist novel that contains a plethora of absurd situations highlighting the disparity between reality and illusion, fact and fiction. By the end, the only way for William to preserve his soul is to return to the small familiar manageable and tranquil world of the country where the truth can be somewhat contained and not so easily manufactured. While much seems to have returned to normal, there is a question of the harmony created at the end. Working on his old local column "Lush Places," William writes that "rodents pilot their furry brood through the stubble," which is not a metaphor of complete fulfillment. As the novel closes, readers are left to pause and give consideration to our own existence in a world that is far from perfect and often tragically comic. The ultimate power of *Scoop* is the power of fiction to remake reality, which is perhaps Waugh's final point.

Source: Daryl McDaniel, Critical Essay on *Scoop*, in *Novels for Students*, The Gale Group, 2003.

Sources

Amsden, David, "Death or Glory: When the stakes are high, British journalist Daniel Jeffreys always gets the story—and he never lets the facts get in the way," in *New York*, May 6, 2002.

Brophy, John, Review of *Scoop*, in *Evelyn Waugh: The Critical Heritage*, edited by Michael Stannard, Routledge &

Kegan Paul, 1984, pp. 198–99, originally published in *Daily Telegraph*, May 13, 1938.

Review of *Scoop*, in *Evelyn Waugh: The Critical Heritage*, edited by Michael Stannard, Routledge & Kegan Paul, 1984, pp. 197–98, originally published in *Times Literary Supplement*, May 7, 1938.

Schlesinger, Arthur J., Jr., "A Man from Mars," in *Atlantic Monthly*, Vol. 279, No. 4, April 1997, pp. 113–18.

Stannard, Michael, *Evelyn Waugh: The Early Years, 1903–1939*, J. M. Dent & Sons, 1986.

Teel, Leonard Ray, Foreword, in *Evelyn Waugh in Ethiopia: The Story behind "Scoop,"* by Michael Brian Salwen, Edwin Mellen Press, 2001, p. v.

Verschoyle, Derek, Review of *Scoop*, in *Evelyn Waugh: The Critical Heritage*, edited by Michael Stannard, Routledge & Kegan Paul, 1984, pp. 199–201, originally published in *Spectator*, May 13, 1938.

Waugh, Evelyn, *Scoop*, Little Brown and Co., 1977, pp. 133, 215.

———, *Waugh in Abyssinia*, Longmans, Green and Company, 1936.

Further Reading

Beaty, Frederick L., *The Ironic World of Evelyn Waugh: A Study of Eight Novels*, Northern Illinois University Press, 1992.

Beaty examines the role that irony plays in Waugh's fiction, in terms of plot, theme, and character. He argues that Waugh's use of irony adds unstated and often crucial meaning to the text.

Crabbe, Kathryn W., *Evelyn Waugh*, Continuum, 1988.

This is a readable survey of Waugh's novels, but in the chapter on *Scoop*, Crabbe makes the error of confusing the two characters Sir Jocelyn Hitchcock and Wenlock Jakes.

Davis, Robert Murray, *Evelyn Waugh, Writer*, Pilgrim Books, Inc., 1981.

This includes a chapter on *Scoop*, in which Davis analyzes the changes Waugh made as he revised the novel from early drafts.

Lane, Calvin W., *Evelyn Waugh*, Twayne English Authors Series, No. 301, Twayne Publishers, 1981.

Lane concentrates on Waugh's fiction, with chapters on all the major novels. He also discusses Waugh's views on the craft of fiction and offers an evaluation of Waugh's achievement as a satiric novelist.

Smilla's Sense of Snow

Peter Høeg
1993

Published in Denmark as *Froken Smillas fornem-melse for sne* in 1992, and appearing in translation as *Smilla's Sense of Snow* in the United States and as *Miss Smilla's Feeling for Snow* in England in 1993, Peter Høeg's novel quickly moved to the top of the bestseller lists in Europe and the United States. Although Høeg had enjoyed modest commercial and critical success in Denmark with his earlier book *Forestilling om det tyvende arhun-drede* (1988), published as *The History of Danish Dreams* in 1995 in the United States, it was his third novel that rocketed Høeg into the international limelight. The book has been published in more than thirty countries, was named the 1993 book of the year by both *Time* and *Entertainment Weekly*, spent twenty-six weeks on the *New York Times* best-seller list, and was made into a film by Danish director Bille August in 1997. In addition to this remarkable popular success, the novel has won favor among literary critics, who note Høeg's careful attention to setting and culture. As Thomas Satterlee notes, "In many of his novels Høeg explores Danish society by deliberately including characters from a wide range of social classes." *Smilla's Sense of Snow* is notable for its treatment of Danish culture, Greenlandic culture, and the inevitable clash of values brought about by the shift from a colonial to postcolonial relationship between the two. In addition, Høeg examines that strange land of the person caught between cultures in the characters of Smilla and Isaiah. Finally, Høeg plays with conventions and expectations in his use

Peter Høeg

and subversion of the murder mystery/suspense novel genre. *Smilla's Sense of Snow* is a complicated and rich novel, a fast-paced thriller, a love story, an anthropological exploration, and a philosophical treatise all in one book. Høeg's accomplishment with this novel has moved him to the top of the list of Danish writers publishing at the beginning of the twenty-first century.

Author Biography

Peter Høeg was born in Copenhagen, Denmark, on May 17, 1957. His father was a lawyer and his mother a classical philologist. Høeg worked as an actor, dancer, drama teacher, and sailor before turning to writing in 1988. Høeg has also traveled extensively throughout the world, most notably in Africa. His wife, Akinyi, is Kenyan, and Høeg and his family visit Africa frequently.

Høeg's first novel *Forestilling om det tyvende arhundrede* was published in Denmark in 1988. Translated as *The History of Danish Dreams*, the book was published in English in 1995. Critics praised the debut novel highly. However, it was not until the publication of his third novel, *Frøken*

Smillas fornemmelse for sne, that Høeg became known internationally. Published simultaneously in 1993 as *Smilla's Sense of Snow* by Farrar, Straus and Giroux in the United States and as *Miss Smilla's Feeling for Snow* in England, the novel immediately won outstanding reviews from critics and readers alike. Tiina Nunnally, the translator of the American version and the primary translator of the English version, along with the pseudonymous "F. David," also won high praise from reviewers for her brilliant rendering of the Danish novel into English. She received an award from the American Translators Association for her translation of the novel. Both *Time* and *Entertainment Weekly* selected *Smilla's Sense of Snow* as their best novel of the year. In 1997, director Bille August released his film rendition of the novel. The novel also won a 1992 Glass Key award from the Crime Writers of Scandinavia. Since its publication, *Smilla's Sense of Snow* has been translated into seventeen languages, testifying to its worldwide appeal.

Høeg's other works include *Tales of the Night*, a collection of short stories, first published in Danish in 1990 and in English in 1997. *Borderliners*, a novel, was published in Denmark in 1993 and in the United States and England in 1994. Finally, *The Woman and the Ape*, a novel, was published in Denmark, the United States, and England in 1996. Høeg established a foundation with the profits from this book to aid women and children in third world countries. At present, Høeg lives in Copenhagen with his wife and two children.

Plot Summary

The City: Part 1

Smilla's Sense of Snow opens in Copenhagen, Denmark, "the city" alluded to in the section title. The very short first chapter locates the scene in a Greenlanders' cemetery during the funeral for Isaiah, a young Inuit boy, killed by falling from the roof of a warehouse. The chapter also introduces the reader to the first-person narrator, Smilla, as well as to Isaiah's mother, Juliane, and the mechanic, later identified as Peter Føjl. Although the chapter is just a little over two pages long, it closes with an important insight for Smilla, an insight that sustains her through the rest of the novel: "All along I must have had a comprehensive pact with Isaiah not to leave him in the lurch, never, not even now."

The story turns in the next chapters to a series of flashbacks. In the first, Smilla recounts returning late one December afternoon to the White Palace, the apartment complex where she, Isaiah, Juliane, and Føjl live, to find Isaiah dead on the ground and police all over the scene. Føjl, the first person to find him, is also there, crying. Although the police call Isaiah's fall an accident, Smilla believes it to be foul play for two important reasons: first, Isaiah was terrified of heights and would never have been on the roof except to escape from someone intent on doing him harm; and second, when Smilla reads the footprints in the snow, she knows he has jumped off the roof, not fallen, for some unknown reason, most probably to escape from someone or something that frightened him badly.

In another set of flashbacks, Smilla tells of meeting Isaiah about a year and a half earlier and of their developing love for each other. Isaiah often turned to both Smilla and to Føjl when Juliane was drunk and unable to care for him. Through these flashbacks, the reader comes to understand the bond between Smilla and the child and to understand her dogged determination to find out what really happened to him.

During this opening section, Smilla begins her investigation into Isaiah's death, talking to the police; to Ravn, an investigator; to Jeanne Pierre Lagermann, the forensic expert who first examines Isaiah's body; and to Johannes Loyen, the powerful director of the Institute for Arctic Medicine. These meetings do nothing to ease Smilla's suspicions about the boy's death. After going through Juliane's papers, she discovers a link between Isaiah and the Cryolite Corporation of Denmark, a firm that both mines and explores Greenland. Isaiah's father was killed during an expedition to Greenland with the Cryolite Corporation, and the company has granted a widow's pension to Juliane.

In the first part of the novel, the reader is also introduced to Peter Moritz Jaspersen, Smilla's father, a very wealthy anesthesiologist and golfer. Smilla and Moritz have a deeply troubled relationship; however, Moritz supports Smilla financially and gathers the information for which she asks him, about Loyen, Tørk, and the Cryolite Corporation. The meeting with Moritz also pushes Smilla to recall her childhood in Greenland and her mother, Ane, a hunter who is now dead.

The reader discovers that Smilla is an expert glaciologist, someone who can read ice and snow better than nearly any other person on the planet. Although she has never finished any advanced degrees, she has published on the subject and is re-

garded as the foremost expert on ice. She also has an uncanny ability to navigate her way through non-navigable conditions in the Arctic.

A final important event of the opening chapters is the growing relationship between Smilla and Føjl. Although neither truly trusts the other, they begin an affair that leads to Smilla falling in love with Føjl.

The City: Part 2

The tension tightens in part two as Smilla follows leads to Loyen; David Ving, an accountant and lawyer who seems to be threatening Juliane in some way; and to Andreas Fine Licht, an expert in Eskimo culture and dialect. All three seem to have some connection to the mysterious expedition to Greenland in 1966 that ended in explosions killing eight people and then a second expedition in 1991 that resulted in Isaiah's father's death. In addition, all three seem to have some connection to yet another expedition being mounted. Føjl also learns that Isaiah was picked up every month by Ving to be examined at a hospital. Smilla discovers the name of Tørk Hiijd. Smilla goes to Licht in order to have a tape she finds in Isaiah's hiding place translated. Licht lives on a boat where The Arctic Museum is housed. Smilla leaves the tape with Licht but returns to the boat when she receives a call from Licht to come at once. She finds Licht murdered just before the boat explodes, and someone tries to kill her. Smilla barely escapes with her life.

The City: Part 3

In the last part of the first section of the novel, more pieces fall into place. Smilla connects Loyen to a conference on "Neocatastrophism." As Moritz explains to her, neocatastrophism is a scientific debate over how great natural catastrophes have affected the evolution of the earth. In addition, she discovers that during the expeditions to Greenland, the divers did not die of botulism as reported by the Cryolite Corporation. Rather, they died from a worm found in the water surrounding a meteorite, a worm that is normally only found in the tropics but that generally does not cause the death of its host. In addition, with help from Føjl's friend, Birgo Lander, she identifies the ship being outfitted for the next secret expedition to Greenland. Lander introduces her to the captain and arranges for her to travel with the expedition as a stewardess. She narrowly misses being picked up by the police at her father's home, but he helps her escape and delivers her to Lander, who takes her to the ship, the *Kronos*.

Media Adaptations

- *Smilla's Sense of Snow* was adapted into a film in 1997 by Twentieth Century Fox. The film was directed by Bille August and starred Julia Ormond as Smilla, Gabriel Byrne as Føjl, and Richard Harris as Moritz. The film is available in both video and DVD formats.

- The soundtrack to the film *Smilla's Sense of Snow* was released on CD by Elektra/Asylum in March of 1997.

- An abridged version of *Smilla's Sense of Snow*, read by Rebecca Pidgeon, was released by Harper Collins in August 1993 as an audiobook.

- A reading group guide for *Smilla's Sense of Snow* is available at www.randomhouse.com/resources/bookgroup/smillassense_bgc.html (last accessed October 2002) along with an interview with the author, discussion questions, an author biography, and links to other sites.

- Another reading group guide for *Smilla's Sense of Snow* is available at www.readinggroupguides.com/guides/smillas_sense_of_snow.asp (last accessed October 2002), including interviews, biography, questions, and links.

The Sea: Part 1

All of the action of the second section of the novel takes place on ship. Smilla meets a variety of dangerous characters, including Jakkelsen, the captain's brother, who is also a heroin addict, and Verlaine, the first mate from some unknown tropical location. She also discovers that there are three mysterious passengers on board who are directing the mission, much to Captain Lukas's displeasure. While on the ship, Smilla continues her investigation, sometimes at great risk to her own safety. She eventually learns that Tørk is one of the secret passengers on board. The trip becomes ever more dangerous as she discovers that the *Kronos* is being used to smuggle drugs by Verlaine. Smilla tries to leave the ship when it stops for refueling and sup-

plies; she is stopped, however, when she finds Jakkelson lying dead at the station platform. She also notes with shock that a new passenger is coming on board; the passenger is none other than Føjl. Although she is uncertain about his loyalty, Smilla returns to the ship because, as she says, "One of the few people who make life worth living is on board the *Kronos*."

However, Smilla's trust is misplaced. Føjl hands her over to Tørk, who says she is under arrest and orders Verlaine to lock her in her cabin. As the section closes, Smilla reveals that she knows she is not under arrest but will be killed: "Verlaine is the one who locks the door. . . . There is something honest about his silence. It tells me that this isn't a cell and I haven't been arrested. This is the beginning of the conclusion, which will happen sometime soon."

The Ice

The last section is the shortest of the book and takes place at Isla Gela Alta, the site of the subterranean cavern, housing the mysterious meteorite. Smilla has learned that Føjl is preparing to dive into the lake to begin preparations for removing the meteorite. She also knows that he will die if he does so. Smilla escapes the ship and races to the location of the work, where Tørk greets her as if he knew she would come. When the conclusion comes, it comes quickly: Lukas shoots Verlaine with a harpoon as Verlaine is about to kill Smilla. Smilla discovers, finally, that Tørk was the one on the roof when Isaiah died and that he pursued him in order to wrest the tape from him. Lukas aims the harpoon at Tørk, but Tørk blows his arm off. Føjl turns on Tørk, who kicks him to the ground. Tørk begins to run for the ship. The book ends with Smilla tracking Tørk, herding him out on to thinner and thinner ice. As Smilla says in the last five words of the book: "There will be no resolution."

Characters

Isaiah Christensen

Although Isaiah is dead as the novel opens, all events of the story circulate around him. The reader comes to know Isaiah through flashbacks narrated by Smilla and Føjl, who calls the child "the Baron." Isaiah is a young Greenlandic child living with his mother in the White Palace apartments in Copenhagen. He is deathly afraid of heights. He is old beyond his years and turns to Smilla and Føjl when his mother is too drunk to care for him. In Isaiah, Smilla sees a younger version of herself, a transplanted Greenlander ill at ease in Danish culture. There is a mystery surrounding Isaiah as well; Smilla learns after his death that powerful men from the Cryolite Corporation and the Arctic Medicine Institute were studying Isaiah and his response to a dangerous parasite that killed his father while diving in Greenland. Indeed, it is Smilla's relationship to Isaiah that leads her to risk her own life in order to understand the boy's death.

Juliane Christensen

Juliane Christensen is Isaiah's mother, a widowed, alcoholic Greenlander living in the White Palace in Copenhagen. Smilla discovers after Isaiah's death that Juliane's living expenses are covered by the Cryolite Corporation, the company for whom her husband was working at the time of his death.

Peter Føjl

Føjl, also referred to throughout the book as "the mechanic," is a large, bear-like man who lives in the same apartment complex with Smilla and Isaiah. He, too, has established a special relationship with Isaiah. Indeed, he is the one who first discovers Isaiah's body. He is a mysterious man, someone who has a variety of talents one would not expect to find in a simple mechanic. In addition, his tastes in food and wine suggest that he has lived outside of Denmark. As he and Smilla begin to cautiously work together to unravel the mystery of Isaiah's death, Føjl and Smilla fall in love, in spite of the fact that neither really trusts the other. Føjl introduces Smilla to Lander, who gets her on board the *Kronos*. Føjl then disappears, only to resurface in Greenland as the fourth secret passenger on the boat. As it turns out, Føjl has been hired by Ving from the very beginning to keep an eye on Isaiah, Juliane, and Smilla. He is also an expert diver, having been a member of an elite Danish navy undercover team similar to the Navy Seals. Tørk has hired him to dive for the meteorite. It is difficult for the reader to truly judge Føjl's loyalties: on the one hand, he was truly devoted to Isaiah, and later to Smilla; on the other, he is greedy and willing to work for those who have murdered Isaiah. This paradox is not resolved by the end of the book.

Tørk Hviid

Tørk, the son of a Danish musician who mistreated him, grows up to be a brilliant scientist of ice and snow. It is he who has discovered a meteorite in a lake on a Greenlandic island and who has attempted to remove the meteorite on at least two previous occasions. He is the mastermind behind Isaiah's death and the current expedition to Greenland. A ruthless man, he is, nonetheless, very attractive to Smilla, even as he plots her death.

Jakkelsen

Lukas's younger brother, Jakkelsen is also a drug addict shipping on the *Kronos* in an attempt by his brother to straighten him out. He takes an interest in Smilla. However, once he discovers a load of drugs on board the ship, his days are numbered. He is murdered when the ship stops at the *Greenland Star* for offshore refueling and restocking.

Ane Jaspersen

Ane is Smilla's mother who dies when Smilla is just seven years old. She is a native Greenland hunter. For Smilla's first seven years, she travels with her mother on hunts. Ane is the great love of Moritz Jaspersen's life. Although she has been dead for many years at the opening of the novel, Smilla flashes back to her mother many times as she considers the differences between Greenlandic and Danish culture.

Jørgen Moritz Jaspersen

Generally referred to as "Moritz," Smilla's father is an extraordinarily wealthy physician and golfer. He met Ane when in Greenland to do research, and fell passionately in love with her. The marriage broke up after four years, but Moritz sent for Smilla after the death of her mother. At the time of the novel, Moritz is married to a ballet dancer thirteen years younger than Smilla. His relationship with his daughter is troubled and ambiguous.

Smilla Qaavigaaq Jaspersen

Smilla Jaspersen is the main character of *Smilla's Sense of Snow*, a thirty-year-old woman living in Denmark, the daughter of a Greenlandic hunter woman and a Danish doctor. Smilla is a solitary, brilliant woman who lives in an apartment complex called the White Palace. A loner, Smilla nevertheless befriends a young Greenlandic boy named Isaiah, caring for him when his alcoholic mother is unable to do so. When Smilla returns to her apartment complex one day to find Isaiah's crumpled body on the pavement, evidently the victim of an accident, Smilla vows to find out what really happened to the boy. She suspects foul play, and her investigation of what turns out to be murder forms the plot of the novel. Smilla is a particularly interesting character. Throughout the novel, she recalls her childhood in Greenland before her mother's death, commenting on the differences between the Inuit culture of her mother and the western, Danish culture of her father. She also reveals the trauma of being brought to Denmark at age seven and placed in boarding schools. Smilla is cynical, rebellious, and brilliant. An expert on ice and snow, she has taken a number of expeditions to Greenland for research. However, her disdain for European culture and her own eccentricities prevented her from finishing an advanced degree, although she has published frequently on the subjects of ice and snow. Indeed, Smilla is recognized by the scientific community as one of the top experts in glacial morphology and ice in the world. In addition, Smilla has a perfect sense of direction. She is able to navigate through fog, ice, and snow without losing her direction. As the first person narrator of the novel, Smilla reveals her love of mathematics, her knowledge of philosophy and physics, and her view of the history of the troubled relationship between Denmark and Greenland. Smilla is at times a paradox, both rough and vulnerable. Through determination and will, she winds her way into the heart of the mystery, placing herself in grave danger, keeping her promise to Isaiah "not to leave him in the lurch, never, not even now."

Jean Pierre Lagermann

Lagermann is a forensic medicine expert who first examines Isaiah's body. He reveals to Smilla that a muscle biopsy has been removed from the body sometime after the child's death.

Birgo Lander

Birgo Lander is a friend of Føjl who owns and directs a shipping firm. He helps Smilla identify the vessel being outfitted for the expedition to Greenland, and he later helps her make contact with Captain Lukas who hires her as a stewardess. Lander also delivers Smilla to the *Kronos*.

Andres Fine Licht

The blind curator of the Arctic Museum, Licht is a professor of Eskimo languages and cultures. Smilla takes him the tape recording she finds in Isaiah's box, and he interprets it for her. A native Greenlander, he is also the person who spoke at Isaiah's funeral. Licht is murdered on the ship housing the Arctic Museum, after summoning Smilla who nearly dies in the resulting fire. Smilla

later learns that Licht was one of the members of the previous expedition to Greenland.

Johannes Loyen

Loyen is the powerful director of the Institute of Arctic Medicine. He performs autopsies of all Greenlandic deaths in Denmark and consequently autopsied Isaiah's body. His interest in Isaiah is deeper than it first appears, however. He is researching the deadly parasite found in the ocean water off Greenland that killed Isaiah's father and that remains inactive in Isaiah's body. He is part of the expedition team that goes to Greenland under deep secrecy to investigate the meteor and the parasite.

Elsa Lübing

Elsa Lübing is the chief accountant of the Cryolite Corporation of Denmark. When Smilla goes through Juliane's papers, she finds a letter from Elsa expressing sympathy over the death of Isaiah's father and informing Juliane that she will be receiving a stipend from the company. When Smilla contacts Elsa, she learns valuable information about the previous two expeditions to Greenland. Elsa is highly religious, and she shares this information because she is concerned about the ethics and morality of the current state of affairs in the Cryolite Corporation.

Sigmund Lukas

Lukas is the captain of the *Kronos*, the ship chartered by Loyen and Tørk for the current expedition to Greenland to try to extricate the meteorite at Gela Alta. A good captain, he is also a compulsive gambler. He thus takes the job because of the money it will bring him, although he is fearful of the purpose of the job and dislikes the secrecy of those who have hired him. He allows Smilla to ship out on *Kronos* disguised as a stewardess.

Ravn

A man who presents himself as an investigator for the district attorney, Ravn actually works in the fraud division. His involvement in the case becomes more complicated when it is revealed that his daughter was involved with the Cryolite Corporation of Denmark and has died in a manner suspiciously like that of Isaiah.

Urs

Urs is the cook on the *Kronos*. He has served time for smuggling, and Smilla uses this information to force more information from him about the *Kronos*.

Verlaine

First mate of the *Kronos*, Verlaine is also a drug smuggler working in cooperation with Tørk. It is he who murders Jakkelsen and tries repeatedly to murder Smilla.

David Ving

Ving is the lawyer and CPA who works with Loyen and Tørk in their cover-up of the earlier expedition and the death of Isaiah's father. Ving picks up Isaiah periodically to take him for medical checkups with Loyen. In addition, Ving is the one who has arranged Juliane and Isaiah's housing and stipend. He is also the one who has hired Føjl to keep an eye on them and, by extension, Smilla.

Themes

Mathematics

Mathematics may seem like an unlikely theme for a book that is about the murder of a young child and the dangerous path the narrator must take to discover the motives of those responsible for the murder. Yet *Smilla's Sense of Snow* is nothing if not unpredictable. Smilla finds in mathematics the certainty and stability she lacks in herself. She says, "I'm not perfect. I think more highly of snow and ice than love. It's easier for me to be interested in mathematics than to have affection for my fellow human beings." In addition, when Smilla first meets Isaiah, she reads to him from Euclid's *Elements*. Smilla says, "There is the feeling that always comes over me at the mere thought of that book: veneration. The knowledge that it is the foundation, the boundary. That if you work your way backwards, past Lobachevsky and Newton and as far back as you can go, you end up at Euclid." Smilla's two great skills are reading snow and direction, two geometrically determined skills. The crystalline structure of a snowflake can be mathematically determined and predicted with absolute regularity in spite of its infinite variety. In addition, navigation requires an intuitive sense of vectors and angles. Tellingly, Smilla's "soul brother" is Newton, not Einstein. Newton's notion of "Absolute Space" is necessary for Smilla's navigation of the world. When she ventures out into the Einsteinian paradoxes of time and space, she loses her orientation. Out on the ice, which she knows so well,

the novel ends unresolved as Smilla flings herself after the villain, leaving foundation and mathematics behind.

Colonialism

One of Høeg's major concerns in *Smilla's Sense of Snow* is the relationship between Denmark and its former colony Greenland. Through Smilla, Høeg recounts the history of this relationship, beginning first in the eighteenth century when the Royal Greenland Trading Company set up a highly protective system of trade with Greenland. As such, the raw materials of the island became the sole property of Denmark, and Greenland became a colony.

The notion of "colonialism," however, is tied up with much more than the history of one nation claiming another as a colony. Rather, it is an exploration of the effects of this relationship on both the colonizer and the colonized. In *Smilla's Sense of Snow*, the days of Greenland as a colony have passed; at the time of the writing of the novel, Greenland was under Home Rule. However, two centuries of colonial exploitation, as well as the two decades of "modernization" that occurred in the 1950s and 1960s, have changed the way that both Greenlanders and Danes think and live.

Smilla informs the reader that in 1964, "The old blatantly colonial policy for Greenland was abandoned.... Making room for the policies of the sixties—the educating of Northern Danes to equal rights." Ironically, the "education" of the Greenlanders took place in Danish, and during the "modernization" large-scale relocation of people from small settlements to larger cities took place. It was also during this period that the Greenlandic language suffered significant destruction. Because so much of cultural identity is tied up with language, the surest way a colonizer can destroy a culture is to limit the use of the native language and insist on the use of the colonizer's language. As Smilla notes, "All money in Greenland is attached to the Danish language and culture. Those who master Danish get the lucrative positions. The others can languish in the filet factories or in unemployment lines. In a culture that has a murder rate comparable to a war zone."

Nevertheless, it would be a mistake to understand colonization as an unambiguously negative event. Indeed, it is the paradox of colonialism that renders any understanding of the situation so very difficult. As Smilla herself reports, "The problem with trying to hate the colonization of Greenland

Topics for Further Study

- Read a short history of the Danish colonization of Greenland in an encyclopedia or another source. Imagine the story of the colonization told from the viewpoint of an Inuit. How do you think the accounts would differ?

- Watch the film version of *Smilla's Sense of Snow* and note how director Bille August chooses to portray the story. What are some of the ways the film conveys the main themes of the novel? Does the film seem "true" to the novel, or are there inexplicable changes?

- Read *Polar Star* by Martin Cruz Smith, a murder mystery that takes place on a fishing boat near the Arctic Circle. What similarities and differences can you find between the two books?

- In what ways do the needs and concerns of Inuit people both clash and coincide with environmental issues? For example, the Inuit traditionally hunt whales, many species of which are endangered. Ought indigenous people be able to follow their traditional ways of living? Or do the needs of the environment outweigh the needs of the culture? How have nations such as Canada and Russia handled this question?

- Smilla's mother, although dead for many years, continues to play an important role in Smilla's life. How has Ane influenced her daughter over the years? How do you think Smilla will come to terms with her mixed heritage?

- Reread the book, noting all references to mathematics, physics, and philosophy. Look up the names of each mathematician and philosopher and learn something about their ideas. How do these allusions contribute to your understanding of Smilla as a character?

---

with a pure hatred is that, no matter what you may detest about it, the colonization irrefutably improved the material needs of an existence that was one of the most difficult in the world." It is within this paradox that Smilla finds herself trapped: nei-

ther fish nor fowl, neither Inuit nor Dane, she struggles to understand both sides of her heritage.

Alienation

Perhaps the most profoundly felt theme running through *Smilla's Sense of Snow* is that of alienation. When a people, or a person, lose(s) a sense of meaning in life or a separation from that which has formerly nurtured them, the result is both a cultural and personal sense of alienation. In many ways, Smilla exemplifies both. Clearly, Smilla is alienated both from her father and Danish society. She often pulls her telephone from its jack and disconnects her doorbell so that she does not have to interact with others in Copenhagen. The root of this alienation is in her forcible transfer from Greenland to Copenhagen after the death of her mother. That she runs away more times than she can remember between the ages of seven and twelve speaks to this deeply felt sense of cultural isolation. By the time she is an adult, Smilla has resigned herself to living at least partially within Danish culture: "I no longer make an effort to keep Europe or Denmark at a distance. Neither do I plead with them to stay. In some way they are part of my destiny. They come and go in my life. I have given up doing anything about it." However, this is the voice of resignation, not integration; even as an adult, Smilla remains alienated from and unable to find meaning in Denmark or Europe.

Smilla's alienation from the culture of her father, however, is not the most distressing alienation in the book. Much earlier, as a small child living with her mother in Greenland, she experiences an even deeper form of alienation. She recalls a hunting and fishing trip she took with her mother and her inability to kill the birds she had trapped:

> The year after—the year before she disappeared—I began to feel nauseated when I went fishing. I was then about six years old. Not old enough to speculate about the reason. But old enough to understand that it was a feeling of alienation toward nature. That some part of it was no longer accessible to me in the natural way that it had been before.

It is this alienation that is truly tragic: Smilla cannot find a place to stand in either Inuit or Danish culture.

On a personal level, however, alienation serves as a defense mechanism for Smilla. Because she keeps everyone at a distance, claiming no people or place as her home, she is able to protect herself from being hurt. Tellingly, her affair with Føjl both awakens her and frightens her. Love, after all, is the cure for all alienation; yet it is the beloved who has the power to wreak the most damage. Likewise, her greatest fear of Tørk is not that he might kill her but that he knows her: "It's the realization that he knew who I was from the very beginning that is so excruciating. Not since my childhood have I felt so strongly in someone else's power." Thus, both knowing and being known occupy the dangerous flip side to the emptiness of alienation and provoke one of the driving questions of the book: is it better to live numbly, without meaning, in a state of alienation, or to live painfully, in the fear that meaning will disappear once found?

Style

Genre

The term "genre" refers to the category of a given literary work in either form or content. In terms of content, certain genres carry with them certain conventions. For example, detective fiction requires both a crime and someone trying to solve the crime. Thus, while a book such as *Smilla's Sense of Snow* is clearly generically a novel, it does not easily fall into any one generic category in terms of content and convention. Indeed, it is almost as if Høeg is playing with the notion of genre itself in his creation of this novel.

The story opens with the trappings of a murder mystery: a death under mysterious circumstances, a protagonist with the information and motive she needs to begin an investigation, a multitude of clues, and a cast of interesting and diverse characters. At the same time, the novel is also of the "thriller/suspense" genre. Because neither Smilla nor the reader has enough information at any one time to solve the case, she is constantly in danger. She cannot know whom to trust. The novel is also a love story, with the unlikely pair of Smilla and Føjl filling the roles of the lovers. The novel is at once tender and tough. Readers who are familiar with conventional love stories expect the relationship between the two to redeem both of them. Høeg dashes this expectation by revealing near the end of the book that Føjl has been collaborating with the villains. Nevertheless, he still appears to love Smilla, and Smilla perhaps continues to love him.

Less obviously, the novel is also a philosophical essay on the nature of mathematics, physics, and metaphysics. Through her ruminations, Smilla reveals that she is engaged in a quest for meaning, looking to philosophy and science to provide her with the answers her experience does not. The novel also functions as both a history and an indictment of Danish colonial policy in Greenland. It is the story of a disenfranchised "other" in the shape of Smilla, a woman who cannot find a place to belong in either culture of her heritage. The book clearly abhors the effects of Western technological capitalism on the environment and the people of the Arctic. The novel then morphs once again and becomes a science fiction thriller, a novel about a strange, alien meteorite and potentially lethal life forms that have killed before and will kill again.

By the end of the novel, Høeg has deliberately destroyed all generic expectations of the reader. For some, these generic twists and turns are both troubling and confusing, as critical comments indicate. However, Høeg's refusal to allow his novel to be generically classified mirrors Smilla's refusal to be classified by ethnicity, gender, or age. As a result, Høeg has produced a postmodern novel that continually slips its boundaries, just as Smilla slips hers.

Setting

Perhaps the most striking feature of *Smilla's Sense of Snow* is its setting. From the deep cold of the Danish winter in the opening scene to the last desperate skate across the ice in Greenland, Høeg uses precise and concrete language to evoke a sense of coldness, ice, and snow, which mirrors Smilla's sense of isolation and alienation.

Specifically, Høeg chooses three separate settings for his novel. The first is the city of Copenhagen, Denmark. For Smilla, the Danish winter is colder than anything she experiences in Greenland. The coldness of urban life also affects her deeply; she lives in an impersonal apartment building called "The White Palace," a place where people can live side by side and never know each other's names. For the transplanted Greenlanders, Copenhagen is a kind of prison, a place where they endure social and physical coldness.

The second section of the book takes place on the open ocean of the North Atlantic. For Smilla, this setting is even more dangerous and frightening than Copenhagen. Ironically, she does not like the sea, although she has grown up with people whose livelihoods come from the sea. The *Kronos*, the ship that transports Smilla from Europe to Greenland, becomes the site of transition for Smilla, a place where she drops her fancy clothes and the veneer of civilization and takes on the clothing of the survivor. In many ways, Smilla loses her footing while she nearly loses her life on the ship; she is much more comfortable with ice than water. For Smilla, the ice is a known and predictable quantity, the crystals shaped into regular and mathematically identifiable crystals. The sea, on the other hand, is always moving, always unpredictable. Likewise, although Smilla has learned how to deal with the Danes in Copenhagen, when she finds herself on the *Kronos*, she discovers that the people aboard are as unpredictable and as dangerous as the ocean itself.

The last section of the novel takes place on the ice of Greenland. Again, Høeg evokes the bitter cold and the alien strangeness of the frozen land. Smilla, however, finds herself on surer footing here. Not only does she have the scientific knowledge of snow and ice that she has learned in Europe, she has the intuitive knowledge of her upbringing. In the final desperate scene, it is Smilla's familiarity with the setting that promises her survival:

> The ice has its own nocturnal hospitality. I have no flashlight now, but I'm running as if it were a level road. Without difficulty, with confidence. My *kamiks* grip the snow in a different way than his boots do.

In the end, it is the setting itself that appears about to kill Tørk: "His strength is about to give out. If you haven't grown up in this landscape, it uses up your strength." The novel ends on the ice, in the dark, without resolution. And at the end, it is the evocation of the story's setting that continues to resonate with the reader long after the closing paragraph.

Historical Context

Understanding the cultural and historical relationship between Greenland and Denmark is essential for an understanding of *Smilla's Sense of Snow*. Although Denmark had granted Greenland Home Rule in 1979, a decade before Høeg began writing his novel, the events leading to this political decision as well as the aftermath of the Home Rule act deeply inform the events of the novel.

People have lived on the island of Greenland for about four thousand years. The first Europeans reached Greenland about 985 CE, when Norwegians settled in two farming colonies. For unknown reasons, these colonies died out. Speculation among scientists suggests that disease or climatic catastrophe may have caused the demise of the Norwegian colonies, a tantalizing link to Høeg's concept of "neocatastrophism." Indeed, Høeg's use of

a giant meteorite as a plot device hints at the possibility of climatic change, while his creation of a fatal parasitic worm suggests that this might have been the cause of the failure of Europeans to sustain life on Greenland. Certainly, Høeg seems to be suggesting that contemporary Europeans ought to take care with what they are willing to unleash on the rest of the world.

There is evidence that the early Europeans had contact with the Inuit people as early as the first settlements. In the sixteenth century, explorers and whalers regularly visited Greenland and had dealings with the Inuit. However, permanent contact was not established until the eighteenth century when Hans Egede traveled to the west coast of Greenland, trying to find the earlier settlements. A Danish-Norwegian priest, Egede acted as both missionary and trader. He and his missionaries learned Inuit and succeeded in converting the indigenous people to Christianity. In 1776, the Danish government established the Royal Greenland Trade Company to control trade with Greenland. For two hundred years, Denmark exerted colonial rule of Greenland, keeping the island both isolated and protected.

Ironically, the abolishment of the colonial relationship in the early 1950s damaged Inuit culture perhaps more than colonization itself. Smilla comments on this period frequently; during the 1950s and 1960s, Greenlanders were considered "Northern Danes" and, as such, beneficiaries of social reform and modernization in the areas of health, education, and welfare. While this led to opportunities for many Greenlanders, it also damaged the language, since "Northern Danes" were expected to learn Danish in school and conduct their affairs in Danish. Many Inuit were forced to leave their traditional homes and ways of life in the Danish effort to move them into the twentieth century.

In *Smilla's Sense of Snow*, the reader learns that Smilla was a member of the Young Greenlander's Council, a group in Denmark comprised of Greenlandic students and dedicated to Home Rule for Greenland. As a result of pressure from this and other radical groups, Denmark established a Home Rule Commission in 1975, and by 1979 Home Rule had been established. Remarkably, the Greenlandic Inuit were the first Inuit people to rule themselves around the world after the advent of colonialism.

As Høeg points out through Smilla, however, even Home Rule is a paradoxical condition. It presupposes that the Inuit adopt European models of self-rule, with a parliament and central government.

Smilla herself sees that Danish involvement in Inuit life is neither clearly good nor evil. Although the introduction of Western technology into Greenland destroyed much of the traditional way of life for the Inuit, as well as destroying many Inuit through disease and alcoholism, the material conditions of the Inuit have improved. Høeg gives Smilla these words to express the paradox:

> The problem with trying to hate the colonization of Greenland with a pure hatred is that, no matter what you may detest about it, the colonization irrefutably improved the material needs of an existence that was one of the most difficult in the world.

Høeg succeeds, then, in initiating the reader into the complexities of the colonial relationship and clearly leads the reader to consider the fate of other polar people across the world. Thus, without historical and cultural background information, the reader loses some of the richness of *Smilla's Sense of Snow* as a postcolonial novel.

Critical Overview

Smilla's Sense of Snow met with both critical and popular praise upon its publication in Danish in 1992 and in English in 1993. In addition to being on many bestseller lists, the novel was reviewed in all major newspapers and magazines in the United States. Most critics hail the book as one of the most important novels to emerge at the end of the twentieth century. Indeed, reviewers commonly compare Høeg to such major writers as John Le Carré, Martin Cruz Smith, Graham Greene, and even Joseph Conrad. While critics agree generally that the novel is of exceptional quality, they nonetheless find that quality in different places. For some, the success of the novel rests in Høeg's construction of the character of Smilla. For others, the plot itself drives the novel. For still other reviewers, the political ramifications of the relationship between Denmark and Greenland are at the core of the book. And for another group of critics, the postmodern characteristics of the novel make it a book worth studying.

Pearl Bell, writing in *Partisan Review*, for example, praises the characterization of Smilla, calling her "truculent, ferociously opinionated, erudite, disorganized, [and a] strangely beguiling woman." Likewise, Lesley Hazelton in the *Seattle Times* writes this of Smilla:

> Bravo Smilla: tough and vulnerable, intelligent and emotional, rational and impulsive, she's her own per-

A monument in Greenland to Hans Egede, an eighteenth-century missionary who converted Inuits to Christianity, an important event in the colonization of Greenland

son, a full person. This Danish writer scarcely takes a false step in creating a multifaceted, believable, brave woman—an amazing achievement when you consider how confused and alienated most American male writers are about women.

Those critics who focus on the plot of the novel include Brad Leithauser in the *New Republic* who writes that Høeg handles "with great deftness" the task of creating a plot for a thriller with "artistic freshness." Richard Eder, writing in the *Los Angeles Times Book Review*, calls "the sinuous turns of [Høeg's] story deeply engrossing," although Eder is not fully satisfied with the book's ending, suggesting that it does not quite make sense. Robert Nathan in the *New York Times Book Review* also praises *Smilla* for both its suspense and "exploration of the heart."

Perhaps the largest group of critics are fascinated by the postcolonial themes of the book and the way Høeg depicts relationships between the Danes and the Greenlanders. Julian Loose in the *London Review of Books* suggests that "what lifts *Miss Smilla* above the ordinary is Høeg's sense of how mixed motives have grotesquely deformed the unequal relationship of Denmark and Greenland."

Novelist Jane Smiley, in a review appearing in the *Washington Post*, points to the "broader political issues, especially the meanings of borders and boundaries between countries and cultures" in Høeg's evocation of the postcolonial relationship between Denmark and Greenland. Likewise, William A. Henry writes in *People* that *Smilla* is "at a deeper level . . . about cultural collisions between the industrial world and more primal places that have fallen under Western sway." Finally, in an interesting review in the *Montreal Gazette*, Merilyn Simonds likens the misunderstandings between the Danes and the Greenlanders to the misunderstandings between Canadians and Inuits living in Canada.

Although some critics find fault with the novel because they have a difficult time classifying it generically, others find this generic fluidity to be a strength, as well as being indicative of postmodern literature. Hans Henrik Møller in an excellent article appearing in *Scandinavian Studies*, for example, identifies Høeg's work as a "pastiche," or a collection of "leftovers." In this, he argues, Høeg's work is bound both to "the literary past" as well to "postmodern écriture." Likewise, Jim McCue, reviewing the book for the *Times Literary Supplement*, applauds Høeg for the books indeterminacy: "Melodrama and slapstick, epic journey and social indictment: the book proudly declines to limit itself."

It is likely that *Smilla's Sense of Snow* will continue to generate critical interest. As a generic hybrid and as an example of postmodernity, the novel elicits a different response with each reading. The wide critical understanding of the book speaks both to its importance as well as its multidimensionality.

Criticism

Diane Henningfeld

Henningfeld is a professor of English literature and composition who has written widely for educational and academic publishers. In this essay, Henningfeld considers Smilla's Sense of Snow *as a postmodern epic.*

In an article for *Scandinavian Studies*, Hans Henrik Møller considers Peter Høeg's work, arguing that it is a "pastiche." According to the writer, pastiche comes from the Italian word for leftovers recombined into a pie. He argues that "pastiche is a radical illustration of the precept that there is nothing new under the sun." Certainly,

Smilla's Sense of Snow fits this description: part suspense thriller, part philosophical treatise, part science fiction story, part psychological study, part postcolonial political novel, the novel does not slip easily into classification. Møller further argues, "Pastiche binds Peter Høeg's writing to the literary past: his books and stories are replete with traces of Karen Blixen, Joseph Conrad and other great and well known authors. It links his growing oeuvre to postmodern écriture. . . . Pastiche is, moreover an exploration of time and the act of storytelling, of re-finding and renewal." Again, *Smilla's Sense of Snow* provides a perfect illustration for these notions. This essay, then, will demonstrate the way that Høeg connects to his literary past through his use of the epic heroic journey and how he manipulates and subverts the journey of the hero in his creation of a postmodern pastiche.

Certainly, one of the most foundational and familiar of all storytelling in Western culture is the epic quest. *The Odyssey* and *The Iliad* provide classic examples of the genre, and *Gawain and the Green Knight* is a well-known early English example. Indeed, the genre is so fundamental to the Western understanding of literature that many writers, including Carl Jung, Joseph Campbell, and Northrup Frye, have identified archetypal characters and structural patterns that function across cultures. To review briefly, the hero is both brave and wise and often the child of an unusual birth. This hero may not recognize himself as a hero (the classic hero is always male) but, through his reluctant acceptance of a challenge, he undertakes a quest that proves his mettle. On this quest, he encounters helpers, tricksters, and figures of evil. Often, his quest requires travel under difficult circumstances. Many attempts are made on his life. Often, the hero is in quest of some valuable and/or mysterious object or is in search of his father. There is always some sort of psychological and physical movement, and the hero often experiences a symbolic death/ rebirth experience.

Even on first reflection, there are clearly a number of ways that *Smilla's Sense of Snow* draws on and uses the epic tradition. Smilla, the protagonist, is both brave and wise. Høeg provides ample evidence that she is a brilliant woman, allowing her to share in her own voice what she knows about life, about mathematics, and about ice. She is an expert in her field, and it is her knowledge of both navigation and ice that allows her to survive in an alien landscape. Certainly, she demonstrates her bravery many times throughout the novel. For example, although Smilla tells the reader directly that she is afraid of open ocean, she nevertheless boards the *Kronos*, a vessel filled with dangerous characters, in order to dig into the truth about Isaiah's death. Furthermore, as the daughter of an Inuit and a European, Smilla's birth in Greenland and her subsequent removal to Denmark qualifies as an unusual background.

There are still other similarities. When Isaiah dies at the opening of the book, Smilla understands that she has an unspoken promise to fulfill: "All along I must have had a comprehensive pact with Isaiah not to leave him in the lurch, never, not even now." It is this pact that begins Smilla's quest through the labyrinth of the Cryolite Corporation of Denmark and finally leads her out to the open ocean and back to her homeland of Greenland. Like a quest hero, Smilla has helpers on her journey. Peter Føjl, the mechanic, provides her with care, information, and love. Jean Pierre Lagermann gives her information about Isaiah's autopsy and about the parasite. Lukas, the captain of the *Kronos*, also reluctantly helps her by allowing her to come on board the ship in the guise of a stewardess.

Smilla nearly dies when she goes to the Arctic Museum and a bomb explodes. She escapes by swimming underwater, a symbolic rebirth. When she emerges from the water, her resolve is firm: she will find the answers she seeks.

Tricksters also abound in the book. Moritz's wife, Benja, fills the role by calling the police on Smilla when she is at their house, causing Smilla to flee. Jakkelsen on the *Kronos* is also a trickster, someone who is not what he seems. After their initial encounter, however, Smilla and he reach an uneasy truce and a strange alliance.

For Smilla, the purpose of the quest is to understand why Isaiah was killed. This information is bound up in the quest for the strange meteorite that gives off heat in the Arctic north. Isaiah's death is inextricably connected to the meteorite that seems to be alive and to the parasite that kills its host. Indeed, the quest for information and the quest for the meteorite merge in the final pages of the book.

Finally, Smilla fights against forces of evil. Tørk, the grand villain, is bent on recovering the meteorite for fame and fortune, regardless of the havoc the accompanying parasite wreaks on the rest of the world. In the final climactic scene, Smilla confronts Tørk, as any good epic hero would do.

However, while it is possible to find the archetypal epic structures in the novel, closer inspection reveals that Høeg has played with these

> ... while it is possible to find the archetypal epic structures in the novel, closer inspection reveals that Høeg has played with these archetypes, just as he has played with generic conventions, to such an extent that he undermines the entire epic project, the triumph of the hero over evil."

archetypes, just as he has played with generic conventions, to such an extent that he undermines the entire epic project, the triumph of the hero over evil.

In the first place, Høeg plays with conventions of gender. As noted earlier, the classic epic hero is always male, and often a male in search of his father. Although Smilla is a woman, she does not even fit easily into that role. Her area of expertise is a male-dominated field. She is aggressive and bold in sex and causes trouble everywhere she goes. Throughout the book, it seems clear that Smilla is in search not of her father but of her mother. Again, Høeg plays with notions of gender by creating Smilla's mother as an androgynous Inuit hunter, a woman who nurses her child at her breast while demonstrating that her arms are as thick as a man's. It is her mother's knowledge and strength that Smilla emulates.

Høeg also creates a false helper for Smilla. Readers of epic literature expect a helper who will fight to the death for the hero. Føjl, Smilla's helper and lover, is not the helper of epic lore, but rather is a betrayer. He has collaborated with the forces of evil in order to help Tørk in his quest. Even here, however, the distinction is not clear. Føjl does not rest easily in the villain's camp; he was devoted to Isaiah and to Smilla, in spite of his duplicitousness. Moreover, Smilla does not seem to be able to reject the mechanic out of hand, even when she sees his betrayal.

Tørk, as the villain, also seems to blur in and out of focus. Smilla finds him breathtakingly handsome and finds herself attracted to him in spite of his murderous intentions. Høeg goes so far as to almost create Smilla's doppelganger, or double, in Tørk: a lonely, precocious child, looking for love, fame, and attention, just like Smilla, who runs away more times than she can count before she is twelve years old. In the final scene, the pair are both running across the ice, each on his or her path to salvation or destruction.

There are other, less obvious details as well. A common motif in the epic quest is the arming of the hero. *Gawain and the Green Knight* provides a well-known example as Gawain puts on his armor as he is about to leave on his search for the Green Knight. In *Smilla's Sense of Snow*, however, Høeg provides an ironic reversal. In Denmark, Smilla is always dressed extravagantly; indeed, her expensive, high-class clothing often allows her to do battle with the Danish establishment. On board the ship, however, as she prepares for what will be her final battle with Tørk, rather than going through an elaborate arming ritual, she takes off her clothing and examines her wounds:

> Anyone interested in death would benefit from looking at me. I've taken off my bandages. There's no skin on my kneecaps. Between my hips there is a wide yellowish-blue patch of blood that has coagulated under the skin where Jakkelsen's marlinspike struck me. The palms of both hands have suppurating lesions that refuse to close. At the base of my skull I have a bruise like a gull's egg. . . . I've been modest enough to keep on my white socks so you can't see my swollen ankle.

It is the ending of the novel, however, that most undermines epic conventions. Most quest stories are of the out and back type. That is, the hero leaves on his quest, defeats evil, retrieves the item of value, and returns to tell his tale, a wiser and stronger man. Høeg both manipulates and subverts this form. The book closes with Smilla tracking Tørk across the snow, herding him onto thinner and thinner ice. Although Smilla knows some of the details of Isaiah's death, she still does not know the truth of it nor the truth of the mysterious meteorite, which will remain where it is, nor the truth of her lover, the mechanic. "Behind us the stone is still there, with its mystery and the questions it has raised. And the mechanic." She considers the story she will tell on her return. Unlike the triumphant tale of the returning hero, however, her tale is one that signifies nothing:

> Tell us, they'll say to me. So we will understand and be able to resolve things. They'll be mistaken. It's only the things you don't understand that you can resolve. There will be no resolution.

By choosing to end his book but not resolve it, Høeg demonstrates the postmodern condition, a condition that allows only pastiche, not epic, only ambiguity, not certainty. Although Smilla can read the ice, she cannot read the truth. As such, she is the postmodern hero, still struggling to find meaning in a darkening world of ice and snow.

Source: Diane Henningfeld, Critical Essay on *Smilla's Sense of Snow*, in *Novels for Students*, The Gale Group, 2003.

Mary Kay Norseng

In the following essay, Norseng explores Høeg's authorial motive in the denouement of Smilla's Sense of Snow.

As *Frøken Smillas fornemmelse for sne* (*Smilla's Sense of Snow*) begins to end, if never to resolve itself, Smilla Qaaviggaaq Jaspersen sets sail for an arctic sea far, far away. In that sea lies as island; on that island there is a glacial cathedral; in that cathedral there is a lake; in that lake there is a black stone; in that stone there is a worm. "Mennesker venter på denne sten. Deres tro og forventning vil gøre den virkelig. Vil gøre den levende, uanset hvordan det ellers forholder sig med den" ("People are waiting for this stone. Their belief and anticipation will make it real. They will make it alive regardless of the true nature of the stone." Tørk, the fictional, murderous plot maker is speaking to Smilla, near the finale, about the public he fully intends to exploit. Is the voice of his creator, Peter Høeg, an equally murderous plot maker, to be heard under Tørk's, albeit with a potentially different public in mind? Inevitably, it would seem, in a novel as self-consciously wrought as this one. Tørk speaks with utter cynicism about our need to believe in the sensational power of the stone. Does Høeg, a most sophisticated, cosmopolitan writer, speak with equal conviction about the need of his late twentieth-century reading public still to believe in the sensational power of the fiction? Does he taunt us, even as he entertains us, with the emptiness of the post-modern novel? Or does he strive to fill it up again? And if so, at what price? Does it become, like Tørk's stone, the commodity in which, in Walter Benjamin's words, "hell rages"? And again, if so, what is that "hell"?

A stone in a lake in an ice cave on an island in an arctic sea far, far away mimics an ancient riddle in Scandinavian folklore.

> "Langt, langt borte i et vann ligger en øy," sa han;
> "på den øya står en kirke; i den kirken er en brønn,

i den brønnen svømmer en and; i den anda er et egg
og i det egget—der er hjertet mitt, du."

("Far, far away in a lake lies an island," he said; "on
that island there's a church; in that church there's a
well, in that well swims a duck; in that duck there's
an egg, and in that egg—that's where my heart is").

This is the riddle at the heart of the Norwegian
folk tale, "Risen som ikke hadde noe hjertet på seg"
(The Giant Who Had No Heart in Him). Askeladd
must find the Giant's heart in order to bring his
brothers and their brides, turned into stone by the
Giant, back to life. What takes Smilla five hundred
pages takes Askeladd two paragraphs in the Asb-
jørnsen and Moe tale. Finally holding the egg en-
veloping the Giant's heart in his hand, Askeladd
squeezes. The Giant cries out in pain. "Klem én
gang til" (Squeeze again), says Askeladd's helpful
sidekick, the Wolf. The Giant begs for his life,
agreeing to do whatever Askeladd wants. "Si at der-
som han skaper om igjen de seks brødrene dine som
han har gjort til stein, og brudene deres, skal han
berge livet" (Say that if he brings back your six
brothers that he has turned into stone, and their
wives, he'll save his life), says the Wolf. The Giant immediately turns stone back into flesh. "Klem
nå sund egget" (Now crush the egg), says the Wolf.
Without hesitation, Askeladd breaks the egg, and
the Giant's heart bursts.

Is there a heart in this novel, and if there is,
does Høeg break it? Without much ado, we can certainly say that he breaks the heart of any notion of
"traditional" closure, quite literally and quite figuratively putting the worm in the stone of the ending, in keeping with post modernism's aesthetic of
failure and fragmentation. And, indeed, the critic
in us may thrill to Smilla's theoretical correctness.
But the reader in us experiences, along with many
others, a dismay as the novel disintegrates, as the
philosophical, European detective fiction spins
seemingly out of control into a Hollywood action-
adventure script. Or as one reviewer wrote:.

Something peculiar happens to *Smilla's Sense of
Snow* as it sails toward its denouement . . . (It) takes
on the trappings of movies like *The Blob* (whose extraterrestrial predator, one recalls, was shipped to the
Arctic), *The Thing* (whose monster preyed on the inhabitants of an Arctic station) and *Them* (which
evoked a world threatened by genetic mutation).

The amorphic movie titles do, indeed, capture
exponentially the "appearance," if not the "essence"
of the second and third parts of *Smilla*, "Havet"
("The Sea") and "Isen" ("The Ice"). Typically, Høeg
gives us warning of the direction his narrative will
take once he and Smilla have left the landscape of

> **Is there a heart in this
> novel, and if there is, does Høeg
> break it? Without much ado, we
> can certainly say that he breaks
> the heart of any notion of
> 'traditional' closure . . . in
> keeping with post modernism's
> aesthetic of failure and
> fragmentation."**

"Byen" or "The City." Only a few hours after Smilla
has gone on board the ship, less than a minute in
fictional time, s/he muses:

Jeg har altid vaeret bange for havet . . . På det åbne
hav findes der ingen landkending, der findes kun en
amorf, kaotisk forskydning af retningsløse vand-
masser, der tårner sig op og bryder og ruller, og hvis
overflade igen brydes af subsystemer der interferer
og danner hvirvler og forsvinder og opstår og tilsidst
forgår sporløst . . . Jeg frygter (havet) fordi det vil
fratage mig orienteringen, mit livs indre gyroskop,
min vished om, hvad der er op og ned, min
forbindelse med absolute space . . . Fra jeg for nogle
timer siden er gået om bord, er nedbrydningen
sat ind.

I've always been afraid of the sea . . . On the open
sea there are no landmarks, there is only an amorphous, chaotic shifting of directionless masses of water that loom up and break and roll, and their surface
is, in turn, broken by subsystems that interfere and
form whirlpools and appear and disappear and finally
vanish without a trace . . . I'm afraid of (the sea) because it will rob me of my orientation, the inner gy-
roscope of my life, my awareness of what is up and
down, my connection to Absolute Space . . . The
process of disintegration started the moment I came
on board several hours ago.

Smilla's loss of connection is reflected everywhere in the fiction henceforward. Characters and
events become increasingly anarchic, narrative
rhythm grows fitful, suspense ebbs and flows, and
the images of the fictional landscape lose both color
and contour, until in the final scene a white fog of
frost is descending, the heroine is losing sight of
the villain, the villain is losing his bearings, the ice
is thinning, the temperature is dropping, and an
obliterating snow storm is coming, returning all, we

might say, to the blank page. As if we have entered into some other, inchoate dimension, philosophically as well as imagistically, we are left to ponder, after all this time, whether Smilla's words are pretentious or profound, empty or full of meaning.

Man kan ikke vinde over isen.

Bag os er stadig stenen, dens gåde, de spørgsmål den bar rejst. Og mekanikeren.

Et sted foran mig bliver den løbende skikkelse langsomt mørkere.

Fortael os, vil de komme og sige til mig. Så vi forstår og kan afslutte. De tager fejl. Det er kun det man ikke forstår, man kan afslutte. Det kommer ikke til nogen afgørelse.

You can't win against the ice.

Behind us the stone is still there, with its mystery and the questions it has raised. And the mechanic.

Somewhere ahead of me the running figure slowly grows darker.

Tell us, they'll say to me. So we will understand and be able to resolve things. They'll be mistaken. It's only the things you don't understand that you can resolve. There will be no resolution.

Does Høeg in the end, like some post-modern Askeladd, break our collective, bourgeois heart? Or has he hidden a heart elsewhere, as the Giant did twice before he was outwitted by the intrepid hero? It would certainly be in keeping with Høeg's fascination with the paradoxical that he play both roles. The folk tale that informs the final phase of the novel is, at least from one point of view, a tale of rebirth. Askeladd tricks the Giant into bringing his family of brothers back to life. Upon my first reading of Smilla the existential thriller, even the extraordinary heroine, even at times the devastating social critique, seemed like masks, Trojan horses, Askeladdian tricks that allowed Høeg to write what he indicated he was writing from the very beginning, a narrative of mourning, a tale of death, loss, and depression, and equally of those flashes of clarity, of white-hot purpose, of the keen sense of being on some right track, as one attempts to trick the Giant, to restore what has been lost, the one who has been lost, if only in another form.

Høeg concludes Smilla with his own riddle. "Det er kun det man ikke forstår, man kan afslutte. Det kommer ikke til nogen afgørelse" ("It is only the things you don't understand that you can resolve. There will be no resolution"). In other words, contrary to what we think we have just read, we have understood it all. I would suggest that the novel is, at heart, about the most common, and the most devastating, of human experiences, those sor-

rows of loss that potentially wean us too soon from this earth. At the risk of being Tørk's fool—and there could be worse fates—the one who would find meaning where there is none, I offer a reading of this novel as a tale of mourning and renewal.

The Corpse

One could say that *Frøken Smillas fornemmelse for sne* is held in the embrace of a child. In the first narrative moments, barely acquainted with our guide, Smilla, we watch her catch sight of a small, dark shadow in the snow early on a December evening in Copenhagen. She runs toward it. The shadow is the corpse of the boy, Isaiah.

Esajas ligger med benene trukket op under sig, og med ansigtet ned i sneen og haenderne omkring hovedet, som skaermer han for den lille projektør der lyser på ham, som er sneen en rude gennem hvilken han har fået øje på noget dybt nede under jorden.

Isaiah is lying with his legs tucked up under him, with his face in the snow and his hands around his head, as if he were shielding himself from the little spotlight shining on him, as if the snow were a window through which he has caught sight of something deep inside the earth.

Nearly five hundred pages later, now all but a double of Smilla, we watch with her as Tørk, the murderer of Isaiah, runs out onto the thinner and thinner ice of the Greenlandic seas. She chases him, running parallel to him.

Han har mistet orienteringen. Han føres ud mod det åbne vand. Mod dér, hvor strømmen har udhulet isen, så den bliver tynd som en hinde, en fosterhinde, og under den er havet mørkt og salt som blod, og et ansigt presser sig nedefra op mod ishinden, det er Esajas' ansigt, den endnu Ufødte Esajas.

He's lost his bearings. He's being led out toward open water. Toward the spot where the current has hollowed out the ice so it's as thin as a membrane, a fetal membrane. Underneath, the sea is dark and salty like blood, and a face is pressing up against the icy membrane from below; it's Isaiah's face, the as-yet-unborn Isaiah.

As if the text were the earth, Isaiah peers back at himself lying lifeless in the snow. How are we to read this fetal embrace? Is it a hole or a whole in a text that ends with the proclamation, "There will be no resolution"? Perhaps it is both, the ever-repeated cycle of meaninglessness and meaning, the failed and the possible, loss and recovery, Isaiah's soothing vision, the vision of newborns and of the extremely old, the gaze of our common humanity, connecting the beginning to the end like a beam of light, providing, one might say, the Absolute Space of the story, the thing for which we long, to which we cling, even as we search for it.

In a review of *Smilla* for *The New Statesman* John Williams began by saying that "It's the corpse that defines a thriller." Isaiah as corpse is particularly poignant. The dead boy bears the name of the greatest of the prophets, who foretold of the coming of the Messiah. His was a prophecy of a paradoxical redemption, made manifest in both a suffering and a reigning Messiah. Does such a namesake have any meaning in a text as profane as this one? Smilla possibly casts doubt. Upon first meeting Elsa Lübing, the novel's elegant, old-fashioned, religious recluse, Smilla remarks, "Jeg har mistet fornemmelsen for, hvordan man tackler troende europaeere" ("I have lost the sense of how to tackle a believing European"). But Miss Lübing, a former "bookkeeping" genius from another era, a woman of conscience, even if she has withdrawn to her windowed penthouse of white and cream, lends credence to the Bible as text. It is the wisdom by which she lives, providing her not only with the language through which she speaks in her daily life, but the secret code through which she and Smilla communicate. Miss Lübing, with her Bible, gives Smilla one of the first keys to unlocking the mystery of Isaiah's death. Her ancient text may also provide a key to the meaning of Høeg's text as well.

Høeg's Isaiah might be said to be both prophet and prophecy. He is a Christ child of sorts, at the center of an albeit highly corrupted nativity myth. Smilla, the quintessential, 1990s vierge moderne,2 in spirit if not in body, thinks of Isaiah as her child. The mechanic, Peter Føjl, plays the carpenter to her Virgin Mary. They are this novel's unholy family. Isaiah dies in December and is fictionally about to be reborn about three months later, roughly corresponding to the Christian feast of the Resurrection. Oddly for a story set in Copenhagen, the boy is often placed by Smilla in an environment of shimmering heat, as if he were in a desert, and he is usually described as being naked, save for the underpants he wears like a loin cloth. His body is pierced by a modern sword, a biopsy needle. And, like Christ, Isaiah turns the other cheek. When lashed out at, abused, hurt, he digs into what Smilla calls "sin naturs ubegraensede reserver" ("the unlimited reserves of his character"). "Tålmodig, tavs, agtpågivende vred han sig bort under de udstrakte haender, og gik sin vej. For, om muligt, at finde en anden løsning" ("Patient, silent, and watchful he would wrench himself away from the outstretched hands and go on his way. In order to find, if possible, some other solution").

Smilla herself sees Isaiah as a potential savior of her cultures, as a Greenlander who could in essence incorporate Denmark, change it to his own, take it backward or forward to something more integrated and whole. Using imagery as eclectic as her boy-hero, she describes his response to her gift of a luxurious, white jacket. The resulting composite is of a hybrid phoenix.

> Esajas var ved at lykkes. Han ville kunne vaere nået frem. Han ville kunne have optaget Danmark i sig, og transformeret det, og vaereblevet både-og.
>
> Jeg fik syet en anorak til ham af hvid silke. Selve mønsteret havde passeret europaeerne. Min far havde engang fået det foraerende af maleren Gitz-Johansen. Han havde fået det i Nordgrønland, da han illustrerede det store standardvaerk om Grønlands fugle. Jeg gav Esajas den på, jeg friserede ham, og så løftede jeg ham op på toiletsaedet. Da han så sig selv i spejlet, skete det. Det tropiske tekstil, den grønlandske andagt ved festdragten, den danske glaede ved luksus, alt. smeltede sammen. Måske betød det også noget, at jeg havde givet ham den.

> Isaiah was on the verge of success. He could have gotten ahead. He would have been able to absorb Denmark and transform it and become both a Dane and a Greenlander.
>
> I had an anorak made for him out of white silk. Even the pattern had been passed down by Europeans. The painter Gitz-Johansen once gave it to my father. He had gotten it in North Greenland, when he was illustrating his great reference work on the birds of Greenland. I put the anorak on Isaiah, combed his hair, and then I lifted him up onto the toilet seat. When he saw himself in the mirror, that's when it happened. The tropical fabric, the Greenlandic respect for fine clothes, the Danish joy in luxury all merged together. Maybe it also meant something that I had given it to him.

The notion of Isaiah being on the verge of success seems blasphemous in a narrative in which he is the ultimate victim of late twentieth century, western culture, a culture of greed, power, and disregard for life. The child of the System's pawns, he is witness to his father's death by explosives and his mother's by alcohol. His body is infected with parasites and his hearing damaged by modern drugs. But as the Biblical Isaiah's Messiah was both sufferer and redeemer, so too is Smilla's young Isaiah both victim and savior, both hollowed out and whole.

One might, in fact, say that Isaiah is the emblematic child sufferer in a sea of suffering. In reviewing Høeg's recently published *The History of Danish Dreams* (1995) for *Nation* John Leonard writes:

How H(ø)eg hates this middle class, whose own children are a Third World, to be colonized, "civilized" and serfed. In his suspicion of science, technology and the very idea of progress, he belongs to a long tradition of those antirationalists who've gone swimming Against the Current ... But H(ø)eg's distinctive contribution to this literature of disenchantment, of subversive subjectivity, is his brilliant focus on the lost child—coveted, abused, eroticized, missing, homeless, inner, emblematic, mode of production, consumer and commodity, Little Mermaid and Ugly Duckling—the orphan in the burning world. No wonder he needed Smilla ... Smilla on her sleigh, who has fled us through dreaming ice to a Winter Palace.

Smilla may have fled. Nevertheless, these lost children lie like an endless chain of corpses on the landscape of *Frøken Smillas fornemmelse for sne*. Like Isaiah they fall from the structures, through the fissures, not only through the corrupted world reflected through the narrative but through the narrative itself, through those expert discourses—economic, scientific, medical, philosophical, aesthetic—that are the building blocks of the fiction.

The novel is really a novel of nothing but children, their adult masks bleeding off like actor's paint, crooks, criminals, and good citizens alike, bleeding into children before Smilla's and our very eyes. Of the dead, to name just a few: Closest to Smilla is her younger brother, who committed suicide when he was forced to transform himself from hunter to dock sweeper, this younger brother, mentioned in an aside here and an aside there, more important in the narrative than he seems, connected somehow to Isaiah through the memory of the shimmering heat of a hot, arctic summer. And there is the investigative detective Ravn's daughter, pushed from another roof, also by Tørk, symbolic of all the children of any class who are forced by violence from the structures of power. Smilla's last communication to the "outside" world is to Ravn about his daughter, and the revenge she takes in the end is certainly in her name as well as Isaiah's. Of the living-dead: There is Benja, the lithe, emotionally stunted, thumbsucking darling of the Royal Ballet and Smilla's abusive doctor/father. There is Landers, the perpetually drunk casino owner whom Smilla calls "En affaldsbarn, en der altid har haft svaert ved at begå sig, og egentlig heller ikke har haft lyst til at laere det" ("A throwaway child, someone who has always had a hard time dealing with the world and hasn't actually wanted to learn how"). No one is exempt, not even the artists, perhaps most particularly not the artists. The murderer, Tørk Hviid, is himself a crucified child, the son of a "great" composer. As a mutual acquaintance condemningly writes to Smilla's father:

> Drengen gik for lud og koldt vand. Huller i tøjet, rødøjet, fik aldrig en cykel, blev pryglet i den lokale proletarskole fordi han var for svag af sult til at forsvare sig. Fordi hans far skulle vaere stor kunstner. I har alle svigtet jeres børn. Og der skal en gammel svans som mig til at fortaelle jer det.

> The boy was totally neglected. Holes in his clothes, red-eyed, never had a bicycle, was beaten at the local proletarian school because he was too weak from hunger to defend himself. Because (his father) was supposed to be a great artist. You've all betrayed your children. And it takes an old queen like me to tell you.

There is also Jakkelsen, the Kronos Captain's drug-addicted younger brother, whom Smilla calls the "sick child." He literally becomes the corpse in the cargo of the ship that takes Smilla to that (w)hole in the ice where she potentially wrecks her revenge on Tørk. Backing Smilla up like some farcical, glacial warrior, Jakkelsen's protective, yet impotent brother, the Captain, steps up behind her, harpoon gun in hand, pointed at Tørk. "Du skal blive gjort ansvarlig" ("You must be held responsible"), he says, just before his arm is shot off. And, of course, there is Smilla, the protagonist, the Greenlandic/Danish hybrid child, whose desires to sink back into her own childhood from the ice-encrusted present continually wash over her like waters, sometimes troubled, sometimes calm, from a sea of memories, even as she pursues the murderer of her beloved child, Isaiah.

Wounded children killing wounded children, wounded children avenging wounded children is the underlying modus operandi of *Frøken Smillas fornemmelse for sne*. In a novel more nakedly about the abused child in contemporary society, *De måske egnede* (1993), the novel that followed *Smilla*, Høeg quotes the god of modern physics who publicly mourned the death of his own childhood, at the same time as he consigned his infant daughter to a similar fate.

> Da Einstein er blevet verdensberømt, og journalister spørger til hans opvaekst, refererer han flere gange selv til den som "liget af min barndom," "The corpse of my childhood".

> Han siger at han sigter til den hårde, indskraenkende borgerlighed der omgav ham.

> Det fremgår tydeligt af hans breve til Mileva Maric, at hans videnskabelige teorier udvikles i protest mod denne borgerlighed ... Den indskraenkning han protesterede mod i sit arbejde, bornertheden, er samtidig den der får ham og Mileva Maric til at sende deres otte måneder gamle datter bort.

"The corpse of my childhood."

When Einstein has become world famous, and journalists ask about his youth, he himself refers to it several times as "the corpse of my childhood."

He says he is referring to the strict, inhibiting bourgeois mentality that surrounded him.

It is clear from his letters to Mileva Maric that his scientific theories are developed in protest against this bourgeois mentality ... At the same time, the inhibition he protested against in his work, the narrowmindedness, is what causes him and Mileva Maric to give away their eight-month-old daughter.

"The corpse of my childhood."

How do we reverse the unending spiral of child corpses? At the heart of much of what Høeg writes is the question, "Can we do it differently?" Those who try, like the boy-murderer, August, in De måske egnede, who ends his own life rather than perpetuate the murderous cycle in which he is caught, are Høeg's twentieth-century, martyred heroes, his messiahs. In the end, as Smilla confronts Tørk on the ice, she recasts herself in the image of Isaiah.

> Det er is der er under mig, jeg er på vej hen over isen, imod ham, som Esajas var på vej vaek fra ham. Det er som om jeg er Esajas. Men nu på vej tilbage. For at gøre noget om. For at prøve, om der skulle findes en anden mulighed.

> There is ice under my feet. I'm on my way across the ice toward him, just as Isaiah was heading away from him. It's as if I am Isaiah. But on his way back now. To do something differently. To see whether there might be an alternative.

The recast Isaiah, the Smilla/Isaiah, would save the child. But which child?

The Character

Preliminarily it must be said that it is the dead child who saves the living, for to bring Isaiah back seems to mean bringing Smilla back, Smilla whose dark love affair with melancholy is far more seductive than her love affair with the mechanic. Death often startles us into living. Isaiah's death sharpens Smilla's senses, like a cup of the mechanic's scalding, tropical tea. She says herself that she has been set free.

> Esajas' død er en uregelmaessighed, en spraengning der har fremkaldt en spalte. Den spalte har sluppet mig fri. For en kort tid, uden at jeg kan forklare hvordan, er jeg kommet i bevaegelse, er jeg blevet et skøjtende fremmedlegeme oven på isen.

> Isaiah's death is an irregularity, an eruption that produced a fissure. That fissure has set me free. For a brief time, and I can't explain how, I have been set

in motion, I have become a foreign body skating on top of the ice.

The death of one child becomes the lifeline of the other.

One can speak of Smilla in this way only, of course, if one can assume that a traditional notion of character has gone into the making of Smilla. Instinctively as readers we seem to believe in her as "real." Brad Leithauser wrote in his review in *The New Republic:*

> At the outset of her tale I was aware that Smilla—as a European, an Eskimo and a woman—stood at three removes from a reader such as myself. All the more striking, then, was the speed with which the sense of distance from her vanished—the speed of arriving on intimate terms with her. And she accomplishes this without being at all forthcoming. She is a taciturn soul. We read nearly 100 pages before we discover that her passion for snow and ice derives not merely from experience but from scholarship. She is a glaciologist, with articles to her credit like "Statistics on Glacial Graphology" and "Mathematical Models for Brine Drainage from Seawater Ice." We believe in this heroine partly because her reticence in no way feels coy. It seems, rather, like the wariness of somebody who, having grown up surrounded by dangers, instinctively seeks to keep predators at bay.

Leithauser's observation touches only the tip of the iceberg. Reticence is Smilla's emotional veneer. Underneath she is a chronically lonely soul, subject to bouts of depression which she records, as only the true melancholic can, with irresistible allure, provoking our desire to follow her into her dark spaces. Depression, I would suggest, is the crack in the personality of this uncommon heroine that allows us, most likely so different from her in most ways, to identify so intuitively with her. Melancholy is, in a sense, our common bond.

For Smilla it seems tantamount to a lost love. Rather than fend it off, she courts it and embraces it with a determined abandon. Momentarily defeated in her search for Isaiah's murderer, she gives herself up to depression with these fighting words:.

> Man kan forsøge at daekke over en depression på forskellige måder. Man kan høre Bachs orgelvaerker i Frelserkirken. Man kan laegge en bane højt humør i pulverform ud på et lommespejl med et barberblad, og tage den ind med et sugerør. Man kan råbe om hjaelp. For eksempel i telefonen, så man har sikret sig, hvem der hører det.

> Det er den europaeiske vej. At håbe på, at man kan handle sig ud af problemerne.

> Jeg tager den grønlandske vej. Den består i at gå ind i det sorte humør. At laegge sit nederlag under mikroskopet og dvaele ved synet.

Julia Ormond as Smilla Jasperson in the film production of Smilla's Sense of Snow

Når det er rigtig galt—som nu—så ser jeg en sort tunnel foran mig. Den går jeg hen til. Jeg laegger mit paene tøj fra mig, mit undertøj, min sikkerhedshjelm og mit danske pas, og så går jeg ind i mørket.

Jeg véd der kommer et tog. Et blyforet damplokomotiv, der transporterer Strontium 90. Jeg går det i møde.

Det kan jeg gøre, fordi jeg er 37 år gammel. Jeg véd, at inde i tunnelen, inde under hjulene, nede mellem svellerne er der et lille punkt af lys.

You can try to cover up depression in various ways. You can listen to Bach's compositions for the organ in Our Saviour's Church. You can arrange a line of good cheer in powder form on a pocket mirror with a razor blade and ingest it with a straw. You can call for help. For instance, by telephone, so that you know who's listening.

That's the European method. Hoping to work your way out of problems through action.

I take the Greenlandic way. It consists of submerging yourself in the dark mood. Putting your defeat under a microscope and dwelling on the sight.

When things are really bad—like now—I picture a black tunnel in front of me. I go up to it. I strip off my nice clothes, my underwear, my hard hat, my Danish passport, and then I walk into the dark.

I know that a train is coming. A lead-lined steam locomotive transporting strontium 90. I go to meet it.

It's possible for me to do this because I'm thirty-seven years old. I know that inside the tunnel, underneath the wheels, down between the ties, there is a little spot of light.

Høeg has taken great pains to give his Smilla a psychologically provocative past, both in the broad sweeps of ancestry and family history and the smaller, more secretive movements of the "soul." During this particular dark mood, literally locked up in her Copenhagen apartment, she consciously evokes a memory that makes her black tunnel even blacker. It is the memory of her second attempt, at the age of twelve, to return to Greenland from Denmark, where her father had forcibly brought her after her mother's death six years prior. She remembers a frantic, winter flight northward, trying to reach Frederikshavn, and from there Oslo, and then Nuuk. First she hitchhikes, then she steals a motorcycle, skids, crashes on lake ice, tears her jacket, breaks her wrist bones, and lands in the hospital, where her father comes to retrieve her. Walking to the car she breaks away, he chases after her and catches her, and she turns on him, her right hand in a cast, her left hand hiding a scalpel that she had stolen from the emergency room. She gashes the palm of his hand. They circle around each other, both ready to strike, when Moritz suddenly straightens up and says, "Du ligner din mor . . . " ("You're just like your mother . . . "). And he starts to cry.

This scene, which begins Part Two of "The City," is key to the novel, an allegory of the greater narrative in which present and past play to and against each other in a drama that stays the same the more it changes. The paradigm of the wandering, violent journey northward, leaving Smilla bloodied but unbowed, is unmistakable. Embedded in it are the complex of forces that compel her to flee, be it to the expanse of the Arctic or to a small, dark room in Copenhagen. Her depression of the present, brought on by her momentary failure to uncover Isaiah's murderer and hence to recover Isaiah, is deeply anchored in the past, in her attempts to return to Greenland, both in body and in spirit, to the home of her mother.

John Bowlby, in his introduction to *Loss: Sadness and Depression* (1980), the third and final volume of his classic study on mourning, *Attachment and Loss*, noted that "bereave" stems from the same root as "rob." Building on earlier studies by Darwin and Strand, he assumed that the attempt of the bereft one to recover what has been lost is instinctive. " . . . a mourner is repeatedly seized, whether he knows it or not, by an urge to call for, to search for and to recover the lost person and . . . not infrequently he acts in accordance with that urge." In Loss he developed his theories of successful versus thwarted mourning, concentrating, in particular, on children who have lost a parent, either through death or separation. The mourning of children would, he contended, reveal the paradigm for adult mourning, which, he further contended, was often founded in childhood. If a child is allowed to/is able to suffer through grief in all its stages, s/he will recover from the loss, will recover what Darwin called "elasticity of mind," but if grieving is thwarted, s/he will be doomed to a repetitive, if disguised search for the dead beloved. Bowlby established an intimate connection between a recent and an earlier loss.

A probable explanation of the tendency for a recent loss to activate or reactivate grieving for a loss sustained earlier is that, when a person loses the figure to whom he is currently attached, it is natural for him to turn for comfort to an earlier attachment figure. If, however, the latter, for example a parent, is dead the pain of the earlier loss will be felt afresh (or possibly for the first time). Mourning the earlier loss therefore follows.

I would suggest that Smilla's search for Isaiah can be interpreted as a repetition of a "life-long," if disguised search for her lost mother. Smilla herself is keenly aware of the need in others to try to hold on to the dead beloved, even if that other is the father she so scorns. In ruminating about her flight toward Greenland, away from Denmark, she recognizes, as both a past and present truth, her father's need to keep her close in order to keep her mother, if only in memory, alive.

Til Danmark havde han hentet mig, fordi jeg var det eneste der kunne minde ham om, hvad han havde mistet. Mennesker der er forelskede, de tilbeder et fotografi. De ligger på knae for et tørklaede. De foretager en rejse for at se på en husmur. Hvad som helst der kan puste til de gløder, der både varmer og forbraender dem.

Med Mortiz var det vaerre. Han var håbløst forelsket i en, hvis molekyler var suget ud i den store tomhed. Hans kaerlighed havde opgivet håbet. Men den havde klamret sig til erindringen. Jeg var den erindring.

He had brought me to Denmark because I was the only thing that could remind him of what he had lost. People in love worship a photograph. They fall on their knees before a scarf. They make a journey to look at the wall of a building. Whatever can ignite the coals that both warm and sear them.

With Moritz it was much worse. He was hopelessly in love with someone whose molecules had been sucked out into the vast emptiness. His love had given up hope. But it had latched on to memory. I was that memory.

The thing that Smilla understands so well about her father, in fact the thing that allows her to understand her father at all, is the thing that drives her with equal ferocity, the need to recover someone who also for Smilla, with even more insidious consequences, was "suget ud i den store tomhed" ("sucked out into the vast emptiness"). What Moritz tries to do through his daughter, Smilla tries to do through her chosen son, Isaiah. After her failed flight at the age of twelve, she never again tried to escape, that is, until Isaiah was murdered. Her return to Greenland may be far more compulsive than the detective novel alone would allow. Smilla as the avenger of the dead child on one level of the narrative, is herself the thwarted child mourner on another.

Smilla was seven years old when her mother disappeared in the Greenlandic seas. The only trace of her was her kayak, which, according to Smilla, led her Inuit kin to conclude that "det havde vaeret en hvalros" ("it must have been a walrus"). There were no further details. Now in her thirty-seventh year, Smilla seems to have made peace with her mother's unknown demise as yet another hard, but natural fact of a hard life. But as so often with Smilla, things are not what they seem. In the context of telling of her mother's disappearance, Smilla detachedly cites two fascinating facts from her seemingly endless list of fascinating facts. First, in Danish waters, compared to Greenlandic waters, due to the warmer temperature, the processes of decomposition cause fermentation of the stomach, giving "selvmordere fornyet opdrift" ("suicides renewed buoyancy"), and causing them to wash up on shore. Second, walruses are unpredictable. They can be transformed from the most sensitive of fish to the most ferocious killers.

> Med de to kindtaender kan de slå en skibsside af faergecement ind. Jeg har engang set fangerne holde en torsk hen til en hvalros de havde fanget levende. Den smalede laeberne til en lille kyssemund, og så sugede den fiskens kød direkte af knoglerne.

> With their two tusks they can stave in the side of a ship made of ferrocement. I once saw hunters holding a cod up to a walrus that they had captured alive. The walrus puckered up his lips as for a kiss and then sucked the meat right off the bones of the fish.

These bits of knowledge are potentially interesting in and of themselves, as are so many of Smilla's multifarious observations. But we should not be fooled. For surely they have a more provocative function in this story of Ane Qaavigaaq's demise. They devilize the unknown waters of her grave. They suggest that Smilla has entertained fantasies of a most violent death, or perhaps even worse for Smilla, a death by her mother's own hand, fantasies that Smilla can only allow herself to express through the detached formula of scientific facts. For the mourning child, Bowlby stressed, it is essential that the child be made aware of two things, "first that the dead parent will never return and secondly that his body is buried in the ground or burned to ashes." Smilla, denied certainty, even of this elementary kind, has lived for thirty years with disembodied ruminations of suicide, dead animals, and lethal walruses, a symptom of what Bowlby called "disordered mourning." Her image of the walrus's kiss of death reveals a truth she cannot see, a fear she cannot feel. It explains her rage with her beloved Isaiah, when she finds him running across the disintegrating ice in Copenhagen harbor. " . . . (jeg) slog . . . ham. Slaget var vel— som vold nu kan vaere det—et destillat af mine føleser for ham. Han holdt sig lige akkurat opre-

jst." (" . . . I hit him. The blow was probably a distillation of my feelings for him, the way violence sometimes is. He barely managed to stay on his feet"). A love more powerful even than her love for Isaiah was distilled in that single blow. For hove could Smilla tolerate even the thought of another loss to the sea?

Smilla does not disguise the centrality of her mother in her life. To the contrary, through memory and fantasy she has created an icon, an androgenous, Inuit god, earth mother and hunter, an almighty presence between whose legs she once lay, at whose breast she once nursed. The image is of a divinity in whose body the fluids of life, milk and blood, flow eternally.

> Hun kysser mig aldrig, og hun rører sjaeldent ved mig. Men i øjeblikke af stor fortrolighed lader hun mig drikke den maelk, der bliver ved med at vaere der, bag huden, som blodet altid er der. Hun spreder sine ben, så jeg kan gå ind imellem dem. Sore de andre fangere går hun i bukser af bjørneskind, som kun garves nødtørftigt. Hun elsker asker, spiser den undertiden direkte ud af bålet, og hun har smurt sig under øjnene meed den. I denne duft af braendt kul og bjørneskind går jeg ind til brystet, der er lysende hvidt, med en stor, sart rosa areola. Der drikker jeg så immuk, min mors maelk.

> She never kisses me, and she seldom touches me. But at moments of great intimacy, she lets me drink from the milk that is always there, beneath her skin, just as her blood is. She spreads her legs so I can come between them. Like the other hunters she wears pants made of bearskin, given only a rudimentary tanning. She loves ashes, sometimes eating them straight from the fire, and she has smeared some underneath her eyes. In this aroma of burned coal and bearskin, I go to her breast, which is brilliantly white, with a big, delicate rose aureole. There I drink immuk, my mother's milk.

But does the all-powerful maternal image conceal a treachery? Smilla's tale of intimate attachment to her mother is contained within a tale of destruction and death. As with the memory of her mother's disappearance, Smilla diverts attention from the actual love object in her mind's eye, not this time through smart, scientific facts, but through her mother's own anecdotal wisdom about the ebb and flow of life in the Arctic. Two years before Ane Qaavigaaq died, Smilla was hunting with her for narwhals and white-breasted auk. Among her mother's kill was a female narwhal and her angel-white pup, not yet born. Smilla herself caught three auk in a flock of black, white-breasted females on their way to their young with worms in a pouch in their beaks. She had them in her net, and she knew how to kill them by pressing on their hearts. She had done it before, but this time she balked.

Og så ser jeg nu alligevel pludselig deres øjne som tunneler, for enden af hvilke ungerne venter, og disse ungers øjne er igen tunneler, og for enden af dem er narhvalungen, hvis blik igen fører ind og bort. Lige så langsomt vender jeg ketcheren, og med en kort eksplosion af støj stiger fuglene til vejrs.

And yet I suddenly see their eyes as tunnels, at the end of which their young are waiting, and the babies' eyes are in turn tunnels, at the end of which is the narwhal pup, whose gaze in turn leads inward and away. Ever so slowly I turn over the net, and with a great explosion of sound, the birds rise into the air.

Seeing her daughter's distress, as if, Smilla recounts, she were seeing her for the first time, Ane, in essence, introduced Smilla to the notion of paradox. Sitting beside her, she said simply, " . . . jeg har båret dig i amaat . . . Alligevel . . . er jeg staerk som en mand" ("I have carried you in amaat . . . And yet, . . . I am as strong as a man"). And then she drew Smilla into her legs and to her breast, comforting her in her generous, fleshy, androgenous way. Later she spoke of the greater paradox of life and death, trying to explain, Smilla says, why one month 3,000 narwhals are gathered in the fjord and the next month they are dead, trapped in the ice. Smilla understood what her mother was trying to tell her, she recounts, "Men det aendrede intet" ("(T)hat didn't change a thing"). The year before her mother's death—Smilla would have been six—she began to feel nauseated when she went fishing.

Clearly, Smilla interprets the memory as her initiation into modern consciousness, the moment forever after which she would harbor "en fremmedhed over for naturen" ("a feeling of alienation toward nature") because it was no longer accessible to her "på den selvfølgelige måde den havde vaeret tidligere" ("in the natural way that it had been before"). "Måske er jeg allered dér begyndt at ønske at forstå isen. At ville forstå er at prøve at generobre noget vi har mistet" ("Perhaps I had even then begun to want to understand the ice. To want to understand is an attempt to recapture something we have lost"). But as Smilla has reconstructed the memory, its real heart is about maternal loss. As that small child Smilla saw herself in the baby birds, whose mothers would never return. She was the narwhal pup, robbed of its own mother, even as it too was robbed of its life. Smilla's image of the dark tunnel of depression, which she enters, stripped of illusion, as an adult, she already saw as

a little girl in the eyes of the baby birds, at the tunnel's end an abandoned child.

Bowlby believed that disordered mourning revealed itself primarily in two variants of behavior, in the one extreme, chronic mourning, and in the other, Smilla's way, a prolonged absence of conscious grieving. "Adults who show prolonged absence of conscious grieving are commonly self-sufficient people, proud of their independence and self-control, scornful of sentiment; tears they regard as a weakness." Smilla is nothing if not in control. Even when she is not, she is looking like she is. She is a character endowed with encyclopedic knowledge, which she imparts with authority and seductive charm. As readers we must become as adept as she is at reading between the lines, decoding the messages, ferreting out the truth in the fissures that suddenly crack open. She is also a character defined by radical self-sufficiency. The very trait that makes her a contemporary, fictional wonder, the perfect heroine for the action-adventure film, is for Smilla as a character in a narrative of mourning, the mask that reveals the true face. Most critically effected, Bowlby maintained, is the mourner's "capacity to make and maintain love relationships (which becomes) more or less seriously impaired or, if already impaired, (is) left more impaired than it was before." By this measure Smilla makes a profound leap toward love when at the end she emotionally embraces the mechanic as part of her future and at the same as part of her return. He is, significantly, waiting "behind" her.

Høeg, in creating Smilla's past, has destined her for grieving. For she has been drubbed by the shattering, sudden, unresolved disappearances of all of her most beloved, her mother by drowning, her brother by suicide, compounded by Isaiah by murder. But Isaiah has left tracks, and for Smilla this seems to make all the difference as the mourning process is compulsively set in motion.

The Search

It would seem that Høeg has been compelled to create not only a character but also a narrative that is, at the very least, illuminated by a theory of mourning, possibly even driven by it. The child Isaiah, Greenlandic, gynandrous, mysteriously gone, is the perfect spark to ignite Smilla's memories both of her mother and of herself as a child, her memories of attachment and, in the same breath, loss, and thus to initiate the search, never completed, to find the mother never truly mourned. At the same time, the very structure of the narrative loosely resembles the four phases of mourning isolated by Bowlby: "numbing," "yearning and searching," "disorganization and despair," and "a greater or lesser degree of reorganization." Smilla seems to be in a phase of numbness as the novel begins, manifest in her rabid self-reliance, her fear of attachment (with, of course, the exception of Isaiah, who may have fooled her because he was "only" a child), and her embrace of the scientific guise, at the same time as she fears it, like the walrus's puckered kiss. The second phase, "yearning and searching," could be the subtitle for "The City," as Smilla begins a series of multi-layered, interconnected, volatile investigations into the murder of the boy, the reluctant love affair with the mechanic, and the memories of the past.

Intermittent hope, repeated disappointment, weeping, anger, accusation, and ingratitude are all features of the second phase of mourning, and are to be understood as expressions of the strong urge to find and recover the lost person. Nevertheless, underlying these strong emotions, which erupt episodically and seem so perplexing, there is likely to coexist deep and pervasive sadness, a response to a recognition that reunion is at best improbable.

Once Smilla leaves land and sets out to sea, both she and the narrative begin to lose their bearings. Smilla's feeling for Absolute Space fails her. Isaiah seems almost forgotten. The mechanic disappears. The target of the investigation seems to shift from a murdered boy to a secret cargo. Bowlby's formulation of the third phase of mourning, "disorganization and despair," may shed critical light on this (often criticized) section of the novel, in which Smilla finds herself quite literally walking and crawling through every inch of the ship, including the dumb waiter, trying, at astounding physical risk, as it turns out, to open locked doors to discover what might be on the other side. "For mourning to have a favourable outcome," Bowlby observed:.

> It appears to be necessary for a bereaved person to endure (a) buffeting of emotion. Only if he can tolerate the pining, the more or less conscious searching, the seemingly endless examination of how and why the loss occurred, and anger at anyone who might have been responsible ... can he come gradually to recognize and accept that the loss is in truth permanent and that his life must be shaped anew.

He cited the English writer, C. S. Lewis, who wrote of his own, overwhelming grief in terms that, when applied to Høeg's narrative, capture the confusion of the section called "The Sea."

> C. S. Lewis (1961) has described the frustrations not only of feeling but of thought and action that griev-

ing entails. In a diary entry after the loss of his wife, H, he writes: "I think I am beginning to understand why grief feels like suspense. It comes from the frustration of so many impulses that had become habitual. Thought after thought, feeling after feeling, action after action, had H for their object. Now their target is gone. I keep on, through habit, fitting an arrow to the string; then I remember and I have to lay the bow down. So many roads lead through to H. I set out on one of them. But now there's an impassable frontier-post across it. So many roads once; now so many culs-de-sac"

Smilla wears her bruised emotions on her body like contemporary body art. As Brad Leithauser described her in her near final phase:

> ... near the close of the book, we glimpse her with her clothes off as she steps into a shower: "There's no skin on my kneecaps. Between my hips there is a wide yellowish-blue patch that has coagulated under the skin where Jakkelsen's marlin spike struck me. The palms of both my hands have suppurating lesions that refuse to close. At the base of my skull I have a bruise like a gull's egg ...."

This is a partial list of wounds. Still to come is the breaking of her nose. The mysterious struggle she is engaged in, against an amorphous circle of thugs and aristocrats, is savage. She might as well be battling one of the bears that she used to come upon in the far north ... Actually, she might be better off with the polar bear. At least she would know who her enemy was and why it wanted her dead.

Leithauser drew no conclusion about the enemy. I speculate that it is the despair of loss, that her wounds and bruises are comic (action-adventure) representations of emotional lacerations she must endure in order to return, if you will, to the house of her mother to enter the final phase of mourning, "a greater or lesser degree of reorganization," as apt, if bland, a description as there could be of the conclusion of *Frøken Smillas fornemmelse for sne*. Smilla herself, toward the end of "The Sea," tells us, as Høeg so often (and, at times, so pedantically) has her do, precisely what is going to happen. She has fled the ship and stumbled into the body of another dead boy, when she suddenly recognizes the mechanic as the fourth passenger.

> Da jeg genkender ham forstår jeg, at jeg bliver nødt til at gå tilbage til Kronos.
>
> Det er ikke fordi det pludselig er blevet lige meget om jeg lever eller dør. Det er snarere fordi problemet er blevet taget ud af haenderne på mig. Det er ikke noget med Esajas alene. Eller med mig selv. Eller med mekanikeren. Ikke engang alene noget med det

der er mellem os. Det er noget større. Måske er det kaerligheden.

When I recognize him, I realize that I'll have to return to the Kronos.

"Not because it suddenly doesn't matter whether I live or die, but because the problem has been taken out of my hands. It no longer has to do with Isaiah alone. Or with me. Or with the mechanic. Or even with what there is between us. It's something much bigger. Maybe it's love.

Smilla returns to her passage through time, at the end, at the edge of the waters that took her mother, embracing for the future both the fetal image of Isaiah and the waiting mechanic, allowing her nemesis, Tørk Hviid, to flee onto the treacherous ice, off the page, and into oblivion.

In elaborating on the phase of "yearning and searching," Bowlby quoted Colin Murray Parks as saying:.

Although we tend to think of searching in terms of the motor act of restless movement towards possible locations of the lost object, (searching) also has perceptual and ideational components . . . Signs of the object can be identified only by reference to memories of the object as it was. Searching the external world for signs of the object therefore includes the establishment of an internal perceptual "set" derived from previous experiences of the object.

In terms of motor action, Høeg has Smilla quite literally get on board a ship that will carry her back to the place of her birth and her deepest loss, and he is not shy with his symbolism. The ship is named Kronos, the classical god of time, associated with change, with melancholy, and with death. In his fine introduction to *Melancholy Dialectics* (1993), his book on the play of mourning in the works of Walter Benjamin, Max Pensky traced the transition of what he calls "the role of melancholia in Western culture" from medical to theological and ethical discourses. The eventual kinship to Kronos is striking.

The original medical texts of late antiquity . . . become associated with astrological bodies and properties. Melancholia becomes connected with Saturn, the cold, dark, and slow planet, and thence the correspondence, Saturn-melancholia, with Chronos, the classical god of time, who is now transfigured into the god of sadness and morbidity, of delay . . . thus the association of melancholy with Saturn, and Saturn with the god Chronos, Chronos with time and universal death . . . "

But Høeg seems to love nothing more than the dialectical, and thus, at the same time as Smilla sails in a ship marked by time, birth imagery abounds: an enclosed vessel, a blind passage through maternal waters, the waiting fetal image. None of this is subtle.

More nuanced, however, is what Bowlby/Parks called the "perceptual and ideational components," or, the external "signs" of the internalized object "as it was." Isaiah is, of course, the most conspicuous sign, but then there is the mechanic. Is Føjl to be read as the English "foil" or the Danish "feel"? Both have connotations. For is he not the perfect, maternal surrogate? (He even shares his own creator's Christian name.) Like Smilla's mother, he is large of body and androgynous of spirit, strong and protective. Like her, too, he is primarily non-verbal, a stutterer, who, nevertheless, is the only one who can cajole Smilla out of her depression. He gives her nourishment, like mother's milk in adult guise, tropical tea and thick espresso, and he takes her between his legs. Time and again, as if she cannot help herself, Smilla connects the mechanic to her childhood. He cooks for her, and she is "mindet om måltidets rituelle betydning. At jeg husker barndommens forening af samvaerets højtidelighed og de store smagsoplevelser . . . Fornemmelsen af, at stort set all i livet er til for at blive delt" ("reminded of the ritual significance of meals. In my childhood I remember associating the solemnity of companionship with great gustatory experiences . . . The feeling that practically everything in life is meant to be shared"). He sleeps with her and she is reminded of a parental kiss. "Munden og naesen vibrerer bløt, som om han dufter til en blomst. Eller skal til at kysse et barn" ("His mouth and nose vibrate gently, as if he were sniffing at a flower. Or were about to kiss a child"). But the mechanic, like Smilla's mother, is also potentially treacherous, a man of secrets who is not necessarily what he seems to be. Most dangerously, he is a man who can mysteriously disappear, as he does, just as Smilla is about to set sail for Greenland. As a "sign" he must be nearly irresistible to her. At the same time he seems to signal a change in her fortune in the narrative of mourning. For when, in the penultimate section, he returns to the Kronos as the fourth passenger, he in effect reverses the series of (three) shattering, mysterious disappearances Smilla has suffered by mysteriously reappearing, significantly in a shower of warm water.

But the most seductive "sign" of all for Smilla is her beloved snow. Smilla authoritatively announces early on, "Jeg synes bedre om sne og is end om kaerligheden" ("I think more highly of snow and ice than love"). Equally authoritatively Høeg cautioned readers not to trust her. "She should not be relied on, because she's hidding her

sensitivity and feelings under a rough surface"
(Lyall). Both statements are misleading, for it is not
so much a matter of snow versus love, but of snow
as Smilla's disguised obsession with the loss of
love. Smilla herself makes the connection, if she
disguises the nature of the loss, when, at the end
of her reminiscence about her mother's intimate
embrace, she muses, "Måske er jeg allerede dér
begyndt at ønske at forstå isen. At ville forstå er at
prøve at generobre noget vi har mistet" ("Perhaps
I had even then begun to want to understand the
ice. To want to understand is an attempt to recapture something we have lost").

Smilla is, she says, "panisk" ("panic-stricken")
at the prospect of loving the mechanic, for fear it
won't last.

> Dér på hans gulv, ved siden af hans seng, kan jeg
> høre noget. Det kommer inde fra mig selv, og det er
> en klynken. Det er frygten for, at det der er givet mig,
> ikke skal vare ved. Det er lyden af alle de ulykkelige
> kaerlighedshistorier jeg aldrig har villet lytte til. Nu
> lyder det, som om jeg selv rummer dem alle.

> Standing there on his floor, next to his bed, I can hear
> something. It's coming from inside me, and it's a
> whimper. It's the fear that what has been given to me
> won't last. It's the sound of all the unhappy love sto-
> ries I've never wanted to listen to. Now it sounds as
> if they're all contained within me.

In her study on melancholy, Soleil Noris: *Depression et melancholie* (1987) (Black Sun: Depression and Melancholia (1989)), Julia Kristeva
wrote early on:

> Le désenchantement, fût-il cruel, que je subis ici et
> maintenant semble entrer en résonance, à l'examen,
> avec des traumas anciens dont je m'aperçois que je
> n'ai jamais su faire le deuil. Je peux trouver ainsi des
> antécédents de mon effondrement actuel dans une
> perte, une mort ou un deuil, de quelqu'un on de
> quelqu'un de chose, que j'ai jadis aimés. La disparition de
> cet être indispensable continue de me priver de la part
> la plus valable de moi-même: je la vis comme une
> blessure ou une privation, pour découvrir, toutefois,
> que ma peine n'est que l'ajournement de la haine ou
> du désir d'emprise que je nourris pour celui ou pour
> celle qui m'ont trahie ou abandonnée. Ma dépression
> me signale que je ne sais pas perdre; peut-être ai-je
> pas su trouver un contrepartie valable à la perte. Il
> s'ensuit que toute perte entraine la perte de mon
> être—et de l'Être lui-même.

> The disenchantment that I experience here and now,
> cruel as it may be, appears, under scrutiny, to awaken
> echoes of old traumas, to which I realize I have never
> been able to resign myself. I can thus discover an-
> tecedents to my current breakdown in a loss, death,
> or grief over someone or something that I once loved.
> The disappearance of that essential being continues
> to deprive me of what is most worthwhile in me; I

> live it as a wound or deprivation, discovering just the
> same that my grief is but the deferment of the hatred
> or desire for ascendency that I nurture with respect
> to the one who betrayed or abandoned me. My de-
> pression points to my not knowing how to lose—I
> have perhaps been unable to find a valid compensa-
> tion for the loss? It follows that any loss entails the
> loss of my being—and of Being itself.

Smilla, afraid to lose, has practiced, she says,
the art of renouncing, "det eneste i denne verden
der er vaerd at laere" ("the only thing in the world
that is worth learning"). Her passion, her yearning
for love and for beauty, she has channeled into the
study of snow and ice, for in her mind they are the
substance of permanence. Ice is the opponent of the
sea. "(D)en daekker vandet og gør det fast, sikkert,
farbart, overskueligt" ("(I)t covers the water and
makes it solid, safe, negotiable, manageable"). The
sea robs Smilla, as we know, of her sense of Absolute Space. She experiences the loss as actual
physical disintegration.

> Langsomt vil denne forvirring arbejde sig ind i mit
> balancesystems vaeskekar og opløse min stedsans,
> den vil kaempe sig ud i mine celler og forskyde deres
> saltkoncentration og dermed nervesystemets led-
> ningsevne, og efterlade mig døv, blind og hjaelpeløs
> . . . Fra jeg for nogle timer siden er gået ombord, er
> nedbrydningen sat ind. Det koger allerede i mine ører,
> i mine slimhinder sker der underlige, umotiverede
> vaeskeskred.

> . . . this confusion will work its way into the cham-
> bers of my inner ear and destroy my sense of orien-
> tation; it will fight its way into my cells and displace
> their salt concentrations and the conductivity of my
> nervous system as well, leaving me deaf, blind, and
> helpless . . . The process of disintegration started the
> moment I came on board several hours ago. There's
> a boiling in my ears, a strange, internal displacement
> of fluids.

This is the experience of dissolving, of dying,
and it is brought on by the very sea that took her
mother.

For Smilla snow is the substance that preserves
form, like Isaiah's tracks. It is the substance of
connection, associated in her mind with winter,
her mother's favorite season, and the visiting of
others. "Vinteren var en tid til samvaer, ikke til jor-
dens undergang" ("Winter was a time for community, not for the end of the world"). Snow is the
substance of certainty. It is the substance of perfection. Like all who mourn, Smilla longs for something that can contain the essence of what is lost,
Keats's Grecian urn, Dinesen's blue vase. Smilla
has found it in her ability to imagine snow. "I den
ydre verden vil der aldrig eksistere en fuldendt dan-
net snekrystal. Men i vores bevidsthed ligger den

glitrende og lydefri viden om den perfekte is" ("In the external world a perfectly formed snow crystal would never exist. But in our consciousness lies the glittering and flawless knowledge of perfect ice"). Smilla seems to find in the ice all that she longs for, life, wildness, beauty, change, and eternal permanence. Nearing Greenland, she describes in the most sensuous terms the creation of the ice cover:

> Det er skabt i skønhed. En oktoberdag er temperaturen faldet 30 grader celcius på fire timer, og havet er blevet stille som et spejl. Det venter på at gengive et skabelsesunder. Skyerne og havet glider nu samme i et forhaeng af grå, fed silke. Vandet bliver tyktflydende og ganske let rødligt, som en likør på vilde baer. En blå tåge af frostrøg gøar sig fri af vandoverfladen, og driver hen over vandspejlet. Så størkner vandet. Op af det mørke hav traekker kulden nu en rosenhave, et hvidt taeppe af lsblomster, dannet af salte og frosne vanddråber. De vil måske leve fire timer, måske to dage.

> It was created in beauty. One October day the temperature drops 50 degrees in four hours, and the sea is as motionless as a mirror. It's waiting to reflect a wonder of creation. The clouds and the sea glide together in a curtain of heavy gray silk. The water grows viscous and tinged with pink, like a liqueur of wild berries. A blue fog of frost smoke detaches itself from the surface of the water and drifts across the mirror. Then the water solidifies. Up out of the dark sea the cold now pulls a rose garden, a white blanket of ice blossoms formed from the salt and frozen drops of water. That may last for four hours or two days.

The ice is endlessly transformed, even as it remains, always, what it is: hexagonal crystals dissolve into new hexagons, to become frazil ice and grease ice and pancake ice and then hiku (permanent ice) and ice floes, blue and black floes, and white glacier ice, ad infinitum.

But, of course, snow is as impermanent as life, the quintessence of impermanence. Touched by the human hand it disappears, as suddenly and completely as Smilla's mother. Only in Smilla's mind is it a constant. Even in its physical construction it is made up of wholes and holes, as illusive a substance as Smilla could have found for her passion, and thus, in essence, the perfect "sign" for her mother, both in her presence and her absence. It is the substance in which she is both to be lost and to be found. Yet, as long as Smilla continues to romanticize snow, she can avoid facing the loss that it hides. She need never lose again.

Kristeva, in her work on mourning, has said that it is the escalating number of signs that is the mourner's true "sign." In summarizing Kristeva's

contribution to the literature of mourning, Max Pensky wrote:

> It is this very proliferation of signs that draws the melancholic's attention, both as the exact schematic representation of the sites of the melancholic's loss and as the only possible medium in which the Thing could be glimpsed. The chaotic mass of symbolic signification—of names—"means" the loss of meaning. It therefore signifies in a double motion. For the melancholic who is able to recover from the paralytic, illogic thrall of loss—who can sublimate it—meaning translates into the continually frustrated fascination with the rifts and discontinuties that remain in the proliferation of signs.

In this light Isaiah's murder is, indeed, the moment that sets Smilla free. For it gives her justification to begin the search, to open up her frozen focus to look for signs of her lost beloved quite literally everywhere, and, as the detective, to explore to the point of obsession, "the rifts and discontinuities" in the case of "the murdered child." At the end Smilla stands on the ice, surrounded by the signs of Isaiah, the mechanic, and the snow, in the landscape of her mother's death, with the possibility of the child—the Smilla/Isaiah—being reborn. And in a Kristevan sense, meaning is reasserted as Smilla poeticizes the ever-expanding rift in the landscape as the white frost of fog hovers overhead and Tørk, driven by her into the distance, disappears on the bluish white ice, destined to be sucked under by the waters running darkly underneath. Smilla has taken her mother up into herself. Like her, she has become the hunter, in the name of the children avenging the deaths of all of those who have been sacrificed.

The Black Stone

To return to the questions provoked by the old folk tale riddle that underlies Høeg's text—is there a heart and does Høeg break it or not?—my answer is only too obvious. In my reading, *Frøken Smillas fornemmelse for sne* is a sentimental narrative about the mourning of the child, a narrative told with a broken heart that the writer attempts to heal. "Min mors forfaedre ville have undret sig over, at universets nøgler for en af deres efterkommere skulle vise sig at vaere skriftlig" ("My mother's forefathers would have been astounded that the key to the universe for one of their descendants would turn out to be in written form"), Smilla/Høeg says. S/he does not seem, to borrow Leithauser's word, to be being "coy." Yet the narrative fact remains that that meteorite, with its deadly worms, lies waiting at the end, just as surely as the mechanic. Smilla, as usual, tells us so herself. "Bag os er stadig stenen, dens gåde, de spørgsmål den har rejst/Og mekanikeren." ("Behind us the stone is still there, with its mystery and the questions it has raised. And the mechanic"). What questions has it raised? we might ask. One certainly is, is this whole tale a showstopping, post-modern pastiche? Another critic, with another bent, could use that worm-filled stone to turn my reading back upon itself. In the short time the stone is present in the text, its meanings shift like sand, particularly as Tørk deconstructs it for Smilla on their walk toward it. It is Inuit myth, science-fiction vision, scientific discovery-of-the-century, ancient source of life, capitalist commodity, waiting plague, narrative signifier, narrative joke, depending on who exploits it. Smilla takes her own turns with it. On first hearing about it from the mechanic, she remarks, "Je håber inderligt, det er et nummer" ("I sincerely hope that it's a hoax"), and later on with Tørk:

> Pludselig er det heller ikke for mig vigtig om den lever. Pludselig er den et symbol. Omkring den udkrystalliseres i dette øjeblik den vestlige naturvidenskabs holdning til verden omkring den. Beregnetheden, hadet, håbet, frygten, forsøget på at instrumentalisere. Og over alt andet, staerkere end nogen følelse for noget levende: pengebegaeret.

> (Suddenly whether the stone is alive or not is no longer important to me, either. Suddenly it has become a symbol. At this moment it becomes the crystallization of the attitude of Western science toward the world. Calculation, hatred, hope, fear, the attempt to measure everything. And above all else, stronger than any empathy for living things: the desire for money.)

In conclusion I would offer my own interpretation of the black stone as yet another "sign" in the narrative of mourning, bearing, of course, in mind the villain's words, "Det er ikke vigtig, hvordan tingene virkelig forholder sig. Det vigtige er, hvad mennesker tror" ("The true reality of things is not important. What's important is what people believe").

"The Giant Who Had No Heart In Him" is only one of many texts, literary and non-, that seem to play in the narrative shadows of *Frøken Smillas fornemmelse for sne*. They are as numerous as readers who have read them, text by Andersen, Benjamin, Conrad, Dinesen, Foucoult, Girard, etc. Yet one that leaps to mind more spontaneously than others is Mary Shelley's *Frankenstein*, the ultimate nineteenth-century critique of a society that gives privilege to the world of science to the exclusion of the world of feeling. At its heart too lies a murdered child, the young boy, William, Dr. Frankenstein's youngest brother, who is the Creature's first victim. The Creature is more literally the young scientist's creation, but Tørk is equally Smilla's double, an arid, white shadow who stalks her, a disembodied voice who talks to her from the other end of the phone, her pursuer as equally as she is his. Their bond is mutually acknowledged.

> (Smilla:) Det er tanken om, at han fra begyndelsen har vidst hvem jeg er, der er ulidelig. Jeg husker ikke, siden jeg var barn, i så høj grad at have følt mig i et andet menneskes vold.

> It's the realization that he knew who I was from the very beginning that is so excruciating. Not since my childhood have I felt so strongly in someone else's power.

> (Tørk:) Du bluffer vidunderligt, siger han.—Jeg ville langt hellere sidde oppe i tønden og høre på at du lyver, end gå rundt blandt alle disse middelmådige sandheder.

> You're a spectacular bluffer . . . I'd much rather sit up in the crow's nest listening to your lies than walk around among all these mediocre truths.

> (Smilla:) Vi er forbundet red en navlestreng, som mor og barn.

> We're connected by an umbilical cord, like mother and child.

Tørk is the frigid mind, the deadened child who, like the deeply wounded Creature, will kill until he is overcome and driven out.

The finale *Frøken Smillas fornemmelse for sne*, Smilla's pursuit of Tørk across the ice and into the distance, has its antecedent in the narrative frame of Frankenstein. The crew of the earlier, fictional ship, temporarily locked in the glacial waters of the Arctic, first spots the Creature fleeing toward the North Pole. As told by the young scholar/explorer:

> . . . a strange sight suddenly attracted our attention, and diverted our solicitude from our own situations. We perceived a low carriage, fixed on a sledge and drawn by dogs, pass on towards the north, at the distance of half a mile; a being which had the shape of a man, but apparently of gigantic stature, sat in the sledge, and guided the dogs. We watched the rapid progress of the traveler with our telescopes until he was lost among the distant equalities of the ice.

In the morning they discover his pursuer, the "melancholy and despairing" Dr. Frankenstein in parallel chase.

> It was, in fact, a sledge, like that we had seen before, which had drifted towards us in the night on a large fragment of ice. Only one dog remained alive; but there was a human being within it, whom the sailors were persuading to enter the vessel. He was not as the other traveler seemed to be, a savage inhabitant of some undiscovered island, but an European.

The novel ends with the horrified, young explorer bearing witness to the Creature's agonized leave-taking of his creator and tormentor, the dead Dr. Frankenstein, and his painful exit from the narrative:

> "But soon," he cried, with sad and solemn enthusiasm, "I shall die, and what I now feel be no longer felt. Soon these burning miseries will be extinct. I shall ascend my funeral pile triumphantly, and exult in the agony of the torturing flames. The light of that conflagration will fade away; my ashes will be swept into the sea by the winds. My spirit will sleep in peace; or if it thinks, it will not surely think thus. Farewell."
>
> He sprung from the cabin window, as he said this, upon the ice-raft which lay close to the vessel. He was soon borne away by the waves, and lost in darkness and distance.

Høeg, reversing the "European" (here Tørk) and "the savage inhabitant" (here Smilla), collapses the chase into the final scene.

> Han ser mig, eller måske set han bare at der står en skikkelse, så søager han ud på isen. Jeg følger ham i en retning der er parallel med hans. Han ser, hvem jeg er. Han maerker at han ikke har overskud til at nå mig . . . Han søger for langt mod højre. Da han instinktivt retter op, ligger skibet 200 meter bag os. Han har mistet orienteringen. Han føres ud mod det øbne vand. Mod dér, hvor strømmen har udhulet isen, så den bliver tynd som en hinde, en fosterhinde . . . Måske vil isen om et øjeblik give efter under ham. Han vil måske føle det som en lettelse, at det kolde vand gør ham vaegtløs og suger ham ned . . . Eller han skifter i stedet retning og søger igen mod højre, ud over isen. Inat vil temperaturen falde yderligere, og der vil komme snestorm. Han vil kun leve et par timer. På et tidspunkt vil han standse op, og kulden vil forvandle ham, som en istap, en frossen skal lukket om et akkurat flydende liv, indtil også pulsen stilner, og han bliver ét med landskabet . . . Et sted foran mig bliver den løbende skikkelse langsomt mørkere.
>
> Then he sees me, or maybe he merely sees a figure, and he heads out onto the ice. I take a path parallel to his. He sees that it's me. He realizes that he doesn't have the strength to reach me . . . He parallel to his. He sees that it's me. He realizes that he doesn't have the strength to reach me . . . He heads too far to the right. When he instinctively corrects his course, the ship is two hundred yards behind us. He's lost his bearings. He's being led out toward open water. Toward the spot where the current has hollowed out the ice so it's as thin as a membrane . . . Maybe in a moment the ice will give way beneath him. Maybe it will seem a relief to have the cold water make him weightless and suck him downward . . . Or maybe he will change direction and head to the right again, across the ice. He'll only survive a couple of hours. At some point he will stop, and the cold will transform him; like a stalactite, a frozen shell will

close around a barely fluid life until even this pulse stops and he becomes one with the landscape . . . Somewhere ahead of me the running figure slowly grows darker.

The death metaphor has been changed from fire to ice, but that Høeg's ending is a deliberate narrative doubling of Shelly's—with a significant twist—calls attention to itself.

Both *Frankenstein* and *Frøken Smillas fornemmelse for sne* are novels of paradises lost, but, metaphorically speaking, Dr. Frankenstein and the Creature flee into a pristine, arctic landscape, only to corrupt it with their footsteps and their corpses. Smilla and Tørk arrive at, one might say, the same place, but it is long since a fallen world, both inner- and extratextually. Tørk and his men have been here before. Isaiah has witnessed his father's destruction here at the hands of the powers of greed. But, too, the Doctor and his Creature fled here, already in 1818. And what they brought with them, and what lies buried with them, is despair. Creator and experiment, they are the precursors of the dark side of the modern, scientific age, where feeling has been sacrificed on the altar of disembodied data. They share the guilt for the symbolic dead child, vying even for the measure of their grief. The Creature parts from the dead Frankenstein with the words, "Blasted as thou were, my agony was still superior to thine; for the bitter sting of remorse will not cease to rankle in my wounds until death shall close them forever." But Frankenstein's earlier words still hang in the air:

> But I, the true murderer, felt the never-dying worm alive in my bosom, which allowed of no hope or consolation . . . Anguish and despair had penetrated into the core of my head; I bore a hell within me which nothing could extinguish.

If only by literary association, might not the mysterious, black stone be the solidification of the Creature's ashes, and might not the worms in the stone be the descendents of "the never-dying worm" in Frankenstein's blasted heart? But in her own narrative Smilla, the hunter/child, is still alive to challenge them. Høeg seems to have been determined to go back, "For at gøre noget om. For at prøve, om der skulle findes en anden mulighed" ("To do something differently. To see whether there might be an alternative"), if only by sheer authorial will.

Source: Mary Kay Norseng, "A House of Mourning: *Frøken Smillas fornemmelse for sne*," in *Scandanavian Studies*, Vol. 69, Winter 1997, pp. 52–83.

Sources

Bell, Pearl, "Fiction Chronicle," in *Partisan Review*, Vol. LXI, No. 1, Winter 1994, pp. 80–95.

Eder, Richard, Review of *Smilla's Sense of Snow*, in *Los Angeles Times Book Review*, September 26, 1993, pp. 3, 11.

Hazleton, Lesley, Review of *Smilla's Sense of Snow*, in the *Seattle Times*, October 3, 1993, p. F2.

Henry, William, III, Review of *Smilla's Sense of Snow*, in *People Weekly*, Vol. 40, No. 14, 1993, p. 32–34.

Kennedy, Thomas E., and Frank Hugus, Introduction, in *Review of Contemporary Fiction*, Vol. 15, No. 1, Spring 1995, pp. 7–10.

Leithauser, Brad, Review of *Smilla's Sense of Snow*, in *New Republic*, Vol. 209, No. 18, November 1, 1992, p. 39.

Loose, Julian, Review of *Miss Smilla's Feeling for Snow*, in *London Review of Books*, Vol. 16, No. 9, May 12, 1994, p. 27.

McCue, John, Review of *Miss Smilla's Feeling for Snow*, in *Times Literary Supplement*, No. 4720, September 17, 1993, p. 20.

Meyer, Michael, Review of *Smilla's Sense of Snow*, in *New York Review of Books*, Vol. XL, No. 19, November 18, 1993, p. 41.

Møller, Hans Henrik, "Peter Høeg or The Sense of Writing," in *Scandinavian Studies*, Vol. 69, Winter 1997, pp. 29–51.

Nathan, Robert, Review of *Smilla's Sense of Snow*, in *New York Times Book Review*, September 26, 1993, p. 12.

Norseng, Mary Kay, "A House of Mourning: *Frøken Smillas Fornemmelse for Sne*," in *Scandinavian Studies*, Vol. 69, No. 1, Winter 1997, pp. 52–83.

Satterlee, Thomas, "Peter Høeg," in *Dictionary of Literary Biography*, Vol. 214: *Twentieth-Century Danish Writers*, edited by Marianne Stecher-Hansen, The Gale Group, 1999, pp. 178–87.

Schaffer, Rachel, "Smilla's Sense of Gender Identity," in *Clues: A Journal of Detection*, Vol. 19, No. 1, Spring–Summer 1998, pp. 47–60.

Shapiro, Laura, Review of *Smilla's Sense of Snow*, in *Newsweek*, Vol. 122, No. 10, September 6, 1993, p. 54.

Simonds, Merilyn, Review of *Smilla's Sense of Snow*, in the *Montreal Gazette*, December 11, 1993, p. 12.

Smiley, Jane, Review of *Smilla's Sense of Snow*, in *Washington Post Book World*, October 24, 1993, pp. 1, 11.

Whiteside, Shaun, Review of *Miss Smilla's Feeling for Snow*, in *Manchester Guardian Weekly*, Vol. 149, No. 19, November 7, 1993, p. 29.

Williams, John, Review of *Miss Smilla's Feeling for Snow*, in *New Statesman and Society*, Vol. 6, No. 268, September 3, 1993, p. 41.

Further Reading

Caufield, Richard A., "The Kalaallit of West Greenland," in *Endangered Peoples of the Arctic: Struggles to Survive and Thrive*, edited by Milton Freeman, Greenwood Press, 2000.
    Caufield presents a readable history of the Inuit peoples of Greenland, from historical past into the twenty-first century.

Nuttal, Mark, "Greenland: Emergence of an Inuit Homeland," in *Polar Peoples: Self-Determination & Development*, edited by Minority Rights Group, Minority Rights Publications, 1994.
    Nuttall's chapter in this longer overview of polar peoples offers the reader a concise history of Danish colonization of Greenland as well as prospects for the future.

Satterlee, Thomas, "Peter Høeg," in *Dictionary of Literary Biography*, Vol. 214: *Twentieth-Century Danish Writers*, edited by Marianne Stecher-Hansen, The Gale Group, 1999, pp. 178–187.
    Satterlee provides an excellent introduction to Peter Høeg's work for the student who wants to know more about the writer.

Schaffer, Rachel, "Smilla's Sense of Gender Identity," in *Clues: A Journal of Detection*, Vol. 19, No. 1, Spring–Summer 1998, pp. 47–60.
    In a readable critical article, Schaffer applies feminist theory to the novel.

Soul Catcher

Frank Herbert
1972

Soul Catcher is a tragic, eye-opening novel about the mistreatment of Native Americans and one man's vengeful attempt to even the cultural score. First published in New York in 1972 when the American Indian Movement (AIM) was just hitting its stride, the book has received surprisingly little critical or popular attention and, in fact, is currently out of print. This may have more to do with the author's other books, however, than with the quality of *Soul Catcher*. Frank Herbert, known worldwide as the author of the immensely popular novel *Dune* and its sequels, is revered as one of science fiction's greatest authors; *Soul Catcher* was his first and only non-science-fiction book that concerned Native Americans, a fact that might have turned off his readers and critics.

Still, the book warrants reading. In the story, Charles Hobuhet, a Native American university student who becomes possessed by the spirit, Soul Catcher, kidnaps David Marshall, the thirteen-year-old son of a powerful politician. Hobuhet has the intention of killing David in revenge for the wrongs that have been visited on Native Americans. He also faces an internal struggle between his tribal identity and the identity that he has acquired in the white—hoquat—world. At the same time, David learns more about his captor's Native American beliefs and way of life, and the two develop a relationship. The powerful themes, which include Native-American religious beliefs, sacrifice, and the meaning of innocence, collectively help to underscore the centuries-old plight of the Native American.

Frank Herbert

Author Biography

Frank Herbert was born on October 8, 1920, in Tacoma, Washington. After attending the University of Washington, Seattle, from 1946 to 1947 Herbert continued working as a reporter, photographer, and editor, work that he had started doing in 1939 at the age of nineteen. Herbert pursued his journalism career for thirty years with many West Coast newspapers, including the *Glendale Star* (California), the *Oregon Statesman*, the *Seattle Star*, and the *San Francisco Examiner*. During this time, Herbert also worked a number of odd jobs and began to sell his first science fiction. His first short story was published in 1952, and his first novel, *The Dragon in the Sea*, was published in 1956.

Although these initial efforts introduced Herbert to science fiction audiences, it was his second novel, 1965's *Dune*, that immediately established Herbert as one of the masters of the field and that spawned a series of books, starting with the sequel, *Dune Messiah* (1970). *Dune* was the first book ever to win both the Hugo (1966) and Nebula (1965) awards, science fiction's two highest honors. The book was also one of the first science-fiction novels to address ecological issues, inspiring other writers to do the same. In 1970, Herbert's interest

in social issues led to his joining the World Without War Council, and in 1971, he served as a consultant in ecological and social studies for the Lincoln Foundation. The same year, he moved to a six-acre farm on Washington's Olympic Peninsula, where he developed an ecological project that demonstrated how people can maintain a high quality of life while using minimal natural resources.

The next year, in 1972, Herbert published *Soul Catcher*, one of his few non-science-fiction stories. Still, through its study of Native-American religion and way of life, the book addressed the theme of ecology that is present in many of his science fiction novels. Following *Soul Catcher*, Herbert wrote more than ten more novels, including four in "The Dune Chronicles" series, which culminated with 1985's *Chapterhouse: Dune*. Herbert died on February 11, 1986, in Madison, Wisconsin.

Plot Summary

The Kidnapping

Soul Catcher begins after David Marshall, the thirteen-year-old son of newly appointed United States Undersecretary of State Howard Marshall, has already been kidnapped. This fact is revealed through public statements, news stories, and notes from the kidnapper, Charles Hobuhet, a university student who is now referring to himself as Katsuk. Hobuhet-Katsuk says that he has taken David as a sacrifice for all of the Native-American innocents who have been murdered by whites. After this choppy beginning, the story then jumps back to the events preceding the kidnapping, including David's preparation for his trip to the Six Rivers Camp and Hobuhet-Katsuk's possession by Soul Catcher. Interspersed with these descriptions, more news stories and statements comment on the kidnapping, a technique that Herbert uses throughout the novel.

A Midnight Journey into the Forest

When Katsuk kidnaps David, he does it by tricking him into thinking that David is taking part in a ritual to become Katsuk's spirit brother. When they have journeyed far into the forest surrounding Six Rivers Camp, Katsuk ties David up and lets him know that he is going to be killed as a sacrifice. He also forces David to use the name "Hoquat," the name that Katsuk says his ancestors had given to David's ancestors when they first settled in North America. In his first attempt to be rescued, David drops his handkerchief on the ground outside the cave where they shelter the first morning, and a helicopter sees it.

Raven

Katsuk realizes what David has done, but instead of being angry, he admires David's resourcefulness. He tells David that Raven, a powerful bird spirit, has hidden them from the helicopter, a fact that is demonstrated for the reader when Katsuk remembers the incident. Katsuk, satisfied that Raven will keep an eye on David, unties the boy. The two set out walking again, and David prays for a helicopter. Meanwhile, Katsuk begins to notice the change in David as David follows Katsuk's lead and adapts to wilderness life, learning the proper times to eat, drink, and rest. At one point, Katsuk proves that Raven will hide them from searchers, when a helicopter flies by and a flock of ravens hides David and Katsuk from sight.

Encounters

On the second day of walking, Katsuk notices that some hikers have passed through and commands David to go hide behind a log. From his position, David watches as Katsuk encounters a hiker (Debay) and kills him so that he cannot report their location. David is horrified at the murder and tries to run away, but Katsuk easily catches him, knocking him out in the process. When David wakes up, Katsuk forces him to hide again while Katsuk conceals Debay's body. Two nights later, David has a spirit dream that tells him he will be granted a wish when he is ready. They talk about Katsuk's religion. The next day as they are walking near a meadow, Katsuk feels the presence of his people who hold a sing that night to lure Katsuk into their camp. Although some of his people—his ex-girlfriend, Tskanay, and his great uncle, Ish—are in the camp and try to stop Katsuk, they are no match for Katsuk's power, which Ish realizes.

No Escape

Tskanay, on the other hand, does not believe that Katsuk is anybody other than Charles Hobuhet. When Katsuk puts David in her care, she encourages the boy to run away. David tries to take the trail that Tskanay has pointed out, but in his efforts to avoid the many ravens on the trail, he veers off and gets lost, getting soaked in the process. Eventually, Ish finds him and takes him back to the camp. David meets Katsuk's aunt Cally, who puts him in a tent and has him take off his wet clothes for her to dry. Tskanay comes into the tent to see David and gives him food to eat. In an attempt to take away

David's innocence, the quality that Katsuk has told them is necessary for the sacrifice, Tskanay steals David's virginity. However, it does not work, since David's shame at the act proves his innocence even more and binds him tighter to Katsuk.

Katsuk Is Shunned

That day, the entire tribe, around twenty people, has a meeting, at which Katsuk tries to garner their support. However, while they agree that they will not try to stop him, they do not agree with Katsuk's plan. Instead, they say that if Katsuk kills David, Katsuk will be just as bad as whites. Later that day, as they are sheltering in an old mine, Katsuk tells David that he will not kill him unless David asks him to. Katsuk plays a song on a willow flute, during which he starts to feel ill. He thinks that his people have tricked him into offending Cedar, a tree spirit, and that he has been infected with Cedar sickness as a result. David falls asleep while Katsuk prays to Cedar. When he wakes up, he and Katsuk leave the mine and head up into the frigid forest region near the timberline. David is freezing, but Katsuk seems fine in his loincloth and moccasins.

Preparation

While David dozes on a riverbank, Katsuk prays for and receives the spirit wood that he needs to make his bow. He gets ready to start cutting the wood into a bow but gets a sign that using a hoquat knife on the wood will remove its power, so he throws David's knife into the river. A few days later, he makes a knife out of obsidian rock. When David finds out Katsuk threw his knife into the river, he says that he hopes Katsuk's Cedar sickness kills him, and he hits Katsuk with a rock. Katsuk begins using his new obsidian knife to carve the wood into a bow, and David asks if he can help him. Katsuk sees this as a sign that Soul Catcher is starting to prepare David to ask for his own death.

Hope and Sickness

While Katsuk is busy carving the bow, David escapes. Katsuk follows him, stopping to make an arrow from a cedar tree that he finds. That night, David finds shelter and makes a fire in the way that Katsuk has taught him, and the next day, he begins to have hope that he will get away. That evening, Katsuk, who is noticeably sick, finds him. His sickness gets worse as the night goes on, and he falls into feverish dreams. When he wakes up the next day, David brings him water and food. Katsuk asks why David is not running away, since it was he that gave Katsuk Cedar sickness, but David tells him he is crazy and that he does not want to leave Katsuk while he is sick. Katsuk gets better, and in one of his dreams, Raven tells him to go downstream, where he finds a search party that is looking for them.

The Sacrifice

The next day, Katsuk announces they will be staying in their shelter. Katsuk is silent, contemplating the meaning of the sacrifice he is about to perform, and his extreme quietness prompts David to ask him questions. Katsuk interprets the questions as further proof that David is preparing himself for the sacrifice, but Katsuk waits for David to ask him for his death. David wakes up when he hears the search party coming and is excited that he is about to be rescued. However, he is also anxious for Katsuk to leave and hide before they catch him and kill him or throw him in jail. Katsuk says that he cannot leave until he has delivered his message, and David tells him to do whatever he needs to do to deliver the message but to hurry before the searchers find him. Katsuk takes this as his sign that David is asking for his death and kills him with the bow and arrow he has constructed. Shortly thereafter, the search party finds Katsuk with the dead boy in his arms, chanting a death song for his lost friend.

<hr>

Characters

Dr. Tilman Barth

Dr. Tilman Barth is one of Hobuhet's professors in the University of Washington anthropology department, who comments on Hobuhet and his beliefs.

Aunt Cally

Cally is Hobuhet's aunt, and she wants him to save his life by releasing David, even though she is proud of her nephew for the kidnapping.

Vince Debay

Vince Debay is the hippie hiker whom Katsuk kills in the forest with David's knife, an act that encourages David to make his first escape attempt. Although Debay recognizes Hobuhet from an anthropology class that they have shared, he thinks it odd that Hobuhet is dressed in traditional Native-American garb, a fact that makes him nervous.

Charles Hobuhet

Charles Hobuhet is a graduate student who becomes possessed by a spirit, kidnaps David Marshall, and ritually sacrifices him as a way to pay back white society for all of the Native Americans they have killed and mistreated. It is the rape of his sister by white loggers and her subsequent suicide that sends him into madness. The madness causes him to go into the forest, where he is possessed by Soul Catcher, a powerful spirit who instructs him to kill an innocent, and where he gets the spirit name of Katsuk. One night, he uses his status as a camp counselor at Six Rivers Camp to lure David away from his bunk, claiming that he is going to make David his spirit brother. Katsuk takes David deep into the forest, then ties him up, and reveals his plan to sacrifice him. Meanwhile, Katsuk has left a number of notes that illustrate the knowledge he has gained in his anthropology degree, his hate for the hoquat—white—world, and his desire to regain lost land and customs. These notes are very angry and often draw on legends from his people.

Katsuk himself draws on the power of legendary spirits such as Soul Catcher, the powerful spirit that possesses him, and Raven, who helps him to hide both him and David from helicopters and search parties. Throughout the story, he prays to many of these spirits, as well as to Alkuntam, the supreme god of his people. After David has his own spirit dream, Katsuk suggests that he pray to Alkuntam. The spirits are both a source of strength and anguish for Katsuk, who faces the internal struggle that results from his beliefs. Katsuk sees a spirit inside David and believes they are engaged in a battle. When Katsuk becomes sick, he thinks that David has infected him with Cedar sickness by encouraging Katsuk to make an arrow from a cedar tree. He also relies on the strength of his spirits to kill a hiker, who could expose their location. Katsuk and his captive eventually form a relationship, which Katsuk sees as a spiritual link. When Katsuk is sick, David takes care of him, and when he gets better, Katsuk thinks that Soul Catcher is helping David's spirit guide the boy to his destiny. When David speaks to him, he starts to hear a hidden meaning, which eventually leads to his belief that David is asking for death, a necessary prerequisite to this traditional sacrifice. Because of this, Katsuk kills David in a ritual sacrifice, with a special bow and arrow that he has made. When David dies, his connection to the spirit world is closed, and Katsuk is just a man again. He is proud of David for his sacrifice and chants a friend's death song for him.

Hobuhet-Katsuk

See Charles Hobuhet

Hoquat

See David Morgenstern Marshall

Agent Norman Hosbig

Special Agent Norman Hosbig of the FBI's Seattle office is the agent assigned to lead the search for Hobuhet and David. He mistakenly believes that Hobuhet has taken David underground in the city and as a result does not concentrate all of his men in the forest. He thinks that Hobuhet is insane and ignores the sacrifice references in Hobuhet's notes, treating David's capture as a standard kidnapping.

Janiktaht

Janiktaht is Hobuhet's sister, whose rape by white loggers and subsequent suicide spark Hobuhet's madness, which in turn leads to his possession by Soul Catcher. Hobuhet has raised Janiktaht in the absence of their deceased parents and loves her very much.

Katsuk

See Charles Hobuhet

Mary Kletnik

Mary Kletnik, also known by her tribal name of Tskanay, is a young Native American who tries to spoil Hobuhet's plans for sacrifice. Tskanay is Hobuhet's ex-girlfriend, and she had hoped to marry him. She is upset when she sees that Hobuhet is too far gone to get married and tries to help David escape. She becomes even angrier when her attempt to steal David's innocence by stealing his virginity—which she thinks will make David an impure sacrifice—does not work. Although she is very Americanized and does not believe in the spirit world anymore, she starts to believe when Hobuhet demonstrates his power.

David Morgenstern Marshall

David Morgenstern Marshall is the thirteen-year-old kidnap victim, who gets ritually murdered by Charles Hobuhet-Katsuk. In the beginning, David is excited about going to the exclusive Six Rivers Camp, where he hopes to see real Indians and learn survival skills. He gets more than he bargains for, when his status as the son of a powerful politician makes him the target of Charles Hobuhet, one of the camp counselors. Hobuhet lures David out of his bunk one night and takes him into the woods, where he makes David call him Katsuk and where he gives David the name Hoquat—the same word that Hobuhet's ancestors used to describe David's ancestors. David tries many times to attract the attention of rescuers or to escape, but it is no use. He is constantly thwarted by the ravens that are summoned by Katsuk's power.

Katsuk chose David for his innocence, something that he demonstrates both in the simplicity in his letters home to his parents and in his conversations with Katsuk. Katsuk tells him in the beginning that he is going to kill David as a sacrifice to even the score between whites and Native Americans, but as they develop a relationship, David thinks that maybe he will survive. At one point, Katsuk tells David that he will not kill him unless David asks him to, and David feels even safer. David feels guilty over the way that his ancestors have treated Katsuk's ancestors, a feeling that is magnified after Tskanay talks him into having sex with her, in an attempt to destroy his innocence. However, this act only binds David to Katsuk more tightly. It is this connection that makes it easier for Katsuk to find David when he escapes. It also prevents David from leaving when he has the chance—instead staying to nurse Katsuk through his sickness. When David hears the search party coming for him, he is worried for Katsuk's safety. In his attempt to help Katsuk escape, he unwittingly gives Katsuk permission to kill him. His last thoughts before he dies are of shock and betrayal.

Mr. Howard Marshall

Mr. Howard Marshall is the newly appointed United States Undersecretary of State, a status that leads to Hobuhet's kidnapping and sacrifice of his son, David.

Mrs. Marshall

Mrs. Marshall is David's mother, who is worried about him bringing a knife to Six Rivers Camp; this is the same knife that Hobuhet uses to kill Vince Debay.

Old Ish

Old Ish is Hobuhet's great uncle on his father's side, and he is one of few who try to stop Hobuhet. After Ish and his people sing in the forest to lead Hobuhet to them, he tries to raise his rifle at Hobuhet but is too scared by the spirit he senses in Hobuhet, which he correctly identifies as Soul Catcher.

Sheriff Mike Pallatt

Sheriff Mike Pallatt is the head of the local law enforcement and leads the search party that finds Hobuhet and David. Pallatt knows about Janiktaht's rape and realizes that this is what caused Hobuhet to go mad. Unlike Agent Hosbig, Pallatt must make do with a very small search party, which he concentrates on the uncharted wilderness area. Pallatt is angry that the news media has pitted him against Hosbig by saying there is a battle to see who will get credit for the case. Pallatt says that his first concern is saving David, and Hobuhet, if he can. In order to do this, he and his deputy camp without a fire so that Hobuhet will not know they are coming. However, it is not until David makes a fire while Hobuhet is sick that Pallat finds their location. Shortly thereafter, Pallatt and a large search party find Hobuhet with a dead David in his arms.

Mrs. Parma

Mrs. Parma is the Marshalls' servant, a woman from India who makes David very uneasy. Before he leaves for camp, David wonders if his "Indian" counselors will look like Mrs. Parma.

Ranger William Redek

Chief Park Ranger William Redek provides the news media with information about the difficulty of the search and the potential dangerous effects from being in the cold weather.

Tskanay

See Mary Kletnik

Themes

Mistreatment of Native Americans

In *Soul Catcher*, Katsuk and others make some very overt references to the struggle between Native Americans and white people in the past. This is his stated reason for sacrificing David: "I want your world to understand something. That an innocent from your people can die just as other innocents have died." Through his captivity, David, an American boy who knows nothing about Native Americans before he goes to camp, learns more than he wishes about the treatment his ancestors have given Native Americans: "His people had stolen this land. He knew Katsuk was speaking the truth. . . . He had even sinned as his ancestors had, with a woman of these people." Katsuk also notes other ways in which early Americans mistreated his

people, such as giving them blankets infested with smallpox: "You hoquat have used sickness blankets on us before." The knowledge of these offenses against Native Americans weighs him down: "David felt himself hostage for all the sins of his kind." Even Sheriff Pallatt, who heads one of the search parties, acknowledges the bad treatment that Native Americans have received at the hands of whites: "This is what comes of sending an Indian to college. He studies how we've been giving his people the s—ty end of the stick. Something happens . . . he reverts to savage."

Native-American Religion

Native-American religion is another key concept in the book. As Katsuk demonstrates, Native-American religion is rooted in respect for nature, which provides the way of life for his people. Throughout the book, Katsuk prays to various spirits, many of which represent natural forces. For example, Raven, named for the birds he commands, serves as a guardian to Katsuk, protecting Katsuk and David from sight when helicopters fly by, as Katsuk proves to David: "The helicopter was high but in plain sight. . . . An occupant would only have to glance this way to see two figures on the high rock escarpment." However, the helicopter does not see them. Shortly after the helicopter flies away, David sees why, when "a single raven flew over the rock where David lay, then another, another."

Katsuk also acknowledges his reliance on other aspects of nature, such as when he prays to Fish, the spirit who controls fish, for forgiveness, when he kills a fish for him and David to eat. The spirits also plague Katsuk, as when he gets sick and attributes it to Cedar sickness, which he believes he has gotten from not praying enough to Cedar. Not all spirits are based in nature. Soul Catcher, the powerful spirit that possesses Katsuk, does not have any specific correspondent in nature. However, when Soul Catcher possesses Katsuk, he does it through the stinger of a bee, another symbol of nature. Even those Native Americans in the story who do not actively practice their religion often remain respectful. When Katsuk walks into the camp of his great uncle, Ish, and his ex-girlfriend, Tskanay, Ish realizes that Katsuk has been possessed and backs down from trying to stop Katsuk: "Don't catch me going up against a real spirit. Soul Catcher's got that one."

Sacrifice

Katsuk lets the outside world know in one of his notes that "I take an innocent of your people to sacrifice for all of the innocents you have murdered. . . . Thus will sky and earth balance." In the beginning, Katsuk reinforces, both to himself and the outside world, that this sacrifice is symbolic in nature. However, occasionally, his thoughts slip to the rape of his sister and her subsequent suicide, at which points the sacrifice becomes a revenge killing. And eventually, the two become one and the same, as he equates his sister's death with all of his ancestors' deaths. Katsuk blames the need for the sacrifice directly on the loggers who raped his sister: "They had killed Janiktaht. . . . They had killed Vince, growing cold up there on the trail. . . . All killed by those drunken hoquat." Katsuk further notes that although Vince's death is not a large enough sacrifice to send a message and even the score, he will still serve as "a preliminary sacrifice, one to mark the way."

Survival

As David becomes a captive of Katsuk in the forest, he starts to learn the Native-American methods of survival. Katsuk notices the change early on: "When it was time to drink, he drank. Hunger came upon him in its proper order. The spirit of the wilderness had seeped into him." After a week with Katsuk, David knows that grubs are "juicy and sweet" and is not above looking inside a stump and "searching for grubs in the rotten wood" when he is hungry. In modern society, eating grubs is not necessary or in many places acceptable. It is David's ability to cast off these modern ways that help him to survive. Likewise, when David escapes from Katsuk and spends a night on his own, he uses the techniques that Katsuk has shown him to make a fire for his shelter:

> With a slab of cedar notched by pounding with a stone, with a shoestring bow to drive the tinder stick, with pitch and cedar splinters, ready at hand, he persisted until he had a coal, then gently blew the coal into flame which he fed with pitch and cedar.

Innocence

Katsuk makes it known to everybody—his people, David, and the outside world—that David must be an innocent to make a proper sacrifice. There are several points in the story when the boy's innocence is threatened. When Katsuk kills the hiker, he sees David's terror over realizing that he will be next: "Hoquat must not let this awareness rise into his consciousness. He must know it while denying it. Too much terror could destroy innocence." Later, as David starts to adapt to his circumstances and gain appreciation for Hobuhet's

Topics for Further Study

- Research the American Indian Movement, which began in the late 1960s, and write a short biography about one of the movement's principal leaders, focusing on this person's background, beliefs, and societal goals. Compare these with the background, beliefs, and societal goals of Charles Hobuhet-Katsuk in the novel.

- In the novel, David Marshall comes to enjoy the types of food that his Native American captor eats. Research other types of traditional foods that Native Americans ate before the arrival of Europeans and compare these foods to the types of foods that Native Americans eat today. How has the changing physical, cultural, and social environment over the last several hundred years affected the way that Native Americans get and prepare their food?

- Research any one of the historical battles between the United States military and a Native-American tribe. Outline the causes of the conflict and the outcome of the battle. Using this information, write one journal entry from the perspective of a Native-American brave and one from the perspective of a United States soldier, the night before the battle begins.

- Living on reservations is one of the few ways in which Native Americans can preserve their traditional way of life in the United States today. However, reservations are also plagued by high rates of alcoholism, gambling, and other problems. Research the history of reservations and discuss how and where these problems first began to arise, as well as any current efforts that are underway to address these issues.

- Throughout the story, Herbert employs a number of fake news stories that comment on the action. However, there is no news story at the end, after Hobuhet-Katsuk has killed David. Write a fake news story that could have gone at the end of the novel, which comments on this ritual sacrifice of David and the reactions that it produces in the community.

way of life, he realizes that Katsuk has eaten a spirit and is surprised by this Native American way of thinking: "David sat up, wondered at such thoughts coming all unbidden into his mind. Those were not the thoughts of childhood." However, though he is beginning to have more adult thoughts, they are not enough to spoil his innocence. Even when Tskanay seduces him, the act of sex is not enough to spoil his innocence, because he feels shame, a quality of innocence. Also, as Katsuk notes to Tskanay when David tries to protect her from being hurt, "You tried to use him against me ... and he still doesn't want you hurt. Is that not innocence?"

Captor/Captive Relationships

When David is kidnapped, Katsuk lures David outside by telling him that they are going to do "a ceremony of spirit brotherhood." When David realizes that he has been kidnapped by Katsuk, he is terrified: "All the horror stories he'd heard about murdered kidnap victims flooded into his mind, set his body jerking with terror." However, as they make their way through the forest, captor and captive start to develop a relationship, and David begins to lose his fear of being killed. In fact, Katsuk feels "a bond being created between himself and this boy," and wonders if it is possible that they "were really brothers" in the spirit world. Although Katsuk feels it is a spiritual bond, relationships between captor and captive have been known to blossom into something resembling friendship. This bond is strengthened to the point where, when David has a chance to escape, he chooses instead to help nurse Katsuk back to health: "I couldn't just leave you. You were sick." When the search party is almost there, David tries desperately to get Katsuk to run and says that if they catch him, "I'll tell 'em I came of my own free will," even though he has not.

Style

Setting

The state of Washington setting is crucial to the story, as it provides a realistic venue for David's kidnapping. Six Rivers Camp is poised on the edge of a huge, uncharted wilderness. Even Chief Park Ranger William Redek notes the difficulty of finding somebody in this area: "we know there are at least six small aircraft crashed somewhere in there. We've never found them. . . . And those aircraft aren't actively trying to hide from us." Besides be-

ing big and secluded, the forest is also the place where Katsuk's powers are their strongest, which he notes when he says that he is not afraid of the search helicopters: "All that lived wild around him helped and guarded him. The new voice of the wilderness spoke to him through every creature, every leaf and rock." For David, the setting is a challenge and provides an appropriate background for his change. In the beginning, he feels that the forest is a place that is "so utterly foreign to the sounds, sights and smells of his usual life that he tried to recall things from other times which would fit here." However, it is only when he begins to work with the forest, not against it, that David learns how to survive, and he matures, gaining a new respect for the Native-American way of life.

Exposition

In the beginning of the novel, Herbert uses several mini chapters that include news stories, statements, and notes from Katsuk. This is a very overt style of exposition—the process by which readers gain information they need to understand the story. This blatant exposition prepares readers for the story they are about to hear. However, when the actual plot progresses and the reader is drawn into the events in the forest with David and Katsuk, the exposition is more subtle. Herbert still uses mini chapters, but now they serve to pull readers out of the story, letting them know: what is going on with the search for David, Katsuk's philosophies, and the views of Katsuk by other people. These outside perspectives do not prepare readers for the story, but they do enhance their reading of it.

Suspense

In the beginning of the story, Herbert gives several different accounts of the kidnapping and then goes back to the events leading up to it. At this point, Herbert is invoking a sense of dread in his readers, who know what is coming. After this point, however, Herbert changes dread for suspense, as he leads readers along, making them guess whether David will live or die. When Katsuk is successful in hiding them from the helicopters by calling on Raven, David starts to realize that Katsuk's powers are for real: "He had the eerie sensation that the birds had spoken to Katsuk in some private way." As a result, David starts to lose hope. However, shortly after this, David makes his first escape attempt, giving both him and the reader some hope that he may survive: "He was running all out now. There was nothing left to do but run." David's escape attempt is cut short when Katsuk comes out of nowhere, catching "the running boy in full stride." The boy's hopes, like the reader's are dashed, at least for now.

Throughout the rest of the story, Herbert employs many more events like this to raise readers' hopes up and send them crashing down. This uncertainty becomes very suspenseful, as Herbert makes it unclear what the outcome is going to be. Katsuk's people try to stand up to him but fail. Tskanay tries to render David an impure sacrifice by sleeping with him—"You're a man now, not a little innocent Katsuk can push around"—but the act only binds him tighter to Katsuk. The ultimate moment of suspense comes at the end of the story, when David can hear the search party coming and thinks he is going home. He tries to encourage Katsuk to leave before the search party catches him, and Katsuk takes the boy's language to mean that he is asking to be sacrificed. For readers, it becomes a race to see if David will be killed by Katsuk or saved by the search party, whose flashlights can be seen "coming through the trees across the river." The slowness of Katsuk's actions increases the suspense of the moment: "Katsuk faded back in the shadows . . . set the bowstring . . . nocked the arrow . . . drew the bow taught . . . released the arrow." These actions take place at an excruciatingly slow pace over a few paragraphs, and it is only when the arrow flies "into the boy's chest," killing him, that the suspense Herbert has built up throughout the novel is finally broken.

Historical Context

American Indian Movement (AIM)

In the late 1960s, Native Americans in both Canada and the United States, reacting to centuries of oppression and mistreatment by whites, began to organize and protest in many isolated regional events, and in 1968 four men established the American Indian Movement (AIM). However, as Vine Deloria, Jr. noted in his book *God is Red: A Native View of Religion*, these smaller events "inspired Indians across the continent to defend their rights, but what was needed was some national symbol, a rallying point, that could launch a national movement." In 1969, Native Americans got their wish. After a convention in San Francisco to discuss Native-American issues, the Indian center where tribal representatives were meeting caught fire and burned to the ground. Realizing that there

were no government funds to build a new Indian center, a group of Native Americans, supported by AIM and calling themselves the Indians of All Tribes, seized Alcatraz, the infamous island-based prison, which had lain empty since 1964, and demanded that the government give them leave to turn the defunct prison into a cultural-educational center.

The majority of the group was university students, like Charles Hobuhet in the novel. In fact, in *Soul Catcher*, Special Agent Hosbig of the FBI mentions that Hobuhet is "a university student" and then ties this into the Alcatraz event: "we've reason to believe he was an Indian militant. He's going to demand that we cede . . . Alcatraz or set up an independent Indian Territory somewhere else." In a statement issued from the Indians of All Tribes in February 1970, they said that they had learned that "violence breeds only more violence" and that because of this, they had "carried on our occupation of Alcatraz in a peaceful manner, hoping that the government will act accordingly." With nationally recognized protests like Alcatraz, the American Indian Movement (AIM) picked up speed.

Native Americans in Higher Education

In the book, Herbert indicates that it was the wish of Hobuhet's people that he get an education. When Katsuk meets his people in the forest, he informs the old man, Ish, that he is there to "show them that my spirit is all powerful." This is not what Ish had hoped for, however: "The old man sighed, said: 'That sure . . . isn't why we sent you to the university.'"

One of the ways in which Native Americans tried to adapt to life in the United States in the twentieth century was by attending American universities. They were aided in this attempt by government programs such as the Higher Education Grant Program, established by the Bureau of Indian Affairs in 1948 to provide educational grants to Native Americans. By 1972, nearly 12,500 Native-American students were receiving $15 million in educational funds. However, like Hobuhet, not all Native Americans wanted to learn in American universities, for fear of losing their heritage. As the Indians of All Tribes noted in their statement, "One of the reasons we took Alcatraz was because the students were having problems in the universities and colleges they were attending . . . . We wanted our own Indian university, so that they would stop whitewashing Indians."

Compare
&
Contrast

- **1970s:** Aided by events like the seizure of Alcatraz, the American Indian Movement gains national recognition. Many Americans, newly aware of growing Native-American activism, initially advocate forced assimilation.

  Today: Through the continued efforts of organizations like the Women of All Red Nations (WARN) and a renaissance in Native-American art and literature, the issues of Native Americans are given more exposure and sympathy.

- **1970s:** Some Native Americans, especially those who are older, choose not to join the American Indian Movement, having gotten used to an American way of life, often on a reservation.

Today: While some Native Americans still live on reservations and try to preserve their heritage, others live in modern suburbs and work in a variety of professional and skilled American trades.

- **1970s:** Hippies and other members of the counterculture glorify nature and a natural way of life, which they see as an escape from corporate America and other areas of the establishment.

  Today: Overworked Americans in corporate America often get away from their hectic lives by taking vacations to natural areas, in some cases taking part in survival camps or other nature programs that teach them how to live off the land.

Native-American Women's Groups

Several groups provided support during the American Indian Movement. Two of the most effective groups were the North American Indian Women's Association (NAIWA), founded in 1970, and the Women of All Red Nations (WARN), founded in 1974. The NAIWA was sponsored by the United States Bureau of Indian Affairs (BIA), and its main goal is exposure for Native-American women across the country, as well as improving communication at both the personal and tribal levels.

WARN, on the other hand, has a slightly different history. Because Native-American women were largely ignored by outsiders—who mainly punished men during the American Indian Movement—the women took the opportunity to band together for their own causes. WARN was founded to address issues among Native-American women, including ending violence against women and increasing educational opportunities. WARN also works with other women's organizations to help improve life for all minority women and provides support on general Native-American issues such as protecting Native-American land and government.

Hippies and Rebellion

In the novel, Katsuk runs into Vince Debay, a hippie, while Debay is hiking through the forest. Debay's hippie status is identified by his "long hair" and by the marijuana that he offers to Katsuk. In his essay, "Youth Protest and the Counterculture," Timothy Miller notes some of the different types of hippies in the 1960s and early 1970s: "Some hippies were escapists who simply favored withdrawal from the prevailing culture; others proposed much more active opposition." Given Debay's easygoing, laid-back attitude, he seems to belong to the former group. In either case, Katsuk is not impressed by Debay's form of protest, as he notes after he has killed the hiker: "Vince had judged his own people harshly, had shared the petty rebellions of his time." Katsuk calls these rebellions, "petty," because they pale in comparison to the type of protest that Katsuk is performing.

Environmentalism

As in other Herbert novels, *Soul Catcher* emphasizes ecological, or environmental, preservation. In the novel, this idea is expressed through the

Native-American way of life, certain aspects which David Marshall becomes used to, and even begins to enjoy, during his captivity. At the time the novel was written, environmental preservation was a hot topic. In 1970, two years before the book was published, President Nixon founded the Environmental Protection Agency (EPA), in large part due to the failure of existing environmental protection laws. Although their duties would eventually encompass a wide range of environmental issues, the EPA's first task was to administer the 1970 Clean Air Act, which sought to reduce air pollution from motor vehicles. As a result of the EPA's efforts, automobile manufacturers began to install catalytic converters in their vehicles, which significantly reduced air-pollution emissions in the next two decades.

Critical Overview

Herbert is a hugely popular author, mainly due to the success of his second novel, *Dune*. *Soul Catcher*, on the other hand, is almost a non-event as far as critical and popular readers are concerned. Published in 1972, the book has since fallen out of print. However, even when it was in print, the book received very little critical attention. In 1974, G. Robert Carlsen notes in the *English Journal*, that the "book builds with spellbinding intensity" and that it is a "moving story." However, while Carlsen also briefly discusses some of the plot elements, in general, one searches in vain for anything more than a line or two about the book. Even in these cases, the book is sometimes talked about for what it is *not*, rather than for what it is. Take, for example, the comment by David M. Miller, in his 1980 book, *Frank Herbert*: "*Soul Catcher* is neither science fiction nor fantasy."

In his entry on Herbert in *Science Fiction Writers*, Willis E. McNelly notes that the book's non-science-fiction status "both puzzled and irritated many" early reviewers. McNelly further notes that, while the book "contains many of Herbert's customary technical devices and is really quite similar to his science fiction," early critics still had difficulty "addressing" the novel, and as a result, "initial reviews of the novel were mixed." Herbert is famous for his science fiction novels with fantastic elements, like *Dune*, so novels that fall into other categories, like *Soul Catcher*, were not widely acknowledged because they deviated from Herbert's style.

Member of the American Indian Movement (AIM) addresses a crowd during the seventies

The lack of critical attention and support could also be due to the fact that it is "a novel about the American Indian," which is all Don D'Ammassa had to say about the book in his 1986 Herbert overview article in *Science Fiction Chronicle*. Of course, the Native-American theme alone would not necessarily prevent the book from being reviewed. In fact, for the past few decades, works about Native-American culture have become increasingly popular. As historian Wilcomb E. Washburn noted in his chapter in *The Cambridge History of the American Peoples, Volume 1: North America, Part 2*, this literary renaissance in Native-American writing began around the same time as the American Indian Movement: "For purposes of emphasis the year 1969 can mark the formal recognition of this phenomenon in the United States." As Washburn says, this was the year that Scott Momaday, "an Indian and professor of English at Stanford University, received the Pulitzer Prize for his novel *House Made of Dawn*."

However, Momaday, and the other popular authors of Native-American literature who followed in his footsteps, has something that Herbert did not—a Native-American heritage. Although Herbert's book champions the Native-American cause, Herbert does not share the background of these other authors. This fact, when coupled with Herbert's overwhelming success in a different genre, may have caused many critics to pass over *Soul Catcher*. McNelly notes, however, that this fact may change in the future and that maybe the book "has yet to achieve the preeminence that a few readers have claimed for it. It is perhaps still seeking its audience."

Criticism

Ryan D. Poquette

Poquette has a bachelor's degree in English and specializes in writing about literature. In the following essay, Poquette examines the reasons why Herbert uses a disjointed narrative in his novel.

Soul Catcher is a shocking story, which grabs the reader on page one and does not let go until its tragic conclusion. Through the characters of Charles Hobuhet-Katsuk and David Marshall, the reader is drawn into a captor-captive tale, in which the captor is hard to hate and the captive is easy to love. In fact, throughout the story, the two develop a relationship that makes the ending even harder to bear. The book has many contradictions, from the modern helicopters that search in the primitive wilderness to the conflicting attitudes toward the characters. The biggest contradiction, however, is Herbert's use of a disjointed narrative, which he uses to complement the action and add to the characterization.

From the very beginning of the novel, readers realize that there is something different about this book from most other books. The first chapter is only a few paragraphs long—a mini chapter—and is followed by three more chapters that are about the same length. With the exception of the first mini chapter, which narrates Howard Marshall's reaction when he finds out his son, David, has been kidnapped, the other three chapters consist entirely of public statements, news stories, and notes about David's kidnapping, which has already happened at this point. Starting with the fifth chapter, which begins with the sentence, "On the day he was to leave for camp, David Marshall had awakened early," Herbert jumps to the past, before David has been kidnapped, and begins to tell the actual story, in chapters that are usually much longer. Herbert jumps between the mini chapters and normal chapters throughout the rest of the book, in most places

alternating one mini chapter with one normal chapter. It is a very obvious technique that Herbert is using, so the reader knows that the author must have good reasons for using it. In fact, this is a common narrative style for Herbert. In this story, he uses it to comment on the action and add to the novel's characterization.

In their entry on Herbert for *Dictionary of Literary Biography*, Robert A. Foster and Thomas L. Wyner note the fact that "Herbert usually employs a fragmented narrative structure, in which relatively brief episodes are introduced by quotations from invented works." On a similar note, in his entry on Herbert for *Science Fiction Writers*, Willis E. McNelly says that the novel "contains many of Herbert's customary technical devices."

As in other Herbert novels, the mini chapter is often used to comment directly on the episode that follows it, as in an example near the beginning of the novel, when a news story reports that the grief-stricken "mother of the kidnap victim arrived at Six Rivers Camp . . . yesterday." This contrasts with the episode that directly follows this mini chapter, which describes the conversation between David and his mother on the morning that he is to leave for Six Rivers Camp. His mother is worried about the knife that David's father has gotten him, even though David tells her he needs it "to cut things, carve wood, stuff like that." His mother is unconvinced, but eventually she relents and lets him take the knife. However, she transfers her dislike for the knife to the camp itself, calling the camp "awful." For the reader, this is a powerful contrast, seeing the mother arrive at the camp where David has been kidnapped and then flashing back to her discussion with David, in which the reader sees her hesitation in letting David go to this "awful" camp.

However, in other cases, the mini chapters also serve to complement the action by "setting up" information that does not ultimately "pay off" until later in the novel. The best example of this also takes place near the beginning of the novel, in the mini chapter where Katsuk announces to his people that he has "done all the things correctly." He goes into detail about the items he has used on the "sacrificial victim," including the "consecrated down of a sea duck." He says that "It was all done in the proper way." In a normal novel, these confessions would serve as a clear foreshadowing of David's death and would tip the reader off to this fact. However, because Herbert is using such a disjointed narrative style and jumps around in his use of time, as he did in the beginning of the book, only the most perceptive readers will recognize that the author is using the past tense, "done," implying that the sacrificial act has already taken place at the time that Katsuk makes this announcement.

In the next chapter, when Katsuk and David stand upon a trail, Katsuk opens his pouch and removes "a pinch of the consecrated white duck down." He thinks to himself that "It must be done correctly" and uses the down to write his name upon the earth, a necessary prerequisite to David's sacrifice. In this way, as in the previous example with David's mother, the mini chapter comments on the episode that follows it. However, unlike the reference to David's mother, which does not appear again in the book, the duck down is referenced again in a few more places. But it is only at the very end of the book that the mini chapter pays off in the reader's mind. In the final scene, the suspense of the book reaches its height as the reader wonders if Sheriff Pallat and his search party can save David from being sacrificed. After David is killed and the suspense is broken, Herbert offers one final detail in the last line of the book. At this point, Katsuk is sitting with "Hoquat's body in his arms," while "The white down of sea ducks floated in the damp air all around them." This line links back to the mini chapter at the beginning of the novel, in which Katsuk lets his people know that everything "was done in the proper way."

Herbert also uses the mini-chapter commentaries in one other way. Foster and Wyner note that Herbert generally uses a fractured narrative because he is "Less concerned with plot and characterization than with setting and ideas." However, in *Soul Catcher*, Herbert deviates from this practice somewhat, because he puts as much emphasis on characterization as the other aspects. The characterization, however, is developed in two ways. First, readers learn aspects of Hobuhet-Katsuk's and David's characters as they follow the two characters on their journey, through the longer episode chapters. This is the normal way that readers learn about their characters, through the actual story itself.

However, in *Soul Catcher*, Herbert uses the mini chapters to introduce many characters that are not found in the actual narrative. In a normal disjointed narrative of this size, these extra characters would decrease readers' understanding of the characters, since they would steal attention away from the two main characters and force the reader to think about other characters, other subplots. But in this book, there is very little information given

> If Hobuhet-Katsuk were depicted only as a crazy person or a lawless militant, the author would be leading his readers to choose one of these ideas as their viewpoint. Instead, Herbert does not give any easy outs."

about these additional characters, which are generally used for the sole purpose of offering outside perspectives of either David or Hobuhet-Katsuk. As a result, the outside world remains very distant, and the reader is forced to focus on David and his captor, who become the two most prominent characters.

Sometimes, these additional characters offer contradictory perspectives. This is true for Hobuhet-Katsuk. For example, in one of the first mini chapters, Dr. Tilman Barth, Hobuhet-Katsuk's old professor, is introduced. "I find this whole thing incredible," says Dr. Barth. "Charles Hobuhet cannot be the mad killer you make him out to be. It's impossible." Dr. Barth's other mini chapter statements also involve Hobuhet-Katsuk and, in fact, serve as some of the few positive views of David's captor. Likewise, Sheriff Pallatt notes in a mini chapter that Charlie's sister was a "good kid" and that Hobuhet has "raised her almost by himself" since their parents died. For this reason, Pallatt is sympathetic about the sister's rape and subsequent suicide, saying that "I'm not surprised Charlie went off his nut." Later on, in another mini chapter, Pallatt also expresses his desire to help Hobuhet: "All I want is to save that kid—and the Indian, if I can."

These positive, or at least supportive, views are important to the narrative, especially since most other statements in the mini chapters are negative. David's father says: "Our Indians were well treated. . . . The man who took David must be insane." Likewise, FBI agent, Norman Hosbig, is cold and stereotypical. Hosbig believes that Hobuhet is either "mentally deranged" or "pretending insanity." He also refuses to believe that the note Hobuhet-Katsuk left was anything but a "ransom note" and sticks doggedly to his idea that

Hobuhet is an "Indian militant" who is going to demand "an independent Indian territory" in exchange for David. This is all that Hosbig knows from his experience. The contradictory viewpoints are intended on Herbert's part. If Hobuhet-Katsuk were depicted only as a crazy person or a lawless militant, the author would be leading his readers to choose one of these ideas as their viewpoint. Instead, Herbert does not give any easy outs. Readers must read all of the accounts of Hobuhet-Katsuk, from both himself and others, and make a decision for themselves as to whether he is evil for his actions.

When it comes to David, however, Herbert does lead the reader into a decisive judgment. David is the good innocent, plain and simple. This is shown in the main narrative, with the way David handles himself during the kidnapping. He feels ashamed at his ancestors' actions, he is embarrassed when he has sex with Tskanay, and he chooses to stay and help Hobuhet-Katsuk get better, even when he has a chance to flee. This characterization of David is strengthened through the depictions of David in the mini chapters. In David's letter home from camp, he uses the short, journalistic-style sentences that an innocent child uses to describe something to someone, in this case his parents: "I am having a lot of fun.... A man from camp met me there. We got on a small bus. The bus drove for a long time. It rained." These short sentences are free from any pretensions or ornamentation whatsoever. They are simply the writings of an innocent who writes about what he sees. Likewise, David's teacher says, "He's a very good student, considerably ahead of most in his form. . . . David is very sensitive . . . the way he studies things." Herbert uses these mini chapters to underscore the pure goodness and innocence of David. With this picture of David in mind, the sacrifice at the end becomes even more painful and tragic.

In the end, Herbert inspires an extreme feeling of uneasiness in the reader, who has just witnessed the horrible death of a true innocent. By contradicting his entire narrative with a second narrative thread, which exists in mini chapters that break up the main narrative, Herbert helps to underscore the fact that the issues surrounding Native Americans are complex, a little chaotic, and not easily solved.

Source: Ryan D. Poquette, Critical Essay on *Soul Catcher*, in *Novels for Students*, The Gale Group, 2003.

Paul Witcover

Witcover is an editor and writer whose fiction and critical essays appear regularly in magazines and online. In the following essay, Witcover discusses myth and religion in Frank Herbert's novel Soul Catcher.

Frank Herbert is justly famed as the author of one of the greatest science fiction epics ever written, the classic *Dune* series. The most popular and successful book in this series was the first, also called *Dune*, but readers who stop there, with the thrilling victory of Paul Atreides, a.k.a. Muad'Dib, over his evil enemies, thus fulfilling the ancient messianic prophecies of the Fremen of his adopted planet, Arrakis, and the secret genetic engineering program of the Bene Gesserit order, miss an extraordinary reversal of fortune for the immensely likeable young hero. In the next two novels, *Dune Messiah* and *Children of Dune*, Herbert boldly and systematically traces Paul's downward path from liberator/messiah to hated tyrant to blinded outcast to mad prophet while simultaneously presenting the journey of his son, Leto, in the opposite direction, with the son not only becoming a more absolute tyrant than his father ever was but finally renouncing his humanity in favor of a monstrous godhood from which Paul had recoiled in horror.

Many readers of *Dune*—who, as Herbert fully intended, had become deeply attached to the charismatic and sympathetic figure of Muad'Dib—recoiled in a kind of horror themselves from the fate to which Herbert subjected him. As critic Timothy O'Reilly notes in his book *Frank Herbert*:

> In the *Dune* trilogy, Herbert portrays a hero as convincing, noble, and inspiring as any real or mythic hero of the past. But as the trilogy progresses, he shows the consequences of heroic leadership for Paul, his followers, and the planet. Anyone devoted to the heroic ideal is apt to be devastated by the conclusion of the trilogy.

The extremity of changes that Herbert puts his characters—and readers—through in the course of these books is very much a conscious choice: a recurring theme in all his work is the inevitability of change and the desirability of aligning oneself and one's culture as far as possible with the inevitable forces of change rather than seeking either to hold them back or to rigidly control them; either of these choices, in Herbert's fiction, is likely to unleash destructive forces on both the personal and cultural level. The virtue Herbert holds highest is that of awareness or consciousness (not to be confused with sheer intelligence); characters like Paul demonstrate a level of consciousness far above and beyond that of normal human beings. This hyper-consciousness is almost always marked by the abil-ity to simultaneously perceive multiple realities or interpretations of reality, which, in its highest form, includes the ability to enter empathetically into the experiences and mindsets of others. As a result, ei-ther willingly or reluctantly, these hyperconscious characters, who often walk a fine line between tran-scendent genius and madness and who remain, de-spite all their advantages, fallible human beings, tend to become powerful leaders, messiah figures to their people. Yet in the process, they unleash forces they cannot control and that seek to control them and that often succeed in doing so in whole or in part. In an interview with *Vertex* magazine, Herbert spoke of the *Dune* series as "a treatment of the messianic impulse in human society" and compared that society, in a characteristic metaphor, to a living organism. Seen in this way, a messiah figure like Paul Muad'Dib is either a virus or a ge-netic mutation in the larger organism. Both can be spurs to healing, adaptation, and evolution. Both can also be fatal.

A dynamic of fiercely contending interests is the norm in Herbert's fictional ecologies. His aim as a writer is not to resolve these conflicts or even judge between them but to compel his readers to evaluate for themselves and make up their own minds. Herbert is not an overtly moralistic writer; he generally does not tell his readers what to think or feel. This is not to say that he doesn't have an opinion or preference himself for solutions to the complex moral, psychological, and emotional situ-ations he presents in his books. On the contrary, but, in keeping with his training as a journalist, Her-bert presents the complexities as objectively as pos-sible, without stacking the deck, then trusts the reader to make an informed choice. A judgment is expected, but it is the reader's to make. In order to make it, Herbert's readers, like his characters, must raise their consciousness. O'Reilly aptly observes that Herbert's novels are "training manuals for ex-actly the kinds of consciousness they describe."

Of course, it is impossible to be completely ob-jective, especially in such an inherently subjective medium as the novel, and Herbert, despite himself, often does subtly, or not-so-subtly, stack the deck. Indeed, a schematic didacticism may be his great-est weakness as a writer; it is a weakness always lurking in his work, though generally counterbal-anced by depth of characterization, vitality of in-tellect, complexity of plot, and that page-turning quality that is the mark of the most skillful fiction.

> **A dynamic of fiercely contending interests is the norm in Herbert's fictional ecologies. His aim as a writer is not to resolve these conflicts or even judge between them but to compel his readers to evaluate for themselves and make up their own minds."**

Herbert's faith in the intelligence of his readers is rarely shaken, and he seldom fails to follow his fic-tional ideas to their logical conclusions, even when those conclusions are likely to be unpopular or un-pleasant.

This is nowhere truer than in Herbert's novel *Soul Catcher*, where rigorous extrapolation of the initial idea leads to a conclusion so viscerally un-pleasant as to be repugnant. Of the twenty-one nov-els that Herbert published in his career, twenty are science fiction; only *Soul Catcher*—published in 1972, midway between the publication of *Dune Messiah* and *Children of Dune*—falls outside the genre. As critic David M. Miller notes in his book *Frank Herbert*, "*Soul Catcher* is neither science fic-tion nor fantasy"; it is, he adds, "an anomaly in Herbert's canon." Yet in some ways it is the most characteristic novel Herbert ever wrote. Again quoting Miller:

> *Soul Catcher* does not add to Herbert's earlier nov-els in the sense of being something new; rather, it steps away from the buffers and props that assured his success in the world of science fiction.... What remains is essential Herbert, without ploy or pretense.

What is *Soul Catcher* if it is neither science fiction nor fantasy? Is it a realistic novel? It can certainly be read that way. On a purely realistic level, the novel is a thriller/horror story recounting the kidnapping of thirteen-year-old David Mor-genstern Marshall, son of a U.S. Undersecretary of State, by Charles Hobuhet, a graduate student in anthropology, who is also a member of the Quin-ault tribes of northwestern Washington state. After evading his pursuers for two weeks in the wilder-ness, Hobuhet—deranged with grief over the recent suicide of his younger sister, following her brutal rape by a gang of white loggers—ritually murders his innocent captive in revenge not only for her death but for the deaths of all Native Americans killed by whites over the centuries. As Hobuhet states in a note left behind after his abduction of David, "I take an innocent of your people to sacrifice for all of the innocents you have murdered."

In this reading, Hobuhet is either a terrorist or a madman (or both), his aim a horrific conflation of personal revenge and grandiose fantasies of a messianic mission to "create a holy obscenity" and "produce for this world a nightmare they will dream while awake." In other words, Hobuhet murders David for the publicity it will bring to the twin causes of justice for his sister and justice for Native Americans, believing—with that naivete peculiar to children, terrorists, and madmen—that the publicity will somehow bring about meaningful change, waking up Native Americans and white Americans alike, albeit in different ways and to different ends.

But such a reading, while defensible on its own terms, is only part of Herbert's design. A purely realistic interpretation of the novel forecloses any judgment of Hobuhet other than terrorist/madman; it would take a sick or perverse individual to view this Hobuhet, whatever the justice of his cause, as a hero of any kind and the cold-blooded murder of a thirteen-year-old boy as justified in any way. What would be the point or challenge to such a novel for a writer of Herbert's distinctive ambitions and interests? No, just as in the *Dune* series, Herbert has larger aims here, and they lie beyond the borders of realistic fiction, in the mist-shrouded realm of the visionary, that space of altered, higher consciousness that is the birthplace of myth and religion. To fully understand *Soul Catcher*, to earn the right to pronounce informed judgment on Hobuhet and his sacrifice of David, rather than simply condemning both with a knee-jerk reaction, readers must, like prophets or shamen, raise their consciousness enough to cross the borders of the realistic and enter the visionary realm. There the possibility—though not the certainty—exists that Hobuhet is in fact a hero, his sacrifice of David an act of supernatural potency that will bear fruit in the worlds of myth and everyday reality. In order to judge, readers must set aside their normal sympathies and moral standards and entertain these fantastic and morally complex possibilities with an open mind. It is not an easy task, but Herbert will use all his considerable skills as a novelist to make it possible.

Before turning to an examination of the visionary realm and a reading of the novel in those terms, it will be useful to give a brief taste of the cultural climate in which Herbert wrote *Soul Catcher*. The late 1960s and early 1970s saw the rise of the American Indian Movement, or AIM, a Native-American civil rights organization dedicated to both redressing the historical wrongs done to Native Americans by the United States and its racist white power structure and reclaiming the lost and/or stolen cultural heritage of Native-American nations and tribes. In 1972, the same year that *Soul Catcher* appeared, AIM led a march on Washington, D.C., that culminated in the occupation of the Bureau of Indian Affairs. In February 1973, local Sioux activists invited AIM to take command of an occupation of Wounded Knee, South Dakota, site of the last major armed conflict between the United States and Native Americans, a brutal and shameful massacre perpetrated by federal troops in 1890. The 1973 occupation would last seventy-one days and again feature armed conflict between Native Americans and the United States, represented this time by local and federal law enforcement and units of the National Guard, with casualties on both sides. The novel—whose plot of kidnapping and murder must seem all-too-believable to readers in the aftermath of the 2001 World Trade Center attack and the 2002 murder of journalist Daniel Pearl by terrorists in Pakistan—would have seemed more like a cautionary tale to readers in the decade of the 1970s, though by no means an impossible one; in fact, it would have seemed less so with each passing year. The fact that history has given *Soul Catcher* a retrospective verisimilitude very much like the prophetic quality occasionally encountered in (and more frequently ascribed to) science fiction is a striking though deeply lamentable bit of tragic irony.

How does a visionary novel in the sense suggested above differ from a fantasy? If the ritual murder of David is invested with supernatural power, doesn't that mean magic is at work? If so, how does that make Hobuhet any different from a wizard? First of all, there are different types of fantasy novels. Some, like the Harry Potter books of J. K. Rowling, feature an escape from the "real" world into one where the usual physical rules or laws are replaced by magical systems. Others, such as J. R. R. Tolkien's Lord of the Rings, take place in magical worlds that either have no connection to the "real" world whatsoever or a tenuous one only: for example, the fantasy world is set in the distant past (Tolkien) or in the far future (Terry

What Do I Read Next?

- Sherman Alexie's *Reservation Blues* (1996), published by Warner Books, features the story of Coyote Springs, an all-Indian Catholic rock band from the Spokane Reservation in eastern Washington. Mixing Native-American mythology and rock 'n' roll, Alexie depicts the individual struggles of the band members as they embark on a national tour.

- Former professional basketball player Larry Colton spent more than a year on the Crow Reservation in Montana, observing Sharon LaForge and other members of the Hardin High School girls' basketball team. Colton's unflinching story, *Counting Coup: A True Story of Basketball and Honor on the Little Big Horn*, reveals that many social conditions such as alcoholism, drug abuse, and low self-esteem continue to plague reservations—and often act as a barrier to success, athletic or otherwise. The book was published by Warner Books in 2000.

- In the story, David Marshall is kidnapped by a Native American. Although this was a rare occurrence in the late twentieth century when the story takes place, it was more common in the previous two centuries. *Captured by Indians: 15 Firsthand Accounts, 1750–1870*, edited by Frederick Drimmer and published by Dover Publications in 1985, collects some of the firsthand stories from these early American captives.

- Herbert is known worldwide for his epic science fiction novel *Dune*, originally published in 1965, which featured the struggles of young Paul Atreides, a messiah-like duke on the desert planet of Arrakis. After he is overthrown by the previous regime, Atreides is cast into the desert to die and must rely on his inner strength, as well as the knowledge of the native tribe of Fremen, to survive and reclaim his throne. The book was reprinted in a twenty-fifth anniversary edition by Ace Books in 1999.

- In many of his novels, such as *Dune* and *Soul Catcher*, Herbert demonstrated his political, ecological, and philosophical beliefs. In *The Maker of Dune: Insights of a Master of Science Fiction*, published by Berkley Publishing Group in 1987, editor Tim O'Reilly collects several essays from Herbert that elaborate on these beliefs.

- Although the majority of books featuring Native-American issues are by Native Americans, Herbert is not the only nonnative to write about these issues. Another prominent example is Tony Hillerman, who has gathered a wide readership for his mysteries featuring Joe Leaphorn and Jim Chee, two Navajo Tribal Police officers. In *The Ghostway*, originally published in 1984, Chee uses his struggles to decide whether or not to leave the tribal police and the reservation for a position with the FBI. At the same time, he must use both his knowledge of his heritage and police procedures to track down a killer and a missing girl.

- Stephen King's *The Girl Who Loved Tom Gordon* (2000), published by Pocket Books, features elements similar to those found in *Soul Catcher*. In the story, a young girl is separated from her family on a nature trip in Maine and becomes lost in the wilderness. While her family, the police, and others form search parties to try to find her, she survives by learning to live off the nature that surrounds her. Meanwhile, she constantly battles her fear of the supernatural forest monster that hunts her by imagining that her favorite baseball player, Tom Gordon, is there guiding her.

- Native-American storytelling has a long history, rooted in oral tradition. In *Coming to Light: Contemporary Translations of the Native Literatures of North America* (1996), published by Vintage Books, editor Brian Swann collects many of these oral stories, songs, prayers, and orations. Each of the pieces in this large anthology is accompanied by an introduction from the translator, which explains the meaning behind each selection, as well as how it was spoken or sung in its time. The literatures represent more than thirty different cultures, including Inuit, Aleut, Iroquois, Lakota, Navajo, and Zuni.

Brooks's Shannara series); more generally, the connection is a metaphorical one. Such fantasies may be pure escapism, religious or political allegories, satires, works of high and serious art, or admixtures of these things. But whatever they are, they are situated at sharp angles to the "real" world; even in the case of allegories or satires, this sharp divergence, which need not take place at every point as long as it occurs at (at least) one significant point, serves to bring differences and similarities into starker relief. Such is not the case with visionary novels. While the magic in a fantasy novel goes against the structure of the "real" world, operating beyond or outside the normal order, visionary novels reach toward a power that invests the "real" world, though often invisibly and secretly. The presence of this power may be known only to a select few or forgotten by all. This power is not magic but the very basis of reality; thus, visionary novels generally are not set at sharp angles to the "real" world but rather lie over or behind it; they permeate the "real" world at every point, just as God is said to do, and they are no more about magic than is the Bible. It is in this sense that *Soul Catcher* may be thought of as a visionary novel, or, more accurately, as a novel employing visionary strategies. It neither seeks nor offers readers (or its characters) an escape from the "real" world; on the contrary, its goal is to awaken readers (and characters) to the real nature of the "real" world.

Throughout the novel, Herbert calls attention to the interpenetrating layers of the visionary and the real. Every character, every event, exists simultaneously in two worlds, on two levels. Hobuhet takes the name of Katsuk, a Quinault word meaning "the center of the universe"; to David, he gives the name Hoquat, a Quinault word meaning "something that floated far out on the water, something unfamiliar and mysterious." Hobuhet/Katsuk sees himself as occupying, and in many ways as being identical with, the fixed point around which the universe revolves, while David/Hoquat is everything that surrounds him at the limits of his perception. Hoquat is not only the name that Katsuk gives to David, it is the name that the Quinault gave to the first whites who appeared on their shores; thus, the relationship between Hobuhet/Katsuk and David/Hoquat is, in microcosm, the relationship between all Native Americans and whites.

Hobuhet receives his mission from his spirit guide, or Tamanawis, which takes the form of a bee whose sting is the trigger that raises his consciousness to a mystical awareness, evolving him

from the human Hobuhet into the more-than-human shaman/warrior Katsuk, "who will set this world afire." David, too, in the course of his ordeal, comes to recognize the truth of the interpenetration of the worlds of everyday reality and myth:

> There were two problems, or one problem with two shapes. One involved his need to escape from the crazy Indian, to get back with people who were sane and could be understood. But there was another part of this thing—a force which tied together two people called Katsuk and Hoquat.

It is important to note that Katsuk and Hoquat, the center and the circumference, together make one thing: the universe. The growing mutual recognition between captor and captive that they are somehow a single thing is an important element of the novel. "Katsuk felt a bond being created between himself and this boy. Was it possible they were really brothers in that other world which moved invisibly and soundlessly beside the world of the senses?" David, too, becomes aware of the bond he shares with Katsuk and comes to trust him. While the Stockholm syndrome is plainly in operation—that is, the psychological process by which a kidnapping victim comes to identify with his or her kidnapper—on the visionary or mythic level, David's recognition is no delusion. Yet this awareness of brotherhood, which both characters come to share, will not move Katsuk to pity; he will not spare his brother Hoquat's life; indeed, the sacrifice becomes all the more potent and sacred because of their brotherhood:

> Katsuk thought: *Any man may emulate the bee. A man may sting the entire universe if he does it properly. He must only find the right nerve to receive his barb. It must be an evil thing I do, with the good visible only when they turn it over. The shape of hate must be revealed in it, and betrayal and anguish and the insanities we all share. Only later should they see the love.*

These are eloquent words, and they may well move readers to sympathy for Katsuk. Indeed, Herbert takes considerable pains to make Katsuk an eloquent and sympathetic character. Again and again, despite Katsuk's repeatedly stated intent to murder David, and despite numerous small cruelties of speech and action, readers find themselves liking the man. Even after Katsuk murders an innocent hiker in cold blood, as a kind of warm-up exercise for the execution of David, readers are loath to label him a monster. This is all the more incredible given the fact that Herbert takes equal if not greater pains to render David sympathetic. Of course, a reader's sympathies will almost always be engaged by an underdog, a child, an innocent victim. But Herbert presents David as a truly exceptional boy: he is brave, intelligent, and compassionate. Though he has been infected with the casual and unexamined racism of his culture, he is himself no racist and even comes to recognize the justice of Katsuk's cause: "Guilt filled David. He thought: *I am Hoquat.* His people had stolen this land. He knew Katsuk was speaking the truth. *We stole his land.*"

Everything readers take for granted about the way that fiction works, everything that exists in the unwritten contract between reader and author, persuades that Katsuk will, in the end, spare David's life. When he does not, readers more than share David's fleeting sense of betrayal as the arrow enters his breast; they feel betrayed by Herbert. And yet, Herbert has not lied. He has not cheated. He has played fair throughout the book. The shock that strikes us at the end of the novel is the same shock that Katsuk is delivering to the connected yet separate worlds of Native Americans and whites. The question is, does the sacrifice succeed in doing what Katsuk intends? What exactly does Katsuk think his sacrifice of David will accomplish anyway?

Katsuk may be mad, but there is method in it. A graduate student in anthropology, Hobuhet is deeply knowledgeable about myths and rituals, not only those of the Quinault culture, but those of cultures from other places, other times. Hobuhet is filled with rage and hate following the rape and suicide of his sister. He longs to take revenge. Yet he cannot do it. Why? Is it because he is weak? Or afraid? No. The reason Hobuhet does not take revenge on the whites who raped his sister is that he recognizes the futility of it. He could kill those men, but would that make a real difference? Would that change the culture in which whites have the power to rape and murder Native Americans both literally and figuratively? It would not. And yet the hatred, the rage, the desire for revenge remain.

Hobuhet's training as an anthropologist comes to his rescue. A symbolic act can provide an outlet for these emotions and desires. What kind of symbolic act? A ritual, of course. But what kind of ritual? Hobuhet cannot answer that question. But Katsuk can. And so Katsuk is born from the sting of a bee. And it is to Katsuk, not Hobuhet, that Tamanawis speaks:

> You must find a white. You must find a total innocent. You must kill an innocent of the whites. Let your deed fall upon this world. Let your deed be a single, heavy hand which clutches the heart. The whites must feel it. They must hear it. An innocent for all of our innocents.

For Hobuhet to kill the rapists of his sister would be a futile and selfish act of personal vengeance; it would not bring his sister back or change the world. Yet for Katsuk to sacrifice an innocent as commanded by Tamanawis, "the greatest of spirits," would be a ritual act of impersonal atonement that could redeem the past and change the future of the world. Hobuhet has created Katsuk to take the vengeance he cannot; yet to disguise the personal nature of that vengeance, he turns it into a ritual of universal, mythic redemption. Such sacrifices bridge the gap between the real and the visionary, breaking through the walls that separate the world of timebound history and the world of timeless myth. But Katsuk cannot simply make up a ritual of his own. There would be no mythic power in such a sacrifice. What makes a sacrifice sacred and potent is the fact that it has always existed, that it enacts—or, rather, reenacts—a timeless action given by divine powers to human beings. The sacrifice of the innocent white must follow the traditional form if it is to have any meaning. Yet the Quinault tribes did not practice human sacrifice; there is no such ritual among the Quinault. Again, Hobuhet the anthropologist comes to the aid of Katsuk the warrior/shaman. The Pawnee tribe, although culturally and linguistically distinct from the Quinault, did practice human sacrifice. And so Katsuk will adopt the Pawnee rite to his own purposes.

The Pawnee ritual involved the sacrifice of captured maidens to the god they called Morning Star. The victims were held in comfort and treated well until the appointed time for the sacrifice, when they were hung on a timber scaffold and pierced with arrows. In Pawnee mythology, the union of the gods Morning Star and Evening Star had produced the first human being, a girl, whom Morning Star placed on Earth to engender the Pawnee people. Thus it was deemed necessary to return a girl to Morning Star in thanks for the god's sacrifice of his daughter.

Katsuk chooses a boy instead of a girl, but the quality of innocence remains of paramount importance. Yet the Pawnee sacrifice that lies behind Katsuk's sacrifice of David is an indication that David, is, among other things, a stand-in for Hobuhet's innocent sister; the sacrifice of David is a recapitulation of the rape and murder of the sister, raised to a mythic level. Hobuhet wants the death of his sister to mean something. He seeks not only retribution, not only transcendence, but the forgiveness of the guilt he carries for not having prevented her death and for not having avenged it.

Yet Herbert is playing a complicated game here. For David's middle name, Morgenstern, means "Morning Star." The name ties him explicitly to the Pawnee sacrifice; he is, in a sense, a born victim. But there is another level of mythic allusion at work. The name also alludes to a passage in the New Testament's Book of Revelation: "I am the root and the offspring of David, and the bright and morning star." (Rev. 22:16.) These words are spoken by Jesus Christ. By "root and offspring of David," Jesus is identifying himself as a descendent of the Jewish king; by "bright and morning star," Jesus is alluding to his death and resurrection, by which sacrifice (in the mythology of Catholicism) he has taken away the sins of the world and shown human beings the path to salvation and eternal life.

In the Pawnee sacrifice, the victim was no scapegoat. The girl was not killed as the bearer of the sins of the Pawnee, thus cleansing them from sin. Nor was she killed as a retributive act, as the embodiment of the sins of the enemies of the Pawnee, from whom she had been stolen. Her death was a mimetic act, a repetition on Earth of a creative sacrifice made at the beginning of time in heaven. It ensured the fertility of the Earth and the continuance of the Pawnee people in the here and now, not in the afterlife.

The role that David plays in Katsuk's sacrifice is closer to that of Jesus. David is innocent. He is a scapegoat; that is, he is the symbolic embodiment of the sins of the whites. He will also carry Hobuhet's guilt. And, like Jesus, he is of the "root and offspring of David"; that is, he is Jewish, a fact entirely overlooked by Katsuk, who, in his fanatical obsession, doesn't see the irony in holding a Jew responsible for the genocide of Native Americans. Yet there are important differences. Jesus willingly and consciously embraced his sacrifice, but that is not true of David. David is manipulated into an agreement that he remains ignorant of making, an agreement that exists only in his murderer's mind. Hobuhet/Katsuk is trying to force together two mythologies that are profoundly, radically different. For all his insistence that he is following the traditions of his people, in fact he is not.

But that doesn't mean his new, hybrid ritual must necessarily fail. Perhaps the violent fusion of Native-American and Judeo-Christian mythologies can spark a new mythological order on heaven and on Earth. Perhaps David's death can serve a purpose, can really be the "artistic act" that Hobuhet/Katsuk envisions: "a refinement of blood revenge, a supreme example to be appreciated by this entire world." Yet if such were the case, Herbert would provide some indication of it in the novel. He does not.

> For David, there was only the sharp and crashing instant of awareness: *He did it*! There was no pain greater than the betrayal. Hunting for a name that was not *Hoquat*, the boy sank into blackness.

This is not sacrifice, but murder. There is no redemption, no resurrection, no renewal. When the search party catches up at last, they find Katsuk "cradling the dead boy like a child, swaying and chanting the death song one sang for a friend." This poignant image cannot erase the bloody fact of what has taken place; instead, it underscores the horror, exposing the banality at the heart of Hobuhet's breathtaking madness. What is shown is not the boundless and all-inclusive embrace of the universe, such as might occur in the aftermath of a successful sacrifice, but the tragic and meaningless result of one man's pathetic delusion. Thus does Charles Hobuhet, a particularly chilling example of what Herbert called "the messianic impulse in human society," take his place among the intelligent monsters of fiction.

Source: Paul Witcover, Critical Essay on *Soul Catcher*, in *Novels for Students*, The Gale Group, 2003.

Joyce Hart

Hart has degrees in English literature and creative writing and focuses her writing on literary themes. In this essay, Hart looks at Herbert's hiker-murder scene to uncover hidden connections between the hiker and the protagonist.

Frank Herbert's *Soul Catcher* was published in 1972, during the heyday of the hippie movement. Although his book is not dated by the inclusion of a hippie-type young man hiking through the woods, the significance of the character of Vince Debay might have carried more weight in the 1970s, when young hippie-types were prevalent on college campuses. Today, Vince's character might represent a young environmentalist or a pot-smoking follower of the Grateful Dead. In the 1970s, however, reader might have seen something more complex in Vince's character and thus something more significant happening between him and the protagonist Charles Hobuhet-Katsuk. They might have understood that this scene represented more than a chance encounter between two young men who, at one time, were college classmates.

Herbert prefaces the scene of Katsuk and Vince's meeting in the forest with an editorial statement that Katsuk had previously sent to the University of Washington's student newspaper. In his statement, Katsuk refers to some of the inspirations of the hippie movement during the 1960s and 1970s, such as the fight for civil rights, but he also accuses the young people of hypocrisy: "You say you would risk anything to achieve equal happiness for all. But your words risk nothing," he wrote. The young people's beliefs, Katsuk held, were "fragmented," because they did not see their own "self-imposed limitations." He continued: "You exist in constant tension between tyranny and victimization."

During those turbulent decades of the 1960s and 1970s, many young college students were caught between tearing down the beliefs of their parents and trying to create new philosophies of their own to replace them. American culture had a relatively short history, so looking backward through time provided the young rebels with very little inspiration. Their American ancestors, for the most part, had come from Europe and Africa, countries that were too far removed from them and therefore did not provide the kind of answers that they were looking for. What developed in this void was a tendency among some youth to look to Native-American culture for answers. There was hope that the Native-American traditional culture might provide a possible alternative to their own lifestyles. Books that explained various aspects of Native-American philosophy and traditional culture such as *Black Elk Speaks* (originally published in 1932), Carlos Castandeda's *Teachings of Don Juan: A Yaqui Way of Knowledge* (1968), and Dee Brown's *Bury My Heart at Wounded Knee* (1971) were widely read and taken to heart, as many young people adopted personal interpretations of Native-American lives and tried to emulate them. The long hair and the wearing of braids and headbands were a direct reflection of more than just a rebellion against the stereotypical teenager of the previous generation. It was also an expression of camaraderie with the Native-American people, albeit a somewhat romantic version, as most youth had little, or no, contact with contemporary Native Americans. Their visions of Native-American life had little to do with the problems of alcoholism, unemployment, and a loss of culture and land, as Herbert's character Katsuk and his people were experiencing.

> " In order to be rid of that self-image, Katsuk therefore had to do more than change his clothes and try to alter himself. He had to get rid of Vince."

So when Katsuk notices Vince bounding down the wilderness trail, he sees a lot more than just a former classmate. Vince, in many ways, represents the hippie movement. He is described as a young man with long hair "bound at the forehead by a red bandanna," which gave him a "curiously aboriginal look." In other words, Vince is portrayed as a pseudo-Indian, or "wanna-be." He might "curiously" bear the look of a Native American, but even David, the thirteen-year-old captive, can see that there are wide gaps in Vince's disguise. First, Vince walks in a marijuana-induced stupor, glancing "neither right nor left," unaware of his surroundings and of the imposing danger that awaits him, so unlike the way that Katsuk moves through the forest. Vince also walks with "a stiff, heel-first stride that jarred the ground," announcing his presence, disturbing the quiet of the forest. In contrast to Katsuk's stalking movements, Vince stomps through the forest. Hence, he plays out Katsuk's reference to the "tension between tyranny and victimization." Vince walks through the wilderness as if he owns it, unaware, and unequipped to deal with, the vast danger that is about to pounce on him in the form of Katsuk. For his part, even David realizes that Vince is incapable of saving himself. Something inside of David comprehends that Vince, maybe even more than David himself, is not a savior but rather is yet another victim.

Just prior to Vince's appearance, Katsuk had "felt an odd fear that he would find his secret name carved some place." As he looked around at his surroundings, he wondered where this name might appear. What form would it take? "He wondered if there were any *thing* in these mountains with the power to set his universe in perfect order once more." Shortly after this statement, Vince shows up. The connection between these two events makes it obvious that in some way Katsuk relates to Vince. Could it be that the name that Katsuk is looking for is written all over Vince? Wasn't Katsuk, at one time, just like Vince? When Katsuk first sees Vince in the woods, he recognizes him, but "it bothered him that he could not name the face." Vince, on the other hand, remembers Katsuk, or rather he remembers him as "Charlie." "We were in that Anthro Three-hundred class together," Vince reminds Katsuk when they finally face one another. Both had been students at the University of Washington. Both had taken upper level anthropology classes, both had been interested in studying people and culture. Both were searching for new definitions of themselves, rejecting many of the beliefs of their parents.

However, that was the old Katsuk, the "Charlie the Chief," as Vince calls him—the white man's description of him. Katsuk had embraced that definition of himself, had tried through an institutionalized educational program to learn about his culture and the white society around him. But just as he had recently taken off the clothes of the "white man" and donned his own traditional costume, Katsuk had also eliminated that version of himself. Vince, therefore, represents not what Katsuk is but rather what he had been. If his name were truly written on Vince, then that name had slipped into the past, and Katsuk's not being able to put a name to Vince's face was proof of it.

Although Katsuk does not immediately remember Vince, he does see something in Vince that immediately angers him. In Vince are "all the defeats of his people. Their sobs and oaths and lamenting echoed within him, a swarm of unavenged shadows." If Katsuk had once been like Vince, then he too was a cause of his people's sorrow, or his people's defeat. In order to be rid of that self-image, Katsuk therefore had to do more than change his clothes and try to alter himself. He had to get rid of Vince. This is the only explanation for why Herbert had Katsuk murder Vince. Why couldn't Katsuk have hidden, like he had ordered David to do, and allowed the hikers to pass by, including Vince? Why did he purposely expose himself to, and confront, Vince? Part of the answer might be explained by the fact that Katsuk was on a mission; and he was obsessed by it. Sometimes his rational thoughts were obscured by his emotions. At other times, he was like an animal, reacting to events on instinct rather than on intellect. He did not want to classify himself among those whom he referred to, in his editorial essay, as people who say they "would risk anything to achieve equal happiness for all" but would never act on their statements. "Words," Katsuk had written, "risk nothing." The old Katsuk might have been a man

of words, but the new Katsuk was a man of action; and his instincts told him that he must kill Vince.

Vince is nervous when Katsuk approaches him. He's not sure why, but he suddenly senses that he is out of his familiar element. He cannot bring Katsuk back to the more recognizable, and light-hearted, "Charlie the Chief." Katsuk is in a place that Vince can only relate to as a game or as a set of an old Western movie in which Katsuk is the "Indian," and Vince is the settler fighting for *his* land. When Vince finally realizes that he has in no way impressed Katsuk and, in fact, might have actually insulted him, he tries to apologize. Even in his asking to be forgiven, Vince has no idea how deeply the offense has actually penetrated Katsuk's psyche. He is not aware of what the true insult is. Surely it has little to do with Vince's inability to recognize that Katsuk is definitely not playing a game. However, maybe it has everything to do with Vince's comment about "Indian" and "settler." Didn't that relationship sum up the whole grievance that Katsuk holds? The history of white people dealing with the Native population, in Katsuk's mind, is a relationship of tyranny. As Katsuk's sister had been raped, Katsuk believed that all Native people had also been raped by the white settlers.

At this point in the story, Vince makes one final attempt to bridge the widening chasm between himself and Katsuk. "You want a little grass?" Vince asks Katsuk. This statement is an ironic twist on the familiar scene in a typical Hollywood cowboy-and-Indian movie in which a Native man offers a white man a peace pipe. The irony does not impress Katsuk, who wants nothing to do with making peace over a shared smoke. However, Vince's gesture illuminates the difference between the two characters. Vince's offer is sincere but, in Katsuk's mind, it is insignificant. Sharing a smoke with this white man would be like putting a bandage on one's body to remove a cancer. When his offer is rejected, Vince tries to evaluate his position in the encounter. So he asks: "What *are* you doing here?" Katsuk's answer only deepens Vince's fear. Katsuk tells him that he is searching "for a deformity of the spirit." Without completely understanding what Katsuk is referring to, Vince finally senses the danger he is in and tries to slip away, but it is too late.

After murdering Vince, Katsuk does a strange thing. Earlier, upon first catching sight of him, Katsuk had criticized Vince for carrying an overloaded backpack. "You have not yet discovered that having too much is no better than having enough," he scolds. However, after burying Vince's body, Katsuk not only takes Vince's backpack, he also puts on Vince's clothes. "Katsuk wore clothes taken from the dead hiker's pack: jeans that were too tight for him over the loincloth, a plaid shirt. He still wore moccasins and the band of red cedar bark around his head." In this passage, Herbert cements the connection between Katsuk and Vince. The murderer has taken what material symbols remain of his victim. He wears Vince's jeans, covering his own traditional costume. He dons the plaid shirt; and although he does not wear Vince's red bandanna, his own headband is the same color as Vince's. Thus immediately after killing him, Katsuk takes on the appearance of Vince. Almost as if memorializing his victim, for a short period of time, Katsuk pays homage to him in wearing his clothes, in using his sleeping bag, in eating his food. A little later, he discards all physical remnants of Vince, re-convinced that the things of the white man are sapping his strength.

Although the two men shared a similar background and a linked fate, they also were dissimilar in significant ways. Vince had risked his life by entering the forest, but he did so without fully understanding the dangers that were waiting for him. He entered the woods, more as an escape, much as he used smoking pot as way of temporarily leaving things behind. Katsuk, however, went to the woods deliberately, consciously aware of every step. He had a mission by which he believed he could avenge his people, and he was willing to risk his life on it.

Herbert neither condones nor explains Katsuk's behavior, especially in this scene between him and Vince. He simply places the two men in full view of one another and describes the action that unfolds, almost as if he, himself, were merely viewing it. The battle between the two young men that ensues from this encounter could be described as an ancient one—a clash of cultures; a clash of beliefs; a clash of misunderstandings. However, Herbert suggests that this conflict might have been something entirely different than it first appears. He implies that it could be interpreted as an interior struggle, fought not between two men but rather between two disparate definitions of self.

Source: Joyce Hart, Critical Essay on *Soul Catcher*, in *Novels for Students*, The Gale Group, 2003.

Allison DeFrees

DeFrees is a published writer and an editor with a bachelor's degree in English from the University of Virginia and a law degree from the University of Texas. In the following essay, DeFrees examines the universality of a story rooted in the genre of science fiction.

> "*Soul Catcher* is a meditation on anger, on what happens when anger has no outlet."

Soul Catcher is a meditation on anger, on what happens when anger has no outlet. It is, in this way, an unwitting metaphor for the root of all terrorist acts: voiceless rage. Katsuk, the self-given Native-American name Charles Hobuhet adopts after denouncing the evils of modern society, is an emblem of a man driven mad—in both senses of the word—by long-standing injustices, by the ridicule he has endured all of his life for being of Native-American descent, and by the history of violence perpetrated against his people, and more specifically, against Katsuk's sister, by white men. *Soul Catcher* covers a time period of ten days, from the day Katsuk abducts David Morgenstern Marshall, a thirteen-year-old boy, until the day Katsuk kills David. In that short span of time, the reader learns about the reasons for Katsuk's actions, about the young boy's changing attitudes about his captive state, and about the outside world's reactions to the kidnapping. Author Frank Herbert uses an omniscient narrator to present a variety of points of view, moving the narration from character to character to tell the story from different vantage points. Herbert assiduously shies away form judging his characters; instead, he allows the reader to decide who may be right and who may be wrong, and whether, in the end, that line may be less clear than it first appears. *Soul Catcher* follows an unforgiving story line—it is the story of anger spun out of control, leaving a tragic aftermath for mourning and the opportunity to examine what may have led to the tragic turn of events.

From the outset of the story, Herbert clearly establishes the work as one of science fiction—it is popularly labeled as a sci-fi novel, for leaps of the imagination are taken almost immediately, demanding that the reader suspend any disbelief. Interestingly, however, nothing that happens in the novel is so far-fetched that it could not happen in society in the present day. By classifying the novel as science fiction, if seems that Herbert is asking his reader to suspend personal values and personal mores in order to delve into the psyches of other humans.

The story is divided into short sections that alternate between viewpoints, relaying the perspectives of a different person or group. The main voices are Katsuk, David, David's father, Katsuk's relatives, David's teachers and counselors, Katsuk's former teacher, the press and the local sheriff's department. The first voice is that of David's father, Howard Marshall, the newly established Undersecretary of State of the United States. Marshall notes that his father before him often hired Indians to work for the family, and paid the Indians wages equal to those paid to other workers. Furthermore, the Indian employees "were well treated. I really don't see how this kidnapping could be aimed at me or my family. The man who took David must be insane." Marshall's logic is incomplete, but it is the first opinion the reader encounters, and first impressions are lasting. Thus, from the outset, Katsuk is presupposed as a "crazy man," rather than as a sane but angry man with a virulent message. Another important thing to note about Marshall's statement is his semantics. He says, "I really don't see how . . . ," which is exactly Katsuk's problem with the "white" society: as Katsuk understands it, white people try to reason everything in legal, logical terms. They try to force reason into visual outlines that work within already established arguments. Katsuk, however, *feels* the impotence of his rage in the face of the white man's arguments, feels the years of oppression that hand-outs from someone like Marshall's father can only conveniently salve, but never heal. Change must come from a far deeper place within the establishment, and Marshall, in his newly ordained place of power within the government, is exactly the target at which Katsuk aims. By kidnapping the son of an important member of the United States government, and one currently earning a great deal of press coverage, Katsuk's message of hate and revenge can reach the largest number of people.

The voice of Professor Tilman Barth, one of Katsuk's university professors, serves as a counterweight to Marshall's voice. Barth claims that Hobuhet is a gentle man, not a "mad killer," and that the kidnapping "could be a monstrous joke." Barth has respect for Hobuhet, who, ironically, throughout the novel expresses nothing but contempt for all of his university professors and

courses. Furthermore, Barth explains that he found Hobuhet to be a bright and eloquent student who expressed himself in such a manner that led Barth to believe that Hobuhet "is capable of great things, as great as any achievements in our Western mythology." In one paper Hobuhet submitted to Barth for Philosophy 200, Hobuhet argues that people in modern society are full of "Words-words-words, no feelings," and "are always running away from your bodies. . . . You try to explain away a civilization which uses trickery, bad faith, lies, and deceit to make its falsehoods prevail *over* the flesh." Later, Katsuk writes on a scrap of paper while at a hideout known as Sam's River shelter:

> When I am confused I listen with as much of my being as I can allow. This was always what my people did. We fell silent in confusion and waited to learn. The whites do a strange thing when they are confused. They run around making much noise. They only add to the confusion and cannot even hear themselves.

Katsuk understands the ways of white men; he lived with them and answered to a name that was given to him while living in "white society." He is not an outside observer who criticizes a world he does not understand. Rather, he has lived the life of white men, and finds it uninhabitable and unnatural. During his educational years, Hobuhet witnessed first hand the methods that white people used to undermine the Native-Americans' right to own land and to live peaceably. He read the derogatory methods the white man used to describe the "Indian," and the ways the white men chose, time and time again, to avoid understanding and honoring the Native-American way of life. *Soul Catcher* is a story for all ages: it outlines the epic story of the taking of the American West by the American government in the nineteenth century, and the attendant usurpation of Native-American land is duplicated in modern United States imperialism with regard to foreign countries. In the novel, after attending the university, Hobuhet worked for a paycheck within the bounds of society, but all the while, his hatred burned, and his heart remained hostile to "the white man." When the chance arose, Hobuhet turned his back on his life within industrialized society, and set out to make the largest statement he could about his anger at the injustices the whites had perpetrated for so long against Native Americans, and in particular against his sister, who, a few months before the events of the novel, had committed suicide after being raped by a brood of white men. Katsuk's carefully planned revenge is not simply a testament to his ancestors—his rage is intimately personal, and it is festering to a bloody boil.

There is, however, a certain extent to which Katsuk's logic falls short in the novel, a crack, as it were, in the pavement of his narrowly carved walk. After a few days in captivity, the innocent, David Marshall, begins to respond to Katsuk's reclaimed way of living in the forest—living in accordance with the rules of nature instead of, as Katsuk had explained in a philosophy class paper, "against nature." Katsuk was angry at white men, and searched for a way to exact revenge on white men for the agony and humiliation they forced his people to suffer. Thus, when Katsuk is stung by a bee during a ritual he created to discover a Native-American name for himself, he claims that the bee is "Soul Catcher." Katsuk believes that the fact that the bee stung him is a sign that he is meant to be a vessel for evil, prompting him to abduct and kill an innocent white person as a ritual sacrifice to boldly show the white men that what they did to his people remains unforgivable. But once captured, David begins to drop the haughty anger that masks his fear, and he grows curious as to the nature of Katsuk and Katsuk's reasons for choosing a primitive life of exile. Katsuk is torn by this change, by his growing admiration for the boy. He "felt a bond being created between himself and this boy." Katsuk harshly dubs David "Hoquat," a derogatory reference to white men, but by the end of Katsuk and David's journey together, Katsuk feels a solidarity with David, and at one point, Katsuk even thinks to himself, "My brother, Hoquat." The reader watches David morph into an ambassador to modern society regarding Katsuk's argument for simplicity and against wanton capitalism, and Katsuk must work harder and harder to keep his warming emotions separate from his ultimate task—to murder the boy he has come to respect. He repeatedly promises that he will not kill David unless David specifically asks him to; in this respect, the reader is allowed to hold out hope that David will be spared, despite Katsuk's common statement to himself that he must sacrifice the boy. Katsuk seems, above all, to be a man of his word, and there is a conflict between his promise to his people and his promise to David. In the end, in the face of clashing promises, Katsuk must make a decision; he chooses the past, rather than the future, and tricks David into saying that he wishes to be killed. As the authorities are closing in on Katsuk and David, David urges Katsuk to run away, to save his life. Katsuk asks David what he should do about his spirit message, and David, not understanding that the message is intimately tied with his own murder, tells Katsuk, "What message? . . . I don't care about your message! Send it! Just don't let them catch you!"

Katsuk interprets David's response to his own purposes, and falsely pretends that David consents to death. Just before he kills David, Katsuk tells him, "Let all men and all spirits learn your qualities, Hoquat." He has taught David the vital importance of living in harmony with nature, but he kills David before David can share his new knowledge to "all men," thus in many ways defeating his very purpose. In his anger, he failed to consider that he might also have something to learn.

Soul Catcher is an interesting study of rage, and how rage and lucidity are commingled in such a way that a person truly angry stands on a delicate precipice of sanity and insanity. Hobuhet becomes Katsuk to live out his rage, but his actions are meditative, willed, and precipitous. The novel ends with the slaughter of an innocent boy, and the answers to the reasons behind Katsuk's terrorist act, and all terrorist acts, and the possible means by which such acts might have been prevented, are left to the reader. Whether what Katsuk did was in any way justified by the history of emotional deprecation and economic depression defies simple logic. Nothing Katsuk does or decides occurs without him first consulting the natural elements. Whether or not this method of consultation—a communion with ravens, bees, the woods—marks a sage man living off the land, both spiritually and physically, or a madman, is left to the individual reader to decide. But what is certain is that Katsuk's actions are deliberate and meticulously thought out, and what is also certain is that he follows through with his plan with exactitude and complete success, despite numerous obstacles standing in his path. His own people rise up against him, but because of the strength of his conviction that he has been chosen by his gods to act out this ritual sacrifice, he is too powerful to be stopped. How this sheds light on the "real world" is effervescently clear: conviction is more potent than might, more powerful than idle words, more dangerous than lies. Science fiction here becomes all too real, in the face of Saddam Hussein, Ayatollah Khomeini, Charles Whitman, Lee Harvey Oswald, suicide bombers, Charles Manson, Cyclops, Hitler—critics may well claim a madness residing in these figures in history, but it is also true that in each case, the act or acts committed were done with dexterous, deliberated planning and extreme precision of thought. There was a sanity, or at least a clear thought process, to the insanity. Katsuk purposely murdered an innocent Caucasian child, a crime far beyond forgiveness in the civilized world. But he did so in strict adherence to his beliefs, and not without painstaking deliberation and sacrifice. With *Soul Catcher*, Herbert does not pronounce judgment on his characters, leaving it to his readers to provide condemnation or approval, leaving a tangled web of history with no square edges, and no straight answers. In this way, Herbert demands that his reader examine the history behind the events in the story. For it is only by unraveling the past that we can begin to examine the present, and only by examining the present that we may begin to understand and act on the possibilities of the future.

Source: Allison DeFrees, Critical Essay on *Soul Catcher*, in *Novels for Students*, The Gale Group, 2003.

Sources

Carlsen, G. Robert, *English Journal*, 1974, p. 91.

D'Ammassa, Don, "Frank Herbert," in *Science Fiction Chronicle*, Vol. 7, No. 7, April 1986, p. 24.

Deloria, Vine, Jr., *God Is Red: A Native View of Religion*, Fulcrum Publishing, 1994, p. 9.

Foster, Robert A., and Thomas L. Wyner, "Frank Herbert," in *Dictionary of Literary Biography*, Vol. 8: *Twentieth-Century American Science-Fiction Writers*, edited by David Cowart, Gale Research, 1981, pp. 232–39.

Herbert, Frank, *Soul Catcher*, Ace Books, 1972.

———, *Soul Catcher*, Berkley Books, 1983.

Indians of All Tribes, "Planning Grant Proposal to Develop an All-Indian University and Cultural Complex on Indian Land, Alcatraz," in *Great Documents in American Indian History*, edited by Wayne Moquin, Praeger Publishers, 1973, pp. 375–77, originally published in *Congressional Record*, 91st Congress, 2d Session.

McNelly, Willis E., "Frank Herbert," in *Science Fiction Writers*, Charles Scribner's Sons, 1982, pp. 377–85.

Miller, David M., *Frank Herbert*, Starmont House, 1980, pp. 10, 50.

Miller, Timothy, "The Counterculture," in *The 1960s*, edited by William Dudley, Greenhaven Press, Inc., 2000, p. 195, originally published in "Introduction," in *The Hippies and American Values*, University of Tennessee Press, 1991.

O'Reilly, Timothy, *Frank Herbert*, Frederick Ungar Publishing Company, 1981, pp. 10, 11.

Turner, Paul, "Vertex Interviews Frank Herbert," in *Vertex*, Vol. 1, Issue 4, October 1973.

Washburn, Wilcomb E., "The Native American Renaissance, 1960–1995," in *The Cambridge History of the American Peoples*, Vol. 1, Pt. 2, *North America*, edited by Bruce G. Trigger and Wilcomb E. Washington, Cambridge University Press, p. 447.

Further Reading

Dubin, Lois Sherr, *North American Indian Jewelry and Adornment*, Harry N. Abrams, 1999.

This comprehensive book on the history of Native-American jewelry follows thousands of years of Native-American adornment, by region and tribe. The book also covers the symbolism and purpose of the various artworks and features detailed photos and graphics.

Eichstaedt, Peter H., *If You Poison Us: Uranium and Native Americans*, Red Crane Books, 1994.

This book details the devastating effects of the uranium radiation that resulted from mining on Navajo Indian lands during America's race to construct the atom bomb. In addition to discussing the struggles that Native Americans in this region have faced when seeking compensation for these effects, the book also talks about how this historic tragedy continues to affect Native Americans.

Lewis, G. Malcolm, *Cartographic Encounters: Perspectives on Native American Mapmaking and Map Use*, University of Chicago Press, 1998.

This book examines the long history of Native Americans and their skill in cartography, starting with the first map that a Native American prepared for the Spaniard Hernando de Alarcó in 1540. The book also discusses the connections among maps, space, and history and examines the maps in light of their importance as archaeological evidence.

Mander, Jerry, *In the Absence of the Sacred: The Failure of Technology and the Survival of the Indian Nations*, Sierra Club Books, 1992.

Mander examines the effects that increasing technology has had on society and advocates a return to a Native-American way of life. In addition, he discusses how some Native Americans who try to maintain their way of life have clashed with the corporate world.

McNaughton, Patrick R., *The Mande Blacksmiths: Knowledge, Power, and Art in West Africa*, Indiana University Press, 1993.

This book uses an anthropological perspective to examine the roles and social context of the blacksmiths of the Mande people in West Africa. These blacksmiths are acknowledged both for their art and the supernatural power they are believed to possess.

Taylor, Collin F., *Native American Weapons*, University of Oklahoma Press, 2001.

This lushly illustrated book serves as an excellent introduction to the study of Native-American weapons. Divided into five categories of weapons—striking, cutting, piercing, defensive, and symbolic—the book examines North American weapons and armor from prehistoric times to the late nineteenth century. The accompanying text describes the weapons and their roles in tribal culture, economy, and politics.

The Time Machine

H. G. Wells
1895

The Time Machine was first published in 1894 as a serial under the name *The Time Traveller* in the *National Observer*. It was brought out as a book the next year under its current name and sold more than six thousand copies in a few months. H. G. Wells was just twenty-seven years old when the story, which came to be called a "scientific romance," was published. Wells's friend, William Henley, edited the *National Observer*, and Wells became part of a group of writers called "Henley's young men." The novel's appeal lies in its attempt to fathom what will become of human beings in the distant future. By making the central character of his story a time traveler who can transport himself back and forth in time with the aid of a machine he invented, Wells is able to explore many of the themes that obsessed him, including class inequality, evolution, and the relationship between science and society. In describing the future world of the effete Eloi and the cannibalistic Morlocks and the world beyond that in which all semblance of human life has been erased, Wells illustrates what he believes may very well be the fate of humanity. The novel's enduring popularity is evident in the three films adapted from the novel and the scores of others inspired by it.

Author Biography

Born in Bromley, England, on September 21, 1866, Herbert George Wells was raised in relative

H. G. Wells

known Wells novels include *The Invisible Man* (1897) and *The War of the Worlds* (1898), the latter of which formed the basis for Orson Welles's infamous radio broadcast on October 30, 1938. In that broadcast, which millions of listeners took seriously, Welles announced that Martians had landed on Earth.

Wells was also passionate about history and politics and developed a reputation as a reformer, joining the Fabian Society, a socialist group whose members included writer George Bernard Shaw, and running for Parliament as a Labour Party candidate. As an internationally celebrated writer, he traveled to countries such as Russia, where he met with Vladimir Lenin and Josef Stalin, and the United States, where he met with President Franklin D. Roosevelt and discussed, among other topics, the implications of *The Time Machine*. Wells was also a supporter of the League of Nations, a precursor to the United Nations, serving on its Research Committee and penning books about its aims.

One of the most prolific and wide-ranging writers of the twentieth century, Wells wrote more than one hundred books, including biology textbooks, collections of short stories and literary criticism, and studies of the world economy, British imperialism, and Russian communism. He continued writing until the end of his life. Some of his later books include *Guide to the New World: A Handbook of Constructive World Revolution* (1941); *The Outlook for Homo Sapiens* (1942); *Phoenix: A Summary of the Inescapable Conditions of World Reorganisation* (1942); *A Thesis on the Quality of Illusion in the Continuity of Individual Life of the Higher Metazoa, with Particular Reference to the Species Homo Sapiens* (1942); *The Conquest of Time* (1942); *Crux Ansata: An Indictment of the Roman Catholic Church* (1944); and *Mind at the End of Its Tether* and *The Happy Turning: A Dream of Life* (1946). At the end of his life, Wells, who had lived through two world wars, became increasingly pessimistic about humanity's future. He died in London on August 13, 1946.

poverty by his father, Joseph Wells, a failed shopkeeper turned professional cricket player, and his mother, Sarah Neal Wells, a housekeeper. Wells, however, used his circumstances as a spur rather than a crutch, reading voraciously as a child in an effort to create a better life for himself. At sixteen, Wells became a student teacher at Midhurst Grammar School and was later awarded a scholarship to the Normal School of Science in London. T. H. Huxley, who, next to Darwin, was the foremost evolutionary theorist of his day, was Wells's biology teacher, and he helped to shape Wells's thinking about humankind's past and its future. Wells taught for three years after taking a bachelor of science degree in 1890, and a few years later he began writing full-time.

His first novel, *The Time Machine*, published in 1895 and hailed as one of the first great works of science fiction, was one of Wells's most popular novels and is one of his most enduring. Its success gave him the confidence to pursue his strategy of using fiction to dramatize scientific concepts such as the fourth dimension, Darwin's theory of natural selection, and Marx's theory of class struggle. In 1896, Wells published *The Island of Dr. Moreau*, about a scientist who experiments in breeding animals with human beings. Other well-

Plot Summary

Chapter 1

The Time Machine begins in the Time Traveller's home at a dinner attended by various friends and acquaintances, including the Medical Man, the Psychologist, the Very Young Man, the Provincial

Mayor, Filby, and Hillyer, the narrator. As the Time Traveller describes how time is the Fourth Dimension, his guests argue with him, claiming that it cannot be a dimension because people cannot move through it as they can through space. The Time Traveller excuses himself and then returns with a machine, which, after the Psychologist pushes its small lever, disappears, allegedly into the Fourth Dimension. The Time Traveller then shows the group a larger version of the time machine and announces he plans to travel through time.

Chapter 2

A week later, Hillyer, the Medical Man, and the Psychologist meet again at the Time Traveller's house, where they are joined by three newcomers: Blank, Dash, and Chose. The group begins dinner but is interrupted by the Time Traveller, who suddenly appears, haggard, thin, and dirty. After refreshing himself and eating, the Time Traveller promises to recount his story of where he has been, asserting that he has lived eight days since four o'-clock that afternoon. The men are skeptical, especially Hillyer, who says, "The fact is the Time Traveller was one of those men who were too clever to be believed."

Chapter 3

In this chapter, the Time Traveller tells his story, beginning with a description of time traveling, which he calls "excessively unpleasant." Traveling faster than a year per minute, the Time Traveller describes the disorientation he feels flying through time as seasons pass in a blur. He finally decides to land, pulling on the lever to bring his machine to a crashing halt in the middle of a hailstorm. Through the hail, the Time Traveller sees an enormous sphinx carved of white marble and huge buildings and a forest. In a frenzied panic, he rushes back to the machine from which he had been thrown, desiring to leave. Just then, a group of strange creatures approaches him. He regains his confidence, and his fear subsides when one of them, four feet tall and dressed in a purple tunic, walks up to him.

Chapter 4

It is 802,701 A.D., and the Time Traveller describes the race of small creatures as being on the intellectual level of five-year-olds. The creatures take him to a large building, where a number of them sit around and eat fruit. He learns they are vegetarian and live communally in one building, with the sexes mingling freely with each other. The

Media Adaptations

- *The Time Machine* has been adapted into film three times. Its first adaptation was released in 1960. Directed by George Pal and starring Rod Taylor, Alan Young, and Yvette Mimieux, this version could be considered the best of the three. The second adaptation, released in 1978, was directed by Henning Schellerup and stars John Beck, Priscilla Barnes, and Andrew Duggan. The most recent adaptation, released in 2002, stars Guy Pearce and Jeremy Irons and is directed by Simon Wells. All three films are widely available in libraries and major video stores.

- In 1997, Simon & Schuster Audioworks released an audiocassette of Star Trek star Leonard Nimoy reading *The Time Traveller* as part of its Alien Voices Presents Series.

Time Traveller becomes frustrated by the creatures' diminishing curiosity about his presence and his inability to communicate with them. Noting the creatures' indolence and the generally dilapidated look of the buildings, the Time Traveller speculates that the creatures evolved from the human race, growing weak because they had managed to decrease their population and to erase all "hardship and vigor" from their existence. His speculation about the creatures echoes both Karl Marx and Darwin's theories of economics and evolution respectively. At the end of the chapter, the Time Traveller signals that his guesses about the creatures are wrong.

Chapter 5

In this chapter, the longest in the novel, the Time Traveller discovers that his machine is missing, and he sets about to find it, guessing that it is in the base of the White Sphinx. However, he cannot open the panel to access it, and the Eloi he asks to help him all refuse. Exploring the Thames River Valley, the Time Traveller sees deep circular wells, and he speculates they are part of a vast ventilation system. Once again, his assumption will later be proved wrong.

Wells further dramatizes Marx's and Darwin's theories, as the Time Traveller learns more about the Eloi, the creatures he is staying with and whose name he learns, and is "introduced" to the Morlocks, a hideous race of underground creatures who resemble apes, with white skin and enlarged eyes, who prey on the Eloi. The Time Traveller learns about the Eloi largely through Weena, a female he rescues from drowning, while other Eloi passively watch. Weena stays with the Time Traveller, sleeping with him at night, even though she is dreadfully afraid of the dark. He later learns her fear is related to the Morlocks, who "harvest" Eloi in the dark to eat. The Time Traveller theorizes that the two races "evolved" out of the working class and the "owning" class of Victorian England. The Morlocks were the working class and had been driven underground, where they continued to work with their machines, while the Eloi were the capitalist class, who had grown dependent on the Morlocks for everything in their lives.

Chapter 6

The Time Traveller discovers a large green building, which he refers to as the Palace of Green Porcelain. He will come back to this building later in the story. For now, he braces himself to explore the underground world of the Morlocks. Weena is too afraid to follow him into the well, but the Time Traveller continues, wending his way through a maze of underground tunnels, eventually coming across a large battery of machines on which the Morlocks are hard at work. As Morlocks come toward him, the Time Traveller scares them off with a match, but he runs out of matches just as he escapes from the underground lair.

Chapter 7

In this chapter, Weena and the Time Traveller begin their journey back to the Palace of Green Porcelain but must sleep outside on a hill because night is descending. The Time Traveller muses on the insignificance of his own existence in relation to the universe and speculates on the nature of the relationship between the Morlocks and the Eloi, concluding that the underground mutants are keeping the Eloi alive both out of habit and for meat. This disgusts him and further spurs him to find his time machine.

This chapter is significant because it marks the only time that the Time Traveller stops his narrative to provide proof of his journey, pulling out

"two withered flowers" that Weena had placed in his jacket pocket and putting them on the table for others to see.

Chapter 8

The Time Traveller and Weena arrive at the Palace of Green Porcelain, which the Time Traveller inspects, discovering that it is a vast museum containing the ruins of "latter day South Kensington," with sections for natural history, paleontology, and geology. When Weena and the Time Traveller leave the museum, the Time Traveller arms himself with a box of matches and a lever he had broken off a machine in the museum with which to defend themselves against the Morlocks.

Chapter 9

In this chapter, Weena and the Time Traveller set out for the White Sphinx, where the latter believes the time machine is being kept. The two are attacked by Morlocks, and the Time Traveller lights matches to ward them off, beating them with a mace. Weary from their fighting and travel, the two fall asleep. They awaken to see frenzied Morlocks running from a raging fire the Time Traveller had set earlier. In the confusion, the Time Traveller leaves Weena behind in the burning forest.

Chapter 10

The Time Traveller finds the bronze panels at the base of the White Sphinx open and the time machine waiting for him. He jumps inside, and the Morlocks lock the doors behind him. After fighting off some of the ape-like creatures, the Time Traveller eventually starts the machine and jets into the fourth dimension.

Chapter 11

The Time Traveller lands at a time of "abominable desolation" in which there is no trace of humanity but plenty of horrendous giant crab-like creatures and enormous centipedes scurrying about in the "inky blackness." The Time Traveller has difficulty breathing and surmises the air is thinner in the future. He travels even further into the future, thirty million years, only to find that all life has vanished, except a ghastly football-sized blob trailing tentacles against the blood-red water.

Chapter 12

The Time Traveller returns to his home and his own time, convinced that because the time machine is at the other end of the laboratory, his experience was real and not a dream. He elicits responses from his guests, all of whom remain skeptical except for Hillyer, who returns the next day for more proof. The Time Traveller tells him that he will travel to the future and return in a half hour with just such evidence. Hillyer sees the Time Traveller disappear in a blur and waits for him to return, but he does not. The story ends with Hillyer saying that it has been three years since the Time Traveller left, and he has not yet returned.

Epilogue

Hillyer speculates on where the Time Traveller might be and notes the Time Traveller's pessimistic view of human progress. Even if the future is bleak, Hillyer says, human beings must live as if it is not while retaining hope for the future. This hope is symbolized by the two flowers that Weena had given the Time Traveller and that now belong to Hillyer.

Characters

Blank

The editor of "a well-known (but unnamed) daily paper," Blank—also referred to as "the Editor"—is a "rare visitor" to the Time Traveller's home. He is skeptical when told of the experiment the week before, and when the Time Traveller appears during dinner, his clothes rumpled and dirty, he makes fun of him, asking, "Hadn't they any clothes brushes in the Future?" The Editor also disbelieves the Time Traveller after he tells his story, remarking, "What a pity it is you're not a writer of stories."

Dash

Attending the second dinner, Dash—also referred to as the Journalist—"is more interested in his own stories than those of the Time Traveller."

The Eloi

Descended from the owning classes of nineteenth-century Britain, the Eloi live in 802,701 A.D. and are small, childlike creatures who spend their days playing and lounging. Vegetarians, they sleep together in large halls as protection against the Morlocks, who prey on them at night. Although initially intrigued by the Time Traveller, they quickly lose interest in him, except for Weena, a female Eloi the Time Traveller rescues from drowning.

Filby

Filby appears in the second chapter and is described as "an argumentative person with red hair." He is a rationalist who does not believe the Time Traveller's claims. He is also not very bright. Hillyer says that if Filby had presented the time machine and explained it instead of the Time Traveller, "a pork-butcher could understand."

Hillyer

Hillyer is the narrator and the only person who believes the Time Traveller's story. The bulk of the novel is the Time Traveller's story, as told to Hillyer. However, Hillyer directly addresses readers in the first, second, and twelfth chapters, and in the epilogue. Unlike the Time Traveller, who is pessimistic about humanity's future, Hillyer maintains hope, saying that even if the Time Traveller's story is true and that humanity is doomed for extinction, "it remains for us to live as though it were not so."

Medical Man

The Medical Man, also referred to as "the Doctor," is one of three guests present at both dinners. The others are Hillyer and the Psychologist. He holds a note from the Time Traveller and a watch and suggests that the group begin dinner on time, as the Time Traveller had instructed. Although he takes the Time Traveller seriously at first, he grows skeptical, believing that the Time Traveller has tricked them with his demonstration in the first chapter.

The Morlocks

In 802,701 A.D., the Morlocks live underground running their machines. Descended from Britain's nineteenth-century working class, the ape-like creatures have large eyes, white skin, and fur, and are fearful of light and fire. They also prey upon the Eloi, whom they use as a food source. They pursue the Time Traveller through the middle of his story, but he eventually beats them off and escapes into the future in his time machine.

Provincial Mayor

The Provincial Mayor is present at the first dinner. He has never heard of the fourth dimension and, in general, does not appear to know much about science.

Psychologist

The Psychologist is present at both dinners and engages the Time Traveller when he explains his theory. He says that historians would find time travel especially useful, noting, "One might travel back and verify the accepted account of the Battle of Hastings, for instance!" The Time Traveller chooses him to pull the lever on the model in the first chapter.

Time Traveller

The Time Machine is comprised mostly of the Time Traveller's story, as told to Hillyer. A well-to-do yet socially conscious inventor and a man of science who lives in Richmond, he creates a machine that allows him to travel in the fourth dimension. He has twinkling gray eyes and a pale face that is usually flushed. Well educated in the leading theories of his day, such as evolution and communism, the Time Traveller moves quickly from observation to speculation but acknowledges when he has been wrong and rethinks his position. The Time Traveller remains excited about the future, even after he learns by traveling in the future that humankind will not survive and that all trace of life will be wiped off the face of the earth. He is also a very witty man who often makes jokes at his own expense. His humor and history of playing practical jokes on his guests is one reason his guests suspect that his story is not true. Hillyer says of him that he "had more than a touch of whim among his elements."

Very Young Man

The very young man is at the first meeting only, participating in the discussion about time travel.

Weena

Weena is an Eloi that the Time Traveller saves from drowning when other Eloi ignore her. A source of information about the Eloi, she accompanies the Time Traveller as he searches for the time machine, and the two develop a strong bond. The night before the Time Traveller returns to the past, she dies in a fire the Time Traveller sets to ward off Morlocks.

Themes

Class Struggle

Prior to the eighteenth century in the West, a person was born into a caste and remained there until he or she died. After the eighteenth century and, with the proliferation of literacy and the standardization of currency, a class system began to emerge. More people had access to old professions, such as medicine and law, and new professions, such as writing and psychology, the latter of which are represented by the Time Traveller's guests. However, with the industrial revolution and the mass migration of rural laborers into the cities, the differences between the haves and the have-nots became more starkly visible. Wells capitalizes on the struggle between these two groups in his depiction of civilization 800,000 years in the future. When he first meets the Eloi, the Time Traveller initially believes society has evolved into a form of communism. However, as he learns more, he realizes that the class struggles of the nineteenth century have continued and are manifested in the relationship between the Eloi and the Morlocks.

Science

In the nineteenth century, science became both a tool of understanding and a means of salvation. Numerous scientific theories and inventions helped science replace religion as the primary way that human beings related to their environment. Marx's theory of labor and capital and Darwin's theory of evolution described human beings as being in a constant struggle for survival, but inventions such as electricity, the telephone, and subways promised to make the struggle easier and people's lives more manageable. *The Time Machine* capitalized on the public's hunger for technology and the promise that technology offered. However, use of the time machine did not make life easier for the Time Traveller or result in any knowledge that could change the future. Rather, the Time Traveller's experiences showed a future of doom, as his journey revealed a world in which the struggles of the 1890s were not resolved but rather exacerbated. His journeys even deeper into the future revealed a world in which humanity had been extinguished from the face of the earth.

Evolution

Evolution, a theory of life's origins and humanity's development, was a groundbreaking idea in the nineteenth century and literally changed the way that people thought about themselves and their place in the world. Biological evolution focuses on changes in a population over time. Wells helped to popularize Darwin's theory of evolution by presenting the scientific theory in a popular form, fiction. The Eloi and the Morlocks represent how human beings have genetically changed in the future as a result of their ability to adapt, or not, to their environments. The Morlocks, representing a mutation of the working class of Wells's day, are

Topics For Further Study

- In groups, draw a timeline with pictures of the evolution of human beings, beginning with prosimians and ending with the large crab-like creatures the Time Traveller encounters towards the end of his adventure. Be sure to include the Morlocks and the Eloi. Present your timeline to the class, and discuss how your timeline of human evolution differs from that of other groups.

- Assume the Time Traveller returns after three years. Write the thirteenth chapter, speculating on the kind of evidence he presents to the narrator about his travels.

- Wells believed that the human race was destined to destroy itself. In class, discuss the possibility of Wells's belief. How might what he said more than a hundred years ago come to pass in your own life or the near future?

- In *The Time Machine*, humanity "evolved" into the Morlocks and the Eloi, each representing a class of people. In groups, discuss other possible ways humanity might evolve in the future, and report your speculations to the class.

- Write a short essay identifying a specific time in the past to which you would like to return, and present reasons for your choice.

- Mark Twain's 1889 novel *A Connecticut Yankee at King Arthur's Court* was the first novel to deal with time travel. However, the hero of that novel has no control over his journeys through time. Compare Wells's novel with Twain's, paying particular attention to the ways in which each uses time travel to satirize popular thinking and public policies. Discuss your comparisons in class.

- Wells's novel has remained popular more than one hundred years after its initial publication. What do you think accounts for its popularity? Be specific with your responses, and discuss as a class.

- The Morlocks represent the devolution of the working class of Wells's day. Many modern and contemporary representations of working class people in film and literature represent them as heroic, yet Wells's demonizes them. In a short essay, account for this choice.

---

ape-like, with large eyes and white skin, features that have evolved because they live underground. They fear the light and love the darkness. Conversely, the Eloi are effete, fragile, and fearful of the dark, a result of thousands of years of not having to work to survive. They represent the owning class. Ironically, the Morlocks rule the Eloi. Wells's genius is "translating" difficult concepts such as natural selection by dramatizing them in fiction.

Style

Scientific Romance

A combination of fantasy and science fiction, *The Time Machine* is an example of a subgenre known as a scientific romance. A popular genre that Wells helped to refine, science fiction's action is often set in the future and examines the relationship between the future and technology. It is also defined by the appearance of characters and setting being dramatically different from those of realistic fiction. For example, the Eloi and Morlocks could not appear in a story by Ernest Hemingway, a realist. Fantasy is also a popular genre but does not necessarily rely on scientific explanations for behavior or action. Rather, fantasy fiction explores supernatural and nonrational phenomena that may or may not exist in realistic settings. J. R. R. Tolkein's *The Lord of the Rings* is a popular example of fantasy fiction. Other scientific romances of Wells's include *The Island of Doctor Moreau* (1896), *The Invisible Man* (1897), and *The War of the Worlds* (1898).

Narrator

The narrator is a speaker through whom the author tells a story. This influences the story's point of view. Wells constructs an ingenious frame for *The Time Machine*, using, in essence, two narrators. The first is the "true" narrator, Hillyer, who introduces the Time Traveller and the other guests present at his house in the first two chapters, and who writes the concluding words in the epilogue. The second narrator is the Time Traveller himself, who takes over the narration, beginning with the third chapter, and who disappears into the future at the end of the twelfth chapter. This narrative technique allows Wells to speculate about the future and at the same time voice his positions on topics such as politics and evolution through the voice of others and within the framework of an adventure story. This strategy makes potentially difficult ideas accessible to more readers. It also gives credibility to the Time Traveller's story, as Hillyer presents the story in the Time Traveller's own words.

Symbolism

Symbols are things or ideas that stand for other things or ideas. The relationship, however, is not one to one but one to many. Wells uses symbols to evoke ideas and emotions and to figuratively stitch together many of the story's themes. For example, the Palace of Green Porcelain, a museum containing artifacts from England of the 1890s, signifies the idea of home, civilization, and extinction—all at once—for the Time Traveller. Other major symbols are the White Sphinx, which evokes the spiritual degradation of the Eloi-Morlock society, and the time machine itself, symbolizing Victorian progress and the promise—and the danger—of technology.

Historical Context

The Time Machine had numerous incarnations, the first of which was a story called "The Chronic Argonauts," which Wells published in *Science Schools Journal* in 1888. The story achieved its final form in 1894. An adherent of evolutionary theory and a staunch advocate of women's suffrage and workers' rights, Wells was deeply influenced by his times. In the 1880s and 1890s, Britain's population was booming, roughly doubling between 1851 and 1901. The rise of industrialization was emptying the farms of residents and rural laborers, as people flocked to the cities and industrial towns to work in factories. By the turn of the century, more than eighty percent of Britain's population lived in urban areas. The shift from an agricultural to an industrial economy meant that England was now dependent on imports to feed its growing population and that the landed gentry who relied on income from renting farmland now had to find another way to make money. As a city dweller and a Progressive, Wells was sensitive to the working conditions of the factory laborer. His description of the Eloi and the Morlocks dramatizes the exploitative relationship between owners and workers in Victorian England.

Wells's time machine itself was a product of an imagination nursed on the extraordinary technological advances of his day, advances that fueled industrial development and changed the complexion of the workforce. In the 1870s, for example, both the typewriter and the telephone were invented. These inventions enabled office work to be done more efficiently, work that fell overwhelmingly to women. Other inventions that altered the daily lives and thinking of Victorians include suspension bridges, the telegraph, subway trains, steamships, buses, automobiles, and electric lights. These inventions made traveling places and moving goods less expensive and opened up vistas of opportunity for entrepreneur and worker alike. Public transportation enabled workers to live farther away from urban centers, which were becoming increasingly crowded, unsafe, and unsanitary. These inventions also sped up the pace of daily life, giving it a kind of urgency previously unknown and adding to the sense that the world was spinning out of control.

England celebrated its domestic progress in 1887 with Queen Victoria's Golden Jubilee and its world empire in 1897 with its Diamond Jubilee. By the late nineteenth century, England controlled a sizeable portion of the world's land, including India, large swaths of Africa and China, Australia, and Canada. Some were outright colonies, while others held "dominion" status. The British rationalized their imperialist policies, in part, not by claiming that their acquisitions were in the military or economic interest of the country (which they were) but by claiming it was their duty as the superior race to "civilize" primitive peoples who were incapable of governing themselves. Rudyard Kipling referred to this duty as "the white man's burden." British Prime Minister Benjamin Disraeli used Darwin's theories to support his claims for racial superiority. However, just as Britain's empire was at its peak, it began to crumble from

Compare & Contrast

- **1890s:** Numerous countries are at war over disputed territory, including China and Japan, the United States and Spain, Turkey and Greece.

  Today: Numerous countries and people feud over disputed territory, including the Palestinians and Israelis and the Pakistanis, and Indians.

- **1890s:** In 1895, T. H. Huxley, a popularizer of Darwin's theory of evolution and Wells's teacher and a primary influence on his thinking and writing, dies.

Today: In 2002, Stephen Jay Gould, perhaps the twentieth century's most prominent proponent of evolutionary theory, dies.

- **1890s:** Wilhelm Roentgen discovers x-rays and Marconi invents radio telegraphy, both of which dramatically change the way people live in the twentieth century.

  Today: The continued development of technology in general, and of computer technology specifically, change the way that millions of people live, work, and play.

---

within, as trying to contain nationalist movements spreading throughout the colonies drained Britain economically and politically.

Critical Overview

Although it sold relatively well when first published, *The Time Machine* was not widely reviewed. When it was, reviewers often likened it to Jules Verne's adventure stories or Robert Louis Stevenson's *Dr. Jekyll and Mr. Hyde*. Over the last century, it has developed a reputation as a science fiction classic. Writers like Isaac Asimov, himself a celebrated writer of science fiction, have praised the novel, noting that Wells "had the trick . . . of explaining the impossible with just the right amount of gravity . . . to induce the reader to follow along joyously." V. S. Pritchett was even more effusive in his praise, claiming in his essay "The Scientific Romances," "Without question *The Time Machine* is the best piece of writing. It will take its place among the great stories of our language." Bernard Bergonzi, a Wells scholar who has introduced thousands of new readers to Wells in his books and essays, argues in his essay, "*The Time Machine*: An Ironic Myth," that the novel has more "romance" than science, and is closer to the romances of nineteenth-century American writers

such as Herman Melville and Nathaniel Hawthorne than it is to the work of Verne. Robert M. Philmus examines the novel for its capacity to satirize various "present ideals." In his essay "The Logic of 'Prophecy' in *The Time Machine*," Philmus reviews a number of articles written about *The Time Machine* before concluding that the Time Traveller's return to the future at the end of the story "reinforces the fiction's claim to integrity." Other critics focus on the novel's action and its ability to entertain. For example, Richard Hauer Costa, author of *H.G. Wells*, a study of Wells's writing and life, calls the novel "a thrilling story of cosmic adventure."

Criticism

Chris Semansky

Semansky is an instructor of English literature and composition and writes on literature and culture for several publications. In this essay, Semansky considers the idea of progress in Wells's novel.

The late nineteenth century was a time when many people believed that progress, especially technological progress, could solve many of humanity's seemingly intractable problems, such as

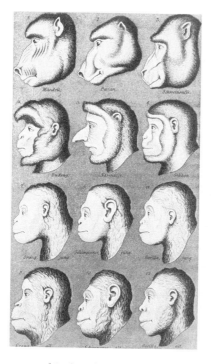

Anthropomorphic facial features depicting the theory of evolution, a formative influence on Wells's The Time Machine

disease, hunger, violence, and exploitation. Wells, a devotee of science, seemingly endorses this view at the beginning of *The Time Machine*, as the Time Traveller, an inventor, creates a machine that travels in the fourth dimension. However, as the story continues, readers see that the Time Traveller discovers a future in which the only thing that has progressed is humanity's savagery and thirst for self-destruction.

The idea of progress emerged contemporaneously with the formation of the sciences and professional scientists and was significantly spurred by the publication of Darwin's *On the Origin of Species* in 1859. Although the notion of evolution was heavily debated before Darwin, Christian beliefs about the creation of the universe held sway in the popular imagination. Holding fast to the Genesis-inspired version of the origins of humanity, the church opposed many ideas of progress put forth by natural historians and scientists because they did not coincide with the church's literal interpretation of the Bible. Such opposition also rationalized the inequality of classes, as humanity was seen as the object, rather than the subject, of change, and people were encouraged to accept their lot in life. Dar-

win's theory of natural selection and Marx's description of history as a class struggle gave many people a new conceptual framework within which to think about change and, more specifically, to view change as progress. They saw in both Darwin and Marx's theories the idea that humankind was improving with time, that its intellect was becoming more sophisticated, and that a classless society was inevitable. Wells, however, did not equate progress with improvement, and the discoveries of the Time Traveller illustrate his belief that evolution does not necessarily mean evolution of morality or of the intellect. Wells's son and literary critic, Anthony West, sums up the writer's thinking on this subject in his essay "H.G. Wells":

> Wells suggests that morals and ethics have their basis in man's behavior as a social animal.... The intellect on the other hand is amoral and ultimately recognizes the single value of efficiency, so that a continuation of the line of development that had made man a reasoning animal might ultimately make him more callous, indifferent, and cruel, not more moral.

The Time Traveller's initial response after landing in the future but prior to meeting the Eloi, underscores this thinking. He worries: "What if cruelty had grown into a common passion? What if in this interval the race had lost its manliness, and had developed into something inhuman, unsympathetic, and overwhelmingly powerful?" His fears partially come true after meeting the creatures, for they have gown weak from not having to work or endure hardship, and since they had all the comforts of the good life provided for them, they had lost the impetus to strive. But the Time Traveller sees this "ruinous splendor" as a kind of paradise, where "One triumph of a united humanity over Nature had followed another." This paradise, however, is not a cause of celebration but a reason for mourning. After learning of the Morlocks' existence, the Time Traveller speculates on what had come to pass:

> I grieved at how brief the dream of human intellect had been. It had committed suicide. It had set itself steadfastly toward comfort and ease, a balanced society with security and permanency as its watchword. It had attained its hopes—to come to this at last.... The rich had been assured of his wealth and comfort, the toiler assured of his life and work.

Wells's depiction of the relationship between the Eloi and the Morlocks can be seen as a critique of the notion that "work" was a problem to be solved, rather than a necessary condition of humanity essential for the intellect to develop. Before Marx drew closer attention to the horrific working conditions of laborers, locating their misery in the historic struggle between capital and labor in writings such as *The Communist Manifesto* (1848), workers were largely resigned to their fate. In *The Annals of Labour: Autobiographies of British Working Class People, 1820–1920*, historian John Burnett sums up their attitude as follows:

> There is a sense of patient resignation to the facts of life, the feeling that human existence is a struggle and that survival is an end in itself. Especially is this so in relation to the early death of wives or children—a fatalistic attitude that 'God gives and God takes away,' and that although one may mourn, one does not inveigh against the Fates which, to us, seem to have treated some so cruelly.

The working class would receive their reward not in this life but in the next. They waited for salvation, not progress, enduring hardship and suffering in their daily lives in the hope of securing a better one after they died. History was merely how one waited for the return of Christ. Wells mocks the Christian notion that life's purpose is to wait for salvation in his image of the winged sphinx, one of the first things the Time Traveller sees after "landing." The Sphinx of Giza, Egypt, has the body of a lion and the head of a king or god and is a symbol of strength and wisdom. By putting wings on it, Wells creates a kind of hybrid angel. Instead of representing God's messengers, however, the statue signifies a degraded civilization on the verge of extinction.

Marx had a different idea of salvation. An atheist who argued that history was evolving towards a classless society in which wealth would be distributed equally, Marx offered hope for millions of people who toiled in factories for low wages, but he also instilled fear in capitalists who benefited from the labor of the working poor. Ironically, Wells, an occasional socialist, parodies communism in the Time Traveller's description of the Eloi, as what he initially sees as the perfect communist society turns out to be little more than an updated and more perverted story of the haves and the have-nots from his own time. Humanity's mistake, Wells implies in the novel, is in believing that through science and technology they had conquered nature. Nature, for Wells, was a stronger force than society, one that could not be subjugated. Overriding Wells's belief in the moral rightness of socialism was his belief that, ultimately, humankind could not contend with the force of nature. The Time Traveller spells this out when he muses on the Eloi:

> I thought of the physical slightness of the people, their lack of intelligence . . . and it strengthened my belief in the perfect conquest of Nature. For after the

What Do I Read Next?

- Charles Darwin's 1859 groundbreaking study of humanity's beginnings, *On the Origin of Species by Natural Selection*, had a profound impact on Wells's intellectual development.

- Like Wells, William Gibson is a science fiction writer. Gibson, however, is interested in the interface between human beings and machines, rather than human beings and animals. His blockbuster novel *Neuromancer* (1984) helped to establish the genre of Cyberpunk literature.

- T. H. Huxley was perhaps the largest single influence on Wells's career as a writer and thinker. Adrian Desmond's biography *Huxley: From Devil's Disciple to Evolution's High Priest* (1997) examines Huxley's role in popularizing Darwin's theory of evolution and in legitimizing science in nineteenth-century Britain.

- Mark Twain's novel *A Connecticut Yankee at King Arthur's Court* (1889) is the first novel to explicitly use time travel in its plot.

- Wells's novel *The Island of Doctor Moreau: A Possibility* (1896), about an island stocked with hybrids of animals and human beings from scientific experiments gone bad, remains one of Wells's more popular works and is particularly relevant today.

---

battle comes Quiet. Humanity has been strong, energetic, and intelligent, and has used all its abundant vitality to alter the conditions under which it lived. And now came the reaction of the altered conditions.

The "reaction," nature's revenge, came in the form of the evolution of two races of "people," neither of which had any exemplary moral traits. By locating progress as a provisional phenomenon contingent upon humanity's capacity to make moral choices, rather than as the purpose of history or evolution, Wells calls attention to the necessity for humankind to change its ways carefully, and with the future in mind. More than a science fiction story or a fantasy tale, *The Time Machine* is a cautionary tale of what may happen if unfettered capitalism is permitted to continue. By making a machine the thing that literally enables time travel, Wells was appealing to the increasing fascination Westerners of the late nineteenth century had for the new and the mechanical. Electricity, steamships, the radio and telephone, and numerous other technological inventions were changing the shape of what was thought possible and, Wells would say, blinding many to their very human responsibilities to use these inventions for the betterment of all rather than for the profit of a few.

Source: Chris Semansky, Critical Essay on *The Time Machine*, in *Novels for Students*, The Gale Group, 2003.

Sources

Asimov, Isaac, Introduction, in *Three Novels of the Future*, Nelson Doubleday Inc., 1979, pp. vii–xii.

Bergonzi, Bernard, "*The Time Machine*: An Ironic Myth," in *H. G. Wells: A Collection of Critical Essays*, edited by Bernard Bergonzi, Prentice-Hall Inc., 1976, pp. 39–56.

Burnett, John, *The Annals of Labour: Autobiographies of British Working Class People, 1820–1920*, Indiana University Press, 1974, p. 14.

Costa, Richard Hauer, *H. G. Wells*, Twayne Publishers, 1967, pp. 31–35.

Philmus, Robert M., "The Logic of 'Prophecy' in *Time Machine*," in *H. G. Wells: A Collection of Critical Essays*, edited by Bernard Bergonzi, Prentice Hall Inc., 1976, pp. 56–69.

Pritchett, V. S., "The Scientific Romances," in *H. G. Wells: A Collection of Critical Essays*, edited by Bernard Bergonzi, Prentice Hall Inc., 1976, pp. 32–39.

Wells, H. G., *The Time Machine and Other Stories*, Scholastic Book Services, 1963, pp. 1–124.

West, Anthony, "H. G. Wells," in *H. G. Wells: A Collection of Critical Essays*, edited by Bernard Bergonzi, Prentice Hall Inc. 1976, pp. 8–25.

Further Reading

Bergonzi, Bernard, *The Early H. G. Wells: A Study of the Scientific Romances*, Manchester University Press, 1961.
    Bergonzi played a large part in establishing Wells's reputation as a great science fiction writer, arguing that Wells's scientific romances such as *The Time Machine*, *The Island of Doctor Moreau*, *The Invisible Man*, and *The War of the Worlds* are classics of the English language.

Coren, Michael, *The Invisible Man: The Life and Liberties of H. G. Wells*, Atheneum, 1993.
    Coren explores the contradictions of Wells's life, claiming that although Wells championed women's suffrage, he was also a misogynist and that although he was sympathetic to the plight of the Jews, he held anti-Semitic views.

Huntington, John, *The Logic of Fantasy: H. G. Wells and Science Fiction*, Columbia University Press, 1982.
    Huntington examines the relationship between Wells's writing and the genre of science fiction and considers how Wells contributed to the emerging form.

MacKenzie, Norman, and Jean MacKenzie, *The Time Traveller: Life of H. G. Wells*, Weidenfeld and Nicolson, 1973.
    The MacKenzies provide a relatively straightforward and uncontroversial account of Wells's life in this accessible biography.

The Tree of Red Stars

Tessa Bridal

1997

Tessa Bridal's *The Tree of Red Stars* takes place during a time of dire political upheaval in Uruguay. Most of the story centers on the activities that occurred during the 1960s and 1970s in Montevideo, Uruguay's capital. Although a fictionalized account, Bridal makes a statement in the front pages of her book that the story was inspired by real people and real events.

After leaving her country, Bridal was surprised to discover that, outside of Uruguay, no one knew what was really happening there. The stories that were being printed in the media of other countries did not correspond to her experiences and memories. She recounts that no one in Uruguay was left untouched by the violence that was occurring there, and her story is told as a way to make sure that the voices of Uruguayans will not be lost. Bridal "uses her book to present a harrowing account of that country's takeover by a military dictatorship, a regime that violently demolished one of Latin America's oldest democracies," wrote Paula Friedman for the *New York Times*.

It was during these troubled times in Uruguay that a citizen's group of urban guerillas, the Tupamaros, was formed to protest the dictatorship government that had set itself in power. *The Tree of Red Stars* tells the story of a young, outspoken girl, Magda, who comes of age in the midst of all this social, political, and economic chaos. Her older friends and some of their parents are secretly involved with the Tupamaros, and as the young girl matures into womanhood, she too takes up the fight

Tessa Bridal

against the corruption that has invaded her life and the lives of her family and friends.

The Tree of Red Stars is Bridal's first novel. It won the Milkweed Prize for fiction and first prize with the Friends of American Writers. It was selected by the New York Public Library for its 1998 Books for the Teenage list, was *Booklist* Editors' choice, and was chosen by *Independent Reader* as one of the five Most Recommended Books for 1997.

Author Biography

Over one hundred years ago, Tessa Bridal's ancestors settled in Uruguay. They had come from Ireland and soon established themselves in the city of Montevideo. It was in Montevideo, the capital city of Uruguay, that Bridal was born and raised.

During her youth, Bridal witnessed the turmoil that occurred in her homeland during the 1960s and 1970s, when Uruguay suffered economic losses and turmoil in the labor sector. The government, which had formerly been very successful in supporting its Uruguayan population, became increasingly corrupt and slid into a form of dictatorship,

which set the scene for the creation of the Tupamaros, an urban guerilla movement. All these elements strongly affected Bridal and play a very significant role in her first novel, *The Tree of Red Stars*.

Bridal eventually left Uruguay. She has since lived in Brazil, Washington, D.C., and in London. For the past twenty years, she has called Minnesota her home. It is in St. Paul, at the Science Museum of Minnesota, that Bridal now spends many hours of her day as the director of public programs, where her responsibilities include producing live theatre performances. For her work in this capacity, she has earned the American Association of Museums Education Committee's Award for Excellence. She has also worked as the artistic director of the Minnesota Theatre Institute of the Deaf.

In 1997, Bridal wrote and published her first novel, for which she won the Milkweed National Fiction Prize. She has also published many articles and short stories, which have been published in various literary journals. In addition, Bridal teaches creative writing classes through The Loft, Borders Books, The Minnesota Center for Arts Education, and at Hamline University in St. Paul and at North Dakota State University.

Currently, Bridal lives outside the Minneapolis-St. Paul cities, in Albertville, with her husband, Randy, and their two daughters, Ana and Kate. She and her husband volunteer their free time for the Humane Society, for which they also run a foster home for animals. They share their home with a dog, a cat, two rabbits, and seventeen birds.

Plot Summary

Prologue–Chapter 1

The Tree of Red Stars begins with a prologue, written almost as a letter to the reader. The protagonist, Magda, is returning to Uruguay after a seven-year exile in Europe. She talks about Marco Aurelio Pereira, who has spent seven years in jail after rescuing her from a similar fate. Statements about the political unrest in Uruguay before Magda left are related, as well as Magda's efforts to secure the release of Marco.

Chapter 1 begins with details about Magda's childhood in Montevideo. The neighborhood is described, with a special emphasis on the poinsettia tree outside of Magda's home, where she and Emilia hide to watch their neighbors. As they sit in the tree, Gabriela, a young woman from the outskirts of town appears, and Magda convince Emilia to hide in the back of Gabriela's wagon to see where she lives. Once at Gabriela's house, which is made of cardboard, newspapers, and plastic, Magda sees a small plate, which she had made in school for her mother, hanging in Gabriela's home. Gabriela is proud of that plate, but Magda is hurt that her mother has given it away. In the meantime, Gabriela, concerned that the police might think she has kidnapped the girls, immediately sets out to return them.

Chapters 2–3

Chapter 2 introduces Cora, a young Jewish girl, whom Magda and Emilia find mysterious. Cora keeps her distance and is always chaperoned by her parents. Also in chapter 2, Josefa, Magda's cook, tells the mythical story about the moon and its present of *mate*, a local, traditional tea that "makes brothers and sisters of all who drink it," a tradition that will soon be shattered as the political upheaval will pit one Uruguayan against another.

In chapter 3, Magda's aunts, or *tías* enjoy a brief discussion of politics and of a woman who insists on her rights in the male-dominated Uruguayan society. Magda carries tidbits of the aunts' conversations to Emilia's house and shares them with Emilia's mother, who proclaims that men "think they know more about being a woman than we do." The rest of the chapter provides further examples of the inequality of women and men in Uruguay.

Chapters 4–5

Magda and Emilia celebrate their twelfth birthday. They discover that Cora is also about to turn twelve. Cora is a romantic image to them, especially in reference to her relationship with her father. Magda's and Emilia's fathers are seldom home and pay little attention to them when they are. They later realize that Cora's father is so attentive because he is afraid Cora will be assaulted for being Jewish.

Señora Francisca is introduced in chapter 5. One night, Magda sees Lilita, Cora's mother, sneaking into Francisca's home. Magda, after intercepting Emilia, insists that the two of them also sneak inside to find out what the two older women are doing. When they overhear the women's conversation, Magda and Emilia realize that the women are involved in the revolution.

Chapters 6–7

Francisca opens the chapter with a loud wailing sound after her husband's mistress appears at her door, telling her about all the money that he spends on her. Francisca is devastated. Although she has given the appearance of having money, her house is all but bare of furnishings. She decides to seek revenge by going on a shopping spree.

In chapter 7, Magda, Emilia, and Cora go to the zoo. After Magda risks danger by climbing over a fence to feed her favorite elephant, Cora yells at her about her careless behavior. Cora fears not only for Magda's life but also for her own, because she is afraid that Magda will one day get her in trouble.

Marco is introduced as Magda goes to his house to visit his mother. Magda describes him and pays special attention to his mouth. "I was too young to understand the hunger it evoked in me," she says, foreshadowing her involvement with him. Marco expounds on his political views, especially his dislike of the United States' intervention in Uruguay.

Chapters 8–9

Che Guevara comes to the university to speak. Magda is forbidden to go but sneaks out anyway and takes Emilia with her. Magda is inspired by Che's talk but, when a gunshot is heard, pandemonium breaks out. Emilia and Magda run into Cora, who has been injured. Magda seeks help, but a policeman corners her and assaults her sexually. She kicks him and runs down the street and is pulled into a doorway by some students, who hide her. They then help her, Emilia, and Cora to get home.

Upon arriving home, Emilia finds that her mother has tried to commit suicide. Lilita is saved and makes Magda promise never to get Emilia into any more trouble.

Chapter 9 takes on a lighter tone as Magda and Emilia celebrate their fifteenth birthdays. At the birthday celebration, Marco dances with Magda and kisses her. He also announces that he has enlisted in the army. Magda also meets a friend of Marco's, Jaime Betancourt, who courts her. As they become more involved, Magda's mother tries to get rid of Jaime, whom she disapproves of because of his social status. She promises to introduce him to people who will help him to find a job in the United States. When this does not work, she tempts Magda with a trip to the United States, hoping Magda will forget Jaime.

Chapters 10–11

Some of the history of Magda's family is portrayed in chapter 10. Her grandfather came from London when he was twenty-four. He arrived in 1902, bought a ranch, and eventually married eighteen-year-old Aurelia Ponce de Aragon, against the wishes of both sets of parents.

There is also mention of the first of Magda's ancestors arriving in Uruguay and of a special ancient agate puzzle that was made by a Charrúa native and which has been handed down over generations in the family. Magda's grandmother imparts this information as she prepares Magda for her trip to the United States.

In chapter 11, both Magda, who lives for one year in Michigan, and Emilia, who spends a year in Missouri, compare life in Uruguay to their experiences in the States.

Chapters 12–13

Chapter twelve is written in the form of several letters sent by Emilia to Magda, Magda to Emilia, Jaime to Magda, and Magda and Marco to one another. In the letters, Magda and Emilia continue to share examples of the strange culture that they are experiencing in the States. Jaime tells Magda how much he misses her and asks her to find out the names of airline executives to whom he can write.

In Magda's letter to Marco, she relates such incidents as the cold winter, the latest Beatles' movie, and sports—typical American topics. In Marco's letter to Magda, however, the tone is more somber, as Marco discusses the student protests in Uruguay.

Magda returns to Uruguay in chapter 13. The mood in Uruguay is rapidly changing, as Brazilians, fleeing their country to escape the military dictatorship there, warn the Uruguayans that the same thing could happen in their country. Marco is now a lieutenant in the army, but he is still involved with covert work that helps the protesters. Magda visits Gabriela, who tells Magda that Marco "has a mission" and that "such men are difficult to love." Magda has broken up with Jaime because both she and Jaime realize that she is really in love with Marco.

Cora elopes with Ramiro, a man she meets at a political gathering. Her parents are devastated.

Chapters 14–15

A friend of Jaime's dies in a plane crash, and Jaime blames his commanding officer, Captain Prego. Jaime believes that Prego was negligent and challenges him to a duel. Prego shoots Jaime in the chest, claiming that Jaime moved into the oncoming bullet. Jaime dies.

As a result of her being at the duel, Magda's picture appears on the front page of the city's newspaper. To avoid scandal, Magda's grandmother takes Magda to Caupolicán, the family ranch. While at the ranch, Magda realizes that her future plans must include Caupolicán. Her grandmother wants to give the ranchland to her, as no one else in the family truly appreciates it. Once back in the city, Magda enters the university in Montevideo and decides to major in economics and land management. One day after attending classes, she runs into Ramiro, who promises to take her to see Cora.

Chapters 16–17

There is a discussion between Cora, Ramiro, and Magda that involves the politics of the day. Russia is hoping that Uruguayans will not promote a capitalistic government, whereas the United States is hoping that there will be no move toward socialism. Ramiro tells Magda that he and Cora are involved with the guerilla group called Tupamaros, a group that wants to ensure that a social democracy is established in Uruguay. Magda decides to become involved.

Magda holds a job at the U.S. Information Services (USIS) because of her fluency in English. She promises the Tupamaros to act as a spy for them. In such a capacity, she discovers that one of her supervisors, Dan Mitrione, teaches Uruguayan police officers how to torture prisoners. Magda and Ramiro plan to kidnap Mitrione and use him to gain the release of political prisoners.

Magda discovers, in chapter 17, that Gabriela had been tortured to death by some of Mitrione's men. She gains permission from her grandmother to bury Gabriela's body at Caupolicán. Magda, Gervasio, and Cora bring Gabriela's body to the ranchland. In the meantime, Mitrione's body is found in the back of a car.

Chapters 18–19

The Tupamaros decide to kidnap the British ambassador, Geoffrey Jackson. In an attempt to gain information about Jackson, Magda must befriend his assistant, Peter Wentworth. Emilia meets Wentworth when she and Magda audition for a play that Wentworth is directing. Emilia and Wentworth fall in love.

The ambassador is kidnapped, Ramiro is arrested, and Cora goes into hiding. Magda and Emilia are invited to Wentworth's home, along with Emilia's parents, who believe that Wentworth is about to propose marriage to their daughter. After they arrive, however, the police show up and arrest Emilia, convinced that she became involved with Wentworth only to find out the comings and goings of the ambassador. Magda confesses that it was she who was a Tupamaro and that Emilia is innocent. The police do not believe her.

Emilia is released three days later. Wentworth, who had set up the arrest, refuses to talk to her. The Uruguayan military is called into force to take over the struggle against the Tupamaros. Marco, now a captain, continues to work with the Tupamaros while keeping his cover as an army officer. He helps political prisoners escape.

Chapter 20–Epilogue

Ramiro escapes prison, and Magda is told where he and Cora are hiding. She brings them food. Emilia insists on helping her. Shortly thereafter, Magda is arrested. She is put in isolation. She often hears, in a room above her, the moans of people being tortured. At one point, she is taken out of her room and brought to a gathering of some old friends, including Ramiro and Cora, whom the police have allowed to be officially married.

Magda remains in her cell for several months. One day Marco, now a colonel, shows up and secretly releases her. He takes her home and Magda's father takes her to Caupolicán.

Marco appears at Caupolicán the first night. He and Magda make love, and then he leaves. Marco is arrested shortly afterward. Magda learns that Ramiro has died and that Cora has disappeared. The next day, Magda escapes to Brazil.

In the Epilogue, Magda and Emilia are waiting for Marco to appear. When he does, he looks frail and tells Magda that he does not have much more time left to live.

Characters

Cora Allenberg

Cora is first introduced as a young girl who moves into Magda's neighborhood. She appears mysterious to both Magda and Emilia because she is always neatly dressed and, whenever she is outside of the home, she is always accompanied by

her parents. Cora eventually is able to throw off the confines of her parents, but she does so through deceit, telling her parents one thing but then doing something quite different. She becomes a good friend of Magda's and Emilia's.

Cora elopes with Ramiro, a young man whom she meets at a political gathering. They both become involved with the Tupamaros and are arrested and tortured. Although they escape, they are recaptured. At the end of the story, no one knows what has happened to Cora. She is listed as a missing person.

Mr. Allenberg

Cora's father, who is overly protective of Cora, afraid that people will offend or assault her because she is Jewish, mourns his daughter after she elopes with Ramiro.

Mrs. Allenberg

Cora's mother, who together with her husband had to flee from Holland in a hearse in order to escape the Nazis, is very suspicious of Magda and Emilia, concerned that they will one day turn on her daughter and call her names because she is Jewish.

Señora Francisca Arteaga

A neighbor of Magda's, Francisca is totally humiliated when her husband's mistress comes to her home and tells her about how much her husband spends on her. After that, Francisca goes out and spends a lot of money on her and her daughters' comfort. Francisca is also involved, covertly, with the Tupamaros. She represents a traditional woman who is going through a transition into a more modern and more independent stance.

Jaime Betancourt

Jaime, Marco's friend, becomes involved in a relationship with Magda. Magda's mother believes that Jaime is trying to use Magda's position in society to make a better name for himself. Jaime's father is a tailor, a profession that Magda's mother looks down upon. Although Jaime professes his love for Magda, he also encourages her to help him find a way to get a job as a pilot with an American airline.

Upon Magda's return from the States, Jaime asks Magda to marry him, but he notices her reluctance and finally makes her admit that she really loves Marco. Jaime graciously backs away.

One of Jaime's colleagues dies in a plane crash, which Jaime blames on his commanding officer and challenges him to a duel. Jaime dies in the contest. While Marco goes through his belongings, he finds a letter addressed, but never sent, to Magda. In the letter, Jaime's true feelings for Magda are revealed.

Charrúas

The Charrúas are native people of Uruguay who initially posed a threat to all pioneering land settlers who came from Europe. One of the Charrúas supposedly had fallen in love with one of Magda's female ancestors, Isabel FitzGibbon, and made her a beautiful agate puzzle, which had been handed down from generation to generation in Magda's family.

Emilia

Emilia moves into Magda's neighborhood while both girls are very young. She and Magda become lifelong friends, sharing their love of climbing into the poinsettia tree and watching people walk by. Although Emilia is included in all of Magda's childish pranks, as the girls grow older, Emilia becomes weary and very concerned that one day Magda's need for adventure will get them both into very serious trouble.

Emilia is described as being very nurturing. She worries about her mother, whose clandestine activities she does not understand. When Emilia's mother tries to commit suicide on the same day that Emilia has followed Magda to hear Che speak, she tells Magda that she no longer wants to be included in any more of Magda's activities. However, when Magda tells Emilia that she is auditioning for a play, Emilia insists on going with her. She meets Peter Wentworth at the audition and immediately falls in love with him. Later, when Peter's boss is kidnapped by the Tupamaros, Emilia is arrested as a suspect and is tortured. After this incident, she becomes involved with the revolution, helping Cora and Ramiro while they are in hiding. At the end of the story, Emilia is involved in the reunion of Magda and Marco.

Charlie FitzGibbon

Charlie is the first male ancestor of Magda's to land in Uruguay from Ireland. Referred to as a "black Irishman," Charlie is Isabel's husband.

Isabel FitzGibbon

The first female ancestor of Magda's to land in Uruguay, Isabel is married to Charlie but is said to have befriended a Charría native who fell in love with her and made a beautiful agate puzzle for her.

Gabriela

Gabriela is a beautiful but poor young girl who lives on the Cerro, a tall hill outside of Montevideo, in a neighborhood of shacks. She is the mistress of a married man. She comes to Magda's neighborhood to beg for food and clothing for her children. During the revolution, she becomes involved with the Tupamaros, is caught, and is tortured to death.

Gervasio

Gervasio is the oldest son of Gabriela. Marco befriends him and encourages Gervasio to attend college. When Gabriela is murdered, Gervasio assists Magda is finding his mother's body and reburying it on Magda's grandmother's ranch.

Carmen Grey

Carmen is one part of Magda's twin cousins. She comes to live with Magda's family after her parents die in a car crash. Because the twins are a little older than Magda, she watches them to see how they act with boys.

Ernest Grey

Ernest is Magda's maternal grandfather, who came from London and fell in love and married Aurelia Ponce de Aragon, against his parents' advice. He and Aurelia reap the benefits of their parents trying to outdo one another in providing wealth to their children. However, his main interest is in sharing his love and life with Aurelia. He is never present in the story, having died prior to the time of narration.

Magdalena Ortega Grey

Magdalena ("Magda") is the protagonist of the story. It is through her that the story is told. Readers learn about her childhood, in which she was always looking for some form of adventure, whether it was soaping the sidewalk so she could watch her neighbors slip and fall or sneaking into her cousins' room to find novels that portray explicit references to sex.

Magda's closest friend is Emilia, whom she has known since elementary school. Magda usually drags Emilia with her, as she seeks out new adventures. Magda loves excitement and going against the sometimes stifling social constraints that her parents try to impose on her due to her family's high standing in the community. Her family can trace their lineage back to one of the oldest European pioneers. Because of their large possessions of land, they belong to the class of the moneyed elite. The family is, therefore, in a general way, the enemy of the Tupamaros, with whom Magda eventually becomes involved.

Magda's reunion with Cora and Ramiro introduces her to the Tupamaros. Since she works for the USIS as a translator, she has access to information that the Tupamaros need. She often bemoans her covert activities, as they are subtle. She would rather be involved in the actual kidnappings, the releasing of prisoners from jail, than the spying that she is told to do. When she does become involved in helping to feed Cora and Ramiro, she is caught and sent to jail. She is tortured there, not physically but psychologically and emotionally. She is secretly released by Marco.

Magda, from an early age, falls in love with Marco. However, because he is older than she and because she creates a romantic image of him in her mind, she has trouble letting her feelings be known. Instead, when she turns fifteen, she becomes involved with Jaime, a friend of Marco's. She is never truly convinced that she loves Jaime, but there is an attraction to him that she does not fully understand. After spending a year in the States, however, she returns to Uruguay and realizes that it is Marco whom she really loves. She breaks up with Jaime shortly before he challenges Prego to a duel in which he dies. Marco, in the meantime, becomes so involved with his rising role in the military and his dual role of working undercover for the Tupamaros that he seldom has time to see Magda. In the end, the two lovers finally admit their strong feelings for one another. However, their paths cross for only a brief time, as Magda is imprisoned and, upon her release, Marco is thrown in jail. They meet again, after a seven-year span, at the end of the story, with Marco having only a few months left to live.

Sofía Grey

Sofía is one part of Magda's twin cousins. She comes to live with Magda's family after being orphaned at the age of seven. The twins are a little more than a year older than Magda. Magda learns about sexual relationships through her cousins by eavesdropping on them.

Geoffrey Jackson

Geoffrey is the British ambassador to Uruguay, whom the Tupamaro kidnap.

Josefa

Josefa is Magda's family cook. She tells Magda local myths about love and the making of *mate*, a local tea. At one point in the story, when Josefa cries over a family incident, Magda relates, "Her tears were a gift of caring." Then Magda continues, "She gave because it was in her nature to give."

Lilita

Lilita is Emilia's mother. She is involved with the Tupamaros from the early development of the movement. She tries to hide her activities from her daughter, but Magda sneaks Emilia into a neighbor's house so they can eavesdrop on a conversation that reveals Lilita's involvement in the revolution. She later talks to Magda about the revolution, warning her that one day she will have to make a decision about which side she wants to take. In the end, she feels bad about having kept so many secrets from her daughter and reveals the truth to her. At the end of the story, Lilita has died.

Mamsita

See Aurelia Ponce de Aragon

Dan Mitrione

Based on a true character, Mitrione was reportedly trained by the FBI and served as a chief of police in the States. He is sent by the State Department to Uruguay to train the local police force. His alleged specialty was torture. Mitrione is the first person that the Tupamaros kidnap. He is later found dead.

Señora Ortega

Magda's mother is typical of the upper-class Uruguayan women of her time. She condescends to her husband, tries to keep her children innocent of adult activities, and wants only that her daughter grow up healthy, well educated, and contented with a rich man. Appearances are very important to her. Only once does she open up to Magda, and that is after her daughter is sexually accosted by a policeman.

Colonel Pereira

The father of Marco, Colonel Pereira encourages his son to enter the army, believing that this will keep him out of trouble. He wields his political power to keep Marco from being put in jail, while Marco, still in his teens, demonstrates alongside of students and laborers who are fighting for more decent wages.

Marco Aurelio Pereira

Marco is a young neighbor and childhood friend of Magda's. He is several years older than she and, as a teenager, he is constantly seeking out ways to join the students and laborers in their protests against the dictatorship of the Uruguayan government.

Marco's father is a military man, and eventually Marco enters the army, thus appeasing his father. However, Marco's real aim is to undermine the army. He senses that it will be the military that will become the strong force of the government, and he wants to be able to inform the Tupamaros of the army's activities. He also wants to rise in rank so that he too will have power, which he will use in favor of the revolution.

Marco is very intelligent and falls in love with Magda at an early age. However, he does not reveal his feelings until Magda is much older. He does educate Magda about what is happening in the government and in the revolution. It is because of Marco that Magda becomes involved in the revolution, although Marco does not know this at first. When he does discover that Magda is working with the Tupamaros, he tries to convince her to stop.

Marco quickly gains the commission of colonel in the army and is responsible for helping political prisoners be released. He is also involved in the satisfactory release of the British ambassador that the Tupamaros have kidnapped. Marco gains the release of Emilia when she is wrongfully accused of having been involved in the ambassador's kidnapping. He also gains Magda's release at the cost of his own imprisonment.

Señora Marta Pereira

Marco's mother, Marta Pereira, is "an ample woman" who likes to cook and to write poetry and dramas for soap operas. She names her sons after characters in Shakespeare's plays. She also befriends Magda when Magda needs someone to talk to.

Aurelia Ponce de Aragon

Aurelia is Magda's maternal grandmother, Mamasita, who was married to Ernest Grey at the young age of seventeen despite her parents' objection. She is a very lively woman, even in her old age. She maintains a large home in the city as well as the ranch called Caupolicán, out in the country, several hours' drive away from Montevideo.

Aurelia rides horses, climbs coconut trees, and tells Magda family secrets and important details about life in general that no one else will convey to her. She speaks openly and honestly to Magda, her favorite grandchild, to whom she wills her estate. She shelters Magda when she is in trouble and encourages her in love.

Captain Prego

Prego is Jaime's commanding officer who agrees to take part in a duel with Jaime, who slaps him in the face with a glove, displaying his anger over the death of a pilot, whom Jaime believes died in a crash due to Captain Prego's negligence. Prego ends up killing Jaime.

Ramiro

Ramiro is a young man who meets Cora at a political rally. He falls in love with Cora, and the couple elopes when Cora's parents try to make her marry a young Jewish man. Ramiro joins the Tupamaros with Cora and becomes involved in two kidnappings, which eventually lead to his arrest. He is tortured and finally released from jail but dies shortly afterward.

Mr. Stelby

Stelby is an English neighbor who is used to show the contrast between European culture and manners and Uruguayan ones. The narrator states, "for reasons no one could fathom, they [the Stelbys] had decided to remain in a country they never stopped reviling."

The Tías

The tías are Magda's mother's sisters: Catalina, Josefina, and Aurora. They come to Magda's house for tea on several occasions, and Magda loves to eavesdrop on their conversations. It is through their talk that she learns inside stories about various neighbors, about men and sex, and about politics.

Tupamaros

The Tupamaros are a group of people who secretly have come together to help to at least embarrass Uruguay's dictatorship. They are referred to as urban guerillas, and it is through them that the revolution against the government is conducted. Although they start peacefully with marches, speeches, and protests, they kidnap one of the men responsible for the torturing of political prisoners and kill him.

Peter Wentworth

Peter works with Ambassador Geoffrey Jackson, and it is through Wentworth that Magda gains information about the ambassador. Wentworth directs the play that Magda and Emilia audition for. When he first sees Emilia, he is captivated by her and falls in love. However, after the ambassador is kidnapped, Wentworth falsely accuses Emilia of being involved and arranges to have her arrested. After she is found innocent, Wentworth continues to refuse to have anything to do with her.

Themes

Oppression

Oppression is a very strong theme in this book, and it is demonstrated to exist in several different areas of the Uruguayan culture. There is the oppression of females from the rules set by the patriarchal society, which encourages its females to gain an education but sets double standards for other aspects of the women's lives. For instance, to have sex before a woman is married is not only discouraged, it is grounds for punishment, possibly a beating. However, it is standard practice for men to have sex before marriage. Not only that, it is common for most married men to have one or more mistresses. For women, once they are married, they are encouraged to stay home; some are even told they must stay in the house all day and are not allowed out unless accompanied by their husbands.

Landowners, at the time of this story, rule in Uruguay. They wield both economic and political power. People who do not own land scrounge for poor-paying jobs, and the population of poor people is growing. Landowners enjoy their elite position and exclude others from their ranks. Daughters are expected to marry within their economic class or to better themselves by marrying into richer families. If a young woman falls in love with someone her parents believe is beneath her, that relationship is thwarted.

There is also the oppression of ideas. Students who have their minds opened to other types of political philosophies and who try to pressure their oppressive government to make changes are imprisoned and tortured. This not only gets rid of the so-called dissidents but attempts to suppress others from speaking out as well. The government uses fear as an oppressor to maintain control over the masses.

Coming of Age

Magda comes of age in many different ways in this story. First, she goes through puberty, turning fifteen in the middle of the novel and awakening to the sexual desires of her body. She is aroused by Marco, but it is Jaime with whom she first encounters sex and mistakes it for love. With Marco, she develops into an understanding of mature love.

She also comes of age in her awareness of the culture around her. At first, she has very little understanding of her own social status. She lives in a privileged world and believes that everyone else does too. Although she visits Gabriela and sees her poverty, she does not fully grasp the hardships that Gabriela must face. Later, when she is rescued from the policeman who tries to sexually assault her, she realizes that the students who befriend her have offered her things that she takes for granted, like a pair of shoes, which she realizes might be the only pair that that particular student owns. When Jaime comments that he cannot afford to go to school, Magda finds the statement unbelievable. School in Uruguay is free. Then she realizes that Jaime has no money to pay for books, housing, food, and the other necessary items that he will need.

In the area of politics, Magda learns to open her mind to different voices, not just those who hand her propaganda about the current government regime. She discovers there is corruption and greed among the officials, which has led to the oppression of many Uruguayans. She comes to a point in her life when she must decide whether to continue to ignore the hardships of those around her or to do something that might be of service to them. Her decisions are made in spite of the difficulties it may cause her own family.

Love

Various forms of love are expressed in this novel. There is the strong friendship between Magda and Emilia that binds them together from their earliest years in elementary school to the end of the story, when Emilia witnesses the reunion of Magda and Marco.

In contrast is the tragic love affair between Magda and Marco, which is intense despite the fact that the two of them are rarely together. They feel their love for one another as teens but are too young to express it. By the time they are more fully matured, their roles in the revolution keep them separated. They make love only once throughout the telling of the story, and then they are torn apart again as Marco sacrifices his own life to save

Topics For Further Study

- U.S. intervention in Uruguay is a topic that is often brought up in Bridal's *The Tree of Red Stars*. Research the role of the United States in Uruguay during the 1950s through today. What kind of investments has the United States made? What, if any, Uruguayan resources are the United States interested in? Has the United States influenced the political climate? Use a broad range of research sources, including, but not exclusively, the *New York Times*, the *Washington Post*, the *Wall Street Journal*, both liberal and conservative news magazines, as well as any publications from Uruguay that are available. The Internet might also offer some rich sources.

- Read the book *Che Guevara: A Revolutionary Life* (1998). Then research the student uprising and the activities of the Tupamaros in Uruguay during the 1960s and 1970s. What kind of speech do you think Guevara might have made at the student gathering mentioned in Bridal's book? Remember that it is Guevara's speech that most inspired Magda. Write and deliver such a speech to your class.

- There have been several reported incidents of police brutality in the United States during the twentieth century. Research some of those incidents and write a report on your findings. You might want to look into the period of time in the South during the Civil Rights Movement. The Rodney King case might also provide material, or do a general search on the Internet for "police brutality." Are there similarities between these cases and what was happening in Uruguay? How are they alike? How are they different?

- Choose one of the more dramatic scenes or events in Bridal's book, and write a poem from the principal character involved, expressing that character's emotions at that time. Suggestions include Emilia after her ordeal in jail, including the loss of John Wentworth's love; Magda while she is in the United States witnessing the differences between the American culture and her Uruguay culture; Marco, sometime during his seven-year prison sentence; Cora, as she sits at her window, wanting desperately to go out and play with Magda and Emilia.

Magda. Once both of them are free, Marco's health is so deteriorated that he has only a few months to live.

There is also the love of country, as expressed by the young men and women who were willing to sacrifice their lives to bring down the dictatorship that was ruining Uruguay. Unable to close their eyes to the poverty and inequalities that existed as a result of the corrupt officials and the ruling elite, the students, the workers, and the poor risked everything that they had to bring about change.

Also represented is the love of the land as seen through Magda and her grandmother and their attachment to the family ranch. It is a love of the ways of nature and of the peace of the open space. It is also a respect for their ancestors who gave them the gift of the land.

Style

Point of View

The story is narrated in the first person, who readers can assume is Magda. Because of the first-person narrative, the story reads as if it has been written specifically for the reader, almost as if the author were writing a letter. The only time the first-person narration is altered is in chapter twelve, when the reader is privy to several actual letters, supposedly written by one character to another. However, even in the letters, of course, the point of view remains first person.

With the first-person narration, the story has a feel of a documentary, giving the plot of the story more authenticity. The narrator sounds as if she is merely relating events that have happened to her, and there is no reason to doubt her. The disadvantage of using the first-person narrator is that the reader has no access to the thoughts of all the other characters in the story. Every character and every event is seen through the eyes of the narrator. Although the narrator may be reliable, she might also be biased. However, the reader has no choice but to witness the events as the narrator remembers them and the way she perceives them. Since a large part of the story involves the memories of a young girl, there is a slight tendency to question some of the narrator's interpretations.

Setting

The setting in *The Tree of Red Stars* is almost a character in itself. The political turmoil of the 1960s and 1970s in Uruguay affects all the characters in the story. It is the setting of the story, as well as the consequences of that setting, that moved the author to write the story in the first place. Most of the characterization is used to put individual faces on the huge conflicts and the chaos that were taking place. Although the reader is pulled in by the stories of the characters' lives, it is the setting that makes this story unique.

Proselytization

The only criticism that has been made against the writing style of this novel is Bridal's occasional slips into a type of proselytization, a seeming attempt to persuade the reader to accept certain beliefs. As the story unfolds, Bridal occasionally ventures into political discussions between her characters. Sometimes these sections read as if she is trying to convince the reader rather than relate a discussion between two characters. The conversations are much longer than other dialogues. The same theme of U.S. intervention in Uruguayan politics is repeated in these specific discussions. Because of this, the discussions feel as if they have been inserted into the story artificially. It is the type of material that is more often found in a documentary than in a novel.

Historical Context

Early History

Uruguay's original populations consisted of the Charrúa Indians. They were a group of hunter-gatherers and, according to most historical accounts, they disliked outsiders. In 1516, when Spaniards first stepped foot into Uruguay, the Charrúa Indians killed Spanish explorer Juan Díaz de Solís and most of his party. Later, in the seventeenth century, the Charrúas became somewhat more friendly and set up trade with the Spanish explorers.

By the latter part of the seventeenth century, a settlement called Colonia was established by the Portuguese at the mouth of the Rio de la Plata. The Spanish, who did not approve of this settlement, built a citadel in Montevideo and later fought the Portuguese and won and then exiled José Artigas, an early Uruguayan hero. In 1828, the Uruguayans, inspired by Artigas, rose up against the Spanish and claimed Uruguay as an independent state.

During most of the nineteenth century, Uruguay had to fight either the Argentines or the Brazilians to maintain their independence. The British arrived in Uruguay and established several new industries, including importing British-raised cattle. Internal politics were made unstable by the two warring political parties, the Blancos and the Colorados, who were responsible for a civil war and several dictatorships.

Modern History

At the beginning of the twentieth century, José Batlle y Ordóñez was elected president. It was under his leadership that Uruguay became what is often referred to as the only welfare state in South America. He served two terms, during which he initiated a wide range of social welfare programs and abolished capital punishment.

Unfortunately, due to Uruguay's lack of natural resources and a slump in the demand for wool and meat, the two principal exports, to refurbish its economy, the country slowly became weighted down by the heavy expenses of Batlle y Ordóñez's social programs. By the 1960s, there was mass unemployment and inflation. Added to this was an overgrown government riddled with corruption. These factors led to a loud outcry from the Uruguayan population who was most affected by the decline in the economy—the unemployed workers, the poor, and the student population. It was during this time that the urban guerrilla movement was created.

The official name for the group was the Movimento de Liberacion Nacional but was known by most people as the Tupamaros, named for the last of the Inca royal family, Tupac Amaru. The movement was founded by Raúl Sendic, a student at the university in Montevideo.

At the beginning of the creation of this group, Uruguayan military and police membership was very low. Uruguay had enjoyed several decades of peace, and it was believed that there was little need to reinforce either establishment. The early goal of the Tupamaros was to embarrass the Uruguayan government. They stole from banks and gun shops. As their membership grew, they began to kidnap government officials.

As the economy grew worse, Montevideo often experienced student rioting. By 1968, a national emergency was declared. In 1970, Dan Mitrione, an American policeman who had been sent to Uruguay from the United States reportedly to teach Uruguayan police forces how to control the rising chaos, was kidnapped and later killed when the government refused to release political prisoners.

The Tupamaros, after the government made it illegal for any radio broadcast or any other media to mention their name, began their own underground media and produced much print and broadcast propaganda. As they grew stronger in force, they made the police look inept. After several policemen were killed, the police force went on strike, demanding better pay and more protection. As the economy continued to fail and after a series of corruption scandals, public support for the government began to diminish.

In 1971, a more liberal political party called the Frente Amplio gained support and looked as if they might actually have a chance to win the election. However, when the Tupamaros came out in favor of the Frente Amplio, the Uruguayan population, still stunned by the murder of Mitrione, turned away from the party and elected Juan María Bordaberry, who immediately suspended civil liberties and declared a state of internal war with the Tupamaros. Toward this end, the army was called into action, and mass arrests, torture, and free-handed search operations ensued. By the end of 1972, the Tupamaros ceased to be a threat.

Once in power, the military demanded that all left-wing political activity be suppressed and the legislature dissolved. For the next eleven years, Uruguay was ruled by one of the most repressive dictatorships in South America.

In 1984, Julio María Sanguinette won the presidential election. Under his leadership, Uruguay returned to democratic traditions. The government issued a massive political amnesty, but no other far-reaching reforms were made. Luis Alberto Lacalle was elected in 1990 but proved unpopular due to

his attempts to restructure the economy. In the following election, Sanguinetti was returned to office.

The year 1999 saw the election of Jorge Batlle, who has promised a return to progressive social programs. He is the first president to call for a search for those people who disappeared during the reign of the Tupamaros. Although the Uruguayan government begins to show signs of a return to democratic rule, there still remain severe restrictions on the Uruguayan press to refrain from publishing any stories that speak out against the government and can be viewed as inciting violence or insulting the nation. Stiff penalties for such crimes range up to a possible three years in jail.

Critical Overview

Bridal realized, upon traveling outside of Uruguay, that the story of her country was little known. Not only did people not know exactly where Uruguay was located, they had little idea of the terrible tragedy that was unfolding there. In writing *The Tree of Red Stars*, Bridal hoped, as Sybil S. Steinberg noted for *Publishers Weekly*, to create a "memorial to lost lives."

Bridal's debut novel won her the Milkweed Prize for fiction, and the overall reaction by critics has been one of praise. Steinberg, for instance, appreciated Bridal's storyline, which she described as "an unblinking exploration of the way absolute power can destroy civilized existence." She also referred to Bridal's "understated prose," which she found capable of permitting "large moments to occur without melodrama, and small ones to build into potent revelations."

In a review for *Library Journal*, Ellen Flexman likened Bridal's first novel to that of Isabel Allende's *The House of the Spirits*. Allende is a fellow South American author, whose family also suffered during an oppressive political regime in Chile. Flexman recommended Bridal's book for its "simple, straightforward plot," which captured "the terror of modern despotism as well as the hope necessary to overcome it."

In general reference to authors from South America, Friedman, in her article for the *New York Times*, stated that Bridal brought "a fresh voice to Latin American literature." Bridal relates her story, Friedman contended, "with a chillingly understated sense of inevitability." A critic for the *Journal of Adolescent & Adult Literacy*, Isabel Schon, called

Students and workers mass together in Montevideo, Uruguay, during the late seventies to protest against the dictatorship of the Uruguayan government

Bridal's story, a "moving, sometimes witty account" of growing up in Montevideo. Schon continued, "this tender story of love and friendship provides an insightful view into the realities of Latin American politics and life."

Criticism

Joyce Hart

Hart has degrees in English literature and creative writing and focuses her writing on literary themes. In this essay, Hart examines the connections between the protagonist Magda and the character Gabriela. Although the two women appear to live worlds apart, the author has built a very strong relationship between them.

In Tessa Bridal's *The Tree of Red Stars*, Magda, the protagonist of the story, grows up in the midst of many female characters. Those closest to her include Emilia, a young girl Magda's age, whom the protagonist has known since elementary school. Emilia has a gentle soul that attracts Magda to her. It is through her that Magda learns to see

people as creatures with emotions, people who need to be nurtured, whereas Magda had tended to view the people around her as mysterious puzzles or strange machines that she would like to take apart to better understand how they work. Emilia is a caretaker, whereas Magda is a scientist. Magda is also an adventurer, often including Emilia in her escapades, with Emilia usually giving in but reluctantly so.

Another childhood friend who influences Magda's early life is Cora, whose exotic family culture lures both Magda and Emilia to want to get to know her. They are awed by Cora's strong connection with her father, something neither Magda nor Emilia enjoys. They soon learn, however, that because of her father's overprotection, Cora remains somewhat a prisoner in her home, denied the free rein that Magda and Emilia enjoy to casually play in the river or to pull childish pranks. It is from Cora that Magda learns a new form of defiance, as Cora slowly moves away from her father's control, deceiving him in order to establish her own identity. Magda also celebrates Cora's decision to elope with a young lover of her choice rather than to marry a man whom her parents have chosen for her.

> " Had Magda not jumped onto that wagon and ridden with Gabriela to the Cerro, poverty might have remained a distant cliché, something talked about but never fully understood."

These girls share Magda's childhood with her on an almost daily basis. They live in her neighborhood, enjoying the same easy lifestyle of comfort afforded by wealth. That neighborhood is many miles away from the Cerro, the tallest hill in Uruguay, abandoned by all but a few soldiers who are stationed at the museum on the summit and "by the city's poorest residents, who lived on the hillside in houses made from the city's leftovers." It is on this hill that Gabriela lives in a house made of cardboard and newspapers, a drastically different environment from that in which Magda lives. However, despite the disparate economics that influence their lives, there are strong similarities that drive Magda toward Gabriela, that make her want to get to know her.

Gabriela is introduced in the first chapter of the novel and is described first by the color of her hair, the only other "redheaded young woman" in the story besides Magda; and, next, there is mention of the fact that she is "driving a rather fine horse," which stands in stark difference to the normally "tough and dusty" horses that other people from the Cerro drive, thus immediately setting Gabriela in a somewhat elevated position. Gabriela is also said to have physical features that "in a different time and place would have made her a movie star." The fact that, immediately following her introduction, Magda devises a plan in which she and Emilia will hide in the back of the young woman's wagon in order to go back to the Cerro to see where Gabriela lives makes the reader aware that this redheaded eighteen-year-old holds great significance.

Gabriela, although still a teen, brings a child with her when she visits Magda's mother. The child is still a very young baby, and Bridal emphasizes that not only is Magda interested in Gabriela, she is also fascinated with the little baby boy that Gabriela carries. In many ways, Gabriela represents exactly the opposite of Magda's potential. Gabriela is the mistress of a married man. She will give birth to several children over the course of the story. For Gabriela, being the mistress of a man of money and social standing might be the most that she can wish for. Her options in the Uruguayan society, during the time of the novel, are slight.

Magda, on the other hand, will fall in love with a neighborhood boy, with whom she will never have children. Her only other sexual relations will be protected, it is subtly suggested, as the issue of condoms is somewhat obliquely mentioned. Magda also not only has the option of going to college, but it is assumed from childhood that she will eventually attain a degree. Magda's options are multiple, given to her because of her family's connections and high standing in a society that at one time was considered one of the most successful welfare states in the world. It is therefore through a comparison of Magda and Gabriela that Bridal characterizes the political, social, and economic changes that have occurred in Uruguay between the early decades of the twentieth century and those of the 1950s through the 1970s, the setting when most of the drama of this novel takes place. The disparity that exists between Magda and Gabriela is the stimulus of the student riots, the labor strikes, and, ultimately, the revolution, the main focus of the story.

However, there is more than just the obvious dissimilarities between Magda and Gabriela. As already mentioned, they both have red hair, a simple fact that could easily be overlooked except that it is so emphasized. Gabriela's red hair is multiplied by her children, a fact that Magda uses later in the story to help her pinpoint Gabriela's whereabouts. She revisits the Cerro but cannot remember where Gabriela lives. Then she notices the redheaded children. She uses the color of their hair as a beacon. In the beginning of the story, it is Magda's red hair that is referred to as a beacon, one that might catch the eye of the soldiers, whom Gabriela fears. So it is with the color of their hair that Bridal first creates a link. Next, it is with a plate that Magda made in school, while quite young, for her mother. Magda's mother gave it away but told Magda that it had broken and had to be discarded. When Magda visits Gabriela, she finds the plate hanging on the wall. Gabriela is proud of the plate, whereas Magda's mother was ashamed of it. Through the plate, Bridal deepens the connection between Magda and Gabriela. With the color of hair, she establishes a sort of sisterhood between them. With the plate, Gabriela takes on a somewhat maternal role.

Magda and Gabriela also share a love of Marco. Once established in the army, Marco provides health benefits to Gabriela and her children. He also helps her children obtain an education. It is through Gabriela that Marco, in turn, understands on a personal level the elements of poverty. They both share political philosophies and are both involved in the revolution.

Magda's love of Marco is on a different level. She is attracted to him physically and emotionally. She is in awe of his intelligence and his commitment. Although it takes Magda a while to recognize her love of Marco, Gabriela notices it immediately. "The two of you are meant for one another," she tells Magda, upon Magda's admission that she loves him. However, she warns Magda that Marco "has a mission" and that such men "are difficult to love." In this role, Gabriela acts as older sister to Magda. She is mature enough to understand love and to recognize not only Marco's personality but also his passion. It is Gabriela who also predicts (and in that way warns Magda) that Marco will never have children and that "a piece of his lifeline is missing." She also tells Magda that his love is very strong.

Although Magda's visits to Gabriela's house cease as she matures into a woman, Gabriela's presence remains throughout the story. While working for the USIS as a translator, Magda is called to the home of Dan Mitrione. While there, acting in her capacity as spy for the Tupamaros, Magda overhears Mitrione discussing techniques of torture and his suggestions of using poor people to practice the new methods on. Later, she discovers photographs of people who have been his victims, and it is through these pictures that she learns that Gabriela has been murdered by Mitrione and his men. Prior to this, Magda had somewhat halfheartedly become involved with the Tupamaros. Once she discovers that Gabriela has suffered a horrendous death, her commitment changes. At first she is outraged and extremely passionate, wanting to kill Mitrione with her own hands. Later, she tempers her emotions, but Gabriela sustains the personal image in her mind, the image that makes Magda willing to sacrifice her own life in order to create changes in her government and in her country.

There is one more poignant scene in this novel that includes Gabriela, and it is through this scene that Magda demonstrates her deep love of Gabriela. With the help of Emilia and Gabriela's oldest son,

Magda locates Gabriela's body and takes it to Caupolicán, Magda's family ranch in the wilderness. Here she reburies her friend, paying her the highest compliment that is possible, given the circumstances. Caupolicán is a place of great beauty and peace for Magda. It represents the part of Uruguay that she most loves. Magda has committed herself to this land, promising her beloved grandmother that she will care for the land in a way that no one else in her family understands. By burying Gabriela here, Magda relays the message to Gabriela's son that she will also care for his mother, giving her peace in her death that she could not give her while she was living.

For Magda, Gabriela was someone to be admired. She was beautiful and self-determining. She was like a goddess of motherhood, fruitful and giving. She was also mature and understanding, qualities that were not dependent on social status, education, or money. However, Gabriela also represented suffering, both from the daily hardships of poverty and from the extreme inhumane conditions of warfare. It was because of these details of her life that she brought Magda out of her sheltered cocoon of privileged prejudice and taught her about the world of inequality and lack of opportunity. Despite the cultured differences of their childhoods and their consequential roles as adults, in the end they shared very similar perspectives on life.

It was through Gabriela that Magda learned to give without expecting anything in return. It was also through her that Magda comprehended that although money provided certain comforts, it was not the highest goal to reach for. Love and friendship went much further. Had Magda not jumped onto that wagon and ridden with Gabriela to the Cerro, poverty might have remained a distant cliché, something talked about but never fully understood. Through Gabriela, in some ways her exact opposite, Magda found herself.

Source: Joyce Hart, Critical Essay on *The Tree of Red Stars*, in *Novels for Students*, The Gale Group, 2003.

David Kelly

Kelly is an instructor of creative writing and literature at several colleges in Illinois. In this essay, Kelly explores the ways in which Magda's gender and social class make her the ideal narrator for the story that she tells.

The triumph of Tessa Bridal's 1997 novel, *The Tree of Red Stars*, is not that it introduces contemporary American readers to the political upheaval in Uruguay in the 1960s and 1970s. In fact, the po-

> As it is, the daily struggle for women to earn a place in society foreshadows the struggle of the poor that turns into a life-or-death struggle by the book's end."

litical situation surrounding the events of the book is somewhat under-explained, left to function as a frightening shadow and not really examined in much detail. Like much in totalitarian countries, the political dynamic that drives the actions of the characters in this novel is shrouded behind a veil of lies and destroyed evidence. Read as a novel about Uruguayan history, this book can only hope to sensitize readers to the signs of what a government is like when it is in the process of turning against its citizens. However, the book is of even more immediate relevance to readers than that. It presents a universal story of how individuals are drawn into revolutionary causes. The natural process that the novel's protagonist, Magdalena Ortega Grey, undergoes is parallel to a political maturation that readers around the world can relate to in their own lives.

At first glance, Magda might seem to be a weak choice to be the narrator of a novel about social upheaval. She comes from a wealthy family, and her parents and extended family make certain that she is trained in the bourgeois values that fit upper-middle-class Uruguayan society. Because of her elevated social status, it would have been very easy to ruin the novel by portraying Magda's concerns falsely.

In every social movement that entails fighting for the rights of the oppressed, there are purists who have a difficult time accepting outsiders who have benefited from the rules made by the oppressors. The rich, according to them, could never experience the social outrage needed of true revolutionaries. Doubtlessly, many who have suffered from brutal regimes like the one described in this book would dismiss Magda. Bridal gives an example of this thinking in Laura, the girl who gives up her only boots when Magda is fleeing from the police. While mocking Magda's wealth, Laura sarcasti-

cally and correctly guesses that the rich girl's parents would never let her come to the area of town where Laura lives. She sees Magda as someone who is dabbling in revolution but is free to flee back to her own sheltered world when things turn bad. Magda, in fact, seems to feel the same way about herself: at the end of the story, when her grandmother tries to convince her that the best way to help free Marco is to go to Europe and publicize the events in Uruguay, Magda feels that leaving the country would be a cowardly act of abandonment.

While a wealthy character in a novel about revolution might be accused of being superficial, there is also the danger that a writer might be tempted to use a wealthy protagonist to overstate the revolutionary cause. A protagonist from the ranks of the oppressed might not allow a writer to bring out the vibrancy of the situation. An impoverished narrator would be familiar with the tactics that are used to keep all of her or his peers from revolting, but such characters would show less dramatic change when taking up the cause. Oppressed people tend to take a world-weary, jaded view toward their own situations, having gradually grown familiar with oppression on a daily basis. For a child raised in privilege, however, the moment of suddenly becoming aware of evil comes as a great shock. It is easy for novelists to shake up their readers by exposing governmental repression to the book's bourgeois protagonist (which, to some extent, actually is the structure of *The Tree of Red Stars*) who then becomes a zealous convert to political activism.

Wisely, Bridal manages to make Magda a credible observer and participant, showing her commitment to political change to be something that, despite her upbringing, she is in fact able to feel sincerely. Used as she is here, the character of an upper-middle-class girl can be an excellent tool for showing readers what is involved in many levels of a society in turmoil.

For one thing, Magda's social position makes her an outsider from the revolution, which is started by the poor. She is only vaguely aware of its existence as a child, putting together the pieces that explain it to her throughout the course of the novel. As a structural technique, Magda's growing awareness of the problems of Uruguay's poor follow the standard "fish out of water" pattern: just as some stories follow a person from a foreign land, or, more recently, an extraterrestrial, learning about a new culture, so Magda's observations about the revolutionary movement are used to introduce the details of the revolution to the book's readership.

What Do I Read Next?

- Isabel Allende wrote her famous work *The House of the Spirits* in 1985. It was her first book and was originally published in Spain. In it, she tells the story of a Chilean family, focusing on three women—a young girl, her mother, and her grandmother—as they struggle to keep their family together during chaotic times. The story is part fiction and part truth, as Allende herself suffered from political oppression while she lived in Chile. Her writing style is highly praised, and she is often referred to as a gifted storyteller.

- Felisberto Hernandez, a Uruguayan, wrote his *Piano Stories* in 1993. This is a collection of tales written in the style of magic realism. The tone of his writing is quite different from that of Bridal, but for a male perspective and another take on creativity from a fellow Uruguayan, his book offers an interesting read. Hernandez is one of the favorite writers of fellow author Gabriel García Márquez.

- *Cane River* (2001) by Lalita Tademy is a family saga that traces the lives of four generations of women born into slavery. The stories are a combination of oral family history and the author's imagination as she pieces together the details of her own Louisiana matriarchal family. The story begins at the early days of slavery, continues through the Civil War, and ends during the fight for civil rights. Tademy, who was a successful corporate executive, quit her job to write this story because she became obsessed with researching her roots. The book includes photographs and reprints of actual documents to attest to its authenticity.

- Rosy Shand wrote the novel *The Gravity of Sunlight* (2001) about life in Uganda, Africa, during Idi Amin's rise to power. Through the telling of the lives of two couples, their successes and failures in love, Shand examines cultural and political conflicts in that country.

- *Coming of Age in Mississippi* (1997) by Anne Moody relates the true story of a young woman living through the 1960s and the beginnings of the Civil Rights movement in the South. The story relates Moody's difficulties in trying to gain a successful education as well as to help others achieve the right to vote in the oppressive political environment of the Deep South.

Perhaps the greatest benefit that Magda's position offers to the book's narrative structure is that it gives her access to many different aspects of Uruguayan society. Throughout the course of the novel, Magda becomes familiar with people of her own social class but also with poor people such as Gabriella and with the revolutionaries of the Tupamaros movement. If Bridal had written Magda as a member of a poorer class, her options for social interaction would have been limited. One of the privileges of wealth is that it is used, in most cases, to shut out those of poorer classes. Bridal shows this in the way that Cora is raised in seclusion, locked away from the rest of the world for her own protection because of her family's experiences as Jews in Europe in the forties. Though the protective shield they throw around her is notably extreme, it is a reflection of the way that all Uruguayan families shelter children of their class. The distinction between the middle class's security and the lower class's defenselessness is actually made clear in the book's very first chapter. When Magda and Emilia disappear to the poor section of town, search parties are formed, and the residents of the Cerro rush to return them home before the situation becomes violent, whereas a few pages later, when Gabriela's baby is missing in the middle-class neighborhood, there is nothing she can do but cry. The social position of Magda's family allows her to cross over into the homes and lives of the poor, but a poor person does not have equal access into the homes of the rich.

If the protagonist of *The Tree of Red Stars* had been poor, Bridal would not have had the means

Che Guevara inspired the Tupamaros as a leader of guerilla movements throughout Latin America

for showing readers how the ruling class thinks. She does this in the form of Magda's gossipy aunts, who consider themselves to be the bearers of traditional standards. In addition, Magda has the opportunity to travel to America as an exchange student and observe firsthand what life is like in a consumer society, where the government is left to carry on unquestioned. Her superb education, including special tutors whom only a few Uruguayans would be able to afford, gains Magda entry into a government position that will eventually expose her to the reality of torture as it is viewed by the torturers: as some sort of game. She lives in the area of town known for its embassies, a fact that in itself gives her a global perspective from her earliest childhood. One final aspect of her social position is her grandmother, a strong-willed landowner, who has ties to the country that are deeper than those of temporary political alliances.

These are the reasons why Magda's social class makes her uniquely qualified to tell this story. The ways in which her social class affects the book's plot are, on the other hand, discussed openly within the novel. An early example of this comes when she is escaping the riot that breaks out during Che Guevara's speech. The young revolution-

aries who rescue her, while mocking her for being from a rich family, also recognize how helpless she is in the unfamiliar situation of police brutality and protect her. Much later, after she is released from jail, Magda's family has the means to send her out of Montevideo and, eventually, out of the country. She is sent to Europe with an heirloom worth a half million dollars and the skill to earn a living in a strange land. If Magda had come from a poor family, Bridal would have had to take her down different paths.

While examining how this novel's narrator allows Bridal to tell a story that could easily have turned too sensationalistic, angry, or superficial, it is important to note the significance of the narrator's gender. Using a girl to tell the story may not even have been a conscious choice: it is quite likely that Bridal did not write about a girl in Uruguay as a storytelling strategy but simply because that is what she knew best and understood. Still, the book makes much about the roles of women and men in the society that it examines, and viewing mid-century Uruguay through the eyes of a maturing woman allows this book to explore its subject to its fullest.

At the time of this novel, change was sweeping through Uruguayan society, redefining gender relationships. This change in gender politics preceded the political revolution and may have been responsible for it to no measurable degree. Regardless of the historical accuracy of the role of women's liberation in bringing about social revolution, the fact that Bridal made such splendid use of their convergence is a mark of extremely intelligent writing. The first third of the book is not explicitly about revolution: it is dedicated to Magda and Emilia's girlhood adventures, and the role models who shaped their views of who they were and could be.

The Uruguay of Magda's youth is a traditional Latin American society, with a double standard regarding sexuality. Men, such as Francisca's husband in the book, are expected to have both a wife and a mistress, while women, like Magda's older cousin Sofía, have their reputations carefully guarded, so that they will not lose their value as material for marriage. This logical inconsistency is obvious to Magda and Emilia, who joke about it.

As the girls grow, they see the double standard change. One force for social change is the progressivism of other countries, particularly America. Magda's aunts pretend to be shocked at the behavior of Miss Newman, an American woman who wears pants and objects openly and violently to the Uruguayan "tradition" of men shouting sexual suggestions at women in the street. Their pretense at disapproving is betrayed by the fact that they talk so much about her, betraying a fascination with Miss Newman's fiery self-assurance.

Though Miss Newman is only a shadowy, vague, talked-about character, Emilia's mother Lilita is quite real in the novel and a strong influence on both girls' lives: she tells Magda outright that she hates men because she is jealous of their freedom. Sofía, chastised because she has been seen in public with a boy, openly flaunts her sexuality, daring Magda's father to beat her again and again if he wants, vowing that the beatings will not change her behavior.

It is easy to see how these role models from the early part of the book influence Magda's behavior in the later chapters. Without them, and the numerous skirmishes against social expectations that Magda and Emilia go through as girls, there would be little point to the novel relating their childhood exploits. As it is, the daily struggle for women to earn a place in society foreshadows the struggle of the poor that turns into a life-or-death struggle by the book's end.

Novels told in the first person are limited by the experiences of their narrators. In addition to its other virtues, *The Tree of Red Stars* has a narrator who has access to a variety of social situations and the drive to explore them. Ultimately, the aspects that make Magda a useful narrative tool trip her up, leading her into situations that endanger the lives of those she loves. She is so uniquely adventurous and capable that Emilia and Marco are unable to keep up with her and are trapped in webs that she has escaped. For readers, the world of this novel would not be as fully realized if it were witnessed through the eyes of any other character.

Source: David Kelly, Critical Essay on *The Tree of Red Stars*, in *Novels for Students*, The Gale Group, 2003.

Bryan Aubrey

Aubrey holds a Ph.D. in English and has published many articles on twentieth-century literature. In this essay, Aubrey discusses the key images in the novel, examines the political context in which they appear, and offers some thoughts about the relevance of the story to the contemporary political world.

Bridal's *The Tree of Red Stars* is a novel of almost infinite delicacy that also possesses the force

> **Although it might be tempting to feel that political events in Uruguay in the 1960s and 1970s have little relevance for today, closer examination suggests otherwise."**

of a sudden, hard punch in the stomach. Its poetic richness includes a few key images—especially the tree and the river—that encapsulate the essence of the novel, while the plot gives much food for thought about the phenomenon of terrorism and the relations between Latin America and the United States.

It is the images that remain indelibly imprinted in the mind long after the reader has finished the novel. The most prominent is that of the old poinsettia tree, which is the "tree of red stars" of the title. This is a reference to the fact that in winter the tree flowers red. Magda thinks it looks like "a hundred small fires holding the cold at bay." This image of the tree that flowers red reverberates at so many levels that it comes to embrace the totality of human life, in pleasure and pain, joy and sorrow, even life and death. It carries the subtlest themes of the novel.

As a young girl, Magda spends many hours sitting in the branches of the poinsettia tree, spending many of those hours with her friend Emilia. The tree is Magda's favorite place, and it is associated in her mind with many of the most important things that have happened in her life, especially the time when she and Emilia "started our journey together into young adulthood." Significantly, these events are often heralded when the tree begins to produce its red flowers. It is in winter, for example, when Magda and Emilia spot from the tree their future friend and Tupamaros comrade, Cora. It is also when the tree flowers red that they first see Ramiro, Cora's future husband, also a future member of the Tupamaros.

What is the significance of the image? The color red is traditionally the color of passion, and it is also the color of blood. The red blossom of the tree therefore symbolizes love and suffering (passion also means suffering, as in the passion of Christ on the cross). This suffering is both mental and physical. Love and suffering are inextricably linked as the two qualities that dominate Magda's life and the lives of the other main characters. It is Magda's love for the beggar Gabriela, and her outrage at the woman's cruel death by torture, that deepens her involvement with the Tupamaros. During Magda's imprisonment, it is her love for the men whom she can hear being tortured in the cell above that sustains both her and the men (as she finds out when she encounters one of them many years later on the riverbank). It is Marco's love for Magda that precipitates his arrest and his premature death, seven long years later, from the injuries inflicted by torture. It is Magda's love for him that motivates her to go into exile to fight for his release. The love of Ramiro and Cora is also presented in romantic terms. Theirs is an ideal, passionate love that endures separation and torture. In every case, love and suffering of the most extreme kind are linked.

The significance of the image of the red-flowering tree does not end there. The young girls perceive the flowers as they gaze upwards from their perch in the lower branches. For Magda, it appears as if the red blossoms are stars in the heavens. After one incident in which she overhears a quarrel between her cousin and her mother, she and Emilia take refuge in the poinsettia tree and happen to look up, where they see that "One perfect star had bloomed a bright, piercing red." This evocative image suggests that if love, suffering (passion), and blood are inextricably mixed, as the two maturing girls will shortly discover, those qualities are also exalted, raised up and woven into the very fabric and heart of life. They express a kind of unshakable, eternal, even glorious perfection, for which the appropriate image can only be a bright red star shining in the heavens.

It might also not be superfluous to mention Magda's comment that whatever sex education she ever had came as a consequence of sitting in the tree, since from her perch she was able to eavesdrop on the conversations of her two older female cousins. The quarrel between Magda's mother and Sofía, which immediately precedes Magda's moment of epiphany when she sees the "red stars," is over sexual matters, and Sofía dares to raise the previously forbidden topic of female sexuality and female sexual needs. This suggests yet another layer of meaning for the color red, since the emergence of sexuality is inseparable from the female menstrual cycle, which is itself a marker of the pas-

sage from childhood to adulthood. Since one of the novel's themes is Magda's coming-of-age, and she directly associates this with the hours spent in the poinsettia tree, there is clearly an association between the physical emergence into womanhood and the condition of exalted love and suffering that the "red stars" represent.

By making the tree of red stars such a significant symbol in the novel, Bridal also taps into a complex of mythological and religious associations conjured up by the tree image. With its roots in the earth and its branches reaching heavenwards, the tree is an apt symbol for human and cosmic life and has been used as such for millennia in Western and Eastern sacred art. In Christian mythology, the Tree of Life in the Garden of Eden is linked to the tree (the wooden cross) on which Christ was crucified. Bridal's red-flowering poinsettia tree provides a close secular equivalent. (In Christian art, the color red is always associated with Christ's passion.) There is also a legend that on the night Christ was born, trees bore fruit and flowers blossomed. Not for nothing, then, from the point of view of the symbolism of the novel, does the poinsettia tree bloom red in early winter—the time of Christ's birth.

If the tree of red stars symbolizes the nobility of love endured through physical and mental suffering, another recurring image in the novel, that of water, represents cleansing and healing. It is associated with the Río de la Plata, the river in Montevideo that Magda has loved since she was a child. She, Emilia, and Marco would often walk along its banks to lighten their cares: "Something about the river's changeable colors and the music of its movement against sand and rock soothed and comforted." At the end of the novel, as Magda walks with Marco along the riverbank, she comments, "It would take time, but the river would heal me, as I had known it would throughout those lonely years of exile." The image of the healing river is also contained in Magda's unforgettable, if distressing, account of the time during her imprisonment when bodily fluids emanating from the men being tortured drip through the wooden ceiling of her cell. Overcoming her natural revulsion at the odor, she comes to regard the liquids as holy, part of a sacred idealism that she reveres. She mops up the liquid with scraps of toilet paper, imagining the faces of the tortured men and repeating their names. Then she shreds the paper slowly, one scrap at a time, and washes it down the sink: "I imagined those scraps being borne down to the river; water to water returned."

The use of the image of the healing river, like the tree image, touches on a vein of religious practice and symbolism common to East and West. Hindu pilgrims, for example, bathe in the waters of the sacred river Ganges as a purification rite. In Christian scriptures, water is used as an image of healing in the New Testament's Revelation, in which John is shown a vision of the new Jerusalem, the redeemed holy city. He sees "the river of the water of life, bright as crystal, flowing from the throne of God and of the Lamb through the middle of the street of the city" (Rev. 22: 1–2). Bridal's Río de la Plata is a secular version of this holy, healing river.

These two powerful images, of the tree and water, cannot be fully appreciated, however, apart from the political context in which they occur. Although it might be tempting to feel that political events in Uruguay in the 1960s and 1970s have little relevance for today, closer examination suggests otherwise. While the United States is currently engaged in a global war on terrorism, it is sobering to note that *The Tree of Red Stars* might also be called "The Making of a Terrorist." It might also be noted that perhaps never before have terrorists been presented in such a sympathetic light. Magda, Marco, Ramiro, and Cora are all deeply appealing figures. They are idealistic, concerned for justice, and remain true to their cause despite torture and death. Yet terrorists they certainly are. Magda is instrumental in the kidnapping of Dan Mitrione, the man she believes to be a FBI agent responsible for training people in the use of torture. Mitrione is then murdered by the Tupamaros.

Mitrione is not a fictional character. He was head of the U.S.-funded Office of Public Safety in Montevideo from 1969 to 1970 and was in charge of a program that trained Uruguayan police officers in counterterrorism methods. These practices included methods of torture, which was widely practiced by the Uruguayan government. In this respect, although it would be comforting to report that Bridal's description of the death by torture of the beggar woman Gabriela is a fictional flourish to enhance the drama of the story, unfortunately this is not so. The Uruguayan government really did test their methods of torture on beggars snatched from the outskirts of Montevideo. It is one of Bridal's most moving achievements that in the character of Gabriela she gives a face to those poor forgotten wretches who were treated like vermin to be experimented on and then disposed of when they had served their purpose.

The military government of Uruguay that crushed the Tupamaros in 1972 was supported by the United States. With the Cold War against the communist Soviet Union at its height, the United States opposed revolutionary socialist movements such as the Tupamaros because it did not want to see left-wing governments established in South America. Unfortunately, the Uruguayan government during the 1970s happened to be one of the most brutal regimes in the world. It had the highest per capita rate of political prisoners in the world (about sixty thousand people, or 2 percent of the population), and torture was practiced as a routine measure. In addition to being brutally tortured, Tupamaros leaders were kept in solitary confinement for more than a decade.

Supporters of American policy might argue (as they do in different circumstances today) that in a war on terrorism, one cannot be too fussy about who one's friends are. Critics, on the other hand, might say (again, as they do today), that in a war on terrorism, it is all the more important to uphold the principles one claims to be defending, and therefore one must be extremely careful about the regimes one supports. In terms of the novel, resentment of what is perceived as American interference in Uruguayan affairs is a prominent theme among the characters who support the Tupamaros, such as Marco and Emilia's mother, Lilita. It is expressed even before the revolutionary movement gathers momentum. Marco, for example, believes that American financial control of many Uruguayan institutions amounts to exploitation masquerading as help. Once again, as with the question of what is an appropriate response to terrorism, this is not a dead issue. Perceptions similar to Marco's about the nature of American involvement overseas are common today in many countries in Latin America, Africa, and Asia. Many Americans may regard such suspicions as unjust, insisting that America's purpose in the world is to defend democracy and promote economic growth. In the novel, this point of view is given a voice in the character of Magda's mother, who does not share Marco's anti-Americanism. She believes that the United States genuinely wishes to help Uruguay.

Seen in this light, *The Tree of Red Stars* not only delves deeply into the spiritual dimensions of suffering and love in a context of political oppression, it also raises issues that remain important for anyone seeking to understand today's complex political world.

Source: Bryan Aubrey, Critical Essay on *The Tree of Red Stars*, in *Novels for Students*, The Gale Group, 2003.

Sources

Flexman, Ellen, Review of *The Tree of Red Stars*, in *Library Journal*, Vol. 122, No. 10, June 1, 1997, p. 144.

Friedman, Paula, Review of *The Tree of Red Stars*, in *New York Times*, November 16, 1997, p. 63.

Schon, Isabel, Review of *The Tree of Red Stars*, in *Journal of Adolescent & Adult Literacy*, Vol. 41, No. 6, March 1998, pp. 501–502.

Steinberg, Sybil S., Review of *The Tree of Red Stars*, in *Publishers Weekly*, Vol. 244, No. 21, May 26, 1997, p. 65.

Further Reading

Anderson, John Lee, *Che Guevara: A Revolutionary Life*, Grove Press, 1998.

> A dashing and dramatic figure, Che Guevara was the son of an aristocratic Argentine family, whose sympathies for the poor and the oppressed turned him into a socialist revolutionary, a friend of Fidel Castro, and a leader of guerilla movements throughout Latin America and Africa. Anderson, a journalist, spent several years gathering research for this book, including gaining access to some of Guevara's personal diaries.

Evans, Malcolm D., and Rod Morgan, *Preventing Torture: A Study of the European Convention for the Prevention of Torture and Inhuman or Degrading Treatment or Punishment*, Clarendon Press, 1999.

> This documentary details the work of the European Committee for the Prevention of Torture and Inhuman and Degrading Treatment or Punishment (the CPT), established in 1989, which represents a new phase in international human rights intervention. The authors, an international lawyer and a criminologist, bring their different analytical perspectives to bear on this innovative human rights mechanism.

Feitlowitz, Marguerite, *A Lexicon of Terror: Argentina and the Legacies of Torture*, Oxford University Press, 1999.

> Feitlowitz spent several years interviewing victims as well as those responsible for what has been called the "dirty war" that took place in Argentina between the years of 1976 and 1983, during which an estimated thirty thousand people were tortured and killed. The political history of Argentina during this time period is similar in some ways to that of Uruguay.

Kimball, Roger, *The Long March: How the Cultural Revolution of the 1960s Changed America*, Encounter Books, 2001.

> From a conservative point of view, Kimball analyzes the cultural revolution of the 1960s, critiques the major players, such as the Beats, Susan Sontag, Norman Mailer, I. F. Stone, Miles Davis, and liberals in general, and shows how the ideas of this period took hold in the United States and changed the lives of its citizens.

Mandela, Nelson, *Long Walk to Freedom: The Autobiography of Nelson Mandela*, Little Brown & Company, 1995.

> Most of this book was written during the twenty-seven years that Nelson Mandela was held as a political prisoner on Robben Island in South Africa. The story of his life demonstrates the strength of his spirit, which remained unbroken despite his imprisonment, his broken marriages, and lack of family life.

What Looks Like Crazy on an Ordinary Day

Pearl Cleage

1997

In an interview in *Black Issues Book Review*, Pearl Cleage reveals that the idea for *What Looks Like Crazy on an Ordinary Day* came from her desire to write about a character whose doctor informs her that she is HIV positive. Cleage was amazed at how many people she saw in denial about HIV and AIDS, so she created a character who has no choice but to deal with it. This character, Ava, not only comes to terms with her HIV-positive status, but she also finds a way to recreate and reclaim her life.

What Looks Like Crazy is Cleage's first novel. Known for her plays and essays, Cleage felt that this particular story required the novel form to explore the culture of Idlewild and the psychological workings of her characters. Idlewild is an actual city in Michigan that was established after the Civil War as an African-American community. The city was a thriving resort during the 1950s and 1960s, but then it began to decline in popularity.

Although Cleage began writing *What Looks Like Crazy* in the third person, she realized that her skills as a playwright would make a first-person point of view a natural choice. She told *Black Issues Book Review*, "As a playwright, I'm used to writing in dialogue."

When Oprah Winfrey chose the novel as one of her book club selections, sales sharply increased, and Cleage quickly reached a wider audience. In 1998, *What Looks Like Crazy* stayed on the *New York Times* bestseller list for almost ten weeks. In 2001, Cleage saw publication of a follow-up novel titled *I Wish I Had a Red Dress*.

Pearl Cleage

In her first novel, *What Looks Like Crazy on an Ordinary Day* (1997), Cleage depicts the life of Ava Johnson, a modern African-American woman struggling with her HIV-positive status. When this novel was selected for talk-show host Oprah Winfrey's book club, Cleage reached a wide and diverse audience. The book stayed on the *New York Times* bestseller list for almost ten weeks in 1998, and Cleage's writing in general attracted a great deal of interest. The success of this novel led to the follow-up, *I Wish I Had a Red Dress* (2001), which takes up the story of Joyce, a character in *What Looks Like Crazy on an Ordinary Day*.

Academics, theatergoers, and readers regard Cleage as an important contemporary African-American writer and feminist. In addition to plays and novels, Cleage has written poetry and essays. She has contributed to magazines such as *Ms.* and *Essence*, and she is a cofounder and editor of the literary magazine *Catalyst*. Today, Cleage continues to write from her home in Atlanta. She is considering another follow-up to *What Looks Like Crazy on an Ordinary Day* that would continue the story of Aretha, one of the young girls in the support group Joyce leads.

Author Biography

Pearl Cleage (pronounced "cleg") was born on December 7, 1948, in Springfield, Massachusetts, to Doris and Reverend Albert B. Cleage, Jr. She was reared in Detroit, where her father's ministry allowed her to hear speakers such as Malcolm X and Martin Luther King, Jr. Cleage graduated from high school and then went to Howard University in Washington, D.C., during the turbulent 1960s. After three years, she transferred to Spelman College in Atlanta, where she graduated in 1971 with a degree in drama.

In 1969, Cleage married Michael Lomax, a politician. The marriage lasted ten years and produced a daughter named Deignan. Cleage remarried in 1994. Her second husband, Zaron Burnett, Jr., is a writer and producing director of Just Us Theatre Company in Atlanta, Georgia, where the couple met. Cleage was the theater's first playwright-in-residence, and she and Burnett collaborated on several works after she became the artistic director in 1992. Another Atlanta theater, The Alliance Theater, is responsible for debuting some of Cleage's most notable plays. Among these is *Flyin' West* (1992), the play credited with gaining Cleage a widespread theatrical audience.

Plot Summary

June

Ava Johnson arrives in Idlewild, her childhood hometown, for a summer-long visit with her older sister. Ava is a successful, single, African-American woman who is HIV positive. She left Atlanta because the news of her virus destroyed her social and professional lives. She plans to go to San Francisco at the end of the summer to start a new life. Her sister, Joyce, became a widow two years ago, when her husband drowned.

Eddie Jefferson, one of Joyce's close friends who also grew up in Idlewild, meets Ava at the airport. He explains that Joyce is with a girl who is having a baby, but she will be back as soon as she can. On the way home, Ava wants to stop at a liquor store. There, she and Eddie see a violent scene between a young man, Frank, and his girlfriend, who is trying to get out of the car in which she and her baby have been riding with Frank. Eddie intervenes, and they take the girl safely home.

Joyce is thrilled to see her younger sister. She tells her all about the girl who just had the baby. She is a crack addict, so Joyce is concerned about the baby but hopes that things will work out for mother and child.

The next day, Joyce learns that the baby is not HIV positive, but the mother has left the hospital. Joyce wants to take care of the baby, so she and Ava go to see the baby's aunt, Mattie, for permission. Mattie lives in a crack house with her brother Frank—the same Frank that Eddie and Ava encountered the day before. They do not want the baby, so Joyce arranges to give her a temporary home.

Joyce tells Ava about the Sewing Circus, a group she formed for the unmarried teenage mothers in her church. The group's name is a twist on "sewing circle," because it meets at the same time the church's sewing circle used to meet. Originally formed to plan a nursery care rotation for Sunday mornings, the group now discusses anything relevant to the girls' lives. Joyce sees this as an opportunity to educate, empower, and guide the girls.

One morning Gerry Anderson, the reverend's wife, arrives at Joyce's house. She tells Ava that she and her husband are unhappy about some of the Sewing Circus's discussion content. Tensions come to a head later, however, when Joyce brings hot dogs and condoms to a meeting to show the girls how to use birth control.

The baby comes to live with Joyce and Ava, and they are surprised at how quiet she is. Joyce names her "Imani," which means "faith" in Swahili.

Ava and Eddie spend time together, sharing meals and talking. Although Ava is attracted to him, she decides that romance is out of the question.

July

Gerry tells Joyce that she can no longer have Sewing Circus meetings on church property. Joyce is disappointed but not altogether surprised.

Aretha, the only member of the Sewing Circus who does not have a baby, stops by to see Joyce one day but finds Ava instead. They talk about Aretha's hopes to attend Interlochen, a private arts school, on a scholarship.

Ava has her prescriptions filled at the Idlewild pharmacy. By the time she picks them up, the pharmacist has already told people, including Gerry, that Ava is HIV positive. Immediately, people start making ignorant and mean-spirited remarks. That night, Ava visits Eddie, and he tells her about his experiences in Vietnam.

Joyce has the Sewing Circus meet at her house. Despite the change in location, turnout is high. She realizes that she needs to find a larger place for their meetings.

The next night, Ava and Eddie watch the violent film *Menace II Society* together. Eddie can only watch a little bit of it, and then he tells Ava about his violent background. After Vietnam, he became part of the violent drug culture and ended up in jail for murder.

A few nights later, Ava goes to Eddie's house for dinner and tells him that she is HIV positive. He is understanding, and they acknowledge their mutual attraction. They begin their physical relationship that night, taking all the precautions necessary.

August

One of the old men in town is selling his house for only ten thousand dollars to a cash buyer, and Eddie thinks the house would be perfect for the Sewing Circus. Ava volunteers to pay the ten thousand dollars, and Joyce is thrilled. Eddie begins renovating the house, and progress is going well until Joyce receives a letter from the state discontinuing funding for her program. Gerry has sent state officials a letter with misleading information about the Sewing Circus, so Joyce must go tell her side of the story.

While Joyce is away, Ava takes care of Imani. One night, Frank and Tyrone (the Andersons' grandson who lives with them) come to the house. They park out front and have sex with Frank's girlfriend in and on their car. When Frank throws his empty beer bottle through one of Joyce's windows, they drive away. Eddie wants to "take care of" Frank and Tyrone, but Ava tells him not to do anything so drastic.

Ava and Joyce file a complaint and meet with Tyrone and Gerry at the sheriff's office. Gerry tells the sheriff that Ava lured the boys to the house to try to seduce them. The sheriff does not believe her story, and the meeting accomplishes nothing.

A few days later, Joyce insists on visiting the Andersons to try to resolve their differences. Reluctantly, Ava goes with her. Gerry is not home, so they talk to the reverend. He is very drunk and difficult to talk to, as he wavers between incoherence and praise of his wife.

Ava goes to help paint the new house, and Eddie proposes to her. Ava retreats for a few days while she processes this possible new future.

Mattie arrives at Joyce's house with a social worker, demanding that they give Imani to her.

Mattie admits that Gerry put her up to this. After weighing her options, Joyce agrees to let Imani go with Mattie for the weekend. On Monday, a hearing will determine where the baby should live, and everyone but Mattie expects that the result will be for Imani to be returned to Joyce.

September

While Imani is with Mattie, Joyce and Ava sit outside the house and listen for signs that Imani needs them. Everything is relatively calm until Sunday, when they hear Imani crying. They rush to the door, but Mattie and Frank tell them to go away. Joyce waits out of sight while Ava goes to get Eddie. While Ava is gone, Joyce goes in after Imani. She hears her screaming frantically, so she enters through the back of the house. She goes in and calls the police and the hospital, and Frank threatens to shoot her in the head. Mattie convinces him that she and Frank should leave before the police arrive. Joyce then discovers that Frank has broken Imani's legs by twisting them. At the hospital, the doctors operate, put Imani in casts, and say she will be fine.

Eddie wants to find Frank and kill him because there is no way to know how far he will go next time. Ava does not try to discourage him this time.

Ava meets a woman who was a member of the Andersons' previous church in Chicago. She reveals that Reverend Anderson left Chicago amidst allegations of inappropriate sexual behavior with some of the boys in the parish. Ava also learns that Tyrone's mother died of AIDS.

Ava confronts Gerry with this information, threatens to make it public, and succeeds in running the Andersons out of town.

November

Ava calls this chapter an epilogue. She says that Imani is healing fine and the casts are off her legs. Police captured Frank and Mattie after they committed a number of robberies to support their drug habits. The church members have embraced the new pastor, Sister Judith, and her husband. Sister Judith married Ava and Eddie in a joyous celebration.

Characters

Geraldine Anderson

See Gerry Anderson

Gerry Anderson

Gerry Anderson is the pastor's wife. She is very involved in the church and in the lives of its members. In fact, the reverend is rarely seen, but Gerry is quite vocal and visible. Gerry is in her late fifties and is usually dressed up more than anyone else is. She wears an elaborately curled hairstyle. She sings in the choir, and her voice is impressive.

Gerry has clear ideas about what is proper and what is not, and she is unwilling to depart from these ideas. Ava characterizes Gerry as condescending, self-righteous, out of touch, and judgmental. When Gerry learns that Joyce is teaching the girls in the Sewing Circus about condom use, she forbids Joyce to meet at the church. She also treats Ava like a leper when she learns that Ava is HIV positive. Her attacks on Joyce and the Sewing Circus become increasingly cruel; she even arranges for Imani, the baby for whom Joyce is caring, to be taken away from Joyce and put into the home of crack-addicted family members. Gerry is also willing to lie to the sheriff and other public officials to get what she wants, and she sends letters to the state to try to have Joyce's funding for the Sewing Circus discontinued.

Ava learns important information about the Andersons' past. Parents of young boys in the reverend's Chicago parish accused him of inappropriate sexual behavior with their sons. The church board sent him away and warned him to avoid all contact with youth. Gerry's attempts to destroy the Sewing Circus are, at least in part, an attempt to keep young people, and the temptation they present, away from her husband. Ava also learns that Gerry and her husband are Tyrone's guardians because their daughter died of AIDS. This explains Gerry's drive to distance herself from Ava, who reminds Gerry of the pain of losing her daughter. In the end, Gerry agrees to move her family away from Idlewild.

Eddie Jefferson

Eddie Jefferson, known in his youth as "Wild Eddie," has returned to Idlewild after serving ten years in prison. When he was young, he went to Vietnam, an experience that left him angry and confused. Once he was back in the United States, he became part of the violent drug culture. As a result, he was sent to prison for murder. In prison, he learned to be introspective and spiritual. He began to meditate and to look for life lessons in his painful experiences. These practices have matured him and given him a peaceful disposition. Ava finds him extremely content and in control. Still, Eddie is protective of those he loves. He is quick to offer to kill anyone who threatens Ava, Joyce, or Imani. He believes that loving someone means being willing to protect her at any cost.

Eddie wears his hair in dreadlocks and wears simple clothes such as sandals and Eastern-inspired shirts. He is a physical person who works as a carpenter and practices martial arts. He is also a spiritual person who enjoys music, tea, and incense. He is thoughtful, sincere, and intense, and he takes time to nurture himself as well as others. Eddie was a close friend of Mitch, Joyce's deceased husband, and Eddie checks on Joyce to be sure she has everything she needs.

Perhaps because of the extreme circumstances of his past, Eddie seems fearless. He is unafraid of the violent, drug-using youth, and he is unafraid of Ava's HIV-positive status. He is never foolish or rash, but he does not allow fear to dictate his decisions in any way. His willingness to fall in love with and marry Ava is evidence that he prioritizes feelings and people over convenience and pleasantness.

Ava Johnson

The main character and narrator of the story, Ava is a single, African-American woman who is HIV positive. She has left Atlanta after ten years because her social life and business (she owned a salon) fell apart when everyone found out about her illness. She has decided to visit her older sister, Joyce, in their hometown of Idlewild, Michigan, on her way to start a new life in San Francisco.

Ava and Joyce share a special bond, and they are able to say things to one another that nobody else can say. Having helped each other through the devastating suicide of their mother, they look to each other for female companionship and guidance.

Ava is direct, sarcastic, sensitive, intelligent, open-minded, and lonely. She accepts responsibility for her disease, but she has trouble dealing with the finality of it. She is often impatient with what the game-playing people do, and she deeply resents the harsh judgments of others. She is also hesitant to get involved with Eddie because she is aware of how her illness would affect him and their relationship, as well as her emotional limitations. A basically selfless person, Ava finds herself torn between surrendering to the romance with Eddie, which she desperately wants, and stopping it before it goes far enough to hurt either one of them. Ultimately, she is able to trust him and believe in

his vision for their future. This is the turning point for Ava; she shifts from pessimism to optimism.

Joyce Mitchell

Joyce is Ava's older sister. She lives in Idlewild, where she has lived her entire life. Joyce is a widow whose husband, Mitch, drowned two years prior to the events of the novel. She has had a hard time coping with her loss but, at the time of the novel, she is beginning to reconnect with her community in meaningful ways. Joyce also lost both of her children, one in infancy and one in childhood. A churchgoer, Joyce identifies a need among the teenage mothers there and begins a weekly meeting with them. The Sewing Circus, as it comes to be called, is a forum for open discussion. It gives the girls a chance to support each other, and it gives Joyce an opportunity to provide guidance and education.

Joyce's drive to make a difference stems from her family environment as a child. She and Ava grew up in a house where their parents cultivated the spirit of the 1960s by planning rallies and drafting handbills with their friends. In addition, Joyce's professional background was as a state caseworker for fifteen years, working with families in the Idlewild area.

Joyce is very nurturing and maternal. The reader's first clue to her character comes when Eddie picks Ava up at the airport because Joyce has driven a woman in labor to the hospital and is staying until she delivers her baby. Joyce's decision to take care of an unwanted baby who is born addicted to crack is not surprising, given her background and her personality. Joyce names the baby Imani, which means "faith" in Swahili. She is also motherly toward Ava and the members of the Sewing Circus. An important part of Joyce's maternal nature is her fierce protectiveness of those she loves. This is evident in her reaction to having Imani taken from her for a weekend and in her fearless confrontation of an armed man high on crack who has hurt Imani.

Aretha Simmons

Aretha is the only member of the Sewing Circus who does not have a baby. She is sixteen years old, intelligent, personable, pretty, and more ambitious than the other girls are. Joyce tells Ava that she believes that Aretha has a chance of making something of her life. Aretha's parents, like Joyce and Ava's parents, were activists hoping to join a community of like-minded African Americans committed to making a difference. When Aretha was twelve, however, they both died in an automobile accident. One of her mother's friends agreed to take her in so she would not have to move to Detroit to live with her grandmother.

Aretha has a vision for her life that includes pursuing a better education than she can receive in Idlewild. She is thrilled at her acceptance to a summer session at Interlochen, a private arts school nearby that hosts a special all-expense-paid program during the summer. Her hard work and talent eventually earn her a scholarship.

Themes

Adversity

All of the novel's main characters have endured adversity prior to the events of the story. Ava learned that she was HIV positive. Joyce suffered the loss of two children and her beloved husband. Eddie was in the military and went to Vietnam, from which he returned angry and confused. As a result, he embarked on a life of crime that ended with a ten-year prison sentence. The younger members of the Sewing Circus also have experienced adversity.

The juxtaposition of these two groups—the adults and the adolescents—reveals Cleage's message that wisdom comes from surviving adversity. At the beginning of the novel, Ava intends to visit her sister for the summer and then go on to San Francisco. What she learns about herself during her visit, however, teaches her that she cannot outrun her HIV-positive status. San Francisco may be more accepting of her, but it will not be an escape. Because of this realization, Ava stops running. Eddie was on a path of destruction and self-destruction until he went to prison, where he met an older, wiser man who told him, "You know what your problem is? You ain't slowed down long enough to see the lessons, youngblood." After serving his sentence, Eddie left prison a wiser, calmer, more focused man who felt peace. The loss of her beloved husband, Mitch, devastated Joyce. This loss came after her two children died, one in infancy from Sudden Infant Death Syndrome (SIDS) and the other by a drunk driver. After Mitch drowned, Joyce lost herself in her grief, gaining weight and detaching from society, until she felt compelled to help the young unwed mothers in her church and her community. She discovered that the surest way to help herself was to help others.

The stories of the three main adult characters illustrate what can come out of adversity. Their stories are very different, but each person has gained wisdom and self-knowledge. This central message is a hopeful one, and it suggests that at least some of the members of the Sewing Circus will endure their hard lot in life and mature into wiser women. Cleage takes this idea a step further with Imani, the baby Joyce takes in after her mother abandons her at the hospital. Holding Imani, Ava explains:

> I ran my hand over her little head again and she snuggled against me in a way that made me feel a surge of what I guess was maternal protectiveness. Imani had already kicked a drug habit cold turkey and outrun the HIV her mama was sending special delivery. She was stronger than she looked, and somehow that made me feel stronger, too.

Ignorance

What Looks Like Crazy depicts the unfortunate results of ignorance. Ava was ignorant and careless in her promiscuous youth, and she contracted a deadly disease. Once people learn that she is HIV positive, Ava finds that not only can her own ignorance hurt her but that the ignorance of others can hurt her. The fear and judgment felt and expressed by others makes her feel rejected, worthless, and alone. The same ignorance that brought about Ava's illness brings about unplanned pregnancies for the teenagers in the Sewing Circus. They, too, are careless and promiscuous, and the result for them is early motherhood. When Joyce teaches them about condoms and how to use them, they are interested because this is mostly new information. Nobody had ever taught them how to protect themselves from pregnancy. They also have no idea that they are at risk for contracting diseases such as AIDS. Ava relates that Joyce "asked them what they thought was the number one killer of young black folks all over America. They guessed homicide, drug overdose, cancer, and car accidents, in that order. When Joyce said AIDS, they thought she was kidding."

The story also shows how ignorance can easily breed intolerance and harsh judgment. Ava endures the judgment of people in Atlanta and people in Idlewild when they learn that she is HIV positive. They treat their wrong ideas as facts and feel justified in treating Ava coldly. She tells that when she first learned of her status, she wrote to everyone she might have exposed to the virus. A furious woman stormed into Ava's salon, demanding that she take back the letter she sent to the woman's husband. She made a scene and slapped Ava. While

Topics for Further Study

- Research the current status of treatment for AIDS. What treatments are most effective, and how expensive are they? What is the prognosis for a person diagnosed with AIDS in the United States today? How long, on average, will that person live, and what will his or her life be like?

- Read Cleage's play *Flyin' West*. Write an essay in which you explore some similarities and differences in the two works.

- Discuss the various religious views of the characters and how these views shape each character's attitudes and actions.

- The resort town of Idlewild is an actual place in Michigan. Do some research to learn about its history. How did it get started as a resort town, what kinds of people lived there and visited there, and why did the town decline? Then discuss why you think Cleage chose to set her story there.

- Write an additional epilogue to the story, telling what Ava, Joyce, Eddie, and Imani are doing ten years after the novel ends. Keep in mind everything that you have learned about the characters and what their approximate ages will be in ten years.

the woman would have been justified to be angry that her husband had been unfaithful, instead she was angry about the letter. Ava recalls: "'All right then,' I said, 'what do you want?' 'I want you to take it back,' she said. 'Take it back?' I was really confused now. What good was that going to do?" The woman wanted to remain ignorant of the risk to her husband's health—and her own. She slapped Ava, not for sleeping with her husband but for sending a letter to inform him that he needed to see his doctor for an HIV screening. Recalling the incident, Ava remarks, "That's when I really started to understand how afraid people can be when they don't have any information."

New Beginnings

Set against the uninspiring backdrop of Idlewild is the theme of new beginnings. Ava visits her sister on her way to make a new beginning for herself in San Francisco. After losing her social status in Atlanta, she is desperate to start over in a new place. What she fails to realize until late in the book is that she can make her fresh start in Idlewild. Her relationship with Eddie and her decision to marry him are very optimistic, an attitude that was foreign to her at the beginning of the book.

Joyce also makes a new beginning when she commits to the Sewing Circus. Delighted at the progress she makes with the girls, she refuses to let the group dissolve just because they can no longer meet at the church. She shifts her focus from her grief at the loss of her husband to figuring out how to continue filling a need in the community. By dedicating herself to the Sewing Circus, she redefines herself. She is no longer just Mitch's widow; she is also a leader and mentor to a group of teenage girls who need a role model. She now has a present and a future as well as a past.

Style

First-Person Narrator

The entire story is told from Ava's perspective in her own voice. Ava is direct, stubborn, and sometimes crass. The reader understands that she is not an objective narrator. For example, she immediately accepts the members of the Sewing Circus and their situations without considering that they bear responsibility for their behavior. As a promiscuous woman herself, Ava does not see the girls as examples of the dangers of promiscuity. Another narrator might perceive them as young women who lack virtue or character. Ava relates her experiences, past and present, and she is open about her feelings and attitudes. The reader really gets to know Ava because Cleage's focus is on maintaining her voice consistently throughout the novel.

As a narrator, Ava is cynical, sarcastic, sensitive, and self-assured. Her sarcasm is established early in the novel. Describing women on television who tell their stories of contracting AIDS, Ava remarks, "There they were, weeping and wailing and wringing their hands, wearing their prissy little Laura Ashley dresses and telling their edited-for-TV life stories."

Time Shifts

As the novel's narrator, Ava reveals her past alongside her present. These time shifts seem natural, as they occur when something in Ava's present reminds her of something in her past. This gives the reader two benefits: first, the reader is able to understand Ava's background and why she came to Idlewild to see her sister; and, second, the reader is able to see how Ava's past relates to what is happening to her at certain moments. When Eartha (Imani's crack-addicted, HIV-positive, teenage mother) leaves the hospital and abandons the baby, Joyce is dumbfounded. Ava, however, remarks, "Homegirl's trying to walk away from that HIV. She's trying to decide if she's going to tell anyone or just keep living her life and see what happens. I used to wish I hadn't taken the test so I still wouldn't know." The result of this kind of merging of the past with the present is intimacy with the main character because the reader knows many of Ava's private memories.

Ava's recollections sometimes shift abruptly from one time period to another. In some cases, Ava breaks off her recollection to return to the present moment. This usually signifies either that the memory is becoming too painful or that the present holds something more promising than the memory. An example of this is when Ava tells the reader about a jazz musician with whom she had a serious relationship. They were involved when she found out she was HIV positive, and her expectations were terribly disappointed. As Ava tells this story, she breaks off suddenly to return to telling about the present:

> When I got the results and told him, he sat there and listened to me tell it all and then he picked up his coat and his horn case and walked out the door. No *good-bye*. No *damn, baby, what we gonna do?* Nothing. One minute he was there, then he was gone. That was it.

Ava abruptly switches from this memory to telling the reader that she went with Joyce to see Eartha's sister, Mattie, about the baby. Her switch from a painful memory to an incident in the present shows that she is eager to stop thinking about the profound disappointments in her past and focus instead on what is happening in the present.

At other times, Ava embraces the present because it offers her something better than her memories offer. Realizing that she will not be around for much of Imani's life, Ava determines to be as focused on the present as possible. She writes:

> So I took a deep breath like they keep saying in this meditation tape and tried to focus on being *right in this room, right in this moment*, and I actually felt better! It was amazing. I dragged that scared part of myself kicking and screaming into *the present moment* and it was so good to be there. I started grinning like an idiot.

Historical Context

HIV and AIDS in America

The U.S. Center for Disease Control (CDC) made its first official announcement regarding Acquired Immune Deficiency Syndrome (AIDS) in 1981. This brought awareness of AIDS and its precursor, Human Immunodeficiency Virus (HIV), to the mainstream. Because the first clusters of cases were among homosexuals, the disease was strongly characterized as a gay disease for many years. In fact, HIV/AIDS was initially known by the acronym GRID, which stood for "gay-related immune deficiency," until heterosexuals began contracting it too. During the early 1980s, the number of AIDS cases rose dramatically every year. By 1988, the CDC was aware of 86,000 cases, compared to only 225 cases reported in 1981.

Although there was a small number of victims who were considered blameless by the general public (such as recipients of blood transfusions and babies of mother with AIDS), the disease retained its social stigma for many years. Ignorance about the disease was also widespread and ingrained. In 1985, for example, a *New York Times*/CBS poll found that about half of Americans thought that AIDS was easily transmitted through casual contact. This attitude is revealed in *What Looks Like Crazy* when Ava picks up her prescriptions from the pharmacy, and the pharmacist handles her bag and her money with great care. In the same scene, Gerry Anderson tells Ava that she does not want her grandson, Tyrone, making pharmacy deliveries to Ava because he is their only grandchild. Headlines around the United States, however, often told more severe stories than Ava's story. In Queens, New York, a girl with AIDS was allowed to attend school, and parents kept twelve thousand children home in protest. Ryan White, a boy in Indiana, became a household name when he was an outcast at school and in town after contracting AIDS from a blood transfusion. In Florida, three boys in one family received tainted blood transfusions and, when they contracted the virus, someone burned their home to the ground.

While some people were hostile toward those with HIV and AIDS, others were simply indifferent to the suffering it caused. Many believed that people with AIDS had brought the disease on themselves and "deserved" it. Some religious fundamentalists claimed that the disease was divine punishment for amoral living. The government was slow to respond to the growing AIDS epidemic in terms of research and education.

In the 1990s, education improved the public's understanding of the disease and helped qualm fears. Announcements by respected athletes with HIV positive status (such as Magic Johnson and Greg Louganis) helped remove the stigma to a certain extent. The generous and vocal support of celebrities brought a sense of urgency to the search for better treatments and a cure. In 1993, Tom Hanks and Denzel Washington starred in *Philadelphia*, a film about a gay attorney who loses his job when his firm learns that he has AIDS. Hanks won an Academy Award for his portrayal of the main character. As the 1990s progressed, AIDS became a part of American culture. Awareness and prevention education expanded, and research continued to improve treatments. Still, perceptions of and reactions to the disease are mixed, and many people with HIV-positive status endure social discrimination.

While HIV and AIDS are a challenge to all of American society, they affect African Americans disproportionately. African Americans make up approximately 14 percent of the American population but comprise 41 percent of all AIDS cases. Of all the women who die of AIDS, fully half of them are African American. Among newly diagnosed women, 64 percent are black, 18 percent are white, and 18 percent are Hispanic. Incidence among black women, especially in the South, rose throughout the 1990s. While some women contract the disease from intravenous drug use, another major factor is heterosexual sex.

Teen Pregnancy and Other Problems

In 1997, when *What Looks Like Crazy* was published, American teenagers faced problems that had been much less common in the generations before them. These issues included teenage pregnancy, drug abuse, violence, and living in single-parent homes. During the 1990s, about one million teenage girls (10 percent of the total U.S. population of girls between the ages of fifteen and nineteen) became pregnant every year. In 1998, almost 13 percent of all births in the United States were to teenage mothers. Teenage pregnancy rates are

higher than those in many other developed countries, and the problem cost the United States seven billion dollars in 1999. Some social commentators assert that teen pregnancy creates a cycle: many girls who become pregnant come from single-parent homes, and then they become single parents. In 1994, almost ten million single mothers were heading households; twenty-five million children were being reared without fathers; and 42 percent of those children had never seen their fathers' houses. In 1998, 26 percent of families with children were headed by single parents, and 42 percent of those single parents had never been married.

Drug abuse was another major issue among teenagers in the 1990s. Nearly 10 percent of adolescents between the ages of twelve and seventeen used illegal drugs in 1998. Most of these teenagers used marijuana, but close to two million admitted to using cocaine and/or inhalants. Although use of drugs such as marijuana, cocaine, and heroin declined through the 1990s, use of "designer" drugs such as ecstasy rose dramatically. Not surprisingly, teenagers who are under the influence of drugs may become violent or sexually uninhibited, both of which often lead to long-term consequences.

Critical Overview

Although Cleage already enjoyed success as a playwright and essayist, in 1997 she ventured into novel writing with *What Looks Like Crazy*. Critics generally deemed her work in fiction as accomplished as her previous work in other forms. *What Looks Like Crazy* earned the acclaim of reviewers for its irreverent tone, relevant social issues, and well-developed characters.

A *Publishers Weekly* reviewer notes that "first-time novelist Cleage, without succumbing to didacticism, delivers a work of intelligence and integrity." The reviewer applauds Cleage for skillfully addressing so many issues that young African-American men and women face, including teenage motherhood, AIDS, drug abuse, unemployment, and inadequate sex education. Vanessa Bush of *Booklist* describes the novel as "riveting," adding that this "funny, irreverent, and hopeful novel is stunningly real and evocative." In *People Weekly*, Laura Jamison writes that the plot developments surrounding the quarrels with the local church can be "a little contrived and overblown." Still, the reviewer finds the book "uplifting" for its central message that a person's fallibility makes him or her

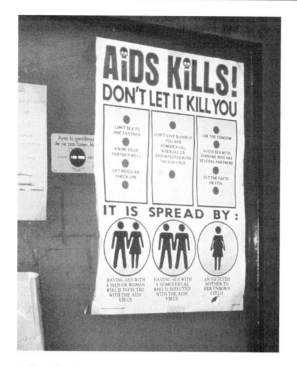

A health education poster instructing people of the safety measures they can take to avoid infection from the AIDS virus

lovable, a message Jamison claims is "delivered with a deft and joyful touch."

Criticism

Jennifer Bussey

Bussey holds a master's degree in interdisciplinary studies and a bachelor's degree in English literature. She is an independent writer specializing in literature. In the following essay, Bussey explores the significance of Ava's revisiting her childhood hometown of Idlewild.

In *What Looks Like Crazy on an Ordinary Day*, Cleage introduces the reader to Ava, a woman whose HIV-positive status ruined her social and professional life in Atlanta. Deciding to start a new life, she chooses San Francisco as her new home but first wants to visit her older sister, Ava, in Idlewild, Michigan, for the summer. Ava and Joyce grew up in Idlewild, and Ava's reaction to the declining resort town is similar to that of most people who revisit their childhood hometowns. She is struck by the changes, but she is also surprised at the things that have not changed and the people

who still live there or who have returned to live there again after some time away. What Ava does not know when she first arrives is that she too is returning for more than just a visit.

Ava comments that in the early days of Idlewild, the town was full of idle men and wild women. Once a popular resort town, Idlewild is now declining and no longer draws tourists. Ava's impression is that the town is stagnating, and there is little evidence of its exciting past. Still, the town's name is fitting; the youth in the town are both idle and wild. With the exception of Aretha, they seem to lack ambition or vision; they do not even have the attitude shared by so many teenagers of being eager to get out of their hometown and see other parts of the world. They expect to stay right where they are and do not even consider other possibilities. The youth are also wild; their lives revolve around sex, drugs, alcohol, and violence.

From Ava's perspective, the frequency of teenage pregnancy and crack use in Idlewild is unexpected. She is stunned because she thought that these problems would be out of her life once she left the big city of Atlanta. Instead, she finds them as commonplace in Idlewild as they are in Atlanta and, probably, San Francisco. Although she may have expected to enjoy a break from urban ills, she learns that these ills are universal. Because she has seen the problems of the urban youth in Atlanta, she quickly recognizes the same defiant attitudes in some of the young men in Idlewild. Commenting on Tyrone, Reverend Anderson's grandson, and his friend Frank, Ava observes:

> I felt sorry for them. I'd seen boys in my Atlanta neighborhood grow into swaggering young men who were suddenly scary until you looked into their still baby faces and realized who they used to be, but I also knew how dangerous they were. I'd seen Frank hit that girl like he didn't care if he broke every bone in her face. I'd seen Tyrone smoking dope right behind his grandmother's back. It was tempting but foolhardy to focus on their vulnerability instead of your own.

Realizing that social ills are everywhere is an important part of Ava's learning that she cannot outrun her HIV-positive status. The same devastation and discrimination she experienced in Atlanta, where she contracted it, will follow her to Idlewild and to San Francisco, where she expects to start a new life. At one point, Ava remarks, "I felt like I was back in Atlanta listening to people talking in tongues, trying not say *HIV*."

Idlewild was once a resort town, a place where people went to escape temporarily the demands of their everyday lives. Tourists came to Idlewild for respite, just as Ava does. She expects to take a break from worrying about her life and its new demands, but she finds that she must still confront her uncertain future and the regrets of her past. In this light, it is appropriate that Idlewild is no longer the haven from the city that it once was; it cannot offer Ava a place to leave her problems behind. Late in the story, she confides that the problem with knowing the truth deep down is that it makes it hard to pretend. She adds that, ever since she arrived in Idlewild, she has been trying to pretend that "this place is so far away from the scene of the crime that the consequences can't catch me."

Ava and Idlewild have three important similarities. The first is that they are seemingly on the decline yet still have much to offer. The second is that their histories demonstrate what is temporary and what is permanent. And the third is that they reflect major social issues of the 1990s. Anyone visiting Idlewild can see that it is a town in decline. Its exciting past contrasts sharply with its troubled present. Although it is no longer a resort town and social problems are a growing issue, it is still rich in history and potential. While some of its residents represent the worst of society, there are also people who represent the best of human nature. In these ways, Idlewild mirrors Ava. She is in decline, waiting for the inevitable destruction of her health and quality of life, but she is still engaged in life and working to improve herself and her community. She has the wisdom and perspective she lacked in her younger years, so she too is rich in history and potential. As a woman who is HIV positive, she embodies a major social problem, but through her loyalty, generosity, and humor she also embodies the resilience and strength of the human spirit. Idlewild is not all good and not all bad, so Ava is not in a position either to give up on it or to declare it perfect. Instead, she is compelled to participate in it, attaching herself to what is good and promising about it and working to repair what is destructive and frightening about it. The more she learns to deal with her HIV-positive status, the more she responds to herself the same way she responds to the town.

The second similarity between Idlewild and Ava is that they illustrate the passing fun of temporary excitement and the stability of lasting character. Idlewild was once a thriving resort town for African Americans. It was rich with entertainment, nightlife, and interesting visitors. Now these elements are gone, but they were never really a fundamental part of the town. Touring entertainers

> It is to Ava's credit that although Idlewild is not where she thought she would find happiness, she is open enough to recognize the opportunity for happiness when it presents itself in the forms of Joyce, Eddie, Imani, and the Sewing Circus."

came and went, the nightlife came alive only when the sun went down, and the interesting visitors finished their stays and returned to their homes. What was always constant about Idlewild was its population of permanent residents. Families like the one in which Joyce and Ava were reared, and notable people like "Wild Eddie" Jefferson, stayed in Idlewild throughout every season. For Ava, the things in her life that were fleeting, such as parties, one-night stands, and alcohol, are now gone. But the permanent fixtures, like her intelligence, wit, perseverance, and family, are still available to her. Idlewild and Ava illustrate the temporary nature of flashy, exciting chapters in the lives of towns and people, and they also show the lasting value of stable, caring people and strong character.

Third, Idlewild and Ava represent important social ills of the 1990s. Ava is surprised to see the same problems in Idlewild that she saw in the urban landscape of Atlanta: teenage pregnancy, domestic abuse, crack addiction, alcoholism, illiteracy, and sexual abuse. Throughout the story, she comments on the blurring line between urban and rural communities' problems. Just as Idlewild represents various social problems of the 1990s, Ava represents one of the most frightening new realities of the time. As a woman who is HIV positive, she serves as a constant reminder to those around her that AIDS is not a disease that attacks only male homosexuals and intravenous drug users. Cleage creates a character who reminds readers that everyone is potentially vulnerable.

Despite Ava's intention to pass through Idlewild and then move on to San Francisco, she finds the new life she desires in Idlewild. The town she was so eager to leave when she was a young woman becomes the perfect place to marry and live out the rest of her life. It is to Ava's credit that although Idlewild is not where she thought she would find happiness, she is open enough to recognize the opportunity for happiness when it presents itself in the forms of Joyce, Eddie, Imani, and the Sewing Circus. When Eddie and Joyce decide that they can buy an old house and renovate it for the Sewing Circus, Ava shares their excitement. She wants to be a part of it, and she says, "San Francisco seemed more and more like somebody else's dream." She adds:

> I felt more alive here than I had for years. I had my sister, the lover of my dreams, a role as part of a long-term project that excited me, and a big-eyed, bald-headed baby girl to take on my morning walks. I was meditating morning and evening, walking three miles a day, and I hadn't had anything stronger than a glass of wine with dinner in a month. It was my *choice* that had brought me back here, and for the first time, it really felt like home.

As if affirming Ava's decision to stay in Idlewild and forget her dreams of San Francisco, the new pastor (a woman named Sister Judith) and her husband come to Idlewild *from* San Francisco. Ava asks her, "Why would anybody leave a city like San Francisco to come to Idlewild?" Sister Judith reminds Ava that she herself left Atlanta to come to Idlewild and asks her, "Then what are you doing here?" Ava tells the reader, "*Watching the sun rise*, I wanted to say. *Walking in the woods. Falling in love. Raising a child. Helping my sister. Protecting my family. Living my life.* 'Planning my wedding,' is what I said." To Ava's surprise, she finds a kinship with Idlewild, and she finds her future within its community. She has no need to see what awaits her in San Francisco or anywhere else. Idlewild mirrors her, suits her, embraces her. It is home, after all.

Source: Jennifer Bussey, Critical Essay on *What Looks Like Crazy on an Ordinary Day*, in *Novels for Students*, The Gale Group, 2003.

Joyce Hart

Hart has degrees in English literature and creative writing and focuses her writing on literary themes. In this essay, Hart compares the three main characters' various uses of religion and spirituality and the specific goals they hope to attain through their beliefs and practices.

In *What Looks Like Crazy on an Ordinary Day*, Pearl Cleage creates three main characters who share a common reliance on a religious, or a spiritual, practice. They each use their own individu-

alized philosophy and ritual to help them overcome tragedies. Despite the fact that the characters' beliefs vary as widely as their motives for observing such practices, Cleage implies that it is through such spiritual practices that the characters confront their challenges and realize an inner peace. Upon discovering this sense of tranquility, the characters are then able to step out of the blindness of their personal suffering and feel compassion for the suffering of others.

The protagonist of this novel, Ava, has many challenges to face, and most of them center around her bout with AIDS. Ava also suffers from alcoholism. In the beginning of the story, she has sold her beauty shop and is leaving Atlanta in search of a new home in a new city, which she hopes will accept her as she is. As the story opens, she has little thought of changing her lifestyle and has resigned herself to an early death. Thoughts about the spiritual side of life, such as praying, would almost be an insult to God, since she has ignored everything religious throughout most of her adulthood. She quit trying to pray because she had figured out that she was just "hedging" her bets. If she was smart enough to come to that conclusion, she believes that "God must know it, too" and probably would not grant her wishes and might even decide that she "needed to be taught a lesson for trying to [bullsh——] him in the first place." With these beliefs in mind, Ava focuses on the physical elements of life and consumes large quantities of alcohol in an attempt to forget that she is dying.

The only remnants of a religious belief that Ava retains are based on her childhood memories of Christianity in the Baptist Church. Her view of religion is that of a powerful figurehead, or god, who exists outside of her and is in control of her life. This spiritual being judges her actions and sends rewards or punishments her way, depending on the decisions she makes on how to live her life. Since she has denied her early Baptist upbringing and has not acquired any spiritual practice to replace it, she is left with only a physical approach to life. In other words, Ava identifies herself only through her body. She says that the reason she is heading for San Francisco is that she believes that that city is progressive enough to accept her on her physical terms: "I wanted to be someplace where I could be my black, female, sexual, HIV-positive self." Because of her inability to see beyond the physical definitions of herself, Ava finds her only sense of relief in dulling her thoughts with large quantities of alcohol. When she is drunk, her thoughts cloud over, removing her, somewhat, from her fears. The most that she gains in her inebriated state is enough distance to temporarily become sarcastic about her condition. However, as soon as the alcohol wears off, she is right back where she started. Only now, she also has a hangover to deal with.

Not until Ava renews her friendship with Eddie, a Vietnam veteran and ex-con who has found solace in a more Eastern approach to spirituality, does Ava find some peace of mind. Through Eddie, Ava learns to meditate and to focus on the present moment through the practice of Tai Chi. In general, this Eastern form of spirituality appeals to the psychology of an individual. Through an understanding of how one's own thoughts influence one's actions, people who practice some Eastern spiritual rituals, such as Tai Chi, believe that the godhead dwells within oneself. By stilling one's thoughts, a person can cultivate an inner peace, which allows a more direct communication with the spiritual aspects of life.

It is through Tai Chi that Ava learns to live in the present moment and to face her fears of death. She does not embrace the Eastern philosophy fully, but rather she mixes the Eastern beliefs with her own Western understanding of religion. She uses Tai Chi to reawaken her sense of spirituality, thus giving her a reason to stop numbing herself with alcohol. Once she begins to cleanse herself of her destructive nature, she becomes more compassionate with the people around her. She takes an interest in her sister's community actions. She opens up her heart to the baby that her sister is trying to adopt. She also allows herself to imagine the possibilities of falling in love with Eddie, rather than simply enjoying the thrills of their sexual relationship. Through the characterization of Ava, Cleage states that it is impossible to run away, or hide, from life's challenges. The best path, Cleage implies, is to confront one's fears. For Ava, this confrontation requires that she use a mixture of beliefs that combine a trust in oneself as well as a faith in a god-figure, whom she describes as a man who reminds her of her grandfather: "tall and tan and like he's been working too hard."

Eddie's story is in many ways similar to Ava's, although the circumstances differ. During his involvement in the Vietnam War, Eddie was taught to kill and was forced to exist in a world of horrid atrocities. "I saw the worst things you can see human beings do to each other," Eddie tells Ava. Upon returning home, he felt lost. He says: "By the time I got back to the world, I was a *bad* man." For

> " Through the characterization of Ava, Cleage states that it is impossible to run away, or hide, from life's challenges. The best path, Cleage implies, is to confront one's fears."

Eddie, like Ava, the spiritual dimension in life had disappeared. He had faced death—both his as well as his victims—and he did not like what he had seen. In an attempt to rid himself of those memories, he too had turned to drugs and sex. He thought that these things would numb him. Instead, they put him in such a desensitized state that he thought nothing of murdering again.

Not until Eddie spends time in jail does he allow all the memories of Vietnam to flood back into his consciousness. When they do, he says they first made him angry. He was angry about having gone to Vietnam, angry about what he was taught to do while he was there, and angry that his subsequent actions, once he returned home, landed him in jail. Fortunately, while in prison, Eddie meets a man who reminds him to slow down and think, not just about what has happened to him but also about the lessons he has learned from all his experiences. It is at this point that Eddie turns to Tai Chi to help him process all the emotions that are stirred by his memories. The ritual of Tai Chi enhances the concept of slowing down, as those who practice it learn to move in very small, concentrated patterns with a full awareness of every muscle that is involved in every little step. With a well-sustained practice, the slow, ritualistic movements become a form of meditation, which helps Eddie to slow down his thoughts, to better understand and accept them, and then to comprehend the lessons behind them.

It is through meditation that Eddie begins to realize his self-destructive nature. His reawakening to the spiritual aspects of life allows him to understand that the fast-paced city life he had been living was counterproductive to his need to be reflective, to learn the lessons of his previous experiences. So, he moves away from Detroit and

What Do I Read Next?

- Jeannie Brewer's *A Crack in Forever* (1996) is the story of how a new romance between a medical student, Eric Moro, and a textbook illustrator, Alexandra Taylor, is put to the test when Eric learns that he has AIDS. Together, they tackle issues of mortality, regret, and family relationships.

- Cleage's *I Wish I Had a Red Dress* (2001) is a follow-up to *What Looks Like Crazy*. The novel features Joyce as she continues her work with the Sewing Circus, finds a love prospect, and explores the conflicting views of men as threatening and protective.

- Cleage's *Flyin' West* (1992) is one of her best-known plays. Set in 1898, it is the story of a group of black women forging new lives for themselves in the American West. Readers will find striking similarities between these turn-of-the-century women and the 1990s women portrayed in *What Looks Like Crazy*.

- Edited by Laura K. Egendorf and Jennifer Hurley, *Teens at Risk* (1998) provides opposing viewpoints in its exploration of various issues related to at-risk teenagers. Topics include violence, divorce, and peer pressure.

- In *Street Soldier: One Man's Struggle to Save a Generation, One Life at a Time* (2000), Joseph Marshall and Lonnie Wheeler tell how Marshall and a man named Jack Jacqua started the Omega Boys Club in San Francisco as a means to save troubled boys from the harsh life of inner-city streets. Critics applaud this book for its exaltation of activism, mentoring, and optimism.

---

reestablishes himself in his hometown of Idlewild. He gives up alcohol and replaces it with herbal teas. He changes his diet to one that is more nurturing and continues his Tai Chi practice.

Eddie knows better than to believe that all his problems are behind him, however. When Ava asks if he has learned all his lessons, he replies: "I'm working on it." He understands that his anger will always be there, just as Ava's HIV-positive status will never go away. Reawakening to spirituality, Cleage states through Eddie, is not some magical pill that one can take to relieve all the pain and rid oneself of all misery. Rather, it is a process. It is a way of coming to terms with life's problems and challenges. Eddie implies that he was not raised in a Christian belief system, so his belief in the Eastern philosophy is more concentrated than Ava's. By focusing on the concept of intentional living— eating the most nutritional foods, meditating to be aware of his thoughts, staying conscious of the present moment—Eddie is able to control his anger and forgive himself for the deaths he has caused. In learning to accept his flaws, to forgive himself, and to learn the lessons of his experiences, Eddie, too, opens up to the community. He is sympathetic to the older folks who are having trouble adjusting to the changing culture that surrounds them, and he is extremely protective of the women around him, willing to risk his own life to protect them.

Ava's sister, Joyce, has a very different list of problems. She also has slightly different ways of dealing with them than Ava and Eddie. Joyce's problems are those of tragedies that have been sent her way without her being an active participant in them. There was nothing that she did other than love her children and her husband and later have to witness their deaths. Her challenge is to accept the losses she has had to suffer through and move on. However, Joyce, too, at first tries to numb herself. Her agent of choice is not drugs or sex. Rather, Joyce turns to food to find solace. When Ava confronts her sister's weight problem, Joyce responds: "I had a couple of months when all that stood between me and taking a tumble was a bowl of Jamoca Almond fudge and some homemade Toll House cookies." Joyce's reference to "tumble" suggests the way that her mother dealt with her father's death. Joyce's mother had committed suicide. To keep herself from falling into that depressive state, Joyce appeases her mourning with sweets. On a psychological level, she might also have seen the extra weight that she gained as a padding that might help to protect her from any more emotional tragedies. Although Joyce's choice of food, on a social scale, might be more easily approved of, it nonetheless falls into the same category as Ava's and Eddie's addictions. Joyce used food to hide behind because she had lost a sense of the spiritual.

It did not take her very long, however, to reunite herself with the church of her childhood. After her husband's death, Joyce started attending services on Sundays, and as Ava explained it, "I think she wanted to pray and she was too self-conscious to do it at home." Whether that was the reason for her return, Joyce admits that her purpose was twofold. Her reacquaintance with the Baptist church was more than a spiritual quest. Joyce, like her sister, believed in a mixture of various philosophies. She was the product of several 1960s concepts, such as those purported by New Age and feminist movements. She was also familiar with many Eastern philosophies and practices. When she had a need to make contact with spirituality, she sought out books on Buddhism, yoga, and meditation. She was also comfortable with creating a godhead figure who might just as well be feminine as masculine. Although she had been struck with tragedies and had temporarily lost sight of the spiritual dimension, she knew, as she later tells her sister, that life was "not just the physical stuff."

Once Joyce regains her equilibrium, her first movement toward recreating her life is to seek out the members in her community who most need her help. She finds them through her church and uses the church as a meeting place until she can find a more liberating one. It is through Joyce's character that Cleage demonstrates the power of helping others in order to heal oneself.

There are many different ways, Cleage seems to imply, to find misery in this life, whether or not one is looking for it. However, there are just as many ways to find one's way through it. In developing these particular characters, Cleage demonstrates that it is not the religious, or spiritual, practice that is important but rather that one finds some way to keep the spiritual and physical balanced.

Source: Joyce Hart, Critical Essay on *What Looks Like Crazy on an Ordinary Day*, in *Novels for Students*, The Gale Group, 2003.

Bryan Aubrey

Aubrey holds a Ph.D. in English and has published many articles on twentieth-century literature. In this essay, Aubrey argues that, although the novel is full of love and compassion and offers a positive approach to solving social problems, the author's didactic purpose makes her characters less effective and real than they might otherwise be.

What Looks Like Crazy on an Ordinary Day was selected in 1998 for the Oprah Winfrey Book Club, which boosted its sales enormously and brought it attention that might otherwise have been

> **"** Going back to her roots in Idlewood, she finds that home can be more than simply the place you come from.**"**

placed elsewhere. There is a certain kind of book that catches Winfrey's eye. Such books often feature women, usually minorities, facing up to difficult, dangerous lives, courageously overcoming obstacles through a sense of solidarity with other women and establishing their independence. A dose of New Age spirituality about taking control of one's life and finding the core of truth within oneself does not go amiss either. Given the talk show host's persona, Cleage's first novel and Oprah's Book Club were a perfect fit. *What Looks Like Crazy on an Ordinary Day*, for all its literary qualities, is a self-help book. It points the way to how to live a productive, useful, happy life, especially for women. It is also a book with a social conscience. It highlights social problems such as AIDS, domestic violence, and the devastation caused by cocaine addiction. In that grim context, it shows women empowering themselves, making better choices about life, and tackling problems themselves when institutional structures (in this case, the local Baptist church) fail them. In fact, when Joyce, the social activist who thinks there is a solution for every problem, writes her statement of purpose for the Sewing Circus, it comes close to the message of the book as a whole: "To create and nurture women who are strong, mentally, physically; free of shackles, both internal and external . . . women who . . . choose their lovers based on mutual respect, emotional honesty and sexual responsibility."

So it is that Ava Johnson, although carrying the weight of being HIV positive, succeeds in making a complete turnaround in her life, both physically and mentally. She is the perfect New Age heroine, the ideal example for everyone who writes or reads those ubiquitous articles in women's magazines that outline a seven- (or eight- or nine- or ten-) point program for physical/mental/spiritual well-being. She begins an exercise program, regularly walking three miles a day; she starts to learn

Tai Chi from Eddie; she meditates twice a day; she and Joyce begin referring, in fashionable New Age feminist style, to "Mother/Father God"; she eats better and virtually eliminates her consumption of alcohol (giving up caffeine, however, proves too big a hurdle). Ava also learns to value what she has and to appreciate the present moment rather than dwelling on the past or worrying about the future. Going back to her roots in Idlewood, she finds that home can be more than simply the place you come from.

Ava is undoubtedly an attractive heroine. Her informal, chatty, confessional, diary-like narration has considerable verve and panache. She is resilient and able to learn. She has an innate decency and a sense of humor that carries her through the most difficult situations—and it is hard to imagine a more difficult situation than being diagnosed HIV positive, which, despite the recent advances in drug therapy, remains a slow death sentence for almost all of its victims.

However, there is an odd paradox about Ava's narration of her story. It is considerably wittier, earthy, irreverent, and entertaining in the early part of the novel, when she is at the height of her alienation from herself and her situation, than it is by the end. At the beginning, when she travels to Michigan and has to get used to living again in Idlewood, there is a gritty edge to her personality, as seen in her frequent use of street-slang, her self-confessions, her defiance, and her refusal to sugarcoat her situation or to lie to herself. All this sounds completely authentic; Ava has a genuine voice of her own. But, as her relationships with Joyce and Eddie deepen and she comes to terms with her situation, valuing the good that is in her life, she softens. She loses that street-smart edge to her language and becomes more bland and predictable. No doubt Cleage softened Ava on purpose, but the result is unfortunate. Instead of the heroine becoming progressively more interesting as the novel unfolds, she becomes considerably less so as she learns to do and say all the "politically correct" and "spiritually correct" things that her creator, who understandably wants to use her to convey a positive social message, requires her to say and do. The result is that Ava loses a quality that few people in real life ever do: the capacity to surprise or startle us.

Just to give one example: when early in the novel Ava describes her inability to adopt the kind of self-help program to reduce stress she sees described in magazine articles, she is humorous and engaging:

I read those articles all the time and I look at the things they recommend and I usually am not doing a single thing on the list. I *consider* doing them all the time, but I rationalize not starting to work on them immediately by thinking how they'd be so *easy* to do if I ever really wanted to do them. This is bulls———, of course, since every one of them would require a major redirecting of energy and since I'm already so guilt-ridden about not having done this stuff a long time ago, I could never just take one at a time. I'd have to tackle the whole righteous group simultaneously, or not at all.

This will surely be familiar to any woman who has been unpleasantly reminded by *Glamour*, *Cosmopolitan*, or any number of other women's magazines of the vast gap between what her life is and what it might be if she were not so lazy—and then decided to do nothing about it. And, how much more interesting, in style and sentiment, are Ava's comments here than her later dutiful remarks about how much better she feels when she finally musters the will to put some of the anti-stress practices into effect!

This is not an unfamiliar problem in literature, since vice, despair, unhappiness, and other negative states of mind are often easier to portray than their opposites. Darkness appears to make more of an impact than light, which is why Dante's *Inferno* is more widely read than his *Paradiso* and why William Blake's *Songs of Experience* are more complex and interesting than his *Songs of Innocence*. Virtue, although undoubtedly good for us, does not always make the most compelling reading.

This slide into virtue (if one may put it that outrageous way) is noticeable in other aspects of Ava's use of language. At first, she peppers her narrative with a commonly used vulgar term that even in these permissive times the *New York Times* refuses to print, referring to it instead as a "barnyard epithet." When, late in the novel, Ava has to find a word for a bodily function for which the barnyard epithet would be the literally correct, if vulgar, choice, she opts instead for the dainty euphemism "call of nature." One suspects that the Ava who waited at the airport in the first chapter of the novel would not be caught dead using such a mealy-mouthed phrase.

In spite of these observations, Ava remains for the most part a genuinely complex and believable character. Such cannot be said, however, of the principal male character, Eddie Jefferson. He may strike many readers as simply too good to be true. In spite of his wild past, he does not appear to have a single flaw. His lifestyle, for example, is beyond reproach. He does not drink or eat meat (he once raised rabbits with the intention of eating them but could not bring himself to kill them); he meditates twice a day; he practices Tai Chi; he grows much of his own food (organic, of course); and he has a habit of showing up on Joyce's doorstep with fresh bread and a smile. He is unfailingly sensitive, wise, tactful, understanding, and protective. He is at home with his emotions; he does not waste words and is often content with silence. Physically, he moves like a dancer, and in Ava's eyes there is a mystical quality about his presence: "There was something really *quiet* about Eddie. I don't mean just not talking. Something about him that was *still*." When Ava describes Eddie physically, she comes within a whisker of sounding like a character from a Harlequin romance novel. Watching him exercising while stripped to the waist, for example, she observes: "Eddie's body was more muscular than I had thought.... I was surprised at the power in his chest and back."

Given that there are no chinks in Eddie's perfection—even his pick-up truck is so clean and polished that Ava can see her reflection in the passenger door—it may come as no surprise to the reader to find a hint that this bearded, long-haired wise-man looks the way Jesus Christ himself might have looked. The hint is repeated when Joyce reports having seen a child in the hospital with a T-shirt bearing the slogan, "Jesus Was a Black Man." Wisely, Cleage refrains from pushing this allusion any further, which would have strained credulity beyond its proper limits.

It is not unusual for an author, in her eagerness to create a positive character who carries the special qualities and virtues that she wishes the story to convey, to fall into a trap such as this. Barbara Kingsolver, in *Animal Dreams* (1990), another book that often appears in the high school curriculum, cannot avoid it either. *Animal Dreams* has a certain amount in common with *What Looks Like Crazy on an Ordinary Day*. In both, the female protagonist (Codi in *Animal Dreams*; Ava in Cleage's novel) returns to the town in which she grew up, much changed from the person she was when she left it. In both novels, the protagonist meets up with a man whom she had known before and who chose to remain living in his hometown. (In *Animal Dreams*, this is Loyd Peregrina.) In both cases, too, the man concerned was a notorious womanizer known also for his anti-social behavior, but he has reformed and calmed down. It takes a while for the protagonists to realize that these men are now very different from what they might have been expected to become, given their wild youth. (This tactic also has the advantage of creating a surprise for the

reader too.) Both men are also representatives of a certain kind of spiritual wisdom. Loyd embodies the wisdom of the Native-American tradition; Eddie has come to a not dissimilar perspective partly through his own introspection and partly through a knowledge of Buddhism. The problem in *Animal Dreams* is that Kingsolver strives to get her spiritual message across. Like Eddie, Loyd is far too perfect; the author's urge to instruct has won out over her instincts as a writer to create multi-dimensional, realistic characters.

Such criticism of *What Looks Like Crazy on an Ordinary Day* may seem harsh. In spite of its faults, this is a novel that is full of compassion and understanding. It makes a valiant attempt to chart a path beyond the depressing realities of many people's lives today: AIDS, domestic violence, drug addiction, and the breakdown of community. Cleage's promotion of AIDS awareness and "safe sex" is laudable, and she makes the emphatic point that a diagnosis of HIV positive does not of itself mean that a person must give up sex entirely. Some sex educators, however, might quarrel with the impression the novel gives that as long as condoms are used during sexual activity, there is no need to fear the transmission of disease. Most experts would agree that this is not a foolproof way to avoid contracting AIDS or any other sexual disease. That caveat aside, the humor with which Cleage deals with the matter is irresistible. The brief comic scene in which the entire Sewing Circus watches as Joyce uses a jumbo hot dog to demonstrate how to use a condom is worthy of John Irving, a master of this kind of irreverent humor.

For all these positives, Cleage deserves credit. Her novel says a large "yes" to life; it refuses to take refuge in fashionable pessimism or nihilism in the name of entertainment. This is shown vividly in the incident when Eddie reacts negatively to the movie that Ava, in a misguided attempt to keep him informed about popular culture, shows him. The movie shows violence as routine. Killing a human being is presented as of no more consequence than swatting a fly. As Eddie puts it, "They're training people to look at this for fun." In that swipe at contemporary Hollywood entertainment, and in many other respects, *What Looks Like Crazy on an Ordinary Day* reaches into the darkness and brings in some badly needed light.

Source: Bryan Aubrey, Critical Essay on *What Looks Like Crazy on an Ordinary Day*, in *Novels for Students*, The Gale Group, 2003.

Sources

Bashir, Samiya A., "Pearl Cleage's Idlewild Idylls," in *Black Issues Book Review*, Vol. 3, No. 4, July 2001, p. 16.

Bush, Vanessa, Review of *What Looks Like Crazy on an Ordinary Day*, in *Booklist*, Vol. 94, No. 7, December 1997, pp. 608–609.

Cleage, Pearl, *What Looks Like Crazy on an Ordinary Day*, Avon, 1997.

Jamison, Laura, Review of *What Looks Like Crazy on an Ordinary Day*, in *People Weekly*, Vol. 49, No. 4, February 2, 1998, p. 30.

Kingsolver, Barbara, *Animal Dreams*, HarperCollins, 1990.

Review of *What Looks Like Crazy on an Ordinary Day*, in *Publishers Weekly*, Vol. 244, No. 46, November 10, 1997, pp. 56–57.

Further Reading

Royster, Jacqueline Jones, *Traces of a Stream: Literacy and Social Change among African-American Women*, Pittsburgh Series in Composition, Literacy, and Culture, University of Pittsburgh Press, 2000.

Royster adopts an interdisciplinary view of rhetoric and social change in this study of the important role played by highly literate African-American women in the late twentieth century. She demonstrates that these women have been able to affect social and political change through speech, books, and periodicals.

Spelman College Museum of Fine Art, *Bearing Witness: Contemporary Works by African American Women Artists*, Vol. 1, Rizzoli International, 1996.

This volume captures the art on display during the title exhibition. Various media were included in the exhibit, and twenty-five notable artists contributed work. The photos of the art are complemented by relevant essays written by such prominent African-American women as Cleage and Maya Angelou.

Stine, Gerald J., *AIDS Update 2002*, Prentice Hall, 2001.

Stine presents a comprehensive overview of AIDS in contemporary society. He addresses its history and its social importance along with the latest medical and biological information available.

Walker, Lewis, and Benjamin C. Wilson, *Black Eden: The Idlewild Community*, Michigan State University Press, 2002.

Walker and Wilson explore the history of Idlewild, including its origins, its status during the civil rights era, its history of entertainment, and efforts to revitalize it. The authors include a selection of primary documents to enhance the book's historical value.

Glossary of Literary Terms

A

Abstract: As an adjective applied to writing or literary works, abstract refers to words or phrases that name things not knowable through the five senses.

Aestheticism: A literary and artistic movement of the nineteenth century. Followers of the movement believed that art should not be mixed with social, political, or moral teaching. The statement "art for art's sake" is a good summary of aestheticism. The movement had its roots in France, but it gained widespread importance in England in the last half of the nineteenth century, where it helped change the Victorian practice of including moral lessons in literature.

Allegory: A narrative technique in which characters representing things or abstract ideas are used to convey a message or teach a lesson. Allegory is typically used to teach moral, ethical, or religious lessons but is sometimes used for satiric or political purposes.

Allusion: A reference to a familiar literary or historical person or event, used to make an idea more easily understood.

Analogy: A comparison of two things made to explain something unfamiliar through its similarities to something familiar, or to prove one point based on the acceptedness of another. Similes and metaphors are types of analogies.

Antagonist: The major character in a narrative or drama who works against the hero or protagonist.

Anthropomorphism: The presentation of animals or objects in human shape or with human characteristics. The term is derived from the Greek word for "human form."

Antihero: A central character in a work of literature who lacks traditional heroic qualities such as courage, physical prowess, and fortitude. Antiheroes typically distrust conventional values and are unable to commit themselves to any ideals. They generally feel helpless in a world over which they have no control. Antiheroes usually accept, and often celebrate, their positions as social outcasts.

Apprenticeship Novel: See *Bildungsroman*

Archetype: The word archetype is commonly used to describe an original pattern or model from which all other things of the same kind are made. This term was introduced to literary criticism from the psychology of Carl Jung. It expresses Jung's theory that behind every person's "unconscious," or repressed memories of the past, lies the "collective unconscious" of the human race: memories of the countless typical experiences of our ancestors. These memories are said to prompt illogical associations that trigger powerful emotions in the reader. Often, the emotional process is primitive, even primordial. Archetypes are the literary images that grow out of the "collective unconscious." They appear in literature as incidents and plots that repeat basic patterns of life. They may also appear as stereotyped characters.

***Avant-garde*:** French term meaning "vanguard." It is used in literary criticism to describe new writing that rejects traditional approaches to literature in favor of innovations in style or content.

B

Beat Movement: A period featuring a group of American poets and novelists of the 1950s and 1960s—including Jack Kerouac, Allen Ginsberg, Gregory Corso, William S. Burroughs, and Lawrence Ferlinghetti—who rejected established social and literary values. Using such techniques as stream of consciousness writing and jazz-influenced free verse and focusing on unusual or abnormal states of mind—generated by religious ecstasy or the use of drugs—the Beat writers aimed to create works that were unconventional in both form and subject matter.

***Bildungsroman*:** A German word meaning "novel of development." The *bildungsroman* is a study of the maturation of a youthful character, typically brought about through a series of social or sexual encounters that lead to self-awareness. *Bildungsroman* is used interchangeably with *erziehungsroman,* a novel of initiation and education. When a *bildungsroman* is concerned with the development of an artist (as in James Joyce's *A Portrait of the Artist as a Young Man*), it is often termed a *kunstlerroman.* Also known as Apprenticeship Novel, Coming of Age Novel, *Erziehungsroman,* or *Kunstlerroman.*

Black Aesthetic Movement: A period of artistic and literary development among African Americans in the 1960s and early 1970s. This was the first major African-American artistic movement since the Harlem Renaissance and was closely paralleled by the civil rights and black power movements. The black aesthetic writers attempted to produce works of art that would be meaningful to the black masses. Key figures in black aesthetics included one of its founders, poet and playwright Amiri Baraka, formerly known as LeRoi Jones; poet and essayist Haki R. Madhubuti, formerly Don L. Lee; poet and playwright Sonia Sanchez; and dramatist Ed Bullins. Also known as Black Arts Movement.

Black Humor: Writing that places grotesque elements side by side with humorous ones in an attempt to shock the reader, forcing him or her to laugh at the horrifying reality of a disordered world. Also known as Black Comedy.

Burlesque: Any literary work that uses exaggeration to make its subject appear ridiculous, either by treating a trivial subject with profound seriousness or by treating a dignified subject frivolously. The word "burlesque" may also be used as an adjective, as in "burlesque show," to mean "striptease act."

C

Character: Broadly speaking, a person in a literary work. The actions of characters are what constitute the plot of a story, novel, or poem. There are numerous types of characters, ranging from simple, stereotypical figures to intricate, multifaceted ones. In the techniques of anthropomorphism and personification, animals—and even places or things—can assume aspects of character. "Characterization" is the process by which an author creates vivid, believable characters in a work of art. This may be done in a variety of ways, including (1) direct description of the character by the narrator; (2) the direct presentation of the speech, thoughts, or actions of the character; and (3) the responses of other characters to the character. The term "character" also refers to a form originated by the ancient Greek writer Theophrastus that later became popular in the seventeenth and eighteenth centuries. It is a short essay or sketch of a person who prominently displays a specific attribute or quality, such as miserliness or ambition.

Climax: The turning point in a narrative, the moment when the conflict is at its most intense. Typically, the structure of stories, novels, and plays is one of rising action, in which tension builds to the climax, followed by falling action, in which tension lessens as the story moves to its conclusion.

Colloquialism: A word, phrase, or form of pronunciation that is acceptable in casual conversation but not in formal, written communication. It is considered more acceptable than slang.

Coming of Age Novel: See *Bildungsroman*

Concrete: Concrete is the opposite of abstract, and refers to a thing that actually exists or a description that allows the reader to experience an object or concept with the senses.

Connotation: The impression that a word gives beyond its defined meaning. Connotations may be universally understood or may be significant only to a certain group.

Convention: Any widely accepted literary device, style, or form.

D

Denotation: The definition of a word, apart from the impressions or feelings it creates (connotations) in the reader.

Denouement: A French word meaning "the un-knotting." In literary criticism, it denotes the resolution of conflict in fiction or drama. The *denouement* follows the climax and provides an outcome to the primary plot situation as well as an explanation of secondary plot complications. The *denouement* often involves a character's recognition of his or her state of mind or moral condition. Also known as Falling Action.

Description: Descriptive writing is intended to allow a reader to picture the scene or setting in which the action of a story takes place. The form this description takes often evokes an intended emotional response—a dark, spooky graveyard will evoke fear, and a peaceful, sunny meadow will evoke calmness.

Dialogue: In its widest sense, dialogue is simply conversation between people in a literary work; in its most restricted sense, it refers specifically to the speech of characters in a drama. As a specific literary genre, a "dialogue" is a composition in which characters debate an issue or idea.

Diction: The selection and arrangement of words in a literary work. Either or both may vary depending on the desired effect. There are four general types of diction: "formal," used in scholarly or lofty writing; "informal," used in relaxed but educated conversation; "colloquial," used in everyday speech; and "slang," containing newly coined words and other terms not accepted in formal usage.

Didactic: A term used to describe works of literature that aim to teach some moral, religious, political, or practical lesson. Although didactic elements are often found in artistically pleasing works, the term "didactic" usually refers to literature in which the message is more important than the form. The term may also be used to criticize a work that the critic finds "overly didactic," that is, heavy-handed in its delivery of a lesson.

Doppelganger: A literary technique by which a character is duplicated (usually in the form of an alter ego, though sometimes as a ghostly counterpart) or divided into two distinct, usually opposite personalities. The use of this character device is widespread in nineteenth- and twentieth-century literature, and indicates a growing awareness among authors that the "self" is really a composite of many "selves." Also known as The Double.

Double Entendre: A corruption of a French phrase meaning "double meaning." The term is used to indicate a word or phrase that is deliberately ambiguous, especially when one of the meanings is risqué or improper.

Dramatic Irony: Occurs when the audience of a play or the reader of a work of literature knows something that a character in the work itself does not know. The irony is in the contrast between the intended meaning of the statements or actions of a character and the additional information understood by the audience.

Dystopia: An imaginary place in a work of fiction where the characters lead dehumanized, fearful lives.

E

Edwardian: Describes cultural conventions identified with the period of the reign of Edward VII of England (1901-1910). Writers of the Edwardian Age typically displayed a strong reaction against the propriety and conservatism of the Victorian Age. Their work often exhibits distrust of authority in religion, politics, and art and expresses strong doubts about the soundness of conventional values.

Empathy: A sense of shared experience, including emotional and physical feelings, with someone or something other than oneself. Empathy is often used to describe the response of a reader to a literary character.

Enlightenment, The: An eighteenth-century philosophical movement. It began in France but had a wide impact throughout Europe and America. Thinkers of the Enlightenment valued reason and believed that both the individual and society could achieve a state of perfection. Corresponding to this essentially humanist vision was a resistance to religious authority.

Epigram: A saying that makes the speaker's point quickly and concisely. Often used to preface a novel.

Epilogue: A concluding statement or section of a literary work. In dramas, particularly those of the seventeenth and eighteenth centuries, the epilogue is a closing speech, often in verse, delivered by an actor at the end of a play and spoken directly to the audience.

Epiphany: A sudden revelation of truth inspired by a seemingly trivial incident.

Episode: An incident that forms part of a story and is significantly related to it. Episodes may be either self-contained narratives or events that depend on a larger context for their sense and importance.

Epistolary Novel: A novel in the form of letters. The form was particularly popular in the eighteenth century.

Epithet: A word or phrase, often disparaging or abusive, that expresses a character trait of someone or something.

Existentialism: A predominantly twentieth-century philosophy concerned with the nature and perception of human existence. There are two major strains of existentialist thought: atheistic and Christian. Followers of atheistic existentialism believe that the individual is alone in a godless universe and that the basic human condition is one of suffering and loneliness. Nevertheless, because there are no fixed values, individuals can create their own characters—indeed, they can shape themselves—through the exercise of free will. The atheistic strain culminates in and is popularly associated with the works of Jean-Paul Sartre. The Christian existentialists, on the other hand, believe that only in God may people find freedom from life's anguish. The two strains hold certain beliefs in common: that existence cannot be fully understood or described through empirical effort; that anguish is a universal element of life; that individuals must bear responsibility for their actions; and that there is no common standard of behavior or perception for religious and ethical matters.

Expatriates: See *Expatriatism*

Expatriatism: The practice of leaving one's country to live for an extended period in another country.

Exposition: Writing intended to explain the nature of an idea, thing, or theme. Expository writing is often combined with description, narration, or argument. In dramatic writing, the exposition is the introductory material which presents the characters, setting, and tone of the play.

Expressionism: An indistinct literary term, originally used to describe an early twentieth-century school of German painting. The term applies to almost any mode of unconventional, highly subjective writing that distorts reality in some way.

F

Fable: A prose or verse narrative intended to convey a moral. Animals or inanimate objects with human characteristics often serve as characters in fables.

Falling Action: See *Denouement*

Fantasy: A literary form related to mythology and folklore. Fantasy literature is typically set in non-existent realms and features supernatural beings.

Farce: A type of comedy characterized by broad humor, outlandish incidents, and often vulgar subject matter.

Femme fatale: A French phrase with the literal translation "fatal woman." A *femme fatale* is a sensuous, alluring woman who often leads men into danger or trouble.

Fiction: Any story that is the product of imagination rather than a documentation of fact. Characters and events in such narratives may be based in real life but their ultimate form and configuration is a creation of the author.

Figurative Language: A technique in writing in which the author temporarily interrupts the order, construction, or meaning of the writing for a particular effect. This interruption takes the form of one or more figures of speech such as hyperbole, irony, or simile. Figurative language is the opposite of literal language, in which every word is truthful, accurate, and free of exaggeration or embellishment.

Figures of Speech: Writing that differs from customary conventions for construction, meaning, order, or significance for the purpose of a special meaning or effect. There are two major types of figures of speech: rhetorical figures, which do not make changes in the meaning of the words, and tropes, which do.

Fin de siecle: A French term meaning "end of the century." The term is used to denote the last decade of the nineteenth century, a transition period when writers and other artists abandoned old conventions and looked for new techniques and objectives.

First Person: See *Point of View*

Flashback: A device used in literature to present action that occurred before the beginning of the story. Flashbacks are often introduced as the dreams or recollections of one or more characters.

Foil: A character in a work of literature whose physical or psychological qualities contrast strongly with, and therefore highlight, the corresponding qualities of another character.

Folklore: Traditions and myths preserved in a culture or group of people. Typically, these are passed on by word of mouth in various forms—such as legends, songs, and proverbs—or preserved in customs and ceremonies. This term was first used by W. J. Thoms in 1846.

Folktale: A story originating in oral tradition. Folktales fall into a variety of categories, including legends, ghost stories, fairy tales, fables, and anecdotes based on historical figures and events.

Foreshadowing: A device used in literature to create expectation or to set up an explanation of later developments.

Form: The pattern or construction of a work which identifies its genre and distinguishes it from other genres.

G

Genre: A category of literary work. In critical theory, genre may refer to both the content of a given work—tragedy, comedy, pastoral—and to its form, such as poetry, novel, or drama.

Gilded Age: A period in American history during the 1870s characterized by political corruption and materialism. A number of important novels of social and political criticism were written during this time.

Gothicism: In literary criticism, works characterized by a taste for the medieval or morbidly attractive. A gothic novel prominently features elements of horror, the supernatural, gloom, and violence: clanking chains, terror, charnel houses, ghosts, medieval castles, and mysteriously slamming doors. The term "gothic novel" is also applied to novels that lack elements of the traditional Gothic setting but that create a similar atmosphere of terror or dread.

Grotesque: In literary criticism, the subject matter of a work or a style of expression characterized by exaggeration, deformity, freakishness, and disorder. The grotesque often includes an element of comic absurdity.

H

Harlem Renaissance: The Harlem Renaissance of the 1920s is generally considered the first significant movement of black writers and artists in the United States. During this period, new and established black writers published more fiction and poetry than ever before, the first influential black literary journals were established, and black authors and artists received their first widespread recognition and serious critical appraisal. Among the major writers associated with this period are Claude McKay, Jean Toomer, Countee Cullen, Langston Hughes, Arna Bontemps, Nella Larsen, and Zora Neale Hurston. Also known as Negro Renaissance and New Negro Movement.

Hero/Heroine: The principal sympathetic character (male or female) in a literary work. Heroes and heroines typically exhibit admirable traits: idealism, courage, and integrity, for example.

Holocaust Literature: Literature influenced by or written about the Holocaust of World War II. Such literature includes true stories of survival in concentration camps, escape, and life after the war, as well as fictional works and poetry.

Humanism: A philosophy that places faith in the dignity of humankind and rejects the medieval perception of the individual as a weak, fallen creature. "Humanists" typically believe in the perfectibility of human nature and view reason and education as the means to that end.

Hyperbole: In literary criticism, deliberate exaggeration used to achieve an effect.

I

Idiom: A word construction or verbal expression closely associated with a given language.

Image: A concrete representation of an object or sensory experience. Typically, such a representation helps evoke the feelings associated with the object or experience itself. Images are either "literal" or "figurative." Literal images are especially concrete and involve little or no extension of the obvious meaning of the words used to express them. Figurative images do not follow the literal meaning of the words exactly. Images in literature are usually visual, but the term "image" can also refer to the representation of any sensory experience.

Imagery: The array of images in a literary work. Also, figurative language.

In medias res: A Latin term meaning "in the middle of things." It refers to the technique of beginning a story at its midpoint and then using various flashback devices to reveal previous action.

Interior Monologue: A narrative technique in which characters' thoughts are revealed in a way that appears to be uncontrolled by the author. The interior monologue typically aims to reveal the inner self of a character. It portrays emotional experiences as they occur at both a conscious and unconscious level. Images are often used to represent sensations or emotions.

Irony: In literary criticism, the effect of language in which the intended meaning is the opposite of what is stated.

J

Jargon: Language that is used or understood only by a select group of people. Jargon may refer to terminology used in a certain profession, such as computer jargon, or it may refer to any nonsensical language that is not understood by most people.

L

Leitmotiv: See *Motif*

Literal Language: An author uses literal language when he or she writes without exaggerating or embellishing the subject matter and without any tools of figurative language.

Lost Generation: A term first used by Gertrude Stein to describe the post-World War I generation of American writers: men and women haunted by a sense of betrayal and emptiness brought about by the destructiveness of the war.

M

Mannerism: Exaggerated, artificial adherence to a literary manner or style. Also, a popular style of the visual arts of late sixteenth-century Europe that was marked by elongation of the human form and by intentional spatial distortion. Literary works that are self-consciously high-toned and artistic are often said to be "mannered."

Metaphor: A figure of speech that expresses an idea through the image of another object. Metaphors suggest the essence of the first object by identifying it with certain qualities of the second object.

Modernism: Modern literary practices. Also, the principles of a literary school that lasted from roughly the beginning of the twentieth century until the end of World War II. Modernism is defined by its rejection of the literary conventions of the nineteenth century and by its opposition to conventional morality, taste, traditions, and economic values.

Mood: The prevailing emotions of a work or of the author in his or her creation of the work. The mood of a work is not always what might be expected based on its subject matter.

Motif: A theme, character type, image, metaphor, or other verbal element that recurs throughout a single work of literature or occurs in a number of different works over a period of time. Also known as *Motiv* or *Leitmotiv*.

Myth: An anonymous tale emerging from the traditional beliefs of a culture or social unit. Myths use supernatural explanations for natural phenomena. They may also explain cosmic issues like creation and death. Collections of myths, known as mythologies, are common to all cultures and nations, but the best-known myths belong to the Norse, Roman, and Greek mythologies.

N

Narration: The telling of a series of events, real or invented. A narration may be either a simple narrative, in which the events are recounted chronologically, or a narrative with a plot, in which the account is given in a style reflecting the author's artistic concept of the story. Narration is sometimes used as a synonym for "storyline."

Narrative: A verse or prose accounting of an event or sequence of events, real or invented. The term is also used as an adjective in the sense "method of narration." For example, in literary criticism, the expression "narrative technique" usually refers to the way the author structures and presents his or her story.

Narrator: The teller of a story. The narrator may be the author or a character in the story through whom the author speaks.

Naturalism: A literary movement of the late nineteenth and early twentieth centuries. The movement's major theorist, French novelist Emile Zola, envisioned a type of fiction that would examine human life with the objectivity of scientific inquiry. The Naturalists typically viewed human beings as either the products of "biological determinism," ruled by hereditary instincts and engaged in an endless struggle for survival, or as the products of "socioeconomic determinism," ruled by social and economic forces beyond their control. In their works, the Naturalists generally ignored the highest levels of society and focused on degradation: poverty, alcoholism, prostitution, insanity, and disease.

Noble Savage: The idea that primitive man is noble and good but becomes evil and corrupted as he becomes civilized. The concept of the noble savage originated in the Renaissance period but is more closely identified with such later writers as

Jean-Jacques Rousseau and Aphra Behn. See also Primitivism.

Novel of Ideas: A novel in which the examination of intellectual issues and concepts takes precedence over characterization or a traditional storyline.

Novel of Manners: A novel that examines the customs and mores of a cultural group.

Novel: A long fictional narrative written in prose, which developed from the novella and other early forms of narrative. A novel is usually organized under a plot or theme with a focus on character development and action.

Novella: An Italian term meaning "story." This term has been especially used to describe fourteenth-century Italian tales, but it also refers to modern short novels.

O

Objective Correlative: An outward set of objects, a situation, or a chain of events corresponding to an inward experience and evoking this experience in the reader. The term frequently appears in modern criticism in discussions of authors' intended effects on the emotional responses of readers.

Objectivity: A quality in writing characterized by the absence of the author's opinion or feeling about the subject matter. Objectivity is an important factor in criticism.

Oedipus Complex: A son's amorous obsession with his mother. The phrase is derived from the story of the ancient Theban hero Oedipus, who unknowingly killed his father and married his mother.

Omniscience: See *Point of View*

Onomatopoeia: The use of words whose sounds express or suggest their meaning. In its simplest sense, onomatopoeia may be represented by words that mimic the sounds they denote such as "hiss" or "meow." At a more subtle level, the pattern and rhythm of sounds and rhymes of a line or poem may be onomatopoeic.

Oxymoron: A phrase combining two contradictory terms. Oxymorons may be intentional or unintentional.

P

Parable: A story intended to teach a moral lesson or answer an ethical question.

Paradox: A statement that appears illogical or contradictory at first, but may actually point to an underlying truth.

Parallelism: A method of comparison of two ideas in which each is developed in the same grammatical structure.

Parody: In literary criticism, this term refers to an imitation of a serious literary work or the signature style of a particular author in a ridiculous manner. A typical parody adopts the style of the original and applies it to an inappropriate subject for humorous effect. Parody is a form of satire and could be considered the literary equivalent of a caricature or cartoon.

Pastoral: A term derived from the Latin word "pastor," meaning shepherd. A pastoral is a literary composition on a rural theme. The conventions of the pastoral were originated by the third-century Greek poet Theocritus, who wrote about the experiences, love affairs, and pastimes of Sicilian shepherds. In a pastoral, characters and language of a courtly nature are often placed in a simple setting. The term pastoral is also used to classify dramas, elegies, and lyrics that exhibit the use of country settings and shepherd characters.

Pen Name: See *Pseudonym*

Persona: A Latin term meaning "mask." *Personae* are the characters in a fictional work of literature. The *persona* generally functions as a mask through which the author tells a story in a voice other than his or her own. A *persona* is usually either a character in a story who acts as a narrator or an "implied author," a voice created by the author to act as the narrator for himself or herself.

Personification: A figure of speech that gives human qualities to abstract ideas, animals, and inanimate objects. Also known as *Prosopopoeia*.

Picaresque Novel: Episodic fiction depicting the adventures of a roguish central character ("picaro" is Spanish for "rogue"). The picaresque hero is commonly a low-born but clever individual who wanders into and out of various affairs of love, danger, and farcical intrigue. These involvements may take place at all social levels and typically present a humorous and wide-ranging satire of a given society.

Plagiarism: Claiming another person's written material as one's own. Plagiarism can take the form of direct, word-for-word copying or the theft of the substance or idea of the work.

Plot: In literary criticism, this term refers to the pattern of events in a narrative or drama. In its simplest sense, the plot guides the author in composing the work and helps the reader follow the work. Typically, plots exhibit causality and unity and have a beginning, a middle, and an end. Sometimes, however, a plot may consist of a series of disconnected events, in which case it is known as an "episodic plot."

Poetic Justice: An outcome in a literary work, not necessarily a poem, in which the good are rewarded and the evil are punished, especially in ways that particularly fit their virtues or crimes.

Poetic License: Distortions of fact and literary convention made by a writer—not always a poet—for the sake of the effect gained. Poetic license is closely related to the concept of "artistic freedom."

Poetics: This term has two closely related meanings. It denotes (1) an aesthetic theory in literary criticism about the essence of poetry or (2) rules prescribing the proper methods, content, style, or diction of poetry. The term poetics may also refer to theories about literature in general, not just poetry.

Point of View: The narrative perspective from which a literary work is presented to the reader. There are four traditional points of view. The "third person omniscient" gives the reader a "godlike" perspective, unrestricted by time or place, from which to see actions and look into the minds of characters. This allows the author to comment openly on characters and events in the work. The "third person" point of view presents the events of the story from outside of any single character's perception, much like the omniscient point of view, but the reader must understand the action as it takes place and without any special insight into characters' minds or motivations. The "first person" or "personal" point of view relates events as they are perceived by a single character. The main character "tells" the story and may offer opinions about the action and characters which differ from those of the author. Much less common than omniscient, third person, and first person is the "second person" point of view, wherein the author tells the story as if it is happening to the reader.

Polemic: A work in which the author takes a stand on a controversial subject, such as abortion or religion. Such works are often extremely argumentative or provocative.

Pornography: Writing intended to provoke feelings of lust in the reader. Such works are often condemned by critics and teachers, but those which can be shown to have literary value are viewed less harshly.

Post-Aesthetic Movement: An artistic response made by African Americans to the black aesthetic movement of the 1960s and early '70s. Writers since that time have adopted a somewhat different tone in their work, with less emphasis placed on the disparity between black and white in the United States. In the words of post-aesthetic authors such as Toni Morrison, John Edgar Wideman, and Kristin Hunter, African Americans are portrayed as looking inward for answers to their own questions, rather than always looking to the outside world.

Postmodernism: Writing from the 1960s forward characterized by experimentation and continuing to apply some of the fundamentals of modernism, which included existentialism and alienation. Postmodernists have gone a step further in the rejection of tradition begun with the modernists by also rejecting traditional forms, preferring the anti-novel over the novel and the antihero over the hero.

Primitivism: The belief that primitive peoples were nobler and less flawed than civilized peoples because they had not been subjected to the tainting influence of society. See also Noble Savage.

Prologue: An introductory section of a literary work. It often contains information establishing the situation of the characters or presents information about the setting, time period, or action. In drama, the prologue is spoken by a chorus or by one of the principal characters.

Prose: A literary medium that attempts to mirror the language of everyday speech. It is distinguished from poetry by its use of unmetered, unrhymed language consisting of logically related sentences. Prose is usually grouped into paragraphs that form a cohesive whole such as an essay or a novel.

Prosopopoeia: See *Personification*

Protagonist: The central character of a story who serves as a focus for its themes and incidents and as the principal rationale for its development. The protagonist is sometimes referred to in discussions of modern literature as the hero or antihero.

Protest Fiction: Protest fiction has as its primary purpose the protesting of some social injustice, such as racism or discrimination.

Proverb: A brief, sage saying that expresses a truth about life in a striking manner.

Pseudonym: A name assumed by a writer, most often intended to prevent his or her identification as the author of a work. Two or more authors may work together under one pseudonym, or an author may use a different name for each genre he or she publishes in. Some publishing companies maintain "house pseudonyms," under which any number of authors may write installations in a series. Some authors also choose a pseudonym over their real names the way an actor may use a stage name.

Pun: A play on words that have similar sounds but different meanings.

R

Realism: A nineteenth-century European literary movement that sought to portray familiar characters, situations, and settings in a realistic manner. This was done primarily by using an objective narrative point of view and through the buildup of accurate detail. The standard for success of any realistic work depends on how faithfully it transfers common experience into fictional forms. The realistic method may be altered or extended, as in stream of consciousness writing, to record highly subjective experience.

Repartee: Conversation featuring snappy retorts and witticisms.

Resolution: The portion of a story following the climax, in which the conflict is resolved. See also *Denouement.*

Rhetoric: In literary criticism, this term denotes the art of ethical persuasion. In its strictest sense, rhetoric adheres to various principles developed since classical times for arranging facts and ideas in a clear, persuasive, appealing manner. The term is also used to refer to effective prose in general and theories of or methods for composing effective prose.

Rhetorical Question: A question intended to provoke thought, but not an expressed answer, in the reader. It is most commonly used in oratory and other persuasive genres.

Rising Action: The part of a drama where the plot becomes increasingly complicated. Rising action leads up to the climax, or turning point, of a drama.

Roman a clef: A French phrase meaning "novel with a key." It refers to a narrative in which real persons are portrayed under fictitious names.

Romance: A broad term, usually denoting a narrative with exotic, exaggerated, often idealized characters, scenes, and themes.

Romanticism: This term has two widely accepted meanings. In historical criticism, it refers to a European intellectual and artistic movement of the late eighteenth and early nineteenth centuries that sought greater freedom of personal expression than that allowed by the strict rules of literary form and logic of the eighteenth-century neoclassicists. The Romantics preferred emotional and imaginative expression to rational analysis. They considered the individual to be at the center of all experience and so placed him or her at the center of their art. The Romantics believed that the creative imagination reveals nobler truths—unique feelings and attitudes—than those that could be discovered by logic or by scientific examination. Both the natural world and the state of childhood were important sources for revelations of "eternal truths." "Romanticism" is also used as a general term to refer to a type of sensibility found in all periods of literary history and usually considered to be in opposition to the principles of classicism. In this sense, Romanticism signifies any work or philosophy in which the exotic or dreamlike figure strongly, or that is devoted to individualistic expression, self-analysis, or a pursuit of a higher realm of knowledge than can be discovered by human reason.

Romantics: See *Romanticism*

S

Satire: A work that uses ridicule, humor, and wit to criticize and provoke change in human nature and institutions. There are two major types of satire: "formal" or "direct" satire speaks directly to the reader or to a character in the work; "indirect" satire relies upon the ridiculous behavior of its characters to make its point. Formal satire is further divided into two manners: the "Horatian," which ridicules gently, and the "Juvenalian," which derides its subjects harshly and bitterly.

Science Fiction: A type of narrative about or based upon real or imagined scientific theories and technology. Science fiction is often peopled with alien creatures and set on other planets or in different dimensions.

Second Person: See *Point of View*

Setting: The time, place, and culture in which the action of a narrative takes place. The elements of setting may include geographic location, characters' physical and mental environments, prevailing cultural attitudes, or the historical time in which the action takes place.

Simile: A comparison, usually using "like" or "as", of two essentially dissimilar things, as in "coffee as cold as ice" or "He sounded like a broken record."

Slang: A type of informal verbal communication that is generally unacceptable for formal writing. Slang words and phrases are often colorful exaggerations used to emphasize the speaker's point; they may also be shortened versions of an often-used word or phrase.

Slave Narrative: Autobiographical accounts of American slave life as told by escaped slaves. These works first appeared during the abolition movement of the 1830s through the 1850s.

Socialist Realism: The Socialist Realism school of literary theory was proposed by Maxim Gorky and established as a dogma by the first Soviet Congress of Writers. It demanded adherence to a communist worldview in works of literature. Its doctrines required an objective viewpoint comprehensible to the working classes and themes of social struggle featuring strong proletarian heroes. Also known as Social Realism.

Stereotype: A stereotype was originally the name for a duplication made during the printing process; this led to its modern definition as a person or thing that is (or is assumed to be) the same as all others of its type.

Stream of Consciousness: A narrative technique for rendering the inward experience of a character. This technique is designed to give the impression of an ever-changing series of thoughts, emotions, images, and memories in the spontaneous and seemingly illogical order that they occur in life.

Structure: The form taken by a piece of literature. The structure may be made obvious for ease of understanding, as in nonfiction works, or may be obscured for artistic purposes, as in some poetry or seemingly "unstructured" prose.

Sturm und Drang: A German term meaning "storm and stress." It refers to a German literary movement of the 1770s and 1780s that reacted against the order and rationalism of the enlightenment, focusing instead on the intense experience of extraordinary individuals.

Style: A writer's distinctive manner of arranging words to suit his or her ideas and purpose in writing. The unique imprint of the author's personality upon his or her writing, style is the product of an author's way of arranging ideas and his or her use of diction, different sentence structures, rhythm, figures of speech, rhetorical principles, and other elements of composition.

Subjectivity: Writing that expresses the author's personal feelings about his subject, and which may or may not include factual information about the subject.

Subplot: A secondary story in a narrative. A subplot may serve as a motivating or complicating force for the main plot of the work, or it may provide emphasis for, or relief from, the main plot.

Surrealism: A term introduced to criticism by Guillaume Apollinaire and later adopted by Andre Breton. It refers to a French literary and artistic movement founded in the 1920s. The Surrealists sought to express unconscious thoughts and feelings in their works. The best-known technique used for achieving this aim was automatic writing—transcriptions of spontaneous outpourings from the unconscious. The Surrealists proposed to unify the contrary levels of conscious and unconscious, dream and reality, objectivity and subjectivity into a new level of "super-realism."

Suspense: A literary device in which the author maintains the audience's attention through the buildup of events, the outcome of which will soon be revealed.

Symbol: Something that suggests or stands for something else without losing its original identity. In literature, symbols combine their literal meaning with the suggestion of an abstract concept. Literary symbols are of two types: those that carry complex associations of meaning no matter what their contexts, and those that derive their suggestive meaning from their functions in specific literary works.

Symbolism: This term has two widely accepted meanings. In historical criticism, it denotes an early modernist literary movement initiated in France during the nineteenth century that reacted against the prevailing standards of realism. Writers in this movement aimed to evoke, indirectly and symbolically, an order of being beyond the material world of the five senses. Poetic expression of personal emotion figured strongly in the movement, typically by means of a private set of symbols uniquely identifiable with the individual poet. The principal aim of the Symbolists was to express in words the highly complex feelings that grew out of everyday contact with the world. In a broader sense, the term "symbolism" refers to the use of one object to represent another.

T

Tall Tale: A humorous tale told in a straightforward, credible tone but relating absolutely impossible events or feats of the characters. Such tales were commonly told of frontier adventures during the settlement of the west in the United States.

Theme: The main point of a work of literature. The term is used interchangeably with thesis.

Thesis: A thesis is both an essay and the point argued in the essay. Thesis novels and thesis plays share the quality of containing a thesis which is supported through the action of the story.

Third Person: See *Point of View*

Tone: The author's attitude toward his or her audience may be deduced from the tone of the work. A formal tone may create distance or convey politeness, while an informal tone may encourage a friendly, intimate, or intrusive feeling in the reader. The author's attitude toward his or her subject matter may also be deduced from the tone of the words he or she uses in discussing it.

Transcendentalism: An American philosophical and religious movement, based in New England from around 1835 until the Civil War. Transcendentalism was a form of American romanticism that had its roots abroad in the works of Thomas Carlyle, Samuel Coleridge, and Johann Wolfgang von Goethe. The Transcendentalists stressed the importance of intuition and subjective experience in communication with God. They rejected religious dogma and texts in favor of mysticism and scientific naturalism. They pursued truths that lie beyond the "colorless" realms perceived by reason and the senses and were active social reformers in public education, women's rights, and the abolition of slavery.

U

Urban Realism: A branch of realist writing that attempts to accurately reflect the often harsh facts of modern urban existence.

Utopia: A fictional perfect place, such as "paradise" or "heaven."

V

Verisimilitude: Literally, the appearance of truth. In literary criticism, the term refers to aspects of a work of literature that seem true to the reader.

Victorian: Refers broadly to the reign of Queen Victoria of England (1837-1901) and to anything with qualities typical of that era. For example, the qualities of smug narrowmindedness, bourgeois materialism, faith in social progress, and priggish morality are often considered Victorian. This stereotype is contradicted by such dramatic intellectual developments as the theories of Charles Darwin, Karl Marx, and Sigmund Freud (which stirred strong debates in England) and the critical attitudes of serious Victorian writers like Charles Dickens and George Eliot. In literature, the Victorian Period was the great age of the English novel, and the latter part of the era saw the rise of movements such as decadence and symbolism. Also known as Victorian Age and Victorian Period.

W

Weltanschauung: A German term referring to a person's worldview or philosophy.

Weltschmerz: A German term meaning "world pain." It describes a sense of anguish about the nature of existence, usually associated with a melancholy, pessimistic attitude.

Z

Zeitgeist: A German term meaning "spirit of the time." It refers to the moral and intellectual trends of a given era.

Cumulative
Author/Title Index

Cumulative Nationality/Ethnicity Index

Crutcher, Chris
   The Crazy Horse Electric Game: V11
Davis, Rebecca Harding
   Margret Howth: A Story of To-Day: V14
Dick, Philip K.
   Do Androids Dream of Electric Sheep?: V5
Dickey, James
   Deliverance: V9
Didion, Joan
   Democracy: V3
Doctorow, E. L.
   Ragtime: V6
Dorris, Michael
   A Yellow Raft in Blue Water: V3
Dos Passos, John
   U.S.A.: V14
Dreiser, Theodore
   An American Tragedy: V17
   Sister Carrie: V8
Ellis, Bret Easton
   Less Than Zero: V11
Ellison, Ralph
   Invisible Man: V2
Emecheta, Buchi
   The Bride Price: V12
Erdrich, Louise
   Love Medicine: V5
Faulkner, William
   Absalom, Absalom!: V13
   As I Lay Dying: V8
   The Sound and the Fury: V4
Fitzgerald, F. Scott
   The Great Gatsby: V2
Flagg, Fannie
   Fried Green Tomatoes at the Whistle Stop Café: V7
Fox, Paula
   The Slave Dancer: V12
Gaines, Ernest J.
   The Autobiography of Miss Jane Pittman: V5
   A Gathering of Old Men: V16
   A Lesson Before Dying: V7
Gardner, John
   Grendel: V3
Gibbons, Kaye
   Ellen Foster: V3
Green, Hannah
   The Dead of the House: V10
Greene, Bette
   Summer of My German Soldier: V10
Guest, Judith
   Ordinary People: V1
Guterson, David
   Snow Falling on Cedars: V13
Harris, Marilyn
   Hatter Fox: V14
Hawthorne, Nathaniel
   The Scarlet Letter: V1

Heller, Joseph
   Catch-22: V1
Hemingway, Ernest
   A Farewell to Arms: V1
   For Whom the Bell Tolls: V14
   The Old Man and the Sea: V6
   The Sun Also Rises: V5
Herbert, Frank
   Soul Catcher: V17
Hijuelos, Oscar
   The Mambo Kings Play Songs of Love: V17
Hinton, S. E.
   The Outsiders: V5
   Rumble Fish: V15
   Tex: V9
   That Was Then, This Is Now: V16
Hurston, Zora Neale
   Their Eyes Were Watching God: V3
Irving, John
   A Prayer for Owen Meany: V14
   The World According to Garp: V12
James, Henry
   The Ambassadors: V12
   The Turn of the Screw: V16
Jewett, Sarah Orne
   The Country of the Pointed Firs: V15
Kerouac, Jack
   On the Road: V8
Kesey, Ken
   One Flew Over the Cuckoo's Nest: V2
Keyes, Daniel
   Flowers for Algernon: V2
Kincaid, Jamaica
   Annie John: V3
Kingsolver, Barbara
   Animal Dreams: V12
   The Bean Trees: V5
   Pigs in Heaven: V10
Kingston, Maxine Hong
   The Woman Warrior: V6
Knowles, John
   A Separate Peace: V2
Le Guin, Ursula K.
   Always Coming Home: V9
   The Left Hand of Darkness: V6
Lee, Harper
   To Kill a Mockingbird: V2
Lewis, Sinclair
   Main Street: V15
London, Jack
   The Call of the Wild: V8
Lowry, Lois
   The Giver: V3
Mailer, Norman
   The Naked and the Dead: V10
Mason, Bobbie Ann
   In Country: V4

McCullers, Carson
   The Heart Is a Lonely Hunter: V6
   The Member of the Wedding: V13
Melville, Herman
   Billy Budd: V9
   Moby-Dick: V7
Méndez, Miguel
   Pilgrims in Aztlán: V12
Mitchell, Margaret
   Gone with the Wind: V9
Momaday, N. Scott
   House Made of Dawn: V10
Mori, Kyoko
   Shizuko's Daughter: V15
Morrison, Toni
   Beloved: V6
   The Bluest Eye: V1
   Song of Solomon: V8
   Sula: V14
Norris, Frank
   The Octopus: V12
Oates, Joyce Carol
   them: V8
O'Connor, Flannery
   Wise Blood: V3
O'Hara, John
   Appointment in Samarra: V11
Plath, Sylvia
   The Bell Jar: V1
Porter, Katherine Anne
   Ship of Fools: V14
Potok, Chaim
   The Chosen: V4
Power, Susan
   The Grass Dancer: V11
Puzo, Mario
   The Godfather: V16
Rand, Ayn
   Atlas Shrugged: V10
   The Fountainhead: V16
Rölvaag, O. E.
   Giants in the Earth: V5
Salinger, J. D.
   The Catcher in the Rye: V1
Sinclair, Upton
   The Jungle: V6
Shange, Ntozake
   Betsey Brown: V11
Steinbeck, John
   The Grapes of Wrath: V7
   Of Mice and Men: V1
   The Pearl: V5
   The Red Pony: V17
Stowe, Harriet Beecher
   Uncle Tom's Cabin: V6
Tan, Amy
   Joy Luck Club: V1
   The Kitchen God's Wife: V13
Toomer, Jean
   Cane: V11
Twain, Mark
   The Adventures of Huckleberry Finn: V1

The Adventures of Tom Sawyer:
V6
Tyler, Anne
The Accidental Tourist: V7
Breathing Lessons: V10
*Dinner at the Homesick
Restaurant:* V2
Updike, John
Rabbit, Run: V12
Vonnegut, Kurt, Jr.
Slaughterhouse-Five: V3
Walker, Alice
The Color Purple: V5
Warren, Robert Penn
All the King's Men: V13
Welty, Eudora
Losing Battles: V15
The Optimist's Daughter: V13
West, Nathanael
The Day of the Locust: V16
Wharton, Edith
The Age of Innocence: V11
Ethan Frome: V5
House of Mirth: V15
Wouk, Herman
The Caine Mutiny: V7
Wright, Richard
Black Boy: V1
Native Son: V7
Zindel, Paul
The Pigman: V14

Asian American
Kingston, Maxine Hong
The Woman Warrior: V6
Tan, Amy
The Joy Luck Club: V1
The Kitchen God's Wife: V13

Asian Canadian
Kogawa, Joy
Obasan: V3

Australian
Clavell, James du Maresq
Shogun: A Novel of Japan: V10
Keneally, Thomas
Schindler's List: V17

Barbadian
Lamming, George
In the Castle of My Skin: V15

Canadian
Atwood, Margaret
Cat's Eye: V14
The Edible Woman: V12
The Handmaid's Tale: V4
Surfacing: V13
Bellow, Saul
Herzog: V14

Kinsella, W. P.
Shoeless Joe: V15
Kogawa, Joy
Obasan: V3
Laurence, Margaret
The Stone Angel: V11
Waugh, Evelyn Arthur St. John
Brideshead Revisited: V13

Chilean
Allende, Isabel
The House of the Spirits: V6

Colombian
García Márquez, Gabriel
Chronicle of a Death Foretold: V10
Love in the Time of Cholera: V1
One Hundred Years of Solitude: V5

Danish
Dinesen, Isak
Out of Africa: V9
Høeg, Peter
Smilla's Sense of Snow: V17

Dominican
Alvarez, Julia
*How the García Girls Lost Their
Accents:* V5
In the Time of Butterflies: V9

English
Adams, Douglas
*The Hitchhiker's Guide to the
Galaxy:* V7
Adams, Richard
Watership Down: V11
Austen, Jane
Persuasion: V14
Pride and Prejudice: V1
Ballard, J. G.
Empire of the Sun: V8
Blair, Eric Arthur
Animal Farm: V3
Bowen, Elizabeth Dorothea Cole
The Death of the Heart: V13
Brontë, Charlotte
Jane Eyre: V4
Brontë, Emily
Wuthering Heights: V2
Burgess, Anthony
A Clockwork Orange: V15
Burney, Fanny
Evelina: V16
Carroll, Lewis
*Alice's Adventurers in
Wonderland:* V7
Chrisite, Agatha
Ten Little Indians: V8
Conrad, Joseph
Heart of Darkness: V2
Lord Jim: V16

Defoe, Daniel
Moll Flanders: V13
Robinson Crusoe: V9
Dickens, Charles
A Christmas Carol: V10
Great Expectations: V4
Oliver Twist: V14
A Tale of Two Cities: V5
du Maurier, Daphne
Rebecca: V12
Eliot, George
The Mill on the Floss: V17
Foden, Giles
The Last King of Scotland: V15
Forster, E. M.
A Passage to India: V3
Howards End: V10
A Room with a View: V11
Golding, William
Lord of the Flies: V2
Greene, Graham
The End of the Affair: V16
Hardy, Thomas
The Mayor of Casterbridge: V15
The Return of the Native: V11
Tess of the d'Urbervilles: V3
Huxley, Aldous
Brave New World: V6
Ishiguro, Kazuo
The Remains of the Day: V13
James, Henry
The Turn of the Screw: V16
Marmon Silko, Leslie
Ceremony: V4
Orwell, George
1984: V7
Animal Farm: V3
Shelley, Mary
Frankenstein: V1
Shute, Nevil
On the Beach: V9
Stevenson, Robert Louis
Dr. Jekyll and Mr. Hyde: V11
Swift, Jonathan
Gulliver's Travels: V6
Thackeray, William Makepeace
Vanity Fair: V13
Tolkien, J. R. R.
The Hobbit: V8
Waugh, Evelyn
Brideshead Revisited: V13
Scoop: V17
Wells, H. G.
The Time Machine: V17
Woolf, Virginia
Mrs. Dalloway: V12
To the Lighthouse: V8

European American
Hemingway, Ernest
The Old Man and the Sea: V6

Stowe, Harriet Beecher
Uncle Tom's Cabin: V6

French

Dumas, Alexandre
The Three Musketeers: V14
Camus, Albert
The Plague: V16
The Stranger: V6
Hugo, Victor
Les Misérables: V5
Flaubert, Gustave
Madame Bovary: V14
Voltaire
Candide: V7

German

Hesse, Hermann
Demian: V15
Siddhartha: V6
Mann, Thomas
Death in Venice: V17
Remarque, Erich Maria
All Quiet on the Western Front: V4

Hispanic American

Cisneros, Sandra
The House on Mango Street: V2
Hijuelos, Oscar
*The Mambo Kings Play Songs of
Love*: V17

Indian

Markandaya, Kamala
Nectar in a Sieve: V13

Italian

Machiavelli, Niccolo
The Prince: V9

Irish

Bowen, Elizabeth Dorothea Cole
The Death of the Heart: V13
Joyce, James
*A Portrait of the Artist as a
Young Man*: V7

Japanese

Ishiguro, Kazuo
The Remains of the Day: V13

Mori, Kyoko
Shizuko's Daughter: V15
Yoshimoto, Banana
Kitchen: V7

Jewish

Bellow, Saul
Herzog: V14
Seize the Day: V4
Kafka, Frank
The Trial: V7
Malamud, Bernard
The Fixer: V9
The Natural: V4
West, Nathanael
The Day of the Locust: V16
Wiesel, Eliezer
Night: V4

Mexican

Esquivel, Laura
Like Water for Chocolate: V5
Fuentes, Carlos
The Old Gringo: V8

Native American

Alexie, Sherman
*The Lone Ranger and Tonto
Fistfight in Heaven*: V17
Dorris, Michael
A Yellow Raft in Blue Water: V3
Erdrich, Louise
Love Medicine: V5
Marmon Silko, Leslie
Ceremony: V4
Momaday, N. Scott
House Made of Dawn: V10

Nigerian

Achebe, Chinua
Things Fall Apart: V3
Emecheta, Buchi
The Bride Price: V12
The Wrestling Match: V14

Norwegian

Rölvaag, O. E.
Giants in the Earth: V5

Polish

Conrad, Joseph
Heart of Darkness: V2
Lord Jim: V16

Kosinski, Jerzy
The Painted Bird: V12

Romanian

Wiesel, Eliezer
Night: V4

Russian

Bulgakov, Mikhail
The Master and Margarita: V8
Dostoyevsky, Fyodor
The Brothers Karamazon: V8
Crime and Punishment: V3
Nabokov, Vladimir
Lolita: V9
Rand, Ayn
Atlas Shrugged: V10
The Fountainhead: V16
Solzhenitsyn, Aleksandr
*One Day in the Life of Ivan
Denisovich*: V6
Tolstoy, Leo
War and Peace: V10
Turgenev, Ivan
Fathers and Sons: V16

South African

Gordimer, Nadine
July's People: V4
Paton, Alan
Cry, the Beloved Country: V3
Too Late the Phalarope: V12

Spanish

Saavedra, Miguel de Cervantes
Don Quixote: V8

Swiss

Hesse, Hermann
Demian: V15

Uruguayan

Bridal, Tessa
The Tree of Red Stars: V17

West Indian

Kincaid, Jamaica
Annie John: V3

Subject/Theme Index